Lecture Notes in Computer Science 4586

Commenced Publication in 1973
Founding and Former Series Editors:
Gerhard Goos, Juris Hartmanis, and .

T0092510

Josef Pieprzyk   Hossein Ghodosi
Ed Dawson (Eds.)

Information Security and Privacy

12th Australasian Conference, ACISP 2007
Townsville, Australia, July 2-4, 2007
Proceedings

 Springer

Volume Editors

Josef Pieprzyk
Macquarie University, Department of Computing
Center for Advanced Computing - Algorithms and Cryptography
Sydney, NSW 2109, Australia
E-mail: josef@ics.mq.edu.au

Hossein Ghodosi
James Cook University
School of Mathematics, Physics, and Information Technology
Townsville, QLD 4811, Australia
E-mail: hossein@cs.jcu.edu.au

Ed Dawson
Queensland University of Technology, Information Security Institute
Brisbane, QLD 4001, Australia
E-mail: e.dawson@qut.edu.au

Library of Congress Control Number: 2007929635

CR Subject Classification (1998): E.3, K.6.5, D.4.6, C.2, E.4, F.2.1, K.4.1

LNCS Sublibrary: SL 4 – Security and Cryptology

ISSN   0302-9743
ISBN-10   3-540-73457-0 Springer Berlin Heidelberg New York
ISBN-13   978-3-540-73457-4 Springer Berlin Heidelberg New York

Springer is a part of Springer Science+Business Media

springer.com

© Springer-Verlag Berlin Heidelberg 2007
Printed in Germany

Typesetting: Camera-ready by author, data conversion by Scientific Publishing Services, Chennai, India
Printed on acid-free paper   SPIN: 12086818   06/3180   5 4 3 2 1 0

Preface

The 12th Australasian Conference on Information Security and Privacy—ACISP2007—was held in Townsville, Queensland, July 2–4, 2007. This was the first conference to be organized outside the traditional three venues: Brisbane and Gold Coast, Melbourne, and Sydney and Wollongong. The conference was sponsored by James Cook University, Center for Advanced Computing – Algorithm and Cryptography at Macquarie University, Information Security Institute at Queensland University of Technology, and the Research Network for Secure Australia. We would like to thank Matthieu Finiasz and Thomas Baignères from EPFL, LASEC, Switzerland for letting us use their iChair software that facilitated the submission and revision processes.

Out of 132 submissions, the Program Committee (PC) selected 33 papers after a rigorous review process. Each paper got assigned to at least three referees. Papers submitted by members of the PC got assigned to five referees. In the first stage of the review process, the submitted papers were read and evaluated by the PC members and then in the second stage, the papers were scrutinized during a three-week-long discussion. We would like to thank the authors of all papers (both accepted and rejected) for submitting their papers to the conference. A special thanks go to the members of the PC and the external referees who gave their time, expertise and enthusiasm in order to select the best collection of papers.

As in previous years, we held a competition for the "best student paper." To be eligible, a paper had to be co-authored by a postgraduate student whose contribution was more than 50%. Eight papers entered the competition. The winner was Norbert Pramstaller from Graz University of Technology, Austria, for the paper "Second Preimages for Iterated Hash Functions and Their Implications on MACs."

This year we had only one invited talk, which was given by Andreas Enge. The title of the talk was "Contributions Cryptographic Curves."

We would like to express our thanks to Springer and in particular, to Alfred Hofmann and Ronan Nugent for their continuing support of the ACISP conference and for help in the conference proceeding production. Further, we thank Michelle Kang, who helped us with the setting up and maintenance of the ACISP Web site, Vijayakrishnan Pasupathinathan, who took care of the iChair server and ACISP mailbox, Adam Shah for installation of the iChair server and Elizabeth Hansford for assisting with conference organization.

July 2007

Josef Pieprzyk
Hossein Ghodosi
Ed Dawson

Organization

ACISP 2007

July 2–4, 2007, Townsville, Queensland, Australia

General Co-chairs

Hossein Ghodosi	James Cook University, Australia
Ed Dawson	QUT, Australia

Program Chair

Josef Pieprzyk	Macquarie University, Australia

Program Committee

Paul Ashley	IBM, Australia
Tuomas Aura	Microsoft, USA
Lynn Batten	Deakin University, Australia
Colin Boyd	QUT, Australia
Andrew Clark	QUT, Australia
Scott Contini	Macquarie University, Australia
Nicolas Courtois	University College London, UK and Gemalto, France
Yvo Desmedt	University College London, UK
Christophe Doche	Macquarie University, Australia
Ed Dawson	QUT, Australia
Hossein Ghodosi	James Cook University, Australia
Jovan Golić	Telecom, Italy
Dieter Gollmann	TUHH, Germany
Peter Gutmann	University of Auckland, New Zealand
Kwangjo Kim	ICU, Korea
Sevin Knapskog	NTNU, Norway
Kaoru Kurosawa	Ibaraki University, Japan
Tanja Lange	TU/e, Netherlands
Javier Lopez	University of Malaga, Spain
Keith Martin	Royal Holloway, UK
Mitsuru Matsui	Mitsubishi Electric, Japan
Paul Montague	Motorola, Australia
Yi Mu	University of Wollongong, Australia
Andrew Odlyzko	University of Minnesota, USA
Eiji Okamoto	University of Tsukuba, Japan
Rafail Ostrovsky	UCLA, USA

David Poincheval ENS, France
Bart Preneel   K.U.Leuven, Belgium
Bimal Roy   ISICAL, India
Rei Safavi-Naini University of Wollongong, Australia
                 University of Calgary, Canada
Jennifer Seberry University of Wollongong, Australia
Igor Shparlinski Macquarie University, Australia
Ron Steinfeld   Macquarie University, Australia
Willy Susilo   University of Wollongong, Australia
Henk van Tilborg TU/e, Netherlands
Serge Vaudenay   EPFL, Switzerland
Huaxiong Wang   Macquarie University, Australia
                 Nanyang Technological University, Singapore
Henry Wolfe   University of Otago, New Zealand

External Reviewers

Ajith Abraham	Avishek Adhikari	Isaac Agudo
Man Ho Au	Joonsang Baek	Vittorio Bagini
Yun Bai	Thomas Baignères	Rana Barua
Daniel J. Bernstein	Peter Birkner	Xavier Boyen
Yang Cui	Jan Camenisch	Christophe De Cannière
Alvaro Cardenas	Dario Catalano	Agnes Chan
Chris Charnes	Benoit Chevallier-Mames	Sherman S. M. Chow
Yvonne Cliff	Tanmoy Das	Pascal Delaunay
Dang Nguyen Duc	Ernest Foo	Pierre-Alain Fouque
Jun Furukawa	Krzysztof M. Gaj	David Galindo
Juan Garay	Danilo Gligoroski	M. Choudary Gorantla
Jens Groth	Kishan Chand Gupta	Goichiro Hanaoka
Kjetil Haslum	Swee-Huay Heng	Jonathan Herzog
Shoichi Hirose	Michael Hitchens	Jeffrey Horton
Xinyi Huang	Laurent Imbert	Sebastiaan Indesteege
Mahabir Prasad Jhanwar	Emilia Käsper	Lars R. Knudsen
Markulf Kohlweiss	Divyan M. Konidala	Takeshi Koshiba
Kerstin Lemke-Rust	Vo Duc Liem	Chu-Wee Lim
Liang Liu	Liang Lu	Anna Lysyanskaya
Mark Manulis	Abe Masayuki	Krystian Matusiewicz
Luke McAven	Miodrag Mihaljevic	Ilya Mironov
Guglielmo Morgari	Sean Murphy	Pablo Najera
Gregory Neven	Antonio Nicolosi	Svetla Nikova
Wakaha Ogata	Jose A. Onieva	Dunkelman Orr
Pascal Paillier	Sylvain Pasini	Kenny Paterson
Maura Paterson	Goutam Paul	Souradyuti Paul
Kun Peng	Slobodan Petrovic	Raphael C.-W. Phan
Le Trieu Phong	Geraint Price	Havard Raddum

Mohammad Reza Reyhanitabar
Chun Ruan
Siamak Shahandashti
Makoto Sugita
Qiang Tang
Toshio Tokita
Frederik Vercauteren
Guilin Wang
Yan Wang
Benne de Weger
Qianhong Wu
Qingsong Ye
Sèbastien Zimmer

Rodrigo Roman
Yasuyuki Sakai
Nicholas Sheppard
Daisuke Suzuki
Christophe Tartary
Jacques Traore
Charlotte Vikkelsoe
Peishun Wang
Yongge Wang
Christopher Wolf
Guangwu Xu
Hongbo Yu

Greg Rose
Somitra Sanadhya
Jason Smith
Katsuyuki Takashima
Clark Thomborson
Pim Tuyls
Martin Vuagnoux
Shuhong Wang
Brent Waters
Hongjun Wu
Bo-Yin Yang
Steve Zdancewic

Table of Contents

Stream Ciphers

An Analysis of the Hermes8 Stream Ciphers   1
    Steve Babbage, Carlos Cid, Norbert Pramstaller, and Håvard Raddum

On the Security of the LILI Family of Stream Ciphers Against
Algebraic Attacks 11
    Sultan Zayid Al-Hinai, Ed Dawson, Matt Henricksen, and
    Leonie Simpson

Strengthening NLS Against Crossword Puzzle Attack 29
    Debojyoti Bhattacharya, Debdeep Mukhopadhyay,
    Dhiman Saha, and D. RoyChowdhury

Hashing

A New Strategy for Finding a Differential Path of SHA-1 45
    Jun Yajima, Yu Sasaki, Yusuke Naito, Terutoshi Iwasaki,
    Takeshi Shimoyama, Noboru Kunihiro, and Kazuo Ohta

Preimage Attack on the Parallel FFT-Hashing Function 59
    Donghoon Chang, Moti Yung, Jaechul Sung, Seokhie Hong, and
    Sangjin Lee

Second Preimages for Iterated Hash Functions and Their Implications
on MACs 68
    Norbert Pramstaller, Mario Lamberger, and Vincent Rijmen

On Building Hash Functions from Multivariate Quadratic Equations . . . 82
    Olivier Billet, Matt J.B. Robshaw, and Thomas Peyrin

Biometrics

An Application of the Goldwasser-Micali Cryptosystem to Biometric
Authentication 96
    Julien Bringer, Hervé Chabanne, Malika Izabachène,
    David Pointcheval, Qiang Tang, and Sébastien Zimmer

Soft Generation of Secure Biometric Keys 107
    Jovan Dj. Golić and Madalina Baltatu

Secret Sharing

Flaws in Some Secret Sharing Schemes Against Cheating 122
    Toshinori Araki and Satoshi Obana

Efficient (k, n) Threshold Secret Sharing Schemes Secure Against
Cheating from $n - 1$ Cheaters 133
  Toshinori Araki

Cryptanalysis

Related-Key Amplified Boomerang Attacks on the Full-Round Eagle-64
and Eagle-128 143
  *Kitae Jeong, Changhoon Lee, Jaechul Sung, Seokhie Hong, and
  Jongin Lim*

Analysis of the SMS4 Block Cipher................................. 158
  *Fen Liu, Wen Ji, Lei Hu, Jintai Ding, Shuwang Lv,
  Andrei Pyshkin, and Ralf-Philipp Weinmann*

Forgery Attack to an Asymptotically Optimal Traitor Tracing
Scheme 171
  Yongdong Wu, Feng Bao, and Robert H. Deng

Public Key Cryptography

TCHo: A Hardware-Oriented Trapdoor Cipher 184
  *Jean-Philippe Aumasson, Matthieu Finiasz, Willi Meier, and
  Serge Vaudenay*

Anonymity on Paillier's Trap-Door Permutation 200
  Ryotaro Hayashi and Keisuke Tanaka

Generic Certificateless Key Encapsulation Mechanism 215
  Qiong Huang and Duncan S. Wong

Double-Size Bipartite Modular Multiplication 230
  Masayuki Yoshino, Katsuyuki Okeya, and Camille Vuillaume

Affine Precomputation with Sole Inversion in Elliptic Curve
Cryptography 245
  Erik Dahmen, Katsuyuki Okeya, and Daniel Schepers

Construction of Threshold (Hybrid) Encryption in the Random Oracle
Model: How to Construct Secure Threshold Tag-KEM from Weakly
Secure Threshold KEM 259
  Takeru Ishihara, Hiroshi Aono, Sadayuki Hongo, and Junji Shikata

Efficient Chosen-Ciphertext Secure Identity-Based Encryption with
Wildcards... 274
  *James Birkett, Alexander W. Dent, Gregory Neven, and
  Jacob C.N. Schuldt*

Authentication

Combining Prediction Hashing and MDS Codes for Efficient Multicast
Stream Authentication 293
    Christophe Tartary and Huaxiong Wang

Certificateless Signature Revisited................................. 308
    Xinyi Huang, Yi Mu, Willy Susilo, Duncan S. Wong, and Wei Wu

Identity-Committable Signatures and Their Extension to
Group-Oriented Ring Signatures 323
    Cheng-Kang Chu and Wen-Guey Tzeng

Hash-and-Sign with Weak Hashing Made Secure 338
    Sylvain Pasini and Serge Vaudenay

"Sandwich" Is Indeed Secure: How to Authenticate a Message with
Just One Hashing 355
    Kan Yasuda

Threshold Anonymous Group Identification and Zero-Knowledge
Proof... 370
    Akihiro Yamamura, Takashi Kurokawa, and Junji Nakazato

Non-interactive Manual Channel Message Authentication Based on
eTCR Hash Functions 385
    Mohammad Reza Reyhanitabar, Shuhong Wang, and
    Reihaneh Safavi-Naini

E-Commerce

A Practical System for Globally Revoking the Unlinkable Pseudonyms
of Unknown Users... 400
    Stefan Brands, Liesje Demuynck, and Bart De Decker

Efficient and Secure Comparison for On-Line Auctions............... 416
    Ivan Damgård, Martin Geisler, and Mikkel Krøigaard

Practical Compact E-Cash 431
    Man Ho Au, Willy Susilo, and Yi Mu

Security

Use of Dempster-Shafer Theory and Bayesian Inferencing for Fraud
Detection in Mobile Communication Networks 446
    Suvasini Panigrahi, Amlan Kundu, Shamik Sural, and
    A.K. Majumdar

On Proactive Perfectly Secure Message Transmission 461
    Kannan Srinathan, Prasad Raghavendra, and
    Pandu Rangan Chandrasekaran

Author Index 475

An Analysis of the Hermes8 Stream Ciphers

Steve Babbage[1], Carlos Cid[2], Norbert Pramstaller[3], and Håvard Raddum[4]

[1] Vodafone Group R&D,
Newbury, United Kingdom
steve.babbage@vodafone.com
[2] Information Security Group,
Royal Holloway, University of London
Egham, United Kingdom
carlos.cid@rhul.ac.uk
[3] IAIK, Graz University of Technology
Graz, Austria
norbert.pramstaller@iaik.tugraz.at
[4] Dept. of Informatics, The University of Bergen,
Bergen, Norway
haavardr@ii.uib.no

Abstract. Hermes8 [6,7] is one of the stream ciphers submitted to the ECRYPT Stream Cipher Project (eSTREAM [3]). In this paper we present an analysis of the Hermes8 stream ciphers. In particular, we show an attack on the latest version of the cipher (Hermes8F), which requires very few known keystream bytes and recovers the cipher secret key in less than a second on a normal PC. Furthermore, we make some remarks on the cipher's key schedule and discuss some properties of ciphers with similar algebraic structure to Hermes8.

Keywords: Hermes8, Stream Cipher, Cryptanalysis.

1 Introduction

Hermes8 is one of the 34 stream ciphers submitted to eSTREAM, the ECRYPT Stream Cipher Project [3]. The cipher has a simple byte-oriented design, consisting of substitutions and shifts of the state register bytes. Two versions of the cipher have been proposed. Originally, the cipher Hermes8 [6] was submitted as candidate to eSTREAM. Although no weaknesses of Hermes8 were found during the first phase of evaluation, the cipher did not seem to present satisfactory performance in either software or hardware [4]. As a result, a slightly modified version of the cipher, named Hermes8F [7], was submitted for consideration during the second phase of eSTREAM. In this paper we present an analysis of the Hermes8 stream ciphers. In Section 2 we present an alternative description of the Hermes8 ciphers. Section 3 describes an attack against the latest version of Hermes8. Section 4 contains some remarks on the key schedule of Hermes8, while we discuss some algebraic properties of the ciphers in Section 5.

J. Pieprzyk, H. Ghodosi, and E. Dawson (Eds.): ACISP 2007, LNCS 4586, pp. 1–10, 2007.

2   Description of Hermes8F

According to [7], Hermes8F is a stream cipher based on the Substitution– Permutation network principle. Hermes8F is defined for two different key lengths: Hermes8F-80 uses 80-bit keys, while Hermes8F-128 uses 128-bit keys. The cipher uses two byte-oriented registers: a 17-byte state register and a 10-byte key register (16 bytes for Hermes8F-128). Additionally, there is a single byte register *Accu*, which seems to have the use of a memory register (Figure 1). The diffusion is provided by moving pointers through both registers, while non-linearity is provided by the AES S-Box [2].

The main operation of the cipher consists of the following steps:

1. XOR the value stored at *Accu* with a byte from the state register and a byte from the key register;

2. Use the previous result as input for the AES S-Box;

3. Replace the state register value used in step 1. by the output of the S-Box;

4. Store the output of the S-Box also in *Accu*;

5. Increment both the state and key register pointers (denoted by $p1$ and $p2$, respectively).

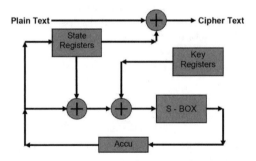

Fig. 1. Hermes8F stream cipher [7]

The steps above are performed at each clocking. A round of the cipher consists of 17 clockings. At every 7 clockings, two bytes of the key register are updated. The updating function is also based on the AES S-Box (Section 4). In the cipher's initialization, the encryption key is loaded into the key register, and the IV is loaded into the state register. The register *Accu* starts with the zero byte as content[1]. The initialization process consists of five rounds (i.e. 85 clockings), and so all the state registers are updated five times before the cipher enters

---

[1] In Hermes8, the initial value of *Accu* is key-dependent; see Section 4.

the normal mode of operation. The first bytes of the keystream are produced after two further rounds. The output consists of 8 bytes from the state register, taken from alternating positions of the register. Further bytes of the output are produced at every two rounds. More details of the algorithm can be found in [7].

2.1 Alternative Description of Hermes8F

We note that it follows from the description above that during the cipher operation, the contents of the registers $Accu$ and state$[p1 - 1]$ are always the same. Thus a more natural description of Hermes8F is given in Figure 2. It consists of the state register R, which is represented as a feedback shift register of length 17, defined as

$$s_i^t = \text{state}[p1 + i] \ , \ \ 0 \le i \le 16,$$

where state$[p1]$ is the byte addressed by pointer $p1$ at time t. This FSR is updated according to the following relations:

$$s_i^{t+1} = s_{i+1}^t \ , \ \ 0 \le i \le 15,$$
$$s_{16}^{t+1} = S(s_0^t \oplus s_{16}^t \oplus k^t),$$

where the byte k^t is the output of the key register K at time t (that is, $k[p2]$), and S represents the AES S-Box.

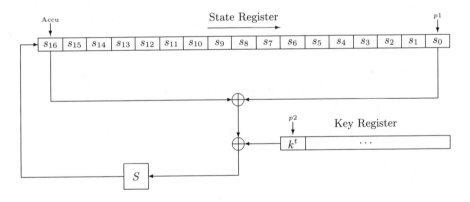

Fig. 2. Hermes8F as a feedback shift register

In our attack, we need to consider the reverse cipher (clocking the generator backwards, and so generating the keystream blocks in reverse order[2]). The relation of the feedback register of the reverse cipher is given by

$$s_0^t = S^{-1}(s_{16}^{t+1}) \oplus s_{16}^t \oplus k^t$$
$$= S^{-1}(s_{16}^{t+1}) \oplus s_{15}^{t+1} \oplus k^t.$$

The inverse cipher is depicted in Figure 3.

---

[2] As pointed out by one of the anonymous referees, the backward keystream was also used in the attack described in [5].

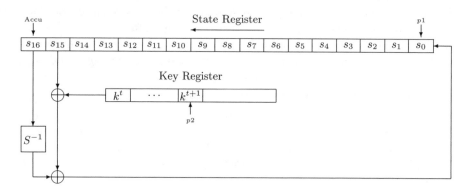

Fig. 3. The inverse of Hermes8F

3   Cryptanalysis of Hermes8F

The attack we describe exploits two features of Hermes8F:

1. In contrast to the forward cipher, the reverse cipher has slow diffusion. (In the forward cipher, the new byte s_{16} contributes to the feedback in the very next clock. But in the reverse cipher, the new byte s_0 has no influence on the feedback until it has shifted all the way along to the s_{15} position.)

2. The IV does not affect the key register.

Let us consider the keystream produced by Hermes8F under a secret key and a random IV, and let B_j be the jth set of 8 bytes output by the cipher. Thus, if we define $T = 34 \cdot j + 85$, we have

$$B_j = [s_0^T, s_2^T, s_4^T, s_6^T, s_8^T, s_{10}^T, s_{12}^T, s_{14}^T].$$

Consider the first two sets of B_1 and B_2, for which T is equal to $7 \times 17 = 119$ and $9 \times 17 = 153$ respectively. Suppose that in addition to the last two bytes of B_2 (that is, s_{12}^{153} and s_{14}^{153}), we also know the values of s_{13}^{153}, k^{150} and k^{149}. Then we have

$$S^{-1}(s_{14}^{153}) \oplus s_{13}^{153} \oplus k^{150} = S^{-1}(s_{16}^{151}) \oplus s_{15}^{151} \oplus k^{150} = s_0^{150}.$$

Likewise, we have that

$$S^{-1}(s_{13}^{153}) \oplus s_{12}^{153} \oplus k^{149} = S^{-1}(s_{16}^{150}) \oplus s_{15}^{150} \oplus k^{149} = s_0^{149}.$$

Now, assuming that we also know k^{133}, we have

$$S^{-1}(s_0^{150}) \oplus s_0^{149} \oplus k^{133} = S^{-1}(s_{16}^{134}) \oplus s_{15}^{134} \oplus k^{133} = s_0^{133} = s_{14}^{119}.$$

We note however that s_{14}^{119} is the last byte of B_1.

Thus consider an attack where we guess on the values of k^{133}, k^{149} and k^{150} and verify against the known byte s_{14}^{119}. The equation we have is

$$S^{-1}(S^{-1}(s_{14}^{153}) \oplus s_{13}^{153} \oplus k^{150}) \oplus S^{-1}(s_{13}^{153}) \oplus s_{12}^{153} \oplus k^{149} \oplus k^{133} = s_{14}^{119}, \quad (1)$$

where the key bytes and s_{13}^{153} are unknown. By setting $c_1 = S^{-1}(s_{14}^{153}) \oplus k^{150}$ and $c_2 = s_{12}^{153} \oplus s_{14}^{119} \oplus k^{149} \oplus k^{133}$ the equation can be more simply written as

$$S^{-1}(s_{13}^{153} \oplus c_1) \oplus S^{-1}(s_{13}^{153}) = c_2. \quad (2)$$

That is, a particular guess of the three key bytes is possible if and only if an input difference of c_1 to S^{-1} can lead to an output difference of c_2. We know that S^{-1} is affinely equivalent to the inverse mapping in $GF(2^8)$, and thus it is rather close to being APN [9]. This means that just under one half of all (c_1, c_2)-values are possible, or equivalently that one half of the guesses of the three key bytes remains as possible after checking them against (1).

Note that since c_2 depends on the sum $k^{149} \oplus k^{133}$ we can never learn the individual values of k^{149} and k^{133} this way, only the sum of them. Hence we are not guessing on 3-byte values but only on 2-byte values, and the complexity of guessing once is 2^{16} and not 2^{24}. By repeating the guessing for several IVs we can remove all wrong guesses, and find two bytes of information - the values of k^{150} and $k^{149} \oplus k^{133}$.

The process above can be repeated using the output bytes s_{12}^{153} and s_{10}^{153} to obtain k^{148} and $k^{147} \oplus k^{131}$, and so on, until we have 14 (or 30 in the case of Hermes8F-128) bytes of information about the key register at times $121 \leq t \leq 150$. It is then not too hard to find the content of the key register at a specific time t, and we can run the key register back to obtain the original encryption key.

The attack requires no more than 16 bytes of output under a few (about 16) distinct IVs. In general, the complexity of the attack is of the order of $7 \times 16 \times 2^{16} < 2^{23}$ very simple operations for Hermes8F-80 (and $15 \times 16 \times 2^{16} < 2^{24}$ for Hermes8F-128). The attack (for Hermes8F-80) has been implemented on a normal workstation, and succeeds in recovering the key in less than a second.

3.1   Analysis of Hermes8

We have considered extending the attack presented above to the original Hermes8 cipher. The main differences between Hermes8 and Hermes8F are the length of the state register (23 bytes and 37 bytes for Hermes8-80 and Hermes8-128, respectively, against 17 bytes for Hermes8F), and the number of rounds between each output of the cipher (three rounds for Hermes8 against two rounds for Hermes8F). Some of the features that we have exploited in our attack, such as the simpler representation of the generator as a shift register, slow diffusion of the reverse clocking cipher, and the fact that the key register is not IV-dependent, apply also to Hermes8. The main difficulty in extending the attack to Hermes8 is the number of rounds between output of the cipher. With three full rounds in Hermes8 between each output, the relations obtained contain a larger number of unknown key and state register bytes. As the state register values are expected to be different for each IV used, we have not been able to obtain a simple equation such as (2) to derive key bits. Therefore a simple extension of the attack does not seem to work against Hermes8. We note however that the increase in the length of the state register alone would in no way have strengthened the cipher against our attack.

4   Equivalent Keys in Hermes8

The key schedule for Hermes8 is described in detail in [6] and is illustrated in Figure 4 (Hermes8F features a similar key scheduling method [7]). The cipher's designer presents a brief analysis of the key schedule and remarks the existence of weak keys for Hermes8. More precisely, keys with equal byte patterns lead to a repetition of byte values in the output of the key scheduling method [6]. In an extreme case, the key defined as $k_i = 63_{\text{hex}}$, for $0 \leq i \leq 9$, is invariant by the key schedule, and it therefore always outputs the byte value 63_{hex} (this follows from the fact that $S(00_{\text{hex}}) = 63_{\text{hex}})$.

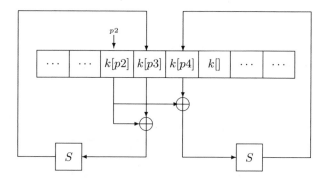

Fig. 4. Hermes8 key schedule

A further property of the Hermes8 key schedule that seemed to have been overlooked by the designer is the existence of equivalent keys. These are keys that for a given IV result in the same keystream. This is an immediate consequence of the structure of the key scheduling method and the key-dependent initialization of the pointers $p1$, $p2$, src, and the $Accu$ register [6].

Consider a key k^*, which results from the byte-wise rotation of the key k. In order to get the same keystream we have to ensure that for both keys, the pointers $p1$, src, and the register $Accu$ have the same value, that is $p1_k = p1_{k^*}$, $src_k = src_{k^*}$, and $Accu_k = Accu_{k^*}$. Additionally, we require that the pointers $p2_k$ and $p2_{k^*}$ address the key register in such a way that the key scheduling method produces the same output for both keys. For instance, consider the 80-bit version of Hermes8 and assume the 10-byte cipher key is given by $k = k_0, \ldots, k_9$. The rotated key $k^* = k_9, k_0, \ldots, k_8$ is *equivalent* to k if the following conditions are satisfied:

$$\text{cond. } p1 : \quad (k_0 \oplus k_1 \oplus k_2) \bmod 23 = (k_0 \oplus k_1 \oplus k_9) \bmod 23 \tag{3}$$

$$\text{cond. } src : \quad (k_0 \oplus k_3 \oplus k_9) \bmod 7 = (k_2 \oplus k_8 \oplus k_9) \bmod 7 \tag{4}$$

$$\text{cond. } Accu : \quad k_6 \oplus k_7 \oplus k_8 = k_5 \oplus k_6 \oplus k_7 \tag{5}$$

$$\text{cond. } p2 : \quad (k_2 \oplus k_3 \oplus k_4) \bmod 10 = ((k_3 \oplus k_4 \oplus k_5) \bmod 10) + 1 \tag{6}$$

Condition (6) ensures that the output of the key schedule is the same for k and k^*. If, in addition, the remaining conditions (3)-(5) are satisfied, then the key stream generation is equivalent for both keys k and k^*. There are approximately

$$2^{80 - (8 - log_2(\lceil \frac{256}{23} \rceil)) - (8 - log_2(\lceil \frac{256}{7} \rceil)) - 8 - (8 - log_2(\lceil \frac{256}{10} \rceil) + log_2(1.109))} \approx 2^{61}$$

keys k satisfying the conditions above, which are therefore essentially equivalent to the key k^* obtained by a simple cyclic shift of its bytes. A similar analysis can be done for other rotation values of the key k, giving us approximately $5 \times 2^{61} \approx 2^{63}$ pairs of equivalent keys. Although this represents a very small fraction of an 80-bit key space, the above argument shows however that Hermes8-80 does not reach the theoretically expected entire 80-bit key space. In fact, if we assume that 80-bit encryption keys are randomly generated, we have that approximately 2^{63} keys effectively occur with twice the expected probability, while 2^{63} keys do not occur at all.

5 Algebraic Structure

Given the highly algebraic structure of Hermes8, it is natural to consider the feasibility of algebraic attacks against the cipher. The only two operations in Hermes8 are the S-Box operation (which is based on the inversion over $GF(2^8)$) and XOR. Thus at each clocking, we can express the resulting register updated through a relation over $GF(2^8)$ (which in turn can be described as a set of multivariate quadratic equations over $GF(2)$). After a number of rounds we should have enough equations to solve the system of equations and therefore recover the secret key. In our estimates however the size of the resulting system appears to be too large to be solved in practice. This is due to the large number of clockings between the cipher output. However it may be possible that one can simplify some of the relations, or exploit this rich algebraic structure in some other way.

We note that the attack presented in section 3 can also be mounted using a more algebraic approach. Due to the algebraic structure of the S-Box, the expressions considered when describing the attack can also be written as a simple system of multivariate equations. If we solve the system (e.g. by computing the corresponding Gröbner basis under the appropriate monomial ordering), requiring that the equations have solutions in $GF(2^8)$, we obtain relations between the key bytes. This corresponds to the bit of information we derived from the relation (2). If we repeat this procedure for a number of IVs, we should obtain enough such relations to allow us to solve the resulting system and recover the respective key bytes. Again, this approach does not seem to work with Hermes8, as we have not been able to obtain relations on the key bytes alone (they always involve at least one unknown register value, which as noted in section 3.1, should change with each different IV). Moreover, this algebraic approach does not seem to be more efficient than the attack described early in this paper.

5.1 Algebraic Structure of a Variant of Hermes8

In this section we consider a slightly modified version of Hermes8, to illustrate how its highly algebraic structure may be exploited. In this modified version, we remove the final affine transformation from the Sbox, so that the variant uses as S-Box the modified *inversion* in the Rijndael field only, that is $S : x \mapsto x^{254}$. We note that the only two operations of the cipher (SBox and XOR) correspond to the exponentiation and addition in the Rijndael field $\mathbb{F} \cong GF(2^8)$, respectively. We also know that the original AES S-Box is affinely equivalent to the inversion, and so this variant of Hermes8 should share much of the security properties with the original Hermes8 cipher.

However the new cipher presents a very interesting property. Let $\tau : \mathbb{F} \to \mathbb{K}$ be any isomorphism from $\mathbb{F}$ to a field $\mathbb{K} \cong GF(2^8)$ (in particular, we may have $\mathbb{K} = \mathbb{F}$ so that τ is an automorphism of $\mathbb{F}$). Then we have

$$S(\tau(x)) = \tau(S(x)) \text{ and } \tau(x \oplus y) = \tau(x) \oplus \tau(y), \ \forall x, y \in \mathbb{F}.$$

If we assume the simplified version of initialization of the cipher's pointers (as with Hermes8F), we can then use these relations to construct a very simple chosen-key algebraic distinguisher against the cipher. Let $KS = \mathcal{E}(k, IV)$ represent the keystream (of length m) generated by the cipher using initialisation vector IV and encryption key k. Then we have

$$\mathcal{E}(\tau(k), \tau(IV)) = \tau(KS),$$

where $\tau(k)$ denotes the application of τ on each byte of the encryption key k (similar for $\tau(IV)$ and $\tau(KS)$).

This property is called *self-duality* [1], and is similar to the complementation property of DES [8]. In particular, it allows us to construct a simple method that reduces the key space when performing exhaustive key search, as following.

Let k be the secret encryption key to be searched, so that an attacker has access to the encryption operation $\mathcal{E}(k, \cdot)$, and can generate the keystream for any IV. Let τ be an automorphism of $\mathbb{F}$.

Prior to performing the exhaustive search, the attacker partitions the key space into equivalence classes

$$k_1 \equiv k_2 \iff k_2 = \tau^r(k_1),$$

and given an IV, computes the set of initialisation vectors

$$\{IV, \tau(IV), \tau^2(IV), \ldots, \tau^{n-1}(IV)\},$$

where n is the order of τ. It can now compute the set of keystreams of length m (for m long enough)

$$KS_i = \tau^{-i}(\mathcal{E}(\tau^i(IV), k)) = \mathcal{E}(IV, \tau^{-i}(k))$$

for $i = 0, \ldots, n - 1$.

To perform the exhaustive key search, for each equivalence class of encryption keys, the attacker selects a key k' and computes the keystream of length m $K = \mathcal{E}(IV, k')$. If $K = KS_i$ for some i, then $\tau^i(k')$ is a candidate for the encryption key k. Otherwise k is not in the equivalence class of k'. This method should reduce the complexity of exhaustive key search by a factor of about n, and is similar to the method that exploits the complementation property of DES (which uses the complementation map of order 2).

For a concrete example, let us consider the Frobenius automorphism defined as $\tau : x \mapsto x^2$. Since the order of τ is 8, this method should reduce the complexity of exhaustive key search to the order of 2^{77} operations (enabling key recovery on average in the order of 2^{76} operations). From the many isomorphisms of fields of order 2^8 [10], this map seems to provide the best reduction for the key space search.

We note however that this property and method of attack does not apply to the original Hermes8 cipher, since the affine operation in the SBox does not commute with the field isomorphisms.

6   Conclusion

We presented in this paper an analysis of the Hermes8 [6] stream cipher, and some of its variants. In particular, we showed how to mount an attack to recover the secret key for the latest version of the cipher (Hermes8F-80) with complexity of around the order of 2^{23} operations, requiring a very small number of known keystream bytes. Although we have not been able to extend the method of attack used to the original version of Hermes8, we note that many of the features that we have exploited - the simpler representation of the generator as a shift register, slow diffusion of the reverse clocking cipher, and the fact that the key register is not IV-dependent - apply also to Hermes8. An interesting topic for further research is whether there are other stream ciphers that may have their security compromised by analysis of the reverse cipher, as with Hermer8F.

Acknowledgments

The work described in this paper has been supported in part by the European Commission through the IST Programme under Contract IST-2002-507932 ECRYPT. We would also like to thank Vincent Rijmen for his suggestion to consider the existence of equivalent keys for the Hermes8 stream ciphers.

References

1. Barkan, E., Biham, E.: In How Many Ways Can You Write Rijndael? Cryptology ePrint Archive, 2002/157, (2002) http://eprint.iacr.org/2002/157/
2. Daemen, J., Rijmen, V.: The Design of Rijndael. Springer, Heidelberg (2002)
3. eSTREAM, the ECRYPT Stream Cipher Project.
   http://www.ecrypt.eu.org/stream/
4. De Cannière, C.: eSTREAM testing framework.
   http://www.ecrypt.eu.org/stream/perf/
5. Golic, J.: Iterative Probabilistic Cryptanalysis of RC4 Keystream Generator. In: Clark, A., Boyd, C., Dawson, E.P. (eds.) ACISP 2000. LNCS, vol. 1841, pp. 220–233. Springer, Heidelberg (2000)
6. Kaiser, U.: Hermes8: A Low-Complexity Low-Power Stream Cipher. Cryptology ePrint Archive, Report, /019. (2006) http://eprint.iacr.org/2006/019.pdf
7. Kaiser, U.: Hermes8F: A Low-Complexity Low-Power Stream Cipher. eSTREAM, the ECRYPT Stream Cipher Project, Second Phase Ciphers.
   http://www.ecrypt.eu.org/stream/p2ciphers/hermes8/hermes8f_p2.pdf
8. Menezes, A.J., Van Oorschot, P.C., Vanstone, S.A.: Handbook of Applied Cryptography. CRC Press, Boca Raton (1996)
9. Nyberg, K.: Diferentially uniform mappings for cryptography. In: Helleseth, T. (ed.) EUROCRYPT 1993. LNCS, vol. 765, pp. 55–64. Springer, Heidelberg (1994)
10. Raddum, H.: More Dual Rijndaels. In: Dobbertin, H., Rijmen, V., Sowa, A. (eds.) Advanced Encryption Standard – AES. LNCS, vol. 3373, pp. 142–147. Springer, Heidelberg (2005)

On the Security of the LILI Family of Stream Ciphers Against Algebraic Attacks

Sultan Zayid Al-Hinai[1], Ed Dawson[1], Matt Henricksen[2], and Leonie Simpson[1]

[1] Information Security Institute (ISI)
Queensland University of Technology (QUT), Australia
[2] Institute for Infocomm Research, Singapore

Abstract. In this paper, we present an algebraic analysis of the LILI family of stream ciphers, and in particular LILI-II, and investigate the security provided against both standard and fast algebraic attacks. We show that the size of the two registers used, the difference between their lengths, the maximum number of times a register is clocked and the degree of the filter function all play important roles in providing resistance against algebraic attacks. Further, we show that the degree 10 filter function used in LILI-II has an algebraic immunity (AI) of 4. Using this, a fast algebraic attack can be performed on LILI-II that significantly reduces the attack complexity, although not to such a degree that it is more efficient than exhaustive key search. These algebraic attacks recover the internal state of the cipher rather than the key bits. We investigate the role of the initialization process in providing resistance to algebraic attacks aimed at key recovery. The investigation shows that, generally, for the LILI family of stream ciphers, the complexity of recovering key bits using algebraic attacks is much worse than exhaustive key search because of the very high degree equations generated during the initialization process.

Keywords: stream ciphers, algebraic attacks, filter function, clock-control, initialization.

1 Introduction

Courtois and Meier introduced algebraic attacks on stream ciphers [11], in which the keystream is used to solve a system of multivariate polynomial equations related to the stream ciphers' initial states. Many linear feedback shift register (LFSR) based stream ciphers have since fallen to algebraic attacks [3, 8, 1, 26, 9, 10, 17, 6]. In this paper we examine the level of resistance of the LILI family of stream ciphers [23] to algebraic attacks. Two well known instances from this family are LILI-128 [14] and LILI-II [7]. These can be viewed as irregularly clocked nonlinear filter generators. Two recent attacks on LILI-128 have been proposed by Molland [21] and Molland and Helleseth [21]. However, applying either of these attacks to LILI-II will result in an attack complexity that is worse than exhaustive key search.

J. Pieprzyk, H. Ghodosi, and E. Dawson (Eds.): ACISP 2007, LNCS 4586, pp. 11–28, 2007.

Courtois and Meier introduced two algebraic attacks on LILI-128 [11]. To date there are no algebraic attacks reported on LILI-II. In this paper we consider the resistance of these and other ciphers in the LILI family to algebraic attacks. We derive a relationship between parameters that provide resistance to algebraic attacks including the size of the registers, the difference in their lengths, the degree of the Boolean function used and the number of times the controlled register is clocked. In particular, for LILI-II, we show that the filter function is not optimal with respect to algebraic attacks because there exist low degree multiples. This has a substantial impact in reducing the overall attack complexity of algebraic attacks on LILI-II. Although as will be shown this complexity is still much greater than exhaustive key search.

In some communication systems, errors occur which require that the entire message be re-sent. When synchronous stream ciphers such as the LILI family are used, then security requires that a different keystream sequence be used. To achieve this, a re-keying algorithm is needed to combine the secret key with a publicly known initialization vector v to form the initial state for keystream generation. If only a single segment of keystream is known, (no re-keying occurs) then to break a particular instance of the cipher, the cryptanalyst must recover the initial internal state S, using knowledge of the structure of the keystream generator and some amount of the keystream, z. In contrast, with resynchronisation occurring, the cryptanalyst has access to related keystream produced under the same k and for different but known v, typically sequential or differing in only a few bits. The cryptanalyst's task is then to recover k, given a set of (v, z) pairs. For security in this scenario, it is required that the re-keying process does not leak information about the key k. In this paper, we investigate the effect of the initialization process of a cipher on the feasibility of algebraic attacks.

In Section 2, we give a description of the LILI family of stream ciphers and of the specific designs for LILI-128 and LILI-II. In Section 3, a general algebraic analysis of the LILI family is outlined. A more specific algebraic analysis of LILI-II is given in Section 4, and we show that the filter function used in LILI-II is not optimal with regards to providing resistance to algebraic attacks. We present a polynomial multiple which significantly reduces the degree of equations generated. A discussion of the importance of initialization for the LILI family of stream ciphers in providing resistance to algebraic attacks is given in Section 5. Section 6 concludes the paper.

2   Description

The LILI family of stream ciphers are keystream generators that use two binary LFSRs and two non-linear functions to generate pseudorandom binary keystream sequences. The feedback polynomials of both LFSRs are chosen to be primitive polynomials. An all-zero state in either register is not permitted. The structure of LILI keystream generators is illustrated in Figure 1.

The components of the keystream generator can be grouped into two subsystems based on the functions they perform: clock control and data generation.

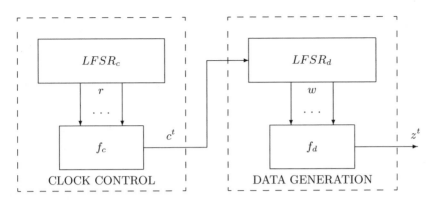

Fig. 1. The LILI Family of Keystream Generators

The l-bit $LFSR_c$ for the clock-control subsystem is regularly clocked. The contents of r stages of $LFSR_c$ are input to a function, f_c. The output of f_c is an integer between 1 and 2^r, inclusive. Denote the sequence of outputs of f_c by $c^t = \{c^t\}_{t=1}^{\infty}$. This is a periodic integer sequence, with period equal to $P_c = 2^l - 1$. The output of the clock-control subsystem controls the clocking of the m-bit $LFSR_d$.

Each time $LFSR_c$ is clocked, $LFSR_d$ is clocked between 1 and 2^r times. The contents of w stages of $LFSR_d$ are input to f_d, a Boolean function of degree d. The binary output of f_d is the keystream bit z^t. At time t, the binary output of f_d is the keystream bit z^t. After z^t is produced the process is repeated to form the sequence $z = \{z^t\}_{t=1}^{\infty}$.

The contents of $LFSR_c$ and $LFSR_d$ at time t are denoted as c_i^t and d_j^t respectively for $1 \leq i \leq l$ and $1 \leq j \leq m$ and $t \geq 1$. The parameters of two specific designs from the LILI family; LILI-128 and LILI-II are shown in Table 1 and described in Sections 2.1 and 2.2 respectively.

Table 1. Parameters for two specific generators from the LILI family

	Length of $LFSR_c$	Period of $LFSR_c$	Length of $LFSR_d$	Period of $LFSR_d$	Algebraic degree of f_d
LILI-128	39 bits	$2^{39} - 1$	89 bits	$2^{89} - 1$	6
LILI-II	128 bits	$2^{128} - 1$	127 bits	$2^{127} - 1$	10

2.1 LILI-128 Keystream Generator

LILI-128 [23] uses registers $LFSR_c$ and $LFSR_d$ of lengths $l = 39$ and $m = 89$ respectively. Thus the internal state size is 128 bits. Keystream generation is performed as follows. At time t, the contents of the $r = 2$ stages 12 and 20 of $LFSR_c$ are used as inputs to the function f_c. The output is calculated by

$f_c(c_{12}^t, c_{20}^t) = 2c_{12}^t + c_{20}^t + 1$. The output is an integer between 1 and 4, inclusive. The $w = 10$ inputs to f_d are taken from the $LFSR_d$ positions (0, 1, 3, 7, 12, 20, 30, 44, 65, 80). We note that the function f_d, given in [23], has an algebraic degree of 6.

LILI-128 is intended for use with a 128-bit key, k, and an initialization vector, v, of up to 128-bits. The re-keying scheme of LILI-128 provided in [13] is as follows. Firstly, use k and v to form an initial internal state value. The initial internal state value is formed by XORing two 128-bit vectors: k and v or a 128-bit vector formed from the concatenation of copies of v, if v is less than 128 bits. Secondly, use the first 39 bits of this sum to form the initial state of $LFSR_c$ and the remaining 89 bits to form the initial state of $LFSR_d$. In [13] the rekeying process is defined with parameters a and b for the number of applications, and the number of lead bits deleted from the outputs, respectively. That is, after the initial loading of the LFSRs, run a applications of the cipher, generating $(128 + b)$ output bits each time, deleting the first b outputs and reloading the LFSRs with the remaining 128 bits. For LILI-128 recommended minimum values are $a = 1$ or $a = 2$ and $b = 32$, but preferably $b = 64$, or $b = 128$. After the rekeying process has been performed the cipher is ready for keystream generation. To align with the initialization process used for LILI-II, we choose $a = 2$ and $b = 0$ to conduct further analysis on the initialization process discussed in Section 5.1.

2.2 LILI-II Keystream Generator

LILI-II [7] uses registers $LFSR_c$ and $LFSR_d$ of lengths $l = 128$ and $m = 127$ respectively. Thus it has an internal state size of 255 bits. Keystream generation is performed as follows. At time t, the contents of the $r = 2$ stages, c_1 and c_{127}, of $LFSR_c$ are used as inputs to the function f_c. The output is calculated by $f_c(c_1^t, c_{127}^t) = 2c_1^t + c_{127}^t + 1$. The output is an integer between 1 and 4, inclusive. The $w = 12$ inputs to f_d are taken from the $LFSR_d$ positions (0, 1, 3, 7, 12, 20, 30, 44, 65, 80, 96, 122). The function selected for f_d and given in [7] has an algebraic degree of 10.

The 255-bit initial state for LILI-II is formed from a 128-bit key k and a 128-bit initialization vector v in a three step process, as follows. Firstly, the 128-bit initial state of $LFSR_c$ is obtained by XORing k and v, and the 127-bit initial state of $LFSR_d$ is obtained by deleting the first bit of k and the last bit of v, and XORing the two resulting 127-bit binary strings. In the second step, the cipher is clocked to produce an output string of length 255 bits. The first 128 bits of this output are used to form a new state for $LFSR_c$, and the remaining 127 bits are used to form a new state for $LFSR_d$. The third step repeats step 2: the cipher is clocked to produce an output string of length 255 bits, of which the first 128 bits are loaded into $LFSR_c$ and the remaining 127 bits are loaded into $LFSR_d$. At this point the generator is ready for the production of keystream.

3   Algebraic Analysis of the LILI Family of Stream Ciphers

Algebraic attacks on stream ciphers involve generating and solving an overdefined system of multivariate polynomial equations relating the stream ciphers' initial state values and known keystream bits. The complexity of an algebraic attack is dominated by the degree of the equations generated, as the lower the degree the more efficient the attack becomes. For LILI keystream generators, the function f_d is central to the generation of equations. Low degree multiples of f_d could be used to reduce the degree of generated equations, and hence the complexity of an algebraic attack. In Section 3.1, we review methods for obtaining low degree multiples of Boolean functions.

There are two existing algebraic attacks on ciphers from the LILI family; both are attacks on LILI-128 [11] and demonstrate time-data tradeoffs. The first attack involves guessing the initial state of $LFSR_c$, then using the known clocking sequence to form equations relating the initial state bits of $LFSR_d$ and the keystream bits and attempting to solve these equations. This attack requires 2^{18} keystream bits and 2^{102} operations. The second attack involves taking a subsequence of keystream bits that are $2^l - 1$ places apart, form equations relating the initial state bits of $LFSR_d$ and these keystream bits and attempting to solve these equations. This attack requires 2^{57} keystream bits and 2^{63} operations. In Sections 3.2 and 3.3 respectively, we review these two attacks on LILI-128, generalizing them to the entire LILI family.

3.1   Finding Low Degree Multiples of f_d

A low degree multiple of an n-input Boolean function f of degree d is obtained by multiplying the Boolean function by a well chosen function such that the product of the two is of degree less than d. For algebraic attacks, finding such low degree multiples reduces the complexity of the attack, possibly to a feasible level. For example, this approach was applied to the Boolean function of the TOYOCRYPT-HS1 [25] stream cipher in [11]. The original TOYOCRYPT output function was of degree 64, but a suitable multiple was found to give a product with degree 3. Note that on average using a low degree multiple in an algebraic attack doubles the keystream required to solve the generated system of equations, as we multiply by a function that could have an output value of either zero or one. This method was applied to f_d of LILI-128 in [11], reducing the degree of the output function from 6 to 4.

In [19], Meier et. al. proposed two algorithms for finding low degree multiples of Boolean functions, both with complexity $O(M^3)$ where $M = \sum_{i=1}^{d} \binom{n}{i}$ is the number of monomials. They also introduce the term algebraic immunity (AI), as a measure of resistance of a function to this approach. A Boolean function g is described as an annihilator of a Boolean function f if g is a nonzero function and the product $fg = 0$ for all inputs. The algebraic immunity of a function f is the minimum degree of all the nonzero annihilators of f and $1 + f$. More efficient algorithms for finding low degree multiples of Boolean functions are given in [4, 27] and [16], which reduce the complexity of finding low degree multiples to $O(M^2), O(n2^n M)$ and $n(n + 1)$ steps, respectively.

For cryptanalytic purposes, finding low degree multiples of output functions for keystream generators is performed in precomputation. The low degree multiple may then be used in an algebraic attack. Note that for high degree Boolean functions with a large number of inputs, the complexity of finding these low degree multiples may exceed that of performing an exhaustive key search, but as this occurs in a precomputation phase, it is a one-off cost which can then be used for multiple key recovery attacks.

3.2   Attack 1 : Guessing the Controlling Register

In the first algebraic attack on LILI-128, the initial internal state of register $LFSR_c$ is guessed, revealing the clocking pattern of $LFSR_d$. For each guess, a system of equations is constructed relating the unknown initial state bits from $LFSR_d$ and the keystream bits. After substituting the keystream bits, an attempt to solve the system of equations is made. If the system of equations is inconsistent then the original guessed $LFSR_c$ state is wrong. Otherwise, the recovered initial state bits can be used to generate a candidate keystream. If this agrees with the observed keystream then the guess is correct.

For other LILI generators, the output function f_d may be of higher degree, potentially providing greater resistance to algebraic attacks. In this case, in a precomputation phase, the lowest degree multiples g of f can be determined, as discussed in Section 3.1. The attack algorithm as shown in Figure 2 is then applied.

As this approach requires guessing the internal state bits of $LFSR_c$, which has a complexity of $2^l - 1$. For each guess, one system of equations needs to be solved, or attempted. This system has $\left[\sum_{i=1}^{d} \binom{m}{d}\right]$ equations. The computational complexity for solving the system of equations in step 1c using Strassen's algorithm [24] is given by M^ω, with $2.807 \leq \omega \leq 3$. In order for this attack to be applied to other members of the LILI family with complexity less than exhaustive key search, the parameters must satisfy the following equation:

$$2^l - 1 \left[\sum_{i=1}^{d} \binom{m}{d}\right]^\omega < (2^k - 1) \tag{1}$$

3.3   Attack 2 : Keystream Decimation

In the second algebraic attack, the attacker targets $LFSR_d$ and avoids guessing the clock control components by taking a regular decimation of the keystream. Let Δ_d denotes the number of times $LFSR_d$ is advanced for one period of $LFSR_c$. It was shown in [14] that

$$\Delta_d = (2^{l-r} - 1) + \sum_{s=2}^{2^r} s \times 2^{l-r} \tag{2}$$

Inputs : Feedback polynomials of $LFSR_c$ and $LFSR_d$; $\sum_{i=1}^{d} \binom{m}{i}$ segments of keystream.
Outputs: Internal state bits of $LFSR_c$ and $LFSR_d$.

1. Guess value for $LFSR_c$.
2. Generate $\sum_{i=1}^{d} \binom{m}{i}$ output bits from $LFSR_c$.
3. Use the output from Step 2 to produce the clocking sequence for $LFSR_d$.
4. Applying this clocking sequence, generate $\sum_{i=1}^{d} \binom{m}{i}$ equations from $LFSR_d$.
5. Substitute the known keystream bits in the appropriate positions in the equations.
6. Solve the system of equations of $LFSR_d$.
7. Use the recovered internal state bits of $LFSR_d$ and guessed bits of $LFSR_c$ to produce a candidate keystream.
8. If candidate keystream matches known keystream go to 9. Otherwise go to 1.
9. Output initial state values for $LFSR_c$ and $LFSR_d$. Terminate.

Fig. 2. Algorithm for algebraic attack based on guessing the controlling register

The attack is performed in two phases: precomputation and a realtime phase. In the precomputation phase, the lowest degree multiple of f_d is computed as discussed in Section 3.1. In addition, $\sum_{i=1}^{d} \binom{m}{i}$ equations are obtained from $LFSR_d$ every Δ_d cycles. In [22], Saarinen suggests stepping $LFSR_d$ Δ_d number of positions using either a vector-matrix multiplication with a precomputed $m \times m$ bit matrix over $GF(2)$, or by using a multiplication algorithm in $GF(2^m)$. In the realtime phase the known keystream bits are substituted into the equations and an attempt to solve the system of equations is made. The steps of the precomputation and realtime phases of this approach are shown in the following algorithm (Figure 3).

For this attack, we need to select keystream bits that are $(2^l - 1)$ apart. Assume that we have found n independent low-degree multiples of f_d. We form $\sum_{i=1}^{d} \binom{m}{d}$ equations relating the initial internal state values for $LFSR_d$ and the known keystream bits, and attempt to solve them. Let T denote the number of keystream bits required for the attack to be successful. Therefore, the total amount of keystream required for a successful attack is

$$T = \left[(2^l - 1) \sum_{i=1}^{d} \binom{m}{d} \right] / n \tag{3}$$

The number of equations that can be generated from $LFSR_d$ can be computed as follows. For each period of $LFSR_c$, use one output or equation formed from $LFSR_d$. In terms of only the initial state bits of $LFSR_d$, the maximum number

Precomputation phase	Realtime phase
Inputs: Feedback polynomial of $LFSR_d$, ANF of f_d. **Outputs**: g, $f_d g = h$ and $\sum_{i=1}^{d} \binom{m}{i}$ equations from $LFSR_d$. 1. Compute the lowest degree multiple of f according to [4]. 2. Compute Δ_d using equation (2). 3. Form $\sum_{i=1}^{d} \binom{m}{i}$ equations by clocking $LFSR_d$ Δ_d cycles at one time. 4. Terminate.	**Inputs**: $\sum_{i=1}^{d} \binom{m}{i}$ Precomputed equations; $\sum_{i=1}^{d} \binom{m}{i}$ bits of keystream **Outputs**: $LFSR_c$ and $LFSR_d$ 1. Substitute known keystream bits into precomputed equations. 2. Solve the resulting system of equations to recover the initial internal state of $LFSR_d$. 3. Use the newly obtained bits of $LFSR_d$ to recover the internal state of $LFSR_c$. 4. Output the initial state values for $LFSR_c$ and $LFSR_d$. 5. Terminate.

Fig. 3. Algorithm for precomputation and realtime phases of the algebraic attack based on keystream decimation

of distinct equations that can be obtained is $2^m - 1$, but this would require an entire period of keystream. The total number of equations E is given by

$$E = (2^m - 1)/gcd((\Delta_d, 2^m - 1)) \qquad (4)$$

The number of equations that can be generated from $LFSR_d$ must be greater or equal to the number of keystream bits required to run the attack.

$$E \geq (2^l - 1) \sum_{i=1}^{d} \binom{m}{d}/n \qquad (5)$$

After recovering the internal state of $LFSR_d$, the cryptanalyst must recover the internal state of $LFSR_c$ to complete the attack, increasing the overall attack complexity. A worst case scenario involves a brute force attack to recover the initial internal state of $LFSR_c$. Alternative methods such as using correlation or embedding attacks could be considered. Depending on the LFSR length and the method used, the complexity of recovering $LFSR_c$ may be less than $2^l - 1$. For the rest of this paper, we denote the complexity of recovering $LFSR_c$ by C_{LFSRc}.

Compared to the attack outlined in Section 3.2, the computational complexity of this attack is lower, but it requires a greater number of keystream bits. The above analysis shows that the resistance of the LILI family of stream ciphers to both of these algebraic attacks depends on the number of times register $LFSR_d$ is clocked, Δ_d, the degree d of the filter function f_d, and the lengths, l and m, of the two registers.

3.4   Fast Algebraic Attacks

Both of the attacks outlined in Sections 3.2 and 3.3 have a common last step, involving solving a system of equations. Fast algebraic attacks [10] aim to reduce the degree of the equations generated in the precomputation phase by linearly combining some specific equations. This has a significant effect in reducing the overall complexity of the attacks. Two algorithms have been proposed for this; one for regularly clocked nonlinear filter generators which utilizes the well known Berlekamp-Massey algorithm [10] and another for combining function generators [2] which makes use of the theory of linear recurring sequences. A modified Berlekamp-Massey algorithm given in [10] is claimed to be best suited for the LILI family of keystream generators.

As with regular algebraic attacks, fast algebraic attacks are performed in two phases: precomputation and a realtime phase. More specifically, in the precomputation phase, an attacker searches for a multiplier g to form a low degree multiple h of f (that is, $fg = h$) with f of degree d and g and h of degree e and d_h respectively where $e, d_h < d$. Using this g, low degree equations in terms of the internal state bits are generated. Then the attacker uses the modified Berlekamp-Massey algorithm to form equations in which all monomials of degree d or higher are eliminated. The number of consecutive keystream bits required in order to find such relations is estimated to be about $T_d + T_e$ where $T_d = \sum_{i=1}^{d_h} \binom{m}{i}$ and $T_e = \sum_{i=1}^{e} \binom{m}{i}$ The complexity of applying the modified Berlekamp-Massey algorithm to find the outputs to be linearly combined is $T_d \cdot log_2^2 T_d$. and the amount of memory required is T_e^2. In the realtime phase, two main steps are involved; the substitution of the keystream bits into the system of equations and solving the system of equations. During the substitution step, monomials of degree higher than e are eliminated. In [18] Hawkes and Rose point out that the original papers on fast algebraic attacks underestimated the complexity of the substitution step and claimed that the best complexity for the substitution step is $2 \cdot T_e \cdot T_d \cdot \log_2 T_d$. The complexity of recovering the internal state is further reduced to the complexity of solving system of equations in T_e only. We apply the analysis presented in this section to evaluate the resistance of LILI-II to these fast algebraic attacks in Sections 4.3.

4 Algebraic Analysis of the LILI-II Stream Cipher

In this section, we first present an algebraic representation of the LILI family of stream ciphers, then compute a low degree multiplier g of f_d and consider using this multiplier in applying the attacks outlined in Section 3 to LILI-II.

4.1 Algebraic Representation for the LILI Family of Stream Ciphers

The relationship between the internal state and the output of the LILI ciphers can be obtained by incorporating the clock control outputs from $LFSR_c$ as variables into $LFSR_d$. Given f_c relations between the two controlling bits c_1^t, c_2^t, the number of times register $LFSR_d$ is clocked and the initial state of $LFSR_d$ can be represented in an algebraic expression as follows:

$$d_i^{t+1} = (c_1^t + 1)(c_2^t + 1)d_{i-1}^t + (c_1^t + 1)c_2^t d_{i-2}^t + c_1^t(c_2^t + 1)d_{i-3}^t + c_1^t c_2^t d_{i-4}^t \quad (6)$$

where d_i^t is the ith stage of $LFSR_d$ at time t. Specifically, the stages c_1^t and c_2^t are c_{12} and c_{20}, respectively, for LILI-128 and c_1 and c_{127}, respectively, for LILI-II.

Equation (6) shows that the degree of the equations in $LFSR_d$ increases by two each time $LFSR_c$ is clocked.

4.2   Algebraic Attacks on LILI-II

The filter function f_d is important in providing resistance to algebraic attacks. The algebraic normal form (ANF) of f_d is computed and presented in appendix A. By inspection of the ANF of f_d, we found a multiplier g of degree $e = 2$, where $g = (x_{11} + 1)(x_7 + 1)$. This results in a product h of degree 4 as shown below.

$$
\begin{aligned}
g \cdot f_d = (x_{11} + 1)(x_7 + 1)f_d = {}& x_2x_4x_7x_{11} + x_3x_7x_8x_{11} + x_1x_7x_9x_{11} + x_7x_{10}x_{11}x_{12} \\
& + x_2x_4x_7 + x_3x_7x_8 + x_1x_7x_9 + x_2x_4x_{11} + x_1x_7x_{11} + x_2x_7x_{11} \\
& + x_3x_7x_{11} + x_4x_7x_{11} + x_5x_7x_{11} + x_6x_7x_{11} + x_3x_8x_{11} + x_7x_8x_{11} \\
& + x_1x_9x_{11} + x_7x_9x_{11} + x_7x_{10}x_{11} + x_7x_{10}x_{12} \\
& + x_{10}x_{11}x_{12} + x_2x_4 + x_1x_7 + x_2x_7 + x_3x_7 + x_4x_7 + x_5x_7 + x_6x_7 \\
& + x_3x_8 + x_7x_8 + x_1x_9 + x_7x_9 + x_7x_{10} + x_1x_{11} + x_2x_{11} + x_3x_{11} \\
& + x_4x_{11} + x_5x_{11} + x_6x_{11} + x_7x_{11} + x_8x_{11} + x_9x_{11} + x_{10}x_{11} + x_{10}x_{12} \\
& + x_1 + x_2 + x_3 + x_4 + x_5 + x_6 + x_7 + x_8 + x_9 + x_{10} + x_{11} + 1
\end{aligned}
\tag{7}
$$

Further examination of f_d using the algorithm outlined in [11] confirmed the multiplier $g = (x_{11} + 1)(x_7 + 1)$ was one of thirty-two degree 2 multipliers that exist for f_d, and the only one of these multipliers that resulted in h of degree 4. Our implementation of the algorithm found the degree 2 multipliers in 82 seconds using Magma 2.11 on the SGI Origin 3000 using CPU at 600 MHz. This demonstrates that f_d of LILI-II has an algebraic immunity of at most 4. In our attack we make use of this by multiplying the initial set of equations by $(x_{11} + 1)(x_7 + 1)$. Note that this implies that z^t is also multiplied by g, so only gives a useful equation when z^t is equal to 1.

Standard Algebraic Attacks of Section 3.2. If we consider applying the attack described in Section 3.2 using the original function f_d of degree 10, then we need to solve equations involving $M = \sum_{i=1}^{10} \binom{127}{i} = 2^{47.7}$ unknowns with a solution complexity of $2^{143.1}$ for $\omega = 3$. From equation (1), this gives a total attack complexity of $2^{128} \cdot 2^{143} = 2^{271}$. However using g of degree 2 to form h of degree 4, rather than f_d of degree 10, reduces the degree of equations generated. This in turn reduces the number of monomials to $2^{23.3}$, and correspondingly the attack complexity to 2^{198}. This is a significant reduction in the complexity of the algebraic attack on LILI-II, and is better than exhaustive search of the initial 255-bit internal state, but is still much worse than exhaustive search on the 128-bit key.

Standard Algebraic Attacks of Section 3.3. Similarly, applying the attack of Section 3.3 using $d = 10$, requires $\Delta_d = 2^{129}$. The complexity of recovering $LFSR_d$ by solving $2^{47.8}$ equations using the linearization approach is 2^{143} with a keystream requirement of $T = 2^{128} \cdot 2^{47.8} = 2^{175.8}$. Since only $E = 2^{127} - 1$

equations can be generated from $LFSR_d$, the amount of keystream required to run the attack is clearly more than the number of independent equations that can be generated. Further, the complexity of recovering the internal state of $LFSR_c$ must be added.

Using the multiplier g to obtain equations of degree 4 reduces the complexity of recovering the initial state of $LFSR_d$ to 2^{70}. Adding the complexity of recovering $LFSR_c$ gives a total attack complexity of $2^{70} + C_{LFSRc}$. There is also the keystream requirement of $(2^{128})(2^{23}) = 2^{151}$ bits, again more than the number of independent equations that can be generated from $LFSR_d$. Therefore, the attack of Section 3.3 cannot be applied successfully to LILI-II for either the case where f_d of degree 10 is used or a reduced gf_d of degree $d = 4$ is used.

Although neither attack is better than exhaustive key search, reducing the degree from 10 to 4 significantly reduces the complexity of an algebraic attack for recovering $LFSR_d$. Table 2 below summarises the requirements for applying the algebraic attacks of Sections 3.2 and 3.3 to both LILI-128 and LILI-II, with the original function f_d of degree 10, and reduced gf_d of degree $d = 4$ respectively.

Table 2. Summary of the algebraic attacks of Sections 3.2 and 3.3 on both LILI-128 and LILI-II

LILI-family	Complexity of attack of Section 3.2		Complexity of attack of Section 3.3		
	Keystream	Operations	Keystream	Max equations	Operations
LILI-128, d=4	2^{18}	2^{102}	2^{57}	$2^{89} - 1$	2^{63}
LILI-II, d=10	2^{48}	2^{271}	2^{176}	$2^{127} - 1$	$2^{143} + C_{LFSRc}$
LILI-II, d=4	2^{23}	2^{198}	2^{151}	$2^{127} - 1$	$2^{70} + C_{LFSRc}$

4.3   Fast Algebraic Attacks on LILI-II

In Section 3.4 it is noted that fast algebraic attacks can be applied to significantly reduce the complexity of solving equations in the realtime phase of the attacks described in Sections 3.2 and 3.3. Table 3 summarises the data obtained when the fast algebraic attack approach is applied in each of these two cases.

The table illustrates the tradeoffs between keystream requirements and attack complexity, and also the significant reduction in the complexity of recovering the internal states for both ciphers when using $e = 2$. However, it can also be seen that with fast algebraic attacks that the complexity of substituting the keystream

Table 3. Attack of Section 3.3 using fast algebraic attacks on both LILI-128 and LILI-II

Attack of	LILI-family	d	e	Keystream	Memory	Precomputation	Substitution	Attack ops
Section 3.2	LILI-128	4	2	2^{21} bits	2^{14} bits	2^{30}	$2^{38.6}$	$2^{39} \cdot 2^{38.6} = 2^{77.6}$
	LILI-II	4	2	$2^{23.3}$	2^{26} bits	$2^{32.4}$	$2^{41.8}$	$2^{41.8} \cdot 2^{127} = 2^{168.8}$
Section 3.3	LILI-128	4	2	2^{60}	2^{14} bits	2^{30}	$2^{38.6}$	2^{30}
	LILI-II	4	2	$2^{151.3}$	2^{26} bits	$2^{32.4}$	$2^{41.8}$	$2^{41.8} + C_{LFSRc}$

bits into the system of equations is higher than the complexity of solving the equations, and that the keystream requirement for the attack of Section 3.3 cannot be met. Although the attack of Section 3.2 requires less keystream bits, its complexity is still more than the exhaustive key search.

5   Initialization and Algebraic Attacks

Most recently proposed stream ciphers use an internal state that is at least twice as large as the key size to provide resistance to attacks such as time/memory/ tradeoff attacks. An initialization process expands the k bit key to fill the internal state, possibly also incorporating initialisation vectors. This is the case for the LILI ciphers. Most algebraic attacks, including those on LILI-128, aim to recover the internal state of the cipher. In this section we consider two aspects of the effect of the initialization process, as outlined in Section 2, on algebraic attacks on the LILI ciphers. Firstly, we examine whether it is possible to recover key bits directly in an algebraic attack, rather than state bits. Secondly, we investigate the possibility that an attacker, having recovered internal state bits through a standard algebraic attack, can extend the attack to key recovery.

5.1   Direct Recovery of Key Bits

If the variables represent the key bits rather than state bits for ciphers with a relatively large internal state size then there are fewer variables to consider. However, generating equations where the variables are the unknown key bits requires consideration of the initialization process. From equation (6) in Section 4.1, it is clear that if the variables are key bit values, rather than the internal state values, the generated system of equations contains k variables with maximum degree of k, and the maximum number of monomials is given by $\sum_{i=1}^{k} \binom{k}{i}$. In contrast, if the variables are the initial internal state values, rather than the key bit values, then the generated system of equations contains $l + m$ variables with maximum degree of $l + d$, where d is the degree of f_d, and the maximum number of monomials formed is equal to $M = \sum_{i=1}^{l+d} \binom{l+m}{i}$.

After initialization, the contents of both registers are high degree functions of all key bits. To recover the key bits of LILI ciphers using the approach outlined in Section 3.2 requires guessing the initial contents of $LFSR_c$. This provides one set of equations. Now the clocking of $LFSR_d$ is known. The attacker then forms another set of equations relating the known keystream values to the filtered outputs of $LFSR_d$. However, each stage of $LFSR_d$ contains a high degree function of key bit variables. To use this approach, the attacker needs to know what these high degree functions are, and also to have the ability to solve them. Therefore, the complexity of this approach is $2^l \cdot \left[\sum_{i=1}^{d} \binom{k}{i} \right]^{\omega}$, for $\frac{k}{2} \le d < k$.

For example, consider applying this to LILI-128 with 128-bit key and initialization vectors, and initialization parameters given by $a = 2$ and $b = 0$. Assume that the degree of the key bit expressions in each stage of the registers after initialization is $64 \le d \le 128$ and $\omega = 3$. Applying the algebraic attack of Section 3.2 requires guessing 39 bits of $LFSR_c$ multiplied with the complexity of solving a system of equations generated using f_d. Note that the equations are a function of all the key bits, therefore there are 128 unknowns in the generated system of equations. The overall attack complexity will be between $2^{39} \left[\sum_{i=1}^{64} \binom{128}{64} \right]^3 \approx 2^{495}$ and $2^{39} \left[\sum_{i=1}^{128} \binom{128}{i} \right]^3 \approx 2^{578.5}$. This exceeds the complexity of exhaustive key search. Similarly, using this approach on LILI-II requires a 128 bit guess of $LFSR_c$, so will also be worse than exhaustive key search. The overall attack complexity will be between $2^{128} \left[\sum_{i=1}^{64} \binom{128}{i} \right]^3 \approx 2^{584}$ and $2^{667.5}$.

Alternatively, we consider the approach outlined in Section 3.3. This requires decimation of the keystream by Δ_d, with a corresponding increase in the degree of the underlying key bit equations. The equations generated from $LFSR_d$ will be of a very high degree, probably the maximum degree. It appears infeasible to generate these high degree equations, let alone solve them. However, assuming this is possible, the overall attack complexity of this approach is $\left[\sum_{i=1}^{d} \binom{k}{i} \right]^\omega$, for $\frac{k}{2} \le d < k$.

For example, consider applying this to LILI-128. The complexity of solving these equations is between $\left[\sum_{i=1}^{64} \binom{128}{i} \right]^3 \approx 2^{456}$ and $\left[\sum_{i=1}^{128} \binom{128}{i} \right]^3 \approx 2^{539.5}$. The same attack complexity will also be applicable to LILI-II when using this approach for recovering the internal state of $LFSR_d$, however, the amount of keystream will be much greater in the case of LILI-II.

Table 4 summarizes the complexity of applying the attacks outlined in Sections 3.3 and 3.2 to LILI-128 and LILI-II after going through the initialization phase. Note that the degree of the filter function f_d used has a minimal effect in increasing the degree of the generated equations, as at the end of initialization, the contents of the stages of each register are high degree equations.

5.2   Recovering the Key Bits Given the Internal State Bits

Consider the initialization processes used in LILI-128 and LILI-II. To align the initialization process for LILI-128 with that used for LILI-II, we choose the parameters $a = 2$ and $b = 0$. Denote the first $l + m$ output bits generated during initialization by $(z_1'' \ldots, z_{l+m}'')$. Each z'' is a high degree function of the key bits. These $(z_1'' \ldots, z_{l+m}'')$ bits are loaded into the cipher registers and the process is repeated to generate another $(l + m)$ bits denoted as $(z_1' \ldots, z_{l+m}')$. This is reloaded and used to generate the keystream bits denoted $\{z^t\}_{t=1}^{\infty}$.

Assume that we have T known keystream bits $(z_1, \ldots z_T)$ and have successfully performed an algebraic attack to recover the initial internal state $(z_1' \ldots, z_{l+m}')$. In order to recover the key bits $(k_1, \ldots, k_{128})$, we need to use $(z_1' \ldots, z_{l+m}')$ as keystream and apply an algebraic attack to recover $(z_1'' \ldots, z_{l+m}'')$. Given this internal state, we can produce the entire keystream sequence for this (k, v_i) pair, but when a new initialization vector is used we will have to repeat the entire attack to generate that keystream. The keystream requirement is approximately

$\sum_{i=1}^{l+m} \binom{l+m}{d}$ bits using the linearization approach. But in this case, there are only $(l+m)$ outputs, which is much less than the needed data. The difficulty of recovering the key bits from the internal state bits is further increased if some output bits are discarded during the initialization.

For example consider applying this to key recovery on LILI-128. Suppose that we have recovered $(z_1' \ldots, z_{128}')$. This attack [11] requires approximately 2^{18} bits. For key recovery, we now need to repeat this attack using $(z_1' \ldots, z_{128}')$ as the keystream bits. But there are only 128 outputs, which is much less than required. Obviously, there is no way to proceed to recover the key bits. Similarly, key recovery cannot be performed on LILI-II as only 255 bits $(z_1' \ldots, z_{255}')$ of keystream are available to recover $(z_1'' \ldots, z_{255}'')$, which is much less than the required keystream bits.

It is evident that the initialization process used in LILI-128 and LILI-II prevents the direct recovery of the key bits using algebraic attacks, and it prevents the recovery of the key bits even if the state bits can be recovered. An interesting exercise is to investigate partial key guessing. That is guessing u-bits of the k-bit secret key. For a carefully selected subset of key bits, this might reduce the degree of the equations generated during initialization so that algebraic attacks may be successfully applied to the reduced system.

Table 4. Summary of requirements for the algebraic attacks of Sections 3.2 and 3.3

LILI-family	Complexity of attack of Section 3.2		Complexity of attack of Section 3.3	
	Keystream	Operations	Keystream	Operations
LILI-128	2^{152} to 2^{179}	2^{495} to $2^{578.5}$	2^{191} to $2^{218.8}$	2^{456} to $2^{539.5}$
LILI-II	2^{152} to 2^{179}	2^{584} to $2^{667.5}$	2^{280} to 2^{307}	2^{456} to $2^{539.5}$

Note that for LILI-128, the key size is equal the internal state size. This is a vulnerability that can be exploited if the initialization process is weak. For example, if the initialization parameters for LILI-128 include $a = 0$, then given the internal state bits at any time t, the cipher can be wound back b clocks to reveal the internal state at the start of initialization. As this is simply the XOR of k and v, and v is known, then k is revealed. Hence the security of LILI-128 against key recovery by known algebraic attacks depends on the choice of a nonzero value for the parameter a.

6 Conclusion

In this paper, we analysed the security of the LILI family of stream ciphers against both standard and fast algebraic attacks. Our analysis provides an increased understanding of algebraic attacks on this type of cipher. It was shown that the size of the two registers used, the difference between their lengths, the maximum number of times a register is clocked and the degree of the filter function all contribute in providing resistance to algebraic attacks. For LILI-128, the internal state bits can be recovered with complexity less than exhaustive keysearch. For LILI-II, a low degree multiplier of the filter function is given, implying the algebraic immunity of the filter function is at most 4. This dramatically reduces the complexity of algebraic attacks, including fast algebraic attacks. However, even the reduced complexity exceeds exhaustive key search.

This paper also examines the role of initialization in reducing the effectiveness of algebraic attacks for key recovery. This is important for applications where rekeying is performed. It was shown that, even assuming a successful algebraic attack has been performed, revealing the internal state for the LILI ciphers, the complexity of recovering the secret key remains worse than exhaustive key search. It appears that the initialization process provides the LILI ciphers with resistance against key recovery attacks.

Acknowledgments. The authors wish to express their appreciation to both Kenneth Wong for implementing the algorithm used in finding the low degree multiple of LILI-II and to the High Performance Computing and Research Support at Queensland University of Technology for providing us with access to their facility.

References

1. Alhinai, S., Batten, L., Colbert, B., Wong, K.: Algebraic attacks on clock controlled stream ciphers. In: Batten, L.M., Safavi-Naini, R. (eds.) ACISP 2006. LNCS, vol. 4058, pp. 1–16. Springer, Heidelberg (2006)
2. Armknecht, F.: Improving fast algebraic attacks. In: Roy, B., Meier, W. (eds.) FSE 2004. LNCS, vol. 3017, pp. 65–82. Springer, Heidelberg (2004)
3. Armknecht, F., Krause, M.: Algebraic attacks on combiners with memory. In: Boneh, D. (ed.) CRYPTO 2003. LNCS, vol. 2729, pp. 162–175. Springer, Heidelberg (2003)
4. Armknecht, F., Carlet, C., Gaborit, P., Kunzli, S., Meier, W., Ruatta, O.: Efficient Computation of Algebraic Immunity for Algebraic and Fast Algebraic Attacks. In: Vaudenay, S. (ed.) EUROCRYPT 2006. LNCS, vol. 4004, pp. 147–164. Springer, Heidelberg (2006)
5. Batten, L., Canteaut, A., Viswanathan, K.: INDOCRYPT 2004. LNCS, vol. 3348, pp. 84–91. Springer, Heidelberg (2004)
6. Berger, T., Minier, M.: Two Algebraic Attacks Against the F-FCSRs Using the IV Mode. In: Maitra, S., Madhavan, C.E.V., Venkatesan, R. (eds.) INDOCRYPT 2005. LNCS, vol. 3797, pp. 143–154. Springer, Heidelberg (2005)
7. Clark, A., Ed Dawson, J., Fuller, J., Golić, J., Lee, H-J., Millan, W., Moon, S-J., Simpson, L.: LILI-II Keystream Generator. In: ACISP 2002. LNCS, vol. 2384, pp. 25–39. Springer, Heidelberg (2002)
8. Cho, J., Pieprzyk, J.: Algebraic attacks on SOBER-t32 and SOBER-t16 without stuttering. In: Roy, B., Meier, W. (eds.) FSE 2004. LNCS, vol. 3017, pp. 49–64. Springer, Heidelberg (2004)
9. Courtois, N.: Cryptanalysis of Sfinks. In: Won, D.H., Kim, S. (eds.) ICISC 2005. LNCS, vol. 3935, pp. 261–269. Springer, Heidelberg (2006)
10. Courtois, N.: Fast algebraic attacks on stream ciphers with linear feedback. In: Boneh, D. (ed.) CRYPTO 2003. LNCS, vol. 2729, pp. 176–194. Springer, Heidelberg (2003)

11. Courtois, N., Meier, W.: Algebraic attacks on stream ciphers with linear feedback. In: Biham, E. (ed.) Advances in Cryptology – EUROCRPYT 2003. LNCS, vol. 2656, pp. 346–359. Springer, Heidelberg (2003)
12. Courtois, N., Pieprzyk, J.: Cryptanalysis of block ciphers with overdefined systems of equations. In: Zheng, Y. (ed.) ASIACRYPT 2002. LNCS, vol. 2501, pp. 267–287. Springer, Heidelberg (2002)
13. Dawson, E., Golić, J., Millan, W., Simpson, L.: Response to Initial Report on LILI-128.NESSIE submission, available at http://www.cryptonessie.org
14. Dawson, E., Clark, A., Golić, J., Millan, W., Penna, L., Simpson, L.: The LILI-128 keystream generator.NESSIE submission. In: The proceedings of the First Open NESSIE Workshop (Leuven, November 2000), available at http://www.cryptonessie.org
15. Dalai, D., Gupta, K., Maitra, S.: Results on Algebraic Immunity for Cryptographically Significant Boolean Functions. In: Canteaut, A., Viswanathan, K. (eds.) INDOCRYPT 2004. LNCS, vol. 3348, pp. 92–106. Springer, Heidelberg (2004)
16. Didier, F.: Using Wiedemanna Algorithm to Compute the Immunity Against Algebraic and Fast Algebraic Attacks. In: Barua, R., Lange, T. (eds.) INDOCRYPT 2006. LNCS, vol. 4329, pp. 236–250. Springer, Heidelberg (2006)
17. Lee, D., Kim, J., Hong, J., Han, J., Moon, D.: Algebraic Attacks on Summation Generators. In: Roy, B., Meier, W. (eds.) FSE 2004. LNCS, vol. 3017, pp. 34–48. Springer, Heidelberg (2004)
18. Hawkes, P., Rose, G.: Rewriting Variables: The Complexity of Fast Algebraic Attacks on Stream Ciphers. In: Franklin, M. (ed.) CRYPTO 2004. LNCS, vol. 3152, pp. 390–406. Springer, Heidelberg (2004)
19. Meier, W., Pasalic, E., Carlet, C.: Algebraic attacks and decomposition of Boolean functions. In: Cachin, C., Camenisch, J.L. (eds.) EUROCRYPT 2004. LNCS, vol. 3027, pp. 474–491. Springer, Heidelberg (2004)
20. Molland, H., Helleseth, T.: An Improved Correlation Attack Against Irregular Clocked and Filtered Keystream Generators. In: Franklin, M. (ed.) CRYPTO 2004. LNCS, vol. 3152, pp. 373–389. Springer, Heidelberg (2004)
21. Molland, H.: Improved linear consistency attack on irregular clocked keystream generators. In: Roy, B., Meier, W. (eds.) FSE 2004. LNCS, vol. 3017, pp. 109–126. Springer, Heidelberg (2004)
22. Saarinen, M.: A Time-Memory Tradeoff Attack Against LILI-128. In: Daemen, J., Rijmen, V. (eds.) FSE 2002. LNCS, vol. 2365, pp. 231–236. Springer, Heidelberg (2002)
23. Simpson, L., Dawson, E., Golić, J., Millan, W.: LILI Keystream Generator. In: Stinson, D.R., Tavares, S. (eds.) SAC 2000. LNCS, vol. 2012, pp. 248–261. Springer, Heidelberg (2001)
24. Strassen, V.: Gaussian Elimination is Not Optimal. Numerische Mathematik 13, 354–356 (1969)
25. Sugimoto, K., Chikaraishi, T., Morizumi, T.: Design criteria and security evaluations on certain stream ciphers. IEICE Technical Report, ISEC2000-69 (September 2000)
26. Wong, K., Colbert, B., Batten, L., Alhinai, S.: Algebraic attacks on clock controlled cascade ciphers. In: Barua, R., Lange, T. (eds.) INDOCRYPT 2006. LNCS, vol. 4329, pp. 32–47. Springer, Heidelberg (2006)
27. Zhang, X., Pieprzyk, J., Zheng, Y.: On Algebraic Immunity and Annihilators. In: Rhee, M.S., Lee, B. (eds.) ICISC 2006. LNCS, vol. 4296, pp. 65–80. Springer, Heidelberg (2006)

A   Algebraic Normal Form of LILI-II Boolean Function

$$f_d(x_1, x_2, \ldots, x_{12}) = x_1 + x_2 + x_3 + x_4 + x_5 + x_6 + x_7 + x_8 + x_9 + x_{10} + x_{11} + x_1 x_9 + x_2 x_4 +$$
$$x_3 x_8 + x_5 x_{11} + x_6 x_7 + x_7 x_{10} + x_7 x_{11} + x_7 x_{12} + x_{10} x_{12} + x_2 x_7 x_{11} + x_2 x_7 x_{12} + x_4 x_7 x_{11} +$$
$$x_4 x_7 x_{12} + x_7 x_{10} x_{11} + x_7 x_{11} x_{12} + x_1 x_2 x_7 x_{11} + x_1 x_2 x_7 x_{12} + x_1 x_3 x_7 x_{11} + x_2 x_7 x_9 x_{11} +$$
$$x_2 x_7 x_9 x_{12} + x_2 x_7 x_{11} x_{12} + x_3 x_4 x_7 x_{11} + x_3 x_7 x_9 x_{11} + x_4 x_7 x_{11} x_{12} + x_7 x_9 x_{11} x_{12} + x_1 x_2 x_3 x_7 x_9 +$$
$$x_1 x_2 x_7 x_{11} x_{12} + x_1 x_3 x_7 x_{11} x_{12} + x_1 x_7 x_9 x_{11} x_{12} + x_2 x_3 x_4 x_7 x_9 + x_2 x_3 x_5 x_7 x_9 + x_2 x_3 x_6 x_7 x_{11} +$$
$$x_2 x_3 x_7 x_8 x_9 + x_2 x_3 x_7 x_9 x_{10} + x_2 x_3 x_7 x_9 x_{11} + x_2 x_3 x_7 x_9 x_{12} + x_2 x_3 x_7 x_{11} x_{12} + x_2 x_3 x_9 x_{11} x_{12} +$$
$$x_2 x_7 x_8 x_9 x_{11} + x_2 x_7 x_8 x_9 x_{12} + x_2 x_7 x_9 x_{10} x_{11} + x_2 x_7 x_9 x_{11} x_{12} + x_3 x_5 x_7 x_{11} x_{12} + x_3 x_7 x_8 x_9 x_{11} +$$
$$x_3 x_7 x_8 x_{11} x_{12} + x_3 x_7 x_9 x_{10} x_{11} + x_4 x_7 x_9 x_{11} x_{12} + x_7 x_8 x_9 x_{11} x_{12} + x_7 x_9 x_{10} x_{11} x_{12} + x_2 x_3 x_4 x_9 x_{11} x_{12} +$$
$$x_2 x_3 x_6 x_7 x_9 x_{11} + x_3 x_4 x_7 x_8 x_9 x_{11} + x_3 x_6 x_7 x_8 x_9 x_{11} + x_2 x_3 x_7 x_{10} x_{11} x_{12} + x_3 x_7 x_9 x_{10} x_{11} x_{12} +$$
$$x_3 x_5 x_7 x_8 x_9 x_{11} + x_1 x_2 x_3 x_7 x_{10} x_{11} + x_2 x_3 x_6 x_9 x_{11} x_{12} + x_2 x_7 x_9 x_{10} x_{11} x_{12} + x_1 x_3 x_4 x_7 x_{11} x_{12} +$$
$$x_1 x_3 x_7 x_{10} x_{11} x_{12} + x_1 x_2 x_3 x_7 x_9 x_{12} + x_2 x_3 x_6 x_7 x_{11} x_{12} + x_3 x_7 x_8 x_9 x_{10} x_{11} + x_2 x_3 x_5 x_7 x_{11} x_{12} +$$
$$x_3 x_5 x_6 x_7 x_9 x_{11} + x_1 x_2 x_3 x_7 x_{11} x_{12} + x_3 x_5 x_6 x_7 x_{11} x_{12} + x_1 x_3 x_7 x_8 x_{11} x_{12} + x_3 x_4 x_7 x_{10} x_{11} x_{12} +$$
$$x_1 x_3 x_5 x_7 x_9 x_{11} + x_2 x_3 x_5 x_7 x_{10} x_{11} + x_2 x_3 x_4 x_7 x_{10} x_{11} + x_2 x_3 x_7 x_8 x_9 x_{12} + x_2 x_3 x_4 x_7 x_9 x_{12} +$$
$$x_2 x_3 x_8 x_9 x_{11} x_{12} + x_3 x_6 x_7 x_8 x_{11} x_{12} + x_4 x_5 x_6 x_7 x_8 x_{11} + x_3 x_5 x_7 x_9 x_{10} x_{11} + x_2 x_3 x_5 x_9 x_{11} x_{12} +$$
$$x_2 x_3 x_9 x_{10} x_{11} x_{12} + x_3 x_7 x_8 x_9 x_{11} x_{12} + x_3 x_4 x_7 x_9 x_{11} x_{12} + x_1 x_2 x_3 x_5 x_7 x_{11} + x_1 x_3 x_4 x_7 x_9 x_{11} +$$
$$x_3 x_5 x_7 x_8 x_{11} x_{12} + x_2 x_3 x_4 x_5 x_7 x_{11} + x_3 x_6 x_7 x_9 x_{11} x_{12} + x_1 x_2 x_3 x_6 x_7 x_{11} + x_2 x_3 x_5 x_7 x_8 x_{11} +$$
$$x_2 x_3 x_5 x_6 x_7 x_{11} + x_1 x_2 x_7 x_9 x_{11} x_{12} + x_2 x_3 x_7 x_8 x_9 x_{11} + x_1 x_2 x_3 x_9 x_{11} x_{12} + x_3 x_4 x_5 x_7 x_9 x_{11} +$$
$$x_3 x_4 x_6 x_7 x_{11} x_{12} + x_3 x_5 x_6 x_7 x_{10} x_{11} x_{12} + x_2 x_3 x_5 x_7 x_8 x_{10} x_{11} + x_1 x_2 x_3 x_6 x_7 x_9 x_{11} + x_1 x_3 x_5 x_7 x_8 x_9 x_{11} +$$
$$x_2 x_3 x_4 x_6 x_7 x_{11} x_{12} + x_2 x_3 x_5 x_7 x_8 x_9 x_{11} + x_2 x_3 x_4 x_5 x_6 x_7 x_{11} + x_2 x_3 x_5 x_7 x_{10} x_{11} x_{12} + x_1 x_3 x_4 x_5 x_7 x_{11} x_{12} +$$
$$x_1 x_3 x_6 x_7 x_9 x_{10} x_{11} + x_3 x_4 x_6 x_7 x_9 x_{10} x_{11} + x_2 x_3 x_4 x_5 x_7 x_{11} x_{12} + x_3 x_5 x_6 x_7 x_9 x_{11} x_{12} + x_1 x_3 x_6 x_7 x_{10} x_{11} x_{12} +$$
$$x_1 x_3 x_6 x_7 x_8 x_{11} x_{12} + x_4 x_5 x_6 x_7 x_8 x_{11} x_{12} + x_2 x_3 x_5 x_6 x_7 x_{11} x_{12} + x_1 x_2 x_3 x_5 x_6 x_7 x_{11} + x_2 x_3 x_4 x_7 x_{10} x_{11} x_{12} +$$
$$x_3 x_5 x_7 x_8 x_9 x_{10} x_{11} + x_2 x_4 x_5 x_6 x_7 x_8 x_{11} + x_1 x_3 x_4 x_7 x_9 x_{11} x_{12} + x_2 x_3 x_4 x_6 x_7 x_9 x_{11} + x_1 x_2 x_3 x_6 x_7 x_{10} x_{11} +$$
$$x_2 x_3 x_4 x_7 x_9 x_{10} x_{11} + x_2 x_3 x_6 x_7 x_8 x_9 x_{11} + x_2 x_3 x_4 x_5 x_7 x_8 x_{11} + x_3 x_5 x_6 x_7 x_9 x_{10} x_{11} + x_1 x_2 x_3 x_7 x_9 x_{10} x_{11} +$$
$$x_4 x_5 x_6 x_7 x_8 x_{10} x_{11} \;+\; x_1 x_2 x_3 x_7 x_8 x_{11} x_{12} \;+\; x_3 x_6 x_7 x_9 x_{10} x_{11} x_{12} \;+\; x_1 x_2 x_3 x_4 x_7 x_{11} x_{12} \;+$$
$$x_2 x_3 x_6 x_7 x_8 x_{11} x_{12} + x_3 x_4 x_5 x_6 x_7 x_8 x_{11} + x_1 x_2 x_3 x_7 x_{10} x_{11} x_{12} + x_1 x_3 x_5 x_7 x_8 x_{11} x_{12} + x_2 x_3 x_4 x_5 x_7 x_{10} x_{11} +$$
$$x_3 x_4 x_6 x_7 x_{10} x_{11} x_{12} + x_3 x_4 x_6 x_7 x_9 x_{11} x_{12} + x_1 x_2 x_3 x_4 x_7 x_9 x_{11} + x_1 x_3 x_5 x_6 x_7 x_9 x_{11} + x_3 x_4 x_7 x_9 x_{10} x_{11} x_{12} +$$
$$x_2 x_3 x_5 x_6 x_7 x_9 x_{11} + x_4 x_5 x_6 x_7 x_8 x_9 x_{11} + x_3 x_5 x_7 x_8 x_9 x_{11} x_{12} + x_1 x_3 x_5 x_6 x_7 x_{11} x_{12} + x_2 x_3 x_5 x_7 x_9 x_{10} x_{11} +$$
$$x_1 x_3 x_4 x_7 x_8 x_{11} x_{12} + x_3 x_4 x_7 x_8 x_{10} x_{11} x_{12} + x_3 x_6 x_7 x_8 x_9 x_{11} x_{12} + x_1 x_3 x_4 x_5 x_7 x_9 x_{11} + x_3 x_5 x_7 x_9 x_{10} x_{11} x_{12} +$$
$$x_1 x_3 x_6 x_7 x_8 x_9 x_{11} + x_1 x_3 x_5 x_7 x_{10} x_{11} x_{12} + x_1 x_3 x_5 x_7 x_9 x_{11} x_{12} + x_1 x_2 x_3 x_4 x_5 x_7 x_{11} + x_1 x_3 x_4 x_6 x_7 x_9 x_{11} +$$
$$x_1 x_3 x_7 x_8 x_9 x_{11} x_{12} + x_2 x_3 x_4 x_6 x_7 x_8 x_{11} x_{12} + x_2 x_3 x_5 x_7 x_9 x_{11} x_{12} + x_3 x_4 x_5 x_7 x_9 x_{10} x_{11} + x_1 x_2 x_3 x_4 x_7 x_8 x_{11} +$$
$$x_1 x_2 x_3 x_4 x_6 x_7 x_{11} \;+\; x_3 x_5 x_7 x_8 x_{10} x_{11} x_{12} \;+\; x_3 x_5 x_6 x_7 x_8 x_{11} x_{12} \;+\; x_3 x_6 x_7 x_8 x_{10} x_{11} x_{12} \;+$$
$$x_3 x_6 x_7 x_8 x_9 x_{10} x_{11} \;+\; x_1 x_2 x_3 x_6 x_7 x_{11} x_{12} \;+\; x_3 x_4 x_5 x_7 x_8 x_{11} x_{12} \;+\; x_1 x_2 x_3 x_4 x_6 x_7 x_9 x_{11} \;+$$
$$x_2 x_4 x_5 x_6 x_7 x_8 x_{10} x_{11} + x_1 x_2 x_3 x_4 x_7 x_8 x_{10} x_{11} + x_1 x_2 x_3 x_4 x_7 x_8 x_9 x_{11} + x_3 x_4 x_5 x_6 x_7 x_8 x_{10} x_{11} +$$
$$x_4 x_5 x_6 x_7 x_8 x_9 x_{11} x_{12} + x_3 x_4 x_7 x_8 x_9 x_{10} x_{11} x_{12} + x_1 x_2 x_3 x_4 x_6 x_7 x_{10} x_{11} + x_2 x_3 x_5 x_7 x_9 x_{10} x_{11} x_{12} +$$
$$x_2 x_3 x_5 x_7 x_8 x_{10} x_{11} x_{12} + x_1 x_2 x_3 x_5 x_6 x_7 x_8 x_{11} + x_1 x_3 x_4 x_7 x_9 x_{10} x_{11} x_{12} + x_1 x_3 x_6 x_7 x_9 x_{10} x_{11} x_{12} +$$
$$x_2 x_3 x_4 x_5 x_7 x_8 x_9 x_{11} + x_3 x_4 x_5 x_7 x_8 x_9 x_{11} x_{12} + x_3 x_4 x_5 x_6 x_7 x_9 x_{10} x_{11} + x_4 x_5 x_6 x_7 x_8 x_9 x_{10} x_{11} +$$
$$x_3 x_4 x_5 x_7 x_9 x_{10} x_{11} x_{12} + x_2 x_3 x_4 x_5 x_7 x_{10} x_{11} x_{12} + x_1 x_2 x_3 x_4 x_5 x_7 x_8 x_{11} + x_1 x_3 x_5 x_6 x_7 x_{10} x_{11} x_{12} +$$
$$x_2 x_4 x_5 x_6 x_7 x_8 x_9 x_{11} + x_2 x_3 x_4 x_5 x_6 x_7 x_{10} x_{11} + x_1 x_2 x_3 x_4 x_6 x_7 x_{11} x_{12} + x_2 x_3 x_4 x_5 x_6 x_7 x_8 x_{11} +$$
$$x_2 x_3 x_5 x_6 x_7 x_8 x_{11} x_{12} + x_1 x_2 x_3 x_5 x_7 x_{10} x_{11} x_{12} + x_1 x_2 x_3 x_6 x_7 x_8 x_{11} x_{12} + x_1 x_2 x_3 x_6 x_7 x_9 x_{10} x_{11} +$$
$$x_2 x_3 x_4 x_7 x_8 x_9 x_{11} x_{12} + x_2 x_3 x_4 x_6 x_7 x_9 x_{10} x_{11} + x_3 x_5 x_6 x_7 x_8 x_9 x_{10} x_{11} + x_1 x_3 x_4 x_5 x_6 x_7 x_{11} x_{12} +$$
$$x_2 x_3 x_4 x_5 x_7 x_8 x_{10} x_{11} + x_3 x_4 x_5 x_6 x_7 x_8 x_9 x_{11} + x_2 x_3 x_4 x_6 x_7 x_8 x_{11} x_{12} + x_1 x_3 x_4 x_7 x_8 x_9 x_{11} x_{12} +$$
$$x_2 x_3 x_6 x_7 x_8 x_{10} x_{11} x_{12} + x_1 x_3 x_5 x_7 x_8 x_9 x_{10} x_{11} + x_1 x_2 x_3 x_6 x_7 x_{10} x_{11} x_{12} + x_1 x_2 x_3 x_4 x_7 x_{10} x_{11} x_{12} +$$
$$x_2 x_3 x_6 x_7 x_8 x_9 x_{10} x_{11} + x_2 x_3 x_4 x_5 x_6 x_7 x_{11} x_{12} + x_1 x_3 x_4 x_6 x_7 x_{10} x_{11} x_{12} + x_2 x_3 x_5 x_7 x_8 x_9 x_{11} x_{12} +$$
$$x_2 x_3 x_4 x_7 x_8 x_{10} x_{11} x_{12} + x_2 x_3 x_6 x_7 x_8 x_9 x_{11} x_{12} + x_2 x_3 x_5 x_6 x_7 x_{10} x_{11} x_{12} + x_1 x_2 x_3 x_5 x_7 x_9 x_{10} x_{11} +$$

$x_2x_3x_6x_7x_9x_{10}x_{11}x_{12}+x_1x_2x_3x_5x_7x_8x_{11}x_{12}+x_1x_2x_3x_4x_7x_9x_{11}x_{12}+x_1x_3x_7x_8x_9x_{10}x_{11}x_{12}+$
$x_2x_3x_5x_6x_7x_9x_{10}x_{11}+x_2x_3x_7x_8x_9x_{10}x_{11}x_{12}+x_2x_3x_4x_5x_6x_7x_9x_{11}+x_1x_2x_3x_6x_7x_8x_9x_{11}+$
$x_2x_3x_5x_6x_7x_8x_9x_{11}+x_1x_2x_3x_5x_6x_7x_9x_{11}+x_3x_4x_6x_7x_8x_9x_{11}x_{12}+x_1x_2x_3x_4x_7x_9x_{10}x_{11}+$
$x_1x_3x_4x_5x_7x_9x_{10}x_{11}+x_1x_3x_5x_6x_7x_9x_{11}x_{12}+x_4x_5x_6x_7x_8x_{10}x_{11}x_{12}+x_2x_3x_5x_6x_7x_9x_{11}x_{12}+$
$x_3x_4x_5x_6x_7x_9x_{11}x_{12}+x_1x_3x_6x_7x_8x_9x_{11}x_{12}+x_2x_3x_5x_7x_8x_9x_{10}x_{11}+x_2x_3x_4x_6x_7x_{10}x_{11}x_{12}+$
$x_2x_4x_5x_6x_7x_8x_{11}x_{12}+x_1x_3x_4x_5x_6x_7x_9x_{11}x_{12}+x_2x_3x_4x_5x_6x_7x_9x_{11}x_{12}+x_2x_3x_4x_7x_8x_9x_{10}x_{11}x_{12}+$
$x_1x_2x_3x_4x_6x_7x_9x_{10}x_{11}+x_1x_2x_3x_4x_5x_7x_8x_9x_{11}+x_2x_3x_4x_5x_7x_8x_9x_{10}x_{11}+x_2x_3x_5x_7x_8x_9x_{10}x_{11}x_{12}+$
$x_1x_2x_3x_4x_7x_9x_{10}x_{11}x_{12}+x_1x_2x_3x_6x_7x_9x_{10}x_{11}x_{12}+x_4x_5x_6x_7x_8x_9x_{10}x_{11}x_{12}+x_1x_2x_3x_5x_7x_8x_9x_{11}x_{12}+$
$x_1x_2x_3x_5x_6x_7x_{10}x_{11}x_{12}+x_1x_2x_3x_4x_5x_7x_9x_{11}x_{12}+x_2x_3x_4x_5x_6x_7x_8x_9x_{11}+x_3x_4x_5x_6x_7x_8x_9x_{10}x_{11}+$
$x_2x_4x_5x_6x_7x_8x_9x_{10}x_{11}+x_1x_2x_3x_4x_5x_6x_7x_{11}x_{12}+x_2x_3x_4x_5x_6x_7x_9x_{10}x_{11}+x_1x_2x_3x_5x_6x_7x_8x_9x_{11}+$
$x_1x_3x_5x_6x_7x_9x_{10}x_{11}x_{12}+x_2x_3x_4x_5x_6x_7x_8x_{10}x_{11}+x_2x_3x_4x_6x_7x_9x_{10}x_{11}x_{12}+x_1x_2x_3x_7x_8x_9x_{10}x_{11}x_{12}+$
$x_1x_3x_4x_6x_7x_9x_{10}x_{11}x_{12}+x_2x_4x_5x_6x_7x_8x_{10}x_{11}x_{12}+x_1x_2x_3x_4x_6x_7x_{10}x_{11}x_{12}+x_2x_3x_4x_6x_7x_8x_9x_{10}x_{11}+$
$x_2x_4x_5x_6x_7x_8x_9x_{11}x_{12}+x_1x_2x_3x_4x_5x_6x_7x_9x_{11}x_{12}+x_1x_2x_3x_4x_6x_7x_9x_{10}x_{11}x_{12}+x_1x_2x_3x_5x_6x_7x_9x_{10}x_{11}x_{12}+$
$x_2x_3x_4x_5x_6x_7x_8x_9x_{10}x_{11}+x_2x_4x_5x_6x_7x_8x_9x_{10}x_{11}x_{12}+1$

Strengthening NLS Against Crossword Puzzle Attack

Debojyoti Bhattacharya[1], Debdeep Mukhopadhyay[2], Dhiman Saha[3],
and D. RoyChowdhury[4]

[1] IIT-Kharagpur, Kharagpur, India
debojyoti.bhattacharya@gmail.com
[2] IIT-Madras, Chennai, India
debdeep@cse.iitm.ernet.in
[3] IIT-Kharagpur, Kharagpur, India
dhimans@cse.iitkgp.ernet.in
[4] IIT-Kharagpur, Kharagpur, India
drc@iitkgp.ac.in

Abstract. NLS is a stream cipher proposal submitted to eSTREAM project. In SAC 2006 Cho and Pieprzyk presented a linear distinguishing attack called Crossword Puzzle attack on NLS where they have shown that the bias of the distinguisher is around $O(2^{-30})$. In this work we have proposed a new function modular *Slash* which is nonlinear in nature and strongly resistant against Linear Cryptanalysis. Replacing the modular addition in the nonlinear filter (NLF) of NLS we have shown that the Crossword puzzle attack presented by Cho and Pieprzyk can be prevented. In the modified NLS the bias of the linear distinguisher reduces to around $O(2^{-60})$. Also we have shown that the implementation cost of modular *Slash*, in terms of hardware and time delay, is less than modular addition. The proposed function could be an interesting alternative to modular addition, due to its better cryptographic properties and lesser implementation cost.

Keywords: Stream ciphers, eSTREAM, Crossword Puzzle attack, Linear Approximations, Modular Addition, NLS.

1 Introduction

A stream cipher project called eSTREAM [1] has been launched by the European Network of Excellence in Cryptography (ECRYPT), to come up with a collection of stream ciphers as de facto standard in industry and government institutions as secure and efficient cryptographic primitives. A variety of different design approaches has been followed by the designers in different submissions and a variety of cryptanalytic techniques are also submitted to cryptanalyze and assess the security of those submitted stream ciphers. In traditional stream ciphers, linear feedback shift register (LFSR) is used as one of the major components. The output of the shift registers are passed to a nonlinear filter (NLF) to produce the keystream. In recent days, modern stream ciphers are using

J. Pieprzyk, H. Ghodosi, and E. Dawson (Eds.): ACISP 2007, LNCS 4586, pp. 29–44, 2007.

nonlinear feedback shift register (NFSR) in place of LFSR. Several ciphers submitted to eSTREAM follow this approach. NLS [2] is one of the stream ciphers submitted to eSTREAM and also a candidate in phase 2, follows this design approach. In [3], Joo Yeon Cho and Josef Pieprzyk studied the NLS cipher and its resistance against linear distinguishing attacks. Though the distinguishing attacks do not allow to recover cryptographic key or any secret element of the cipher under observation, the attack is important in the sense that it helps to distinguish the cipher under attack from a truly random cipher.

In [3], Joo Yeon Cho and Josef Pieprzyk proposed an excellent linear distinguishing attack namely **"Crossword Puzzle attack"** (CP attack) against NLS where they derived linear approximations for both the NFSR and the nonlinear filter (NLF) and combined those approximations to build a linear distinguisher to distinguish the output key-stream generated by NLS from a truly random cipher. They showed that the bias of the distinguisher is around $O(2^{-30})$ for NLSv1 and hence the complexity of the attack is $O(2^{60})$ keystream words. They also extend their attack to NLSv2 where the bias of the distinguisher is found to be around $O(2^{-48})$. Hence they claimed that the security margin of NLS is small to guarantee the claimed security level in future.

In this paper, we propose a new boolean function named *Slash* (denoted by $\oslash$) which offers high non-linearity keeping the hardware implementation overhead small. We cryptanalyzed our proposed function to show that it offers high security against Linear Cryptanalysis. We modified NLS by replacing the modular addition used in the nonlinear filter (NLF) by modular *Slash* and showed theoretically that the **CP** attack proposed in [3] fails. The bias of the linear distinguisher built in the method of Joo Yeon Cho and Josef Pieprzyk reduces to a value of around $O(2^{-60})$ and hence the complexity of the attack increases to around $O(2^{120})$ keystream words. We show our computations only for NLSv1. We also give the hardware architectural comparison of modular *Slash* function with modular addition to show that both the hardware complexity and the time delay to realize modular *Slash* are less than modular addition.

The rest of the work is organised as follows. Section 2 discusses some preliminaries required for this work. Section 3 explores our proposed function. Performance of the proposed function against Linear Cryptanalysis has been discussed in Section 4. Section 5 briefly describes the NLS cipher and our suggested modification. A brief description of the framework of the CP attack has been discussed in Section 6. The analysis of the linear approximations for the NFSR and the NLF for both the original NLS and the modified NLS are given in Section 7. In Section 8 the complexity comparison of the CP attack on the original NLS and the modified NLS has been discussed. Hardware and time delay comparison of the new function with addition modulo 2^n are given in Section 9. Section 10 concludes the work.

2   Preliminaries

Some basic definitions and notations have been discussed in this section. A boolean function of n variables $g(x)$ is a map $g(x): F_2^n \to F_2$, where F_2^n is a vector space defined over F_2. The operation $x \oplus y$ on two binary strings x and y is the bitwise exclusive OR operation between the strings x and y. The Hamming weight of a binary string x is the number of 1's in the string and is denoted by $wt(x)$. The Hamming distance between two binary strings of equal length (say x and y) is the number of positions where x and y differ and is measured by $wt(x \oplus y)$.

Definition 1. *A boolean function $g(x)$, where x is an n variable binary string, can be uniquely written as a sum (XOR) of products (AND). This is known as Algebraic Normal Form (ANF). $g(x_1, x_2, \ldots, x_n) = p_0 \oplus p_1 x_1 \oplus p_2 x_2 \oplus \ldots$ $p_n x_n \oplus p_{1,2} x_1 x_2 \oplus p_{n-1,n} x_{n-1} x_n \oplus \ldots \oplus p_{1,2,\ldots,n} x_1 x_2 \ldots x_n$. The values of $(p_0, p_1, \ldots, p_{1,2,\ldots,n} \in \{0,1\})$ uniquely represent a boolean function.*

Definition 2. *An n variable boolean function $g(x_1, x_2, \ldots, x_n)$ is said to be an affine function if the ANF of g is of the form $g(x_1, x_2, \ldots, x_n) = \oplus_{i=0}^{n} p_i x_i \oplus q$ for $p_i, q \in \{0,1\}$. If q is 0, then the function is said to be linear.*

Definition 3. *Non-linearity of an n variable boolean function g is defined as the minimum Hamming distance from the set of all affine functions of n variables, i.e., $N_f = min_{a \in A_n} d_H(g,a)$, where Hamming distance is defined as, $d_H(g,a) = \{\#x | g(x) \neq a(x)\}$. A_n is the set of all n variable affine functions.*

Definition 4. *[4] A boolean function $g(x)$ of n variable, where n is even, is called a Bent function if it has a non-linearity value $2^{n-1} - 2^{\frac{n}{2}-1}$. This is the highest possible non-linearity for an n variable boolean function if n is even.*

Theorem 1. *[5] The boolean function $g(x_{n-1}, x_{n-2}, \ldots, x_0) = x_{n-1} x_{n-2} \oplus x_{n-3} x_{n-4} \oplus \ldots \oplus x_3 x_2 \oplus x_1 x_0$ is a bent function having nonlinearity value $2^{n-1} - 2^{\frac{n}{2}-1}$, where 'n' is even and $x_n, x_{n-1}, \ldots, x_0$ are n independent random boolean variables.*

Definition 5. *A bias $\epsilon(a,b)$ is defined as $P = \frac{1}{2}(1 + \epsilon)$, $|\epsilon| > 0$ where P is the probability that an approximation holds.*

Piling-up Lemma. [6] If we have n independent approximations having biases $\epsilon_1, \ldots, \epsilon_n$, then the bias of the approximation combining these n approximations becomes $\prod_{i=1}^{n} \epsilon_i$.

3   Proposed Boolean Operator: Slash

Definition 6. Slash: *It is defined as an operation '$\oslash$' which operates on two 1 bit boolean variables A and B and produces a 2 bit output C_{out}, O such that $A \oslash B = C_{out} \| O$. The output bits are defined as, $O = A \oplus B$ and $C_{out} = AB$. For three 1 bit boolean variables, $A, B,$ and C_{in} the definition extends to $A \oslash B \oslash C_{in}$ and the output bits are expressed as $O = A \oplus B \oplus C_{in}$ and $C_{out} = AB \oplus C_{in}$.*

We present a function modular *Slash* using *Slash* operator below with proof of its reversibility.

- **Forward:** Let $X = (x_{n-1}, x_{n-2}, \ldots, x_0)$ and $Y = (y_{n-1}, y_{n-2}, \ldots, y_0)$ be two n-bit data and $Z = (z_{n-1}, z_{n-2}, \ldots, z_0)$ be the n-bit output, where x_0, y_0, z_0 denote the LSBs and $x_{n-1}, y_{n-1}, z_{n-1}$ denote the MSBs. We define the function $Z = F(X, Y)$ as below:

$$z_i = x_i \oplus y_i \oplus c_{i-1}$$
$$c_i = x_i y_i \oplus c_{i-1}$$
$$c_{-1} = 0$$

c_i is the carry term propagating from i^{th} bit position to $(i+1)^{th}$ bit position. The definition of c_i is recursive as shown in the equation. The end carry c_{n-1} is neglected. This defines the operation $Z = F(X, Y) = (X \oslash Y) \bmod 2^n$ (Definition 6).

- **Inverse:** Let $Z = (z_{n-1}, z_{n-2}, \ldots, z_0)$ be an n-bit input, $Y = (y_{n-1}, y_{n-2}, \ldots, y_0)$ be another n-bit input and $X = (x_{n-1}, x_{n-2}, \ldots, x_0)$ be the n-bit output, notation of LSB and MSB being the same as of the forward. We define the inverse function $X = G(Z, Y)$ as below:

$$x_i = z_i \oplus y_i \oplus d_{i-1}$$
$$d_i = x_i y_i \oplus d_{i-1}$$
$$d_{-1} = 0$$

d_i is the carry term propagating from i^{th} bit position to $(i+1)^{th}$ bit position. The definition of d_i is recursive as shown in the equation. It can be noted here that $d_i = (z_i \oplus y_i \oplus d_{i-1})y_i \oplus d_{i-1} = z_i y_i \oplus y_i \oplus d_{i-1}y_i \oplus d_{i-1} = y_i(\neg z_i) \oplus d_{i-1}(\neg y_i)$. This definition of d_i has been used in the hardware design and result is shown in Table 2. The end carry d_{n-1} is neglected.

Theorem 2. *If X, Y, Z be three n-bit data such that $Z = F(X, Y)$, where $z_i = x_i \oplus y_i \oplus c_{i-1}, c_i = x_i y_i \oplus c_{i-1}$ and $c_{-1} = 0$ and G is defined as $X = G(Z, Y)$, where $x_i = z_i \oplus y_i \oplus d_{i-1}, d_i = x_i y_i \oplus d_{i-1}$ $(\forall \, 0 \leq i < n)$ and $d_{-1} = 0$ then G is the inverse function of F.*

Proof. Let, $z_i \oplus y_i \oplus d_{i-1} = p_i$
Given that, $c_i = x_i y_i \oplus c_{i-1}$

$$\therefore c_{i-1} = x_{i-1} y_{i-1} \oplus c_{i-2}$$
$$= x_{i-1} y_{i-1} \oplus \ldots \oplus c_0$$
$$= x_{i-1} y_{i-1} \oplus \ldots \oplus x_0 y_0$$

According to the definition of F, $z_i = x_i \oplus y_i \oplus c_{i-1}$
According to the definition of G, $d_i = x_i y_i \oplus d_{i-1}$

$$\therefore d_{i-1} = x_{i-1} y_{i-1} \oplus d_{i-2}$$
$$= x_{i-1} y_{i-1} \oplus \ldots \oplus d_0$$
$$= x_{i-1} y_{i-1} \oplus \ldots \oplus x_0 y_0$$
$$= c_{i-1}$$

$$\therefore p_i = z_i \oplus y_i \oplus d_{i-1}$$
$$= z_i \oplus y_i \oplus c_{i-1}, (\text{ putting value of } d_{i-1})$$
$$= (x_i \oplus y_i \oplus c_{i-1}) \oplus y_i \oplus c_{i-1}$$
$$= x_i$$

Hence the proof.

The following corollary follows from the definition of $F(X, Y)$.

Corollary 1. *If X and Y are two n-bit numbers, then the operation F is commutative, i.e $F(X, Y) = F(Y, X)$.*

4   Performance of *Slash* Against Linear Cryptanalysis

In this section we give the performance measurement of our proposed function against Linear Cryptanalysis (LC). Throughout the analysis we will consider $X = (x_{n-1}, \ldots, x_0)$ and $Y = (y_{n-1}, \ldots, y_0)$ are two mutually independent random variables of n bits each and each of the n bits of X and Y are mutually independent random boolean variables.

Theorem 3. *If two n bit numbers, $X = (x_{n-1}, x_{n-2}, \ldots, x_0)$ and $Y = (y_{n-1}, y_{n-2}, \ldots, y_0)$ generate an n bit number $Z = (z_{n-1}, z_{n-2}, \ldots, z_0)$ such that, $Z = F(X, Y)$, then the probability p_i of denoting z_i, each output bit of Z by the linear function $x_i \oplus y_i$ is $p_i = \frac{1}{2}(1 + (\frac{1}{2})^i)$ and p_i lies in the range $\frac{1}{2} < p_i \leq 1$ as i lies in $0 \leq i < n$.*

Proof. We denote the carry propagated from the ith bit position to $(i+1)^{th}$ bit position as c_i. As per the definition of F, $c_{-1} = 0$. Hence $z_0 = x_0 \oplus y_0$ with probability 1. Therefore $p_0 = 1$. Now, $z_1 = x_1 \oplus y_1$ if there is no carry c_0. But, $c_0 = 0$ holds with a probability of $\frac{3}{4}$ as $c_0 = x_0 y_0$. Hence $p_1 = \frac{3}{4}$.
Let p_i be the probability of denoting z_i as $z_i = x_i \oplus y_i$. Similarly z_{i+1} can be expressed linearly with a probability of p_{i+1}.

Fact: It is clear hereby that, z_{i+1} can be expressed linearly if the carry term from i^{th} bit position, $c_i = 0$.
   This scenario can be expressed as the union of the following two cases.

  - **Event A:** This is the case when $c_{i-1} = 0$ and $x_i \oslash y_i$ generates a carry. If $c_{i-1} = 0$, then z_i could have been expressed linearly (using the **Fact** stated above) and the probability of that by definition is p_i. Hence, the probability that A is true is $\frac{1}{4}.p_i$.
  - **Event B:** This is the case where $c_{i-1} = 1$ and $x_i \oslash y_i$ generates a carry. The probability that event B is true is $\frac{3}{4}.(1 - p_i)$.

From the above two events it is clear that z_{i+1} cannot be expressed linearly if the event $(A \cup B)$ occurs. By definition the probability of this event is $(1 - p_{i+1})$, as p_{i+1} is the probability that z_{i+1} can be expressed linearly.

$$\therefore (1 - p_{i+1}) = P(A \cup B)$$
$$= P(A) + P(B)(\text{A and B are mutually}$$
$$\text{exclusive events})$$
$$= \frac{1}{4}.p_i + \frac{3}{4}.(1 - p_i)$$
$$\Rightarrow p_{i+1} = \frac{1}{4} + \frac{1}{2}.p_i$$

Using the above recurrence relation we can write,

$$p_{i+1} = \frac{1}{4} + \frac{1}{2}.p_i$$
$$= \frac{1}{4} + \frac{1}{2}.(\frac{1}{4} + \frac{1}{2}.p_{i-1})$$
$$= \frac{1}{4}.(1 + \frac{1}{2}) + (\frac{1}{2})^2 p_{i-1}$$
$$\vdots$$
$$= \frac{1}{4}.(1 + (\frac{1}{2}) + \ldots + (\frac{1}{2})^i) + (\frac{1}{2})^{i+1} p_0$$
$$= \frac{1}{2}.(1 + (\frac{1}{2})^{i+1}), \text{ as } p_0 = 1$$

Hence, $p_i = \frac{1}{2}.(1 + (\frac{1}{2})^i)$.

Therefore, $p_i = 1$, when $i = 0$ and p_i tends to $\frac{1}{2}$ for high value of i. Hence the proof.

From Theorem 3 it can be inferred that the bias of the linear approximation relating to the ith bit position is $(\frac{1}{2})^i$. In the following theorem, the maximum value of the biases of all possible linear approximations of the output bits is computed.

Theorem 4. *If two n bit numbers $X = (x_{n-1}, x_{n-2}, \ldots, x_0)$ and $Y = (y_{n-1}, y_{n-2}, \ldots, y_0)$ generate an n bit number $Z = (z_{n-1}, z_{n-2}, \ldots, z_0)$ such that, $Z = F(X,Y)$, then the bias of the best linear approximation of the ith output bit of Z is 2^{-i}.*

Proof. From the definition of F it is evident that $z_i = x_i \oplus y_i \oplus c_{i-1}$, where c_{i-1} is the carry propagated from i^{th} bit position. The carry c_{i-1} is the only nonlinear term of the equation. Therefore, in order to obtain various linear approximations for the nonlinear part, linear approximations have to be found out for the carry term. Each possible approximation of c_{i-1}, denoted by L_{i-1} will give rise to different biases which are equal to the bias of a linear approximation of z_i. By the definition of c_i, we know that, $c_i = x_i y_i \oplus x_{i-1} y_{i-1} \oplus \ldots \oplus x_0 y_0$, i.e. c_i is a boolean function of $2(i + 1)$ variables. It has been proved in Theorem 1, that c_i is a bent function. Hence, it has a nonlinearity value $2^{2(i+1)-1} - 2^{\frac{2(i+1)}{2}-1}$. Hence, the probability of match for the best linear approximation of c_i is :

$1 - \frac{2^{2(i+1)-1}-2^{2(i+1)/2-1}}{2^{2(i+1)}} = \frac{1}{2}+2^{-(i+2)}$. Therefore the output, $z_i = x_i \oplus y_i \oplus c_{i-1}$ can be approximated by a linear equation, $z_i' = x_i \oplus y_i \oplus L_{i-1}$, where L_{i-1} is the best linear approximation for c_{i-1}. Now, the largest probability that L_{i-1} matches c_{i-1} is $\frac{1}{2}+2^{-(i-1+2)} = \frac{1}{2}+2^{-(i+1)} = \frac{1}{2}(1+2^{-i})$. Thus, the largest bias of the best linear approximation for c_{i-1} and hence z_i is 2^{-i}.

We observe from the above theorems that the bias of any linear approximations reduces considerably and makes the finding of linear approximations in the cipher with a large bias more difficult.

5 Brief Description of NLS Stream Cipher

NLS key-stream generator uses NFSR whose outputs are given to a nonlinear filter NLF that produces output key-stream bits. Detail of the cipher can be found in [2].

NLS has two components, one NFSR and one NLF whose work is synchronised by a clock. The state of NFSR at time t is denoted by $\sigma_t = (r_t[0], \ldots, r_t[16])$ where $r_t[i]$ is a 32-bit word. The state is determined by 17 words. The transition from the state σ_t to the state σ_{t+1} is defined as follows :

1. $r_{t+1}[i] = r_t[i+1]$ for $i = 0, \ldots, 15$;
2. $r_{t+1}[16] = f((r_t[0] \lll 19) \boxplus (r_t[15] \lll 9) \boxplus Konst) \oplus r_t[4]$;
3. if $t = 0 (\mod f16), r_{t+1}[2] = r_{t+1}[2] \boxplus t$;

where $f16$ is 65537 and $\boxplus$ is the addition modulo 2^{32}. The $Konst$ value is a 32-bit key dependent constant. The function $f \colon \{0,1\}^{32} \to \{0,1\}^{32}$ is constructed using an S-box with 8-bit input and 32-bit output and defined as $f(a) = \text{S-box}(a_H) \oplus a$ where a_H is the most significant 8 bits of 32-bit word a. Each output key-stream word ν_t of NLF is obtained as

$$\nu_t = NLF(\sigma_t) = (r_t[0] \boxplus r_t[16]) \oplus (r_t[1] \boxplus r_t[13]) \oplus (r_t[6] \boxplus Konst). \qquad (1)$$

The cipher uses 32-bit words to ensure a fast keystream generation.

5.1 Suggested Modification

The NLS key-stream generator has two components, one NFSR and one NLF. We keep the NFSR same and change the Non-Linear Filter (NLF) only. We replace the modular additions used in the NLF by our proposed *Slash* function. We use *Slash* modulo 2^{32}. Hence in the modified NLS the output key-stream word ν_t' is obtained as :

$$\nu_t' = NLF'(\sigma_t) = (r_t[0] \oslash r_t[16]) \oplus (r_t[1] \oslash r_t[13]) \oplus (r_t[6] \oslash Konst). \qquad (2)$$

Here $\oslash$ is *Slash* modulo 2^{32}.

6   Brief Description of Crossword Puzzle (CP) Attack

The CP attack proposed in [3] is based on linear distinguisher [7] which uses linear approximations of both the NFSR and the NLF. The roles of the two nonlinear components are :

- NFSR transforms the current state σ_i to the next state σ_{i+1} using some function $NF1$, $\sigma_{i+1} = NF1(\sigma_i)$.
- NLF produces an output ν_i from the current state σ_i through a function $NF2$, $\nu_i = NF2(\sigma_i)$.

The basic steps of the attack are :

1. Find a linear approximation of the non-linear state transition function used by NFSR : $l_1(\sigma_i) = \sigma_{i+1}$ with bias of ϵ_1.
2. Find a linear approximation of the non-linear function applied by NLF : $l_2(\sigma_j) \oplus l_3(\nu_j) = 0$ with bias of ϵ_2.
3. Obtain two sets of clock I and J such that $\sum_{i \in I}(l_1(\sigma_i) \oplus \sigma_{i+1}) = \sum_{j \in J} l_2(\sigma_j)$.
4. Build a distinguisher by computing

$$\sum_{i \in I}(l_1(\sigma_i) \oplus \sigma_{i+1}) \oplus \sum_{j \in J}(l_2(\sigma_j) \oplus l_3(\nu_j)) = \sum_{j \in J} l_3(\nu_j) = 0$$

which has bias of $\epsilon^{|I|} \cdot \epsilon^{|J|}$.

This is the basic outline of the attack. The attackers obtained linear approximations of both the NFSR and the NLF and combined them to build a linear distinguisher with high bias value. In the following subsections we introduce our suggested modification and show that how the attack can be thwarted using this modification. We show that in the modified version the bias of the distinguisher decreases to such a low value that any practical attack using this linear distinguisher is impossible.

7   Analysis of NFSR and NLF

As we have not changed the structure of the NFSR, the analysis given in [3] holds. We briefly describe the analysis of NFSR here. Let α_t be a 32-bit output of the S-box that defines the transition function f. Then, the following equation holds for the least significant bit.

$$\alpha_{t,(0)} \oplus r_t[0]_{(13)} \oplus r_t[15]_{(23)} \oplus Konst_{(0)} \oplus r_t[4]_{(0)} \oplus r_{t+1}[16]_{(0)} = 0 \qquad (3)$$

where $\alpha_{t,(i)}$ and $x_{(i)}$ stand for the i-th bit off the 32 bit words α_t and x respectively.(Throughout the paper, this notation will be used). To make the analysis simpler initially $Konst$ is taken as zero.

7.1 Linear Approximation of $\alpha_{t,(0)}$ and NFSR

In Table 1 the linear approximations for $\alpha_{t,(0)}$ has been given. For detail, reader can refer to [3]. Linear approximation of the NFSR can be obtained using the

Table 1. Linear approximations for $\alpha_{t,(0)}$ when $Konst = 0$

$r_t[0]_{(10)} \oplus r_t[0]_{(6)} \oplus r_t[15]_{(20)} \oplus r_t[15]_{(16)} \oplus r_t[15]_{(15)}$	$\frac{1}{2}(1 + 0.048828)$
$r_t[0]_{(10)} \oplus r_t[0]_{(6)} \oplus r_t[0]_{(5)} \oplus r_t[15]_{(20)} \oplus r_t[15]_{(16)}$	$\frac{1}{2}(1 + 0.048828)$
$r_t[0]_{(12)} \oplus r_t[15]_{(22)}$	$\frac{1}{2}(1 - 0.045410)$
$r_t[0]_{(12)} \oplus r_t[0]_{(11)} \oplus r_t[0]_{(10)} \oplus r_t[15]_{(22)} \oplus r_t[15]_{(21)} \oplus r_t[15]_{(20)}$	$\frac{1}{2}(1 - 0.020020)$

linear approximation for $\alpha_{t,(0)}$. If the first approximation from Table 1 is chosen, then the following linear equation :

$$\alpha_{t,(0)} = r_t[0]_{(10)} \oplus r_t[0]_{(6)} \oplus r_t[15]_{(20)} \oplus r_t[15]_{(16)} \oplus r_t[15]_{(15)} \qquad (4)$$

holds with bias $0.048828 = 2^{-4.36}$. Combining equations (3) and (4), the following approximation for NFSR holds

$$r_t[0]_{(10)} \oplus r_t[0]_{(6)} \oplus r_t[15]_{(20)} \oplus r_t[15]_{(16)} \oplus r_t[15]_{(15)} =$$
$$r_t[0]_{(13)} \oplus r_t[15]_{(23)} \oplus Konst_{(0)} \oplus r_t[4]_{(0)} \oplus r_{t+1}[16]_{(0)} \qquad (5)$$

with bias $2^{-4.36}$.

7.2 Linear Approximation of Modular Addition [3]

As the least significant bits are linear for modular addition $\boxplus$ so the following equation holds with probability 1.

$$(r[x] \boxplus r[y])_{(0)} = r[x]_{(0)} \oplus r[y]_{(0)} \qquad (6)$$

$x_{(i)}$ stands for i^{th} bit of 32-bit word x. All consecutive bits $i > 0$ of $\boxplus$ are nonlinear. Consider the function $(r[x] \boxplus r[y])_{(i)} \oplus (r[x] \boxplus r[y])_{(i-1)}$. The function has a linear approximation as follows

$$(r[x] \boxplus r[y])_{(i)} \oplus (r[x] \boxplus r[y])_{(i-1)} = r[x]_{(i)} \oplus r[y]_{(i)} \oplus r[x]_{(i-1)} \oplus r[y]_{(i-1)} \qquad (7)$$

that has the bias 2^{-1}.

In a similar way, the function $(r[x] \boxplus r[y])_{(i)} \oplus (r[x] \boxplus r[y])_{(i-1)} \oplus (r[x] \boxplus r[y])_{(i-2)} \oplus (r[x] \boxplus r[y])_{(i-3)}$ has the following approximation. For $i > 2$,

$$(r[x] \boxplus r[y])_{(i)} \oplus (r[x] \boxplus r[y])_{(i-1)} \oplus (r[x] \boxplus r[y])_{(i-2)} \oplus (r[x] \boxplus r[y])_{(i-3)} =$$
$$r[x]_{(i)} \oplus r[y]_{(i)} \oplus r[x]_{(i-1)} \oplus r[y]_{(i-1)} \oplus r[x]_{(i-2)} \oplus r[y]_{(i-2)} \oplus r[x]_{(i-3)} \oplus r[y]_{(i-3)} \qquad (8)$$

that has a bias of 2^{-2}.

7.3   Linear Approximation of Modular Slash

Let us look at the change in bias due to the introduction of modular *Slash* in place of modular addition. Let $r[z] = r[x] \oslash r[y]$. As the least significant bits are linear so the following equation holds with probability 1.

$$(r[x] \oslash r[y])_{(0)} = r[x]_{(0)} \oplus r[y]_{(0)} \tag{9}$$

which is same as of equation (6). All consecutive bits $i > 0$ are nonlinear.

The function $(r[x] \oslash r[y])_{(i)} \oplus (r[x] \oslash r[y])_{(i-1)}$ having a linear approximation as follows

$$(r[x] \oslash r[y])_{(i)} \oplus (r[x] \oslash r[y])_{(i-1)} = r[x]_{(i)} \oplus r[y]_{(i)} \oplus r[x]_{(i-1)} \oplus r[y]_{(i-1)} \tag{10}$$

has bias of at most 2^{-i} (theorem 4), considering this as the best linear approximation of the output bit $r[z]_{(i)}$.

In a similar way the function $(r[x] \oslash r[y])_{(i)} \oplus (r[x] \oslash r[y])_{(i-1)} \oplus (r[x] \oslash r[y])_{(i-2)} \oplus (r[x] \oslash r[y])_{(i-3)}$ has the following approximation. For $i > 2$,

$$(r[x] \oslash r[y])_{(i)} \oplus (r[x] \oslash r[y])_{(i-1)} \oplus (r[x] \oslash r[y])_{(i-2)} \oplus (r[x] \oslash r[y])_{(i-3)} =$$
$$r[x]_{(i)} \oplus r[y]_{(i)} \oplus r[x]_{(i-1)} \oplus r[y]_{(i-1)} \oplus r[x]_{(i-2)} \oplus r[y]_{(i-2)} \oplus r[x]_{(i-3)} \oplus r[y]_{(i-3)})_{(i-3)} \tag{11}$$

has a bias of at most 2^{-i} (theorem 4), considering this as the best linear approximation of the output bit $r[z]_{(i)}$.

7.4   Linear Approximation for NLF

Equation (1) defines the output key-stream generated by the original NLF and equation (2) defines the output key-stream generated by the modified NLF. The relation for the least significant bits of both the original and the modified NLF having the following form holds with probability one (as observed from equation (6) and (9)).

$$\nu_{t,(0)}/\nu'_{t,(0)} = (r_t[0]_{(0)} \oplus r_t[16]_{(0)}) \oplus (r_t[1]_{(0)}$$
$$\oplus r_t[13]_{(0)}) \oplus (r_t[6]_{(0)} \oplus Konst_{(0)}) \tag{12}$$

For $2 \le i \le 31$ and using equation (7), the original NLF function has linear approximation of the following form :

$$\nu_{t,(i)} \oplus \nu_{t,(i-1)} = (r_t[0]_{(i)} \oplus r_t[16]_{(i)} \quad \oplus r_t[0]_{(i-1)} \oplus r_t[16]_{(i-1)})$$
$$\oplus (r_t[1]_{(i)} \oplus r_t[13]_{(i)} \quad \oplus (r_t[1]_{(i-1)} \oplus r_t[13]_{(i-1)})$$
$$\oplus (r_t[6]_{(i)} \oplus Konst_{(i)} \quad \oplus r_t[6]_{(i-1)} \oplus Konst_{(i-1)}) \tag{13}$$

with the bias of $(2^{-1})^2 = 2^{-2}$ under the condition that $Konst = 0$ [3], when modular addition has been used in the Filter function.

When modular *Slash* has been used in the filter function, for $2 \leq i \leq 31$ and using equation (10), the modified NLF function has linear approximation of the following form :

$$
\begin{aligned}
\nu'_{t,(i)} \oplus \nu'_{t,(i-1)} = {} & (r_t[0]_{(i)} \oplus r_t[16]_{(i)} && \oplus r_t[0]_{(i-1)} \oplus r_t[16]_{(i-1)}) \\
& \oplus (r_t[1]_{(i)} \oplus r_t[13]_{(i)} && \oplus (r_t[1]_{(i-1)} \oplus r_t[13]_{(i-1)}) \\
& \oplus (r_t[6]_{(i)} \oplus Konst_{(i)} && \oplus r_t[6]_{(i-1)} \oplus Konst_{(i-1)}) \quad (14)
\end{aligned}
$$

with the bias of $(2^{-i})^2 = 2^{-2i}$ under the condition, $Konst = 0$.

In case of modular addition, applying approximation (8), for $i > 2$ the following expression holds

$$
\begin{aligned}
\nu_{t,(i)} \oplus \nu_{t,(i-1)} & \oplus \nu_{t,(i-2)} \oplus \nu_{t,(i-3)} = \\
(r_t[0]_{(i)} \oplus r_t[0]_{(i-1)} & \oplus r_t[0]_{(i-2)} \oplus r_t[0]_{(i-3)} \oplus r_t[16]_{(i)} \oplus r_t[16]_{(i-1)} \\
\oplus r_t[16]_{(i-2)} \oplus r_t[16]_{(i-3)}) & \oplus (r_t[1]_{(i)} \oplus r_t[1]_{(i-1)} \oplus r_t[1]_{(i-2)} \oplus r_t[1]_{(i-3)} \quad (15) \\
\oplus (r_t[13]_{(i)} \oplus r_t[13]_{(i-1)} & \oplus r_t[13]_{(i-2)} \oplus r_t[13]_{(i-3)}) \oplus (r_t[6]_{(i)} \oplus r_t[6]_{(i-1)} \\
\oplus r_t[6]_{(i-2)} \oplus r_t[6]_{(i-3)}) & \oplus Konst_{(i)} \oplus Konst_{(i-1)} \oplus Konst_{(i-2)} \oplus Konst_{(i-3)})
\end{aligned}
$$

with the bias $(2^{-2})^2 = 2^{-4}$ when $Konst = 0$.

In case of modular *Slash*, applying approximation (11), for $i > 2$ the following expression holds

$$
\begin{aligned}
\nu'_{t,(i)} \oplus \nu'_{t,(i-1)} & \oplus \nu'_{t,(i-2)} \oplus \nu'_{t,(i-3)} = \\
(r_t[0]_{(i)} \oplus r_t[0]_{(i-1)} & \oplus r_t[0]_{(i-2)} \oplus r_t[0]_{(i-3)} \oplus r_t[16]_{(i)} \oplus r_t[16]_{(i-1)} \\
\oplus r_t[16]_{(i-2)} \oplus r_t[16]_{(i-3)}) & \oplus (r_t[1]_{(i)} \oplus r_t[1]_{(i-1)} \oplus r_t[1]_{(i-2)} \oplus r_t[1]_{(i-3)} \quad (16) \\
\oplus (r_t[13]_{(i)} \oplus r_t[13]_{(i-1)} & \oplus r_t[13]_{(i-2)} \oplus r_t[13]_{(i-3)}) \oplus (r_t[6]_{(i)} \oplus r_t[6]_{(i-1)} \\
\oplus r_t[6]_{(i-2)} \oplus r_t[6]_{(i-3)}) & \oplus Konst_{(i)} \oplus Konst_{(i-1)} \oplus Konst_{(i-2)} \oplus Konst_{(i-3)})
\end{aligned}
$$

with bias $(2^{-i})^2 = 2^{-2i}$, when $Konst = 0$.

8   Complexity Comparison of CP Attack on the Original and Modified NLS

The main idea behind the CP attack is to find the best combination of approximations for both NFSR and NLF, while the state bits of the shift register vanish and the bias of the resulting approximation is as big as possible [3]. The case for $Konst = 0$ has been studied at first and then the attack has been extended to $Konst \neq 0$. We show that for non-zero $Konst$, even if we assume all zero values for the lower 3 bytes of the $Konst$, the attack proposed in [3] does not work on the modified NLS.

8.1   Case for $Konst = 0$

We first describe here the approximation chosen by the attacker in [3] and then we show that in modified NLS, how the bias of this approximation decreases to a low value such that any practical attack become impossible.

The linear approximations of $\alpha_{t,(0)}$ are given in Table 1. The third approximation from the table has been chosen which is

$$\alpha_{t,(0)} = r_t[0]_{(12)} \oplus r_t[15]_{(22)} \tag{17}$$

and the bias of this approximation is $0.045410 = 2^{-4.46}$. By combining equations (3) and (17) the following approximation has been obtained

$$r_t[0]_{(12)} \oplus r_t[15]_{(22)} \oplus r_t[0]_{(13)} \oplus r_t[15]_{(23)} \oplus r_t[4]_{(0)} \oplus r_{t+1}[16]_{(0)} = 0 \tag{18}$$

which has the same bias.

Approximation (18) has been divided into two parts : the least significant bits and the other bits as

$$l_1(r_t) = r_t[4]_{(0)} \oplus r_{t+1}[16]_{(0)}$$
$$l_2(r_t) = r_t[0]_{(12)} \oplus r_t[0]_{(13)} \oplus r_t[15]_{(22)} \oplus r_t[15]_{(23)} \tag{19}$$

Clearly, $l_1(r_t) \oplus l_2(r_t) = 0$ with the bias $2^{-4.46}$. Since, $l_1(r_t)$ has only the least significant bit variables, approximation (12) can be applied which is true with probability one. The following set of approximations are obtained.

$$l_1(r_t) = r_t[4]_{(0)} \oplus r_{t+1}[16]_{(0)}$$
$$l_1(r_{t+1}) = r_{t+1}[4]_{(0)} \oplus r_{t+2}[16]_{(0)}$$
$$l_1(r_{t+6}) = r_{t+6}[4]_{(0)} \oplus r_{t+7}[16]_{(0)} \tag{20}$$
$$l_1(r_{t+13}) = r_{t+13}[4]_{(0)} \oplus r_{t+14}[16]_{(0)}$$
$$l_1(r_{t+16}) = r_{t+16}[4]_{(0)} \oplus r_{t+17}[16]_{(0)}$$

Adding up all approximations of (20) and by applying approximation (12), the following equation can be written

$$l_1(r_t) \oplus l_1(r_{t+1}) \oplus l_1(r_{t+6}) \oplus l_1(r_{t+13}) \oplus l_1(r_{t+16}) = \nu_{t+4,(0)} \oplus \nu_{t+17,(0)} \tag{21}$$

since $r_{t+p}[0] = r_t[p]$.

Now focusing on $l_2(r_t)$, where the bit positions involved are 12, 13, 22 and 23,

$$l_2(r_t) = r_t[0]_{(12)} \oplus r_t[0]_{(13)} \oplus r_t[15]_{(22)} \oplus r_t[15]_{(23)}$$
$$l_2(r_{t+1}) = r_{t+1}[0]_{(12)} \oplus r_{t+1}[0]_{(13)} \oplus r_{t+1}[15]_{(22)} \oplus r_{t+1}[15]_{(23)}$$
$$l_2(r_{t+6}) = r_{t+6}[0]_{(12)} \oplus r_{t+6}[0]_{(13)} \oplus r_{t+6}[15]_{(22)} \oplus r_{t+6}[15]_{(23)} \tag{22}$$
$$l_2(r_{t+13}) = r_{t+13}[0]_{(12)} \oplus r_{t+13}[0]_{(13)} \oplus r_{t+13}[15]_{(22)} \oplus r_{t+13}[15]_{(23)}$$
$$l_2(r_{t+16}) = r_{t+16}[0]_{(12)} \oplus r_{t+16}[0]_{(13)} \oplus r_{t+16}[15]_{(22)} \oplus r_{t+16}[15]_{(23)}$$

Since, $r_{t+p}[0] = r_t[p]$, the above approximations are presented as follows.

$$l_2(r_t) = r_t[0]_{(12)} \oplus r_t[0]_{(13)} \oplus r_{t+15}[0]_{(22)} \oplus r_{t+15}[0]_{(23)}$$
$$l_2(r_{t+1}) = r_t[1]_{(12)} \oplus r_t[1]_{(13)} \oplus r_{t+15}[1]_{(22)} \oplus r_{t+15}[1]_{(23)}$$
$$l_2(r_{t+6}) = r_t[6]_{(12)} \oplus r_t[6]_{(13)} \oplus r_{t+15}[6]_{(22)} \oplus r_{t+15}[6]_{(23)} \tag{23}$$
$$l_2(r_{t+13}) = r_t[13]_{(12)} \oplus r_t[13]_{(13)} \oplus r_{t+15}[13]_{(22)} \oplus r_{t+15}[13]_{(23)}$$
$$l_2(r_{t+16}) = r_t[16]_{(12)} \oplus r_t[16]_{(13)} \oplus r_{t+15}[16]_{(22)} \oplus r_{t+15}[16]_{(23)}$$

For original NLS, approximations (13) and (23) are combined which leads to the following approximation.

$$l_2(r_t) \oplus l_2(r_{t+1}) \oplus l_2(r_{t+6}) \oplus l_2(r_{t+13}) \oplus l_2(r_{t+16}) =$$
$$\nu_{t,(12)} \oplus \nu_{t,(13)} \oplus \nu_{t+15,(22)} \oplus \nu_{t+15,(23)} \qquad (24)$$

By combining the approximations (21) and (24) the final approximation has been obtained that defines the distinguisher in [3], i.e.

$$l_1(r_t) \oplus l_1(r_{t+1}) \oplus l_1(r_{t+6}) \oplus l_1(r_{t+13}) \oplus l_1(r_{t+16})$$
$$\oplus l_2(r_t) \oplus l_2(r_{t+1}) \oplus l_2(r_{t+6}) \oplus l_2(r_{t+13}) \oplus l_2(r_{t+16}) \qquad (25)$$
$$= \nu_{t,(12)} \oplus \nu_{t,(13)} \oplus \nu_{t+15,(22)} \oplus \nu_{t+15,(23)} \oplus \nu_{t+4,(0)} \oplus \nu_{t+17,(0)}$$
$$= 0$$

As approximation (18) has been used five times and approximation (13) twice, the bias of the approximation (25) is $(2^{-4.46})^5 \cdot (2^{-2})^2 = 2^{-26.3}$. Therefore, the complexity of the attack is $2^{52.6}$. For the modified NLS, to obtain the same distinguisher defined above, we have to combine approximation (14) and (23) which leads to the following approximation.

$$l_2(r_t) \oplus l_2(r_{t+1}) \oplus l_2(r_{t+6}) \oplus l_2(r_{t+13}) \oplus l_2(r_{t+16}) =$$
$$\nu'_{t,(12)} \oplus \nu'_{t,(13)} \oplus \nu'_{t+15,(22)} \oplus \nu'_{t+15,(23)} \qquad (26)$$

By combining the approximations (21) (as same expression holds for ν' also) and (26) the final approximation is obtained that defines the distinguisher

$$l_1(r_t) \oplus l_1(r_{t+1}) \oplus l_1(r_{t+6}) \oplus l_1(r_{t+13}) \oplus l_1(r_{t+16})$$
$$\oplus l_2(r_t) \oplus l_2(r_{t+1}) \oplus l_2(r_{t+6}) \oplus l_2(r_{t+13}) \oplus l_2(r_{t+16}) \qquad (27)$$
$$= \nu'_{t,(12)} \oplus \nu'_{t,(13)} \oplus \nu'_{t+15,(22)} \oplus \nu_{t+15,(23)} \oplus \nu'_{t+4,(0)} \oplus \nu'_{t+17,(0)}$$
$$= 0$$

As approximation (18) has been used five times and approximation (14) twice, the bias of the approximation (27) is $(2^{-4.46})^5 \cdot (2^{-13}) \cdot (2^{-23}) = 2^{-58.3}$ (as bit positions 13 and 23 are used in the approximation). Therefore, the complexity of the attack for the modified NLS is $2^{116.6}$. Since the specification of the NLS cipher allows the adversary to observe up to 2^{80} keystream words per one key/nonce pair [2], the attack is not successful for the modified NLS as bias of the distinguisher is less than 2^{-40}.

8.2   Case for $Konst \neq 0$

The biases of linear approximations of both $\alpha_{t,(0)}$ and the NLF vary with $Konst$ as it occurs as a parameter. Bias of the linear distinguisher has been explored in [3] and it has been showed that with non-zero $Konst$ the bias reduces. According to [3] the $Konst$ has been divided into two parts as

$Konst = (Konst_{(H)}, Konst_{(L)})$ where $Konst_{(H)} = (Konst_{(31)}, \ldots, Konst_{(24)})$, and $Konst_{(L)} = (Konst_{(23)}, \ldots, Konst_{(0)})$. The biases of linear approximations of $\alpha_{t,(0)}$ depend on $Konst_{(H)}$ and those of NLF depend on $Konst_{(L)}$. Here we have explored only the case where $Konst_{(H)} \neq 0$ and $Konst_{(L)} = 0$.

Since the most significant 8-bits of $Konst$ contribute to the form of $\alpha_{t,(0)}$, bias of approximation (17) fluctuates according to the value of $Konst_{(H)}$. The bias of (17) becomes smallest when $Konst_{(H)}$ is around 51 or 179 and the biggest when $Konst_{(H)}$ is around 127 or 255. The average bias of approximation (17) with $Konst_{(H)}$ is $2^{-5.19}$ [3].

As explained in [3], for the original NLS, bias of the NLF with non-zero $Konst_{(L)}$ decreases and the bias of (13) is around 2^{-3} for any $i > 0$. Hence the bias of the distinguisher (25) with non-zero $Konst$ becomes $(2^{-5.19})^5 \cdot (2^{-3}) = 2^{-31.95}$.

In case of the modified NLS, even if we consider $Konst_{(L)} = 0$ and $Konst_{(H)} \neq 0$, combining approximations (17) and (14), the bias of distinguisher (27) becomes $(2^{-5.19})^5 \cdot (2^{-13}) \cdot (2^{-23}) = 2^{-61.95}$, which is low enough to thwart any linear distinguishing attack.

8.3   Multiple Distinguisher

For original NLS the bias of the distinguisher (25) is very small for some values of $Konst_{(H)}$ [3]. In order to address this problem, the attackers took the fourth approximation from Table 1 which is

$$\alpha_{t,(0)} = r_t[0]_{(12)} \oplus r_t[0]_{(11)} \oplus r_t[0]_{(10)} \oplus r_t[15]_{(22)} \oplus r_t[15]_{(21)} \oplus r_t[15]_{(20)} \quad (28)$$

having average bias of $2^{-6.2}$. Using approximation (28), another approximation of NFSR has been built which is

$$r_t[0]_{(10)} \oplus r_t[0]_{(11)} \oplus r_t[0]_{(12)} \oplus r_t[0]_{(13)} \oplus r_t[15]_{(20)} \oplus r_t[15]_{(21)} \oplus r_t[15]_{(22)}$$
$$\oplus r_t[15]_{(23)} \oplus Konst_{(0)} \oplus r_t[4]_{(0)} \oplus r_{t+1}[16](0) = 0 \quad (29)$$

By combining approximations (15) and (29) a new distinguisher has been built having a bias of $2^{-37.8}$. The distinguisher is as follows

$$\nu_{t,(10)} \oplus \nu_{t,(11)} \oplus \nu_{t,(12)} \oplus \nu_{t,(13)} \oplus \nu_{t+15,(20)} \oplus \nu_{t+15,(21)} \oplus \nu_{t+15,(22)} \oplus \nu_{t+15,(23)}$$
$$\oplus \nu_{t+4,(0)} \oplus \nu_{t+17,(0)} = 0 \quad (30)$$

By observing two distinguishers together and selecting always the better bias among them, the success rate of the distinguishing attack has been improved.

For the modified NLS approximation (16) and (29) must be combined to obtain the above distinguisher. The new distinguisher is

$$\nu'_{t,(10)} \oplus \nu'_{t,(11)} \oplus \nu'_{t,(12)} \oplus \nu'_{t,(13)} \oplus \nu'_{t+15,(20)} \oplus \nu'_{t+15,(21)} \oplus \nu'_{t+15,(22)} \oplus \nu'_{t+15,(23)}$$
$$\oplus \nu'_{t+4,(0)} \oplus \nu'_{t+17,(0)} = 0 \quad (31)$$

Distinguisher (31) has a bias $(2^{-6.2})^5 \cdot (2^{-13}) \cdot (2^{-23}) = 2^{-67}$ (the calculation is similar as in section 8.1). Here we observe that for both the distinguisher mentioned in [3], the bias is too low for any attack in case of the modified NLS. The data complexity in both the cases are well above 2^{80}. As only 2^{80} key-stream words per key/nonce pair is allowed to be observed by an adversary (as per the specification of NLS), the linear distinguishing attack or CP attack mentioned in [3] can be resisted by the proposed modification.

9   Hardware and Time Complexity

We have analyzed the gate count and time delay of our proposed key mixing function slash. Comparison and gate count and time delay is shown in Table 2. Time delay is given in terms of AND gate delay. Delay of 1 XOR gate is considered to be equivalent to 1.5 AND gate delay [8] and delay of 1 AND gate and 1 OR gate are considered to be equal.

Table 2. Comparison of Gate Count and Time Delay

Function	Forward				
	Gate Count				Time Delay
	$\#XOR$	$\#AND$	$\#OR$	$\#NOT$	
Addition modulo 2^n	$(2n-1)$	$(2n-3)$	$(n-2)$	-	$2.5n + .5\ AND$ gate
Slash modulo 2^n	$3(n-1)$	$n-1$	-	-	$1.5n\ AND$ gate
	Reverse				
	Gate Count				Time Delay
	$\#XOR$	$\#AND$	$\#OR$	$\#NOT$	
Subtraction modulo 2^n	$(3n-1)$	$(2n-3)$	$(n-2)$	-	$2.5n + 2\ AND$ gate
Reverse Slash modulo 2^n	$3(n-1)$	$(2n-3)$	-	$2(n-1)$	$3(n-1)\ AND$ gate

10   Conclusions

In this work we have modified the stream cipher NLS which is a candidate of the eSTREAM project to prevent it against the Crossword Puzzle attack [3]. We modified the nonlinear filter (NLF) of NLS by replacing the modular addition with a new boolean operator modular *Slash*. The paper shows that the complexity of the CP attack against the modified NLS has been increased to around $O(2^{120})$ keystream words from $O(2^{60})$ keystream words as published in [3] against the original cipher. As the specification of the NLS allows only 2^{80} keystream words to be observed per key/nonce pair [2], this attack becomes impractical against the modified NLS. We also showed that both the hardware cost and time delay of modular *Slash* is less than modular addition. To summarize, the paper shows that by suitably modifying the modular addition with modular *Slash*, the stream cipher NLS could be strengthened against the CP attack at a lower hardware cost.

References

1. eSTREAM project. http://www.ecrypt.eu.org/stream/
2. Rose, G., Hawkes, P., Paddon, M., de Vries, M.W.: Primitive specification for nls. (April 2005) http://www.ecrypt.eu.org/stream/nls.html
3. Cho, J.Y., Pieprzyk, J.: Crossword Puzzle Attack on NLS. In: SAC 2006 (2006)
4. Rothaus, O.S.: On "Bent" Functions. Journal of Combinatorial Theory 20(A), 300–305 (1976)
5. Macwilliams, F.J., Sloane, N.J.A.: The Theory of Error-Correcting Codes. North Holland (January 1983)
6. Matsui, M.: Linear Cryptanalysis method for DES cipher. In: Helleseth, T. (ed.) EUROCRYPT 1993. LNCS, vol. 765, pp. 386–397. Springer, Heidelberg (1994)
7. Golic, J.D.: Linear models for keystream generators. IEEE Transactions on Computers 45(1), 41–49 (1996)
8. Uyemura, J.P.: Introduction to VLSI Circuits and Systems. John Wiley & Sons, New York (2002)

A New Strategy for Finding a Differential Path of SHA-1

Jun Yajima[1], Yu Sasaki[2], Yusuke Naito[2], Terutoshi Iwasaki[3],
Takeshi Shimoyama[1], Noboru Kunihiro[2], and Kazuo Ohta[2]

[1] FUJITSU LABORATORIES LTD.
4-1-1, Kamikodanaka, Nakahara-ku, Kawasaki, 211-8588, Japan
{jyajima,shimo}@labs.fujitsu.com
[2] The University of Electro-Communications
1-5-1, Chofugaoka, Chofu-shi, Tokyo, 182-8585, Japan
{yu339,tolucky,kunihiro,ota}@ice.uec.ac.jp
[3] Chuo University
1-13-27, Kasuga, Bunkyou-ku, Tokyo, 112-8551, Japan
teiwasak@chao.ise.chuo-u.ac.jp

Abstract. In this paper, we propose a new construction algorithm for finding differential paths of Round 1 of SHA-1 for use in the collision search attack. Generally, the differential path of Round 1 is very complex, and it takes much time to find one by hand. Therefore, we propose a new search algorithm that consists of three sub searches, naming the forward search, the backward search, and the joint search, so that we can find a differential path by computers. By implementing our new algorithm and doing some experiments on a computer, we actually found 383 differential paths in the joint search that are different from Wang's. Since it is designed by quite a new policy, our algorithm can search a range of space that was not examined by existing algorithms.

1 Introduction

The hash function plays an important role in modern cryptology from both the theoretical and the practical viewpoints, e.g., provably secure digital signature schemes or time-stamp business services. Its important property is *collision resistance*, that is, it is infeasible to find different messages with the same hash value. Among developed hash functions, SHA-1 has been a widely used scheme since it was issued by NIST as a Federal Information Processing Standard in 1995 [1].

The progress of collision attacks against SHA-1 is summarized as follows: Wang et al.[2] pointed out the weakness of compression functions of SHA-1. It is called the local collision (hereafter LC for short). The disturbance vector (DV) [2] was introduced in order to find an appropriate combination of LCs for SHA-1. Three conditions were required for DV for SHA-1 (see Table 2 of [3]). They were several obstacles of attacks of SHA-1. The attack discussed in [4] is only applicable to the reduced 53-step SHA-1.

J. Pieprzyk, H. Ghodosi, and E. Dawson (Eds.): ACISP 2007, LNCS 4586, pp. 45–58, 2007.
© Springer-Verlag Berlin Heidelberg 2007

Paper [3] removed these obstacles and finally succeeded in attacking the full 80-step SHA-1 with 2^{69} complexity, by adjusting the differential path of Round 1 to another possible differential path, and adopting the multi-block collision technique introduced in [4,5].

Recently Wang et al. improved their attack with the complexity of $2^{61} \sim 2^{62}$ by a new DV and advanced message modification techniques in [6,7].

Roughly speaking, their attack consists of the following procedures [3]: Obtaining message differentials $\Delta M = M' - M$ from DVs, locating differential paths which are the differences between two sequences of chaining variables yielded by the calculation of $H(M)$ and $H(M')$, deriving the sufficient conditions of chaining variables for the result of $H(M) = H(M')$, and executing collision search by constructing M using message modification (MM) so that M efficiently satisfies all the chaining variable conditions (CVCs) and message conditions (MCs). Message modification consists of basic and advanced message modifications (BMM and AMM, respectively). The former is applied to steps 1 to 16, and the latter is applied to steps larger than 16.

The followings remained unclear even after the previous studies: 1) How to select good disturbance vectors, 2) How to locate differential paths, and derive CVCs and MCs, and 3) How to perform advanced message modification.

Recently, many researches have discussed these unclear points. On 1), Wang et al. propose a new DV as explained in the above that was found with heuristic approach [6,7]. On 2), Hawkes et al. are trying to find a differential path by the exhaustive search, but have not succeeded yet [8]. Cannière et al. proposed on automated construction method of the differential path more efficient than exhaustive search and have succeeded in case of 64-step SHA-1 [9]. And they studied the characteristics of full-step SHA-1 in [10]. On 3), a heuristic approach proposed by Wang et al. is currently most efficient. In [6,7], they extend applicable steps of AMM from step 21 to 24.

Contribution of this paper

We propose a new algorithm for constructing a differential path and deriving CVCs and MCs of full-step SHA-1. The features of our algorithm are, 1) It consists of 3 sub-searches of the forward search, the backward search, and the joint search. 2) In the backward search, differential path candidates that are combined of LCs are generated as far as possible. 3) In the forward search, the differential path candidates are generated as many as possible. 4) In the joint search, the differential path is generated by joining the results of the forward search and the backward search. And in this search, we use the technique of carry expansion. We implemented the automatic path generation software tool using our algorithm. And by using this tool, we found 383 differential paths different from Wang's from the same DV. As far as we know, this is a first work for the algorithm to find the differential path by automated search and succeeded it in PC experiment. Moreover, our algorithm can be used to find a differential path from another DV.

This paper is organized as follows: In Section 2 we describe the algorithm of SHA-1. In Section 3 we explain the collision attack proposed by Wang et al.

In Section 4 we explain our strategy and propose our original algorithm for finding the differential path of SHA-1. In Section 5 we explain how to implement our algorithm, and report the result of our experiment. Finally, in Section 6 we conclude and survey future work.

2   Description of SHA-1[1]

SHA-1 input is an arbitrary length message M, and SHA-1 output is 160-bit data $H(M)$. The message is padded to realize a multiple of 512 bits. Padded message M is divided into several messages M_i each 512 bits long $(M = (M_1||M_2||...||M_n))$. These divided messages are input to the compression function. In this paper, we call the calculation performed in a single run of the compression function 1 block. We next explain the structure of the compression function of SHA-1. All calculations in this are 32-bit. Hereafter, we exclude the description of "mod 2^{32}".

(i). Divide the input message M_j into 32-bit messages $m_0, m_1, ..., m_{15}$.
(ii). Calculate m_{16} to m_{79} by $m_i = (m_{i-3} \oplus m_{i-8} \oplus m_{i-14} \oplus m_{i-16}) \lll 1$.
(iii). Calculate chaining variables a_i, b_i, c_i, d_i, e_i in step i by the following procedures.

$$a_i = (a_{i-1} \lll 5) + f(b_{i-1}, c_{i-1}, d_{i-1}) + e_{i-1} + m_{i-1} + k_{i-1},$$
$$b_i = a_{i-1}, c_i = b_{i-1} \lll 30, d_i = c_{i-1}, e_i = d_{i-1}.$$

(iv). $(a_0+a_{80}, b_0+b_{80}, c_0+c_{80}, d_0+d_{80}, e_0+e_{80})$ is the output of the compression function.

Symbol "$\lll j$" denotes left cyclic shift by j bits. The above process of (ii) to (iii) is repeated 80 times. Initial values a_0, b_0, c_0, d_0, e_0 for the compression function of the first block are the initial values of SHA-1. a_0, b_0, c_0, d_0, e_0 for the compression function from the second block are the output values of the previous block. Steps 1-20 are called the Round 1. Steps 21-40, 41-60, and 61-80 are Round 2, Round 3 and Round 4, respectively, k_i is a constant defined in each round. Function f is a Boolean function defined in each round, $(b \wedge c) \vee (\neg b \wedge d)$ in the Round 1, $b \oplus c \oplus d$ in the Round 2 and the Round 4 and $(b \wedge c) \vee (c \wedge d) \vee (d \wedge b)$ in the Round 3.

2.1   Notations

Δa :   An Arithmetic differential value of a $(a' - a)$.
∇a :   differential values of each bit in a [1].

---

[1] For example, $a' = $ 0x5E50CA8B , $b' = $ 0x4223594C s.t. $a = $ 0x1E4FCAAB , $b = $ 0x0222596C, and $\Delta a = \Delta b = $ 0x4000FFE0, ∇a and ∇b are as follows.
$\nabla a = \{0, +, 0, 0, 0, 0, 0, 0, 0, 0, 0, 0, +, -, -, -, -, 0, 0, 0, 0, 0, 0, 0, 0, 0, -, 0, 0, 0, 0, 0\}$,
$\nabla b = \{0, +, 0, 0, 0, 0, 0, 0, 0, 0, 0, 0, 0, 0, 0, 0, +, 0, 0, 0, 0, 0, 0, 0, 0, 0, -, 0, 0, 0, 0, 0\}$.
('+' shows the change from 0 to 1, and '−' shows the change from 1 to 0.) We define "carry expansion" as exchanging a nabla representation from a certain parameter ∇x to another nabla representation ∇x_{exp} with respect to $\#\nabla x < \#\nabla x_{exp}$ and $\Delta x = \Delta x_{exp}$, where $\#\nabla x$ is the number of non-zero elements of ∇x. For example, the above ∇a is a carry-expansion of ∇b (3-bit carry expansion).

δa :   XOR differential value of a ($a' \oplus a$).
CVC(a) :   Chaining Variable Condition of a [2].
HW(Δa) :   Hamming Weight of Δa [3].
$\#carry(\nabla a)$:   Length of Carry Expansion of ∇a [4].

3   The Outline of Wang's Attack

In this section, we introduce the collision search technique proposed by Wang et al.[3,6,7]. One of features of their technique is to derive a collision message pair at not one hash block but two consecutive blocks (Fig. 1). In their technique, following conditions are needed for each block of a collision search.

1. Disturbance Vector(DV).
2. Differential Path, Chaining Variable Conditions(CVCs) and Message Conditions(MCs) corresponding to the DV.
3. Message Modification(MM) corresponding to the result of 2

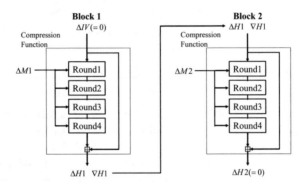

Fig. 1. The outline of Wang's attack in collision search phase

In [3,6,7], they describe (a part of) construction methods and results of 1-3 for the 1st block. Especially, the differential path is derived with a heuristic [11] approach. For the 2nd block, they only estimate the complexity. Constitution of 1-3 for the 2nd block must be done with respect to each result of collision search for the 1st block. There are too much heuristic operations to construct the differential path easily. Therefore, we propose the new algorithm for the construction of the differential path with automated approach. Our algorithm is described in the next section.

---

[2] CVC is a condition that must be satisfied for collision search [3]. It exists in each bit of each variable. For example, there are '0', '1', '=', and 'N'(no condition), etc,...

[3] We define the hamming weight of Δa as the number of terms of essential differential values. For example, $HW(2^{31}) = 1$, $HW(2^{31} - 2^2) = 2$ and $HW(2^5 - 2^4 - 2^3) = HW(2^3) = 1$.

[4] We define the length of carry expansion of ∇a as the number $\#\nabla a - HW(\Delta a)$.

4   Proposed Strategy for Finding Differential Path

We propose an algorithm for constructing a differential path of Round 1. It is well known that differential paths for Round 2 to 4 can be plainly constructed from a DV (just arrange the LCs that are determined by the DV), it is very important to find an efficient algorithm for Round 1.

4.1   Strategy

Our goal is to construct the differential path and to derive CVCs and MCs of Round 1 with a given DV. To construct it, the following parameters are needed.

- DV
- ∇IV
- δm_i for $i = 0, ..., 19$ (derived by the DV)
- Differential values from Round 2($\nabla a_{20}, \nabla a_{19}, \nabla a_{18}, \nabla a_{17}, \nabla a_{16}$)

We construct the differential path, CVCs and MCs by searching on a computer. When a differential path is searched from step 1 straightforwardly (forward search), the search space becomes huge in several steps. (An image of the search is shown at the Fig.2(a).) Hence, we try to reduce the search space. In order to execute AMM effectively, a differential path should have CVCs with a small number of conditions in step 11 to 20. We note that such differential path is achieved by combining LCs with the backward search procedure from step 20. When a differential path in intermediate step has CVCs with large number of conditions, the path is excluded from this search. In our algorithm, we compare the current path with the path made by LCs and give up the path if the difference grows too much. Using this excluding algorithm, the search space is efficiently reduced. However, if this search is continued back to step 1, the search space is too large to find a differential path that has input differential value ∇IV. (The image of the search is shown at the Fig.2(b).)

Consequently, we take the strategy of joining the results of the forward search and the backward search. Then, we execute the forward search to find the candidates of differential path of step 1 to n, and we join the results of the forward search and the backward search by using the joint search in the middle of Round 1 (step $n+1 \sim n+5$). In the joint search, for ($\Delta a_n, \Delta b_n, \Delta c_n, \Delta d_n, \Delta e_n$) taken from the output of the forward search and ($\Delta a_{n+6}, \Delta b_{n+6}, \Delta c_{n+6}, \Delta d_{n+6}, \Delta e_{n+6}$) taken from the output of the backward search, we look for a path whose input differentials are ($\Delta a_n, \Delta b_n, \Delta c_n, \Delta d_n, \Delta e_n$) and whose outputs differentials are ($\Delta a_{n+6}, \Delta b_{n+6}, \Delta c_{n+6}, \Delta d_{n+6}, \Delta e_{n+6}$). We use for carry-expansion technique for generating many candidates, which helps join the results of the two searches. An image of the forward search is shown at the left of Fig.2(a). And the total search range of our algorithm is shown at the right of Fig.2(c).

4.2   Proposed Algorithm

Our algorithm consists of three sub-searches. In our proposal algorithm, we execute the forward search(step $1 \sim n$) and the backward search(step $20 \sim$

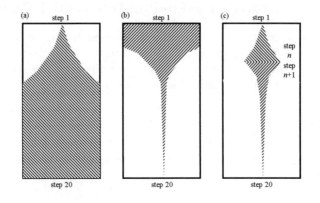

Fig. 2. An illustration of the search range of our algorithm

$n + 6$) independently. And we input the results of the both searches to the joint search(step $n + 1 \sim n + 5$). In the joint search, carries of ∇a_n and ∇a_{n+1} are expanded in order to join the results of the forward search and the backward search. The value of n is defined previously.

Forward search
In this search, many differential paths, CVCs and MCs for step 1 to n are constructed from DV and ΔIV. This search derives all candidates of the differential path, CVCs and MCs in considering variations of the followings.

- CVCs of ∇a_i in each step i.
- Signs of each bit in message differentials.
- Output differential values of rotation operation.
- Carries of ∇a_i in each step i.

When we consider all variations mentioned the above, the number of results becomes very huge. Therefore, it is infeasible to derive whole of the candidates by this search. Hence we introduce the following parameters as thresholds.

- $(MAX\_CARRY(i))$: The maximum values of $\#carry(\nabla a_i)$ in each step i.
- $(MAX\_HW(i))$: The maximum values of $HW(\Delta a_i)$ in each step i.

The procedure at step i is as follows. The procedure is executed for $i = 1$ to n.

1. Take a sign $(+, -)$ on each non-zero bit in the message differential in step i and set MCs.
2. Take a $\{(\nabla a_{i-1}, \nabla b_{i-1}, \nabla c_{i-1}, \nabla d_{i-1}, \nabla e_{i-1})$ and CVCs of $(a_{i-1}, b_{i-1}, c_{i-1}, d_{i-1}, e_{i-1})\}$ from the result of the previous step.
3. Calculate all variations of $f_f = \{\Delta f(b_{i-1}, c_{i-1}, d_{i-1})$ and CVCs of $(b_{i-1}, c_{i-1}, d_{i-1})\}$. Discard all f_f whose CVCs contradict the CVCs calculated in the above steps.

4. Calculate all variations of $\Delta a_i = (\Delta a_{i-1} \lll 5) + \Delta f(b_{i-1}, c_{i-1}, d_{i-1}) + \Delta m_{i-1} + \Delta e_{i-1}$ [5]. Set ∇a_i in the nabla expression of Δa_i whose $\#\nabla a_i$ is the smallest.
5. Discard Δa_i when $HW(\Delta a_i) > MAX\_HW(i)$.
6. Expand carries of ∇a_i up to $MAX\_CARRY(i)$. And calculate CVC corresponds with the expanded ∇a_i. Calculate all variations of these $\{\nabla a_i$ and CVC of $a_i\}$.
7. Output $FS_{out} = \{(\nabla a_i, \nabla b_i, \nabla c_i, \nabla d_i, \nabla e_i)$ and CVCs of $(\nabla a_i, \nabla b_i, \nabla c_i, \nabla d_i, \nabla e_i)\}$ as a result of the search at step i.
8. Execute 1-7 for all variations at step i.

Backward search
In this search, several differential paths, CVCs and MCs for step 20 to $n + 6$ are constructed from a DV and the differential values from Round 2. To execute AMM efficiently, we construct the differential paths whose number of CVCs of step 20 to $n+6$ is small. Such differential paths are constructed by arranging the LCs that are determined by a DV. However, such differential paths cannot be constructed for some values of DV. For example, when DV has "1" in the same bit position in consecutive 2 steps, we cannot construct such differential paths for any CVC according to LC technique in Round 1. Then we use reference-differential paths for excluding useless candidates. Let a reference-differential path be a differential path simply constructed from LCs associated with given DV. The values of $MAX\_HW(i)$ must be defined at the beginning of the procedure. The procedure is as follows.

1. Take a sign $(+, -)$ on each non-zero bit in the message differentials and set MCs in step $n+6$ to 20. And make a reference-differential path corresponds with the message differentials.
2. For $i = 20$ to $n + 6$, execute 3-7.
3. Take a $\{(\nabla a_i, \nabla b_i, \nabla c_i, \nabla d_i, \nabla e_i)$ and CVCs of $(a_i, b_i, c_i, d_i, e_i)\}$ from the result of the step $(i + 1)$.
4. Calculate $\Delta f_{obj} = \Delta e_{i-1} - \Delta a_i - (\Delta a_{i-1} \lll 5) - \Delta m_{i-1}$. Δe_{i-1} is taken from the reference-differential path.
5. Calculate all variations of $f_b = \{\Delta f(b_{i-1}, c_{i-1}, d_{i-1})$ and CVCs of $(b_{i-1}, c_{i-1}, d_{i-1})$ $\}$ Discard all f_b whose CVCs contradict the CVCs calculated in the following steps. And discard all f_b if $HW(\Delta f(b_{i-1}, c_{i-1}, d_{i-1}) - \Delta f_{obj}) > MAX\_HW(i)$
6. Output $BS_{out} = (\nabla a_{i-1}, \nabla b_{i-1}, \nabla c_{i-1}, \nabla d_{i-1}, \nabla e_{i-1})$ and CVCs of $(\nabla a_{i-1}, \nabla b_{i-1}, \nabla c_{i-1}, \nabla d_{i-1}, \nabla e_{i-1})\}$ as a result of the search at step i.
7. Execute 3-6 for all variations of the output at step i.

Joint search
In this search, the results of the forward search(step 1-n) and the backward search(step 20-$n + 6$) are joined in step $(n+1 \sim n+5)$. An image of this search is shown as Fig.3. In the figure, gray marks mean the result of the forward search, and white marks mean the result of the backward search.

---

[5] We note that $\Delta a_{i-1} \lll 5$ is not always equal to $(a'_{i-1} \lll 5) - (a_{i-1} \lll 5)$.

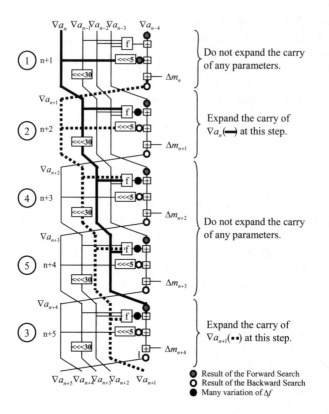

Fig. 3. An outline of the joint search

We think that when we have many candidates of Δf in each step, the results of the forward search and the backward search are joined easily. To obtain many candidates of Δf, we expand carries of $\nabla a_n, \nabla a_{n+1}$. This increases the variations of the differential values of Δf in step $n+2 \sim n+5$ (black marks). We note that the values of Δa_n and Δa_{n+1} are stable while carries of ∇a_n and ∇a_{n+1} are expanded. Therefore, no change of the differential paths found by the forward search and the backward search is caused. In step $n+1$, we try to join the results of the both searches by simple comparing of Δa_{n+1}.

The processing order of these 5 steps is $n + 1$, $n + 2$, $n + 5$, $n + 3$, and $n + 4$. This order is efficient for the computer search. We explain the effectiveness of this order in the next section. The values of $MAX\_CARRY\_J(n)$ and $MAX\_CARRY\_J(n + 1)$ must be defined at the beginning of the procedure.

1. Read FS_{out} from the result of the forward search. If all $FS_{out} = \emptyset$, stop this procedure as "FAILURE".
2. Read BS_{out} from the result of the backward search. If all $BS_{out} = \emptyset$, go back to 1.
3. Execute from 4 to 8, for $i = n + 1, n + 2, n + 5, n + 3, n + 4$.

4. If $i = n + 2$, expand carries of ∇a_n to $MAX\_CARRY\_J(n)$ and calculate CVC corresponds with the ∇a_n. Calculate all variations of these $\{\nabla a_n$ and CVC of $a_n\}$. If $i = n+5$, expand carries of ∇a_{n+1} to $MAX\_CARRY\_J(n+1)$ and calculate CVC corresponds with the ∇a_{n+1}. Calculate all variations of these $\{\nabla a_{n+1}$ and CVC of $a_{n+1}\}$. (If $i = n+1, n+3, n+4$, carry expansion is not executed.)

5. Calculate all variation of $f_j = \{\Delta f(b_{i-1}, c_{i-1}, d_{i-1})$ and CVCs of $(b_{i-1}, c_{i-1}, d_{i-1})\}$ Discard f_js whose CVCs contradict the CVCs calculated in the another steps.

6. Take a sign $(+, -)$ on each non-zero bit of message differentials in step i and set MCs. If all variations of sign are taken, go back to 2.

7. Calculate all variations of $\Delta x_i = \Delta a_i - \Delta m_{i-1} - (\Delta a_{i-1} \ggg 5) - \Delta a_{i-5}$. If all variations of Δx_i are taken, go back to 6.

8. If the result of 5 and 7 are the same, go to 3 to continue the loop. If they are not, go back to 7 to calculate the next candidate.

If this procedure is completed without any contradiction, the differential path from step $n+1$ to $n+5$ is constructed successfully. Finally, the differential path, CVCs, and MCs of all steps in Round 1 are completely constructed.

5   Implementation and Experiment

We implemented the three sub-searches proposed in section 4. In implementing each search, we adopted the composition whose search space can be adjusted at the execution time. We explain the details in each paragraph. We also implemented efficient techniques to treat the operations of the arithmetic differential value(Δa), the arithmetic differential value of each bit(∇a), the XOR differential values (δa), and CVCs.

5.1   Implementation of Sub-Searches

Forward search
In this search, the number of search results at each step increases in exponential according to the step. Therefore, this may cause the memory overflow. Then, we implemented by the following policies in order to save the memory requirement.

– We implemented this search that we can control the amount of input data at each step in the path search phase. (We input a part of results from previous step in the path search phase.)
– We implemented this search that works just 1 step. (We execute this implementation n times repeatedly, in the path search phase.)

We treat the variables $MAX\_HW(i)$ and $MAX\_CARRY(i)$ that can be modifiable in the path search phase to manage the search space. It is not always satisfy $(\Delta a_{i-1} \lll 5) \neq (a'_{i-1} \lll 5) - (a_{i-1} \lll 5)$. We discard ∇a_{i-1} related Δa_{i-1} that doesn't satisfy this equation for simplify the implementation. When

Table 1. The range of each sub-search

Forward search	step1 - step8
Backward search	step14 - step20
Joint search	step9 - step13

we want to expand the search space in the path search phase, we adjust the variables $MAX\_HW(i)$ and $MAX\_CARRY(i)$. The satisfaction of the equation is checked between the item 6 and 7 in the forward search algorithm described in §4.2.

Backward search

In this search, It is not always satisfy $(\Delta a_{i-1} \lll 5) \neq (a'_{i-1} \lll 5) - (a_{i-1} \lll 5)$. We discard ∇a_{i-1} related Δa_{i-1} that doesn't satisfy this equation for simplify the implementation like the forward search.

Joint search

In this search, carries of ∇a_n and ∇a_{n+1} are expanded as described in §4.2. This enables easy to join the result of the forward search and the backward search. But this also greatly increases the variations of CVCs outputted at each step and the number of states that should be stored into the memory. Especially, the number of states depends on the variations of ∇a_n and ∇a_{n+1}.

We implemented in order of step $n+1, n+2, n+5, n+3$ and $n+4$ as shown in Fig.3. According to this order, we can discard many of candidates at once whose ∇a_n or ∇a_{n+1} cannot connect the FS_{out} and BS_{out}. Then, we can save greatly the memory requirement and reduce the number of dependencies of each CVC. In addition, the maximum length of carry-expansion of ∇a_n and ∇a_{n+1} can be modifiable in the path search phase.

5.2   Experiment

We searched a differential path by using the automatic path generation software implemented in the previous sub-section. In this experiment, we used the data described in [3] as input data, and we operated each sub-search with the following ranges in Table 1. As a result of the experiment, we confirmed three sub-searches independently worked correctly. The computer environment is as follows.

Computer environment
    PC   Fujitsu FMV LIFEBOOK Q8220
    OS   Microsoft Windows XP SP2
    CPU Intel Core Solo U1400 1.2GHz
    RAM DDR2 SDRAM PC2-4200 1GB

Forward search

In this experiment, we set the parameters as follows. As a result, we could obtain millions of the output at step 8. The processing time from step 1 to 3 is shown

Table 2. The results of the forward search

Step	#search results	Time
1	9	4.7 msec
2	2050	266 msec
3	257306	17.3 sec

in table 2. After step 4, number of obtained data becomes very huge when we input all the results of the previous step. Then, we input partial data from the previous step after step 4 to 8, and this partial search worked tens of hours until the search was finished.

Parameters
step1-step3 : $MAX\_HW(step) = 4, MAX\_CARRY(step) = 3$
step4-step8 : $MAX\_HW(step) = 3, MAX\_CARRY(step) = 0$

Backward search
In this experiment, we set all the parameter $MAX\_HW(i)$ to 2. As a result, we could obtain 10 outputs at step 14. This search worked in about half a second.

Joint search
In this experiment, we set the parameters of carry expansion length of ∇a_8 and ∇a_9 to 16. We inputted data (the arithmetic differential value, the each bit differential values and CVCs) described in [3]. In about CVCs, we reset some bits to be 'N' that seems to be no condition theoretically when we start this search. As a result, we could obtain 384 patterns of differential path, CVCs and MCs. 383 in them were original paths, CVCs and MCs that are different from Wang's. It took 13.3 seconds for each input of a pair; one output of the forward search and one output of the backward search.

6   Conclusion

In this paper, we proposed an new algorithm for the constructing differential paths for a collision attack against SHA-1. The algorithm outputs a differential path, CVCs and MCs of Round 1 corresponding with a given DV, a differential value from Round 2 and ∇IV. By this algorithm, we can automatically construct a differential path from various DV and ∇IV. There are three sub-searches in our algorithm: the backward search, forward search, and joint search. In the forward search, the search space is limited by the hamming weight and the carry length of the differential values of output at each step. And in this condition, the algorithm calculates all variation of the differential values, CVCs and MCs for step 1 through n (ex.$n = 8$). In the backward search, it finds differential paths whose number of CVCs is as few as possible at step 20 to $n + 6$ so that it can make AMM efficiently to execute. Finally, the carry of two parameters are expanded in the joint search, and both search results are tried to join in step $n + 1$ to $n + 5$.

We implemented our proposal algorithm on the computer and executed computer experiment by using the DV in [3]. We executed the forward search from step 1 to 8, the backward search from step 20 back to 14 and the joint search from step 9 to 13. As a result, we succeeded in obtaining millions outputs in the forward search, 10 outputs in the backward search and 384 outputs in the joint search. We found 383 patterns of paths with CVCs and MCs by the joint search that are our original and differed from Wang's. The processing time were tens of hours in the forward search, half a second in the backward search and about thirteen seconds to find a differential in the joint search. By these results, we can confirm the correctness of our strategy, search algorithms and implementations.

In the future, we will try to find a collision message pair of SHA-1. In [7], Wang insisted that the complexity to find a collision message pair is $2^{61} \sim 2^{62}$. We think that this complexity may be difficult to execute by present computers. In order to much reduce the complexity, another DV different from Wang's might needed we think. Our algorithm and implementation can be used to find a differential path from such the DVs .

References

1. NIST. Secure hash standard. Federal Information Processing Standard, FIPS180-1, (April 1995)
2. Wang, X.: The Collision Attack on SHA-0. (in Chinese) (to appear) http://www.infosec.edu.cn
3. Wang, X., Yin, Y.L., Yu, H.: Finding Collisions in the Full SHA-1. In: Shoup, V. (ed.) CRYPTO 2005. LNCS, vol. 3621, pp. 17–36. Springer, Heidelberg (2005)
4. Biham, E., Chen, R., Joux, A., Carribault, P., Lemuet, C., Jalby, W.: Collisions in SHA-0 and Reduced SHA-1. In: Cramer, R.J.F. (ed.) EUROCRYPT 2005. LNCS, vol. 3494, pp. 36–57. Springer, Heidelberg (2005)
5. Wang, X., Yu, H.: How to Break MD5 and Other Hash Functions. In: Cramer, R.J.F. (ed.) EUROCRYPT 2005. LNCS, vol. 3494, pp. 19–35. Springer, Heidelberg (2005)
6. Wang, X., Yao, A.C, Yao, F.: Cryptanalysis on SHA-1 Hash Function. Keynote Speech at CRYPTOGRAPHIC HASH WORKSHOP
7. Wang, X.: Cryptanalysis of Hash functions and Potential Dangers. Invited Talk at CT-RSA (2006)
8. Hawkes, P., Paddon, M., Rose, G.: Automated Search for Round 1 Differentials for SHA-1: Work in Progress. NIST SECOND CRYPTOGRAPHIC HASH WORK-SHOP (August 2006)
9. Cannière, C.D., Rechberger, C.: Finding SHA-1 Characteristics. ASIACRYPT (2006)
10. Cannière, C.D., Rechberger, C.: Finding SHA-1 Characteristics: General Results and Applications. NIST SECOND CRYPTOGRAPHIC HASH WORKSHOP (August 2006)
11. Wang, X.: Private Communication in Japan

Appendix. An Example of the Results of the Joint Search

Table 3 and Table 4 show an example of the results of the joint search by using the data described in [3]. Our original part of the differential path is step 9 to 13 and CVCs are a_5 to a_{11}. (The data from step 1 to 8 and from step 14 to 20 are as same as Wang's.) We found such 384 differential paths. (One of them is the same as Wang's.)

Table 3. An example of our path(step9-13)

step	x_{i-1}	Δm_{i-1}	Δa_i(no carry)	∇a_i(with carry)
1	40000001	$29, 30$	$29, 30$	$29, 30$
2	2	$-1, -3, 5, -29, -30, 31$	$1, 5, 29$	$-1, 2, -5, -6, 7, -29, -30, 31$
3	2	$0, 1, -6, 29$	$-0, 3, 10$	$-0, 3, -10, -11, -12, 13$
4	80000002	$6, 28, -29, -31$	$-1, 8, 15, -31$	$-1, 8, -15, -16, -17, 18, -31$
5	1	$0, -1, -4, 6, 28, 30, 31$	$-5, 20, 27$	$4, -5, -20, 21, 27$
6	0	$-1, -5, 28, 30, 31$	$10, 15, 25$	$-10, -11, 12, -15, 16, -25, 26$
7	80000001	29	$0, -4, -5, 31$	$0, -3, 5, -6, 31$
8	2	$-1, -4, -5, 29, 30$	-18	$18, ..., -25$
9	2	$0, -1, -6, -\mathbf{29}, 30$	$-2, -9$	$-1, 9, ..., -19$
10	2	$6, -29$	1	1
11	0	$1, -6, \mathbf{29}, 30, \mathbf{31}$	8	$-8, 9$
12	0	$1, -29, \mathbf{30}$	-3	-3
13	1	$0, 31$	0	0
14	0	-5		
15	80000002	$-0, 1$	-31	-31
16	2	$+1, 4, -6, -30$	1	1
17	80000002	$-6, 30$	$-1, 31$	$-1, 31$
18	0	$-1, -4, 6, 29, 30, 31$		
19	2	$29, 31$	1	1
20	0	$-6, 31$		

Table 4. CVCs of the original path(a_5-a_{11})

Chaining variable	Conditions on bits			
	31-24	23-16	15-8	7-0
a_1	a00-----	--------	1-----aa	1-0a11aa
a_2	01110---	------1-	0aaa-0--	011-001-
a_3	0-100---	-0-aaa0-	--0111--	01110-01
a_4	10010---	a1---011	10011010	10011-10
a_5	001a0---	--01-000	10001111	-010-11-
a_6	1-0-0011	1-1001-0	111011-1	a10-000-
a_7	0---1011	1a0111--	101--010	-10-11-0
a_8	-01---10	000000aa	001aa111	---01-1-
a_9	-10-----	10001000	0000000-	---11-1-
a_{10}	1-------	**0000000-**	11100000	0-----0-
a_{11}	1-------	------10	11111101	1-a-----
a_{12}	0-------	--------	--------	10--11--
a_{13}	--------	--------	--------	11----10
a_{14}	-0------	--------	--------	----0-1-
a_{15}	10------	--------	--------	----1-0-
a_{16}	--1-----	--------	--------	----0-0-
a_{17}	0-0-----	--------	--------	------1-
a_{18}	--1-----	--------	--------	----a---
a_{19}	--b-----	--------	--------	------0-
a_{20}	--------	--------	--------	-------1

The notation 'a' stands for the condition $a_{i,j} = a_{i-1,j}$ and 'b' denotes the condition $a_{19,30} = a_{18,32}$ as same as in [3].

Preimage Attack on the Parallel FFT-Hashing Function[*]

Donghoon Chang[1], Moti Yung[2], Jaechul Sung[3], Seokhie Hong[1],
and Sangjin Lee[1]

[1] Center for Information Security Technologies(CIST), Korea University, Korea
{dhchang,hsh,sangjin}@cist.korea.ac.kr
[2] RSA Laboratories and Department of Computer Science, Columbia University, New
York, USA
moti@cs.columbia.edu
[3] Department of Mathematics, University of Seoul, Korea
jcsung@uos.ac.kr

Abstract. The parallel FFT-Hashing function was designed by C. P.
Schnorr and S. Vaudenay in 1993. The function is a simple and light
weight hash algorithm with 128-bit digest. Its basic component is a multi-
permutation which helps in proving its resistance to collision attacks.

In this work we show a preimage attack on the parallel FFT-Hashing
function using $2^{t+64} + 2^{128-t}$ time complexity and 2^t memory, which
is less than the generic complexity 2^{128}. Specifically, when $t = 32$, we
can find a preimage using 2^{97} time and 2^{32} memory. Our method can
be described as "disseminative-meet-in-the-middle-attack". we actually
use the properties of multi-permutation (helpful against collision attack)
to our advantage in the attack. Overall, this type of attack (beating the
generic one) demonstrates that the structure of the parallel FFT-Hashing
function has some weaknesses when preimage attack is considered (and
relevant). To the best of our knowledge, this is the first attack on the
parallel FFT-Hashing function.

Keywords: Cryptographic Hash Function, Preimage Attack, the Parallel FFT-Hashing function.

1 Introduction

Nowadays, motivated by the breaking of the MD4-style hash functions family,
novel constructions of cryptographic hash functions are required as are better
understanding of their design principles.

[*] This research was supported by the MIC(Ministry of Information and Communication), Korea, under the ITRC(Information Technology Research Center) support
program supervised by the IITA(Institute of Information Technology Advancement)
(IITA-2006-(C1090-0603-0025)). Part of this work was done while the first author
visited Columbia University.

J. Pieprzyk, H. Ghodosi, and E. Dawson (Eds.): ACISP 2007, LNCS 4586, pp. 59–67, 2007.
© Springer-Verlag Berlin Heidelberg 2007

The parallel FFT-Hashing function is an example of a potential novel construction. This paper investigates this function, suggested by Schnorr and Vaudenay in 1993 [4] (improving and correcting previously broken designs [2,3,1,6,5]). The parallel FFT-Hashing function uses a simple component called 'multipermutation' repeatedly. The designers proved that the parallel FFT-Hashing function is collision resistant when the black box multi-permutations are given by the oracle. On the other hand, the designers did not say anything about other security notions such as preimage resistance and second preimage resistance. Unlike MD4-style hash function whose compression function is not invertible, the parallel FFT-Hashing function has a step function which is invertible. For the parallel FFT-Hashing function (the MD4-style hash function), each message string is applied only to one step function (one compression function). Also the internal size of the parallel FFT-Hashing function is twice the output size. Thus, one may think that the parallel FFT-Hashing function can be secure against preimage attacks. Further, the FFT-Hashing function seems to be even secure against time-memory trade-off attacks.

In this paper, however, we give an attack that finds a preimage with complexity $2^{t+64} + 2^{128-t}$ and memory 2^t, which is less than the cost of its (generic) exhaustive search complexity (2^{128}). This attack, therefore, demonstrates some weaknesses in the structure of the design, at least when considered in settings where protection against preimage finding is crucial. We note that our attack exploits the properties of the multi-permutation components, i.e., we capitalize on exactly the property that helps preventing collision attacks in finding the preimage.

General Meet-in-the-Middle Attack. Our attack method is different from the general meet-in-the-middle attack. To show this, we explain the general meet-in-the-middle attack on the parallel FFT-Hashing function. Given a hash output o, we want to find its preimage. The parallel FFT-Hashing function can be described as in Fig. 1. The size of the internal state is 256 bits and the output size is 128 bits. f (corresponding to a step function of the parallel FFT-Hashing function) and g (corresponding to the last s steps which is the constant related to the collision resistance property) can be inverted with complexity 1.

We choose randomly $x_{i+1} \sim x_l$ and compute the corresponding value r in Fig. 1 and store them in table. This is repeated to get 2^t cases. Similarly, from $x_1 \sim x_i$ we compute the corresponding value s in Fig. 1. If s is stored in the table (i.e., we meet in the middle), we get a preimage of o. According to the

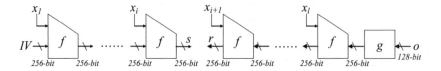

Fig. 1. The Structure of the parallel FFT-Hashing function. f and g are invertible.

birthday paradox, in order to get one preimage we have to compute s from random $x_1 \sim x_i$ 2^{256-t} times. Therefore, we can get a preimage with complexity $2^t + 2^{256-t}$ and memory size 2^t. On the other hand, this paper's attack shows that we can find a preimage with complexity $2^{t+64} + 2^{128-t}$ and memory 2^t.

2   The Parallel FFT-Hashing Function

In this section, we describe the parallel FFT-Hashing function [4]. The size of each word is 16 bits. Here $+$ is the addition modulo 2^{16} and $a \odot b = (a'b' \bmod 2^{16} + 1) \bmod 2^{16}$ where for $a \neq 0$ and $b \neq 0$ $a' = a$ and $b' = b$ and for $a=0$ and $b=0$ $a' = 2^{16}$ and $b' = 2^{16}$. L means the one-bit circular left shift on 4-bit strings and R^j is the j-bit circular right shift on 16-bit strings. Further, $c = 0000000011111111$ is a 16-bit constant and $s = 5$ is the constant related to the number of steps in Fig. 2, which guarantees the collision resistance. In our attack, we can find a preimage for any s (even for big s). The initial value is $(c_0, c_1, \cdots, c_{15})$ which is 16 words. $(c_0, c_1, c_2, c_3):=$(0xef01, 0x2345, 0x6789, 0xabcd), $(c_4, c_5, c_6, c_7):=$(0xdcba, 0x9876, 0x5432, 0x10fe), $c_{8+i}:=\overline{c_i}$ for $i=0,...,7$ where $\overline{c_i}$ is the bitwise logical negation of c_i. Each step of the parallel FFT-Hashing is depicted in Fig. 3.

PaFFTHashing$(M) = o_0||o_1|| \cdots ||o_7$

M is the padded message for which $M = m_0||m_1|| \cdots ||m_{n-1} \in E^n$

1.   For $i = 0, ... ,15$ Do $e_i := c_i$ ($c_0|| \cdots ||c_{15}$ is the initial value.)
2.   For $j = 0, ... ,\lceil n/3 \rceil$+s-2 Do   (: Step j)
    2.1   For $i = 0, ... ,11$ Do
            If $m_{3j+(i \bmod 3)}$ is defined,
            $e_{L(i)} := e_{L(i)} + m_{3j+(i \bmod 3)}$ for even i.
            $e_{L(i)} := e_{L(i)} \odot m_{3j+(i \bmod 3)}$ for odd i.
    2.2   For $i = 0, ... ,7$ Do in parallel
        $e_{2i} := e_{L(2i)} \oplus e_{L(2i+1)}$, $e_{2i+1} := e_{L(2i)} \oplus (e_{L(2i+1)} \wedge c) \oplus R^{2i+1}(e_{L(2i+1)})$
    2.3   For $i = 0, ... ,15$ Do $e_i := e_i \odot c_i$
3.   Output $h_4(M) := o_0||o_1|| \cdots ||o_7$ for which $o_i = e_{L(2i)} \odot e_{L(2i+1)}$.

Fig. 2. The parallel FFT-hashing function

3   Attack Strategy and Several Properties

In this section, we describe the strategy of our preimage attack on the parallel FFT-Hashing function. See Fig. 4. Our target is to find a padded preimage $m_0||m_1|| \cdots ||m_{47}$ when a hash output $o_0||o_1|| \cdots ||o_7$ is given. This strategy consists of 4 phases.

In the first phase, we choose a constant $w_0||w_1|| \cdots ||w_6||w_7$. In the second phase, we show how to find a message $m_0||m_1|| \cdots ||m_{23}$ such that the last 4 words of output of step 7.5 are $w_4||w_5||w_6||w_7$ with complexity 1 (time complexity 1 means the time required to simulate 7.5 steps in this case, and the time of computing the entire function once, in general).

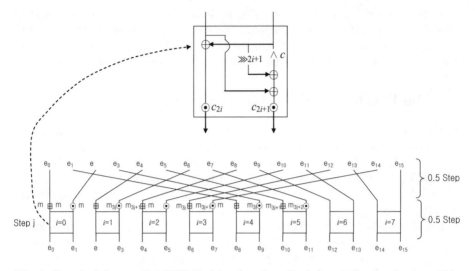

Fig. 3. Step j of the parallel FFT-Hashing function. Each box indicates the invertible multi-permutation which is explained in property 2 in Section 3.

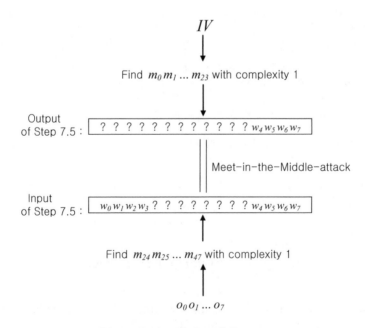

Fig. 4. Preimage Attack Strategy

In the third phase, given hash output $o_0||o_1|| \cdots ||o_7$, we show how to find a message $m_{24}||m_{25}|| \cdots ||m_{47}$ such that the first 4 words of the input of step 7.5 and the last 4 words of the input of step 7.5 are $w_0||w_1||w_2||w_3$ and $w_4||w_5||w_6||w_7$ with complexity 1, respectively (time complexity 1 means more precisely here the

time required to simulate 7.5+s steps). In the fourth phase, we find a preimage
with the meet-in-the-middle-attack method on the results of phases 2 and 3.
We can call this type of meet-in-the-middle-attack "disseminative-meet-in-the-
middle-attack" (i.e., partial values are first disseminated through the function
structure and the rest is completed employing man-in-the-middle).

We want to describe useful three properties which help us to find a preimage
of the parallel FFT-Hashing function.

Property 1: In each step, the last two words of the output e_{13}, e_{15} depend only
on the input words $e_9, e_{11}, e_{13}, e_{15}$. See Fig. 3.

A permutation $B : E^2 \rightarrow E^2$, $B(a, b) = (B_1(a, b), B_2(a, b))$, is a *multi-
permutation* if for every $a, b \in E$ the mappings $B_i(a, *)$, $B_i(*, b)$ for $i = 1, 2$
are permutations on E.

Property 2: Each box of Fig. 3 is an invertible multi-permutation [5] ($E =
\{0, 1\}^{16}$). For example, for any b and i, if $B_i(*, b)$ is fixed, then $*$ and
$B_{i+1 \bmod 2}(*, b)$ are determined automatically. And for any a, $a \odot *$ and $* \odot a$
are invertible permutations on $\{0, 1\}^{16}$.

Property 3: For any $a, b, c, d, a', b', c', d', t$ and all cases of Fig. 5, if we choose
the value of m, m' and m^* are determined automatically by property 2 and then
the undefined values are also determined.

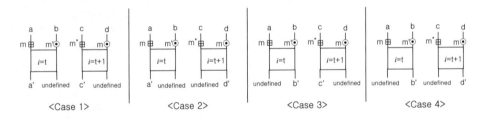

<Case 1>   <Case 2>   <Case 3>   <Case 4>

Fig. 5. Four Cases of Property 3

4   Preimage Attack on the Parallel FFT-Hashing Function

In this section, we show how to get a preimage for a given hash output
$o_0||o_1|| \cdots ||o_7$. The original preimage is $m_0||m_1|| \cdots ||m_{42}$. After the preimage
is padded, the padded preimage is $m_0||m_1|| \cdots ||m_{47}$ where the last four words
$w_{44}||w_{45}||w_{46}||w_{47}$ indicate the message length and m_{43} is '1000000000000000'.
Our attack idea is a disseminative-meet-in-the-middle attack in the location of
output of Step 7.5.

<u>First Phase</u> (Choice of a constant $w_0||w_1|| \cdots ||w_6||w_7$) See Fig. 6. We can de-
scribe the relations among (0)~(35) like table 1. In table 1, $a \rightarrow b$ means that
the value of b is determined by the value of a. (0) ~ (3) [the last 4 entries into
step 0 layer in Fig. 6] are already fixed values because they are initial values. So,

Table 1. Relations among (0)~(35) in Fig 6

(0),(1),(2),(3) → (20),(21)	(20),(21) → (23)
(4),(5) → (22)	(22),(23) → (25)
(6),(7) → (24)	(24),(25) → (27)
(8),(9) → (26)	(26),(27) → (29)
(10),(11) → (28)	(28),(29) → (31)
(12),(13) → (30)	(30),(31) → (33)
(14),(15) → (32)	(32),(33) → (35)
(16),(17) → (34)	

if we choose values of (4) ~ (17), then the values of (20) ~ (35) are determined (via computation) by property 1 as we describe in table 1. And we choose the values of (18) and (19). Finally, we let $w_4||w_5||w_6||w_7$ be (18)||(19)||(34)||(35) and let $w_0||w_1||w_2||w_3$ be any fixed value.

<u>Second Phase</u> (find a message $m_0||m_1||\cdots||m_{23}$ which keeps the last 4 words of output of step 7.5 as a 4-word constant $w_4||w_5||w_6||w_7$ with complexity 1) See Fig. 6. We can describe the relations among $m_0 \sim m_{23}$ as the following table 2 : Once m_2 is fixed, m_0 and m_1 are determined by property 3 because (4) and (5) are already fixed. Likewise, once m_5 is fixed, m_3 and m_4 are also determined by property 3 because (6) and (7) are already fixed. Similarly, we can find $m_0 \sim m_{23}$ satisfying the values of (4) ~ (19). Since we can assign m_{3i+2} random values for $0 \leqslant i \leqslant 7$, we know that there are 2^{128} $m_0 \sim m_{23}$ satisfying the values of (4) ~ (19).

Table 2. Relations among $m_0 \sim m_{23}$ in Fig 6

m_2	→	m_0,m_1
m_5	→	m_3,m_4
m_8	→	m_6,m_7
m_{11}	→	m_9,m_{10}
m_{14}	→	m_{12},m_{13}
m_{17}	→	m_{15},m_{16}
m_{20}	→	m_{18},m_{19}
m_{23}	→	m_{21},m_{22}

<u>Third Phase</u> (given the hash output $o_0||o_1||\cdots||o_7$, we show how to find a message $m_{24}||m_{25}||\cdots||m_{47}$ which makes the first 4 words of the input of step 7.5 and the last 4 words of the input of step 7.5 '$w_0||w_1||w_2||w_3$' and '$w_4||w_5||w_6||w_7$' with complexity 1.) See Fig. 7. Given a hash output $o_0||o_1||\cdots||o_7$, by property 2, we can invert $o_0||o_1||\cdots||o_7$ up-to the output of step 11 by giving arbitrary random value to $m_{36} \sim m_{42}$. As described in the first paragraph of Section 4, $m_{43} \sim m_{47}$ are already fixed. And $w_0 \sim w_7$ are already fixed in the first phase, so (40)~(45) are determined as well. Further, since we know the output of step

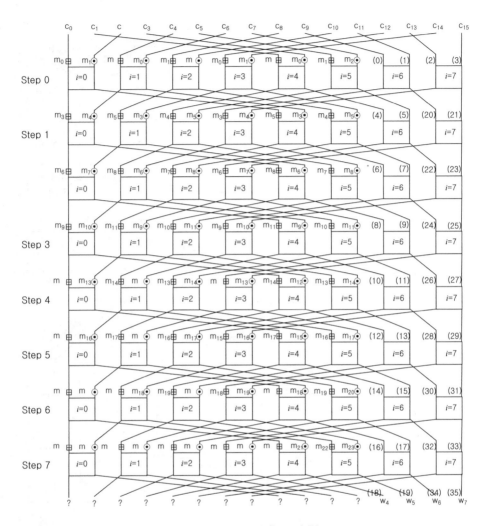

Fig. 6. The First and Second Phases

11, (46) is also fixed through the inverting process. Then m_{34} is determined by property 2 because (45) and (46) are already fixed. At this point we give arbitrary random values to m_{33} and m_{35}. Now we have the output of Step 10. Then m_{31} is determined by (44), at which point we give arbitrary random values to m_{30} and m_{32}. Then m_{27} and m_{28} are determined by (40) and (42). Then (36), (38) and (39) are also determined, while m_{26} and m_{24} are also determined by (38) and (39). Then, employing the property of multi-permutation, m_{25} is determined by (36). Then (37) is automatically determined, so m_{29} is also determined by (37). Therefore, we can get $m_{24} \sim m_{47}$ satisfying $w_0 \sim w_7$ with complexity 1. Since we can assign m_{30}, m_{32}, m_{33} and $m_{35} \sim m_{42}$ random values, we know that there are 2^{176} $m_{24} \sim m_{47}$ cases.

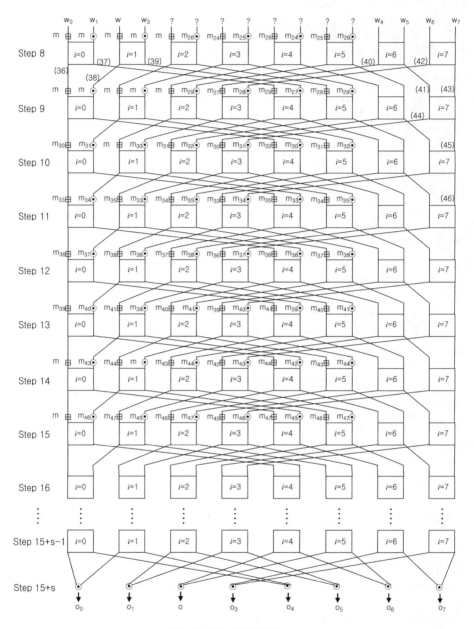

Fig. 7. The Third Phase

<u>Fourth Phase</u> (Meet-in-the-Middle-attack) We repeat the second phase 2^{t+64} times. Then we can get 2^t $m_0 \sim m_{23}$ which make the first 4-word of the output of step 7.5 $w_0||w_1||w_2||w_3$. We store these 2^t $m_0 \sim m_{23}$ and the output of step 7.5 for each $m_0 \sim m_{23}$. We repeat the third phase 2^{128-t} times. According to the birthday attack complexity, given a hash output $o_0||o_1||\cdots||o_7$, we can find a

padded preimage $m_0 \sim m_{47}$ with $2^{t+64} + 2^{128-t}$ time complexity and 2^t memory. This concludes our attack.

Note that our attack does not depend on the value of s which is the constant related to the number of steps guaranteeing the collision resistance property. Also our attack can be used in any word size case (in this paper, we only consider 16-bit word size).

5 Conclusion

In this paper, we described a preimage attack on the parallel FFT-Hashing function which is the first attack on this design. For example we can find a preimage with 2^{97} time complexity and 2^{32} memory which is less than the generic preimage attack complexity of 2^{128}.

References

1. Baritaud, T., Gilbert, H., Girault, M.: FFT Hashing is not Collision-free. In: Rueppel, R.A. (ed.) EUROCRYPT 1992. LNCS, vol. 658, pp. 35–44. Springer, Heidelberg (1993)
2. Schnorr, C.P.: FFT-Hashing: An Efficient Cryptographic Hash Function. In: Presented at the rump session of the Crypto'91
3. Schnorr, C.P.: FFT-Hash II, efficient hashing. In: Rueppel, R.A. (ed.) EUROCRYPT 1992. LNCS, vol. 658, pp. 45–54. Springer, Heidelberg (1993)
4. Schnorr, C.P., Vaudenay, S.: Parallel FFT-Hashing. In: Anderson, R. (ed.) Fast Software Encryption. LNCS, vol. 809, pp. 149–156. Springer, Heidelberg (1994)
5. Schnorr, C.P., Vaudenay, S.: Black Box Cryptanalysis of Hash Networks based on Multipermutations. In: De Santis, A. (ed.) EUROCRYPT 1994. LNCS, vol. 950, pp. 47–57. Springer, Heidelberg (1995)
6. Vaudenay, S.: FFT-Hash II is not yet Collision-free. In: Brickell, E.F. (ed.) CRYPTO 1992. LNCS, vol. 740, pp. 587–593. Springer, Heidelberg (1993)

Second Preimages for Iterated Hash Functions and Their Implications on MACs

Norbert Pramstaller, Mario Lamberger, and Vincent Rijmen

Institute for Applied Information Processing and Communications (IAIK)
Graz University of Technology, Austria
{Mario.Lamberger,Norbert.Pramstaller,Vincent.Rijmen}@iaik.tugraz.at

Abstract. In this article, we focus on second preimages for iterated hash functions. More precisely, we introduce the notion of a b-block bypass which is closely related to the notion of second preimage but specifies additional properties. We will then give two examples of iterated hash functions to which this notion applies: a double-block length hash function and a single-block length hash function. Furthermore, we look at NMAC and HMAC and show the implications of a b-block bypass regarding forgery attacks. As a result it turns out that the impact of second preimages for NMAC and HMAC heavily depends on how the second preimages are constructed.

Keywords: iterated hash functions, double block-length hash functions, block-cipher based hash functions, differential cryptanalysis, second preimage.

1 Introduction

A cryptographic hash function maps a binary string of arbitrary length to a fixed length binary string, called hash value. A cryptographic hash function H has to be secure against the following attacks:

- **Collision attack:** Find two different messages m and $m^* \neq m$ such that $H(m) = H(m^*)$
- **Preimage attack:** For a given hash value h, find a message m such that $H(m) = h$
- **Second preimage attack:** For a given message m, find a second message $m^* \neq m$ such that $H(m) = H(m^*)$

Based on the birthday paradox the expected complexity for a collision attack is about $2^{n/2}$ hash computations, where n is the size of the hash value. For a preimage attack and a second preimage attack the complexity is about 2^n hash computations. If, for a given hash function H, collisions and (second) preimages can be found with a complexity less than $2^{n/2}$ and 2^n, respectively, the hash function is considered to be broken.

Recently, a lot of progress has been made in the cryptanalysis of hash functions. Especially the breakthrough results of Wang *et al.* showing how to construct collisions for MD5 and SHA-1 [15,16], have drawn a lot of attention to

J. Pieprzyk, H. Ghodosi, and E. Dawson (Eds.): ACISP 2007, LNCS 4586, pp. 68–81, 2007.
© Springer-Verlag Berlin Heidelberg 2007

the analysis of hash functions in the research community. To date, most of the attacks focus on collisions for iterated hash functions. Collisions are considered to be less devastating than second preimages since the adversary needs to control both messages. Kelsey and Schneier [7] have recently presented a new generic second preimage attack on iterated hash functions following the Merkle-Damgård construction (cf. [4,13]). As a result, second preimages can be found in much less than the theoretically expected 2^n hash computations for very long messages.

Besides the cryptanalysis of hash functions it is of high interest to understand the implications of these recent advances for applications employing hash functions. For instance, which implications does a collision attack on a hash function have for message authentication codes such as NMAC and HMAC? Recently, some answers to this question have been published in [3,10,14].

Being motivated by these new results, we will look at the implications of second preimages for NMAC and HMAC. We will start by introducing a new notion for iterated hash functions, namely a b-block bypass, in Section 2. This notion is closely related to the definition of a second preimage but specifies more details on how the second preimage can be constructed. To justify the newly introduced notion we discuss two hash functions for which a b-block bypass can be constructed. In Section 3, we analyze a double-block length hash function presented at FSE 2006 [6], referred to as DBLH. We will show that if this hash function scheme is instantiated with a block cipher following the FX construction [9] we can construct a 2-block, respectively 3-block, bypass. As another example, we will discuss the SMASH design strategy [11] in Section 4. We will show that the second preimage attack presented by Lamberger et al. in [12] satisfies the definition of a b-block bypass. In Section 5, we analyze NMAC and HMAC employing these hash functions. Finally, we present conclusions in Section 6.

2   The Notion of b-Block Bypass

In this section, we introduce a new property of iterated hash functions and show which implications it has. For the remainder of this article, we assume without loss of generality that we have message lengths that are a multiple of the block length. Furthermore, we assume that the blocks required for MD strengthening have been removed.

Definition 1. *(b-Block Bypass) Let H be an iterated hash function. We say that we can construct a b-block bypass for H, if for any b-block message $m = m_1, \ldots, m_b$ we can find a b-block message $m^* = m_1^*, \ldots, m_b^* \neq m$ such that for any initial value h_0 the following holds:*

$$H(h_0; m_1, \ldots, m_i) \neq H(h_0; m_1^*, \ldots, m_i^*) \quad for \; i = 1, \ldots, b-1$$
$$H(h_0; m_1, \ldots, m_b) = H(h_0; m_1^*, \ldots, m_b^*) \tag{1}$$

Remark 1. It follows directly from Definition 1 that the notions of b-block bypass and second preimage are closely related. To be more precise, if we can construct a b-block bypass for an iterated hash function then it is possible to construct a second preimage m^* for any given message $m = m_1, \ldots, m_t \neq m^*$ with $t \geq b$. Furthermore, both the second preimage m^* and the message m are of equal length. Hence, a b-block bypass provides additional details such as the dependency on the chaining value.

Lemma 1. *Let H be an iterated hash function for which we can construct a b-block bypass. Then, for every message $m = m_1, \ldots, m_t$ with $t \geq b \geq 1$, we can construct at least*

$$\sum_{j=1}^{\lfloor t/b \rfloor} \binom{t - j(b-1)}{j} \tag{2}$$

distinct second preimages.

Proof. From Definition 1 it follows immediately that it doesn't matter which b consecutive blocks of the message m are taken to construct a second preimage m^* (cf. Figure 1).

If $\lfloor t/b \rfloor \geq 2$, we can apply Definition 1 not only for one b-block sub-message of m but for j sub-messages, with j ranging from $1, \ldots, \lfloor t/b \rfloor$. An illustration of this fact is also shown in Figure 1. The problem of counting all these possible second preimages of m boils down to counting the number of possibilities of putting $t - jb$ indistinguishable balls into $j + 1$ distinguishable urns. This number is known to be

$$\binom{t - j(b-1)}{j},$$

cf. [5, page 38, Eq. (5.2)]. Summing over all $j = 1, \ldots, \lfloor t/b \rfloor$ proves (2).   □

Remark 2. The result of Lemma 1 seems intuitive. However, Lemma 1 does not necessarily apply to the notion of second preimage but it always holds for the notion of b-block bypass. Therefore, the notion of b-block bypass enables a better insight on the possibilities for constructing a second preimage.

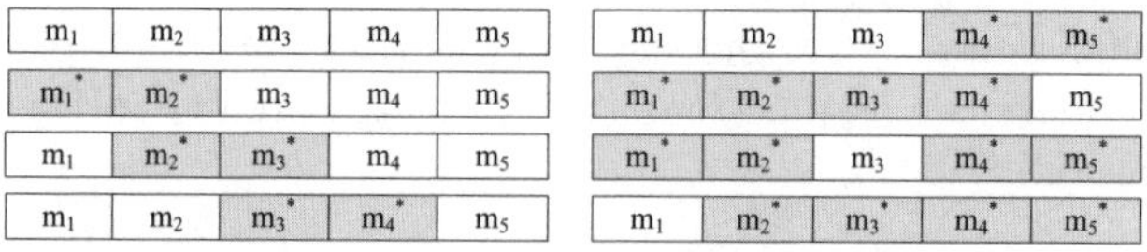

Fig. 1. For a 2-block bypass we can construct for any 5-block message $m = m_1, \ldots, m_5$ seven distinct second preimages. The shadowed rectangles show which blocks of the original message m have been modified to construct the second preimage.

3   The Double Block-Length Hash Proposal DBLH

We start this section by introducing some notation. For the concatenation of two variables, we write $a \| b$. Addition modulo 2 (XOR) is denoted by $a \oplus b$. The bit length of variable a is denoted by $|a|$. We stick to the convention of [2] to denote a difference by $u' = u \oplus u^*$. Furthermore, we write $F_k(x)$ for the encryption of the input x with an arbitrary block cipher F under the key k. The cipher F processes blocks of n bits and the key length is denoted by $|k|$.

Shoichi Hirose proposed a double block-length hash function at FSE 2006 [6]. It is an iterated, block cipher based hash function. The compression function is defined as follows:

$$
\begin{aligned}
g_i &= F_{h_{i-1}\|m_i}(g_{i-1}) \oplus g_{i-1} \\
h_i &= F_{h_{i-1}\|m_i}(g_{i-1} \oplus c) \oplus g_{i-1} \oplus c,
\end{aligned}
\tag{3}
$$

where c is an arbitrary constant ($c \neq 0$), F_k ($k = h_{i-1}\|m_i$) is an arbitrary block cipher, and $h_i\|g_i$ is the chaining value with $h_0\|g_0$ the initial value (cf. Figure 2). After t message blocks have been processed, the final hash value is the concatenation $h_t\|g_t$. As it can be seen in (3), the key length of the underlying block cipher F_k has to be greater than the block length. This is due to the fact that $|k| = |h_{i-1}| + |m_i|$, where $|h_{i-1}|$ is the block length of the cipher. In [6], Hirose proved the security of DBLH in the ideal cipher model.

3.1   Block Ciphers Following the FX Construction

The block cipher DESX [9] was proposed by Rivest to protect DES against exhaustive key search attacks. Kilian and Rogaway proved the security of the DESX construction in [8,9] against a key-search adversary. However, DESX is not an *ideal cipher*. The general form of this construction is referred to as FX [8,9], where F can be any block cipher with block length n and key length $|k|$. The FX construction is defined as follows:

$$
\mathrm{FX}_{k\|k_1\|k_2}(x) = F_k(x \oplus k_1) \oplus k_2 ,
\tag{4}
$$

where $|k_1| = |k_2| = n$.

3.2   DBLH with FX

For DBLH with underlying block cipher $\mathrm{FX}_{k\|k_1\|k_2}(x)$, we can construct the following three configurations (see Figure 2), where $m_i = l_i\|r_i$.

> Configuration I:
> $k\|k_1\|k_2 = l_i\|h_{i-1}\|r_i$, where $|l_i| = |k|, |h_{i-1}| = |r_i| = n$
>
> Configuration II:
> $k\|k_1\|k_2 = h_{i-1}\|l_i\|r_i$, where $|h_{i-1}| = |k|, |l_i| = |r_i| = n$ (5)
>
> Configuration III:
> $k\|k_1\|k_2 = l_i\|r_i\|h_{i-1}$, where $|l_i| = |k|, |r_i| = |h_{i-1}| = n$

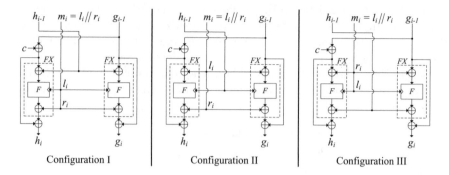

Fig. 2. Three possible configurations of DBLH with FX as underlying block cipher. The hatch denotes the key input of the block cipher F.

For each configuration, we can interchange l_i and r_i. However, without loss of generality, we take the configurations defined in (5) for the further analysis. Note that if F is a block cipher with $|k| < n$ then, for Configuration II, the chaining variable h_{i-1} needs to be truncated to match the key length $|k|$. Which bits are truncated does not have any impact on the analysis. For the remainder of this section, we assume that F is a block cipher with $|k| = n$.

For the sake of simplicity, we will write DX to denote the instantiation of DBLH with FX as underlying block cipher. If we speak of a specific configuration, we append the number of the configuration. For instance for DBLH with FX in Configuration II, we write DX-II.

3.3   Second Preimages for DX Based on a b-Block Bypass

We now demonstrate how to construct second preimages based on a 3-block bypass for Configuration II of DX.

Theorem 1. *For the iterated hash function DX-II we can construct a 3-block bypass, since for every 3-block message $m = m_1, m_2, m_3$ the following message m^* satisfies the conditions of Definition 1:*

$$m^* = m_1 \oplus (0\|u'), m_2 \oplus (v'\|w'), m_3 \oplus (z'\|z') \ , \tag{6}$$

where $m_i = l_i\|r_i$, $|l_i| = |r_i| = n$, u', v' any value with $|u'| = |v'| = n$, and 0 is the n-bit all-zero binary string. Let t' be the output difference of the left F instance in iteration 2:

$$t' = [F_{h_1}(g_1 \oplus c \oplus l_2)] \oplus [F_{h_1 \oplus u'}(g_1 \oplus u' \oplus c \oplus l_2 \oplus v')] \tag{7}$$

Then, $w' = u' \oplus t'$ and the difference z' in (6) is defined as

$$z' = [F_{h_1}(g_1 \oplus l_2) \oplus r_2 \oplus g_1] \oplus$$
$$[F_{h_1 \oplus u'}(g_1 \oplus u' \oplus l_2 \oplus v') \oplus r_2 \oplus w' \oplus g_1 \oplus u']. \quad (8)$$

Furthermore, for an arbitrary message $m = m_1, \ldots, m_t$ with $t \geq 3$, we can find at least

$$\sum_{j=1}^{\lfloor t/3 \rfloor} \binom{t - 2j}{j}$$

second preimages based on this 3-block bypass.

Proof. We show that for the 3-block messages m and m^*, where

$$m = m_1, m_2, m_3 = (l_1 \| r_1), (l_2 \| r_2), (l_3 \| r_3)$$
$$m^* = m_1 \oplus (0 \| u'), m_2 \oplus (v' \| w'), m_3 \oplus (z' \| z') = (l_1^* \| r_1^*), (l_2^* \| r_2^*), (l_3^* \| r_3^*)$$
$$l_1^* = l_1 \oplus 0, \quad r_1^* = r_1 \oplus u'$$
$$l_2^* = l_2 \oplus v', \quad r_2^* = r_2 \oplus w'$$
$$l_3^* = l_3 \oplus z', \quad r_3^* = r_3 \oplus z',$$

the output difference equals zero after three iterations. After one iteration, we have

$$g_1 = g_0 \oplus F_{h_0}(g_0 \oplus l_1) \oplus r_1$$
$$g_1^* = g_0 \oplus F_{h_0}(g_0 \oplus l_1) \oplus r_1 \oplus u' = g_1 \oplus u'$$
$$h_1 = g_0 \oplus c \oplus F_{h_0}(g_0 \oplus c \oplus l_1) \oplus r_1$$
$$h_1^* = g_0 \oplus c \oplus F_{h_0}(g_0 \oplus c \oplus l_1) \oplus r_1 \oplus u' = h_1 \oplus u'.$$

After two iterations, chaining variable h_2 is computed as follows

$$h_2 = g_1 \oplus c \oplus F_{h_1}(g_1 \oplus c \oplus l_2) \oplus r_2$$
$$h_2^* = g_1 \oplus u' \oplus c \oplus F_{h_1 \oplus u'}(g_1 \oplus u' \oplus c \oplus l_2 \oplus v') \oplus r_2 \oplus w'.$$

With $w' = u' \oplus t'$ and t' as defined in (7), we get

$$h_2^* = g_1 \oplus u' \oplus c \oplus F_{h_1 \oplus u'}(g_1 \oplus u' \oplus c \oplus l_2 \oplus v') \oplus r_2 \oplus u'$$
$$\oplus \underbrace{F_{h_1}(g_1 \oplus c \oplus l_2) \oplus F_{h_1 \oplus u'}(g_1 \oplus u' \oplus c \oplus l_2 \oplus v')}_{t'}$$
$$= g_1 \oplus u' \oplus c \oplus r_2 \oplus u' \oplus F_{h_1}(g_1 \oplus c \oplus l_2)$$
$$= h_2.$$

The difference in chaining variable g_2 after two iterations is

$$g_2^* = g_2 \oplus z',$$

where z' is defined in (8). After three iterations, we get

$$g_3 = g_2 \oplus F_{h_2}(g_2 \oplus l_3) \oplus r_3$$
$$g_3^* = g_2 \oplus z' \oplus F_{h_2}(g_2 \oplus z' \oplus l_3 \oplus z') \oplus r_3 \oplus z'$$
$$= g_2 \oplus F_{h_2}(g_2 \oplus l_3) \oplus r_3$$
$$= g_3$$
$$h_3 = g_2 \oplus c \oplus F_{h_2}(g_2 \oplus c \oplus l_3) \oplus r_3$$
$$h_3^* = g_2 \oplus z' \oplus c \oplus F_{h_2}(g_2 \oplus z' \oplus c \oplus l_3 \oplus z') \oplus r_3 \oplus z'$$
$$= g_2 \oplus c \oplus F_{h_2}(g_2 \oplus c \oplus l_3) \oplus r_3$$
$$= h_3 \ .$$

Therefore, after three iterations the differences in the chaining variables are $g_3' = g_3 \oplus g_3^* = 0$ and $h_3' = h_3 \oplus h_3^* = 0$. Since the difference of the chaining variables $g_0' = h_0' = 0$, we have constructed a 3-block bypass for DX-II.

The final statement of the theorem is an immediate consequence of Lemma 1 with $b = 3$. □

For Configuration I and III, we can prove similar theorems.

Theorem 2. *For the iterated hash function DX-I, we can construct a 2-block bypass, since for every two block message $m = m_1, m_2$ the following message m^* satisfies the conditions of Definition 1:*

$$m^* = m_1 \oplus (0\|u'), m_2 \oplus (0\|u') \ , \tag{9}$$

where $m_i = l_i\|r_i$, $|l_i| = |k|$, $|r_i| = n$, u' any value with $|u'| = n$, and 0 is the $|k|$-bit all-zero binary string.
Furthermore, for an arbitrary message $m = m_1, \ldots, m_t$ with $t \geq 2$, we can find at least

$$\sum_{j=1}^{\lfloor t/2 \rfloor} \binom{t-j}{j}$$

second preimages based on this 2-block bypass.

Theorem 3. *For the iterated hash function DX-III, we can construct a 3-block bypass, since for every 3-block message $m = m_1, m_2, m_3$ the following message m^* satisfies the conditions of Definition 1:*

$$m^* = m_1 \oplus (u'\|v'), m_2 \oplus (0\|z'), m_3 \oplus (0\|(w' \oplus z')) \ , \tag{10}$$

where $m_i = l_i\|r_i$, $|l_i| = |k|$, $|r_i| = n$, u', v' any value with $|u'| = |k|$ and $|v'| = n$, and 0 is the $|k|$-bit all-zero binary string. Once the values u', v' have been chosen for the given input message block m_1, the differences w' and z' can be computed:

$$w' = [g_0 \oplus c \oplus F_{l_1}(g_0 \oplus c \oplus r_1) \oplus h_0]$$
$$\oplus [g_0 \oplus c \oplus F_{l_1 \oplus v'}(g_0 \oplus c \oplus r_1 \oplus u') \oplus h_0] \ ,$$
$$z' = [g_0 \oplus F_{l_1}(g_0 \oplus r_1) \oplus h_0]$$
$$\oplus [g_0 \oplus F_{l_1 \oplus v'}(g_0 \oplus r_1 \oplus u') \oplus h_0]$$

Furthermore, for an arbitrary message $m = m_1, \ldots, m_t$ with $t \geq 3$, we can find at least

$$\sum_{j=1}^{\lfloor t/3 \rfloor} \binom{t - 2j}{j}$$

second preimages based on this 3-block bypass.

The proof of Theorem 2 and Theorem 3 works along the same lines as the proof of Theorem 1 and is given in Appendix A and B.

4   The Hash Function Design Strategy SMASH

In [11], Knudsen presented a new design strategy for iterated hash functions. For a message $m = m_1, m_2, \ldots, m_t$ consisting of t blocks of length n, the hash output h_{t+1} gets computed via

$$h_0 = f(iv) + iv \tag{11}$$

$$h_i = f(h_{i-1} + m_i) + h_{i-1} + \theta m_i \quad \text{for } i = 1, \ldots, t \tag{12}$$

$$h_{t+1} = f(h_t) + h_t, \tag{13}$$

where f denotes a bijective, non-linear n-bit mapping. Note that "$+$" and multiplication by θ is defined as an operation in the finite field $GF(2^n)$ with the only restriction that $\theta \notin \{0, 1\}$. In [11], also two instantiations of SMASH have been proposed, namely SMASH-256 and SMASH-512 which produce a 256-bit, respectively 512-bit output.

Let us for now consider a slightly reduced variant of SMASH-n by omitting the final step (13) in the definition of SMASH-n. The main result of [12] is a method to effectively construct preimages for this reduced variant. Their method makes use of the following simple observation (which was already pointed out in [11]): Let h_i and h_i^* be two intermediate hash values and let m_i be an arbitrary n-bit message block. Then, if we set $m_i^* = m_i + h_{i-1} + h_{i-1}^*$ we have

$$h_i + h_i^* = (1 + \theta)(h_{i-1} + h_{i-1}^*).$$

This can be used to derive an equation of the form:

$$h_t = a + b \sum_{j=1}^{t} \delta_j (1 + \theta)^{t-j}, \tag{14}$$

where $1 \leq t \leq n$, a, b are values depending on the used initial value and compression function f, and the $\delta_i \in \{0, 1\}$ are unknowns on which the respective blocks of the preimage $m^* = m_1^*, \ldots, m_n^*$ will depend. Equation (14) can be interpreted as an inhomogenous system of n linear equations in t variables over $GF(2)$.

For the solvability of this system we have to look on the element θ. If $(1 + \theta)$ is not contained in a proper subfield of $GF(2^n)$, then the elements $(1 + \theta)^i$ are linearly independent for $0 \leq i \leq n - 1$. For SMASH-256 and SMASH-512, it is easy to show that this condition is satisfied. In most applications we will have $n = 2^\ell$. Then, a randomly selected θ fulfills this requirement with probability $1 - 2^{-n/2}$.

Thus, if we set $t = n$ in equation (14) we are guaranteed a unique solution $\delta_1, \ldots, \delta_n$ from which an n-block preimage m^* can be constructed. For a more detailed description of the method we refer to [12].

Remark 3. To clarify the multiple use of n we recapitulate: SMASH-n operates on n-bit blocks but since we need exactly n variables to derive a unique solution for the system (14) the method of [12] also produces a preimage consisting of n blocks.

Because of (13) this preimage attack cannot be augmented to the full variant of SMASH-n. However, we can use this result to construct an n-block bypass for an arbitrary message $m = m_1, m_2, \ldots, m_n$. Let h_n denote the chaining value computed after n applications of (12) starting from our initial message m. Then, the technique described above leads to a message m^* such that $h_n^* = h_n$ and therefore $h_{n+1}^* = h_{n+1}$. The method shown in [12] guarantees that the constructed second preimage m^* differs from m at least in the first message block. Since this can be carried out independent of the choice of h_0 we arrive at the following theorem:

Theorem 4. *For almost all instantiations of SMASH-n, we can construct an n-block bypass. Especially, we can construct a 256-block, respectively 512-block bypass for the hash functions SMASH-256, respectively SMASH-512.*

5   Implications of a b-Block Bypass for NMAC and HMAC

In this section, we will look at the implications if one of the hash functions described in Section 3 and Section 4 is employed in applications such as message authentication codes. In particular, we will focus on NMAC and HMAC [1]:

$$\mathrm{NMAC}_{k_1,k_2}(m) = H(k_1, H(k_2, m)) \tag{15}$$

$$\mathrm{HMAC}_k(m) = H(H(iv, k \oplus opad), H(H(iv, k \oplus ipad), m)) , \tag{16}$$

where $H(cv, m)$ denotes the application of the iterated hash function H with chaining value cv (iv or k_i) and t-block message $m = m_1, \ldots, m_t$. For HMAC, two appropriate padding methods $ipad$ and $opad$ for the secret key k are required (see [1] for further details). Both constructions are depicted in Figure 3.

For NMAC the initial value and for HMAC the chaining value of the iterated hash function H processing the message m are not known to an adversary unless he/she knows the secret key k. Therefore, a second preimage attack on an iterated

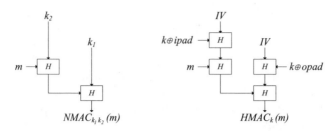

Fig. 3. The NMAC (left) and HMAC (right) construction based on an iterative hash function H

hash function for which the attacker needs to know certain chaining values will not lead to an immediate forgery. On the other side, if the second preimage attack is independent of the initial chaining value, an adversary will always succeed in forging an authenticated message: for any given valid message-MAC pair $\{m, MAC_k(m)\}$ he/she can construct a second valid message-MAC pair by just replacing m with the second preimage m^*. If we look at the hash functions described in Section 3 and Section 4, we can now conclude the following:

Fact 1. *The second preimages based on the 3-block bypass for DX-II and DX-III, as well as the n-block bypass for SMASH-n cannot directly be exploited to mount a forgery attack on NMAC and HMAC. This is an immediate consequence of the fact that certain chaining values need to be known by the adversary for constructing the second preimage.*

Fact 2. *For the DX-I construction we see that the second preimage based on the 2-block bypass can be constructed in a pure differential way, i.e. it is independent of the chaining values. Therefore, both NMAC and HMAC with DX-I as underlying hash function are vulnerable to forgery attacks.*

From these facts we observe that even if we can construct second preimages for both hash functions in all configurations, the implications for the security of hash-based MACs depend heavily on how the second preimage is constructed.

6   Conclusion

In this article, we have introduced the notion of b-block bypass for iterated hash functions, which is closely related to the notion of second preimage. A b-block bypass is more accurate in the sense that the structure of second preimages based on a b-block bypass is more clear. We presented two entirely different hash functions for which we can construct a b-block bypass. Even if we can construct second preimages deterministically for both hash functions, we have shown that if we look at NMAC/HMAC the implications are different. It turned out that

for NMAC/HMAC it is important how the second preimage is constructed: the
DX construction in Configuration I implies immediate forgery, whereby DX in
Configuration II and III as well as the SMASH construction do not lead to a
forgery attack on NMAC/HMAC. We can derive from our results that a weak
hash function does not necessarily imply a weak application employing this hash
function. Therefore, it makes sense to not only define properties for the hash
function but to specify additional properties concerning the application in which
a hash function is employed.

Acknowledgements

The authors wish to thank Florian Mendel, Christian Rechberger, and the anonymous referees for useful comments and discussions.

The work in this paper has been supported in part by the Austrian Science
Fund (FWF), project P18138 and by the European Commission through the
IST Programme under contract IST2002507 932 ECRYPT. The information in
this paper is provided as is, and no guarantee or warranty is given or implied
that the information is fit for any particular purpose. The user thereof uses the
information at its sole risk and liability.

References

1. Bellare, M., Canetti, R., Krawczyk, H.: Keying Hash Functions for Message Authentication. In: Koblitz, N. (ed.) CRYPTO 1996. LNCS, vol. 1109, pp. 1–15.
   Springer, Heidelberg (1996)
2. Biham, E., Shamir, A.: Differential Cryptanalysis of DES-like Cryptosystems. Journal of Cryptology 4(1), 3–72 (1991)
3. Contini, S., Yin, Y.L.: Forgery and Partial Key-Recovery Attacks on HMAC and
   NMAC Using Hash Collisions. In: Lai, X., Chen, K. (eds.) ASIACRYPT 2006.
   LNCS, vol. 4284, pp. 37–53. Springer, Heidelberg (2006)
4. Damgård, I.: A Design Principle for Hash Functions. In: Brassard, G. (ed.)
   CRYPTO 1989. LNCS, vol. 435, pp. 416–427. Springer, Heidelberg (1990)
5. Feller, W.: An introduction to probability theory and its application, 3rd edn.
   vol. I. John Wiley & Sons, New York (1968)
6. Hirose, S.: Some Plausible Constructions of Double-Block-Length Hash Functions.
   In: Robshaw, M. (ed.) FSE 2006. LNCS, vol. 4047, pp. 210–225. Springer, Heidelberg (2006)
7. Kelsey, J., Schneier, B.: Second Preimages on n-bit Hash Functions for Much less
   than 2^n Work. In: Cramer, R.J.F. (ed.) EUROCRYPT 2005. LNCS, vol. 3494, pp.
   474–490. Springer, Heidelberg (2005)
8. Kilian, J., Rogaway, P.: How to Protect DES Against Exhaustive Key Search. In:
   Koblitz, N. (ed.) CRYPTO 1996. LNCS, vol. 1109, pp. 252–267. Springer, Heidelberg (1996)

9. Kilian, J., Rogaway, P.: How to Protect DES Against Exhaustive Key Search (an Analysis of DESX). J. Cryptology 14(1), 17–35 (2001)
10. Kim, J., Biryukov, A., Preneel, B., Hong, S.: On the Security of HMAC and NMAC Based on HAVAL, MD4, MD5, SHA-0 and SHA-1 (Extended Abstract). In: De Prisco, R., Yung, M. (eds.) SCN 2006. LNCS, vol. 4116, pp. 242–256. Springer, Heidelberg (2006)
11. Knudsen, L.R.: SMASH - A Cryptographic Hash Function. In: Gilbert, H., Handschuh, H. (eds.) FSE 2005. LNCS, vol. 3557, pp. 228–242. Springer, Heidelberg (2005)
12. Lamberger, M., Pramstaller, N., Rechberger, C., Rijmen, V.: Second Preimages for SMASH. In: Abe, M. (ed.) CT-RSA 2007. LNCS, vol. 4377, pp. 101–111. Springer, Heidelberg (2006)
13. Merkle, R.C.: One Way Hash Functions and DES. In: Brassard, G. (ed.) CRYPTO 1989. LNCS, vol. 435, pp. 428–446. Springer, Heidelberg (1989)
14. Rechberger, C., Rijmen, V.: On Authentication with HMAC and Non-Random Properties. In: Financial Cryptography and Data Security, 11th International Conference, FC, Lowlands, Scarborough, Trinidad/Tobago, February 12–15, 2007 (to appear in LNCS)
15. Wang, X., Yao, A., Yao, F.: New Collision Search for SHA-1. In: Shoup, V. (ed.) CRYPTO 2005. LNCS, vol. 3621, Springer, Heidelberg (2005)
16. Wang, X., Yu, H.: How to Break MD5 and Other Hash Functions. In: Cramer, R.J.F. (ed.) EUROCRYPT 2005. LNCS, vol. 3494, pp. 19–35. Springer, Heidelberg (2005)

A   Proof of Theorem 2

Proof. Assume, we have the following 2-block messages m, m^*, where:

$$m = m_1, m_2 = (l_1 \| r_1), (l_2 \| r_2)$$
$$m^* = m_1^*, m_2^* = m_1 \oplus (0 \| u'), m_2 \oplus (0 \| u') = (l_1^* \| r_1^*), (l_2^* \| r_2^*)$$
$$l_1^* = l_1 \oplus 0 = l_1, \quad r_1^* = r_1 \oplus u'$$
$$l_2^* = l_2 \oplus 0 = l_2, \quad r_2^* = r_2 \oplus u'$$

After one iteration, we have

$$g_1 = g_0 \oplus F_{l_1}(g_0 \oplus h_0) \oplus r_1$$
$$g_1^* = g_0 \oplus F_{l_1}(g_0 \oplus h_0) \oplus r_1 \oplus u' = g_1 \oplus u' \text{ , and}$$
$$h_1 = g_0 \oplus c \oplus F_{l_1}(g_0 \oplus c \oplus h_0) \oplus r_1$$
$$h_1^* = g_0 \oplus c \oplus F_{l_1}(g_0 \oplus c \oplus h_0) \oplus r_1 \oplus u' = h_1 \oplus u' \text{ .}$$

The outputs after two iterations are

$$g_2 = g_1 \oplus F_{l_2}(g_1 \oplus h_1) \oplus r_2$$
$$g_2^* = g_1 \oplus u' \oplus F_{l_2}(g_1 \oplus u' \oplus h_1 \oplus u') \oplus r_2 \oplus u'$$
$$= g_1 \oplus F_{l_2}(g_1 \oplus h_1) \oplus r_2 = g_2 \text{ , and}$$

$$h_2 = g_1 \oplus c \oplus F_{l_2}(g_1 \oplus c \oplus h_1) \oplus r_2$$
$$h_2^* = g_1 \oplus u' \oplus c \oplus F_{l_2}(g_1 \oplus u' \oplus c \oplus h_1 \oplus u') \oplus r_2 \oplus u'$$
$$= g_1 \oplus c \oplus F_{l_2}(g_1 \oplus c \oplus h_1) \oplus r_2 = h_2 \ .$$

Hence, $g_2' = g_2 \oplus g_2^* = 0$ and $h_2' = h_2 \oplus h_2^* = 0$. Since the difference of the chaining variables $g_0' = h_0' = 0$, we have constructed a 2-block bypass for DX-I. The final statement of the theorem is an immediate consequence of Lemma 1 with $b = 2$.   □

B   Proof of Theorem 3

As for the proof of Theorem 1 and Theorem 2, we show that for the 3-block messages m and m^*, where $m = m_1, m_2, m_3 = (l_1\|r_1), (l_2\|r_2), (l_3\|r_3)$ and

$$m^* = m_1 \oplus (u'\|v'), m_2 \oplus (0\|z'), m_3 \oplus (0\|(w' \oplus z')) = (l_1^*\|r_1^*), (l_2^*\|r_2^*), (l_3^*\|r_3^*)$$
$$l_1^* = l_1 \oplus u', \quad r_1^* = r_1 \oplus v'$$
$$l_2^* = l_2 \oplus 0, \quad r_2^* = r_2 \oplus z'$$
$$l_3^* = l_3 \oplus 0, \quad r_3^* = r_3 \oplus (w' \oplus z') \ ,$$

the output difference equals zero after three iterations, *i.e.* $g_3' = h_3' = 0$. After the first iteration, we have

$$g_1 = g_0 \oplus F_{l_1}(g_0 \oplus r_1) \oplus h_0$$
$$g_1^* = g_1 \oplus z', \text{where}$$
$$z' = [g_0 \oplus F_{l_1}(g_0 \oplus r_1) \oplus h_0]$$
$$\oplus [g_0 \oplus F_{l_1 \oplus v'}(g_0 \oplus r_1 \oplus u') \oplus h_0] \ , \text{and}$$
$$h_1 = g_0 \oplus c \oplus F_{l_1}(g_0 \oplus c \oplus r_1) \oplus h_0$$
$$h_1^* = h_1 \oplus w', \text{where}$$
$$w' = [g_0 \oplus c \oplus F_{l_1}(g_0 \oplus c \oplus r_1) \oplus h_0]$$
$$\oplus [g_0 \oplus c \oplus F_{l_1 \oplus v'}(g_0 \oplus c \oplus r_1 \oplus u') \oplus h_0] \ .$$

The difference of the chaining variables after two iterations is

$$g_2 = g_1 \oplus F_{l_2}(g_1 \oplus r_2) \oplus h_1$$
$$g_2^* = g_1 \oplus z' \oplus F_{l_2}(g_1 \oplus z' \oplus r_2 \oplus z') \oplus h_1 \oplus w'$$
$$= g_2 \oplus (w' \oplus z') \ , \text{and}$$
$$h_2 = g_1 \oplus c \oplus F_{l_2}(g_1 \oplus c \oplus r_2) \oplus h_1$$
$$h_2^* = g_1 \oplus z' \oplus c \oplus F_{l_2}(g_1 \oplus z' \oplus c \oplus r_2 \oplus z') \oplus h_1 \oplus w'$$
$$= h_2 \oplus (w' \oplus z') \ .$$

The output difference after three iterations is computed as follows. For the sake of clearness, we write $y' = w' \oplus z'$:

$$g_3 = g_2 \oplus F_{l_3}(g_2 \oplus r_3) \oplus h_2$$
$$g_3^* = g_2 \oplus y' \oplus F_{l_3}(g_3 \oplus y' \oplus r_3 \oplus y') \oplus h_2 \oplus y'$$
$$= g_3 \text{ , and}$$
$$h_3 = g_2 \oplus c \oplus F_{l_3}(g_2 \oplus c \oplus r_3) \oplus h_2$$
$$h_3^* = g_2 \oplus y' \oplus c \oplus F_{l_3}(g_2 \oplus y' \oplus c \oplus r_3 \oplus y') \oplus h_2 \oplus y'$$
$$= h_3$$

Hence, $g_3' = g_3 \oplus g_3^* = 0$ and $h_3' = h_3 \oplus h_3^* = 0$. Since the difference of the chaining variables $g_0' = h_0' = 0$, we have constructed a 3-block bypass for DX-III.

The final statement of the theorem is an immediate consequence of Lemma 1 with $b = 3$. $\qquad\square$

On Building Hash Functions from Multivariate Quadratic Equations*

Olivier Billet, Matt J.B. Robshaw, and Thomas Peyrin

France Telecom R&D, Issy-les-Moulineaux, France
{forename.name}@orange-ftgroup.com

Abstract. Recent advances in hash functions cryptanalysis provide a strong impetus to explore new designs. This paper describes a new hash function MQ-HASH that depends for its security on the difficulty of solving randomly drawn systems of multivariate equations over a finite field. While provably achieving pre-image resistance for a hash function based on multivariate equations is relatively easy, naïve constructions using multivariate equations are susceptible to collision attacks. In this paper, therefore, we describe a mechanism—also using multivariate quadratic polynomials—yielding the collision-free property we seek while retaining provable pre-image resistance. Therefore, MQ-HASH offers an intriguing companion proposal to the provably collision-free hash function VSH.

1   Introduction

Cryptographic hash functions are essential components within the information security infrastructure. A cryptographic hash function HASH$(\cdot)$ is a function that takes an arbitrary length input and generates a fixed length output of n bits. Classically, there are three main properties of such functions which can be loosely described in the following way [19]:

1. *Pre-image resistance.* Given an output y it is computationally hard to find any input x such that HASH$(x) = y$;
2. *Second pre-image resistance.* Given an input and output pair (x, y) so that HASH$(x) = y$, it is computationally hard to find an input x' distinct from x such that HASH$(x') = y$;
3. *Collision resistance.* It is computationally hard to find any two inputs x and x' such that HASH$(x) = $ HASH(x').

While there have been a variety of different hash function proposals over the years, most currently deployed hash functions are closely built around design principles which go back to MD4 [28]. Probably the most popular hash functions in use today are MD5 [29] and SHA-1 [22]. However recent cryptanalytic advances [32,33] have shown weaknesses that allow collisions to be computed

---

* This work has been supported in part by the French government through the SAPHIR and MAC projects.

J. Pieprzyk, H. Ghodosi, and E. Dawson (Eds.): ACISP 2007, LNCS 4586, pp. 82–95, 2007.

for these hash functions much faster than by brute force. A more recent family of hash functions [22] has been standardised by NIST in the U.S., but these are closely related to SHA-1 and confidence in their construction is somewhat undermined by recent cryptanalytic work on MD5 and SHA-1. An alternative approach has been to build hash functions around a secure block cipher, see for example [19,27] and more recently [26], and the widespread deployment of the AES [21] may well provide new opportunities in this direction.

In this paper we consider a third approach and we base the security of a hash function on a hard mathematical problem. Until recently this approach was very limited, but there has been considerable success with VSH [8] which relates the difficulty of finding collisions to a hard problem built around the mechanics of current factoring techniques. A variant based on the discrete logarithm problem VSH-DL has also been proposed [17] and other proposals include the FSB hash function [2] that is related to fast syndrome-based decoding problems and LASH [6] which is based on problems in lattice theory.

The new hash function in this paper, MQ-HASH, is built around the problem of solving a system of multivariate quadratic equations. This is the same problem that underpins the security of the stream cipher QUAD [4] and we will find it useful to appeal to some of the results that feature in that design.

Designing a pre-image resistant compression function from a set of multivariate quadratic polynomials without a care for collision-resistance is quite easy, because it is enough to rely on the hard problem MQ. However, such naïve constructions give rise to collision-full hash functions. So the difficult part in building a hash function based on sets of multivariate quadratic polynomials is in providing collision-resistance in a plausible way, but without sacrificing any pre-image resistance or its proof. This is the purpose of the current paper.

Our paper is structured as follows. In the next section we provide some background on hash function design and the use of systems of quadratic polynomials. We illustrate the difficulty of using quadratic polynomials directly by demonstrating an intrinsic weakness. In Section 3 we describe our construction MQ-HASH while we prove its structural security in Section 4 and its instantiated security with explicit parameter values in Section 5. The performance of our proposal and some variants are considered in Section 5.3 and we close by highlighting open problems and drawing our conclusions in Section 6.

2 Hash Functions and Quadratic Equations

In this paper we consider the problem of building a hash function from one particular hard problem, namely that of solving a system of multivariate equations over a finite field $\mathbf{F}$. The natural one-wayness of this primitive, together with its computational efficiency, provides an interesting starting point for a new hash function proposal.

While evaluating a random set of m multivariate polynomials in n variables is of polynomial complexity with respect to n, finding a common root of this set of polynomials is well known to be an NP-hard problem. This remains true even when restricted to quadratic polynomials or to the case of two equations [12].

The problem of solving multivariate quadratic equations over a finite field $\mathbf{F}$ is known as the MQ-problem. It is a hard problem, but also one that permits efficient schemes. Consequently it has been used in the design of several cryptographic applications. See [34] for an overview along with some additional information that can be found in [4].

A tuple of multivariate quadratic polynomials consists of a finite ordered set of polynomials of the form:

$$q(x_1, \ldots, x_n) = \sum_{1 \leq i \leq j \leq n} a_{i,j}\, x_i x_j + \sum_{1 \leq k \leq n} b_k\, x_k + c ,$$

where the constants are in a finite field $\mathbf{F}$. The MQ problem can then be stated as follows:

Problem 1 (MQ). Given a tuple $q = (q_1, \ldots, q_m)$ of m multivariate quadratic polynomials in n unknowns defined over $\mathbf{F}$, and the image $y = (q_1(z), \ldots, q_m(z))$ of an element z randomly chosen from $\mathbf{F}^n$ through q, find an element x of $\mathbf{F}^n$ such that $y = (q_1(x), \ldots, q_m(x))$.

Solving a set of randomly chosen quadratic equations in several variables over a finite field is a well-known hard problem [13]. That it is conjectured to be very difficult not only asymptotically and in worst case, but already for well chosen practical values of m and n makes it very attractive as a cryptographic building block. Apart from degenerate parameters like $n \ll m$ or $n \gg m$ (see [31]) or low rank polynomials, the complexity of the best known algorithms for solving the problem are exponential in $\min(m, n)$, (see [3,31]).

This leads to the following naïve construction for a compression function based on the evaluation of multivariate quadratic polynomials:

Attempt 1 (naïve and flawed). Let $\mathbf{F}$ be a finite field of size q and, assume that we wish to compress a fixed-length input of $\rho = r \log_2 q$ bits to give an output of $\nu = n \log_2 q$ bits. A compression function g can be obtained by randomly choosing a tuple $(g_1, \ldots, g_n)$ of n quadratic polynomials in r variables defined over $\mathbf{F}$:

$$\mathbf{F}^r \longrightarrow \mathbf{F}^n$$
$$x = (x_1, \ldots, x_\rho) \longmapsto g(x) = \big(g_1(x), \ldots, g_\nu(x)\big) .$$

While the one-way property of Attempt 1 is straightforward to establish, it is very easy to find collision and it would not be, in itself, an acceptable way to build a cryptographic hash function. In the next section, therefore, we investigate more closely the problem of collision resistance in the setting of multivariate quadratic polynomials.

2.1   About Collision Resistance

Unfortunately there is no collision-resistance when using a system of quadratic equations directly and it is hard to achieve this property in a simple way for the following reason. For polynomial equations of degree d, any differential of order $d-1$ is an affine application. Thus, in the special case of sets of quadratic polynomials, this amounts to saying that the set of first order differentials of any quadratic polynomial in the original set is a set of affine mappings. This simple fact has previously been used for instance by Fouque, Granboulan, and Stern to attack an asymmetric multivariate scheme [11].

Theorem 1. *Let Q be a tuple of e quadratic equations $f_1, \ldots, f_e$ in u variables over a finite field $\mathbf{F}$. For every value $\delta = (\delta_1, \ldots, \delta_u)$, it is possible to give, with time complexity $O(eu^2)$, a parametrized description of the set of inputs $x = (x_1, \ldots, x_u)$ and $y = (y_1, \ldots, y_u)$ colliding through Q and such that $y - x = \delta$, if any.*

Proof. Given δ, one computes a linear system $L_\delta(z) = 0$ in the indeterminate z where L_δ is the affine mapping defined by $L_\delta : z \mapsto Q(z + \delta) - Q(z)$. Thus, any colliding pair $(x, y) = (x, x + \delta)$ for Q with prescribed difference δ translates into a solution x of a linear system, and any standard algorithm for solving linear system recovers the set of solutions of the collision equation $Q(z) = Q(z + \delta)$. $\square$

Theorem 1 thus basically implies that collisions can be easily constructed for any naïve design like the one described in Attempt 1. Further, a hash function design facilitating the analysis of differences might be subject to attack. It is therefore reasonable to ask whether there is any way to plausibly achieve collision resistance when using sets of multivariate quadratic polynomials, and yet to provably retain the original one wayness property? The following sections answer this question positively.

3   Construction of MQ-HASH

We now present one particular approach to using multivariate quadratic polynomials in the design of a hash function. While we do so with general parameter sets, we propose some concrete values in Section 5.3.

3.1   Preliminaries

While recent analysis [14,15] has provided new insight into the Merkle-Damgård paradigm [9,20], our goal has been to design a secure compression function for use in this familiar way. The Merkle-Damgård construction requires the specification of an $(\mu + \nu)$-bit to ν-bit compression function COMPRESS. The compression function will be used repeatedly to hash the input message M in a component-wise manner. We denote the block of a message being hashed at the i-th iteration by B_i, where each block is of constant length μ bits. Clearly this requires padding and the standard Merkle-Damgård or MD-hardening is assumed. Thus we append a single bit '1' followed by as many '0' as required to leave the message

64 bits short of a multiple of μ. The remaining 64 bits are then used for a representation of the length of the input message M in bits[1]. We will assume that the message M requires t blocks after padding and so $M = B_1 || \cdots || B_t$.

3.2   The Compression Function of MQ-HASH

At iteration i, for $1 \leq i \leq t$, the compression function is used to update the value v_{i-1} of an ν-bit *chaining variable* to v_i. The initial value of the chaining variable v_0 is specified and fixed. Thus, at iteration i of the compression function we have that $v_i = \text{COMPRESS}(v_{i-1}, B_i)$. At the end of the iteration process, the last chaining variable is used as the output of the hash function.

Figure 1 shows the compression function MQ-HASH. It uses two non-invertible components with the first component f providing a stretching function while the second, g, provides a shrinking function. These are embodied by randomly chosen tuples of multivariate quadratic polynomials. Thus, in the process of proving the necessary security properties, we have a construction that shares features with the work of Aiello, Haber, and Venkatesan [1].

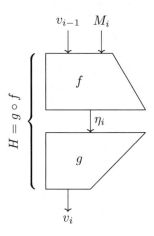

Fig. 1. Schematic description of the compression function of MQ-HASH, where v_i denotes the chaining variable and B_i the message block being hashed at iteration i

The compression function of MQ-HASH takes as input a message block B_i of μ bits and a chaining variable v_{i-1} of ν bits. Let $\mathbf{F}$ be a finite field of size q so that μ and ν are multiples of $\log_2 q$, say $\mu = m \log_2 q$ and $\nu = n \log_2 q$. We also fix another integer $\rho = r \log_2 q$ so that $r \geq m + n$. Then the stretching function consists of a randomly chosen tuple $(f_1, \ldots, f_r)$ of r quadratic polynomials in $n + m$ variables defined over $\mathbf{F}$. That is, f is given by:

---

[1] Thus the maximum length of a message that can be hashed using MQ-HASH is 2^{64} as for many other hash functions [29,22].

$$\mathbf{F}^{n+m} \longrightarrow \mathbf{F}^r$$
$$x = (c_1, \ldots, c_n, b_1, \ldots, b_m) \longmapsto f(x) = \big(f_1(x), \ldots, f_r(x)\big) \ ,$$

where $(b_1, \ldots, b_m)$ stands for the μ-bit message block split into m elements of $\mathbf{F}$, and $(c_1, \ldots, c_n)$ stands for the ν-bit chaining variable split into n elements of $\mathbf{F}$. The shrinking stage is, in turn, defined by a randomly chosen tuple $(g_1, \ldots, g_n)$ of n quadratic polynomials in r variables. That is, g is given by:

$$\mathbf{F}^r \longrightarrow \mathbf{F}^n$$
$$\eta = (\eta_1, \ldots, \eta_r) \longmapsto g(\eta) = \big(g_1(\eta), \ldots, g_n(\eta)\big) \ .$$

The final compression function is then defined to be the composition of f and g and $v_i = g \circ f(v_{i-1}, B_i)$. For the construction to be secure, we will show that:

- the two functions f and g must be hard to invert;
- the *stretch factor* $\frac{r}{m+n}$ in the first step must lie within a certain range.

The value of the stretch factor will be discussed in Section 5 and it will depend on the number of bits hashed at each compression function iteration as well as the length of the chaining variable.

In order to ease the exposition, we will assume for the rest of the paper that the ground field $\mathbf{F}$ is the binary field $GF(2)$ and it follows that $m = \mu$, $n = \nu$, and $r = \rho$.

4   The Security of MQ-HASH

The work of Merkle and Damgård allows us to concentrate on the properties of the compression function $g \circ f$. We first give elements of provable security for the first pre-image resistance of MQ-HASH. Then we discuss the collision resistance of MQ-HASH.

4.1   Preliminaries to the Study of Pre-image Resistance

In what follows, U_k denotes the uniform distribution over $\{0,1\}^k$. We say that two distributions X and Y over the binary strings of size k are distinguishable in time T with advantage ε if there exists a probabilistic algorithm D running in time less than T such that:

$$\left| \Pr_{x \in X}[D(x) = 1] - \Pr_{y \in Y}[D(y) = 1] \right| \geq \varepsilon \ .$$

We describe a pseudo-random number generator as a deterministic polynomial-time algorithm G from $\{0,1\}^l$ to $\{0,1\}^k$ with $k > l$ such that $G(U_l)$ cannot be distinguished from U_k in reasonable time (for instance with a time complexity lower than 2^s for some security level s) and with a non-negligible advantage.

We say that a function g is non-invertible in time T with probability ε if for any probabilistic algorithm $\mathcal{B}$ running in time less than T:

$$\left| \Pr_{z \in U_r} \left[g\big(\mathcal{B}(g(z))\big) = g(z) \right] \right| < \varepsilon .$$

An important aspect to our proofs will be the fact that a tuple of multivariate quadratic equations with a small stretching factor is in effect acting as a pseudo-random number generator. This ensures that the outputs from the stretching function f does not have noticeable specific properties. Since this is a property that underpins the design of QUAD, it is not surprising to find some of the fundamental components for our work covered in [4].

Theorem 2. *Let $\mathcal{A}$ be an algorithm that, on input a randomly chosen tuple f of r multivariate quadratic equations in $n + m$ binary unknowns distinguishes the distribution $\{f_1(x)\| \cdots \| f_r(x)\}_{x \in U_{n+m}}$ over the binary strings of length r from the uniform distribution U_r in time T and with advantage ε. Then $\mathcal{A}$ can be converted into an algorithm $\mathcal{B}$ that inverts a tuple g of r randomly chosen multivariate quadratic equations in $n + m$ binary unknowns with probability $\varepsilon/2$ (over both g and the inputs) in time less than:*

$$\tilde{T}(T, n, m, \varepsilon) = \frac{128(n+m)^2}{\varepsilon^2} \left(T + \log \left(\frac{128(n+m)}{\varepsilon^2} \right) + r(n+m) + 2 \right) .$$

Proof. The proof is a direct application of Theorems 2 and 3 from [4].   □

The above theorem gives rise to two comments. First, the choice of the base field is GF(2). However no obstacles to generalisations over other fields are anticipated, though the reduction would obviously lead to another value of $\tilde{T}$. Second, the reduction achieved by Theorem 2 is not very tight. However this is enough for us to derive secure parameters in Section 5.

4.2   Pre-image Resistance of MQ-HASH

The next theorem reduces the pre-image resistance of MQ-HASH's compression function to the problem of inverting random multivariate quadratic systems. Let T_f (resp. g) be the time required to evaluate f (resp. g) on its input.

Theorem 3. *Let $\mathcal{A}$ be an algorithm inverting $g \circ f$ in time T with probability ε, where f is a randomly chosen tuple of r multivariate quadratic polynomials in $n + m$ binary unknowns and g is a randomly chosen tuple of m multivariate quadratic polynomials in n binary unknowns. Then $\mathcal{A}$ can be either converted into an algorithm inverting g in time $T + T_f + T_g$ with probability ε or into an algorithm that can invert randomly chosen tuples of r multivariate quadratic polynomials in $n + m$ binary unknowns in time $\tilde{T}(T + T_f + 3T_g, n, m, \varepsilon)$ with probability $\varepsilon/2$.*

Proof. Let us define $\tilde{\mathcal{A}}(x) = f(\mathcal{A}(g(x)))$. By the assumption on algorithm $\mathcal{A}$

$$\left| \Pr_{x \in U_{n+m}} \left[g \circ f \left(\mathcal{A}(g \circ f(x)) \right) = g \circ f(x) \right] \right| \geq \varepsilon \ .$$

Thus g can be inverted by $\tilde{\mathcal{A}}$ in time $T + T_f + T_g$ with probability ε when queried with the distribution $f(U_{n+m})$. So either g can be inverted in time $T + T_f + T_g$ with probability ε or $f(U_{n+m})$ can be distinguished from U_r in time $T + T_f + 3T_g$. The theorem then follows from a direct application of Theorem 2. □

Thus, assuming that g and f are hard to invert and that f is a pseudo-random number generator, we deduce that their composition $g \circ f$, that is MQ-HASH's compression function, is pre-image resistant.

4.3 Collision and Second Pre-image Resistance of MQ-HASH

There are two sets of multivariate quadratic polynomials corresponding to functions f and g and it is their composition that gives the compression function in MQ-HASH. Intuitively, the function g provides the actual compression. However, Theorem 1 demonstrated the potential ease of finding collisions when using g on its own. So in a first step we use a non-invertible function f. This ensures that lifting collisions in g to yield pre-images for f is hard. However, finding collisions for f must not be easy, or even better, f must be an injection. This will be the rational behind what we term the *stretch* requirement for f.

The construction used in MQ-HASH is a close analogue to the construction of Aiello, Haber, and Venkatesan [1]. Their claims for collision-resistance apply equally to our own construction. Consider the compression function $g \circ f$. We know that g has collisions since it compresses but there can be no collisions in f if f is an injection. For any collisions across g to be useful for the entire compression function, they must (a) lie in the range of f and (b) be invertible through f. The choice of stretch factor ensures that (a) is unlikely while the choice of hard problem prevents (b).

Of course, this is not a proof, and a proof for the collision resistance in the standard model remains an open problem. Nevertheless, it is possible to prove this conjecture in the *random oracle model*, which, while less appealing than the standard model, provides some evidence that the overall construction is not completely flawed. It is interesting to note that this is one difference between MQ-HASH and VSH. While both proposals are able to provide a classical hash function property in a provable manner, the remaining classical properties are still conjectured to hold for MQ-HASH.

5 Establishing Parameters for MQ-HASH

While several elements of provable security for MQ-HASH were given in Section 4, the limitations of such proofs are exposed when we instantiate the general constructions in practice. In this section, therefore, we study the security and performance of MQ-HASH and illustrate the different trade-offs possible.

Our proofs in Section 4 required that f be an injection; this was the basis for the stretching role of f. But our construction also requires that solving a random system of multivariate quadratic equations is a hard problem. Thus, we observe that there are two conflicting practical constraints:

- A sufficiently large stretch is needed to ensure (to a degree of certainty that is consistent with the intended security level) that there are no collisions in the first part of the compression function.
- The system of equations that results, which will have more equations than variables, must remain computationally non-invertible.

5.1   On the Injectivity of f

The following theorem provides a bound on the stretch factor needed for the first stage f, embodied by a system of quadratic equations, to ensure its injectiveness.

Proposition 1. *The probability that a tuple f of e randomly chosen quadratic polynomials in u unknowns over a finite field $\mathbf{F}$ of size q, with $e > u$, is not an injection is lower than q^{2u-e}.*

Proof. The linear part of the affine application $A_\delta(z) = f(z + \delta) - f(z)$ is a matrix of size $e \times u$ and is defined over a finite field $\mathbf{F}$ of size q. So A_s is of rank less than u. But the probability that any matrix of size $e \times u$ and of rank u has a uniformly randomly chosen element in its image is less than q^{u-e}. Writing the tuple f as $f = f^{(2)} + f^{(1)} + f^{(0)}$ where $f^{(i)}$ denotes the homogeneous part of degree i, we see that for a randomly drawn value δ the constant $f^{(2)}(\delta) + f^{(1)}(\delta)$ is uniformly randomly distributed in $\mathbf{F}^e$, independently of the coefficients of $f^{(2)}$. Expanding the expression of A_δ as $A_\delta(z) = \beta_{f^{(2)}}(\delta, z) + f^{(2)}(\delta) + f^{(1)}(\delta)$ where $\beta_{f^{(2)}}$ is the bilinear form associated to f, one see that:

$$\Pr_{\delta \in U_u}\big[\mathrm{Ker}(A_\delta) \neq \{0\}\big] = \Pr_{\delta \in U_u, c \in U_e}\big[c \in \mathrm{Im}(A_\delta)\big] \leq q^{u-e} \ .$$

The corresponding tuple f thus has less than q^{u-e} chances of providing a collision pair of the form $(x, x + \delta)$ for any randomly chosen δ. Running through all possible values for δ, we have that the probability of f being an injection is greater than $(1 - q^{u-e})^{q^u}$ and thus the probability of f not being an injection is lower than q^{2u-e}. □

Interpreting this result and assuming that we seek a security level s, we have the constraint $2^{2u-e} < 2^{-s}$, or $e > 2u + s$ over the binary field as ground field $\mathbf{F}$. Hence, our construction will asymptotically show a stretch factor of two in the case of the binary field.

5.2   On the Hardness of Inverting f

The hardness of the system solving problem is closely related to the ratio between the number of equations and the number of variables. So we need to study the complexity of solving randomly generated quadratic equation systems over the field GF(2) when there are more equations than variables. This has been studied in detail [3] and we summarize the results in our very special case.

Theorem 4. *Solving a random system of e quadratic equations in u unknowns over the field GF(2) by the best Gröbner basis algorithm requires $\binom{u}{d}^{\omega}$ operations where $\omega \approx 2.3$ and*

$$d = \frac{u}{2} - e + \frac{e}{2}\sqrt{2 - \left(\frac{u}{e}\right)^2 - 10\frac{u}{e} + 2\sqrt{8\left(\frac{u}{e}\right)^3 + 12\left(\frac{u}{e}\right)^2 + 6\frac{u}{e} + 1}} \ .$$

Proof. The proof is available in [3]. □

Since we expect to use a stretch factor slightly bigger than two for our construction, the complexity of solving with the best Gröbner basis methods will be about $\binom{u}{u/20}^{\omega}$. For the values proposed in Section 5.3 this complexity is much higher than the security level.

# variables	80	128	160	256	512
time complexity	2^{47}	2^{74}	2^{99}	2^{153}	2^{323}

5.3 Performance Considerations

In this section, we investigate how the security requirements impact the performances of MQ-HASH. For conservative settings and aiming at 80-bit security, the use of the base field $\mathbf{F} = GF(2)$ seems mandatory. In this case, the chaining variable could be 160 bits in length, the message block at each iteration could be 32 bits in length, and the intermediate output from f should be around 464 bits. This would leave us with the parameter set $n = \nu = 160$, $m = \mu = 32$, and $r = \rho = 464$ which are consistent with the security levels implied by Theorem 4. The storage requirements for the first part of the computation, the evaluation of f, is about 1 MB while the storage for the evaluation of g is less than 2.2 MB. The total amount of storage is more than 3 MB of memory, so it will not fit in the cache of contemporary processors, incurring a big performance penalty that will severely restrict its practical use.

As usual, the property of provable security comes at a price. Crude estimates for the performance of MQ-HASH show that it might be expected to run thousands of times slower than SHA-1. However, we foresee that various modifications can be made to the design of MQ-HASH so as to lower the gap of performance with usual hash functions like SHA-1. We leave this question as an open research subject.

5.4 Deploying Random Systems

One issue with using quadratic systems might be a concern about weak instances. This is of special interest in the case of multivariate quadratic systems since trapdoors for this environment have been proposed as a fundamental feature of several asymmetric schemes [16,23,24,25]. However, this is not such an unusual issue in cryptographic deployment and shared equation systems can be generated using a variety of techniques so as to allay suspicion. See, for example, the case of DSS [30].

5.5   Alternative Approaches

Our proposal MQ-HASH might be viewed as a first attempt to build a practical hash function that relies for its security on multivariate quadratic equations. There are several ways the work might be extended.

For instance, we might consider some slight variants to the structure of MQ-HASH. It would be very natural to replace the *fixed* tuple f of multivariate polynomials with tuples that are randomly re-generated at each iteration of the compression function. Such a variant, outlined below, allows the tuple f to be modified via some transformation of the chaining variable.

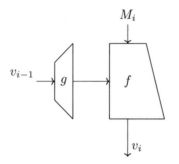

It is interesting to observe that this approach, that we denote RMQ-HASH, can be viewed as bringing us closer to some established block-cipher constructions such as *Matyas-Meyer-Oseas* [7,27]: the one-way function f would be akin to a block cipher with feed-forward and the treatment of the chaining variable would be analogous to a (very) unusual key-schedule. While there are some intriguing challenges in this approach, early analysis suggests that such a scheme would allow for a more compact system of equations with accompanying performance advantages. This may well be an interesting structure to consider in future work.

6   Conclusions

In this paper we have introduced a new hash function MQ-HASH. The security of this hash function is based on the difficulty of solving systems of multivariate quadratic equations, a problem that is well-studied and used elsewhere in cryptography. The hash function MQ-HASH is provably pre-image resistant in the standard model, and there is good evidence to support the conjecture that MQ-HASH is collision-free and second pre-image resistant. However a proof in the standard model remains an area of open research.

We believe there to be considerable promise in using multivariate quadratic equations as a hard problem in symmetric cryptography. This is something that has been pioneered with QUAD, and we anticipate similar success in the design of other primitives. With regards to hash functions, however, there are some particular challenges in using multivariate quadratic equations. In particular one is forced to adopt a more complex construction than one might initially like, and one must act carefully so as retain provable pre-image resistance. This may well result in a wide variety of alternative constructions. In this paper we have considered one particular approach and establishing a broader range of designs with alternative security/performance trade-offs remains a topic of ongoing research.

References

1. Aiello, W., Haber, S., Venkatesan, R.: New Constructions for Secure Hash Functions. In: Vaudenay, S. (ed.) FSE 1998. LNCS, vol. 1372, pp. 150–167. Springer, Heidelberg (1998)
2. Augot, D., Finiasz, M., Sendrier, N.: A Family of Fast Syndrome Based Cryptographic Hash Functions. In: Dawson, E., Vaudenay, S. (eds.) Mycrypt 2005. LNCS, vol. 3715, pp. 64–83. Springer, Heidelberg (2005)
3. Bardet, M., Faugère, J.-C., Salvy, B.: On the complexity of Gröbner basis computation of semi-regular overdetermined algebraic equations. In: ICPSS, pp. 71–74 (2004)
4. Berbain, C., Gilbert, H., Patarin, J.: QUAD: A Practical Stream Cipher with Provable Security. In: Vaudenay, S. (ed.) EUROCRYPT 2006. LNCS, vol. 4004, pp. 109–128. Springer, Heidelberg (2006)
5. Berbain, C.: Personal communication (November 21, 2006)
6. Bentahar, K., Page, D., Silverman, J.H., Saarinen, M.-J.O., Smart, N., LASH (2006) Available from: http://csrc.nist.gov/pki/HashWorkshop/2006/
7. Black, J., Rogaway, P., Shrimpton, T.: Black-Box Analysis of the Block-Cipher-Based Hash-Function Constructions from PGV. In: Yung, M. (ed.) CRYPTO 2002. LNCS, vol. 2442, pp. 320–335. Springer, Heidelberg (2002)
8. Contini, S., Lenstra, A.K., Steinfeld, R.: VSH, an Efficient and Provable Collision-Resistant Hash Function. In: Vaudenay, S. (ed.) EUROCRYPT 2006. LNCS, vol. 4004, pp. 165–182. Springer, Heidelberg (2006)
9. Damgård, I.: A Design Principle for Hash Functions. In: Brassard, G. (ed.) CRYPTO 1989. LNCS, vol. 435, pp. 416–427. Springer, Heidelberg (1990)
10. Ding, J., Schmidt, D.: Rainbow, a New Multivariable Polynomial Signature Scheme. In: Ioannidis, J., Keromytis, A.D., Yung, M. (eds.) ACNS 2005. LNCS, vol. 3531, pp. 164–175. Springer, Heidelberg (2005)
11. Fouque, P.-A., Granboulan, L., Stern, J.: Differential cryptanalysis for multivariate schemes. In: Cramer, R.J.F. (ed.) EUROCRYPT 2005. LNCS, vol. 3494, pp. 341–353. Springer, Heidelberg (2005)

12. Fraenkel, A.S., Yesha, Y.: Complexity of Problems in Games, Graphs, and Algebraic Equations. Discr. Appl. Math. 1, 15–30 (1979)

13. Garey, M.R., Johnson, D.S.: Computers and Intractability: A Guide to the Theory of NP-Completeness. W.H. Freeman & Co. New York (1979)

14. Joux, A.: Multicollisions in Iterated Hash Functions. Application to Cascaded Constructions. In: Franklin, M.k. (ed.) CRYPTO 2004. LNCS, vol. 3152, pp. 306–316. Springer, Heidelberg (2004)

15. Kelsey, J., Schneier, B.: Second Preimages on n-Bit Hash Functions for Much Less than 2^n Work. In: Cramer, R.J.F. (ed.) EUROCRYPT 2005. LNCS, vol. 3494, pp. 474–490. Springer, Heidelberg (2005)

16. Kipnis, A., Patarin, J., Goubin, L.: Unbalanced Oil and Vinegar Signature Schemes. In: Stern, J. (ed.) EUROCRYPT 1999. LNCS, vol. 1592, pp. 206–222. Springer, Heidelberg (1999)

17. Lenstra, A.K., Page, D., Stam, M.: Discrete logarithm variants of VSH. In: Nguyen, P.Q. (ed.) VIETCRYPT 2006. LNCS, vol. 4341, pp. 229–242. Springer, Heidelberg (2006)

18. Lidl, R., Niederreiter, H.: Finite Fields. Cambridge University Press, Cambridge (1997)

19. Menezes, A.J., Vanstone, S.A., Van Oorschot, P.C.: Handbook of Applied Cryptography. CRC Press, Boca Raton (1996)

20. Merkle, R.C.: One Way Hash Functions and DES. In: Brassard, G. (ed.) CRYPTO 1989. LNCS, vol. 435, pp. 428–446. Springer, Heidelberg (1989)

21. National Institute of Standards and Technology. FIPS 197: Advanced Encryption Standard (November 2001) Available from: http://csrc.nist.gov

22. National Institute of Standards and Technology. FIPS 180-2: Secure Hash Standard (August 2002) http://csrc.nist.gov

23. Patarin, J.: Hidden Fields Equations (HFE) and Isomorphisms of Polynomials (IP): Two New Families of Asymmetric Algorithms. In: Maurer, U.M. (ed.) EUROCRYPT 1996. LNCS, vol. 1070, pp. 33–48. Springer, Heidelberg (1996)

24. Patarin, J., Courtois, N.T., Goubin, L.: QUARTZ, 128-Bit Long Digital Signatures. In: Naccache, D. (ed.) CT-RSA 2001. LNCS, vol. 2020, pp. 282–297. Springer, Heidelberg (2001)

25. Patarin, J., Courtois, N.T., Goubin, L.: FLASH, a Fast Multivariate Signature Algorithm. In: Naccache, D. (ed.) CT-RSA 2001. LNCS, vol. 2020, pp. 298–307. Springer, Heidelberg (2001)

26. Peyrin, T., Gilbert, H., Muller, F., Robshaw, M.J.B.: Combining Compression Functions and Block Cipher-based Hash Functions. In: Lai, X., Chen, K. (eds.) ASIACRYPT 2006. LNCS, vol. 4284, pp. 315–331. Springer, Heidelberg (2006)

27. Preneel, B.: Analysis and design of cryptographic hash functions. Ph.D. thesis. Katholieke Universiteit Leuven (1993)

28. Ronald, L.: Rivest. RFC 1320: The MD4 Message-Digest Algorithm (April 1992)http://www.ietf.org/rfc/rfc1320.txt

29. Rivest, R.L.: RFC 1321: The MD5 Message-Digest Algorithm (April 1992) http://www.ietf.org/rfc/rfc1321.txt

30. Smid, M.E., Branstad, D.K.: Response to Comments of the NIST Proposed Digital Signature Standard. In: Brickell, E.F. (ed.) CRYPTO 1992. LNCS, vol. 740, pp. 76–88. Springer, Heidelberg (1993)

31. Courtois, N., Goubin, L., Meier, W., Tacier, J.-D.: Solving Underdefined Systems of Multivariate Quadratic Equations. Public Key Cryptography, 211–227 (2002)
32. Wang, X., Yin, Y.L., Yu, H.: Finding Collisions in the Full SHA-1. In: Ziarko, W., Yao, Y. (eds.) RSCTC 2000. LNCS (LNAI), vol. 2005, pp. 17–36. Springer, Heidelberg (2001)
33. Wang, X., Yu, H.: How to Break MD5 and Other Hash Functions. In: Cramer, R.J.F. (ed.) EUROCRYPT 2005. LNCS, vol. 3494, pp. 19–35. Springer, Heidelberg (2005)
34. Wolf, C., Preneel, B.: Taxonomy of Public Key Schemes based on the problem of Multivariate Quadratic equations. http://eprint.iacr.org/

An Application of the Goldwasser-Micali Cryptosystem to Biometric Authentication[*]

Julien Bringer[1], Hervé Chabanne[1], Malika Izabachène[2], David Pointcheval[2], Qiang Tang[2], and Sébastien Zimmer[2]

[1] Sagem Défense Sécurité
[2] Departement d'Informatique, École Normale Supérieure
45 Rue d'Ulm, 75230 Paris Cedex 05, France

Abstract. This work deals with the security challenges in authentication protocols employing volatile biometric features, where the authentication is indeed a comparison between a fresh biometric template and that enrolled during the enrollment phase. We propose a security model for biometric-based authentication protocols by assuming that the biometric features to be public. Extra attention is paid to the privacy issues related to the sensitive relationship between a biometric feature and the relevant identity. Relying on the Goldwasser-Micali encryption scheme, we introduce a protocol for biometric-based authentication and prove its security in our security model.

Keywords: Authentication, biometrics, privacy.

1 Introduction

Security protocols generally rely on exact knowledge of some data, such as a cryptographic key, however there are particular applications where environment and human participation generate variability. In biometric-based cryptosystems, when a user identifies or authenticates himself using his biometrics, the biometric feature, which is captured by a sensor (e.g. a camera for iris biometrics), will rarely be the same twice. Thus, traditional cryptographic handling such as a hash value is not suitable in this case, since it is not error tolerant. As a result, the identification or authentication must be done in a special way, and moreover precaution is required to protect the sensitivity (or privacy) of biometrics.

We here consider a practical environment where a human user wants to authenticate himself to a database using his biometrics. A typical scenario is that some reference biometric data is stored inside a database, through which the server authenticates the user by checking whether or not a "fresh" biometric template sent by the sensor matches with the reference one. Our main focus is about biometrics such as iris [4], which can be extracted into binary strings. Therefore, an authentication leads to a comparison between two binary vectors. If the Hamming distance is adopted, then a comparison consists of computing

---

[*] Work partially supported by french ANR RNRT project BACH.

J. Pieprzyk, H. Ghodosi, and E. Dawson (Eds.): ACISP 2007, LNCS 4586, pp. 96–106, 2007.

the Hamming distance between the reference data and the fresh template and comparing this to a threshold.

To enforce privacy, we wish biometric data after their capture to be hidden in some way so that an adversary is unable to find out who is the real person that is trying to authenticate himself. Note that a live person is uniquely identified by his biometrics and we want to hide the relationship between biometrics and the identity (used in an application). To achieve this goal, an application dependent identity is used and biometric matching is made over encrypted data. Moreover, to retrieve data to be compared with from the database, we introduce a new protocol to hide the index of record from the database.

1.1   Related Works

In [8] Juels and Wattenberg start the pioneering work by combining error correction codes with biometrics to construct fuzzy commitment schemes. Later on two important concepts about, i.e., secure sketch and fuzzy extractor, are widely studied. In [9], a number of secure sketch schemes have been proposed. In [6], Dodis *et al.* formalize the concept of fuzzy extractor, and propose to use for symmetric key generation from biometric features. In [2], Boyen *et al.* propose applications to remote biometric authentication using biometric information. Moreover, the work of Linnartz and Tuyls [10] investigates key extraction generated from continuous sources. In these schemes, biometric features are treated to be secret and used to derive general symmetric keys for traditional cryptographic systems.

There are a number of papers which deal with the secure comparison of two binary strings without using error correcting codes. In the protocol proposed by Atallah *et al.* [1], biometric features are measured as bit strings and subsequently masked and permuted during the authentication process. The comparison of two binary vectors modified following the same random transformation leads then to the knowledge of the Hamming distance. The main drawback of their protocol is that the client needs to store a number of secret values and update them during every authentication process, as the security relies mainly on these transformations.

Cryptographic protocols using homomorphic encryption may also allow us to compare directly encrypted data. For instance, Schoenmakers and Tuyls improve Paillier's public encryption protocol and propose to use it for biometric authentication protocols by employing multi-party computation techniques [12].

In summary, most of these protocols, except the work of [11] which uses biometry for Identity-Based Encryption, rely on the assumption that biometric features belonging to live users are private information. However, this assumption is not true in practice. As a user's biometric information, such as fingerprint, may be easily captured in daily life. In this paper, we assume that the biometric information is public, but the relationship between a user's identity and its biometric information is private.

1.2   Our Contributions

In this paper we propose a general security model for biometric-based authentication. The model possesses a number of advantages over the existing ones: The first is that we lower the level of trust on the involved individual principals. The second is that extra attention has been paid to the privacy issues related to the sensitive relationship between a biometric feature and the relevant identities. Specifically, this relationship is unknown to the database and the matcher.

We propose a new biometric authentication protocol which is proved secure in our security model. Our protocol follows a special procedure to query the database, which, as in the case of Private Information Retrieval (PIR) protocol [3], allows to retrieve an item without revealing which item is retrieved. The protocol heavily exploits the homomorphic property of Goldwasser-Micali public-key encryption scheme [7], its ability to treat plaintext bit after bit, and the security is based on its semantic security, namely the quadratic residuosity assumption.

1.3   Organization of This Work

The rest of the paper is organized as follows. In Section 2, we describe our security model for (remote) biometric-based authentication. In Section 3, we describe a new protocol for biometric authentication. In Section 4, we give the security analysis of the new protocol in the new security model. In Section 5, we conclude the paper.

2   A New Security Model

For a biometric-based remote authentication system, we assume the system mainly consists of two parts: the client part and the server part. At the client side, we distinguish the following two types of entities:

- A human being U_i, for any $i \geq 1$, who registers his reference biometric template b_i at the server side, and provides fresh biometric information in order to obtain any service from the authentication server.
- A sensor S which is capable of capturing the user's biometric and extracting it into a binary string, namely a fresh template.

In practice, the template extraction process may involve a number of components, nonetheless, here we assume that the sensor implements all these functionalities. Implicitly, we assume that the sensor can communicate with the server.

At the server side, we distinguish the following three types of entities:

- An authentication server, denoted $\mathcal{AS}$, which deals with the user's service requests and provides the requested service.
- A database $\mathcal{DB}$, which stores users' biometric templates.
- A matcher $\mathcal{M}$, which helps the server to make a decision related to a user's request of authentication.

Fig. 1 below illustrates this model.

Fig. 1. Our model

Like most existing biometric-based systems (and many traditional cryptosystems), in our security model, a biometric-based authentication protocol consists of two phases: an enrollment phase and a verification phase.

1. In the enrollment phase, U_i registers its biometric template b_i at the database $\mathcal{DB}$ and its identity information ID_i at the server $\mathcal{AS}$.
2. In the verification phase, U_i issues an authentication request to the server $\mathcal{AS}$ through the sensor $\mathcal{S}$. The server $\mathcal{AS}$ retrieves U_i's biometric information from the database $\mathcal{DB}$ and makes its decision with the help of $\mathcal{M}$.

We assume that a "liveness link" is always available between the sensor $\mathcal{S}$ and the authentication server $\mathcal{AS}$ to ensure $\mathcal{AS}$ that the biometric it receives is from a present living person. The possible methods to achieve this liveness link are beyond the scope of this paper, but one can think about organizational measures or technical anti-spoofing countermeasures as those described in [5]. In addition, classical cryptographic challenge / response may also be used. This liveness link ensures that the server do not receive fake or replayed data. Since the sensor $\mathcal{S}$ is responsible for processing the biometric features, hence, it should be fully trusted and extensively protected in practice. Implicitly, the communications at the server side are also properly protected in the sense of authenticity. We further assume that all principals in the system will not collude and be honest-but-curious, which means they will not deviate from the protocol specification. In practice, certain management measures may be used to guarantee this assumption.

Let $\mathcal{H}$ be the distance function in the underlying metric space, for instance the Hamming space in our case. We regard soundness as a pre-requisite of any useful protocol. Formally, we have the following requirement.

Requirement 1. *The matcher $\mathcal{M}$ can faithfully compute the distance $\mathcal{H}(b_i, b'_i)$, where b_i is the reference biometric template and b'_i is the fresh biometric template sent in the authentication request. Therefore, $\mathcal{M}$ can compare the distance to a given threshold value d and the server $\mathcal{AS}$ can make the right decision.*

Our main concern is the sensitive relationship between U_i's identity and its biometrics. We want to guarantee that any principal except for the sensor $\mathcal{S}$ cannot find any information about the relationship. Formally, we have the following requirement.

Requirement 2. *For any identity ID_{i_0}, two biometric templates b'_{i_0}, b'_{i_1}, where $i_0, i_1 \geq 1$ and b'_{i_0} is the biometric template related to ID_{i_0}, it is infeasible for any of $\mathcal{M}$, $\mathcal{DB}$, and $\mathcal{AS}$ to distinguish between (ID_{i_0}, b'_{i_0}) and (ID_{i_0}, b'_{i_1}).*

We further want to guarantee that the database $\mathcal{DB}$ gets no information about which user is authenticating himself to the server. Formally, we have the following requirement.

Requirement 3. *For any two users U_{i_0} and U_{i_1}, where $i_0, i_1 \geq 1$, if U_{i_β} where $\beta \in \{0, 1\}$ makes an authentication attempt, then the database $\mathcal{DB}$ can only guess β with a negligible advantage. Suppose the database $\mathcal{DB}$ makes a guess β', the advantage is $|\Pr[\beta = \beta'] - \frac{1}{2}|$.*

3   A New Biometric-Based Authentication Protocol

3.1   Review of the Goldwasser-Micali Scheme

The algorithms $(\mathcal{K}, \mathcal{E}, \mathcal{D})$ of Goldwasser-Micali scheme [7] are defined as follows:

1. The key generation algorithm $\mathcal{K}$ takes a security parameter 1^ℓ as input, and generates two large prime numbers p and q, $n = pq$ and a non-residue x for which the Jacobi symbol is 1. The public key pk is (x, n), and the secret key sk is (p, q).
2. The encryption algorithm $\mathcal{E}$ takes a message $m \in \{0, 1\}$ and the public key (x, n) as input, and outputs the ciphertext c, where $c = y^2 x^m \mod n$ and y is randomly chosen from $\mathbb{Z}_n^*$.
3. The decryption algorithm $\mathcal{D}$ takes a ciphertext c and the private key (p, q) as input, and outputs the message m, where $m = 0$ if c is a quadratic residue, $m = 1$ otherwise.

It is well-known (cf. [7]) that, if the quadratic residuosity problem is intractable, then the Goldwasser-Micali scheme is semantically secure. In other words an adversary $\mathcal{A}$ has only a negligible advantage in the following game.

$$\mathbf{Exp}_{\mathcal{E},\mathcal{A}}^{\text{IND-CPA}}$$
$$\left|\begin{array}{rl} (sk, pk) & \leftarrow \mathcal{K}(1^\ell) \\ (m_0, m_1) & \leftarrow \mathcal{A}(pk) \\ c & \leftarrow \mathcal{E}(m_\beta, pk), \ \beta \leftarrow \{0, 1\} \\ \beta' & \leftarrow \mathcal{A}(m_0, m_1, c, pk) \\ \text{return } \beta' \end{array}\right.$$

At the end of this game, the attacker's advantage $\mathbf{Adv}_{\mathcal{E},\mathcal{A}}^{\text{IND-CPA}}$ is defined to be

$$\mathbf{Adv}_{\mathcal{E},\mathcal{A}}^{\text{IND-CPA}} = \left| Pr[\mathbf{Exp}_{\mathcal{E},\mathcal{A}}^{\text{IND-CPA}} = 1 | \beta = 1] - Pr[\mathbf{Exp}_{\mathcal{E},\mathcal{A}}^{\text{IND-CPA}} = 1 | \beta = 0] \right|.$$

Moreover the encryption protocol possesses a nice homomorphic property, for any $m, m' \in \{0, 1\}$ the following equation holds.

$$\mathcal{D}(\mathcal{E}(m, pk) \times \mathcal{E}(m', pk), sk) = m \oplus m'$$

Note that the encryption algorithm encrypts one bit at a time, hence, in order to encrypt a binary string we need to encrypt every bit individually. We thus have the following property.

Lemma 1 ([7]). *Given any $M \geq 1$, the attacker's advantage in the following game is negligible based on the quadratic residuosity assumption.*

$$\mathbf{Exp}_{\mathcal{E},\mathcal{A}'}^{P\text{-}IND\text{-}CPA}$$

$$
\begin{vmatrix}
& (sk, pk) & \leftarrow \mathcal{K}(1^{\ell}) \\
((m_{0,1}, \ldots, m_{0,M}), (m_{1,1}, \ldots, m_{1,M})) & \leftarrow \mathcal{A}'(pk) \\
& c & \leftarrow (\mathcal{E}(m_{\beta,1}, pk), \ldots, \mathcal{E}(m_{\beta,M}, pk)), \ \beta \leftarrow \{0,1\} \\
& \beta' & \leftarrow \mathcal{A}'((m_{0,1}, \ldots, m_{0,M}), (m_{1,1}, \ldots, m_{1,M}), c, pk) \\
& return \ \beta'
\end{vmatrix}
$$

3.2 Enrollment Phase

In the protocol we treat U_i's biometric template b_i as a binary vector of the dimension M, i.e. $b_i = (b_{i,1}, b_{i,2}, \ldots, b_{i,M})$.

In the enrollment phase, U_i registers (b_i, i) at the database $\mathcal{DB}$, and (ID_i, i) at the authentication server $\mathcal{AS}$, where ID_i is U_i's pseudonym and i is the index of the record b_i in $\mathcal{DB}$. Let N denotes the total number of records in $\mathcal{DB}$.

The matcher $\mathcal{M}$ possesses a key pair (pk, sk) for the Goldwasser-Micali scheme $(\mathcal{K}, \mathcal{E}, \mathcal{D})$, where $pk = (x, n)$ and $sk = (p, q)$.

3.3 Verification Phase

If the user U_i wants to authenticate himself to the authentication server $\mathcal{AS}$, the procedure below is followed:

1. The sensor $\mathcal{S}$ captures the user's biometric data b_i', and sends $\mathcal{E}(b_i', pk)$ together with the user's identity ID_i to the authentication server $\mathcal{AS}$, where

$$\mathcal{E}(b_i', pk) = (\mathcal{E}(b_{i,1}', pk), \mathcal{E}(b_{i,2}', pk), \ldots, \mathcal{E}(b_{i,M}', pk)).$$

   Note that a "liveness link" is available between $\mathcal{S}$ and $\mathcal{AS}$ to ensure that data coming from the sensor are indeed fresh and not artificial.
2. The server $\mathcal{AS}$ retrieves the index i using ID_i, and then sends $\mathcal{E}(t_j, pk)$ $(1 \leq j \leq N)$ to the database, where $t_j = 1$ if $j = i$, $t_j = 0$ otherwise.
3. For every $1 \leq k \leq M$, the database $\mathcal{DB}$ computes $\mathcal{E}(b_{i,k}, pk)$, where

$$\mathcal{E}(b_{i,k}, pk) = \prod_{j=1}^{N} \mathcal{E}(t_j, pk)^{b_{j,k}} \mod n,$$

   Then it sends these $\mathcal{E}(b_{i,k}, pk)$ $(1 \leq k \leq M)$ to the authentication server $\mathcal{AS}$.
4. The authentication server $\mathcal{AS}$ computes ν_k $(1 \leq k \leq M)$, where

$$
\begin{aligned}
\nu_k &= \mathcal{E}(b_{i,k}', pk)\mathcal{E}(b_{i,k}, pk) \mod n \\
&= \mathcal{E}(b_{i,k}' \oplus b_{i,k}, pk)
\end{aligned}
$$

It then makes a random permutation among ν_k $(1 \leq k \leq M)$ and sends the permuted vector λ_k $(1 \leq k \leq M)$ to the matcher $\mathcal{M}$.

5. The matcher $\mathcal{M}$ decrypts the λ_k $(1 \leq k \leq M)$ to check if the Hamming weight of the corresponding plaintext vector is equal to or less than d, and sends the result to $\mathcal{AS}$.

6. The authentication server $\mathcal{AS}$ accepts or rejects the authentication request accordingly.

To sum up, $\mathcal{S}$ stores the public key pk, $\mathcal{AS}$ stores the public key pk and a table of relations (ID_i, i) for $i \in \{1, \ldots, N\}$, $\mathcal{DB}$ contains the enrolled biometric data $b_1, \ldots, b_N$, and $\mathcal{M}$ possesses the secret key sk, then the protocol runs following Fig. 2.

$\mathcal{S}$	$\xrightarrow{\mathcal{E}(b'_i, pk), ID_i}$	$\mathcal{AS}$
Capture b'_i from U_i		

$\mathcal{AS}$	$\xrightarrow{(\mathcal{E}(t_j, pk))_{1 \leq j \leq N}}$	$\mathcal{DB}$
Choose $t_j = \delta_{i,j}$		

$\mathcal{AS}$	$\xleftarrow{(\mathcal{E}(b_{i,k}, pk))_{1 \leq k \leq M}}$	For $1 \leq k \leq M$, compute $\prod_{j=1}^{N} \mathcal{E}(t_j, pk)^{b_{j,k}} \mod n = \mathcal{E}(b_{i,k}, pk)$

Compute
$$\nu_k = \mathcal{E}(b'_{i,k}, pk)\mathcal{E}(b_{i,k}, pk) \mod n = \mathcal{E}(b'_{i,k} \oplus b_{i,k}, pk)$$

$\xrightarrow{\lambda_1, \ldots, \lambda_M}$

$\mathcal{M}$
Check the weight of
$(\mathcal{D}(\lambda_1, sk), \ldots, \mathcal{D}(\lambda_M, sk))$

Take a random permutation σ,
compute $\lambda_k = \nu_{\sigma(k)}$

$\mathcal{AS}$	$\xleftarrow{\text{OK / NOK}}$	$\mathcal{DB}$

Fig. 2. The Authentication protocol

It is easy to verify that the sensor $\mathcal{S}$ performs at most $2M$ modular multiplications, the server performs $2N$ modular multiplications in step 2 (which can be pre-computed) and M modular multiplications in step 4. The database needs to perform $\frac{MN}{2}$ modular multiplications in step 3, if we assume that 0 and 1 are equally distributed in the set $\{b_{j,k}\}_{1 \leq j \leq N, 1 \leq k \leq M}$. The matcher performs M modular exponentiations to check quadratic residuosity modulo p. And the overall communication complexity is linear on the number N of records in the database.

4 Security Analysis of the Protocol

The introduction of the matcher $\mathcal{M}$, which holds the decryption key, effectively limits the access to users' biometric information. The matcher $\mathcal{M}$ can only obtain the Hamming distance between two measurements of any user's biometrics, which actually can be thought of being public information. The server does not store any biometric information, hence, compromise of the server leaks no information to an outside attacker. Moreover, biometrics are almost always handled in an encrypted form.

Indeed the biometric templates are stored in plaintext in the database $\mathcal{DB}$, however, without any relevant identity information. In case that the database is compromised, no sensitive relationship information would be leaked, though we consider encrypting the biometric templates in the database is an interesting future research topic.

In the next section we show that the protocol satisfies the requirements described in Section 2.

4.1 Fulfillment of Our Requirements

In step 4 of the protocol, we show that $\nu_k = \mathcal{E}(b'_{i,k} \oplus b_{i,k}, pk)$ for $1 \leq k \leq M$. Obviously, the Hamming distance between b_i and b'_i, $\mathcal{H}(b_i, b'_i)$, is equal to the Hamming weight of the plaintext vector corresponding to $(\nu_1, \ldots, \nu_M)$ and $(\lambda_1, \ldots, \lambda_M)$. Hence, it is straightforward to verify that **Requirement 1** is fulfilled.

We next show that the authentication protocol satisfies **Requirement 2** under the quadratic residuosity assumption.

Theorem 1. *For any identity ID_{i_0} and two biometric templates b'_{i_0}, b'_{i_1}, where $i_0, i_1 \geq 1$ and b'_{i_0} is the biometric template related to ID_{i_0}, any of $\mathcal{M}$, $\mathcal{DB}$, and $\mathcal{AS}$ can only distinguish between (ID_{i_0}, b'_{i_0}) and (ID_{i_0}, b'_{i_1}) with a negligible advantage.*

Proof. It is clear that the matcher $\mathcal{M}$ and the database $\mathcal{DB}$ have advantage 0 in distinguishing between (ID_{i_0}, b'_{i_0}) and (ID_{i_0}, b'_{i_1}), because they have no access to any information about users' identities.

As to the server $\mathcal{AS}$, the proof follows. From (ID_{i_0}, b'_{i_β}) with $\beta \in \{0, 1\}$, if the database $\mathcal{AS}$ can guess β with a non-negligible advantage δ, then we construct an attacker $\mathcal{A}$ for the Goldwasser-Micali scheme (as defined in Lemma 1) which has the advantage δ. The attacker simulates the protocol executions for the server $\mathcal{AS}$.

Suppose $\mathcal{A}$ receives pk from the challenger and gets a challenge $c_d = \mathcal{E}(m_{i_d}, pk)$ for $m_{i_0} \neq m_{i_1}$, where d is a random bit chosen by the challenger. $\mathcal{A}$ simulates the protocol executions by assuming that the matcher $\mathcal{M}$ and the database $\mathcal{DB}$ take pk as the public key. Then $\mathcal{A}$ registers m_{i_0} and m_{i_1} in the database.

Note that it is straightforward to verify that the protocol execution for $\mathcal{AS}$ can be faithfully simulated by $\mathcal{A}$, and the knowledge of private key sk is not needed. If the server $\mathcal{AS}$ outputs a guess β', then $\mathcal{A}$ outputs the guess bit $d' = \beta'$ for d. As $\mathcal{A}$ wins if $\mathcal{AS}$ wins, the theorem now follows from Lemma 1.   □

Now we prove that the authentication protocol also satisfies **Requirement 3** under the quadratic residuosity assumption.

Theorem 2. *For any two users U_{i_0} and U_{i_1}, where $i_0, i_1 \geq 1$, if U_{i_β} where $\beta \in \{0,1\}$ makes an authentication attempt, then the database $\mathcal{DB}$ can only guess β with a negligible advantage.*

Proof. If the database $\mathcal{DB}$ can guess β with a non-negligible advantage δ, then we construct an attacker $\mathcal{A}$ for the Goldwasser-Micali scheme which has the advantage δ.

Suppose $\mathcal{A}$ receives pk from the challenger and gets a challenge $c_d = \mathcal{E}(m_d, pk)$ for $m_0 = 0, m_1 = 1$, where d is a random bit chosen by the challenger. In addition, $\mathcal{DB}$ takes pk as the matcher's public key. For any $i_0, i_1 \geq 1$ and $i_0 \neq i_1$, $\mathcal{A}$ issues a query with $\mathcal{E}(t_j, pk)$ $(1 \leq j \leq N)$, where $\mathcal{E}(t_{i_1}, pk) = c_d$, $\mathcal{E}(t_{i_0}, pk) = y^2 x c_d$ where y is randomly chosen from $\mathbb{Z}_n^*$, and $t_j = 0$ for all $1 \leq j \leq N, j \neq i_0, j \neq i_1$. If the database $\mathcal{DB}$ outputs a guess β', then $\mathcal{A}$ outputs the guess bit $d' = \beta'$ for d. And it is straightforward to verify that $\mathcal{A}$ wins if $\mathcal{DB}$ wins.   □

4.2   Advantages of the Protocol

To emphasize the interest of our protocol, we further compare it with one recent protocol of Atallah et al. [1] which also allows the comparison between two binary biometric templates.

In the protocol of Atallah et al. [1] two entities are involved: a server which stores some information about the reference data b and a client (with a biometric sensor) which sends other information derived from the measured data b'. In the initialization phase, the client stores a random permutation Π_1 of $\{0,1\}^n$ and three random boolean vectors s_1, s_2, r_1. The client then sends $s_1 \oplus \Pi_1(b_1 \oplus r_1), H(s_1), H(s_1, H(s_2))$ to the server for backup, where H is a hash function and b_1 is the user's biometric data. When measuring a new features vector b_2, the client sends $s_1, \Pi_1(b_2 \oplus r_1)$ to the server which could then verify the value of $H(s_1)$ and compute the Hamming distance of b_1, b_2 to check if it is in an acceptable range. Thereafter, the remaining vectors are used to renew all the information stored at the client and the server sides for a future authentication.

The main drawback of this protocol is that the client needs to store secret values. Once these values are compromised, the attacker would be able to compute a user's biometric template easily by passively eavesdropping on the communication channel. It is also possible to show that an active attacker could impersonate the client to the server. Finally, it is also clear that the user's privacy is not ensured against the server. Therefore, it makes sense for us to explore new protocols that avoid these drawbacks.

Hence, the most important points that make our protocol more appropriate for biometrics authentication protocols are the following. Firstly, no secret information storage is required at the client side. Secondly, the protocol guarantees the privacy of the relationship between the user's identity and its biometric data, and the privacy of the user's biometric information.

5   Conclusion

In this paper, we considered a biometric authentication protocol where confidentiality is required for biometric data solely for privacy reasons. We captured these notions into a security model and introduced a protocol which is proved secure in this security model. It remains an interesting issue to improve its performance. For a better acceptability, we also want to look at an extension of this work where biometric data inside the database are also encrypted.

Acknowledgment

We would like to thank Michel Abdalla for the fruitful discussions.

References

1. Atallah, M.J., Frikken, K.B., Goodrich, M.l.T., Tamassia, R.: Secure biometric authentication for weak computational devices. In: Patrick, A.S., Yung, M. (eds.) FC 2005. LNCS, vol. 3570, pp. 357–371. Springer, Heidelberg (2005)
2. Boyen, X., Dodis, Y., Katz, J., Ostrovsky, R., Smith, A.: Secure remote authentication using biometric data. In: Cramer, R.J.F. (ed.) EUROCRYPT 2005. LNCS, vol. 3494, pp. 147–163. Springer, Heidelberg (2005)
3. Chor, B., Kushilevitz, E., Goldreich, O., Sudan, M.: Private information retrieval. J. ACM 45(6), 965–981 (1998)
4. Daugman, J.: How iris recognition works. ICIP (1), 33–36 (2002)
5. Daugman, J.: Iris recognition and anti-spoofing countermeasures. In: 7-th International Biometrics Conference (2004)
6. Dodis, Y., Reyzin, L., Smith, A.: Fuzzy extractors: How to generate strong keys from biometrics and other noisy data. In: Cachin, C., Camenisch, J.L. (eds.) EUROCRYPT 2004. LNCS, vol. 3027, pp. 523–540. Springer, Heidelberg (2004)
7. Goldwasser, S., Micali, S.: Probabilistic encryption and how to play mental poker keeping secret all partial information. In: Proceedings of the Fourteenth Annual ACM Symposium on Theory of Computing, May 5-7, 1982, San Francisco, California, USA, pp. 365–377. ACM Press, New York (1982)
8. Juels, A., Wattenberg, M.: A fuzzy commitment scheme. In: ACM Conference on Computer and Communications Security, pp. 28–36 (1999)
9. Li, Q., Chang, E.: Robust, short and sensitive authentication tags using secure sketch. In: MM&Sec '06: Proceeding of the 8th workshop on Multimedia and security, pp. 56–61. ACM Press, New York (2006)

10. Jean-Paul, M., Linnartz, J.P., Tuyls, P.: New shielding functions to enhance privacy and prevent misuse of biometric templates. In: Kittler, J., Nixon, M.S. (eds.) AVBPA 2003. LNCS, vol. 2688, pp. 393–402. Springer, Heidelberg (2003)
11. Sahai, A., Waters, B.: Fuzzy identity-based encryption. In: Cramer, R.J.F. (ed.) EUROCRYPT 2005. LNCS, vol. 3494, pp. 457–473. Springer, Heidelberg (2005)
12. Schoenmakers, B., Tuyls, P.: Efficient binary conversion for Paillier encrypted values. In: Vaudenay, S. (ed.) EUROCRYPT 2006, vol. 4004, pp. 522–537. Springer, Heidelberg (2006)

Soft Generation of Secure Biometric Keys

Jovan Dj. Golić and Madalina Baltatu

Security Innovation, Telecom Italia
Via Reiss Romoli 274, 10148 Turin, Italy
{jovan.golic, madalina.baltatu}@telecomitalia.it

Abstract. A new, soft two-level approach for the generation of multiple and revocable biometric keys, adapted to the analog nature of biometric signals, is proposed. It consists of a novel soft code-offset construction for the Euclidean metric, applied at the first level, and a code-redundancy construction for the Hamming metric, preferably based on a Reed-Solomon code, applied at the second level. The Shannon entropy analysis shows that the new construction achieves maximal possible security. It is also shown that the previously proposed constructions for the Euclidean metric are vulnerable to biometric template reconstruction in the multiple-key scenario.

Keywords: Biometric key, biometric authentication, template protection, Shannon entropy, Euclidean metric, Reed-Solomon codes.

1 Introduction

Biometric identification is a strong form of user authentication based on various biometric data reflecting unique personal features, such as a person's fingerprint, face, voice, or iris or retina eye scan. Biometric data have an intrinsic lifetime nature, but are prone to limited variations, both inherently and due to imperfect measurement. A biometric key can repeatedly be reproduced from live biometric data and, as such, does not have to be stored. It is uniquely linked to biometric data inasmuch as it should be unlikely to reproduce the key from biometric data of other persons. Biometric keys can be used both for user authentication and as cryptographic keys for various cryptographic applications. In a system for biometric authentication or biometric key generation, for privacy and identity theft concerns, it is highly desirable to avoid storage of biometric reference templates. As some auxiliary information, which can be called a sketch [5], related to original biometric data has to be stored, a basic requirement is the property of biometric template protection, that is, if the sketch is compromised, then the residual uncertainty/entropy about the biometric data and the corresponding key should be sufficiently high. The sketch can be stored in a centralized tamper-proof database or locally, in a tamper-proof hardware token, such as a smart card, possessed by the user. For a wide deployment of systems for biometric authentication and key generation, the second option is preferable.

Another important requirement for biometric keys is the property of key revocability and key diversity. Namely, it should be possible to have different keys

J. Pieprzyk, H. Ghodosi, and E. Dawson (Eds.): ACISP 2007, LNCS 4586, pp. 107–121, 2007.

for different applications and to revoke and renew some keys without affecting the others. Clearly, as all these keys are linked to essentially the same biometric data, this property requires some internal randomization in the key generation algorithm. Yet another important prerequisite for biometric keys is that the compromise of the biometric data, which is a realistic assumption [7], should not compromise the biometric keys, neither those generated in the past nor those to be generated in the future, of course, under the condition that no sketch is compromised. This also requires some internal randomization.

The property of biometric key invariance under natural variations of biometric samples, i.e., error tolerance, is relative to the underlying metric in the space of biometric samples. The common metrics [5] considered in the literature are the Hamming distance between two discrete feature vectors of equal length, the edit distance between two discrete feature vectors of different length, and the set difference between two sets of discrete feature vectors [10]. On the other hand, the property of biometric template protection is relative to the information-theoretic criterion used to measure the entropy. Both properties are captured in the notions of secure fuzzy sketches and fuzzy extractors introduced in [5]. The entropy measure proposed in [5] and used in the follow-up papers is the so-called (average) min-entropy, which is equivalent to the (average) minimal probability of decision error and is related to randomness extraction. For a given fuzzy sketch construction, the objective is then to derive a lower bound on the min-entropy of the biometric template when conditioned on a given sketch.

The main construction for the Hamming metric over discrete spaces is known as the fuzzy commitment scheme [8] and, according to [5], is here referred to as the code-offset construction. For a concrete example regarding iris biometric data, see [7]. This construction can be regarded as a randomized generalization of a previous construction [4], which is here referred to as the code-redundancy construction. Both constructions are based on error-correcting codes, which are necessarily linear in [4], and the error tolerance is provided by the error-correcting capability of the code used. The analysis from [5] shows that the scheme [8] is a secure fuzzy sketch with a decrease in the security level upper-bounded by the number of redundancy symbols. However, it is later shown in [1] that nonlinear codes do not necessarily maintain their security if multiple sketches in the key diversity scenario are compromised. We point out that this insensitivity of the min-entropy is due to the fact that the conditional min-entropy does not characterize the statistical independence of random variables, like the Shannon entropy. For this reason, it is interesting to analyze the information-theoretic security of the code-offset construction for the Hamming and other metrics by using the Shannon entropy. We also discuss more general security criteria and, in particular, explain in more detail why randomized constructions are better suited for biometric key generation than the non-randomized ones.

The main problems considered in this paper relate to the analysis and the design of code-offset constructions for the Euclidean metric over real-valued or integer-valued vector spaces. These constructions are significant in practice, as the Euclidean metric is inherently adapted to measure variations in analog biometric signals resulting from practical measurements. We describe some previously proposed constructions, namely, [9], [14], and [11], and point out that they are variations of the basic construction [9]. Note that the construction [2] also uses the Euclidean metric, but in a different, essentially single-key setting, adapted to the set difference metric, where the biometric templates are represented as well-separated sets of integer-valued feature vectors. Starting from the Shannon entropy analysis, we first demonstrate that the construction [9] is vulnerable to biometric template reconstruction in the multiple-key scenario. We then define an appropriate modification of the code-offset construction by introducing the wrap-around subtraction/addition for defining the sketch as an offset vector and conduct the Shannon entropy analysis to show that the new construction achieves maximal possible security, also in the multiple-key setting.

Then, we propose a new, so-called soft two-level approach for biometric key generation. At the first level, the new soft (randomized) wrap-around code-offset construction for the Euclidean metric is applied. As opposed to usual discretization/quantization algorithms, this soft code-offset construction enables one to keep the false rejection rate for each individual feature at a small, controllable level. At the second level, a (non-randomized) code-redundancy construction for the Hamming metric, preferably based on a Reed-Solomon code, is then applied. Thanks to the first level soft construction, the second level construction has to deal with a significantly reduced number of errors, and this renders the new approach more effective than the usual hard approach, in which the discrete features are obtained by quantization algorithms. Moreover, the security level is controllable and maximal possible and allows key revocation and key diversity.

The code-offset constructions for the Hamming and Euclidean metrics are described in Sections 2 and 3, respectively. General security criteria related to biometric key generation are discussed in Section 4, whereas the information-security analysis of the known code-offset construction for the Euclidean metric and the corresponding attack in the multiple-key scenario are presented in Section 5. The wrap-around code-offset construction for the Euclidean metric is introduced and analyzed in Section 6. The soft two-level approach for biometric key generation is proposed in Section 7. Conclusions are given in Section 8.

The full version of the paper [6] contains a more detailed discussion of the notions of entropy, statistical independence, and randomness extraction as well as the Shannon entropy analysis of a general code-offset construction for the Hamming metric which allows a nice characterization and differentiation among the codes with respect to the level of biometric template protection in the multiple-key scenario. In addition, the new approach is illustrated by an experiment related to face biometrics.

2 Code-Offset Construction for Hamming Metric

According to [8], [9], let the user biometric templates be represented as vectors in a vector space $\mathcal{F}^n$ over a finite field $\mathcal{F}$ and let $\mathcal{F}^n$ be regarded as a metric space induced by the Hamming distance, i.e., the number of coordinates in which two vectors differ. Let $C \subseteq \mathcal{F}^n$ be an $[n, k, d]$ error-correcting block code over $\mathcal{F}$ which is capable of correcting any t errors and let there exist an efficient decoding algorithm for correcting any t errors. Here, $d = 2t + 1$ is the minimum distance of C (i.e., the minimum Hamming distance between two different codewords) and $k = \log_{|\mathcal{F}|} |C|$ (i.e., the number of codewords is $|C| = |\mathcal{F}|^k$). A code C is linear if it is closed under addition and multiplication by a scalar, i.e., if C is a vector subspace of $\mathcal{F}^n$.

The code-offset construction is randomized: during the enrollment, given a biometric template $x = (x_i)_{i=1}^n$, select a random codeword $z = (z_i)_{i=1}^n$ and then compute and store a sketch of x as the shift/offset vector $w = x - z$, whereas, during the recovery or authentication, given a live biometric sample x' and the sketch w, compute $z' = x' - w$ and then decode z' to z. (Alternatively, compute $w = z - x$ and $z' = x' + w$.) The procedure works provided that $\mathrm{dist}(x', x) \leq t$, because $z' - z = x' - x$ then implies that $\mathrm{dist}(z', z) \leq t$, in view of the fact that the Hamming distance is preserved under the addition of a constant vector (i.e., $\mathrm{dist}(x, y) = \mathrm{dist}(x + v, y + v)$ and, in particular, $\mathrm{dist}(x, y) = \mathrm{dist}(x - y, 0)$, which is called the Hamming weight of $x - y$ and usually denoted as $\|x - y\|$). Here, the recovered z is used for user authentication and key generation. For user authentication, one may equivalently use x, recovered as $x = z - w$.

When the code C is linear, it is pointed out in [5] that one may alternatively work in the syndrome domain and thus obtain a non-randomized construction with a shorter sketch, $n - k$ instead of n symbols long. Recall that a syndrome of a vector v with respect to C, $\mathrm{syn}(v)$, is a vector of parity-check values on v corresponding to a set of $n - k$ linearly independent parity checks, i.e., codewords of the dual code $C^\perp$. (Accordingly, $v \in C \Leftrightarrow \mathrm{syn}(v) = 0$.) More precisely, the sketch of x is computed as $w = \mathrm{syn}(x)$ and x is recovered from x' as $x = x' - e$, where e is the unique vector of the Hamming weight $\leq t$ such that $\mathrm{syn}(e) = \mathrm{syn}(x') - w$, which is obtained by the decoding algorithm. The recovered x can then be used for key generation via randomness extraction. Alternatively, as suggested in [4], one can use x as the information part of a codeword of length $n' > n$ and compute the sketch of x as the redundancy part according to a set of $n' - n$ linearly independent parity checks. The two constructions are here called *the syndrome and the code-redundancy constructions*, respectively. The syndrome construction is equivalent to a non-randomized version of the code-offset construction in which x is mapped to any fixed codeword z in a linear code possibly depending on x (e.g., the closest codeword or the zero codeword) and the key is derived from x. However, the syndrome construction is not equivalent to the randomized version described above in which the key is derived from the random codeword z instead of the template x. For more details, see Section 4.

3   Code-Offset Construction for Euclidean Metric

In [8], the authors concentrated on the binary case $\mathcal{F} = \{0, 1\}$, but they also suggested that the code-offset construction can as well be applied to other spaces supplied with an appropriate metric. In particular, when $\mathcal{F}$ is the set of real numbers $\mathcal{R}$ and the metric is Euclidean, they suggested in [9] to use as a (countably infinite) code the lattice of all the vectors in $\mathcal{R}^n$ whose coordinates are integer multiples of a given positive real number q and to apply, as a decoding algorithm, rounding off each coordinate to the closest integer multiple of q. Then, for the ith coordinate, $z_i' - z_i = x_i' - x_i$ implies that z_i can be recovered if $|z_i' - z_i| < q/2$ and this is true iff $|x_i' - x_i| < q/2$, where $|\cdot|$ denotes the absolute value. The same randomized construction is also proposed in [14], except that the parameter q can vary over different coordinates proportionally to the standard deviation of the corresponding feature for a given user, but no efficient decoding algorithm is indicated.

A similar, but non-randomized construction is proposed in [11], with the only difference that the coordinates of codewords are additively shifted by $q/2$ and the key is extracted in a different way. More precisely, for each coordinate, in the enrollment, the offset is essentially computed with respect to the closest instead of a randomly selected codeword coordinate and, in the recovery, the closest codeword coordinate is recovered and only one key bit is then extracted depending on whether the recovered coordinate value corresponds to an even or odd multiple of q.

It is not noted in [8], [9], [14], and [11] that, for the lattices of real vectors whose ith coordinate is an integer multiple of a given real number q_i, decoding to the closest codeword with respect to the Euclidean distance is equivalent to decoding each coordinate to the closest codeword coordinate. The same is true if the codeword coordinates are additively shifted by $q/2$ (or by any other real number, possibly depending on i). Shifting by $q_i/2$ enables one to simplify the round-off algorithm to computing the integer part of z_i'/q_i, i.e., $\lfloor z_i'/q_i \rfloor$.

A security analysis of these constructions presented in Sections 4 and 5 shows that all of them suffer from serious security weaknesses.

4 Security Aspects

The main components of a system for biometric user authentication and key generation are a feature vector x representing a biometric template, a randomized or non-randomized sketch w of x, a live biometric sample x', and the key key. The system should be such that a user can be authenticated by recovering the same key from w and all x' that are close to x with respect to some metric adapted to the features. Here, both x and w are produced during the enrollment, but only w is stored. The main security requirement is that of biometric template protection, which means that the stored sketch w should not contain essential information about the original biometric template x, if compromised to an attacker. At the same time, w should contain enough information for recovering the same key from all x' close to x.

The template protection requirement can be put into precise mathematical terms by defining the amount of information by using an appropriate entropy measure. There have been a couple of papers dealing with the Shannon entropy, such as [11] and [13], but the majority of papers in this area, following up [5], have been using the so-called (average) min-entropy, which itself is equivalent, i.e., monotonically functionally related to the (average) minimal probability of decision/classification error and has a meaning with respect to randomness extraction. When considered as a measure of uncertainty of one random variable conditioned on another random variable, it reflects only the one-step guessing/deciding about the random variable, whereas it can be shown that the conditional Shannon entropy is closer to the logarithm of the minimal average number of trials [12] required to correctly guess a random variable. Recall that the average conditional Shannon entropy is called equivocation. All these measures of uncertainty have different practical interpretations and may achieve considerably different values of average conditional uncertainties, but the differences become smaller if the unconditional probability distribution is close to being uniform. Moreover, what in fact matters is the entropy/uncertainty loss or mutual information defined as the (nonnegative) difference between the unconditional and average conditional entropies/uncertainties and, in this respect, one may use any of these uncertainty measures to obtain essentially similar results.

However, the Shannon mutual information has an advantage that it can be regarded as a measure of statistical independence of two random variables, that is, they are (statistically) independent iff the mutual information is equal to zero, whereas in terms of the min-entropy, the analogous condition is necessary, but not sufficient. In a system for biometric key generation, this implies that, when a sketch is compromised, a small upper bound on the Shannon entropy loss, i.e., mutual information implies a small upper bound on the min-entropy loss, whereas the converse is not true. Moreover, this also implies that the Shannon entropy is more sensitive than the min-entropy for describing the entropy loss when multiple sketches are disclosed, in the scenario of multiple enrollments. In particular, the definition [5] of a secure sketch does not differentiate well among different $[n, k, d]$ error-correcting block codes in the code-offset construction [8] and it is later shown in [1] that nonlinear codes need not remain secure under multiple enrollments, meaning that a relatively large lower bound on the min-entropy need not be preserved under multiple compromised sketches. The Shannon entropy is thus more suitable for the multiple-key scenario and it turns out that it nicely differentiates between secure and insecure code-offset constructions with respect to multiple enrollments.

If a sketch or sketches are not compromised, then there is no need for randomness extraction, because one can obtain uniformly distributed biometric keys by using internal (secret) random variables, as pointed out in this paper. In the opposite, much less likely case, the generated biometric keys remain secret, but are no longer uniformly distributed. However, even in this case, randomness extraction for obtaining approximately uniformly distributed keys is not necessary in many cryptographic applications.

In the setting of fuzzy sketches and fuzzy extractors, [5] and the follow-up papers concentrate on the uncertainty of x given w as a security criterion. In this case, it is not important whether the sketch is randomized or not. However, as rightfully pointed out in [7], it is also important to consider the scenario when the biometric data x or x' are compromised and w remains secret, e.g., securely stored on a smart card, namely, whether false user authentication and key recovery are then possible. Unlike the randomized sketches, where key and x can be statistically independent, non-randomized sketches completely fail in this scenario. A similar situation is encountered if key is compromised (e.g., through a weak cryptographic algorithm) and w remains secret. In this case, for a randomized sketch, key can be revoked and a new one issued, whereas for a non-randomized sketch, the key revocation is not possible.

To avoid that key uniquely determines x and still use a non-randomized sketch, one may be tempted to derive key from x by using a simple many-to-one function, e.g., the least significant bit of the closest codeword, as suggested in [11]. On one hand, this does not enable key revocation and, on the other, introduces another security weakness, i.e., given x, it is then easy to produce one or many biometric templates y, very much different from x and, as such, possibly corresponding to other users, that give rise to the same key or to an arbitrarily chosen modification of key, even if key is unknown. We thus arrive at another meaningful security criterion, which can be regarded as a kind of information-theoretic collision resistance for biometric keys. Namely, given x and key_x, the probability of producing another pair y and key_y, where y is not close to x with respect to the metric considered and where $key_y = key_x$ is a valid key for y should be negligible. This criterion cannot be sasified by a non-randomized sketch, whereas, for a randomized sketch, it is desirable to avoid simple many-to-one functions, such as extracting the bits, when deriving key from the internally produced random variables, e.g., a random codeword z in a code-offset construction. Furthermore, deriving key directly from z instead of x is advantageous, because x is then never used in the recovery algorithm.

5 Security of Euclidean Metric Construction

According to the constructions proposed in [9], [14], and [11], consider a randomized Euclidean metric code-offset construction over $\mathcal{R}$, where the code is a Euclidean lattice $L = \{(s_1 q_1, \ldots, s_n q_n) | (s_1, \ldots, s_n) \in \mathcal{Z}^n\}$, with $q_1, \ldots, q_n$ being positive real numbers and $\mathcal{Z}$ denoting the set of integers. In particular, $\mathcal{R}$ can be replaced by the set of rational numbers $\mathcal{Q}$ or by $\mathcal{Z}$, corresponding to a finite-precision arithmetic used in practice. More generally, we can also consider a shifted lattice $L = \{(s_1 q_1 + a_1, \ldots, s_n q_n + a_n) | (s_1, \ldots, s_n) \in \mathcal{Z}^n\}$, where $0 \leq a_i < q_i, 1 \leq i \leq n$. Let (X, Z, W) be a triple of random variables corresponding to a randomized Euclidean metric code-offset construction over $\mathcal{R}$, where X is a random biometric template (randomly chosen over different users and for each user, over different measurements), Z is a random codeword from L, chosen independently of X according to some probability distribution, and $W = X - Z$ is the corresponding random sketch. For the calculus of the Shannon entropies, it is assumed that X, like Z, follows a discrete probability distribution over a finite or countably infinite subset of $\mathcal{R}^n$ and that the entropies $H(X)$ and $H(Z)$ are both finite.

Consequently, we have $H(Z|X) = H(Z)$ and $H(X|Z) = H(X)$. For practical distributions of X, we generally have $H(X - Z|X) = H(Z) < H(X - Z)$, meaning that $X - Z$ and X are not independent. In other words, W necessarily contains some information about X and we also have $H(X|W) < H(X)$. Our objective is to determine a useful lower bound on $H(X|W) = H(X|X - Z)$, which measures the average uncertainty about the original biometric template x used in the enrollment, given a compromised value of the sketch w.

The bottom line of our analysis is the so-called code-offset representation of x, $x = (\hat{x}, x^{\text{off}})$, where $\hat{x}$ is the unique codeword obtained by rounding off the ith coordinate of x to the closest integer multiple of q_i shifted by a_i and x^{off} is the vector of the corresponding residues satisfying $-q_i/2 \leq x_i^{\text{off}} < q_i/2$, for every $1 \leq i \leq n$, where in the case of ambiguity, a coordinate is rounded off to the bigger number. If $a_i = q_i/2$, then rounding off to the closest codeword coordinate simplifies to computing the integer part of z_i'/q_i, i.e., $\lfloor z_i'/q_i \rfloor + q_i/2$. As x uniquely determines $(\hat{x}, x^{\text{off}})$ and vice versa, we have $H(X) = H(\hat{X}, X^{\text{off}})$, where $(\hat{X}, X^{\text{off}})$ is the corresponding pair of random variables uniquely representing X.

Consequently, L can be regarded as a perfect code and it follows that for every $x \in \mathcal{R}^n$, $w = \hat{x} - z + x^{\text{off}}$ uniquely determines $(\hat{x} - z, x^{\text{off}})$. More precisely, x^{off} is uniquely determined by w^{off} and $\hat{x} - z$ is then uniquely determined as $w - x^{\text{off}} = \hat{w} + w^{\text{off}} - x^{\text{off}}$. In particular, if $a_i = 0$, $1 \leq i \leq n$, then $x^{\text{off}} = w^{\text{off}}$ and $\hat{x} - z = \hat{w}$. As $(\hat{x} - z, x^{\text{off}})$ uniquely determines w, we thus get

$$H(X|W) = H(X|\hat{X} - Z, X^{\text{off}}). \tag{1}$$

By using the calculus of conditional entropies, we can further derive

$$H(X|\hat{X} - Z, X^{\text{off}}) = \left(H(X) - H(X^{\text{off}})\right) - \left(H(\hat{X} - Z|X^{\text{off}}) - H(Z)\right). \tag{2}$$

The first term on the right-hand side of (2) is independent of Z and satisfies $H(X) - H(X^{\text{off}}) = H(X|X^{\text{off}}) = H(\hat{X}|X^{\text{off}})$, and the second term is the mutual information between $\hat{X} - Z$ and $\hat{X}$ when conditioned on X^{off}, i.e., $H(\hat{X} - Z|X^{\text{off}}) - H(Z) = I(\hat{X} - Z; \hat{X}|X^{\text{off}}) \geq 0$, where we used $H(\hat{X} - Z|, \hat{X}, X^{\text{off}}) = H(Z)$, which follows from Z and X being independent. The mutual information will be equal to zero iff $\hat{X} - Z$ and $\hat{X}$ are independent when conditioned on X^{off}, which is equivalent to $\hat{X} - Z$ and $\hat{X}$ being independent, because Z is independent of X. However, they are here always statistically dependent, for all the probability distributions of Z and $\hat{X}$, where Z and $\hat{X}$ are independent, because perfect masking or perfect secret sharing do not exist over countably infinite sets [3].

Theorem 1. *For a Euclidean metric code-offset construction over $\mathcal{R}$, we have*

$$H(X|W) = H(X) - H(X^{\text{off}}) - \left(H(\hat{X} - Z|X^{\text{off}}) - H(Z)\right), \tag{3}$$

where

$$H(\hat{X} - Z|X^{\text{off}}) - H(Z) > 0. \tag{4}$$

In the multiple-key scenario, consider the case, which intuitively seems to be the best for cryptanalysis, when the same biometric template is used in a number, m, of different enrollments, with independently selected random codewords z_j from the same code L, to yield a number of sketches $w_j = x - z_j$ of the same x, and assume that all the sketches are compromised. The corresponding $H(X|(W_j)_{j=1}^m)$, is then lower-bounded by

$$H(X|(W_j)_{j=1}^m) = H(X) - H(X^{\text{off}}) - \left(H((\hat{X} - Z_j)_{j=1}^m | X^{\text{off}}) - H(Z) \right), \quad (5)$$

where $H((\hat{X}-Z_j)_{j=1}^m | X^{\text{off}}) - H(Z) > 0$. Accordingly, X^{off} is uniquely determined by any W_j^{off} and the information about $\hat{X}$ contained in $\hat{X} - Z_j$, when conditioned on X^{off}, accumulates with multiple enrollments, which causes the conditional entropy $H(X|(W_j)_{j=1}^m)$ in (5) to decrease with m, possibly to zero.

Let us now consider a particular case, suitable for practical implementation, when Z has the uniform probability distribution over a finite subset of codewords

$$C = \{(s_1 q_1 + a_1, \ldots, s_n q_n + a_n) \mid s_i \in \mathcal{Z}, 0 \le s_i \le K_i - 1, 1 \le i \le n\}. \quad (6)$$

In this case, in the ith coordinate, for any given $\hat{x}_i$, the probability distribution of $\hat{x}_i - z_i$ is uniform over the set $\{\hat{x}_i - s_i q_i - a_i | s_i \in \mathcal{Z}, 0 \le s_i \le K_i - 1\}$ and as such is dependent on $\hat{x}_i$.

Moreover, the information about $\hat{x}_i$ that is contained in $\hat{x}_i - z_i$ (i.e., w_i) can be rendered practically useful by using multiple enrollments. Let w_i^{min} and w_i^{max} denote the minimal and maximal values of w_i in all the enrollments, respectively. Then, by using $x_i = w_i + z_i$ and $a_i \le z_i \le (K_i - 1)q_i + a_i$, we get

$$a_i + w_i^{\text{max}} \le x_i \le (K_i - 1)q_i + a_i + w_i^{\text{min}}. \quad (7)$$

So, the range of possible values for $\hat{x}_i$ is narrowing down with multiple enrollments to only $K_i - (w_i^{\text{max}} - w_i^{\text{min}})/q_i = K_i - (z_i^{\text{max}} - z_i^{\text{min}})/q_i$ discrete values, the more so if the minimal and maximal values of randomly chosen codeword coordinates, z_i^{min} and z_i^{max}, are closer to a_i and $(K_i - 1)q_i + a_i$, respectively. In addition, a practical estimate of x_i can be computed by using the arithmetic mean, w_i^{av}, of the values w_i resulting from different enrollments, as

$$x_i^{\text{est}} = a_i + 0.5(K_i - 1)q_i + w_i^{\text{av}}, \quad (8)$$

and $\hat{x}_i^{\text{est}}$ is then computed by rounding off x_i^{est}.

6   Code-Offset Euclidean Metric Construction with Wrap-Round Arithmetic

An interesting problem to be addressed is whether it is possible to remedy the code-offset construction for the Euclidean metric so as to avoid the accumulated information leakage resulting from multiple enrollments. In this section, it is shown that this is possible by using the finite code C defined by (6), but, instead of dealing with the usual addition/subtraction over the real numbers as in Sections 3 and 5, we introduce a modified, so-called wrap-around subtraction/addition, adapted to the code in question. For convenience, we choose $a_i = q_i/2$, $1 \leq i \leq n$, i.e.,

$$C = \{(s_1 q_1 + q_1/2, \ldots, s_n q_n + q_n/2) \mid s_i \in \mathcal{Z}, 0 \leq s_i \leq K_i - 1, 1 \leq i \leq n\}. \quad (9)$$

Therefore, there is an one-to-one correspondence between the codewords $z = (z_i)_{i=1}^n$ and the integer vectors $s = (s_i)_{i=1}^n$. The codewords z from C or, equivalently, the vectors s are chosen uniformly at random and independently of the biometric template vectors x.

The main distinction of the new code-offset construction is in the binary operation defining a sketch w of x in terms of x and z. To this end, for every $y = (y_i)_{i=1}^n \in \mathcal{R}^n$, let $[y] = ([y_i])_{i=1}^n$, where $[y_i]$ is equal to the unique real number in $[0, K_i q_i)$ such that $K_i q_i$ divides $y_i - [y_i]$, which can be called the residue of y_i modulo $[0, K_i q_i)$. During the enrollment, a sketch of a biometric template x is then computed and stored as $w = [x - z]$, whereas, during the recovery, a live biometric sample x' and the sketch w are combined into $z' = [x' - w]$, which is then decoded to the closest codeword $\tilde{z}$, by applying $\tilde{s}_i = \lfloor z_i'/q_i \rfloor$, for each $1 \leq i \leq n$. In other words, for the ith coordinate, provided that $x_i \in [0, K_i q_i]$, we have that $w_i = x_i - z_i$ if $x_i \geq z_i$ and $w_i = x_i - z_i + K_i q_i$ if $x_i < z_i$ and hence the name wrap-around subtraction/addition.

Accordingly, we have that $z' = [z + [x' - x]]$ and we are interested in characterizing the conditions for a successful recovery, i.e., for $\tilde{z} = z$. It follows that for each $1 \leq i \leq n$,

$$\tilde{z}_i = z_i \Leftrightarrow -\frac{q_i}{2} \leq z_i' - z_i < \frac{q_i}{2} \Leftrightarrow \left([x_i' - x_i] < \frac{q_i}{2} \vee [x_i' - x_i] \geq K_i q_i - \frac{q_i}{2}\right), \quad (10)$$

so that z can be recovered from z' if $q_i/2 \leq [x_i'] - x_i < q_i/2$. Moreover, if the probability distribution of X is such that $\Pr\{x_i \in [q_i/2, K_i q_i - q_i/2)\} = 1$, then

$$-\frac{q_i}{2} \leq z_i' - z_i < \frac{q_i}{2} \Leftrightarrow -\frac{q_i}{2} \leq [x_i'] - x_i < \frac{q_i}{2}. \quad (11)$$

This means that z can be recovered from z' iff $[x']$ is close to x in the Euclidean metric, provided that the range covered by the codewords is slightly bigger than the range of x, to avoid wrap-around effects. Even if we allow $x_i = K_i q_i - q_i/2$, we would have $|z_i' - z_i| < q_i/2 \Leftrightarrow |[x_i'] - x_i| < q_i/2$.

We now show that the wrap-around code-offset construction overcomes the security weakness of previous code-offset constructions for the Euclidean metric explained in Section 5. We proceed along similar lines as in Section 5, by using the code-offset representation of x with respect to the whole lattice L instead of just the subset C. The first point to note is that the sketch $w = [\hat{x} - z + x^{\text{off}}]$ uniquely determines $([\hat{x} - z], x^{\text{off}})$ and vice versa, for every $x \in \mathcal{R}^n$. Namely, x^{off} is uniquely determined by w^{off} and $[\hat{x} - z]$ is then uniquely determined as $[w - x^{\text{off}}]$. Consequently, we similarly get

$$H(X|W) = H(X|[\hat{X} - Z], X^{\text{off}}) =$$
$$H(X) - H(X^{\text{off}}) - \left(H([\hat{X} - Z]|X^{\text{off}}) - H(Z)\right). \quad (12)$$

The second point to note is that, due to the wrap-around subtraction/addition, the probability distribution of $[\hat{x} - z]$ is uniform over the same set

$$C' = \{(s_1q_1, \ldots, s_nq_n)|s_i \in \mathcal{Z}, 0 \leq s_i \leq K_i - 1, 1 \leq i \leq n\}, \qquad (13)$$

for each $\hat{x} \in L$, because z is chosen uniformly at random and independently of x and $\{[\hat{x} - z]|z \in C\} = C'$ for each $\hat{x} \in L$. This means that $[\hat{X} - Z]$ and $\hat{X}$ are independent, i.e., since Z and X are independent, that $[\hat{X} - Z]$ and $\hat{X}$ are independent when conditioned on X^{off}. As a consequence, their mutual information is equal to zero, i.e.,

$$I([\hat{X} - Z]; \hat{X}|X^{\mathrm{off}}) = H(\hat{X} - Z|X^{\mathrm{off}}) - H(Z) = 0 \qquad (14)$$

and, hence, $H([\hat{X} - Z]|X^{\mathrm{off}}) = H(Z)$. Together with (12), this yields the following theorem.

Theorem 2. *For the wrap-around Euclidean metric code-offset construction over $\mathcal{R}$, we have*

$$H(X|W) = H(X) - H(X^{\mathrm{off}}). \qquad (15)$$

The advantage of the derived Shannon entropy bound is that it also relates to multiple enrollments. Namely, the behavior of $H(X|([X - Z_j])_{j=1}^m)$ as m increases depends on whether $H([\hat{X} - Z]|X^{\mathrm{off}}) \geq H(Z)$ holds with equality or not. In the case of equality, $[\hat{X} - Z_j]$ and $\hat{X}$ are independent and since $(Z_j)_{j=1}^m$ are independent even when conditioned on X, it follows that $([\hat{X} - Z_j])_{j=1}^m$ and $\hat{X}$ are also independent. Accordingly, (14) remains to hold even for multiple enrollments. We thus obtain the following corollary to Theorem 2.

Corollary 1. *For the wrap-around Euclidean metric code-offset construction over $\mathcal{R}$ and multiple enrollments, we have*

$$H(X|(W_j)_{j=1}^m) = H(X) - H(X^{\mathrm{off}}) \qquad (16)$$

or, in terms of the mutual information,

$$I(X; (W_j)_{j=1}^m) = H(X) - H(X|(W_j)_{j=1}^m) = H(X^{\mathrm{off}}). \qquad (17)$$

Accordingly, X^{off} is uniquely determined by any W_j^{off} and $[\hat{X} - Z_j]$ resulting from multiple enrollments do not contain any information about $\hat{X}$. So, the only information about X leaked out through the sketches is that X^{off} is uniquely determined by any of the sketches, and this holds for any probability distribution of X. Due to inherent variations of biometric templates for a given user, the information contained in X^{off} can be regarded as marginal, whereas the information contained in $\hat{X}$ is characteristic and essential for a given user. In this sense, one can regard the template protection achieved by the described construction as being ideal, that is, maximal possible.

For any given w, $[x]$ uniquely determines z and vice versa, through $z = [[x]-w]$ and $[x] = [z + w]$. Therefore, $H(Z|W) = H([X]|W) \leq H(X|W)$, with equality iff $\Pr\{x_i \in [0, K_i q_i)\} = 1$, $1 \leq i \leq n$, i.e., iff $[X] = X$. Since both x and $[x]$ have the same x^{off} in the code-offset representation, it follows that Theorem 2 and Corollary 1 remain to hold if $[X]$ is substituted for X. Then, (15) and (16) relate to the equivocations of the key $H(Z|W) = H([X]|W)$ and $H(Z|(W_j)_{j=1}^m) = H([X]|(W_j)_{j=1}^m)$, respectively, (17) relates to $I([X]; (W_j)_{j=1}^m)$, whereas for $I(Z; (W_j)_{j=1}^m)$, we have

$$I(Z; (W_j)_{j=1}^m) = H(Z) - H([X]|(W_j)_{j=1}^m) = H(Z) - H([X]) + H(X^{\mathrm{off}}). \quad (18)$$

We also have $H([X]|W) = H(Z|W) \leq H(Z) = \sum_{i=1}^n \log K_i \leq \sum_{i=1}^n k_i$, where $k_i = \lceil \log K_i \rceil$ is the number of bits in the binary representation of s_i, $1 \leq i \leq n$. If we choose $K_i = 2^{k_i}$, which means that the codeword parameter s_i is a uniformly distributed k_i-bit nonnegative integer, then we have $H(Z) = \sum_{i=1}^n k_i$.

The mutual information $H(X^{\mathrm{off}})$ depends on the probability distribution of X and can be upper bounded if the coordinates of x are represented as finite-precision integers or rational numbers by a finite number of bits. In a practical biometric key generation process, for each given user, the code parameter q_i should preferably be chosen to be proportional to the standard deviation of the coordinate x_i for that user. The whole process is then essentially invariant under scaling and shifting of the coordinates of x, independently of the users. Then, without loss of generality, we can assume that x_i and q_i are represented as nonnegative integers, where q_i is even and positive. In this case, in view of (11), the key can be recovered if the ith coordinate of the biometric template is perturbed by less than $q_i/2$, for any $1 \leq i \leq n$, and the information leakage satisfies

$$H(X^{\mathrm{off}}) \leq \sum_{i=1}^n \log q_i, \quad (19)$$

which, in practice, can be made negligible in comparison with $H(X)$ or $H([X])$.

7   Soft Two-Level Construction

In a real biometric key generation system, during the enrollment of a given user, a training set of real-valued feature vectors is first obtained by the biometric data acquisition and feature extraction subsystems. A biometric template vector x is then computed as the arithmetic mean of all the feature vectors, whereas the code parameters q_i are computed as $q_i = 2c\sigma_i$, where σ_i is the standard deviation of the ith feature over the training set, for each $1 \leq i \leq n$. Here, the parameter c may depend on the biometric data and features chosen and, e.g., may satisfy $1 \leq c \leq 3$. In view of (11), c essentially determines the false rejection rate (FRR) for each individual feature, e.g., under the normal distribution assumption. The FRR for the feature vector as a whole then depends on the number, n, of features.

Unlike the template vector x, the code parameters q_i are not essential to the user and may as well be chosen as user independent.

In the proposed wrap-around code-offset construction for the Euclidean metric, both user authentication and key generation are based on the codeword $\tilde{z}$ or, equivalently, the codeword parameter vector $\tilde{s}$, recovered from a live biometric sample x' and the sketch w of x computed and stored during the enrollment. A user is assumed to be authenticated correctly iff $\tilde{s} = s$, where s is the value computed in the enrollment. In practice, this condition is checked by a known one-way collision-resistant hash function h via testing if $h(\tilde{s}) = h(s)$, where $h(s)$ is computed and stored in the enrollment. If the user is successfully authenticated, the key is then generated as $key = \tilde{s}$ or as $key = f(\tilde{s})$, where f is a known one-way collision-resistant key derivation function, which, preferably, should in addition be pseudorandom. By using $key = f(\tilde{s})$ instead of $key = \tilde{s}$, one does not expose key through a possibly weak cryptographic algorithm. In addition to $\tilde{s}$, the inputs to h and/or f can also include user-specific information such as personal data and secret PINs and passwords.

If the number of features, n, is relatively large, then the overall FRR will be unacceptably high, as each coordinate of s has to be recovered successfully (see (11)). Consequently, in a real biometric key generation system, we have to introduce further error tolerance, not with respect to the Euclidean metric, but with respect to the Hamming metric related to coordinates of s. In other words, we need to allow a successful user authentication even if $\tilde{s}$ and s differ from each other in at most t coordinates. This can be done by applying another code-offset construction, but adapted to the Hamming instead of Euclidean metric. As this construction does not have to be randomized, we can use either the syndrome construction, where s is regarded as a noisy codeword, or the code-redundancy construction, where s is considered as the information part of a codeword. The underlying error-correcting code should necessarily be symbol based, as the errors to be corrected intrinsically relate to the symbols, i.e., blocks of bits representing the coordinates of s.

The new sketch computed at the second level is then attached to the first sketch resulting from the Euclidean metric code-offset construction, applied at the first level. However, as the second level sketch is not randomized, it reduces the entropy of s by revealing substantial information about s. While this is not important for user authentication, for key generation it is desirable to remove from s the amount of information leaked out through the second level sketch. This can be done elegantly if the code applied at the second level is a maximum distance separable code such as a Reed-Solomon code. In this case, the coordinates of s are regarded as elements of $\mathcal{F} = \mathrm{GF}(2^k)$, where $k \geq \max\{k_i | 1 \leq i \leq n\}$ and, if $k_i < k$, then s_i of length k_i is extended to common length k by fixed dummy bits. In the code-redundancy construction, to achieve an error tolerance of t errors, the second level sketch v is composed of $2t$ k-bit blocks that are computed as parity symbols according to a Reed-Solomon code. The amount of information leaked out through the parity sketch v can then be removed from s simply by discarding any $2t$ coordinates of s (with the largest bit lengths k_i), to obtain $\hat{s}$ of length $n - 2t$, to be used for key generation in place of s. Then, v may even be allowed to be compromised, e.g., publicly known. The entropy of s is thus reduced by no more than $2tk$ bits. If the offset sketch w is not compromised, then $\hat{s}$ is uniformly distributed, even if x or x' are compromised. Otherwise, the entropy of s is reduced to $H(Z|W) = H([X]) - H(X^{\mathrm{off}})$ and, hence, the residual entropy of $\hat{s}$ is lower-bounded by $H([X]) - \sum_{i=1}^{n} \log q_i - 2tk$, if we work over the integers. If the key needs to be uniformly distributed even if w is compromised, then one may apply randomness extraction techniques as in [5].

During the recovery, the sketches are used in the same order in which they are produced during the enrollment, i.e., $\tilde{s}$ is first obtained from a live biometric sample x' and the offset sketch w in the same way as before, and $\tilde{s}'$ is then reconstructed from $\tilde{s}$ and the parity sketch v by a fast decoding algorithm for a Reed-Solomon code capable of correcting up to t errors in the coordinates of $\tilde{s}$. A user is assumed to be successfully authenticated iff $\tilde{s}' = s$ and this holds iff $d(\tilde{s}, s) \leq t$. The FRR can be reduced to an acceptable level by adjusting the error tolerance level t. In a real application, since the false acceptance rate (FAR) generally increases as t increases, a tradeoff between FRR and FAR is required.

The proposed combined code-offset construction, for the soft Euclidean metric at the first level and the discrete Hamming metric at the second level, can be referred to as a *soft two-level construction*. The Euclidean metric relates to each individual feature and, as a measure of closeness, is adapted to the analog nature of features stemming from practical measurements. The Hamming metric relates to sets of features representing individual users and, as a measure of closeness, allows for a successful key recovery even if, due to a large variation of features, a number of key coordinates are erroneously reconstructed at the first level.

Alternatively, one may take a common *hard approach*, which, instead of the first level construction, uses a discretization/quantization algorithm to convert analog features into discrete values and then a randomized code-offset construction for the Hamming or some other discrete metric. However, the error tolerance level then has to be much higher. Namely, the FRR for each individual feature then depends on the offset of the biometric template with respect to quantization levels and generally increases as the offset increases. The importance of the first level offset sketch is that it enables one to keep the FRR for each individual feature at a small, controllable level, which is not possible without the additional information provided by the offset sketch. In conclusion, the proposed *soft two-level approach* is important for improving the effectiveness and security of practical systems for biometric user authentication and key generation.

8   Conclusions

Systems for biometric authentication and key generation are very important in practice due to their capacity to strongly authenticate users, not only in terms of what they know or possess, but also in terms of their unique physical features, which are typically difficult to counterfeit, and due to their potential to reproduce unique and yet multiple secret keys from live biometric samples without a need for storing sensitive data or the keys themselves. The systems that provide biometric key invariance under the variations of biometric data according to the Euclidean metric are especially important, due to analog measurements. In this paper, it is shown that the previously proposed systems of this type are insecure in the multiple-key scenario and a new construction achieving maximal possible security, even if the biometric data are compromised, is proposed. A new combined, soft two-level approach that allows a number of coordinates of the key to be erroneously reconstructed at the first level and then corrected at the second level is also introduced.

References

1. Boyen, X.: Reusable cryptographic fuzzy extractors. In: Proc. 11th ACM Conference on Computer and Communications Security, pp. 82–91 (2004)
2. Chang, E.-C., Li, Q.: Hiding secret points amidst chaff. In: Vaudenay, S. (ed.) EUROCRYPT 2006. LNCS, vol. 4004, pp. 59–72. Springer, Heidelberg (2006)
3. Chor, B., Kushilevitz, E.: Secret sharing over infinite domains. In: Quisquater, J.-J., Vandewalle, J. (eds.) EUROCRYPT 1989. LNCS, vol. 434, pp. 299–306. Springer, Heidelberg (1990)
4. Davida, G.I., Frankel, Y., Matt, B.J.: On enabling secure applications through off-line biometric identification. In: Proc. IEEE Symposium on Security and Privacy, pp. 148–157 (1998)
5. Dodis, Y., Reyzin, L., Smith, A.: Fuzzy extractors: How to generate strong keys from biometrics and other noisy data. In: Cachin, C., Camenisch, J.L. (eds.) EUROCRYPT 2004. LNCS, vol. 3027, pp. 523–540. Springer, Heidelberg (2004)
6. Golić, J.Dj., Baltatu, M.: Entropy analysis and new constructions of biometric key generation systems (submitted)
7. Hao, F., Anderson, R., Daugman, J.: Combining cryptography with biometrics effectively, Technical Report UCAM-CL-TR-640, University of Cambridge (July 2005)
8. Juels, A., Wattenberg, M.: A fuzzy commitment scheme. In: Proc. 6th ACM Conference on Computer and Communications Security, pp. 28–36 (1999)
9. Juels, A., Wattenberg, M.: A fuzzy commitment scheme. Patent Application WO 00/51244 A1 (August 2000)
10. Juels, A., Sudan, M.: A fuzzy vault scheme. In: Proc. IEEE International Symposium on Information Theory, p. 408 (2002)
11. Linnartz, J.-P., Tuyls, P.: New shielding functions to enhance privacy and prevent misuse of biometric templates. In: Proc. 4th International Conference on Audio- and Video-Based Biometric Person Authentication, pp. 393–402 (2003)
12. Sundaresan, R.: Guessing under source uncertainty. IEEE Trans. Inform. Theory 53, 269–287 (2007)
13. Tuyls, P., Goseling, J.: Capacity and examples of template-protecting biometric authentication systems. In: Maltoni, D., Jain, A.K. (eds.) BioAW 2004. LNCS, vol. 3087, pp. 158–170. Springer, Heidelberg (2004)
14. Wu, Y.D.: Method of using biometric information for secret generation. Patent Application WO 02/078249 A1 (March 2001)

Flaws in Some Secret Sharing Schemes Against Cheating

Toshinori Araki and Satoshi Obana

NEC Corporation
{t-araki@ek,obana@bx}.jp.nec.com

Abstract. In this paper, we point out flaws in existing secret sharing schemes against cheating. Namely, we show that a scheme proposed by Ghodosi and Pieprzyk presented at ACISP 2000 and a one by Obana and Araki presented at Asiacrypt 2006 are both insecure against single cheater. We further show that the scheme by Obana *et al.* can be made secure by slight modification.

1 Introduction

A secret sharing scheme is a cryptographic primitive used to distributedly share a secret among participants in such a way that only a qualified set of participants can recover the secret. It is a fundamental building block for many cryptographic protocols, and because of its importance, it is still being studied actively for more than a quarter century since the seminal papers presented by Shamir [13] and Blakley [1].

Cheating prevention is one of the most important issues in secret sharing schemes [15]. Tompa and Woll have pointed out that in Shamir's k-out-of-n threshold secret sharing scheme is vulnerable to cheating. Namely, they showed that even a single user can make other participants reconstruct incorrect secret by submitting invalid shares. They also proposed a scheme which can detect the fact of cheating when invalid shares are submitted at that point.

The work of [15] has been followed by various literatures. Ogata, Kurosawa and Stinson presented an efficient scheme for detecting cheating [11]. The size of shares in their scheme is proven to be optimum when the secret is uniformly distributed. Ghodosi and Pieprzyk also presented scheme which is only one bit longer compared to the lower bound [7]. Cabello, Padró and G. Sáez presented a near-optimum scheme which is secure even when cheaters *know* the secret [5]. Recently, Obana and Araki presented schemes based on a special class of universal hash families [10].

In this paper, we showed some of these schemes are insecure. Namely, we showed that a scheme in [7] and one in [10] can be broken by only single cheater. We also show that the flaw in [10] can be easily fixed by introducing *"constant padding"* to the underlying universal hash family.

The rest of the paper is organized as follows. In Section 2, we briefly review models of secret sharing schemes capable of detecting cheating. In Sections 3

J. Pieprzyk, H. Ghodosi, and E. Dawson (Eds.): ACISP 2007, LNCS 4586, pp. 122–132, 2007.
© Springer-Verlag Berlin Heidelberg 2007

and 4, we present attacks against the scheme given in [7] and [10], respectively. in Section 5, we show a modified version of [10] in which the proposed attack no longer works. In Section 6, we summarize our work.

2   Preliminaries

2.1   Secret Sharing Schemes

In secret sharing schemes, there are n participants $\mathcal{P} = \{P_1, \ldots, P_n\}$ and a dealer D. The dealer D is in charge of generating partial information v_i $(1 \leq i \leq n)$ of the secret. Each v_i is called a *share* and is given to a participant P_i. The set of participants who are allowed to reconstruct the secret is characterized by an *access structure* $\Gamma \subseteq 2^{\mathcal{P}}$; that is, participants $P_{i_1}, \ldots, P_{i_k}$ are allowed to reconstruct the secret if and only if $\{P_{i_1}, \ldots, P_{i_k}\} \in \Gamma$ (for instance, the access structure of a k-out-of-n threshold secret sharing scheme is defined by $\Gamma = \{\mathcal{A} \mid \mathcal{A} \in 2^{\mathcal{P}}, |\mathcal{A}| \geq k\}$.) A model consists of two algorithms: ShareGen and Reconst. Share generation algorithm ShareGen takes a secret $s \in \mathcal{S}$ as input and outputs a list of shares $(v_1, v_2, \ldots, v_n)$. Secret reconstruction algorithm Reconst takes a list of shares and outputs a secret $s \in \mathcal{S}$.

A secret sharing scheme is called *perfect* if the following two conditions are satisfied for the output $(v_1, \ldots, v_n)$ of ShareGen$(\hat{s})$ where the probabilities are taken over the random tape of ShareGen.

1. if $\{P_{i_1}, \ldots, P_{i_k}\} \in \Gamma$ then $\Pr[\mathsf{Reconst}(v_{i_1}, \ldots, v_{i_k}) = \hat{s}] = 1$,
2. if $\{P_{i_1}, \ldots, P_{i_k}\} \notin \Gamma$ then $\Pr[\mathcal{S} = s \mid \mathcal{V}_{i_1} = v_{i_1}, \ldots, \mathcal{V}_{i_k} = v_{i_k}] = \Pr[\mathcal{S} = s]$
for any $s \in \mathcal{S}$.

2.2   Secret Sharing Schemes Secure Against Cheating

A secret sharing schemes capable of detecting cheating was first presented by Tompa and Woll [15]. They considered the scenario in which cheaters who do not belong to the access structure submit forged shares in the secret reconstruction phase. Such cheaters will succeed if another participants in the reconstruction accepts an incorrect secret[1]. There are two different models for secret sharing schemes capable of detecting such cheating. Carpentieri, De Santis and Vaccaro [3] first considered a model in which cheaters who *know* the secret try to make another participant reconstruct an invalid secret. As in [10], we call this model the *"CDV model."* Recently, Ogata, Kurosawa and Stinson [11] introduced a model with weaker cheaters who *do not* know the secret in forging their shares. We call this model the *"OKS model."*

Each of these models consists of two algorithms. A share generation algorithm ShareGen is the same as that in the ordinary secret sharing schemes. A secret reconstruction algorithm Reconst is slightly different: it takes a list of

---

[1] Please note that here we focus on the problem of *detecting* the fact of cheating with unconditional security. Neither secret sharing schemes which *identify* cheaters [2,8] nor *verifiable secret sharing schemes* [12,4] are within the scope of this paper.

shares as input and outputs either a secret or the special symbol $\perp$ ($\perp \notin \mathcal{S}$.) Reconst outputs $\perp$ if and only if cheating has been detected. We follow the security definition of [10]; that is, we define the following simple game for any (k, n) threshold secret sharing scheme $\mathbf{SS} = (\mathsf{ShareGen}, \mathsf{Reconst})$ and for any (not necessarily polynomially bounded) Turing machine $\mathsf{A} = (\mathsf{A}_1, \mathsf{A}_2)$, where A represents cheaters $P_{i_1}, \ldots, P_{i_{k-1}}$ who try to cheat P_{i_k}.

Game($\mathbf{SS}, \mathsf{A}$)
```
        s ← S;     // according to the probability distribution over S.
        (v₁,...,vₙ) ← ShareGen(s);
        (i₁,...,i_{k-1}) ← A₁(X);
        // set X = s for the CDV model, X = ∅ for the OKS model.
        (v'_{i₁},...,v'_{i_{k-1}}, i_k) ← A₂(v_{i₁},...,v_{i_{k-1}}, X);
```

The advantage of cheaters is expressed as $Adv(\mathbf{SS}, \mathsf{A}) = \Pr[s' \in \mathcal{S} \wedge s' \neq s]$, where $s' = \mathsf{Reconst}(v'_{i_1}, v'_{i_2}, \ldots, v'_{i_{k-1}}, v_{i_k})$ and the probability is taken over the distribution of $\mathcal{S}$, and over the random tapes of $\mathsf{ShareGen}$ and A.

Definition 1. *A (k, n) threshold secret sharing scheme $\mathbf{SS}$ is called a (k, n, ϵ)-secure secret sharing scheme if $Adv(\mathbf{SS}, \mathsf{A}) \leq \epsilon$ for any adversary A.*

3   An Attack Against a Scheme in [7]

In this section, we present an attack against a k-out-of-n threshold secret sharing scheme against cheating presented by Ghodosi and Pieprzyk in §4 of [7]. The share generation algorithm and secret reconstruction algorithm of the target scheme is described as follows.

Share Generation: On input a secret $s \in GF(p)$, the share generation algorithm $\mathsf{ShareGen}$ outputs a list of shares $(v_1, \ldots, v_n)$ as follows:

1. Generate a random polynomial $f_s(x) \in GF(p)[X]$ of degree $2k - 2$ such that $f_s(0) = s$.
2. Compute $v_i = (f_s(x_{2i-1}), f_s(x_{2i}))$ and output $(v_1, \ldots, v_n)$ where x_i ($1 \leq i \leq 2n$) are distinct elements of $GF(p)$.

Secret Reconstruction and Validity Check: On input a list of k shares $(v_{i_1}, \ldots, v_{i_k})$ where $v_{i_j} = (v_{2i_j-1}, v_{2i_j})$, the secret reconstruction algorithm $\mathsf{Reconst}$ outputs a secret s or $\perp$ as follows:

1. Reconstruct $\hat{f}_s(x)$ from $2k - 1$ pieces $(v_{2i_1-1}, v_{2i_1}), \ldots, (v_{2i_{k-1}-1}, v_{2i_{k-1}})$ and v_{2i_k-1} using Lagrange interpolation.
2. Output $\hat{f}_s(0)$ if $v_{2i_k-1} = \hat{f}_s(x_{2i_k})$ holds. Otherwise, $\mathsf{Reconst}$ outputs $\perp$.

In [7], it is claimed that the above scheme is $(k, n, 1/p)$-secure secret sharing scheme in the OKS model. We will show it is incorrect by showing a simple attack in which a single cheater can cheat the other participants with probability 1.

An Attack Against the Scheme: Without loss of generality, we can assume P_1 is cheater and it tries to fool the other participants $P_2, \ldots, P_k$. The aim of P_1 is to make reconstruction algorithm Reconst reconstruct a secret s' such that $s' \neq s$. Since all shares $v_1, \ldots, v_k$ are generated by polynomial $f_s(x)$, the following equality holds.

$$f_s(x) = \sum_{i=1}^{2k} \prod_{\substack{1 \leq j \leq 2k \\ j \neq i}} \frac{x - x_j}{x_i - x_j} \cdot v_i$$

Now suppose that P_1 forges its share from (v_1, v_2) to (v_1', v_2') then a polynomial $f_s'(x)$ reconstructed from $v_1' = (v_1', v_2')$ and remaining $k-1$ shares $v_i = (v_{2i-1}, v_{2i})$ $(2 \leq i \leq k)$ can be described as follows:

$$f_s'(x) = \sum_{i=1}^{2} \prod_{\substack{1 \leq j \leq 2k \\ j \neq i}} \frac{x - x_j}{x_i - x_j} \cdot v_i' + \sum_{i=3}^{2k} \prod_{\substack{1 \leq j \leq 2k \\ j \neq i}} \frac{x - x_j}{x_i - x_j} \cdot v_i$$

It is easy to see that cheater succeed in cheating if it can generate $v_1' = (v_1', v_2')$ such that the polynomial $f_s'(x)$ computed above satisfies $f_s'(0) \neq f_s(0)$ and $\deg(f_s'(x)) = 2k - 2$ (i.e. all the $2k$ pieces are consistent with a polynomial of degree $2k - 2$.)

Now we consider a polynomial $\Delta f_s(x) = f_s'(x) - f_s(x)$ described as follows where Δv_i $(i = 1, 2)$ is defined by $\Delta v_i = v_i' - v_i$:

$$\Delta f_s(x) = \sum_{i=1}^{2} \prod_{\substack{1 \leq j \leq 2k \\ j \neq 1}} \frac{x - x_j}{x_i - x_j} \cdot \Delta v_i = \prod_{\substack{1 \leq j \leq 2k \\ j \neq 1}} \frac{x - x_j}{x_1 - x_j} \cdot \Delta v_1 + \prod_{\substack{1 \leq j \leq 2k \\ j \neq 2}} \frac{x - x_j}{x_2 - x_j} \cdot \Delta v_2$$

The following two observations are straightforward.

1. $\deg(f_s'(x)) = 2k - 2$ if and only if the coefficient of x^{2k-1} equals 0 in $\Delta f_s(x)$ (since $\deg(f_s(x)) = 2k - 2$.)
2. $f_s'(0) \neq f_s(0)$ if and only if $\Delta f_s(0) \neq 0$.

The coefficient c_{2k-1}, c_0 of x^{2k-1} and x^0 (i.e. constant term) of $\Delta f_s(x)$ can be respectively described as:

$$c_{2k-1} = \prod_{\substack{1 \leq j \leq 2k \\ j \neq 1}} \frac{1}{x_1 - x_j} \cdot \Delta v_1 + \prod_{\substack{1 \leq j \leq 2k \\ j \neq 2}} \frac{1}{x_2 - x_j} \cdot \Delta v_2,$$

$$c_0 = \prod_{\substack{1 \leq j \leq 2k \\ j \neq 1}} \frac{-x_j}{x_1 - x_j} \cdot \Delta v_1 + \prod_{\substack{1 \leq j \leq 2k \\ j \neq 2}} \frac{-x_j}{x_2 - x_j} \cdot \Delta v_2.$$

Therefore, by solving the following equations for arbitrarily chosen Δs ($\neq 0$), P_1 can successfully cheat the other participants $P_2, \ldots, P_k$ with probability 1.

$$\begin{cases} \prod_{\substack{1 \leq j \leq 2k \\ j \neq 1}} \frac{1}{x_1 - x_j} \cdot \Delta v_1 + \prod_{\substack{1 \leq j \leq 2k \\ j \neq 2}} \frac{1}{x_2 - x_j} \cdot \Delta v_2 = 0 \\ \prod_{\substack{1 \leq j \leq 2k \\ j \neq 1}} \frac{-x_j}{x_1 - x_j} \cdot \Delta v_1 + \prod_{\substack{1 \leq j \leq 2k \\ j \neq 2}} \frac{-x_j}{x_2 - x_j} \cdot \Delta v_2 = \Delta s \end{cases}$$

Note that the above equations have a unique solution $(\Delta v_1, \Delta v_2)$ for any $\Delta s \neq 0$ since $\prod_{\substack{1 \leq j \leq 2k \\ j \neq 1}} (-x_j)$ and $\prod_{\substack{1 \leq j \leq 2k \\ j \neq 2}} (-x_j)$ are distinct.

An Example of the Proposed Attack: Consider the following 2-out-of-3 threshold scheme in which a secret $s = 1$ is chosen from $GF(7)$ and the dealer chooses $f_s(x) = 1 + x + x^2$ of degree $2 (= 2k - 2)$ to generate shares and $x_i = i$ holds for $1 \leq i \leq 6$.

Suppose P_1 try to cheat P_2 by forging their share $(v_1, v_2) = (f_s(1), f_s(2)) = (3, 0)$. As in the description of the proposed scheme, what P_1 has to do is to solve the following equations (Note that coefficients of the following equations can be constructed only from the public data.)

$$\begin{cases} \prod_{\substack{1 \leq j \leq 4 \\ j \neq 1}} \frac{1}{x_1 - x_j} \cdot \Delta v_1 + \prod_{\substack{1 \leq j \leq 4 \\ j \neq 2}} \frac{1}{x_2 - x_j} \cdot \Delta v_2 = \Delta v_1 + 4 \Delta v_2 = 0 \\ \prod_{\substack{1 \leq j \leq 4 \\ j \neq 1}} \frac{x_j}{x_1 - x_j} \cdot \Delta v_1 + \prod_{\substack{1 \leq j \leq 4 \\ j \neq 2}} \frac{x_j}{x_2 - x_j} \cdot \Delta v_2 = 4 \Delta v_1 + \Delta v_2 = \Delta s \end{cases}$$

Let $\Delta s = 1$ then $(\Delta v_1, \Delta v_2) = (4, 6)$ is the solution of above equations.

Now suppose cheater P_1 submits $(v_1', v_2') = (v_1 + \Delta v_1, v_2 + \Delta v_2) = (0, 6)$ to the reconstruction algorithm. With input $(v_1', v_2') = (0, 6)$ and $(v_3, v_4) = (6, 0)$, the reconstruction algorithm first reconstructs a polynomial $\hat{f}_s(x) = 2 + x + 4x^2$ which is consistent with $\hat{f}_s(1) = 0, \hat{f}_s(2) = 6$ and $\hat{f}_s(3) = 6$. We can verify that $\hat{f}_s(4) = 2 + 4 + 4 \cdot 4^2 = 0 = f_s(4)$ holds, which means that P_1 succeeds in cheating P_2.

4 An Attack Against a Scheme in [10]

In this section, we present an attack against a k-out-of-n threshold secret sharing scheme against cheating presented by Obana and Araki in §3.2 of [10]. The scheme is designed to ensure security in the CDV model (i.e. cheaters know the secret in forging their shares.) The basic idea of the scheme is to use a class of universal hash families. Namely, they showed that if there exists an efficiently samplable ϵ-SKDU$_2$ hash family H whose domain is a set of secret $\mathcal{S}$, then there exists (k, n, ϵ)-secure secret sharing scheme. Where the hash family ϵ-SKDU$_2$ is defined as follows.

Definition 2. [10]   *A family of hash functions $H : \mathcal{A} \to \mathcal{B}$ is called a strongly key-differential universal ϵ-SKDU$_2$ if there exists $\hat{b} \in \mathcal{B}$ such that for any distinct $a, a' \in \mathcal{A}$ and for any $c \in \mathcal{E}$,*

$$\frac{|\{h_e \mid e \in \mathcal{E}, \ h_e(a) = \hat{b}, \ h_{e+c}(a') = \hat{b}\}|}{|\{h_e \mid e \in \mathcal{E}, \ h_e(a) = \hat{b}\}|} \leq \epsilon. \tag{1}$$

Further, ϵ-SKDU$_2$ is called an "efficiently samplable" if there exists an efficient (i.e. polynomial time) algorithm to choose $e \in \mathcal{E}$ randomly from the set $\{e \in \mathcal{E} \mid h_e(a) = \hat{b}\}$ for any $a \in \mathcal{A}$.

In [10], the following hash family $H : GF(p)^N \to GF(p)$ is presented as an example of N/p-SKDU$_2$ and a secret sharing scheme against cheating which we will break is constructed based on it.

$$H = \left\{ h_{e_0, e_1} \ \middle| \ h_{e_0, e_1}(s_1, \ldots, s_N) = e_0 - \sum_{j=1}^{N} s_j \cdot e_1^j, \ e_i \in GF(p) \right\} \tag{2}$$

The share generation algorithm and secret reconstruction algorithm of the target scheme is described as follows.

Share Generation: On input a secret $s = (s_1, \ldots, s_N) \in GF(p)^N$, the share generation algorithm ShareGen outputs a list of shares $(v_1, \ldots, v_n)$ according to the following procedure. Please note that we sometimes regard $s = (s_1, \ldots, s_N)$ as an element of $GF(p^N)$ instead of $GF(p)^N$.

1. Choose random $e_0, e_1 \in GF(p)$ such that $e_0 - \sum_{j=1}^{N} s_j e_1^j = 0$.
2. Generate a random polynomials $f_s(x) \in GF(p^N)[X]$ and $f_{e_0}(x), f_{e_1}(x) \in GF(p)[X]$ of degree $k - 1$ such that $f_s(0) = s$, $f_{e_0}(0) = e_0$ and $f_{e_1}(0) = e_1$.
3. Compute $v_i = (f_s(i), f_{e_0}(i), f_{e_1}(i))$ and output $(v_1, \ldots, v_n)$.

Secret Reconstruction and Validity Check: On input a list of k shares $(v_{i_1}, \ldots, v_{i_k})$, the secret reconstruction algorithm Reconst outputs a secret s or $\perp$ as follows:

1. Reconstruct $\hat{s}, \hat{e}_0$ and $\hat{e}_1$ from $v_{i_1}, \ldots, v_{i_k}$ using Lagrange interpolation.
2. Output s if $\hat{e}_0 - \sum_{j=1}^{N} \hat{s}_j \hat{e}_1^j = 0$ holds. Otherwise Reconst outputs $\perp$.

An Attack against the Scheme: The proposed attack is straightforward from the following lemma which shows the hash family H used to construct the above scheme does *not* satisfy the conditions of ϵ-SKDU$_2$ when $\hat{b} = 0$.

Lemma 1. *Let H be the universal hash family defined by eq. (2) and $\mathcal{E} = (e_0, e_1) \in GF(p)^2$. Then, for any $s = (s_1, \ldots, s_N) \in GF(p)^N$, there exists a constant $(c_0, c_1) \in GF(p)^2$ and $s' = (s'_1, \ldots, s'_N) \in GF(p)^N$ such that $s' \neq s$ and*

$$\frac{|\{h_{(e_0, e_1)} \in H \mid h_{(e_0, e_1)}(s) = 0, \ h_{(e_0 + c_0, e_1 + c_1)}(s') = 0\}|}{|\{h_{(e_0, e_1)} \in H \mid h_{(e_0, e_1)}(s) = 0\}|} = 1$$

Proof. It suffices to show that there exist constants c_0, c_1 and $s' \neq s$ such that $h_{(e_0 + c_0, e_1 + c_1)}(s')$ is equivalent to $h_{(e_0, e_1)}(s)$ where $h_{(e_0, e_1)}(s)$ and $h_{(e_0 + c_0, e_1 + c_1)}(s')$ are described as follows:

$$h_{(e_0, e_1)}(s) = e_0 - \sum_{j=1}^{N} s_j e_1^j, \qquad h_{(e_0 + c_0, e_1 + c_1)}(s') = (e_0 + c_0) - \sum_{j=1}^{N} s'_j (e_1 + c_1)^j$$

Fix $c_1 = \hat{c}_1 (\neq 0)$ arbitrarily and let $s_N = s'_N$, then we have the following equalities since each coefficients of e_1^j $(0 \leq j \leq N)$ must be identical.

$$\sum_{j=i}^{N} \binom{j}{i} s'_j \hat{c}_1^{j-i} = s_i \ \text{(for } 1 \leq i \leq N), \qquad e_0 + c_0 - \sum_{j=1}^{N} s'_j \hat{c}_1^j = e_0$$

The former equalities can be rewritten as follows:

$$s'_i = s_i - \sum_{j=i+1}^{N} \binom{j}{i} s'_j \hat{c}_1^{j-i} \tag{3}$$

Therefore, starting from $s'_N = s_N$, all s'_j $(j = N-1, N-2, \ldots, 1)$ can be computed using recurrent formula of eq. (3). Finally, c_0 can be computed by

$$c_0 = \sum_{j=1}^{N} s'_j \hat{c}_1^j. \tag{4}$$

$\square$

Based on Lemma 1, we will present an attack by a single cheater who know the secret in forging its share. As in the attack presented in §3, we can assume P_1 is a cheater who tries to fool the other participants $P_2, \ldots, P_k$. Since P_1 knows the secret s, it can compute $s' \neq s$ and (c_0, c_1) such that

$$(e_0 + c_0) - \sum_{j=1}^{N} s'_j (e_1 + c_1)^j = 0.$$

On the other hand, P_1 knows that the following equations hold for its original share $v_1 = (v_{s,1}, v_{e_0,1}, v_{e_1,1})$ where $v_i = (v_{s,i}, v_{e_0,i}, v_{e_1,i})$ $(2 \leq i \leq k)$ is a share of P_i and $L_i = \prod_{\substack{1 \leq j \leq k \\ j \neq i}} \frac{-j}{i-j}$ be a Lagrange coefficient.

$$s = L_1 v_{s,1} + \sum_{j=2}^{k} L_j v_{s,j}, \quad e_0 = L_1 v_{e_0,1} + \sum_{j=2}^{k} L_j v_{e_0,j}, \quad e_1 = L_1 v_{e_1,1} + \sum_{j=2}^{k} L_j v_{e_1,j}$$

P_1 also knows that the following s', e'_0 and e'_1 are reconstructed if it submits forged share $v'_1 = (v'_{s,1}, v'_{e_0,1}, v'_{e_1,1})$.

$$s' = L_1 v'_{s,1} + \sum_{j=2}^{k} L_j v_{s,j}, \quad e'_0 = L_1 v'_{e_0,1} + \sum_{j=2}^{k} L_j v_{e_0,j}, \quad e'_1 = L_1 v'_{e_1,1} + \sum_{j=2}^{k} L_j v_{e_1,j}$$

Therefore, the following equalities hold where $\Delta e_i = e'_i - e_i$ $(i = 0,1)$, $\Delta v_{s,1} = v'_{s,1} - v_{s,1}$ and $\Delta v_{e_i,1} = v'_{e_i,1} - v_{e_i,1}$ $(i = 0,1)$.

$$s' - s = L_1 \cdot \Delta v_{s,1}, \quad \Delta e_0 = L_1 \cdot \Delta v_{e_0,1}, \quad \Delta e_1 = L_1 \cdot \Delta v_{e_1,1}$$

It is easy to see that when we set $\Delta e_0 = c_0$, $\Delta e_1 = c_1$ and compute $\Delta v_{s,1}$, $\Delta v_{e_0,1}$, $\Delta v_{e_1,1}$ then resulting $v'_{s,1}, v'_{e_0,1}, v'_{e_1,1}$ will yield s', e'_0, e'_1 satisfying

$$e'_0 - \sum_{j=1}^{N} s'_j e_1'^j = (e_0 + c_0) - \sum_{j=1}^{N} s'_j (e_1 + c_1)^j = 0,$$

which shows that the cheater P_1 successfully cheats $P_2, \ldots, P_k$ with probability 1. Note that all of $v'_{s,1}, v'_{e_0}$ and v'_{e_1} can be locally computed by P_1.

An Example of the Proposed Attack: Consider the following 2-out-of-3 threshold scheme in which a secret $s = (s_1, s_2) = (1,1)$ is chosen from $GF(5) \times GF(5)$ and the dealer chooses $f_s(x) = (1 + \alpha) + (1 + \alpha)x \in GF(5^2)[X]$ of degree 1 to generate shares for the secret. Also suppose that the dealer chooses $e_0 = 3$ and $e_1 = 1$ among pairs of (e_0, e_1) satisfying $e_0 + s_1 e_1 + s_2 e_1^2 = 0$ and it chooses polynomials $f_{e_0}(x) = 3 + x$ and $f_{e_1}(x) = 1 + x$ to generate shares of e_0 and e_1, respectively.

Suppose P_1 who *knows* the secret $s = (1, 1)$ try to cheat P_2 by forging their share $(v_{s,1}, v_{e_0,1}, v_{e_1,1}) = ((2, 2), 4, 2)$. As in the description of the proposed scheme, P_1 first computes c_0, c_1, and s_1', s_2' such that

$$e_0 + s_1 e_1 + s_2 e_1^2 = (e_0 + c_0) + s_1'(e_1 + c_1) + s_2'(e_1 + c_1)^2 \tag{5}$$

holds for any e_0 and e_1. This can be done by assigning $c_1 = 1$ (arbitrary element of $GF(5)$,) $s_2' = s_2(= 1)$ and compute s_1' and c_0 from s_1 and s_2 according to eq. (3) and eq. (4) as follows:

$$s_1' = s_1 - \sum_{j=2}^{2} \binom{j}{1} s_j' c_1^{j-1} = s_1 - \binom{2}{1} s_2' c_1 = 1 - 2 \cdot 1 \cdot 1 = 4,$$

$$c_0 = \sum_{j=1}^{2} s_j' c_1^j = 4 \cdot 1 + 1 \cdot 1 = 0.$$

The following equation shows that eq. (5) holds for any e_0 and e_1.

$$(e_0 + c_0) + s_1'(e_1 + c_1) + s_2'(e_1 + c_1)^2$$
$$= e_0 + 4(e_1 + 1) + (e_1 + 1)^2 = e_0 + e_1 + e_1^2 = e_0 + s_1 e_1 + s_2 e_1^2$$

Once P_1 computes c_0, c_1, s_1' and s_2', it can computes

$$\Delta v_{s,1} = \frac{s'-s}{L_1} = \frac{3+0 \cdot \alpha}{2} = (4, 0), \quad \Delta v_{e_0,1} = \frac{c_0}{L_1} = \frac{0}{2} = 0, \quad \Delta v_{e_1,1} = \frac{c_1}{L_1} = \frac{1}{2} = 3$$

and $v_{s,1}' = v_{s_1} + \Delta v_{s,1} = (1, 2)$, $v_{e_0,1}' = v_{e_0,1} + \Delta v_{e_0,1} = 4$ and $v_{e_0,1}' = v_{e_0,1} + \Delta v_{e_0,1} = 0$.

Now suppose cheater P_1 submits $v_1' = (v_{s,1}', v_{e_0,1}', v_{e_1,1}') = ((1, 2), 4, 0)$ to the reconstruction algorithm. With input v_1' and $v_2 = ((3, 3), 0, 3)$, the reconstruction algorithm first reconstructs $\hat{s} = (4, 1)$, $\hat{e}_0 = 3$ and $\hat{e}_1 = 2$ and outputs $(4, 1)$ as a correct secret since $\hat{e}_0 + s_1 \hat{e}_1 + s_2 \hat{e}_1^2 = 0$ holds, which means that P_1 succeeds in cheating P_2.

5 Fixing the Flaw in [10]

In this section, we fix the flaw of the scheme attacked in the previous section. More precisely, we slightly modify the family of hash family H defined by eq. (2) in a way that it satisfies the properties of ϵ-SKDU$_2$. Since the following proposition has been proven in [10], we can easily construct (k, n, ϵ)-secure secret sharing scheme based on this modified hash family.

Proposition 1. [10] *If there exist linear secret sharing schemes over $\mathcal{S}$ and $\mathcal{E}$ for a common access structure Γ and an efficiently samplable ϵ-SKDU$_2$ H : $\mathcal{S} \to \mathcal{B}$ with the set of key $\mathcal{E}$, then there exists a secret sharing scheme capable of detecting cheating for the access structure Γ in the CDV model such that the successful cheating probability is equal to ϵ for arbitrary secret distribution.*

The modification to the hash family H defined by eq. (2) is simple. The modified hash family $\hat{H}$ is defined as follows:

$$\hat{H} = \left\{ h_{e_0,e_1} \middle| h_{e_0,e_1}(s_1,\ldots,s_N) = e_0 - s_N \cdot e_1^{N+1} - \sum_{j=1}^{N-1} s_j \cdot e_1^j, \ e_i \in GF(p) \right\}$$

(6)

We can easily check that for $h \in H$ ($H : GF(p)^{N+1} \to GF(p)$), $\hat{H} : GF(p)^N \to GF(p)$ can be also defined by

$$\hat{H} = \{\hat{h}_{e_0,e_1} \mid \hat{h}_{e_0,e_1}(s_1,\ldots,s_N) = h_{e_0,e_1}(s_1,\ldots,s_{N-1},0,s_N), \ h_{e_0,e_1} \in H\}.$$

Therefore, modified hash family $\hat{H}$ can be viewed as "H with a *constant padding*." Now we will prove the following theorem:

Theorem 1. *The family of hash function $\hat{H} : GF(p)^N \to GF(p)$ defined by eq. (6) is ϵ-SKDU$_2$ with $\epsilon = \frac{N+1}{p}$.*

Proof. First, it is easy to see that, for any $s = (s_1,\ldots,s_N) \in GF(p)^N$, there exist p hash functions $h_{e_0,e_1} \in \hat{H}$ such that $h_{e_0,e_1}(s) = 0$. This is because for any fixed e_1, such e_0 is uniquely determined by $e_0 = s_N \cdot e_1^{N+1} + \sum_{j=1}^{N-1} s_j \cdot e_1^j$. Therefore, what we need to prove is the following: for any $s, s' (\neq s)$ and for any c_0 and c_1,

$$|\{h_{(e_0,e_1)} \in H \mid h_{(e_0,e_1)}(s) = 0, \ h_{(e_0+c_0,e_1+c_1)}(s') = 0\}| \leq N+1.$$

We will prove the following equivalent statement.

$$|\{h_{(e_0,e_1)} \in H \mid h_{(e_0,e_1)}(s) = 0, \ h_{(e_0+c_0,e_1+c_1)}(s') - h_{(e_0,e_1)}(s) = 0\}| \leq N+1.$$

There are two cases to be considered. In the first case, suppose $c_1 = 0$. In this case $h_{(e_0+c_0,e_1+c_1)}(s') - h_{(e_0,e_1)} = h_{(e_0+c_0,e_1)}(s') - h_{(e_0,e_1)} = 0$ can be written as follows:

$$c_1 - (s'_N - s_N) \cdot e_1^{N+1} - \sum_{j=1}^{N-1} (s'_j - s_j) \cdot e_1^j = 0$$

For any fixed s, s' and c_1, the above equation can be viewed as univariate polynomial $\Delta h(e_1)$ of degree at most $N+1$. Since $\Delta h(e_1)$ have at most $N+1$ roots and, for each root $\hat{e}_1$, there exists unique $\hat{e}_0$ such that $h_{(\hat{e}_0,\hat{e}_1)}(s) = 0$. Therefore, we see that $|\{h_{(e_0,e_1)} \in H \mid h_{(e_0,e_1)}(s) = 0, \ h_{(e_0+c_0,e_1+c_1)}(s') = 0\}| \leq N+1$ holds in this case.

Now consider the second case in which $c_1 \neq 0$. In this case we consider the number of roots of the following univariate polynomial $\Delta h(e_1)$ for any fixed $s, s'(\neq s)$ and $c_1 \neq 0$:

$$\Delta h(e_1) = c_0 - s'_N(e_1 + c_1)^{N+1} - s \cdot e_1^{N+1} - \sum_{j=1}^{N-1} \left(s'_j(e_1 + c_1)^j - s_j \cdot e_1^j \right) = 0$$

Further, there are two cases to be considered. In the first case, suppose $s_N \neq s'_N$. In this case, $\Delta h(e_1)$ becomes a polynomial of degree $N+1$, which means that the number of roots is at most N and, consequently, $|\{h_{(e_0,e_1)} \in H \mid h_{(e_0,e_1)}(s) = 0, \ h_{(e_0+c_0,e_1+c_1)}(s') = 0\}| \leq N+1$ holds. Now we consider the second case where $s'_N = s_N$ and $c_1 \neq 0$. In this case, the coefficient of e^N of $\Delta h(e_1)$ becomes $(N+1) \cdot c_1 \neq 0$. Therefore, there are at most N roots for $\Delta h(e_1)$, which shows that $|\{h_{(e_0,e_1)} \in H \mid h_{(e_0,e_1)}(s) = 0, \ h_{(e_0+c_0,e_1+c_1)}(s') = 0\}| \leq N+1$ holds also in this case. Since we have seen that $|\{h_{(e_0,e_1)} \in H \mid h_{(e_0,e_1)}(s) = 0, \ h_{(e_0+c_0,e_1+c_1)}(s') = 0\}| \leq N+1$ holds in all cases, the theorem has been proven. □

Putting Proposition 1 and Theorem 1 together, we can construct $(k, n, \frac{N+1}{p})$-secure secret sharing scheme such that $|S| = p^N$, $|V_i| = p^{N+2} (= \frac{|S|(\log_p |S|-1)^2}{\epsilon^2})$. The complete description of the scheme is as follows:

Share Generation: On input a secret $s = (s_1, \ldots, s_N) \in GF(p)^N$, the share generation algorithm ShareGen outputs a list of shares $(v_1, \ldots, v_n)$ according to the following procedure. Please note that we sometimes regard $s = (s_1, \ldots, s_N)$ as an element of $GF(p^N)$ instead of $GF(p)^N$.

1. Choose random $e_0, e_1 \in GF(p)$ such that $e_0 - s_N e_1^{N+1} - \sum_{j=1}^{N-1} s_j e_1^j = 0$.
2. Generate a random polynomials $f_s(x) \in GF(p^N)[X]$ and $f_{e_0}(x)$, $f_{e_1}(x) \in GF(p)[X]$ of degree $k-1$ such that $f_s(0) = s$, $f_{e_0}(0) = e_0$ and $f_{e_1}(0) = e_1$.
3. Compute $v_i = (f_s(i), f_{e_0}(i), f_{e_1}(i))$ and output $(v_1, \ldots, v_n)$.

Secret Reconstruction and Validity Check: On input a list of k shares $(v_{i_1}, \ldots, v_{i_k})$, the secret reconstruction algorithm Reconst outputs a secret s or $\perp$ as follows:

1. Reconstruct $\hat{s}, \hat{e}_0$ and $\hat{e}_1$ from $v_{i_1}, \ldots, v_{i_k}$ using Lagrange interpolation.
2. Output s if $\hat{e}_0 - \hat{s}_N \hat{e}_1^{N+1} - \sum_{j=1}^{N-1} \hat{s}_j \hat{e}_1^j = 0$ holds. Otherwise Reconst outputs $\perp$.

6   Conclusion

In this paper, we point out flaws in existing secret sharing schemes against cheating. Namely, we show that the scheme proposed by Ghodosi and Pieprzyk presented at ACISP 2000 and the one by Obana and Araki presented at Asiacrypt 2006 are both insecure against single cheater. We further show that the scheme by Obana *et al.* can be made secure by slight modification.

References

1. Blakley, G.R.: Safeguarding cryptographic keys. In: Proc. AFIPS 1979, National Computer Conference, vol. 48, pp. 313–317 (1979)
2. Carpentieri, M.: A Perfect Threshold Secret Sharing Scheme to Identify Cheaters. Designs, Codes and Cryptography 5(3), 183–187 (1995)
3. Carpentieri, M., De Santis, A., Vaccaro, U.: Size of Shares and Probability of Cheating in Threshold Schemes. In: Helleseth, T. (ed.) EUROCRYPT 1993. LNCS, vol. 765, pp. 118–125. Springer, Heidelberg (1993)
4. Cramer, R., Damgård, I., Maurer, U.M.: General Secure Multi-party Computation from any Linear Secret-Sharing Scheme. In: Preneel, B. (ed.) EUROCRYPT 2000. LNCS, vol. 1807, pp. 316–334. Springer, Heidelberg (2000)
5. Cabello, S., Padró, C., Sáez, G.: Secret Sharing Schemes with Detection of Cheaters for a General Access Structure. Designs, Codes and Cryptography 25(2), 175–188 (2002)
6. den Boer, B.: A Simple and Key-Economical Unconditional Authentication Scheme. Journal of Computer Security 2, 65–71 (1993)
7. Ghodosi, H., Pieprzyk, J.: Cheating Prevention in Secret Sharing. In: Clark, A., Boyd, C., Dawson, E.P. (eds.) ACISP 2000. LNCS, vol. 1841, pp. 328–341. Springer, Heidelberg (2000)
8. Kurosawa, K., Obana, S., Ogata, W.: t-Cheater Identifiable (k, n) Secret Sharing Schemes. In: Coppersmith, D. (ed.) CRYPTO 1995. LNCS, vol. 963, pp. 410–423. Springer, Heidelberg (1995)
9. MacWilliams, F., Sloane, N.: The Theory of Error Correcting Codes. North Holland, Amsterdam (1977)
10. Obana, S., Araki, T.: Almost Optimum Secret Sharing Schemes Secure against Cheating for Arbitrary Secret Distribution. In: Lai, X., Chen, K. (eds.) ASIACRYPT 2006. LNCS, vol. 4284, pp. 364–379. Springer, Heidelberg (2006)
11. Ogata, W., Kurosawa, K., Stinson, D.R.: Optimum Secret Sharing Scheme Secure against Cheating. SIAM Journal on Discrete Mathematics 20(1), 79–95 (2006)
12. Pedersen, T.: Non-Interactive and Information-Theoretic Secure Verifiable Secret Sharing. In: Feigenbaum, J. (ed.) CRYPTO 1991. LNCS, vol. 576, pp. 129–149. Springer, Heidelberg (1992)
13. Shamir, A.: How to Share a Secret. Communications of the ACM 22(11), 612–613 (1979)
14. Stinson, D.R.: On the Connections between Universal Hashing, Combinatorial Designs and Error-Correcting Codes. Congressus Numerantium 114, 7–27 (1996)
15. Tompa, M., Woll, H.: How to Share a Secret with Cheaters. Journal of Cryptology 1(3), 133–138 (1989)

Efficient (k, n) Threshold Secret Sharing Schemes Secure Against Cheating from $n - 1$ Cheaters

Toshinori Araki

NEC Corporation
t-araki@ek.jp.nec.com

Abstract. In (k, n) threshold secret sharing scheme, Tompa and Woll consider a problem of cheaters who try to make another participant reconstruct invalid secret. Later, the model of such cheating is formalized in some researches. Some schemes secure against cheating of these models are proposed. However, in these models, the number of colluding participants is restricted to $k - 1$ or less. In this paper, we consider k or more colluding participants. Of course, secrecy is not maintained to such participants. However, if considering detecting the fact of cheating, we need to consider a cheating from k or more colluding participants. In this paper, we propose a (k, n) threshold secret sharing scheme that is capable of detecting the fact of cheating from $n - 1$ or less colluding participants. A scheme proposed by Tompa and Woll can be proven to be a (k, n) threshold secret sharing scheme that is capable of detecting the fact of cheating from $n - 1$ or less colluding participants. However, our proposed scheme is much more efficient with respect to the size of shares.

1 Introduction

Background. A (k, n) threshold secret sharing scheme [1,10] is a cryptographic primitive used to distribute a secret s to n participants in such a way that a set of k or more participants can recover the secret s and a set of $k - 1$ or less participants cannot obtain any information about s. A piece of information held by participant is called a share.

Various problems in (k, n) threshold secret sharing schemes are considered. Above all, the problem of cheaters in threshold schemes is considered in various researches.

Tompa and Woll [11] considered the following cheating scenario. Suppose that colluding participants want to cheat another participant by submitting forged shares in the reconstruction. They succeed if the reconstructed value is different from the original secret. Later, a model of such cheating is formalized in [3,8]. Some schemes secure against cheating of these models are proposed [2,7,8,11].

Our Contribution. In the models of [3,8], the number of colluding participants is restricted to $k - 1$ or less. However, we can consider k or more colluding

J. Pieprzyk, H. Ghodosi, and E. Dawson (Eds.): ACISP 2007, LNCS 4586, pp. 133–142, 2007.

participants. Of course, secrecy is not maintained to such participants. However, if considering detecting the fact of cheating, we need to consider a cheating from k or more colluding participants. In this paper, we construct a (k, n) threshold secret sharing scheme that is capable of detecting the fact of cheating from $n - 1$ or less colluding participants.

Schemes in [2,7,8] are not capable of detecting the fact of cheating from k or more colluding participants. Scheme in [11] is capable of detecting the fact of cheating from $n - 1$ colluding participants. However our proposed scheme is much more efficient with respect to the size of shares. Particularly, the size of the share in the proposed scheme is a few bit longer than lower bound of [7] when parameter k,n are small and $|\mathcal{S}|^1$ is smaller than $1/\epsilon$, where ϵ denotes the successful probability of cheating and $\mathcal{S}$ denotes the set of secrets.

Organization. The rest of the paper is organized as follows. In Section 2, we briefly review the models of secret sharing schemes capable of detecting cheating, and we discuss previous works done on them. In Section 3, we introduce a new model of cheating from $n-1$ or less colluding cheaters. In Section 4, we present an efficient scheme secure in the new model. In Section 5, we consider the problem of forged reconstruction result. In Section 6, we summarize our work.

2   Preliminaries

2.1 (k, n) Threshold Scheme

In secret sharing schemes, there are n participants $\mathcal{P} = \{P_1, \ldots, P_n\}$ and a dealer D.

A model consists of two algorithms: ShareGen and Reconst. Share generation algorithm ShareGen takes a secret $s \in \mathcal{S}$ as input and outputs a list $(v_1, v_2, \ldots, v_n)$. Each v_i is called a *share* and is given to a participant P_i. Ordinarily, ShareGen is invoked by the D. Secret reconstruction algorithm Reconst takes a list of shares and outputs a secret $s \in \mathcal{S}$. In a (k, n) threshold scheme [1,10], any k or more participants can recover s but no subset of less than k participants can determine any partial information about s.

2.2   Secret Sharing Schemes Secure Against Cheating

A secret sharing scheme capable of detecting cheating was first presented by Tompa and Woll [11]. They considered the scenario that $k - 1$ or less cheaters submit forged shares in the secret reconstruction phase. Such cheaters will succeed if another participant in the reconstruction accepts an incorrect secret[2].

There are two different models for secret sharing schemes capable of detecting such cheating. Carpentieri, De Santis, and Vaccaro [4] first considered a model

---

[1] Throughout the paper, the cardinality of the set $\mathcal{X}$ is denoted by $|\mathcal{X}|$.

[2] Please note that here we focus on the problem of *detecting* the fact of cheating with unconditional security. Neither secret sharing schemes which *identify* cheaters [3,6] nor *verifiable secret sharing schemes* [9,5] are within the scope of this paper.

in which cheaters who *know* the secret try to make another participant reconstruct an invalid secret. We call this model the *"CDV model."* Recently, Ogata, Kurosawa, and Stinson [8] introduced a model with weaker cheaters who *do not know* the secret in forging their shares. We call this model the *"OKS model."*

As in ordinary secret sharing schemes, each of these models consists of two algorithms. A share generation algorithm ShareGen is the same as that in the ordinary secret sharing schemes. A secret reconstruction algorithm Reconst is slightly changed: it takes a list of shares as input and outputs either a secret or the special symbol $\perp$ ($\perp \notin S$.) Reconst outputs $\perp$ if and only if cheating has been detected. To formalize the models, we define the following simple game for any (k, n) threshold secret sharing scheme $\mathbf{SS} = (\mathsf{ShareGen}, \mathsf{Reconst})$ and for any (not necessarily polynomially bounded) Turing machine $\mathsf{A} = (\mathsf{A}_1, \mathsf{A}_2)$, where A represents cheaters $P_{i_1}, \ldots, P_{i_{k-1}}$ who try to cheat P_{i_k}.

Game($\mathbf{SS}$, A)
```
    s ← S;      // according to the probability distribution over S.
    (v₁,...,vₙ) ← ShareGen(s);
    (i₁,...,i_{k-1}) ← A₁(X);
    // set X = s for the CDV model, X = ∅ for the OKS model.
    (v'_{i₁},...,v'_{i_{k-1}}, i_k) ← A₂(v_{i₁},...,v_{i_{k-1}}, X);
```

The advantage of cheaters is expressed as $Adv(\mathbf{SS}, \mathsf{A}) = \Pr[s' \in S \wedge s' \neq s]$, where s' is a secret reconstructed from $v'_{i_1}, v'_{i_2}, \ldots, v'_{i_{k-1}}, v_{i_k}$ and the probability is taken over the distribution of S and over the random tapes of ShareGen and A.

Definition 1. *A (k, n) threshold secret sharing scheme $\mathbf{SS}$ is called a (k, n, ϵ)-secure secret sharing scheme if $Adv(\mathbf{SS}, \mathsf{A}) \leq \epsilon$ for any adversary A.*

2.3 Previous Work

In this subsection, we briefly review the known bounds and constructions of (k, n, ϵ)-secure secret sharing schemes.

Tompa and Woll have proposed a scheme [11] that can be proven to be a $(k, n, \epsilon_{\mathsf{CDV}})$-secure secret sharing scheme in the CDV model. Where $\mathcal{V}_i$ denotes the set of shares, the size of share $|\mathcal{V}_i|$ is as large as $(\frac{(|S|-1)(k-1)}{\epsilon_{\mathsf{CDV}}} + k)^2$.

A lower bound for the size of shares in the CDV model is described as follows:

Proposition 1. *[4] In the CDV model, the size of shares for $(k, n, \epsilon_{\mathsf{CDV}})$-secure secret sharing schemes is lower bounded by $|\mathcal{V}_i| \geq \frac{|S|}{\epsilon_{\mathsf{CDV}}}$.*

Ogata *et al.* improved this bound when the secret is uniformly distributed:

Proposition 2. *[8] In the CDV model, if the secret is uniformly distributed, then the size of shares $|\mathcal{V}_i|$ for $(k, n, \epsilon_{\mathsf{CDV}})$-secure secret sharing schemes is lower bounded by $|\mathcal{V}_i| \geq \frac{|S|-1}{\epsilon_{\mathsf{CDV}}^2} + 1$.*

Ogata *et al.* also presented the lower bound for the size of shares for $(k, n, \epsilon_{\text{OKS}})$-secure secret sharing scheme in the OKS model as follows.

Proposition 3. [8] *In the OKS model, the size of shares for $(k, n, \epsilon_{\text{OKS}})$-secure secret sharing schemes is lower bounded by $|\mathcal{V}_i| \geq \frac{|S|-1}{\epsilon_{\text{OKS}}} + 1$.*

Within the OKS model, Ogata *et al.* have proposed a $(k, n, \epsilon_{\text{OKS}})$-secure secret sharing schemes that satisfies the bound of Proposition 3 with equality [8]. However, this scheme is proven to be secure only if the secret is uniformly distributed. Within the CDV model, Cabello *et al.* have proposed a $(k, n, \epsilon_{\text{CDV}})$-secure secret sharing scheme [2]. The size of share is a little longer than the lower bound of Proposition 2. Further, the scheme is secure for arbitrary secret distribution, but , in this scheme, the successful cheating probability is uniquely determined from the size of the secret. Obana *et al.* have generalized this result in [7]. In this scheme, the successful cheating probability can be chosen without regard to the size of secret.

3   New Model of Secret Sharing Schemes Secure Against Cheating

Some kinds of cheating are not covered by the OKS(CDV) model. For example, cheaters who know k or more shares are not considered. Schemes in [2,7,8] are proven to be secure in the CDV model or OKS model. However, if cheaters know k or more shares, these schemes are not secure. The successful cheating probability is one.

Actually, cheating from k or more colluding participants exists. Of course, secrecy is not maintained to such participants. However, if considering detecting the fact of cheating, we need to consider a cheating from k or more colluding participants. Therefore, it is highly desired to construct secret sharing schemes capable of detecting cheating from k or more colluding participants with unlimited computational power. To this end, we define new models : the OKS^{n-1} model and the CDV^{n-1} model which are slight modifications of the OKS model and the CDV model, respectively. Cheaters in the new models are allowed to know $n - 1$ shares. To characterize such cheaters, a game is defined as follows.

Game($\textbf{SS}, \textbf{B}$)
    $s \leftarrow \mathcal{S}$;   // according to the probability distribution over $\mathcal{S}$.
    $(v_1, \ldots, v_n) \leftarrow \textsf{ShareGen}(s)$;
    $(i_1, \ldots, i_{n-1}) \leftarrow \textsf{B}_1(X)$;
    // set $X = s$ for the CDV^{n-1} model, $X = \emptyset$ for the OKS^{n-1} model.
    $(v'_{i_1}, \ldots, v'_{i_{k-1}}, i_n) \leftarrow \textsf{B}_2(v_{i_1}, \ldots, v_{i_{n-1}}, X).$;

The advantage of cheaters is redefined by $Adv(\textbf{SS}, \textbf{B}) = \Pr[s' \in \mathcal{S} \wedge s' \neq s]$, where s' is a secret reconstructed from $v'_{i_1}, v'_{i_2}, \ldots, v'_{i_{k-1}}, v_{i_n}$ and the probability is taken over the distribution of $\mathcal{S}$ and over the random tapes of $\textsf{ShareGen}$ and B. In CDV^{n-1} model, s seems to be non-valuable information for $\textsf{B}_2$, because k

or more colluding cheaters can reconstruct secret . However, in the case of (n, n) threshold structure, s is valuable for B_2 .

Please note that the CDV^{n-1} model is the most powerful model of cheating. Because, now, target participant's share is the only information that cheaters don't know. Besides, please note that all the bounds for the OKS (CDV) model (e.g. Propositions 1-3) are also valid for OKS^{n-1} (CDV^{n-1}) since a scheme secure in the OKS^{n-1} (CDV^{n-1}) model is also secure in the OKS (CDV) model.

However, the schemes secure in the OKS(CDV) model are not necessarily secure in the OKS^{n-1}(CDV^{n-1}) model. For example, the schemes presented in [2,7,8] are not secure in the OKS^{n-1}(CDV^{n-1}) model. In these schemes, k or more cheaters can know any other participant's share v_{i_n}. So, they can adjust $v'_{i_1}, v'_{i_2}, \ldots, v'_{i_{k-1}}$ such that reconstructed result from $v'_{i_1}, v'_{i_2}, \ldots, v'_{i_{k-1}}, v_{i_n}$ is the value which they want.

However, the schemes presented in [11] can be proven to be secure in the CDV^{n-1} model.

Next, we briefly review the scheme presented in [11].

3.1   The Tompa and Woll Scheme[11]

The share generation algorithm ShareGen and the share reconstruction algorithm Reconst is described as follows[3].

Share Generation. On input a secret $s \in \{0, \ldots, |\mathcal{S}| - 1\}$, the share generation algorithm ShareGen outputs a list of shares $(v_1, \ldots, v_n)$ as follows. Here, q is a prime such that $q > (|\mathcal{S}| - 1)(k - 1)/\epsilon + n$:

1. Generate random polynomial $f(x)$ of degree $k-1$ over Z_q such that $f(0) = s$.
2. Choose n distinct elements $r_1, \ldots, r_n$ uniformly and randomly from $\{1, \ldots, q - 1\}$.
3. Compute $v_i = (f(r_i), r_i)$ and output $(v_1, \ldots, v_n)$.

Secret Reconstruction and Validity Check. On input a list of k shares $(v_{i_1}, \ldots, v_{i_k})$, the secret reconstruction algorithm Reconst outputs a secret s or $\perp$ as follows:

1. Reconstruct $\hat{f(0)}$ from $v_{i_1}, \ldots, v_{i_k}$ using Lagrange interpolation.
2. Output $\hat{f(0)}$ if $\hat{f(0)} < |\mathcal{S}|$ holds. Otherwise Reconst outputs $\perp$.

In this scheme, k or more cheaters can't know any other participant's share r_{i_n}. This scheme can be proven to be a (k, n, ϵ)-secure secret sharing scheme in the CDV^{n-1} model, and the size of share $|V_i|$ is $q^2 = (\frac{(|\mathcal{S}|-1)(k-1)}{\epsilon} + n)^2$. Further, the scheme is secure for arbitrary secret distribution.

---

[3] We made slight modification to the parameter of [11]. Because, the parameters in [11] are the parameters considering at most $k-1$ cheaters. We change the parameters to the parameters considering at most $n - 1$ cheaters.

4   Proposed Scheme

Tompa and Woll scheme's *Validity Check algorithm* check whether reconstructed secret is in range. This is the reason why their scheme needs very large field for polynomial which distributes secret. In proposed scheme, we use one more polynomial for distributing secret. Comparing two reconstructed secret, proposed scheme's *Validity Check algorithm* can check whether reconstructed secret is a particular value. Then, the size of the field for polynomial can be made small. Consequently, though proposed scheme uses two polynomials, the size of the share is smaller than Tompa and Woll scheme.

In this section, we propose an efficient (k, n, ϵ)-secure secret sharing scheme in the CDV^{n-1} model that is proven to be secure for any secret distribution.

The share generation algorithm ShareGen and the share reconstruction algorithm Reconst are described as follows where p is a prime power and q is a prime power such that $q > \max((k-1)/\epsilon + n, p)$.

Share Generation. On input a secret $s \in \{0, \ldots, p-1\}$, the share generation algorithm ShareGen outputs a list of shares $(v_1, \ldots, v_n)$ as follows:

1. Generate random polynomial $f(x)$ of degree $k-1$ over $GF(q)$ such that $f(0) = s$, and $g(x)$ of degree $k-1$ over $GF(p)$ such that $g(0) = s$.
2. Choose n distinct elements $r_1, \ldots, r_n$ uniformly and randomly from $\{1, \ldots r\}$, $r \leq q - 1$.
3. Compute $v_i = (f(r_i), g(i), r_i)$ and output $(v_1, \ldots, v_n)$.

Secret Reconstruction and Validity Check. On input a list of k shares $(v_{i_1}, \ldots, v_{i_k})$, the secret reconstruction algorithm Reconst outputs a secret s or $\perp$ as follows:

1. Reconstruct $f(\hat{0})$ and $g(\hat{0})$ from $v_{i_1}, \ldots, v_{i_k}$ using Lagrange interpolation.
2. Output $f(\hat{0})$ if $f(\hat{0}) = g(\hat{0})$ holds. Otherwise Reconst outputs $\perp$.

the properties of this scheme is summarized by the following theorem.

Theorem 1. *The scheme of §4 is a (k, n, ϵ)-secure secret sharing scheme in the CDV^{n-1} model with parameters $|\mathcal{S}| = p, \epsilon = (k-1)/(r-n+1)$ and $|\mathcal{V}_i| = p \cdot q \cdot r \simeq \max(|S|^2(\frac{k-1}{\epsilon} + n + 1), |S|(\frac{k-1}{\epsilon} + n + 1)^2)$. Further, the scheme is secure for arbitrary secret distribution.*

Proof. Without loss of generality, we can assume $P_1, \ldots, P_{n-1}$ are cheaters and they try to cheat P_n who has $v_n = (f_n, g_n, r_n)$ by forging their shares $v_i = (f_i, g_i, r_i)$ (for $1 \leq i \leq k-1$.)

Now, suppose that cheaters try to cheat P_n by forging their shares to $v_i = (f'_i, g'_i, r'_i)$(for $1 \leq i \leq k-1$.), $(r'_1, f'_1), \ldots, (r'_{k-1}, f'_{k-1}), (r_n, f_n)$ define a polynomial $\hat{f}$ and $(1, g'_1), \ldots, (k-1, g'_{k-1}), (n, g_n)$ define a polynomial $\hat{g}$. They succeed in cheating P_n if $f(\hat{0}) = g(\hat{0})$. In the other words, they succeed in cheating if $(r'_1, f'_1), \ldots, (r'_{k-1}, f'_{k-1}), (r_n, f_n), (0, g(\hat{0}))$ are passing through the same polynomial f' of degree $k-1$ such that $f'(0) = g(\hat{0})(\neq s)$. The cheaters can obtain polynomial g from $(0, s), (1, g_1), \ldots, (k-1, g_{k-1})$. We can rewrite $g(\hat{0})$ by

$g(\hat{0}) = L_n g(n) + \sum_{j=1}^{k-1} L_j g'_j$ (L_j is a Lagrange coefficient), so cheaters can control the value $g(\hat{0})$ as they want by adjusting their shares. Now suppose a polynomial f' that is passed by the points $(r'_1, f'_1), \ldots, (r'_{k-1}, f'_{k-1}), (0, g(\hat{0})(\neq s))$. The cheaters succeed in cheating if $f'(r_n) = f(r_n)$. The f' is different polynomial from f, because $f'(0) = g(\hat{0}) \neq s = f(0)$. So, f' can intersect f in at most $k-1$ points. Here, r_n is a random element of $\{1, \ldots, r\} - \{r_1, \ldots, r_{n-1}\}$. Thus, the probability that $f'(r_n) = f(r_n)$ is at most $(k-1)/(r-n+1)$. So $\epsilon = (k-1)/(r-n+1)$. □

5   Validity Check of Reconstruction Result

In previous work, participants can identify the fact of cheating only when they participate in the reconstruction.

In some situation, participants want to verify whether there was cheating from only reconstruction result. In this section, we consider the scenario that cheaters forge the reconstruction result. Such cheaters will succeed if another participants accepts an incorrect secret.

We define new models for secret sharing schemes capable if detecting such cheating. These model consist of three algorithms: ShareGen, Reconst, and a validity checking algorithm Check. The share generation algorithm ShareGen is the same as that in the ordinary secret sharing schemes. A secret reconstruction algorithm Reconst is slightly changed: it takes a list of shares as input and outputs either a pair of secret s and "check data" c or the special symbol $\perp$ ($\perp \notin \mathcal{S}$.) Reconst outputs $\perp$ if and only if cheating has been detected. "check data" c is a value for checking the validity of the reconstructed secret. Check takes a secret s, check data c, and one share v_i and outputs either a secret s or the special symbol $\perp$ ($\perp \notin \mathcal{S}$.) Check outputs $\perp$ if and only if cheating has been detected. To formalize the models, we define the following simple game for threshold secret sharing scheme $\mathbf{SS} = (\mathsf{ShareGen}, \mathsf{Reconst}, \mathsf{Check})$ and for any (not necessarily polynomially bounded) Turing machine $\mathsf{C} = (\mathsf{C}_1, \mathsf{C}_2)$, where C represents cheaters $P_{i_1}, \ldots, P_{i_{n-1}}$ who try to cheat P_{i_n}.

Game($\mathbf{SS}, \mathsf{C}$)
    $s \leftarrow \mathcal{S}$;   // according to the probability distribution over $\mathcal{S}$.
    $(v_1, \ldots, v_n) \leftarrow \mathsf{ShareGen}(s)$;
    $(i_1, \ldots, i_{n-1}) \leftarrow \mathsf{C}_1(X)$;
    // set $X = s$ for the CDV^{n-1} model, $X = \emptyset$ for the OKS^{n-1} model.
    $(s', c') \leftarrow \mathsf{C}_2(v_{i_1}, \ldots, v_{i_{n-1}}, X)$;

The advantage of cheaters is expressed as $Adv(\mathbf{SS}, \mathsf{C}) = \Pr[s' \in \mathcal{S} \wedge s' \neq s]$, where $s' = \mathsf{Check}(s', c', v_{i_n})$ and the probability is taken over the distribution of $\mathcal{S}$ and over the random tapes of ShareGen and C.

Definition 2. *A (k, n) threshold secret sharing scheme $\mathbf{SS}$ is called a $(k, n, \epsilon_1, \epsilon_2)$-secure secret sharing scheme with Validity check of reconstruction result* *if* $Adv(\mathbf{SS}, \mathsf{B}) \leq \epsilon_1$ *for any adversary* B *and* $Adv(\mathbf{SS}, \mathsf{C}) \leq \epsilon_2$ *for any adversary* C.

Easily, we can construct a $(k, n, \epsilon_1, \epsilon_2)$-secure secret sharing scheme with Validity check of reconstruction result from the scheme of Section 4.

Using reconstruction algorithm which outputs all inputs as check data, all participants can check the validity of a reconstruction result by inputing $k - 1$ shares from check data and a share which they have to the reconstruction algorithm.

But, in this scheme, the size of check data is very large. However, by slight modification to the scheme of Section 4, we can construct more efficient scheme.

5.1   Modified Proposed Scheme

In this section, we propose a $(k, n, \epsilon_1, \epsilon_2)$-secure secret sharing scheme with Validity check of reconstruction result. This scheme is a slightly modified scheme of the scheme of Section 4 and the check data is much smaller than trivial scheme.

The share generation algorithm ShareGen, the share reconstruction algorithm Reconst, and the validity checking algorithm Check are described as follows where p is a prime power and q is a prime power such that $q > \max\left((k-1)/\epsilon_l + n, p\right)$ (for $l = 1, 2$).

Share Generation. On input a secret $s \in \{0, \ldots, p-1\}$, the share generation algorithm ShareGen outputs a list of shares $(v_1, \ldots, v_n)$ as follows:

1. Generate random polynomial $f(x)$ of degree $k - 1$ over $GF(q)$ such that $f(0) = s$, and $g(x)$ of degree $k - 1$ over $GF(p)$ such that $g(0) = s$.
2. Choose n distinct elements $r_1, \ldots, r_n$ uniformly and randomly from $\{1, \ldots r\}$ $r \leq q - 1$.
3. Compute $v_i = (f(r_i), g(i), r_i)$ and output $(v_1, \ldots, v_n)$

Secret Reconstruction and Validity Check. On input a list of k shares $(v_{i_1}, \ldots, v_{i_k})$, the secret reconstruction algorithm Reconst outputs a secret s or $\perp$ as follows:

1. Reconstruct $\hat{f}$ and $g(\hat{0})$ from $v_{i_1}, \ldots, v_{i_k}$ using Lagrange interpolation.
2. Output $f(\hat{0})$ as secret and $\hat{f}$ as check data if $f(\hat{0}) = g(\hat{0})$ holds. Otherwise Reconst outputs $\perp$.

Validity check of Reconstruction result. On input a polynomial $f(x)$ of degree $k - 1$ over $GF(q)$ and a share $v_i = (f_i, g_i, r_i)$, the validity checking algorithm Check outputs a secret s or $\perp$ as follows:

– Output $f(0)$ if $f(r_i) = f_i$ holds. Otherwise Reconst outputs $\perp$.

In this validity check algorithm, f can be regarded not only as secret but also as check data.

The properties of this scheme is summarized by the following theorem.

Theorem 2. *The scheme of §5.1 is $(k, n, \epsilon_1, \epsilon_2)$-secure secret sharing scheme in the CDV^{n-1} model with parameters $|\mathcal{S}| = p, \epsilon_1 = \epsilon_2 = (k-1)/(r-n+1)$, and $|\mathcal{V}_i| = p \cdot q \cdot r \simeq max\left(|S|^2(\frac{k-1}{\epsilon_1} + n + 1), |S|(\frac{k-1}{\epsilon_1} + n + 1)^2\right)$. Further, the scheme is secure for arbitrary secret distribution.*

Proof. Firstly, ϵ_1 is proven to be $(k-1)/(r-n+1)$ by similar discussion to the proof of Theorem 1. Next, we will show that $\epsilon_2 = (k-1)/(r-n+1)$. Without loss of generality, we can assume $P_1, \ldots, P_{n-1}$ are cheaters and they try to cheat P_n who has $v_n = (f_n, g_n, r_n)$ by forging their check data to f' such that $f'(0) \neq s$.

They succeed in cheating P_n if $f'(r_n) = f_n$. In other words, they succeed in cheating P_n if $f'(r_n) = f(r_n)$. The f' is different polynomial from f, because $f'(0) \neq s$. Here, r_n is a random element of $\{1, \ldots, r\} - \{r_1, \ldots, r_{n-1}\}$. Thus, the probability that $f'(r_n) = f(r_n)$ is at most $(k-1)/(r-n+1)$. So $\epsilon_2 = (k-1)/(r-n+1)$. □

In proposed scheme, the size of check data is only one polynomial representation of degree $k-1$ over $GF(q)$. This is much smaller than the check data of trivial scheme.

6 Conclusion

In this paper, we proposed an efficient (k, n) threshold secret sharing scheme capable of detecting cheating from $n-1$ or less colluding participants.

Table 1 and Table 2 below compares the bit length of shares for the various security parameters where the access structure considered is 3-out-of-5 threshold access structure.

Compared to the scheme of [11] the size of the share in the proposed scheme is smaller for all the security parameters. When $|\mathcal{S}| < 1/\epsilon$ and k, n are small,

Table 1. Comparison of the bit length of the shares (for $\epsilon = 2^{-128}$)

$|S|$	Known Bound	Proposed Scheme	Tompa and Woll
2^{64}	321	324	388
2^{128}	385	388	516
2^{256}	503	642	772
2^{512}	769	1154	1284

Table 2. Comparison of the bit length of the shares (for $\epsilon = 2^{-256}$)

$|S|$	Known Bound	Proposed Scheme	Tompa and Woll
2^{64}	577	580	644
2^{128}	641	644	772
2^{256}	769	772	1026
2^{512}	1025	1282	1540

the size of the share in the proposed scheme is a few bits longer than the lower bound of [7].

Finding more efficient (k, n, ϵ)-secure secret sharing schemes in the CDV^{n-1} model will be future work.

Acknowledgement

We thank the anonymous referees for useful and datailed comments.

References

1. Blakley, G.R.: Safeguarding cryptographic keys. In: Proc. AFIPS 1979, National Computer Conference, vol. 48, pp. 313–137 (1979)
2. Cabello, S., Padró, C., Sáez, G.: Secret Sharing Schemes with Detection of Cheaters for a General Access Structure. Designs, Codes and Cryptography 25(2), 175–188 (2002)
3. Carpentieri, M.: A Perfect Threshold Secret Sharing Scheme to Identify Cheaters. Designs, Codes and Cryptography 5(3), 183–187 (1995)
4. Carpentieri, M., De Santis, A., Vaccaro, U.: Size of Shares and Probability of Cheating in Threshold Schemes. In: Helleseth, T. (ed.) EUROCRYPT 1993. LNCS, vol. 765, pp. 118–125. Springer, Heidelberg (1994)
5. Cramer, R., Damgård, I., Maurer, U.M.: General Secure Multi-party Computation from any Linear Secret-Sharing Scheme. In: Preneel, B. (ed.) EUROCRYPT 2000. LNCS, vol. 1807, pp. 316–334. Springer, Heidelberg (2000)
6. Kurosawa, K., Obana, S., Ogata, W.: t-Cheater Identifiable (k, n) Secret Sharing Schemes. In: Coppersmith, D. (ed.) CRYPTO 1995. LNCS, vol. 963, pp. 410–423. Springer, Heidelberg (1995)
7. Obana, S., Araki, T.: Almost Optimum Secret Sharing Schemes Secure Against Cheating for Arbitrary Secret Distribution. In: Lai, X., Chen, K. (eds.) ASIACRYPT 2006. LNCS, vol. 4284, pp. 364–379. Springer, Heidelberg (2006)
8. Ogata, W., Kurosawa, K., Stinson, D.R.: Optimum Secret Sharing Scheme Secure against Cheating. SIAM Journal on Discrete Mathematics 20(1), 79–95 (2006)
9. Pedersen, T.: Non-Interactive and Information-Theoretic Secure Verifiable Secret Sharing. In: Feigenbaum, J. (ed.) CRYPTO 1991. LNCS, vol. 576, pp. 129–149. Springer, Heidelberg (1992)
10. Shamir, A.: How to Share a Secret. Communications of the ACM 22(11), 612–613 (1979)
11. Tompa, M., Woll, H.: How to Share a Secret with Cheaters. Journal of Cryptology 1(3), 133–138 (1989)

Related-Key Amplified Boomerang Attacks on the Full-Round Eagle-64 and Eagle-128[*]

Kitae Jeong[1], Changhoon Lee[1], Jaechul Sung[2], Seokhie Hong[1],
and Jongin Lim[1]

[1] Center for Information Security Technologies(CIST),
Korea University, Seoul, Korea
{kite,crypto77,hsh}@cist.korea.ac.kr, jilim@korea.ac.kr
[2] Department of Mathematics, University of Seoul, Seoul, Korea
jcsung@uos.ac.kr

Abstract. In this paper we show that the full-round Eagle-64 and Eagle-128 are vulnerable to the related-key amplified boomerang attack. The attack on the full-round Eagle-64 requires 2^{65} full-round Eagle-64 decryptions with 2^{37} related-key chosen ciphertexts, while the attack on the full-round Eagle-128 requires about $2^{154.51}$ full-round Eagle-128 encryptions with $2^{94.83}$ related-key chosen plaintexts. These works are the first known attacks on Eagle-64 and Eagle-128.

Keywords: Block Ciphers, Eagle-64, Eagle-128, Data-Dependent Operations, Related-key Amplified Boomerang Attack.

1 Introduction

Recently, several DDP-based ciphers have been proposed for hardware implementations with low cost, such as SPECTR-H64[4], the CIKS family - CIKS-1[13], CIKS-128[2] and CIKS-128H[17], and Cobra family - Cobra-S128[3], Cobra-F64a[3] and Cobra-F64b[3], Cobra-H64[16] and Cobra-H128[16]. Since all of them use very simple key schedules in order to have no time consuming key preprocessing, they are suitable for the applications of many networks requiring high speed encryption in the case of frequent change of keys. However, most of them have been cryptanalyzed because of a linearity of DDP and simply designed key scheduling algorithms[6,7,8,9,10,11,12].

So, in order to eliminate a linearity of DDP and improve the security of DDP-based ciphers, DDO-based ciphers, which use nonlinear CE (controlled elements) boxes, Eagle-64 and Eagle-128 are proposed in [15,14], respectively. Eagle-64 and

[*] This research was supported by the MIC(Ministry of Information and Communication), Korea, under the ITRC(Information Technology Research Center) support program supervised by the IITA(Institute of Information Technology Advancement) (IITA-2006-(C1090-0603-0025)) and the second author was supported by the Korea Research Foundation Grant funded by the Korean Government(MOEHRD)(KRF-2005-908-C00007).

J. Pieprzyk, H. Ghodosi, and E. Dawson (Eds.): ACISP 2007, LNCS 4586, pp. 143–157, 2007.
© Springer-Verlag Berlin Heidelberg 2007

Eagle-128 are 64-bit and 128-bit block ciphers with 128-bit and 256-bit secret keys, respectively. They have better efficiency than conventional block ciphers in both FPGA and ASIC implementations[14,15].

In this paper, however, we present the structural properties of the nonlinear DDO used in Eagle-64 and Eagle-128, which allow us to make full-round related-key amplified boomerang distinguishers. We then present related-key amplified boomerang attacks on the full-round Eagle-64 and Eagle-128. The attack on the full-round Eagle-64 requires 2^{65} full-round Eagle-64 decryptions with 2^{37} related-key chosen ciphertexts, while the attack on the full-round Eagle-128 requires about $2^{154.51}$ full-round Eagle-128 encryptions with $2^{94.83}$ related-key chosen plaintexts. These works are the first known attacks on Eagle-64 and Eagle-128. Table 1 summarizes our results.

This paper is organized as follows; In Section 2, we briefly describe DDO-boxes, used in Eagle-64 and Eagle-128, and the related-key amplified boomerang attack. Section 3 describes Eagle-64, Eagle-128 and their structural properties. In Sections 4 and 5, we present related-key amplified boomerang attacks on Eagle-64 and Eagle-128, respectively. Finally, we conclude in Section 6.

Table 1. Results of our attacks on Eagle-64 and Eagle-128

Block Cipher	Number of Attacked Rounds	Data/Time Complexity
Eagle-64	8 (full)	2^{37} RK-CC / 2^{65} decryptions
Eagle-128	10 (full)	$2^{94.83}$ RK-CP / $2^{154.51}$ encryptions

RK-CC: Related-Key Chosen Ciphertexts, RK-CP: Related-Key Chosen Plaintexts

2   Preliminaries

In this section, we introduce some notations and DDO-boxes which are components of Eagle-64 and Eagle-128 and the related-key amplified boomerang attack. Following notations are used throughout the paper. A bit index will be numbered from left to right, starting with bit 1. If $P = (p_1, p_2, \cdots, p_n)$ then p_1 is the most significant bit and p_n is the least significant bit.

- $e_{i,j}$: A binary string in which the i-th and j-th bits are one and the others are zeroes, e.g., $e_{1,3} = (1, 0, 1, \cdots, 0)$.
- $\oplus$: Bitwise-XOR operation.
- $\ggg$: Right cyclic rotation.

2.1   DDO-Boxes

In general, a DDO-box can be performed with nonlinear controlled element (CE) boxes, which are defined as follows.

Definition 1. *Let* $F(X, V, Z)$ *be a three-variable function* $F : \{0,1\}^n \times \{0,1\}^{\frac{m}{2}} \times \{0,1\}^{\frac{m}{2}} \to \{0,1\}^n$. F *is called a* $n \times m$ *DDO-box, if* $F(X, V, Z)$ *is a bijection for any fixed* $\frac{m}{2}$*-bit control vectors, V and Z.*

The $n \times m$ DDO-Box, denoted by $F_{n/m}$, is constructed as a superposition of the elementary building box $F_{2/2}$. As shown in Fig. 6(b) and 6(c) of Appendix A, the $F_{2/2}$ is controlled by two bits (v, z) and outputs two bits (y_1, y_2), represented as a pair of two boolean functions with four variables $y_1 = f_1(x_1, x_2, v, z)$ and $y_2 = f_2(x_1, x_2, v, z)$. The followings are two elementary DDO-boxes $F_{2/2}$ and $F'_{2/2}$ used in Eagle-64 and Eagle-128.

○ $F_{2/2}(x_1, x_2, v, z) = (y_1, y_2)$,
   where $y_1 = vzx_2 \oplus vx_2 \oplus vx_1 \oplus zx_1 \oplus z \oplus x_2$,
         $y_2 = vzx_1 \oplus vz \oplus vx_2 \oplus zx_1 \oplus zx_2 \oplus x_1$.

○ $F'_{2/2}(x_1, x_2, v, z) = (y_1, y_2)$,
   where $y_1 = vzx_1 \oplus vzx_2 \oplus vx_1 \oplus vx_2 \oplus zx_1 \oplus zx_2 \oplus z \oplus v \oplus x_2$,
         $y_2 = vzx_1 \oplus vzx_2 \oplus vz \oplus vx_1 \oplus vx_2 \oplus zx_1 \oplus zx_2 \oplus x_1$.

Fig. 6(d) of Appendix A shows the structure of $F_{n/n}$ implemented as a active cascade containing $\frac{n}{2}$ $F_{2/2}$, and Fig. 6(e)((f)) and Fig. 7 of Appendix A depict DDO-boxes $F_{8/24}(F_{8/24}^{-1})$, $F_{32/96}(F_{32/96}^{-1})$ and $F_{64/192}(F_{64/192}^{-1})$, respectively. Because of their symmetric structure, the mutual inverses of $F_{n/m}$ and $F_{n/m}^{-1}$ differ only in the distribution of controlling bits over $F_{2/2}$, e.g., $F_{32/96}(\cdot, (V, Z))$ and $F_{32/96}^{-1}(\cdot, (V', Z'))$ are mutual inverse when $(V, Z) = (V_1, Z_1, V_2, Z_2, V_3, Z_3)$ and $(V', Z') = (V_3, Z_3, V_2, Z_2, V_1, Z_1)$.

2.2   The Related-Key Amplified Boomerang Attack

The related-key amplified boomerang attack[1,5] treats a block cipher $E : \{0, 1\}^n \times \{0, 1\}^k \to \{0, 1\}^n$ as a cascade of two sub-cipher $E = E^1 \circ E^0$. With the chosen plaintext attack scenario, the related-key amplified boomerang distinguisher works as follows. Note that the plaintext is just replaced with the ciphertext in the chosen ciphertext attack scenario.

1. Choose two random n-bit plaintexts P, P' and compute two other plaintexts $P^* = P \oplus \alpha$ and $P'^* = P' \oplus \alpha$ for a constant α.
2. With a chosen plaintext attack scenario, obtain the corresponding ciphertexts $C = E_K(P), C^* = E_{K^*}(P^*), C' = E_{K'}(P')$ and $C'^* = E_{K'^*}(P'^*)$, where $K^* = K \oplus \Delta K, K' = K \oplus \Delta K', K'^* = K \oplus \Delta K \oplus \Delta K'$ (i.e., $K \oplus K^* = K' \oplus K'^* = \Delta K$ and $K \oplus K' = K^* \oplus K'^* = \Delta K'$) and $\Delta K, \Delta K'$ are key differences chosen by the attacker.
3. Check if $C \oplus C' = C^* \oplus C'^* = \delta$ or $C \oplus C'^* = C^* \oplus C' = \delta$.

As stated, the related-key amplified boomerang distinguisher checks if two pairs chosen from a ciphertext quartet have the same difference δ. If this difference δ holds with a higher probability than for a random cipher, then the related-key amplified boomerang distinguisher can be applied effectively to the underlying cipher. If the plaintext quartet (P, P^*, P', P'^*) satisfies the last δ-test, we call such a quartet a *right quartet*.

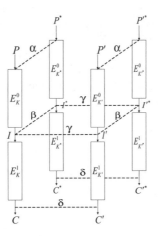

Fig. 1. Related-Key Amplified Boomerang Distinguisher

The related-key amplified boomerang distinguisher can be formed by building quartets of plaintexts (P, P^*, P', P'^*) that satisfy the following four differential conditions.

- Differential Condition 1: $P \oplus P^* = P' \oplus P'^* = \alpha$.
- Differential Condition 2: $I \oplus I^* = I' \oplus I'^* = \beta$ (for some β).
- Differential Condition 3: $I \oplus I' = \gamma$ (or $I \oplus I'^* = \gamma$) (for some γ).
- Differential Condition 4: $C \oplus C' = C^* \oplus C'^* = \delta$ (or $C \oplus C'^* = C^* \oplus C' = \delta$).

where $I = E_K^0(P), I^* = E_{K^*}^0(P^*), I' = E_{K'}^0(P')$ and $I'^* = E_{K'^*}^0(P'^*)$. In these four differential conditions, α, δ, β and δ represent specific differences. Note that differential conditions 2 and 3 imply $I^* \oplus I'^* = \gamma$ (or $I^* \oplus I' = \gamma$) with probability 1. If these four differential conditions are satisfied, such a quartet (P, P^*, P', P'^*) is a right quartet. See Fig. 1 for a schematic description of right quartets.

To begin with, we assume that we have m_1 pairs of (P, P^*) and m_2 pairs of (P', P'^*) with difference α, where P, P^*, P' and P'^* are encrypted with the keys K, K^*, K' and K'^*, respectively. Then about $m_1 \cdot p$ and $m_2 \cdot p$ pairs will satisfy the related-key differential characteristic $\alpha \to \beta$ for E_0 under the key difference ΔK. Here, the probability p is computed as follows;

$$p = Pr_{P,K} \left[E_K^0(P) \oplus E_{K^*}^0(P^*) = \beta \mid P \oplus P^* = \alpha, K \oplus K^* = \Delta K \right].$$

Thus, we have about $m_1 \cdot m_2 \cdot p^2$ quartets satisfying differential conditions 1 and 2. Moreover, we get $I \oplus I' = \gamma$ with probability 2^{-n}. These assumptions enable us to obtain about $m_1 \cdot m_2 \cdot 2^{-n} \cdot p^2$ quartets satisfying differential conditions 1, 2 and 3. As stated above, differential conditions 2 and 3 allow us to get $I^* \oplus I'^* = \gamma$ with probability 1, and each of the pairs (I, I') and (I^*, I'^*) satisfies the related-key differential characteristic $\gamma \to \delta$ for E^1 with probability q. Here, q is computed as follows.

$$q = Pr_{I,K} \left[E_K^1(I) \oplus E_{K'}^1(I') = \delta \mid I \oplus I' = \gamma, K \oplus K' = \Delta K' \right].$$

Therefore, the expected number of right quartets is about $m_1 \cdot m_2 \cdot 2^{-n} \cdot p^2 \cdot q^2$. On the other hand, for a random cipher the expected number of right quartets is about $m_1 \cdot m_2 \cdot 2^{-2n}$. Thus, if $p \cdot q > 2^{-n/2}$, then the related-key amplified boomerang distinguisher can distinguish E from a random cipher.

3   Eagle-64 and Eagle-128

In this section, we describe Eagle-64, Eagle-128 and their structural properties. Eagle-64 and Eagle-128 use a same iterative structure and are composed of the round function $Crypt^{(e)}$ and the final transformation (FT), where $e = 0(e = 1)$ denotes encryption(decryption) mode. The following is the r-round encryption($e = 0$) procedure of Eagle-64 and Eagle-128.

1. An input block P is divided into two subblocks P_L and P_R;
2. $(L, R) \leftarrow (P_L, P_R)$
3. For $j = 1$ to $r - 1$ do :
   - $(L, R) \leftarrow Crypt^{(0)}\left(L, R, Q_j^{(0)}\right)$, where $Q_j^{(0)}$ is the j-th round key;
   - Swap data subblocks : $(L, R) \leftarrow (R, L)$;
4. $j = r$ do : $(L, R) \leftarrow Crypt^{(0)}\left(L, R, Q_r^{(0)}\right)$;
5. Perform the final transformation : $(L, R) \leftarrow \left(L \oplus Q_{r+1}^{(0)}, R \oplus Q_{r+1}^{(0)}\right)$;
6. $(C_L, C_R) \leftarrow (L, R)$;
7. Return the ciphertext block $C = (C_L, C_R)$.

In the decryption mode, P and $Q_j^{(0)}$ are just replaced with C and $Q_j^{(1)}$, respectively.

3.1   Description of Eagle-64

Eagle-64 encrypts 64-bit data blocks with an 128-bit secret key by iterating a round function $Crypt^{(e)}$ 8 times. The round function $Crypt^{(e)}$ is specified in Fig. 2(a). Here, three DDO-boxes $F_{32/96}, F_{32/96}^{-1}$ and $F_{16/16}$ are constructed by using the $F_{2/2}$ as depicted in Fig. 6 and Fig. 7 of Appendix A.

Two 96-bit controlling vectors V and V' corresponding to $F_{32/96}$ and $F_{32/96}^{-1}$ boxes are formed with the extension box E described as follows;

$$E(X) = V = (V_1, Z_1, V_2, Z_2, V_3, Z_3),$$
$$V_1 = X, Z_1 = X^{\ggg 2}, V_2 = X^{\ggg 6}, Z_2 = X^{\ggg 8}, V_3 = X^{\ggg 10}, Z_3 = X^{\ggg 12}.$$

The permutational involution I_1 is performed as follows;

$$I_1 = (1)(2,9)(3,17)(4,25)(5)(6,13)(7,21)(8,29)(10)(11,18)(12,26)$$
$$(14)(15,22)(16,30)(19)(20,27)(23)(24,31)(28)(32).$$

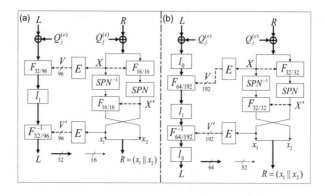

Fig. 2. One round of Eagle-64 (a) and Eagle-128 (b)

As shown in Fig. 3(a), SPN are composed of eight 4×4 S-boxes $S_0, \cdots, S_7$. See [15] for the detail description of S-boxes. Two permutational involutions I_2, I_3 are as follows;

$$I_2 = (1)(2,10)(3)(4,12)(5)(6,14)(7)(8,16)(9)(11)(13)(15),$$
$$I_3 = (1)(2,5)(3,9)(4,13)(6)(7,10)(8,14)(11)(12,15)(16).$$

Eagle-64 uses a simple key schedule. An 128-bit secret key K is divided into four 32-bit blocks, i.e., $K = (K_1, K_2, K_3, K_4)$ and then subkeys K_i $(1 \le i \le 4)$ are directly in procedure $Crypt^{(e)}$ as specified in Table 2.

Table 2. Key schedule of Eagle-64

Round (j)	1	2	3	4	5	6	7	8	9
$Q_j^{(0)}$ (encryption)	K_1	K_2	K_3	K_4	K_1	K_4	K_2	K_3	K_2
$Q_j^{(1)}$ (decryption)	K_2	K_3	K_2	K_4	K_1	K_4	K_3	K_2	K_1

$Q_9^{(0)}, Q_9^{(1)}$: round keys of the final transformation

3.2   Description of Eagle-128

Eagle-128 encrypts 128-bit data blocks with an 256-bit secret key by iterating a round function $Crypt^{(e)}$ 10 times. The round function $Crypt^{(e)}$ is specified in Fig. 2(b). These components are a little bit different from those of Eagle-64. Note that two DDO-boxes $F_{64/192}$ and $F_{64/192}^{-1}$ consist of the $F_{2/2}$, while the $F_{32/32}$ consists of the $F_{2/2}'$.

Given an input X, the output of E, V and V' corresponding to $F_{64/192}$ and $F_{64/192}^{-1}$ boxes, are formed as follows;

$$E(X) = V = (V_1, Z_1, V_2, Z_2, V_3, Z_3),$$
$$V_i = X^{\ggg 10(i-1)}, Z_i = X^{\ggg 10i-5} \ (i = 1, 2, 3).$$

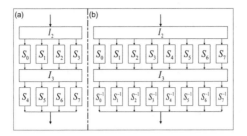

Fig. 3. SPN used in Eagle-64 (a) and Eagle-128 (b)

Two permutational involutions I_0 and I_1 are performed as follows;

$$I_0 = (1)(2,34)\cdots(2i-1)(2j,2j+32)\cdots(63)(32,64),$$

$$\begin{aligned}I_1 = {}&(1)(2,9)(3,17)(4,25)(5,33)(6,41)(7,49)(8,57)(10)(11,18)(12,26)\\&(13,34)(14,42)(15,50)(16,58)(19)(20,27)(21,35)(22,43)(23,51)\\&(24,59)(28)(29,36)(30,44)(31,52)(32,60)(37)(38,45)(39,53)\\&(40,61)(46)(47,54)(48,62)(55)(56,63)(64).\end{aligned}$$

SPN are defined in Fig. 3(b), in which 4×4 S-boxes $S_0,\cdots,S_7$ are equal to those used in Eagle-64 and two permutational involutions I_2, I_3 used in SPN, SPN^{-1} are performed as follows;

$$\begin{aligned}I_2 = {}&(1)(2,18)(3)(4,20)(5)(6,22)(7)(8,24)(9)(10,26)(11)(12,28)(13)\\&(14,30)(15)(16,32)(17)(19)(21)(23)(25)(27)(29)(31),\end{aligned}$$

$$\begin{aligned}I_3 = {}&(1)(2,5)(3,9)(4,13)(6)(7,10)(8,14)(11)(12,15)(16)(17)(18,21)\\&(19,25)(20,29)(22)(23,26)(24,30)(27)(28,31)(32).\end{aligned}$$

The key schedule of Eagle-128 is also simple. As shown Table 3, subkeys $K_i \in \{0,1\}^{64}$ of the 256-bit secret key $K = (K_1, K_2, K_3, K_4)$ are used directly in procedure $Crypt^{(e)}$.

Table 3. Key schedule of Eagle-128

Round (j)	1	2	3	4	5	6	7	8	9	10	11
$Q_j^{(0)}$ (encryption)	K_1	K_2	K_3	K_4	K_2	K_1	K_3	K_4	K_3	K_2	K_1
$Q_j^{(1)}$ (decryption)	K_1	K_2	K_3	K_4	K_3	K_1	K_2	K_4	K_3	K_2	K_1

$Q_{11}^{(0)}, Q_{11}^{(1)}$: round keys of the final transformation

3.3   Properties of Eagle-64 and Eagle-128

In this subsection, we describe some properties for components of $Crypt^{(e)}$ of Eagle-64 and Eagle-128, which allow us to construct related-key amplified boomerang distinguishers. To begin with, we present several basic properties of DDO-boxes (*Property* 1 and 2) and then, some differential probabilities of S-boxes and $SPN(SPN^{-1})$ (*Property* 3 and 4).

Property 1. Let $Pr_{(CE)}(\Delta Y/\Delta X, (\Delta V, \Delta Z))$ be a probability to have the output difference ΔY, where $CE \in \{F_{2/2}, F'_{2/2}\}$, the input difference is ΔX and the difference at the controlling input is $(\Delta V, \Delta Z)$. Then we have the followings;

a) $Pr_{(F_{2/2})}((0,0)/(0,0), (0,0)) = 1$.
b) $Pr_{(F_{2/2})}(\Delta Y/\Delta X, (1,0)) = Pr_{(F_{2/2})}(\Delta Y/\Delta X, (0,1)) = 2^{-2}$ for any $\Delta Y, \Delta X$.
c) $Pr_{(F'_{2/2})}((0,0)/(0,0), (0,0)) = 1$.
d) $Pr_{(F'_{2/2})}(\Delta Y/\Delta X, (1,0)) = Pr_{(F'_{2/2})}(\Delta Y/\Delta X, (0,1)) = 2^{-2}$ for any $\Delta Y, \Delta X$.
e) $Pr_{(F'_{2/2})}(\Delta Y/(0,1), (0,0)) = Pr_{(F'_{2/2})}(\Delta Y/(1,0), (0,0)) = 2^{-1}$, where $\Delta Y \in \{(0,1), (1,0)\}$.

The above properties are also extended into the following properties.

Property 2. Let $Pr_{(CE)}(\Delta Y/\Delta X, (\Delta V, \Delta Z))$ be a probability to have the output difference ΔY, where $CE \in \{F_{n/m}, F_{n/m}^{-1}, F_{n/n}\}$, the input difference is ΔX and the difference at the controlling input is $(\Delta V, \Delta Z)$. Then we have the followings;

a) $Pr_{(F_{64/192}^{-1})}((e_1)/(0), (e_{1,43,85}, e_{6,48,90})) = 2^{-12}$.
b) $Pr_{(F_{16/16})}((0)/(0), (e_1, 0)) = 2^{-2}$.
c) $Pr_{(F_{32/32})}((0)/(0), (e_1, 0)) = 2^{-2}$.
d) $Pr_{(F_{32/32})}((e_{5,7,9,11,22,26})/(e_{5,7,9,11,22,26}), (0,0)) = 2^{-6}$.

Property 3. Let $DP^S(\alpha \rightarrow \beta)$ be a differential probability of 4×4 S-boxes S_i $(i = 0, \cdots, 7)$ to have the output difference β when the input difference is α. Then we have the followings;

a) $DP^{S_i}(0x0 \rightarrow 0x0) = DP^{S_j^{-1}}(0x0 \rightarrow 0x0) = 1$ $(i, j = 0, \cdots, 7)$.
b) $DP^{S_1}(0xE \rightarrow 0x8) = DP^{S_2}(0xE \rightarrow 0x8) = 3 \cdot 2^{-3}$.
c) $DP^{S_0^{-1}}(0x6 \rightarrow 0x8) = 2^{-3}$.

The above properties are also extended into the following properties.

Property 4. Let $DP^{SPN}(\alpha \rightarrow \beta)$ be a differential probability of SPN to have the output difference β when the input difference is α. Then we have the followings;

a) $DP^{SPN}(0x0 \rightarrow 0x0) = DP^{SPN^{-1}}(0x0 \rightarrow 0x0) = 1$.
b) $DP^{SPN}(0xAA00440 \rightarrow 0x80000000) = 9 \cdot 2^{-9}$.

4   Related-Key Amplified Boomerang Attack on Eagle-64

In this section, we describe a full-round(8 rounds) related-key amplified boomerang distinguisher of Eagle-64 and use it to attack the full-round Eagle-64. This attack works through the decryption process of Eagle-64. We consider the case that $K = K'^*$ and $K' = K^*$ in this attack.

Table 4. Two Related-Key Differential Characteristics of Eagle-64

Round (i)	ΔI_i	$\Delta Q_i^{(1)}$	Probability
1	$(e_1, e_1) = \alpha$	e_1	1
2	$(0,0)$	0	1
Output	$(0,0) = \beta$	$\cdot$	$\cdot$
3	$(e_1, e_1) = \gamma$	e_1	1
4	$(0,0)$	0	1
5	$(0,0)$	0	1
6	$(0,0)$	0	1
7	$(0,0)$	0	1
8	$(0,0)$	e_1	2^{-2}
FT (Round 9)	$(?||?, 0||?)$	0	1
Output	$(?||?, 0||?) = \delta$	$\cdot$	$\cdot$

ΔI_i: the i-th round input difference, $\Delta Q_i^{(1)}$: the i-th round key difference

4.1 A Full-Round Related-Key Amplified Boomerang Distinguisher of Eagle-64

As stated before, the key schedule of Eagle-64 is very simple, i.e., round keys are only 32-bit parts of a 128-bit secret key, and there are many useful properties of $F_{32/96}$, $F_{32/96}^{-1}$, $F_{16/16}$, SPN and SPN^{-1} which allow us to construct a good related-key amplified boomerang distinguisher.

We consider the situation that we decrypt ciphertexts $C = (C_L, C_R), C^* = (C_L^*, C_R^*), C' = (C_L', C_R')$ and $C'^* = (C_L'^*, C_R'^*)$ under keys K, K^*, K^*, K such that $\alpha = C \oplus C^* = C' \oplus C'^* = (e_1, e_1)$, $\Delta K = K \oplus K^* = (0, e_1, 0, 0)$, respectively. Then, as shown in Table 4, we construct the first 2-round related-key differential characteristic $\alpha \to \beta$ for rounds 1-2 (E^0) with probability $1(= p)$, where $\beta = (0,0)$. Note that round i in Table 4 means round $9 - i$ in encryption process of Eagle-64 ($i = 1, \cdots, 8$).

The second 6-round related-key differential characteristic is similar to the first one. We decrypt intermediate values $I = (I_L, I_R), I^* = (I_L^*, I_R^*), I' = (I_L', I_R')$ and $I'^* = (I_L'^*, I_R'^*)$ under keys K, K^*, K^*, K such that $\gamma = I \oplus I' = I^* \oplus I'^* = (e_1, e_1)$ and $\Delta K = K \oplus K^* = (0, e_1, 0, 0)$, respectively. Then we construct a 6-round related-key differential characteristic $\gamma \to \delta$ for rounds 3-8 (E^1) with probability $2^{-2}(= q)$, where $\delta = (?||?, 0||?)$ (see Table 4). Here, "?" denotes a 16-bit unknown difference. The propagation of the difference in round 8 is specified in Fig. 4. The input difference of the first $F_{16/16}$ in the right branch is 0. According to *Property 2-b)*, the output difference of the first $F_{16/16}$ in the right branch is 0 with probability 2^{-2}. Thus, according to *Property 4-a)*, the output difference of SPN is 0 with probability 1. So the output difference of round 8 is $(?||?, 0||?)$ with probability 2^{-2}.

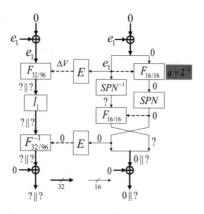

Fig. 4. Propagation of the difference in the last round ($\Delta V = (e_1, e_{19}, e_{39}, e_{57}, e_{75}, e_{93})$)

4.2   Key Recovery Attack on the Full-Round Eagle-64

We are now ready to show how to exploit the above full-round distinguisher to attack the full-round Eagle-64. We assume that Eagle-64 cipher uses the secret key K and the related key K^* with difference $\Delta K = K \oplus K^* = (0, e_1, 0, 0)$. Our attack procedure is as follows.

1. Choose a pool of 2^{36} ciphertext pairs (C_j, C_j^*) with the difference $\alpha = (e_1, e_1)$ $(j = 1, \cdots, 2^{36})$ and construct 2^{71} ciphertext quartets $(C_i, C_i^*, C_i', C_i'^*)$ $(i = 1, \cdots, 2^{71})$. With a chosen ciphertext attack, $(C_i, C_i^*, C_i', C_i'^*)$ are decrypted using the keys K, K^*, K^*, K, respectively, to get the corresponding plaintext quartets $(P_i, P_i^*, P_i', P_i'^*)$. We keep all these plaintexts in a table.
2. Check that $P_i \oplus P_i' = P_i^* \oplus P_i'^* = (?||?, 0||?)$ for each i.
3. Guess a 32-bit subkey pair (K_1, K_1^*) of final transformation, where $K_1^* = K_1$, and do the following;
   (a) Partially encrypt all plaintext quartets $(P_i, P_i^*, P_i', P_i'^*)$ passing Step 2 with the guessed subkey pair (K_1, K_1^*) to get input values of $F_{32/96}, SPN$ and SPN^{-1} in the last round. We denote these 64-bit quartets by $(T_i, T_i^*, T_i', T_i'^*)$, where $T_i = (T_{i,L}, T_{i,R})$ and $T_{i,L}$ is the 32-bit input value of $F_{32/96}$ and $T_{i,R}$ is the concatenation of 16-bit input value of SPN and 16-bit input value of SPN^{-1} in the last round. Finally, check that $T_i \oplus T_i' = T_i^* \oplus T_i'^* = (e_1, e_1)$ for each i.
   (b) If the number of quartets passing Step 3-(a) is greater than or equal to 6, output the guessed subkey pair (K_1, K_1^*) as the right 32-bit subkey pair. Otherwise, go to Step 3.

This attack requires a pool of 2^{36} ciphertext pairs and thus the data complexity of this attack is 2^{37} related-key chosen ciphertexts. The required memory for this attack is about $2^{40}(= 2^{36} \cdot 2 \cdot 8)$ memory bytes.

The time complexity of Step 1 is 2^{37} full-round Eagle-64 decryptions. Each ciphertext quartet can pass Step 2 with probability $2^{-32}(= (2^{-16})^2)$. So only

$2^{39} (= 2^{71} \cdot 2^{-32})$ ciphertext quartets pass Step 2. The time complexity of Step 3-(a) is $2^{65} (= 2^{32} \cdot 2^{37} \cdot \frac{1}{2} \cdot \frac{1}{8})$ full-round Eagle-64 decryptions on average. Therefore, the time complexity of this attack is about $2^{65} (\approx 2^{37} + 2^{65})$ full-round Eagle-64 decryptions.

The probability that Step 3 outputs a wrong subkey quartet is $2^{-319.49} (\approx \sum_{i=6}^{t} (\binom{t}{i} \cdot (2^{-64 \cdot 2})^i \cdot (1 - (2^{-64 \cdot 2}))^{t-i}) \cdot (2^{32} - 1))$. Here, $t = 2^{71}$ represents the number of all possible ciphertext quartets generated by a pool of 2^{36} ciphertext pairs. Thus the possibility that the output of the above attack algorithm is a wrong subkey pair is very low; Due to $p \cdot q = 2^{-2}$ in this attack, the expected number of quartets for the right subkey is about $8 (\approx 2^{71} \cdot 2^{-64} \cdot (2^{-2})^2)$ and the probability that the number of quartets for the right subkey is no less than 6 is $0.81 (\approx \sum_{i=6}^{t} (\binom{t}{i}) \cdot (2^{-64} \cdot (2^{-2})^2)^i \cdot (1 - 2^{-64} \cdot (2^{-2})^2)^{t-i}))$. Therefore, with the success probability of 0.81, our related-key amplified boomerang attack can break the full-round Eagle-64.

5   Related-Key Amplified Boomerang Attack on Eagle-128

In this section, we briefly describe a related-key amplified boomerang attack on the full-round(10 rounds) Eagle-128. Note that our attack on Eagle-128 works through the encryption process of Eagle-128 and we consider the case that $K = K'^*$ and $K' = K^*$ in our attack.

5.1   A Full-Round Related-Key Amplified Boomerang Distinguisher of Eagle-128

As shown in Table 5, if we encrypt plaintexts P, P^*, P' and P'^* under keys K, K^*, K^*, K such that $\alpha = P \oplus P^* = P' \oplus P'^* = (0, e_{37,39,41,43,54,58})$, $\Delta K = K \oplus K^* = (0, e_1, 0, 0)$, respectively. Then we construct the first 4-round related-key differential characteristic $\alpha \to \beta$ for rounds 1-4 (E^0) with probability $9 \cdot 2^{-29} (= p)$, where $\beta = (0, 0)$. The second 6-round related-key differential characteristic is constructed as follows; we encrypt intermediate values I, I^*, I' and I'^* under keys K, K^*, K^*, K such that $\gamma = I \oplus I' = I^* \oplus I'^* = (e_1, e_1)$ and $\Delta K = K \oplus K^* = (0, e_1, 0, 0)$, respectively. Then we construct a 6-round related-key differential characteristic $\gamma \to \delta$ for rounds 5-10 (E^1) with probability $2^{-2} (= q)$, where $\delta = (?||?, 0||?)$. Here, "?" denotes a 32-bit unknown difference.

5.2   Key Recovery Attack on the Full-Round Eagle-128

We assume that Eagle-128 cipher uses the secret key K and the related key K^* with difference $\Delta K = K \oplus K^* = (0, e_1, 0, 0)$. Our attack procedure is as follows.

1. Choose a pool of $2^{93.83}$ plaintext pairs (P_j, P_j^*) with the difference $\alpha = (0, e_{37,39,41,43,54,58})$ ($j = 1, \cdots, 2^{93.83}$) and construct $2^{186.66}$ plaintext quartets $(P_i, P_i^*, P_i', P_i'^*)$ ($i = 1, \cdots, 2^{186.66}$). With a chosen plaintext attack,

Table 5. Two Related-Key Differential Characteristics of Eagle-128

Round (i)	ΔI_i	$\Delta Q_i^{(0)}$	Probability
1	$(0, e_{37,39,41,43,54,58}) = \alpha$	0	$9 \cdot 2^{-29}$
2	(e_1, e_1)	e_1	1
3	$(0,0)$	0	1
4	$(0,0)$	0	1
Output	$(0,0) = \beta$	·	·
5	$(e_1, e_1) = \gamma$	e_1	1
6	$(0,0)$	0	1
7	$(0,0)$	0	1
8	$(0,0)$	0	1
9	$(0,0)$	0	1
10	$(0,0)$	e_1	2^{-2}
FT (Round 11)	$(?||?, 0||?)$	0	1
Output	$(?||?, 0||?) = \delta$	·	·

ΔI_i: the i-th round input difference, $\Delta Q_i^{(0)}$: the i-th round key difference

$(P_i, P_i^*, P_i', P_i'^*)$ are encrypted using the keys K, K^*, K^*, K, respectively, to get the corresponding ciphertext quartets $(C_i, C_i^*, C_i', C_i'^*)$. We keep all these ciphertexts in a table.

2. Check that $C_i \oplus C_i' = C_i^* \oplus C_i'^* = (?||?, 0||?)$ for each i.

3. Guess a 64-bit subkey pair (K_1, K_1^*) of the final transformation, where $K_1^* = K_1$, and do the following;

   (a) Partially decrypt all ciphertext quartets $(C_i, C_i^*, C_i', C_i'^*)$ passing Step 2 with the guessed subkey pair (K_1, K_1^*) to get input values of $F_{64/192}$, SPN and SPN^{-1} in the last round. We denote these 128-bit quartets by $(U_i, U_i^*, U_i', U_i'^*)$, where $U_i = (U_{i,L}, U_{i,R})$ and $U_{i,L}$ is the 64-bit input value of $F_{64/192}$ and $U_{i,R}$ is the concatenation of 32-bit input value of SPN and 32-bit input value of SPN^{-1} in the last round. Finally, check that $U_i \oplus U_i' = U_i^* \oplus U_i'^* = (e_1, e_1)$ for each i.

   (b) If the number of quartets passing Step 3-(a) is greater than or equal to 6, output the guessed subkey pair (K_1, K_1^*) as the right 64-bit subkey pair. Otherwise, go to Step 3.

This attack requires a pool of $2^{93.83}$ plaintext pairs and thus the data complexity of this attack is $2^{94.83}$ related-key chosen plaintexts. The required memory for this attack is dominated by ciphertext pairs, which is approximately $2^{98.83}(= 2^{93.83} \cdot 2 \cdot 16)$ memory bytes.

The time complexity of Step 1 is $2^{94.83}$ full-round Eagle-128 encryptions. Each plaintext quartet can pass Step 2 with the probability $2^{-64}(= (2^{-32})^2)$. So only $2^{122.66}(= 2^{186.66} \cdot 2^{-64})$ plaintext quartets pass Step 2. The time complexity of Step 3-(a) is $2^{154.51}(\approx 2^{64} \cdot 2^{94.83} \cdot \frac{1}{2} \cdot \frac{1}{10})$ full-round Eagle-128 encryptions on average. Therefore, the time complexity of this attack is about $2^{154.51}(\approx 2^{94.83} + 2^{154.51})$ full-round Eagle-128 encryptions.

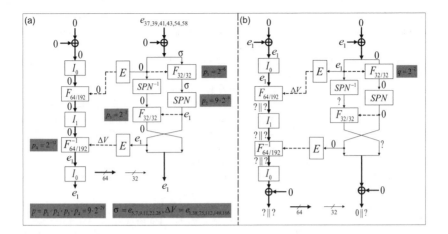

Fig. 5. Propagation of the difference in the first round (a) and the last round (b)

The probability that the output of the above attack algorithm is a wrong subkey pair is $2^{-361.53}(\approx \sum_{i=6}^{t}(\binom{t}{i}\cdot(2^{-128\cdot2})^i\cdot(1-(2^{-128\cdot2}))^{t-i})\cdot(2^{64}-1))$. Here, $t = 2^{186.66}$ represents the number of all possible ciphertext quartets generated by a pool of $2^{93.83}$ ciphertext pairs. Because of the probability $p\cdot q = 9\cdot2^{-31}$, the expected number of quartets for the right subkey is $8(\approx 2^{186.66}\cdot2^{-128}\cdot(9\cdot2^{-31})^2)$ and the probability that the number of quartets for the right subkey is no less than 6 is $0.81(\approx \sum_{i=6}^{t}(\binom{t}{i}\cdot(2^{-128}\cdot(9\cdot2^{-31})^2)^i\cdot(1-2^{-128}\cdot(9\cdot2^{-31})^2)^{t-i}))$. Therefore, the success rate of this attack is 0.81.

6   Conclusion

In this paper, we have presented the first known cryptanalysis results of the full-round Eagle-64 and Eagle-128 by using related-key amplified boomerang attacks. As summarized in Table 1, our attacks on Eagle-64 and Eagle-128 requires about 2^{65} time complexity and $2^{154.51}$ time complexity smaller than the exhaustive search, respectively. These results imply that Eagle-64 and Eagle-128 are still vulnerable to the related-key attack, though Eagle-64 and Eagle-128 are designed to advance conventional DDP-based ciphers which are vulnerable to the related-key attack.

References

1. Biham, E., Dunkelman, O., Keller, N.: Related-Key Boomerang and Rectangle Attacks. In: Cramer, R.J.F. (ed.) EUROCRYPT 2005. LNCS, vol. 3494, pp. 507–525. Springer, Heidelberg (2005)
2. Goots, N., Izotov, B., Moldovyan, A., Moldovyan, N.: Modern cryptography: Protect Your Data with Fast Block Ciphers, Wayne, A-LIST Publish. (2003)

3. Goots, N., Moldovyan, N., Moldovyanu, P., Summerville, D.: Fast DDP-Based Ciphers: From Hardware to Software. In: 46th IEEE Midwest International Symposium on Circuits and Systems (2003)
4. Goots, N., Moldovyan, A., Moldovyan, N.: Fast Encryption Algorithm Spectr-H64. In: Gorodetski, V.I., Skormin, V.A., Popyack, L.J. (eds.) MMM-ACNS 2001. LNCS, vol. 2052, pp. 275–286. Springer, Heidelberg (2001)
5. Hong, S., Kim, J., Lee, S., Preneel, B.: Related-Key Rectangle Attacks on Reduced Versions of SHACAL-1 and AES-192. In: Gilbert, H., Handschuh, H. (eds.) FSE 2005. LNCS, vol. 3557, pp. 368–383. Springer, Heidelberg (2005)
6. Ko, Y., Hong, D., Hong, S., Lee, S., Lim, J.: Linear Cryptanalysis on SPECTR-H64 with Higher Order Differential Property. In: Gorodetsky, V., Popyack, L.J., Skormin, V.A. (eds.) MMM-ACNS 2003. LNCS, vol. 2776, pp. 298–307. Springer, Heidelberg (2003)
7. Ko, Y., Lee, C., Hong, S., Lee, S.: Related Key Differential Cryptanalysis of Full-Round SPECTR-H64 and CIKS-1. In: Wang, H., Pieprzyk, J., Varadharajan, V. (eds.) ACISP 2004. LNCS, vol. 3108, pp. 137–148. Springer, Heidelberg (2004)
8. Ko, Y., Lee, C., Hong, S., Sung, J., Lee, S.: Related-Key Attacks on DDP based Ciphers: CIKS-128 and CIKS-128H. In: Canteaut, A., Viswanathan, K. (eds.) INDOCRYPT 2004. LNCS, vol. 3348, pp. 191–205. Springer, Heidelberg (2004)
9. Lee, C., Hong, D., Lee, S., Lee, S., Yang, H., Lim, J.: A Chosen Plaintext Linear Attack on Block Cipher CIKS-1. In: Deng, R.H., Qing, S., Bao, F., Zhou, J. (eds.) ICICS 2002. LNCS, vol. 2513, pp. 456–468. Springer, Heidelberg (2002)
10. Lee, C., Kim, J., Hong, S., Sung, J., Lee, S.: Related-Key Differential Attacks on Cobra-S128, Cobra-F64a, and Cobra-F64b. In: Dawson, E., Vaudenay, S. (eds.) Mycrypt 2005. LNCS, vol. 3715, pp. 245–263. Springer, Heidelberg (2005)
11. Lee, C., Kim, J., Sung, J., Hong, S., Lee, S.: Related-Key Differential Attacks on Cobra-H64 and Cobra-H128. In: Smart, N.P. (ed.) Cryptography and Coding. LNCS, vol. 3796, pp. 201–219. Springer, Heidelberg (2005)
12. Lu, J., Lee, C., Kim, J.: Related-Key Attacks on the Full-Round Cobra-F64a and Cobra-F64b. In: De Prisco, R., Yung, M. (eds.) SCN 2006. LNCS, vol. 4116, pp. 95–110. Springer, Heidelberg (2006)
13. Moldovyan, A., Moldovyan, N.: A cipher Based on Data-Dependent Permutations. Journal of Cryptology 15(1), 61–72 (2002)
14. Moldovyan, N., Moldovyan, A., Eremeev, M., Sklavos, N.: New Class of Cryptographic Primitives and Cipher Design for Networks Security. International Journal of Network Security 2(2), 114–225 (2006)
15. Moldovyan, N., Moldovyan, A., Eremeev, M., Summerville, D.: Wireless Networks Security and Cipher Design Based on Data-Dependent Operations: Classification of the FPGA Suitable Controlled Elements. In: Proceedings of the CCCT'04, vol. VII, pp. 123–128, Texas, USA (2004)
16. Sklavos, N., Moldovyan, N., Koufopavlou, O.: High Speed Networking Security: Design and Implementation of Two New DDP-Based Ciphers. In: Mobile Networks and Applications-MONET, vol. 25(1-2), pp. 219–231. Kluwer Academic Publishers, Mobile Networks and Applications-MONET (2005)
17. Sklavos, N., Moldovyan, N., Koufopavlou, O.: A New DDP-based Cipher CIKS-128H: Architecture, Design & VLSI Implementation Optimization of CBC-Encryption & Hashing over 1 GBPS. In: proceedings of The 46th IEEE Midwest Symposium on Circuits & Systems, December 27-30, Cairo, Egypt (2003)

A   DDO-boxes

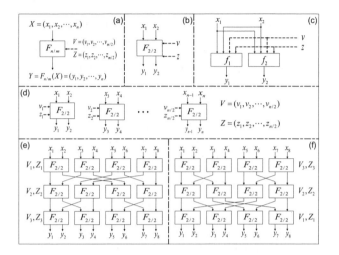

Fig. 6. (a) $F_{n/m}$, (b) $F_{2/2}$, (c) $F_{2/2}$, (d) $F_{n/n}$, (e) $F_{8/24}$ and (f) $F_{8/24}^{-1}$

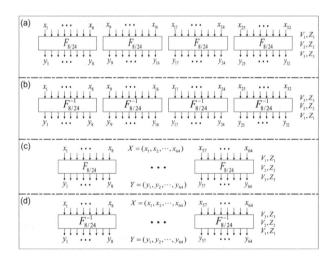

Fig. 7. (a) $F_{32/96}$, (b) $F_{32/96}^{-1}$, (c) $F_{64/192}$ and (d) $F_{64/192}^{-1}$

Analysis of the SMS4 Block Cipher

Fen Liu[1], Wen Ji[1], Lei Hu[1], Jintai Ding[2],
Shuwang Lv[1], Andrei Pyshkin[3,*], and Ralf-Philipp Weinmann[3]

[1] State Key Laboratory of Information Security,
Graduate School of Chinese Academy of Sciences,
Beijing 100049, China
[2] Department of Mathematical Sciences,
University of Cincinnati,
Cincinnati, OH, 45221, USA
[3] Fachbereich Informatik,
Technische Universität Darmstadt,
64289 Darmstadt, Germany

Abstract. SMS4 is a 128-bit block cipher used in the WAPI standard for providing data confidentiality in wireless networks. In this paper we investigate and explain the origin of the S-Box employed by the cipher, show that an embedded cipher similar to BES can be obtained for SMS4 and demonstrate the fragility of the cipher design by giving variants that exhibit 2^{64} weak keys.

We also show attacks on reduced round versions of the cipher. The best practical attack we found is an integral attack that works on 10 rounds out of 32 rounds with a complexity of 2^{18} operations; it can be extended to 13 rounds using round key guesses, resulting in a complexity of 2^{114} operations and a data complexity of 2^{16} chosen pairs.

Keywords: block ciphers, cryptanalysis, UFN, algebraic structure.

1 Introduction

The Wired Authentication and Privacy Infrastructure (WAPI) standard is an alternative to the security mechanisms for wireless networks that are specified in IEEE 802.11i. It has been submitted to the International Standards Organization (ISO) by the Chinese Standards Association (SAC). Although it was subsequently rejected by the ISO in favour of IEEE 802.11i, WAPI still is officially mandated for securing wireless networks within China.

For protecting data packets, the WAPI standard references a 128-bit block cipher called SMS4 which initially was kept secret. In January 2006, the specification of this block cipher however was declassified and published [6]. Other than a differential power attack [11] in a Chinese journal, no analysis of this cipher has appeared in the open literature.

This document sheds light on the design of this block cipher and present a preliminary analysis of its strength against cryptanalytic attacks.

---

* Supported by a stipend of the Marga und Kurt-Möllgaard-Stiftung.

J. Pieprzyk, H. Ghodosi, and E. Dawson (Eds.): ACISP 2007, LNCS 4586, pp. 158–170, 2007.

In Section 2 we give a description of the SMS4 cipher. In Section 3 we show how the SMS4 S-Box can be derived algebraically and how an embedding of SMS4 similar to the Big Encryption System (BES) can be obtained. Section 4 describes an practical integral attack on a 10-round version of SMS4 that can be extended to a theoretical attack on 13 rounds. Our results in Section 5 demonstrate the fragility of SMS4; we show that modifications of the round constants can lead to a large subspace of weak keys. Finally, in Section 6 we conclude this paper and summarize our findings.

1.1 Notation

In the following, we agree on the conventions used throughout the rest of this paper.

Since all operations of the cipher are defined on either 8-bit, 32-bit or 128-bit quantities, we shall use the following terminology: 8-bit values will simply be called *bytes*, 32-bit values *words* and 128-bit values will be called *blocks*. Word and block values shall be considered to be in big-endian order, i.e. the most-significant bit is in the leftmost position when writing the value as a bitstring.

Let $w \lll r$ denote a cyclic shift of the word w by r positions to the left. Sometimes we will need to write down blocks or words in which certain bytes are unknown. In these cases the symbol $\star$ shall denote bytes with unknown values.

To concatenate multiple byte values into a word and multiple word values into a block, we define a vector of bytes or words to be equivalent to a word respectively block value. To access individual bit ranges of a value w we shall use the notation $w_{[i...j]}$ to extract bits i to j, e.g. for $w \in \mathbb{Z}_{2^{32}}$ the expression $w_{[7...0]}$ denotes the lowestmost byte of the word value w.

2 Description of the SMS4 Block Cipher

In this section we will give a top-down description of the SMS4 block cipher.

SMS4 is a 32 round unbalanced Feistel network; both the block and the key size are 128 bits. Following the terminology of [10], the cipher is a homogeneous, complete, source-heavy (96:32) UFN with 8 cycles.

Let the internal state be denoted by $\mathcal{S} = (S_1, S_2, S_3, S_4)$ where $S_i \in GF(2)^{32}$. The round keys of the cipher shall be denoted by $K_i \in GF(2)^{32}$.

Define the linear diffusion function λ as

$$\lambda : GF(2)^{32} \rightarrow GF(2)^{32}$$
$$x \mapsto x \oplus (x \lll 2) \oplus (x \lll 10) \oplus (x \lll 18) \oplus (x \lll 24)$$

and the brick-layer function γ applying an 8-bit S-Box to the input 4 times in parallel as:

$$\gamma : GF(2)^{32} \rightarrow GF(2)^{32}$$
$$x \mapsto (\rho(x_{[31...24]}), \rho(x_{[23...16]}), \rho(x_{[15...8]}), \rho(x_{[7...0]}))$$

The F-function then simply is the composition of these two functions

$$F : GF(2)^{32} \times GF(2)^{32} \to GF(2)^{32}$$
$$(X, K_i) \to \lambda(\gamma(X \oplus K_i))$$

and the round function R that maps S_i to S_{i+1} under the round key K_i as:

$$R : GF(2)^{128} \times GF(2)^{32} \to GF(2)^{128}$$
$$(S_1, S_2, S_3, S_4, K_i) \mapsto (S_2, S_3, S_4, S_1 \oplus F(S_2 \oplus S_2 \oplus S_3, K_i))$$

The key schedule. of the cipher operates in a manner similar to the encryption function. In total, 32 round key words k_i are generated from a 128-bit cipher key. For the key schedule a function F' is used that is almost identical to the round function; the only thing changed is the linear transform. Instead of λ, the following mapping λ' is used:

$$\lambda' : GF(2)^{32} \to GF(2)^{32}$$
$$x \mapsto x \oplus (x \lll 13) \oplus (x \lll 23)$$

In order to obtain the round keys, the cipher key K is first masked with a so-called system parameter

$$T = \texttt{0xA3B1BAC656AA3350677D9197B27022DC}$$

as follows:

$$k_{-4} = K_{[127..96]} \oplus T_{[127..96]}$$
$$k_{-3} = K_{[95..64]} \oplus T_{[95..64]}$$
$$k_{-2} = K_{[63..32]} \oplus T_{[63..32]}$$
$$k_{-1} = K_{[31..0]} \oplus T_{[31..0]}$$

The reasoning behind the masking of the cipher key is not explained in the design document. The round key of the i-th round is computed as follows:

$$k_i = k_{i-4} \oplus \lambda'(\gamma(k_{i-3} \oplus k_{i-2} \oplus k_{i-1} \oplus \kappa_i))$$

where κ_i are key constants. The key constants κ_i are of the form

$$\kappa_i = ((28 \cdot i), (28 \cdot i + 7), (28 \cdot i + 14), (28 \cdot i + 21))$$

where each component of the above vector is a byte, the operators $\cdot$ and $+$ denote the multiplication respectively addition in $\mathbb{Z}_{256}$.

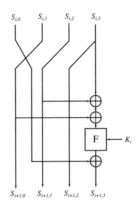

Fig. 1. One round of the SMS4 Unbalanced Feistel Network

3   Algebraic Structure of SMS4

In the SMS4 specification [6], the origin of the S-box is not explained. All the reader is left with is a table with 256 entries. However, we had a hunch that the designers of the cipher had chosen an S-Box design similar to Rijndael; namely that they used an inversion-based mapping. We were confirmed when we looked at the difference distribution table and the linear charateristics of the SMS4 S-Box. These fit our assumption.

3.1   The SMS4 S-Box

We initially assumed the S-Box to be either of the form

$$S(x) = I(x) \cdot A + C, \tag{1}$$

or of the form

$$S(x) = I(x \cdot A + C)$$

where I is the patched inversion over $GF(2^8)$. The matrix $A \in GL(8, 2)$, the vector $C \in GF(2)^8$ and the irreducible polynomial defining the finite field are all undetermined. Experimentally we found that for none of the 30 irreducible polynomials of degree 8, the above expression could be fulfilled for all values of the SMS4 S-Box. However, for a simple permutation of the output bits, we obtained a significant amount of coincident entries between an assumed S-Box of the structure of equation 3.1 and the actual SMS4 S-Box.

The, next idea was to test S-Boxes of the form

$$S(x) = I(x \cdot A_1 + C_1) \cdot A_2 + C_2, \tag{2}$$

with $A_1, A_2 A \in GL(8, 2)$ and $C_1, C_2 \in GF(2)^8$. An exhaustive search for A_1 and C_1 is impractical, because the total number of the 8×8 invertible matrixes is

$$N = \prod_{i=0}^{7}(2^8 - 2^i) \approx 5.348 \times 10^{18} \approx 2^{62}.$$

Because the affine matrix in the algebraic expression of the S-Box in AES is a cyclic matrix, we decided to restrict ourselves to cyclic matrices for A_1 and A_2. Cyclic matrices are determined by their first row. Since there are 255 non-zero binary cyclic 8×8 matrices, we get a total complexity of less than $2^8 \times 2^8 \times 2^8 \times 30 < 2^{29}$, which is practical. In fact, a cyclic matrix with first row $(a_0, a_1, \cdots, a_{n-1})$ is a invertible matrix if and only if the polynomial $a_0 + a_1 x + \cdots + a_{n-1} x^{n-1}$ and $x^n - 1$ are relatively prime. If $n = 8$, this condition is equal to $a_0 + a_1 + \cdots + a_{n-1} \neq 0$. Thus there exist only 2^7 invertible cyclic 8×8 matrices, causing the search complexity to decrease to less than 2^{27}.

Our experiments finally validated the structure of equation 2. We successfully obtained a tuple (A_1, A_2, C_1, C_2) for which all elements of the S-Box all satisfy equation 2. The irreducible polynomial is

$$f(x) = x^8 + x^7 + x^6 + x^5 + x^4 + x^2 + 1,$$

the cyclic matrices in the algebraic expression are

$$A_1 = A_2 = \begin{pmatrix} 1\,1\,1\,0\,0\,1\,0\,1 \\ 1\,1\,1\,1\,0\,0\,1\,0 \\ 0\,1\,1\,1\,1\,0\,0\,1 \\ 1\,0\,1\,1\,1\,1\,0\,0 \\ 0\,1\,0\,1\,1\,1\,1\,0 \\ 0\,0\,1\,0\,1\,1\,1\,1 \\ 1\,0\,0\,1\,0\,1\,1\,1 \\ 1\,1\,0\,0\,1\,0\,1\,1 \end{pmatrix},$$

and the row vectors are

$$C_1 = C_2 = (1, 1, 0, 0, 1, 0, 1, 1).$$

The results presented can also be obtained with less computational effort by using the Affine Equivalence Algorithm for S-Boxes described in [2]. This algorithm in turn is based on the To and Fro algorithm for the isomorphism of polynomials [8].

3.2 Embedding SMS4

Similar to the embedding defined by Murphy and Robshaw for AES–128 [7], we can embed SMS4 into a more elegant and structured cipher ESMS4 in which all operations are performed over the finite field $GF(2^8)$. In this section we will show how this can be done. First note that the description we give is probabilistic, since we do not allow the inversion of the value 0 to occur. The overall number of S-Boxes in the cipher and key schedule is 256, henceforth the probability that an arbitrary plaintext can be encrypted under an arbitrary key without causing a zero inversion can be approximated by $\left(\frac{255}{256}\right)^{256} \approx 1/e \approx 36.7\%$.

First of all, let F denote the field ESMS4 will be defined over:

$$F = GF(2^8) = \frac{GF(2)[x]}{x^8 + x^7 + x^6 + x^5 + x^4 + x^2 + 1} = GF(2)(\theta)$$

The state space, the key space and the message space of ESMS4 then are F^{128}, the round key space is F^{32}. In accordance with [7] we define a vector conjugate mapping ϕ that maps an element $a \in F$ to an 8-tuple $a \in F^8$

$$\phi(a) = \left(a^{2^0}, a^{2^1}, a^{2^2}, a^{2^3}, a^{2^4}, a^{2^5}, a^{2^6}, a^{2^7} \right)$$

and analogously maps a vector $A \in F^n$ to $A' \in F^{8n}$. The inverse of ϕ, $Im(\phi)$ shall be called extraction mapping. For a $GF(2)$-linear function L operating on a byte $b := (b_8, b_7, b_6, b_5, b_4, b_3, b_2, b_1)$ we obtain a F-linear function $\mathcal{L}$ that performs the equivalent operation on the vector $\phi(b)$ by first computing the coefficients $\beta_1, \dots, \beta_8$ of the the linearized polynomial

$$\mathcal{L}(b) = \sum_{k=1}^{8} \beta_k a^{2^{k-1}}$$

and then computing the matrix $M_{\mathcal{L}} = (\alpha_{i,j})$ with $\alpha_{i,j} = \beta_{1+((j-i) \bmod 8)}^{2^{i-1}}$. The function $\mathcal{L}$ then is defined as $\mathcal{L} : F^8 \to F^8, v \to M_{\mathcal{L}} \cdot v$. We call $M_{\mathcal{L}}$ the *linearized polynomial matrix form* of L.

The S-Box layer. From Section 3.1 we know that the S-Box of SMS4 can be decomposed into the form $A \circ I \circ A$, with A an affine-linear function over $GF(2)$. Analogously, for ESMS4, the S-Box operation can be performed by $\mathcal{A} \circ \mathcal{I} \circ \mathcal{A}$, with $\mathcal{A}$ being an affine-linear transform over F and $\mathcal{I}$ being the componentwise inversion of elements on a vector $v \in F^8$. The linear part of $\mathcal{A}$ can be expressed by multiplication of the linearized polynomial matrix form $M_{\mathcal{A}} \in F^{8 \times 8}$ of the linear part of A, whilst the constant can simply be embedded using ϕ. We define $\widetilde{C} = (\phi(C_1), \phi(C_1), \phi(C_1), \phi(C_1))$ and $\widetilde{A} = \text{Diag}_4(M_{\mathcal{A}})$.

The linear transform λ. Let $P \in GF(2)^{32 \times 32}$ be the permutation matrix such that for $v \in GF(2)^{32}$, the product $P \cdot v$ corresponds to a cyclic shift of elements of v by one position to the left. This matrix can be decomposed into the following form

$$P = \begin{pmatrix} M_1 & 0 & 0 & M_2 \\ M_2 & M_1 & 0 & 0 \\ 0 & M_2 & M_1 & 0 \\ 0 & 0 & M_2 & M_1 \end{pmatrix}, \quad M_1, M_2 \in GF(2)^{8 \times 8}$$

By computing the linearized polynomial matrix forms for M_1, M_2

$$\widetilde{M_1} = \mathcal{L}(M_1), \quad \widetilde{M_2} = \mathcal{L}(M_2)$$

we obtain the following matrix that performs the equivalent action on a 32-tuple of elements representing 4 bytes of the state:

$$
P = \begin{pmatrix} \widetilde{M_1} & 0 & 0 & \widetilde{M_2} \\ \widetilde{M_2} & \widetilde{M_1} & 0 & 0 \\ 0 & \widetilde{M_2} & \widetilde{M_1} & 0 \\ 0 & 0 & \widetilde{M_2} & \widetilde{M_1} \end{pmatrix}, \quad \widetilde{M_1}, \widetilde{M_2} \in F^{8 \times 8}
$$

Then the transformation λ is equivalent to the multiplication from the left with the matrix

$$
\Lambda_1 = P^0 + P^2 + P^{10} + P^{18} + P^{24}
$$

whilst for λ' the corresponding matrix is

$$
\Lambda_2 = P^0 + P^{13} + P^{24}.
$$

The round function. The F-function function of the cipher ESMS4 can be expressed as:

$$
\widetilde{F} : F^{32} \times F^{32} \rightarrow F^{32},
$$
$$
(\widetilde{X}, \widetilde{K}) \mapsto \Lambda_1 \cdot \left(\widetilde{A} \cdot \mathcal{I} \left(\widetilde{A} \cdot \left(\widetilde{X} + \widetilde{K} \right) + \widetilde{C} \right) + \widetilde{C} \right)
$$

The key schedule. The key generation function of ESMS4 is defined in the same way as the F-function except for replacing Λ_1 by Λ_2.

The existence of the embedding stems from the fact that SMS4 uses only $GF(2)$-linear operations and an inversion over $GF(2^8)$. Since the number of S-Boxes per cipher round is only a quarter of that of BES–128, we expect ESMS4 to be more amenable to experimenting with algebraic attacks without resorting to scaling down the field or block size.

4   A Reduced-Round Attack Using Integrals

Integral cryptanalysis is a powerful cryptanalytic method that was first used to break a reduced version of SQUARE [3], a predecessor of Rijndael. In following we will use the notation of [5]. We will use $[A_1, A_2, A_3, A_4]$ to denote a block and (a_1, a_2, a_3, a_4) to denote a word.

Our attack is based on the following difference pairs for the round function of SMS4:

$$[\Delta, 0, 0, 0] \rightarrow [0, 0, 0, \Delta] \qquad\qquad [0, 0, \Delta, \Delta] \rightarrow [0, \Delta, \Delta, 0]$$
$$[0, \Delta, \Delta, 0] \rightarrow [\Delta, \Delta, 0, 0] \qquad\qquad [0, \Delta, 0, \Delta] \rightarrow [\Delta, 0, \Delta, 0]$$

All these difference pairs are of probability one.

Table 1. Propagation of the 8 round integral

round no. (r)	$S_{r,1}$	$S_{r,2}$	$S_{r,3}$	$S_{r,4}$
0	(C,C,C,A)	(C,C,C,A)	(C,C,C,A)	(C,C,C,C)
1	(C,C,C,A)	(C,C,C,A)	(C,C,C,C)	(C,C,C,A)
2	(C,C,C,A)	(C,C,C,C)	(C,C,C,A)	(C,C,C,A)
3	(C,C,C,C)	(C,C,C,A)	(C,C,C,A)	(C,C,C,A)
4	(C,C,C,A)	(C,C,C,A)	(C,C,C,A)	(A,A,A,A)
5	(C,C,C,A)	(C,C,C,A)	(A,A,A,A)	(S,S,S,S)
6			(S,S,S,S)	(⋆,⋆,⋆,⋆)
7		(S,S,S,S)	(⋆,⋆,⋆,⋆)	
8	(S,S,S,S)	(⋆,⋆,⋆,⋆)		

Let $P = [P_1, P_2, P_3, P_4]$ be a plaintext. Then the following collection of 256 plaintexts will allow us to attack the 9th round key of SMS4:

$$[P_1 \oplus \delta, \; P_2 \oplus \delta, \; P_3 \oplus \delta, \; P_4],$$

where δ ranges from 0 to 255.

A trace of this integral through the cipher is depicted in Table 1. Each letter C denotes a distinct constant byte value whilst the letter A ranges over all possible byte values. In our case, the letter S means that the sum of all bytes after the γ function is zero. This integral will allow us to determine four key bytes of the last round key.

Moreover, since

$$\gamma(S_{8,2} \oplus S_{8,3} \oplus S_{8,4} \oplus K_i) = \lambda^{-1}(S_{8,1} \oplus S_{9,4}),$$

each key byte can be found independently.

Following the ideas of [4], this attack can be extended by an additional round at the beginning using the following integral:

$$\Delta \; (C, C, C, A) \; (C, C, C, A) \; (C, C, C, A)$$

where $\Delta = \lambda(0, 0, 0, \tilde{A}) \oplus (C, C, C, C)$; with $\tilde{A}$ independently ranging over all byte values. Using a structure of 2^{16} plaintexts allows us to parallelly determine all bytes of the the 10th round key. We have implemented and experimentally verified this attack.

The attack can be extended without increasing the data complexity by guessing additional round keys. A theoretical attack on 13 rounds is thus possible with a complexity of about 2^{114} cipher operations. Generic attacks on Feistel networks with the structure of SMS4 (96:32 UFN) work on a significantly smaller number of rounds, namely up to 7 rounds [9,10].

5   Weak Keys for Modified Round Key Constants

In this section we show that for slightly modified round key constants in the key schedule, the cipher will exhibit a class of 2^{64} weak keys. For all of these keys, the cipher exhibits an invariant property over an arbitrary number of rounds. This invariance can be used to effectively distinguish the encryption function from a random permutation. Once the use of a weak key is detected, the key search space for an attacker of course shrinks from 2^{128} to 2^{64}. The property shows an unexpected fragility of the cipher design and in our opinion casts serious doubt on its strength.

Definition 1. *Let $a \in GF(2)^{2n}$. If $a = b||b$ for an element $b \in GF(2)^n$, then we say that the element a has a 1/2-repetition property; alternatively a may be called 1/2-repeated.*

Theorem 1. *Let $(s_1, \ldots, s_k) \in \mathbb{Z}^k$ be a vector of shift offsets. Any 2n-bit function $g : GF(2)^{2n} \to GF(2)^{2n}$ of the form*

$$x \mapsto \bigoplus_{i=1}^{k} (x \lll s_i)$$

preserves the 1/2-repetition property.

Proof. Obviously the invariance condition is preserved under addition if it holds for all elements of the sum. By induction the invariance condition for n-bit cyclic shifts can be derived for 1-bit shits. □

Modifying all round key constants κ_i to be 1/2-repeated, we obtain 2^{64} cipher keys for which all round keys possess the 1/2-repetition property; note that due to the masking of the cipher key with the system parameter in the key generation the 2^{64} actual cipher keys are not 1/2-repeated though. Both the round key function and the round function preserve the invariance for these keys. From this follows that for plaintexs in which each word is 1/2-repeated, we obtain ciphertexts that also are 1/2-repeated. Henceforth, these cipher variants are insecure.

6   Conclusions

We have given a detailed analysis of SMS4. Its design seems to be clearly influenced by Rijndael, although the UFN structure makes for a much simpler implementation. We decomposed the S-Box into two affine linear transforms and an inversion and have given an embedding to the cipher similar to BES. An practical attack on 10 rounds of SMS4 has been demonstrated and the fragility of the key schedule has been exposed. We think that our results are only a first step in the cryptanalysis of SMS4 and that further improvements can be made. Especially the point of algebraic cryptanalysis – for which this cipher is an excellent target – has not been addressed in this paper. This will be discussed in a future paper.

References

1. Barkan, E., Biham, E.: In How Many Ways Can You Write Rijndael? In: Zheng, Y. (ed.) ASIACRYPT 2002. LNCS, vol. 2501, pp. 160–175. Springer, Heidelberg (2002)
2. Biryukov, A., De Cannière, C., Braeken, A., Preneel, B.: A Toolbox for Cryptanalysis: Linear and Affine Equivalence Algorithms. In: Biham, E. (ed.) Advances in Cryptology – EUROCRPYT 2003. LNCS, vol. 2656, pp. 33–50. Springer, Heidelberg (2003)
3. Daemen, J., Knudsen, L.R., Rijmen, V.: The Block Cipher Square. In: Biham, E. (ed.) FSE 1997. LNCS, vol. 1267, pp. 149–165. Springer, Heidelberg (1997)
4. Ferguson, N., Kelsey, J., Lucks, S., Schneier, B., Stay, M., Wagner, D., Whiting, D.: Improved Cryptanalysis of Rijndael. In: Schneier, B. (ed.) FSE 2000. LNCS, vol. 1978, pp. 213–230. Springer, Heidelberg (2000)
5. Knudsen, L.R., Wagner, D.: Integral Cryptanalysis. In: Daemen, J., Rijmen, V. (eds.) FSE 2002. LNCS, vol. 2365, pp. 112–127. Springer, Heidelberg (2002)
6. Beijing Data Security Technology Co. Ltd. Specification of SMS4 (in Chinese) (2006) http://www.oscca.gov.cn/UpFile/,21016423197990.pdf
7. Murphy, S., Robshaw, M.J.B.: Essential Algebraic Structure within the AES. In: Yung, M. (ed.) CRYPTO 2002. LNCS, vol. 2442, pp. 1–16. Springer, Heidelberg (2002)
8. Patarin, J., Goubin, L., Courtois, N.: Improved algorithms for isomorphisms of polynomials. In: Nyberg, K. (ed.) EUROCRYPT 1998. LNCS, vol. 1403, pp. 184–200. Springer, Heidelberg (1998)
9. Patarin, J., Nachef, V., Berbain, C.: Generic Attacks on Unbalanced Feistel Schemes with Contracting Functions. In: Lai, X., Chen, K. (eds.) ASIACRYPT 2006. LNCS, vol. 4284, pp. 396–411. Springer, Heidelberg (2006)
10. Schneier, B., Kelsey, J.: Unbalanced Feistel Networks and Block Cipher Design. In: Gollmann, D. (ed.) Fast Software Encryption. LNCS, vol. 1039, pp. 121–144. Springer, Heidelberg (1996)
11. Zhang, L., Wu, W.: Difference Fault Attack on the SMS4 Encryption Algorithm (in Chinese). Chinese Journal of Computers 29(9) (2006)

Appendix A: The SMS4 S-Box

Below you find the entries of the SMS4 S-Box in hexadecimal notation. For example, for an input of 0xef the corresponding output can be read off in the row labelled with the value e and the column labelled with f: 0x84.

	0	1	2	3	4	5	6	7	8	9	a	b	c	d	e	f
0	d6	90	e9	fe	cc	e1	3d	b7	16	b6	14	c2	28	fb	2c	05
1	2b	67	9a	76	2a	be	04	c3	aa	44	13	26	49	86	06	99
2	9c	42	50	f4	91	ef	98	7a	33	54	0b	43	ed	cf	ac	62
3	e4	b3	1c	a9	c9	08	e8	95	80	df	94	fa	75	8f	3f	a6
4	47	07	a7	fc	f3	73	17	ba	83	59	3c	19	e6	85	4f	a8
5	68	6b	81	b2	71	64	da	8b	f8	eb	0f	4b	70	56	9d	35
6	1e	24	0e	5e	63	58	d1	a2	25	22	7c	3b	01	21	78	87
7	d4	00	46	57	9f	d3	27	52	4c	36	02	e7	a0	c4	c8	9e
8	ea	bf	8a	d2	40	c7	38	b5	a3	f7	f2	ce	f9	61	15	a1
9	e0	ae	5d	a4	9b	34	1a	55	ad	93	32	30	f5	8c	b1	e3
a	1d	f6	e2	2e	82	66	ca	60	c0	29	23	ab	0d	53	4e	6f
b	d5	db	37	45	de	fd	8e	2f	03	ff	6a	72	6d	6c	5b	51
c	8d	1b	af	92	bb	dd	bc	7f	11	d9	5c	41	1f	10	5a	d8
d	0a	c1	31	88	a5	cd	7b	bd	2d	74	d0	12	b8	e5	b4	b0
e	89	69	97	4a	0c	96	77	7e	65	b9	f1	09	c5	6e	c6	84
f	18	f0	7d	ec	3a	dc	4d	20	79	ee	5f	3e	d7	cb	39	48

Appendix B: Equivalent Forms of the S-Box

Just as for the Rijndael S-Box [1], different equivalent representations of the SMS4 S-Box can be obtained. The S-Box constructed by equation 2 in Section 3.1 is a composition of two affine transformations and a mapping I in the vector space. I is a mapping in the vector space obtained from an inversion mapping in $GF(2^8)$, it is related to the chosen basis of the finite field. The basis defining I in equation 2 is a polynomial basis $\{\beta^7, \cdots, \beta, 1\}$ (β is a root of the polynomial), which is defined by the irreducible polynomial $x^8 + x^7 + x^6 + x^5 + x^4 + x^2 + 1$.

Below we study the equivalent forms of algebraic expression of the S-Box, namely we find other algebraic expressions when the inversion mapping of the finite field is represented in different bases. We do not limit ourselves to polynomial bases, we consider general bases of finite fields.

If $\{\alpha_{n-1}, \cdots, \alpha_1, \alpha_0\}$ and $\{\beta_{n-1}, \cdots, \beta_1, \beta_0\}$ are two bases of $GF(2^n)$ over $GF(2)$, there must be a $n \times n$ invertible matrix M that satisfies the equation below

$$\begin{pmatrix} \alpha_{n-1} \\ \vdots \\ \alpha_0 \end{pmatrix} = M \begin{pmatrix} \beta_{n-1} \\ \vdots \\ \beta_0 \end{pmatrix}.$$

M is a transformation matrix from the basis $\{\beta_{n-1}, \cdots, \beta_1, \beta_0\}$ to the basis $\{\alpha_{n-1}, \cdots, \alpha_1, \alpha_0\}$.

Lemma 1. Let $I_1, I_2 : GF(2)^n \to GF(2)^n$ be mappings corresponding to I under the basis $\{\alpha_{n-1}, \cdots, \alpha_1, \alpha_0\}$ and $\{\beta_{n-1}, \cdots, \beta_1, \beta_0\}$ respectively. Then

$$I_1(x) = I_2(x \cdot M) \cdot M^{-1}$$

Proof. For any $x \in GF(2^n)$, if the denotation of x under two bases are

$$x = (x_{n-1}, \cdots, x_0) \begin{pmatrix} \alpha_{n-1} \\ \vdots \\ \alpha_0 \end{pmatrix} = (y_{n-1}, \cdots, y_0) \begin{pmatrix} \beta_{n-1} \\ \vdots \\ \beta_0 \end{pmatrix},$$

then

$$(x_{n-1}, \cdots, x_0) \cdot M = (y_{n-1}, \cdots, y_0). \tag{3}$$

While

$$I_1(x_{n-1}, \cdots, x_0) \begin{pmatrix} \alpha_{n-1} \\ \vdots \\ \alpha_0 \end{pmatrix} = I(x) = I_2(y_{n-1}, \cdots, y_0) \begin{pmatrix} \beta_{n-1} \\ \vdots \\ \beta_0 \end{pmatrix},$$

namely that

$$I_1(x_{n-1}, \cdots, x_0) \cdot M \begin{pmatrix} \beta_{n-1} \\ \vdots \\ \beta_0 \end{pmatrix} = I_2(y_{n-1}, \cdots, y_0) \begin{pmatrix} \beta_{n-1} \\ \vdots \\ \beta_0 \end{pmatrix},$$

so

$$I_1(x_{n-1}, \cdots, x_0) \cdot M = I_2(y_{n-1}, \cdots, y_0).$$

Substituting equation 3 into the formula above, we obtain

$$I_1(x_{n-1}, \cdots, x_0) \cdot M = I_2((x_{n-1}, \cdots, x_0) \cdot M),$$

namely for any $x \in GF(2)^n$,

$$I_1(x) = I_2(x \cdot M) \cdot M^{-1}$$

Corollary 1. *Select* $\{\beta_7, \cdots, \beta_1, \beta_0\}$ *as the polynomial basis defined by the irreducible polynomial* $x^8 + x^7 + x^6 + x^5 + x^4 + x^2 + 1$. *Let* $\{\alpha_7, \cdots, \alpha_1, \alpha_0\}$ *be another polynomial basis of* $GF(2^8)$ *and* M *be the transformation matrix from* $\{\beta_7, \cdots, \beta_1, \beta_0\}$ *to* $\{\alpha_7, \cdots, \alpha_1, \alpha_0\}$. *Then under the basis* $\{\alpha_7, \cdots, \alpha_1, \alpha_0\}$, *the algebraic expression of the SMS4 S-Box is*

$$S(x) = I_1(xA_1M + C_1M)M^{-1}A_2 + C_2. \tag{4}$$

For convenience, A_1, A_2 of the equation 2 are called generator matrices of the S-Box. According to Corollary 1, under the basis $\{\alpha_{n-1}, \cdots, \alpha_0\}$ the generator matrices of the S-Box are A_1M and $M^{-1}A_2$.

There are 30 irreducible polynomials of degree 8 over $GF(2)$. Every irreducible polynomial can define 8 different bases. Therefore there are $30 \times 8 = 240$ algebraic expressions of the S-Box with different generator matrices. If we do not limit ourselves to polynomial bases, the generator matrix A_1M in the algebraic expression of the S-Box can be any invertible matrix (correspondingly, $M^{-1}A_2$ is another matrix).

Next we will prove that if we limit ourselves to cyclic matrices for A_1, A_2 under a polynomial basis, the basis must be the one mentioned in the previous section. In this sense the algebraic expression presented in 3.1 is the simplemost form that can be obtained.

Proposition 1. *If restrict A_1, A_2 to be cyclic matrices, the algebraic expression of the S-Box (A_1, A_2, C_1, C_2) presented in Section 3.1 is uniquely defined.*

Proof. According to Corollary 1, for the other tuple

$$S(x) = I_1(x \cdot A_1^T \cdot M + C_1 \cdot M) \cdot M^{-1} \cdot A_2^T + C_2. \tag{5}$$

holds. Assume that $(A_1^T \cdot M)$ and $(M^{-1} \cdot A_2^T)$ are cyclic matrices, while A_1, A_2 are cyclic matrices as well. Then M^T and M must also be cyclic matrixes, namely we get

$$\begin{pmatrix} \alpha^{n-1} \\ \vdots \\ 1 \end{pmatrix} = \begin{pmatrix} c_0 & c_1 & c_2 & c_3 & c_4 & c_5 & c_6 & c_7 \\ c_7 & c_0 & c_1 & c_2 & c_3 & c_4 & c_5 & c_6 \\ c_6 & c_7 & c_0 & c_1 & c_2 & c_3 & c_4 & c_5 \\ c_5 & c_6 & c_7 & c_0 & c_1 & c_2 & c_3 & c_4 \\ c_4 & c_5 & c_6 & c_7 & c_0 & c_1 & c_2 & c_3 \\ c_3 & c_4 & c_5 & c_6 & c_7 & c_0 & c_1 & c_2 \\ c_2 & c_3 & c_4 & c_5 & c_6 & c_7 & c_0 & c_1 \\ c_1 & c_2 & c_3 & c_4 & c_5 & c_6 & c_7 & c_0 \end{pmatrix} \begin{pmatrix} \beta^{n-1} \\ \vdots \\ 1 \end{pmatrix}$$

We then can get a system of linear equations,

$$\begin{cases} 1 = c_0 + c_1\beta + \cdots + c_7\beta^7 \\ \alpha = c_0\beta + \cdots + c_6\beta^7 + c_7 \\ \vdots \\ \alpha^7 = c_0\beta^7 + c_1 + \cdots + c_6\beta^5 + c_7\beta^6 \end{cases}$$

which can be transformed into:

$$\begin{cases} \alpha - \beta = c_7(1 - \beta^8) \\ \alpha(\alpha - \beta) = c_6(1 - \beta^8) \\ \vdots \\ \alpha^6(\alpha - \beta) = c_1(1 - \beta^8) \end{cases}$$

From this follows that

$$\alpha = \frac{c_6}{c_7} = \frac{c_5}{c_6} = \frac{c_4}{c_5} = \frac{c_3}{c_4} = \frac{c_2}{c_3} = \frac{c_1}{c_2}.$$

Since we know that $(\alpha^7, \cdots, \alpha, 1)^T$ is a polynomial basis, it is impossible for α to satisfy the above form. Hence our initial assumption is wrong. From this follows that for generator matrices limited to cyclic matrices, the generator tuple of the SMS4 S-Box is unique.

Forgery Attack to an Asymptotically Optimal Traitor Tracing Scheme

Yongdong Wu[1], Feng Bao[1], and Robert H. Deng[2]

[1] Institute for Infocomm Research ($\mathbf{I^2R}$), A-Star, Singapore
{wydong, baofeng}@i2r.a-star.edu.sg
[2] School of Information Systems, Singapore Management University
robertdeng@smu.edu.sg

Abstract. In this paper, we present a forgery attack to a black-box traitor tracing scheme [2] called as CPP scheme. CPP scheme has efficient transmission rate and allows the tracer to identify a traitor with just one invalid ciphertext.

Since the original CPP scheme is vulnerable to the multi-key attack, we improved CPP to thwart the attack. However, CPP is vulnerable to a fatal forgery attack. In the forgery attack, two traitors can collude to forge all valid decryption keys. The forged keys appear as perfect genuine keys, can decrypt all protected content, but are untraceable by the tracer. Fortunately, we can patch this weakness with increasing the decoder storage.

1 Introduction

With the advent and rapid development of networks, piracy is becoming a great threat to the content service vendors. For example, the annual report by the Cable and Satellite Broadcasting Association of Asia (CASBAA)[3], which studied TV markets across 11 Asian countries, predicted the number of illegal connections is expected to rise 20% to $5.2 million in 2006, and pay-TV piracy in Asia is estimated to cost the industry $1.13 billion in 2006, up 6.6% from 2005. It is apparent that the need for broadcast encryption systems is urgent and challenging. In the broadcast encryption system, each authorized user has a legal decoder embedded with a unique decryption key. A content distributor encrypts broadcast content such that only authorized users can decode protected content with their legal decoders. However, a group of legal users may conspire to violate copyright protection policies by reverse-engineering the legal decoders (*e.g.*, [4]), sharing their decryption keys, constructing and distributing pirate decoders. In this pirate process, the legal user who gives her key to construct the pirate decoder is called as a traitor, while the person who has illegally access to protected content is called as pirate, and the device of a pirate is a pirate decoder.

Kiayias and Yung [5,6] categorized the pirate-decoders according to their self-protection capabilities. If a pirate decoder employs an internal reactive mechanism, it is called "abrupt", otherwise, it is called "available". One "abrupt" method is the "aggressive action" mechanism [5] which crashes the host tracing

J. Pieprzyk, H. Ghodosi, and E. Dawson (Eds.): ACISP 2007, LNCS 4586, pp. 171–183, 2007.
© Springer-Verlag Berlin Heidelberg 2007

system, or releases a virus. The weakness of this method is that it is not able to entirely prohibit tracing, especially in a virtual-machine protection environment where the decoder code is run in a restrict manner. Another "abrupt" method is the "shutting down" mechanism [7] which erases all internal decryption keys in order to halt the tracing process. This "suicidal" approach apparently renders the decoder useless. If the broadcaster can disseminate messages to permanently shut down pirate decoders, the copyright protection goal of the broadcaster is almost achieved. The "aggressive action" method has more impact on software decoders, while the "shutting down" mechanism is more effective on hardware decoders. Yet another "abrupt" method is the "blind" mechanism [8] which outputs ambiguous messages to confuse the tracer. To this end, a pirate decoder analyzes the input messages, and then takes defensive actions. For example, if the decoder detects invalidate ciphertexts in its input (*e.g.*, in [9]), it outputs garbage. This mechanism is applicable to both software and hardware decoders.

A broadcast encryption and traitor tracing (BETT) system is an effective tool to frustrate pirates. Assume that each pirate decoder has at least one key for decrypting encrypted messages, a tracer in BETT extracts at least one key from a pirate decoder so as to incriminate at least one traitor. A BETT has two important performance parameters: traceability (*i.e.*, number of tolerable traitors) and transmission rate (*i.e.*, the ratio between ciphertext size and plaintext size). Clearly, a BETT system targets for high traceability, but low transmission rate. Intuitively, it is not easy to achieve both goals for a BETT system. For example, a naïve BETT system which assigns the same key to all users has the best transmission rate (*i.e.*, transmission rate is 1) but the worst traceability (*i.e.*, traceability is 0); the combinatorial-key schemes [10]-[12] can tolerate t traitors with the transmission rate $O(t^4 \log n)$ where n is the number of users and $t \ll n$; the hybrid scheme [13] enables full-public-traceability when its enabling block size is linear to n, while the fully collusion resistant traitor tracing schemes [14,15] are able to defeat $t = n$ traitors with a transmission rate $O(\sqrt{n})$ but they are vulnerable to the Denial-of-Trace (DOT) attack [16].

Since broadcast content is usually very large (e.g., 2M bit/s in MPEG2 movie), any BETT scheme can be used in hybrid encryption system [17] such that the entire system has asymptotically optimal transmission rate without reducing the BETT traceability. Concretely, the broadcaster selects a random key K for content M, and generates the protected content as $< \mathcal{E}_1(PK, K), \mathcal{E}_2(K, M) >$, where PK is the BETT encryption key, $\mathcal{E}_1(\cdot)$ is the BETT encryption algorithm, and $\mathcal{E}_2(\cdot)$ is a standard cipher such as RC4. Obviously, the transmission rate of the above hybrid encryption system is close to 1, and its traceability is the same as that of the original BETT. Nonetheless, hybrid encryption has one weakness that the traitors may prefer to directly disclosing content key K on-line instead of distributing pirate decoders off-line. Since the content key is known to all legal users, it can not be used to identify traitors. To prevent traitors from disclosing the content key, the broadcaster need directly encrypt content and broadcast the ciphertext to the users, given that traitors are unwilling to disseminate decrypted content in real-time due to high bandwidth requirement and legal risk.

Kiayas and Yung [1] propose the first BETT algorithm (called as KY scheme) which directly encrypts content at constant transmission rate. Following the same system model as the KY scheme, Chabanne, Phan and Pointcheval [2] propose an asymptotically optimal BETT scheme (called as CPP scheme) with transmission rate close to 1. Suppose that each pirate decoder has a unique key, both KY scheme and CPP scheme have the same traitor tracing algorithm: generating an invalid ciphertext and feeding it a pirate decoder, extracting a word from the pirate decoder, and adopting collusion-secure code Γ [18] to arrest at least one traitor. The traitor tracing algorithms in [1,2] are very efficient since they can identify a traitor with just one ciphertext.

1.1 Our Contribution

The present paper investigates the security of KY and CPP schemes. Our major contributions can be summarized as follows.

(1) Since CPP scheme inherit the KY scheme, both are vulnerable to the multi-key attack [8]. Recently, Papers [19,20] found the weakness of KY scheme but fixed it. This paper improved CPP scheme so as to defeat multi-key attack too. Concretely, to trace a pirate decoder, the tracer crafts and sends multiple invalid ciphertexts to the decoder such that decryption keys are traced independently. Since pirate decoders can not always distinguish tracing ciphertexts from broadcasting ciphertexts, the tracer is able to extract some of the decryption keys using the indistinguishable tracing ciphertexts. The extracted keys suffice to identify a traitor.
(2) We introduce a novel forgery attack to CPP scheme. The forgery attack allows two traitors produce a forged key set which is a permutation of a genuine key set. The pirate decoder embedded with the forged key set is able to decrypt all encrypted content, but prevents the tracer from identifying any one of the traitors. In addition, we describe a countermeasure which is asymptotically Optimal in terms of transmission rate.

The rest of the paper is organized as follows. Section 2 introduces some preliminaries. Sections 3 describes the upgraded CPP scheme. Section 4 presents our forgery attack and countermeasure. In Section 5, we discuss practical issues in traitor tracing schemes. The last section draws a conclusion.

2 Preliminaries

This section reviews the basic concepts used in the KY [1] and CPP [2] traitor tracing schemes. Most of them are based on the definitions in [18]. For ease of exposition, notations in this paper are listed in Table 1.

2.1 Marking Assumption

Definition 1. A set $\Gamma_0 = \{W^{(1)}, W^{(2)}, \ldots, W^{(n)}\}$ is called an (l, n)-code where $W^{(i)} = <w_1^{(i)}, w_2^{(i)}, \cdots, w_l^{(i)}>$ is a codeword consisting of l binary symbols. The codeword $W^{(i)}$ is assigned to user U_i.

Table 1. Notations

Γ	a collusion-secure code
$W^{(i)}$	a codeword in Γ
U_i	the ith user with a unique codeword $W^{(i)}$
$\mathbf{T}$	the set of the traitors
$\mathbb{F}(\mathbf{T};\Gamma)$	a feasible set for $\mathbf{T}$
$\mathbf{R_T}$	undetectable position set for $\mathbf{T}$
n	the number of users
l	the length of a codeword
t	the maximum number of tolerable traitors
ϵ	the error probability of collusion-secure code Γ
M	plaintext message

Let $\mathbf{T}$ be a set of codewords. For $1 \le j \le l$, we say that position j is undetectable for $\mathbf{T}$ if all the codewords in $\mathbf{T}$ are identical in the jth position. Formally, suppose $\mathbf{T} = \{U_1, U_2, \ldots, U_t\}$, position j is undetectable if $w_j^{(1)} = w_j^{(2)} = \cdots = w_j^{(t)}$. Let $\mathbf{R_T}$ be the set of undetectable positions for $\mathbf{T}$, $i.e.$, $\mathbf{R_T} = \{j \mid w_j^{(1)} = w_j^{(2)} = \cdots = w_j^{(t)}, 1 \le j \le l\}$. Assume that the users in $\mathbf{T}$ can not change the symbols in $\mathbf{R_T}$, $i.e.$, they can only construct a set of words based on the *marking assumption* [18]:

Marking assumption:
Given two codewords $W^{(1)} = \{w_1^{(1)}, w_2^{(1)}, \ldots, w_l^{(1)}\}$ and $W^{(2)} = \{w_1^{(2)}, w_2^{(2)}, \ldots, w_l^{(2)}\}$, $\mathbf{T} = \{W^{(1)}, W^{(2)}\}$, $\mathbf{R_T}$ is their undetectable position set. Word $Z = \{z_1, z_2, \ldots, z_l\}$ created from $W^{(1)}$ and $W^{(2)}$ must be
$$z_j = w_j^{(1)} \text{ if } j \in \mathbf{R_T}, \text{ or } z_j = \text{"?"}.$$
where "?" represents random.

2.2   Feasible Set

When a coalition creates new words according to the *marking assumption*, the resulting set of words is called the feasible set of the coalition.

Definition 2 [18]. Let Γ_0 be an (l, n)-code, $\mathbf{T}$ be a coalition of users, and $\mathbf{R_T}$ be the set of undetectable positions for $\mathbf{T}$. Define the feasible set of $\mathbf{T}$ as

$$\mathbb{F}(\mathbf{T};\Gamma_0) = \{Z \in \{0, 1, ?\}^l \ \ s.t. \ \ Z \mid_{\mathbf{R_T}} = W^{(u)} \mid_{\mathbf{R_T}}, \exists U_u \in \mathbf{T}\}$$

where "?" represents random, $Z \mid_{\mathbf{R_T}}$ are the symbols of Z in position set $\mathbf{R_T}$. In summary, the feasible set contains all words which match the coalition's undetectable bits, and the *marking assumption* states that any coalition of users is only capable of creating a word which lies in the feasible set of the coalition.

2.3   Collusion-Secure Code

Given a word $W \in \mathbb{F}(\mathbf{T}; \Gamma)$, where the size of $\mathbf{T}$ is at most t, if one can confirm at least one member $U \in \mathbf{T}$, we say that user U is identified, and the code Γ is refereed to as t-collusion-secure.

Definition 3. If an (l, n)-code Γ allows a collusion of up to t users and has a tracing algorithm that succeeds with probability $1 - \varepsilon$, Γ is refereed to as a (l, n, t, ε)-collusion-secure code.

2.4   Traitor Tracing System

The participants in a BETT system are: authority, broadcaster, tracer, user and pirate. An authority generates and delivers the encryption key PK, decryption keys SK's and tracing key TK; a broadcaster is a service provider which encrypts the content and broadcasts the encrypted content to users; each legal user has an authorized decoder embedded with a unique decrypting key SK for consuming the encrypted content, traitors are legal users who conspire to create a pirate decoder; a tracer runs a traitor tracing algorithm with tracing key TK to extract a token from a confiscated decoder and then identify a traitor with the token. To identify a traitor, a tracer with white-box tracing algorithm must know the internals of the pirate decoder, but a tracer with black-box tracing system knows nothing of the decoder's internals.

3   The Upgraded CPP Scheme

KY scheme is the first traitor tracing scheme with constant transmission rate. Based on the same architecture as KY, CPP scheme achieves asymptotically optimal transmission rate. Without loss of generality, we will in the rest of the paper focus on CPP scheme unless stated otherwise.

CPP scheme is designed to broadcast encrypted messages at the optimal transmission rate 1, and identify at least one traitor from a confiscated pirate decoder. To achieve the objectives, the authority first sets up a 2-user 1-traitor BETT system S. The authority then constructs a multi-user BETT system from l-instantiations of S with (l, n, t, ϵ)-collusion-secure code Γ.

3.1   Two-User System

In a 2-user traitor tracing system S, there are two users U_1 and U_2, and each user has an authorized decoder which is embedded with a unique decryption key SK. If the broadcaster sends a valid ciphertext to the two users, the resulting outputs of the two decoders are identical; however, if the input ciphertext to the two decoder are invalid, their outputs will be different. The different results enable the tracer to identify the user's key unambiguously assuming that there is at most one traitor. The CPP scheme includes the following modules: Setting up, Encrypting $\mathcal{E}(\cdot)$, Decrypting $\mathcal{D}(\cdot)$ and Traitor tracing.

- **Setting up:** First, the authority selects the system parameters: a prime q and two groups $\mathcal{G}_1, \mathcal{G}_2$ of order q, an admissible bilinear map $\hat{e} : \mathcal{G}_1 \times \mathcal{G}_1 \rightarrow \mathcal{G}_2$, a generator $P \in \mathcal{G}_1$, and sets $g = \hat{e}(P, P)$ which is a generator of $\mathcal{G}_2$. Next, the authority picks two random numbers $a, z_1 \in Z_q^*$, a one-way function $\mathcal{H}$, and then calculates $Q = aP$, $Z_1 = g^{z_1}$. The public key is $PK = \langle g, Q, Z_1 \rangle$. The authority key is $\langle a, z_1 \rangle$. Subsequently, the authority creates a random matrix

$$K = \begin{pmatrix} k_{10} & k_{11} \end{pmatrix}_{1 \times 2},$$

  where $k_{1w_1} = \langle d_{1w_1}, f_{1w_1} \rangle$ such that $d_{1w_1} + af_{1w_1} = z_1 \mod q, w_1 = 0, 1$. For each user U_{1+w_1}, her decoder key is $SK = \langle d_{1w_1}, f_{1w_1}P \rangle$.

- **Encrypting:** To encrypt a message M_1, the broadcaster generates a random r, and then creates the ciphertext

$$\langle A, B, C_1 \rangle = \langle rP, r^2Q, M_1 \oplus \mathcal{H}(Z_1^{r^2}) \rangle \tag{1}$$

  which will be broadcast to all the users.

- **Decrypting:** Upon receiving a ciphertext $\langle A, B, C_1 \rangle$, the decoder will extract its decoder key $\langle d_{1w_1}, f_{1w_1}P \rangle$, then calculate

$$v_1 = \hat{e}(d_{1w_1}A, A) \cdot \hat{e}(f_{1w_1}P, B) = \hat{e}(d_{1w_1}rP, rP) \cdot \hat{e}(f_{1w_1}P, r^2aP)$$
$$= g^{d_{1w_1}r^2 + af_{1w_1}r^2} = g^{(d_{1w_1}+af_{1w_1})r^2} = g^{z_1 r^2} = Z_1^{r^2}$$

  and recover the original message as $m_1 = C_1 \oplus \mathcal{H}(v_1)$.

- **Traitor tracing:** CPP scheme has public traceability, *i.e.*, its tracing key TK is known to all. The tracer first selects random numbers $r_1 \in Z_q$ and $r_2 \in Z_q$, and then constructs an invalid ciphertext $\langle A, B, C_1 \rangle = \langle r_1P, r_2^2Q, C_1 \rangle$. Secondly, he sends the invalid ciphertext to a pirate decoder, and records the output m of the decoder. Thirdly, he calculates

$$v_{10} = \hat{e}(d_{10}P, r_1^2P) \cdot \hat{e}(Q, r_2^2 f_{10}P) = g^{d_{10}r_1^2 + af_{10}r_2^2}$$
$$v_{11} = \hat{e}(d_{11}P, r_1^2P) \cdot \hat{e}(Q, r_2^2 f_{11}P) = g^{d_{11}r_1^2 + af_{11}r_2^2}$$
$$w_1 = \begin{cases} 0 : m = C_1 \oplus \mathcal{H}(v_{10}) \\ 1 : m = C_1 \oplus \mathcal{H}(v_{11}) \\ ? : \text{otherwise} \end{cases}$$

Finally, user U_{1+w_1} is identified as guilty if $w_1 \neq \text{"?"}$.

3.2   Multi-user System

As shown in Fig.1, the multi-user BETT system is constructed by repeatedly using l-instantiations of two-user system $S_j, j = 1, 2, \ldots, l$. Concretely, the functions in the broadcast encryption algorithms are as follows.

- **Key setup.** After selecting the same system parameters $\langle q, g, P, \mathcal{G}_1, \mathcal{G}_2, \mathcal{H}, \hat{e} \rangle$ as those in the two-user system, the authority picks a random $a \in Z_q^*$ and l elements $z_j \in Z_q^*$, computes $Q = aP$, $Z_j = g^{z_j}$, $j = 1, 2, \ldots, l$. The public key is $PK = <g, Q, Z_1, Z_2, \ldots, Z_l>$, and the key of the authority is $<a, z_1, z_2, \ldots, z_l>$. Thirdly, the authority creates a secret key matrix K as

$$K = \begin{pmatrix} k_{10} & k_{11} \\ k_{20} & k_{21} \\ \vdots & \vdots \\ k_{l0} & k_{l1} \end{pmatrix}_{l \times 2}$$

where sub-key $k_{jw_j} = <d_{jw_j}, f_{jw_j}P>$ such that

$$d_{jw_j} + af_{jw_j} = z_j \mod q, \quad w_j = 0, 1. \tag{2}$$

Any k_{jw_j} which satisfies Eq.(2) is a valid key of 2-user system S_j. From an (l, n, t, ϵ)-collusion-secure code Γ, the authority randomly selects a binary codeword $W = <w_1, w_2, \ldots, w_l>$ and assign W to a user U such that her decoder key is $SK = <k_{1w_1}, k_{2w_2}, \ldots, k_{lw_l}>$.

- **Encrypt.** To encrypt a message $M = <M_1, M_2, \ldots, M_l>$, the broadcaster selects a random r, and generates the ciphertext

$$<A, B, C_1, \cdots, C_l> = <rP, r^2Q, M_1 \oplus \mathcal{H}(Z_1^{r^2}), \cdots, M_l \oplus \mathcal{H}(Z_l^{r^2})> \tag{3}$$

which is broadcast to all the users.

- **Decrypt.** After receiving a ciphertext $<A, B, C_1, C_2, \ldots, C_l>$, for each $j \in [1, l]$, the sub-decoder of 2-user system S_j embedded with a sub-key $k_{jw_j} = <d_{jw_j}, f_{jw_j}P>$ calculates

$$v_j = \hat{e}(d_{jw_j}A, A) \cdot \hat{e}(f_{jw_j}P, B) = \hat{e}(d_{jw_j}rP, rP) \cdot \hat{e}(f_{jw_j}P, r^2aP)$$
$$= g^{d_{jw_j}r^2 + af_{jw_j}r^2} = g^{(d_{jw_j} + af_{jw_j})r^2} = g^{z_jr^2} = Z_j^{r^2}$$
$$M_j = C_j \oplus \mathcal{H}(v_j)$$

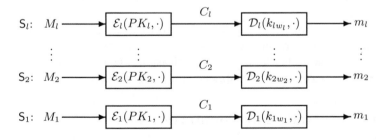

Fig. 1. Multi-user broadcast encryption. The entire decoder consists of l sub-decoders

3.3   Multi-user Traitor Tracing

Although Chabanne, Phan and Pointcheval [2] elaborate their traitor tracing method for 2-user system, they do not explicitly address the traitor tracing algorithm for multi-user system. However, they mention that their scheme shares the same black-box tracing capability as KY scheme [1]. Hence, to analyze the multi-user tracing algorithm of CPP scheme, we adapt the KY scheme to CPP scheme by merely customizing the encryption function. Since the original traitor tracing scheme in [1] is vulnerable to the multi-key attack [8], in the following, we fix the weakness in CPP. Specifically, in order to prevent a multi-key pirate decoder from detecting the presence of a tracing process, the tracer creates l invalid ciphertexts, and performs tracing on each 2-user system independently. That is to say, the tracer

- Randomly selects numbers $r_1 \in Z_q$, $r_2 \in Z_q$, $r \in Z_q$ and $t \in [1, l]$.
- Constructs a ciphertext $< A_t, B_t, C_t >=< r_1 P, r_2^2 Q, C_t = M_t \oplus \mathcal{H}(Z_t^{r_1^2} >$ for S_t, and generates $< A, B, C_j >=< rP, r^2 Q, C_j = M_j \oplus \mathcal{H}(Z_j^{r^2}) >$ for other S_j, $j \in [1, t-1] \cup [t+1, l]$.
- Sends the invalid ciphertexts

$$< t, A_t, B_t, C_t, A, B, C_1, C_2, \ldots, C_{t-1}, C_{t+1}, \ldots, C_l > \qquad (4)$$

to the pirate decoder.
- Obtains the output m_t of the decoder, and calculates

$$v_{t0} = \hat{e}(d_{t0}P, r_1^2 P) \cdot \hat{e}(Q, r_2^2 f_{t0} P) = g^{d_{t0}r_1^2 + af_{t0}r_2^2}$$

$$v_{t1} = \hat{e}(d_{t1}P, r_1^2 P) \cdot \hat{e}(Q, r_2^2 f_{t1} P) = g^{d_{t1}r_1^2 + af_{t1}r_2^2}$$

$$w_t = \begin{cases} 0 : m_t = C_t \oplus \mathcal{H}(v_{t0}) \\ 1 : m_t = C_t \oplus \mathcal{H}(v_{t1}) \\ ? : \text{otherwise} \end{cases}$$

After repeating the above tracing method by scanning each word position at least once, the tracer can obtain all the symbols in the word $W \in \{0, 1, ?\}^l$. Based on the security of the 2-user system and the *marking assumption*, $W \in \mathbb{F}(\mathbf{T}; \mathbf{\Gamma})$. Thus, the tracer can identify at least one traitor based on the collusion-secure code (e.g., [18]).

Note that the ciphertext in Eq.(3) in the broadcast process should be changed to that given in Eq.(4) assuming $r_1 = r_2 \neq r$, in order that the tracing message is indistinguishable from the normal broadcast message; otherwise, the pirate decoder will be alerted from the abnormal message format.

4   Forgery Attack and Countermeasure

Section 3 fixes a security flaw of KY and CPP schemes such that they are free from our multi-key attack. However, we will show in this section that CPP tracing scheme is still vulnerable to a new forgery attack. This forgery attack allows traitors to create perfect valid, and hence untraceable, decryption keys.

4.1 Forging Decryption Key

In the key setup stage of CPP scheme, each user is assigned a unique codeword from the collusion-secure code Γ. Therefore, for any two users, their codewords are different in at least one symbol. Without loss of generality, assume that the different symbols is in the first position. Thus, the traitors have sub-keys $k_{10} = <d_{10}, f_{10}P>$ and $k_{11} = <d_{11}, f_{11}P>$ that must satisfy

$$\begin{cases} d_{10} + af_{10} = z_1 \mod q \\ d_{11} + af_{11} = z_1 \mod q \end{cases}$$

Denote $\Delta_d = d_{10} - d_{11}$ and $\Delta_f = f_{10} - f_{11}$. Thus $\Delta_d + a\Delta_f = 0 \mod q$. To fabricate a decryption key, the two traitors select a word $W = <w_1, \ldots, w_l> \in \mathbb{F}(\mathbf{T}; \Gamma)$ randomly, hence $k_{jw_j} = <d_{jw_j}, f_{jw_j}P>$ is one sub-key of one of the traitors. Denote $K_j = \{<d_j^*, f_j^*P> | s_j \in Z_q\}, j = 1, 2, \ldots, l$, where

$$\begin{cases} d_j^* = d_{jw_j} + s_j\Delta_d \\ f_j^*P = f_{jw_j}P + s_jf_{10}P - s_jf_{11}P = f_{jw_j}P + s_j\Delta_fP = (f_{jw_j} + s_j\Delta_f)P \end{cases} \quad (5)$$

Theorem. For all $j \in [1, l]$, K_j is the whole key set for 2-user system S_j.

Proof.

(1)*Soundness*: For any $j \in [1, l]$, assume that $<d_j^*, f_j^*P> \in K_j$ is generated with a random $s_j \in Z_q$ according to Eq.(5). Then,

$$d_j^* + af_j^* = d_{jw_j} + s_j\Delta_d + a(f_{jw_j} + s_j\Delta_f)$$
$$= (d_{jw_j} + af_{jw_j}) + s_j(\Delta_d + a\Delta_f) = d_{jw_j} + af_{jw_j} = z_j \mod q$$

Given a valid encryption $<A = rP, B = r^2Q, C_j = M_j \oplus \mathcal{H}(Z_j^{r^2})>$ of any message M_j, a pirate decoder embedded with $<d_j^*, f_j^*P>$ will compute

$$v_j^* = \hat{e}(d_j^*A, A) \cdot \hat{e}(f_j^*P, B) = \hat{e}(d_j^*rP, rP) \cdot \hat{e}(f_j^*P, r^2aP)$$
$$= \hat{e}(p, p)^{d_j^*r^2} \cdot \hat{e}(P, P)^{af_j^*r^2} = g^{(d_j^* + af_j^*)r^2} = g^{z_jr^2} = Z_j^{r^2}$$
$$M_j = C_j \oplus \mathcal{H}(v_j^*)$$

Hence, the pirate decoder can decrypt any valid message correctly, *i.e.*, every element in K_j is a valid decrypting key for S_j.

(2)*Completeness*: For any legal key $<d_j, f_jP>$ generated by the authority for 2-user system S_j, according to Eq.(2), $d_j + af_j = z_j \mod q$. Since a and q are co-prime, there are q legal keys in total for each 2-user system S_j. On the other hand, since s_j is randomly selected from Z_q, the number of elements in K_j is also q. Therefore, the traitors can generate the same number of legal keys as the authority.

Moreover, for any d_j, $\exists s_j = (d_j - d_{jw_j})\Delta_d^{-1} \mod q$ such that $d_j^* = d_j$, *i.e.*, the traitors and the authority produce the same legal keys for each 2-user system S_j. $\square$

Obviously, the traitors and the authority produce the same legal keys for the whole multi-user system since all the K_j are constructed independently. We should mention that the traitors do not know f_j^* although they can construct the legal sub-key $<d_j^*, f_j^*P>$.

4.2   Evading Tracing

Given a confiscated pirate decoder, the tracer produces an invalid ciphertext $< t, r_1P, r_2^2Q, C_t, rP, rQ, C_j >$ as Eq. (4) for tracing, $j = 1, 2, \ldots, t-1, t+1, \ldots, l$. Upon receiving the above invalid ciphertext, the decoder calculates

$$v_t^* = \hat{e}(d_t^*A, A) \cdot \hat{e}(f_t^*P, B) = \hat{e}(d_t^*r_1P, r_1P) \cdot \hat{e}(f_t^*P, r_2^2aP)$$
$$= \hat{e}(p, p)^{d_t^*r_1^2} \cdot \hat{e}(P, P)^{af_t^*r_2^2} = g^{(d_t^*r_1^2 + af_t^*r_2^2)}$$
$$= g^{d_{tw_t}r_1^2 + af_{tw_t}r_2^2} \cdot g^{s_t(\Delta_d r_1^2 + \Delta_f r_2^2)}$$
$$m_t^* = C_t \oplus \mathcal{H}(v_t^*)$$

According to Eq.(4), the tracer will set $w_t = $ "?" since he does not know v_t^* due to random number s_t. Consequently, no traitor will be identified.

4.3   Countermeasure

The present attack crucially depends on the shared secret a among all the sub-systems S_j, $j = 1, \ldots, l$. To defeat the attack, all the a_j in S_j is independently selected. We called this upgraded scheme as CPP'. Since the sub-systems S_j' in CPP' are independently, the transmission rate of CPP' is almost 3 and hence it has the same performance as KY scheme. An improvement for managing stateless decoder is to independently build a CPP scheme for broadcasting only and a CPP' scheme for both broadcasting and tracing, then merge them together. Concretely, in the broadcast and/or tracing stage, the provider randomly selects the t-th sub-system S_t' from CPP' and $l - 1$ sub-systems $\{S_1, S_2, \ldots, S_{t-1}, S_{t+1}, \ldots, S_l\}$ from CPP. In this case, the transmission rate is still asymptotically optimal, but the storage of the decoder is doubled.

5   Discussion

In a BETT system, a traitor has a decryption key, and hence she can always obtain the decrypted content and distribute it off line. As a result, BETT is only applicable to protection of on-line content dissemination, assuming that traitors are unwilling to distribute decrypted content in real time due to high bandwidth limitation and legal risk. In practical applications, we should take the following issues into consideration.

5.1   Structured Messages

Decoders are usually designed to process formatted messages which are compliant to international or industrial standards. For example, content sent to VCD decoders follows MPEG format. Thus, messages transmitted in either normal broadcast mode or traitor tracing mode must have clearly specified format or structure. If a pirate decoder decrypts a ciphertext into an unstructured messages, it knows that a tracing is underway and then takes action. For this reason, traitor tracing schemes in [1,2] seem to be impractical since they assume that a pirate decoder is not able to distinguish random data from broadcast content.

5.2   Stateless Assumption

Many traitor tracing schemes assume stateless pirate decoders. However, this stateless assumption seems too restrictive for several reasons.

- Nowadays, memory is getting cheaper. Embedding a few bytes of non-volatile memory, which essentially costs nothing, makes a decoder stateful.
- Most decoders require non-volatile memory to store private data and to keep track of history information. For example, in order to decode MPEG video, a VCD decoder has to store recently decoded pictures in rendering a movie.
- Many authors assume that a traitor tracing scheme for stateless decoders can be converted into a tracing scheme for stateful decoders using the conversion algorithm [5]. Since the conversion algorithm increases the transmission rate substantially, the total transmission rate is far from satisfactory if the tracer attempts to defeat stateful pirate decoders.

If the pirate decoder is stateful by embedding several bytes, a lot of traitor tracing algorithms including [1,2] are in trouble.

5.3   Codeword Length

In KY scheme [1] and CPP scheme [2], the length l of codeword is usually large. Let's evaluate l with the optimal collusion-secure code in [21], where
$$l = 100t^2 \cdot \log(n/\epsilon).$$
Assuming conservative parameters $n = 1000, \epsilon = 0.001, t = 10$, each codeword is of $l = 1.38 \times 10^5$ bits. Clearly, the length of a codeword is very long. The large l has the following disadvantages:

- Each decoder has to store $l = 1.38 \times 10^5$ sub-keys. Since it's very costly to store hundreds of Mega-bytes of sub-keys in a tamper-resistant device, large key size makes the sub-keys easily exposed to traitors.
- On account of all-or-nothing decryption mechanism, for one BETT cipher-text, the decoder in both KY and CPP schemes must perform public-key decryption l times, and it can not render the content until the last decryption is finished. This mechanism incurs a long rendering delay, and requires lots of memory for storing the decrypted content.
- Packet loss or error is almost inevitable during delivery of a BETT ciphertext (up to 10^4 packets assume the plaintext M_j is of 1024 bits). As long as one packet is not received correctly, the decoder can not render the rest. Therefore, large key size adversely affects the quality of service (QoS) of a broacast system.

6   Conclusion

Designed as a black-box traitor tracing scheme with efficient transmission rate, CPP scheme [2] directly encrypts broadcast content with public-key cryptosystems, and identifies at least one traitor with just one invalid ciphertext. Although security properties of CPP scheme is proved in theory, this paper points out that a multi-key attack can foil the CPP traitor tracing algorithm. It also presented an efficient countermeasure to the multi-key attack.

Albeit CPP scheme can be improved to prevent the multi-key attack, it is vulnerable to a more severe forgery attack which is able to thwart even white-box tracing. In the forgery attack, two traitors can collude to forge valid decoder keys. The forged key appears as perfect genuine keys, can decrypt all protected content, but is untraceable by the tracer.

We also discussed several important technical issues in practical broadcast encryption and traitor tracing systems, such as structured messages. Most traitor tracing schemes assume that a pirate decoder can not tell random data from structured content, and require a tracer to send unstructured invalid ciphertexts to the pirate decoder during a tracing process. This assumption is too restrictive since in practice decoders can only interpret formatted data. Thus, an important challenge for future research is to design traitor tracing schemes against format-aware pirate decoders.

References

1. Kiayias, A., Yung, M.: Traitor Tracing with Constant Transmission Rate. In: Knudsen, L.R. (ed.) EUROCRYPT 2002. LNCS, vol. 2332, pp. 450–465. Springer, Heidelberg (2002)
2. Chabanne, H., Phan, D.H., Pointcheval, D.: Public Traceability in Traitor Tracing Schemes. In: Cramer, R.J.F. (ed.) EUROCRYPT 2005. LNCS, vol. 3494, pp. 542–558. Springer, Heidelberg (2005)
3. CASBAA, Pay-TV Piracy on the Rise in Asia: Study, AsiaMedia Media News Dialy (October 24, 2006), http://news.yahoo.com/s/afp/20061024/ennew_afp/asiatvindustrycrime_061024162529
4. Evers, J.: Breaking Through Apple's FairPlay, http://news.com.com/Breaking+through+Apples+FairPlay/2008-1025_3-6129420.html
5. Kiayias, A., Yung, M.: On Crafty Pirates and Foxy Tracers. In: Sander, T. (ed.) DRM 2001. LNCS, vol. 2320, pp. 22–39. Springer, Heidelberg (2002)
6. Kiayias, A., Yung, M.: Self Protecting Pirates and Black-Box Traitor Tracing. In: Kilian, J. (ed.) CRYPTO 2001. LNCS, vol. 2139, pp. 63–79. Springer, Heidelberg (2001)
7. Pfitzmann, B.: Trails of Traced Traitors. In: Anderson, R. (ed.) Information Hiding. LNCS, vol. 1174, pp. 49–64. Springer, Heidelberg (1996)
8. Yan, J.J., Wu, Y.: An Attack on a Traitor Tracing Scheme, http://eprint.iacr.org/2001/067
9. Boneh, D., Franklin, M.: An Efficient Public Key Traitor Tracing Scheme. In: Wiener, M.J. (ed.) CRYPTO 1999. LNCS, vol. 1666, pp. 338–353. Springer, Heidelberg (1999)
10. Chor, B., Fiat, A., Naor, M.: Tracing Traitors. In: Desmedt, Y.G. (ed.) CRYPTO 1994. LNCS, vol. 839, pp. 257–270. Springer, Heidelberg (1994)
11. Chor, B., Fiat, A., Naor, M., Pinkas, B.: Tracing Traitors. IEEE Transactions on Information Theory 46(3), 893–910 (2000)
12. Naor, M., Pinkas, B.: Threshold Traitor Tracing. In: Krawczyk, H. (ed.) CRYPTO 1998. LNCS, vol. 1462, pp. 502–517. Springer, Heidelberg (1998)

13. Phan, D., Safavi-Naini, R., Tonien, D.: Generic Construction of Hybrid Public Key Traitor Tracing with Full-Public-Traceability. In: Bugliesi, M., Preneel, B., Sassone, V., Wegener, I. (eds.) ICALP 2006. LNCS, vol. 4052, pp. 264–275. Springer, Heidelberg (2006)
14. Boneh, D., Sahai, A., Waters, B.: Fully Collusion Resistant Traitor Tracing With Short Ciphertexts and Private Keys. In: Vaudenay, S. (ed.) EUROCRYPT 2006. LNCS, vol. 4004, pp. 573–592. Springer, Heidelberg (2006)
15. Boneh, D., Waters, B.: A Fully Collusion Resistant Broadcast, Trace and Revoke System. In: ACM CCS, pp. 211–220 (2006)
16. Wu, Y., Deng, R.H.: A Multi-Key Pirate Decoder against Traitor Tracing Schemes. Submission to IEEE Transactions on Information Forensics and Security (February 2007)
17. Bao, F., Deng, R., Feng, P., Guo, Y., Wu, H.: Secure and Private Distribution of Online Video and several Related cryptographic Issues. In: Varadharajan, V., Mu, Y. (eds.) ACISP 2001. LNCS, vol. 2119, pp. 190–205. Springer, Heidelberg (2001)
18. Boneh, D., Shaw, J.: Collusion-Secure Fingerprinting for Digital Data. IEEE Trans. on Information Theory 44(5), 1897–1905 (1998)
19. Wu, Y., Bao, F., Deng, R.H.: Attacks to and Improvement of Two Traitor Tracing Schemes. Submission to Eurocrypto 2007 (November 7, 2006)
20. Kiayias, A., Yung, M.: Copyrighting Public-key Functions and Applications to Black-box Traitor Tracing (December 3, 2006) http://eprint.iacr.org/2006/458
21. Tardos, G.: Optimal Probabilistic Fingerprint Codes. STOC, pp. 116–125 (2003)

TCHo: A Hardware-Oriented Trapdoor Cipher

Jean-Philippe Aumasson[1,*], Matthieu Finiasz[2], Willi Meier[1,**],
and Serge Vaudenay[3]

[1] FHNW, Windisch, Switzerland
[2] ENSTA, Paris, France
[3] EPFL, Lausanne, Switzerland
http://lasecwww.epfl.ch/

Abstract. This paper improves the Finiasz-Vaudenay construction of
TCHo, a hardware-oriented public-key cryptosystem, whose security relies on the hardness of finding a low-weight multiple of a given polynomial,
and on the decoding of certain noisy cyclic linear codes. Our improvement
makes it possible to decrypt in polynomial time (instead of exponential
time), to directly prove semantic security (instead of one-wayness), and
to achieve pretty good asymptotic performances. We further build IND-
CCA secure schemes using the KEM/DEM and Fujisaki-Okamoto hybrid
encryption frameworks in the random oracle model. This can encrypt an
arbitrary message with an overhead of about 5 Kb in less than 15 ms, on
an ASIC of about 10 000 gates at 4 MHz.

Keywords: public-key cryptosystem, post-quantum cryptography, hardware, linear feedback shift register, polynomial multiples.

1   Introduction

Since the introduction of public-key cryptography [12,13], dozens of cryptosystems appeared, based on hard problems like integer factorization, discrete logarithms, lattice reduction, knapsacks, *etc.*, in various algebraic structures. But
their non-trivial constructions made their use somewhat difficult in constrained
environments (PDAs, RFID tags, *etc.*), where stream ciphers used to rule. In that
sense, a secure public-key cryptosystem with stream cipher-like design would be
a breakthrough. Furthermore, studying alternate designs for public-key encryption not based on factoring or discrete logarithm is an important duty for the
academic research community to prepare a post-quantum era [25].

In [14], Finiasz and Vaudenay introduced a new public-key cryptosystem
called TCHo, where the public key is a high-degree binary polynomial, and the
private key a sparse multiple of the latter. Security relies on the *ad-hoc* problem
of finding a low-weight multiple of a certain degree. This problem, or its variants, has been important in LFSR cryptanalysis since some attacks are possible

* Supported by the Swiss National Science Foundation under project number 113329.
** Supported by Hasler Foundation http://www.haslerfoundation.ch under project
number 2005.

J. Pieprzyk, H. Ghodosi, and E. Dawson (Eds.): ACISP 2007, LNCS 4586, pp. 184–199, 2007.
© Springer-Verlag Berlin Heidelberg

only when the feedback polynomial or one of its multiples is sparse [24]. A few works [16,18,22] study the distribution of multiples of a given weight.

In this article, TCHo1 designates the original cryptosystem from [14] whereas TCHo2 designates our variant. By default, TCHo refers to TCHo2.

TCHo1 encryption is probabilistic, and can be roughly described as the transmission of a codeword over a noisy channel: one small LFSR encodes the message, while a large one randomly initialized, along with a source of biased random bits, produces the noise. A ciphertext is a XOR of the three bitstreams. The private key is used to "delete" the bitstream of the large LFSR by a kind of convolution product, thereby reducing the noise over the coded message, so as to be able to decode the cyclic linear code spanned by the first LFSR. Although the design of TCHo1 is very simple and well fitted for hardware, some major disadvantages are its prohibitive decryption time complexity, of exponential cost, the absence in [14] of an estimate of incorrect decryption probability, and the lack of asymptotic complexities. In this paper, we

- propose a variant leading us to polynomial decryption time,
- estimate the error probability in decryption,
- study asymptotic parameters,
- prove semantic security of this new scheme, under certain assumptions,
- and suggest two hybrid constructions to reach IND-CCA security.

Finally we present performances of TCHo in a software implementation.

2   Preliminaries

2.1   Notations

The logarithm in base 2 is denoted $\log_2$, and log is the natural logarithm.

A *bitstring* x is a sequence of bits. Its *length* $|x|$ is its number of bits, and may be finite or infinite. Its *Hamming weight*, or simply *weight*, is its number of ones. The concatenation of x and y is $x\|y$. The sum over $\mathbb{F}_2$ is denoted $+$, and the product $\times$. A bitstring x can be written $(x_1, x_2, \ldots, x_n)$, and $(0, \ldots, 0)$ can simply be denoted 0. The sum (also denoted $+$) of two bitstrings of equal length produces a bitstring of same length, and is defined as a bitwise sum. A *bitstream* is a bitstring of unspecified (possibly infinite) length produced by some device or bit source, and shall be denoted by the symbol $\mathcal{S}$ with contextual subscript. The symbol $\mathcal{S}^\ell$ refers to the bitstream $\mathcal{S}$ truncated to its first ℓ bits.

The degree of a polynomial P in $\mathbb{F}_2[X]$ is denoted $\deg(P)$, and its *weight* is its number of non-zero coefficients.

If we speak about *random* bits, or random sequence, *etc.*, it is either uniform or biased randomness, and the distribution is specified only where the meaning can be ambiguous. A random source of independent bits with bias γ produces a zero with probability $\frac{1}{2}(1 + \gamma)$ (and a one with probability $\frac{1}{2}(1 - \gamma)$). The produced bitstream is denoted $\mathcal{S}_\gamma$, and $\mathcal{S}_\gamma(r)$ if we specify the seed r of the generator. $\mathcal{S}_0$ is a uniform random bitstream.

When no probability distribution or space is explicitly set, *randomly chosen* means randomly chosen among all the objects of this kind, with respect to a uniform probability law.

A linear feedback shift register (LFSR) is entirely characterized by its feedback function, defined by a *feedback polynomial* $P = \sum_{i=0}^{\infty} p_i X^i$, the size of the LFSR being the degree of this polynomial. We use the notation $\mathcal{L}_P$ for the LFSR with feedback polynomial P. The bitstream determined by the initial state $s = (s_0, \ldots, s_{\deg(P)-1})$ is denoted $\mathcal{S}_{\mathcal{L}_P(s)} = (s_0, \ldots, s_i, \ldots)$, such that $s_{i+\deg(P)} = \sum_{k=0}^{\deg(P)-1} p_k s_{i+k}$.

We define the product of a binary polynomial $K = \sum_{i=0}^{\infty} k_i X^i$ of degree d and a bitstream $\mathcal{S}^{d+N} = (s_0, \ldots, s_{d+N-1})$ as

$$K \otimes \mathcal{S}^{d+N} = (s'_0, \ldots, s'_{N-1})$$

with $s'_i = s_i k_0 + s_{i+1} k_1 + \cdots + s_{i+d} k_d$. The operator thus defined is distributive over the bitstring sum, it verifies $(PQ) \otimes \mathcal{S} = P \otimes (Q \otimes \mathcal{S})$ and $P \otimes \mathcal{S}_{\mathcal{L}_P(x)} = 0$, for all $P, Q \in \mathbb{F}_2[X]$, $x \in \mathbb{F}_2^{\deg(P)}$, and $\mathcal{S}$. As a consequence, if P divides K, for any ℓ, x, s we have $K \otimes (\mathcal{S}^\ell_{\mathcal{L}_P(x)} + s) = K \otimes s$.

We shall use the acronyms CCA, CPA, IND, OW, respectively standing for the usual notions of Adaptive Chosen Ciphertext Attack, Chosen Plaintext Attack, Indistinguishability, and One-Wayness.

2.2 Computational Problem

Like TCHo1, the main problem on which TCHo relies can be stated as follows:

LOW WEIGHT POLYNOMIAL MULTIPLE (LWPM)
Parameters: Three naturals w, d and d_P, such that $0 < d_P < d$ and $w < d$.
Instance: $P \in \mathbb{F}_2[X]$ of degree d_P.
Question: Find a multiple K of P of degree at most d and weight at most w.

In [14] the authors suggest several strategies to solve this problem (namely birthday paradox [28], syndrome decoding [6,21], and exhaustive search). Inspired from this, we make the following average-case assumption:[1]

Assumption 1. *Let* Gen *be a random generator which generates a random polynomial K of degree d_K and weight w_K until it has an irreducible factor P whose degree d_P is in a given interval $[d_{\min}, d_{\max}]$. The output of* Gen *is P. We assume that $w_K \log_2 \frac{d_K}{d_{\max}} \geq \lambda$. For any d and w such that $\binom{d}{w-1} \leq 2^{d_{\min}}$ and $w \log_2 \frac{d}{d_{\max}} \geq \lambda$, the* LWPM *problem for an instance generated by* Gen *needs at least 2^λ operations to solve.*

More concretely, the best algorithm to find one solution has a complexity within the order of $(d/d_P)^{w-1}$ when the existence of a solution is unexpected and $2^{d_P}(d/d_P)^{w-1}/\binom{d}{w-1}$ when many solutions exist.

---

[1] In [14], P is assumed to be primitive. Here, we only assume that it is irreducible as discussed later.

As a nominal example, we will use $w_K = \Theta(\lambda)$, $d_{\min} = \Theta(\lambda^2)$, $d_{\max} = \Theta(\lambda^2)$, and $d_K = \Theta(\lambda^3)$. The assumption seemingly suggests that the problem needs exponential time (in λ) to solve LWPM with w and d asymptotically equivalent to the parameters of K. Hence, K can be used as a hidden trapdoor.

3   Description of the TCHo Scheme

3.1   Presentation

Just like TCHo1, TCHo uses a polynomial K of degree d_K and weight w_K as a secret key; a polynomial P of degree $d_P \in [d_{\min}, d_{\max}]$ as a public key; it produces ciphertexts of ℓ bits and uses a random source of bias γ. We use in TCHo a new parameter k (which replaces the old d_Q from TCHo1 because it is no longer the degree of a polynomial). It is the length of the plaintext.

TCHo differs from TCHo1 in the coding applied to the plaintext. In TCHo1, a code spanned by an LFSR with an arbitrary primitive polynomial Q was used, leading to an expensive decryption procedure. We can generalize TCHo1 and use an arbitrary code C of dimension k and length ℓ for which an efficient decoding procedure exists, and denote $C(x)$ the codeword of x in C. This code is subject to many constraints and cannot be chosen at random. In the decryption process of TCHo1, the ciphertext is multiplied by K to suppress $\mathcal{S}^\ell_{\mathcal{L}_P}$. In this process, the noise source $\mathcal{S}^\ell_\gamma$ becomes like $\mathcal{S}^{\ell-d_K}_{\gamma^{w_K}}$. In the general case, the multiplication by K being a linear operation, we will have $K \otimes C(x) = \tilde{C}(x)$, where $\tilde{C}$ is a new linear code of dimension k and length $\ell - d_K$. This means that when decrypting a ciphertext, one will have to decode in the modified code $\tilde{C}$. The only case where decoding in $\tilde{C}$ can be efficient for an arbitrary K is when C is a truncated cyclic linear code, that is, C is the output of an LFSR.[2] In that case, as for TCHo1, $K \otimes C(x)$ is equal to $C(x')$ truncated to $\ell - d_K$ bits, where x' is obtained from x exactly as with TCHo1. TCHo is a particular instance of this generalized TCHo1 construction with a repetition code. These codes offer straightforward encoding and decoding algorithms.

Another innovation of TCHo is that the need for P to be primitive is obviated; let n be the order of the polynomial P. In [14] primitivity is required so as not to have $X^n + 1$ as a trivial solution of LWPM, when $n \le \ell$. However, for randomly chosen P, the order n is smaller than ℓ with probability about $\ell/2^{d_P}$, which is close to zero. Hence LWPM may remain as hard when P is a random irreducible polynomial, not necessarily primitive.

Parameters. A security parameter λ defines a parameter vector

$$(k, d_{\min}, d_{\max}, d_K, w_K, \gamma, \ell).$$

Key Generation. We generate a random polynomial K of degree d_K and weight w_K with constant term 1 until it has a primitive factor P of degree d_P belonging to the interval $[d_{\min}, d_{\max}]$. This works just like TCHo1, in time

---

[2] Appendix A provides more discussion on the code selection.

$\mathcal{O}\left(\frac{d_{\max}}{d_{\max}-d_{\min}}d_K^2\log d_K\log\log d_K\right)$ using the Cantor-Zassenhaus algorithm [8] and the probabilistic primitivity test from [14].

Encryption. TCHo encrypts a plaintext x of length k in the following way:

$$\mathsf{TCHo_{enc}}(x, r_1\|r_2) = C(x) + \mathcal{S}^\ell_{\mathcal{L}_P(r_1)} + \mathcal{S}^\ell_\gamma(r_2).$$

The codeword $C(x)$ of a bitstring x of length k is formed of contiguous repetitions of x truncated to ℓ bits, and so the minimum distance of the code is $\lfloor \ell/k \rfloor$. It has length ℓ and the code has dimension k. Complexity is $\mathcal{O}(\ell \cdot d_P)$, provided that the random generator has no higher complexity. The ciphertext length is ℓ. Note that ℓ/k is the expansion factor of the message.

Decryption. Given $y = \mathsf{TCHo_{enc}}(x, r_1\|r_2)$, decryption works as follows:

1. K is used to delete $\mathcal{S}_{\mathcal{L}_P}$ in y:[3]

$$K \otimes y \approx \tilde{C}(x) + \mathcal{S}^{\ell-d_K}_{\gamma^{w_K}}$$

   where $\tilde{C}(x)$ is equal to a truncated codeword $C(x')$, with $x' = f(x)$ for some linear map f. Complexity is $\mathcal{O}(w_K \cdot \ell)$ for this operation only.
2. $K \otimes y$ is decoded to find x'. Decoding is performed using majority logic decoding (MJD), which is equivalent to maximum likelihood decoding for these codes, but runs in time $\mathcal{O}(\ell - d_K)$, instead of $\mathcal{O}(k \cdot 2^k)$. It allows to encrypt larger blocks.
3. $\mathsf{TCHo_{dec}}(y) = f^{-1}(x') = x$ is computed. This operation takes $\mathcal{O}(k^3)$ complexity. Note that the matrix of f^{-1} can be precomputed from K and C.

The overall decryption complexity thus becomes $\mathcal{O}(w_K \cdot \ell + k^3)$.

3.2   Reliability

Here $\tilde{C}$ has minimum distance $\delta = \lfloor (\ell - d_K)/k \rfloor$, but decoding more than $\lfloor (\delta - 1)/2 \rfloor$ errors will of course be possible. The probability of erroneous decoding is exactly the probability that at least one bit is more frequently erroneous than correct, that is (under the heuristic assumption that the correlation in $K \otimes \mathcal{S}^\ell_\gamma$ is similar to the correlation in $\mathcal{S}^{\ell-d_K}_{\gamma^{w_K}}$),

$$\rho \approx 1 - \left(\sum_{i=\lceil \delta/2\rceil}^\delta 2^{-\delta}(1+\gamma^{w_K})^i(1-\gamma^{w_K})^{\delta-i}\binom{\delta}{i}\right)^k. \tag{1}$$

---

[3] Each bit of the word obtained after multiplying by K by $\mathcal{S}^\ell_\gamma$ is the sum of w_K bits with bias γ. Hence they have a bias of γ^{w_K}. However, the noisy bits are correlated, depending on the offsets of the non-zero coefficients of K, but experiment shows that $K \otimes \mathcal{S}^\ell_\gamma$ behaves mostly like $\mathcal{S}^{\ell-d_K}_{\gamma^{w_K}}$. So we write $K \otimes \mathcal{S}^\ell_\gamma \approx \mathcal{S}^{\ell-d_K}_{\gamma^{w_K}}$.

This probability can also be expressed using the central limit theorem (summing k times on the δ bits), and we get

$$\rho \approx k \cdot \varphi \left(-\sqrt{\frac{\gamma^{2w_K}}{1 - \gamma^{2w_K}}} \times \frac{\ell - d_K}{k} \right). \tag{2}$$

where φ is the cumulative distribution function of a normal distribution:

$$\varphi(z) = \frac{1}{\sqrt{2\pi}} \int_{-\infty}^{z} e^{-t^2/2} dt.$$

Table 1. Examples of TCHo parameters vectors

	k	$d_{\min}$–$d_{\max}$	d_K	w_K	γ	$\frac{1}{2}(1 - \gamma^{w_K})$	ℓ	ρ
I_{65}	128	5 800–7 000	25 820	45	0.981	0.289	50 000	$2^{-26.5}$
II_{65}	128	8 500–12 470	24 730	67	0.987	0.292	68 000	$2^{-48.5}$
III	128	3 010–4 433	44 677	25	$1 - \frac{3}{64}$	0.349	90 000	$2^{-22.4}$
IV	128	7 150–8 000	24 500	51	0.98	0.322	56 000	$2^{-22.9}$
V	128	6 000–8 795	17 600	81	$1 - \frac{3}{128}$	0.427	150 000	$2^{-13.0}$
VI	128	9 000–13 200	31 500	65	$1 - \frac{1}{64}$	0.320	100 000	$2^{-54.7}$

3.3 Selecting the Parameters

Table 1 shows some parameters suiting the security constraints for $\lambda = 80$.
Asymptotically, we choose the parameters in terms of λ and k as follows.

$$w_K = \Theta(\lambda) \quad d_K = \Theta(\lambda^2 \cdot k) \quad \ell = \Theta(\lambda^2 \cdot k)$$
$$d_{\min} = \Theta(\lambda^2) \quad d_{\max} = \Theta(\lambda^2) \quad \gamma = 1 - \Theta(\tfrac{1}{\lambda})$$

In addition to this, the plaintext length k must satisfy $k = \mathcal{O}(\lambda)$. We do not provide any fixed relation between k and λ because, depending on the application, we may either want to encrypt a constant-size plaintext (*i.e.* $k = \mathcal{O}(1)$) or a plaintext as long as possible (*i.e.* $k = \Theta(\lambda)$). With those parameters

- key generation takes $\mathcal{O}\left(\lambda^4 \cdot k^2 \cdot \log \lambda \cdot \log \log \lambda\right)$,
- encryption takes $\mathcal{O}\left(\lambda^4 \cdot k\right)$,
- decryption takes $\mathcal{O}\left(\lambda^3 \cdot k\right)$,
- the unreliability is $\rho = \mathcal{O}\left(\frac{k}{\lambda} \cdot 2^{-\lambda^2}\right)$ (heuristically),
- the private key length is $w_K \log_2 d_K = \mathcal{O}(\lambda \log \lambda)$,
- the public key length is $d_P = \mathcal{O}(\lambda^2)$,
- the plaintext length is k,
- the ciphertext length is $\ell = \mathcal{O}(\lambda^2 \cdot k)$.

4   Security

Clearly, TCHo is not OW-CCA secure: given a valid ciphertext, it suffices to modify one bit and ask an oracle to decrypt it to get with high probability the plaintext corresponding to the original ciphertext. Thus it is not IND-CCA secure either. Like RSA, TCHo is malleable, given a single ciphertext: if y is a ciphertext of x, then $y + C(\tilde{x})$ is a valid ciphertext of $x + \tilde{x}$, for any $\tilde{x} \in \{0,1\}^k$. In what follows we study semantic security.

Lemma 2. *There exists a constant ν such that for any λ, t, ε and TCHo parameters, if, for a random P generated by TCHo key generation, $S^\ell_{\mathcal{L}_P} + S^\ell_\gamma$ cannot be distinguished from S^ℓ_0 in time t with an advantage larger than ε, then TCHo encryption is $(t - \nu \cdot \ell, \varepsilon)$-IND-CPA secure.*

On the asymptotic side, letting t be polynomial and ε be exponentially small in terms of λ, we obtain that TCHo is IND-CPA secure.

Proof. We proceed by reduction: let $\mathcal{A}^{\text{ror}} = (\mathcal{A}^{\text{ror}}_1, \mathcal{A}^{\text{ror}}_2)$ be an adversary in a real-or-random game, which, given a chosen plaintext $x = \mathcal{A}^{\text{ror}}_1(1^\lambda)$ and a bitstring z of length ℓ, decides whether z is a ciphertext of x or of an unknown randomly chosen plaintext x'; this adversary returns $\mathcal{A}^{\text{ror}}_2(z) \in \{0,1\}$, and succeeds with an advantage ε, in time t. Since a ciphertext of TCHo consists of some bitstring noised with a random source, the ciphertexts space is equal to $\{0,1\}^\ell$, so there are no trivial instances of the problem, and every element of $\{0,1\}^\ell$ can be a ciphertext of one or several messages.

   We build a distinguisher between $S^\ell_{\mathcal{L}_P} + S^\ell_\gamma$ and S^ℓ_0 in the following way: given an unknown instance $S^\ell_\star$, choose a plaintext $x = \mathcal{A}^{\text{ror}}_1(1^\lambda)$ independently of $S^\ell_\star$, and compute $z = C(x) + S^\ell_\star$, then return $\mathcal{A}^{\text{ror}}_2(z)$. If $S^\ell_\star$ is random, then so is z, otherwise z is a valid ciphertext of x, therefore we got an adversary distinguishing a noised LFSR stream from random with exactly the same advantage than a real-or-random one, in time greater than t. As real-or-random security implies [5] semantic security, TCHo is IND-CPA secure.

   The cost of simulation is $\mathcal{O}(\ell)$ so if $\mathcal{A}^{\text{ror}}$ has complexity $t - \nu \cdot \ell$, for ν large enough, the distinguisher has complexity bounded by t.   □

Let P be a random polynomial of degree $d_P \in [d_{\min}, d_{\max}]$ and weight w_P. In order to determine whether a bitstring is $S^\ell_{\mathcal{L}_P} + S^\ell_\gamma$ or S^ℓ_0, one strategy consists in multiplying the stream by P, and deciding whether the obtained stream has bias γ^{w_P} or not. It is infeasible to distinguish a random source with bias γ^{w_P} from a uniform one as soon as $\gamma^{w_P} < 2^{-\lambda/2}$. Instead of multiplying by P, one can multiply by multiples of P of lower weight and degree less than ℓ and use the obtained bits. For a random P there are on average $\binom{d-1}{w-2} 2^{-d_P}$ multiples of weight w and degree d with non-zero constant term. Hence the total number of bits of bias γ^w one can obtain using all the multiples of weight w is approximately

$$N_w \approx 2^{-d_P} \sum_{d=w-1}^{\ell-1} (\ell - d) \binom{d-1}{w-2} = 2^{-d_P} \binom{\ell}{w}.$$

When there are too many such bits, we must reduce this number. Let N be the number of used bits. We have $N \leq N_w$. If γ^w is small, the advantage of the best distinguisher using N bits is [4] $\mathsf{Adv} \approx \gamma^w \sqrt{N/(2\pi)}$. The complexity of the distinguisher using these N bits can be lower-bounded by the sum of

- wN (we have to calculate all bits),
- the cost of finding at least one multiple of P with degree up to ℓ and weight w, which can be lower bounded by $(\ell/d_P)^{w-1} \times 2^{d_P} / \binom{\ell}{w-1}$ (we use here the lower bound for syndrome decoding from [14]).

By optimizing over the choice of w and N, the best advantage-over-complexity ratio for this strategy is

$$R = \max_{\substack{w \in [0, d_P] \\ N \geq 1}} \frac{\gamma^w / \sqrt{2\pi}}{w\sqrt{N} + \frac{1}{\sqrt{N}} \left(\frac{\ell}{d_P}\right)^{w-1} \times \frac{2^{d_P}}{\binom{\ell}{w}}}.$$

Given the optimal w, the maximum in dependence of N is reached when

$$N = \max\left(1, \left(\frac{\ell}{d_P}\right)^{w-1} \times \frac{2^{d_P}}{w\binom{\ell}{w}}\right).$$

By using the approximation $\binom{\ell}{w} \approx \ell^w / w!$ and the Stirling approximation we can show that for $w \in [0.33 d_P, 1.88 d_P]$ this N is equal to 1. But then, R is bounded by $\gamma^w / w\sqrt{2\pi}$ which is maximal for the smallest w. On the other hand, for $w < 0.33 d_P$ we can show that the R ratio increases with w so the best ratio is for the threshold w such that N decreases to 1. We deduce that $R = \mathcal{O}\left(\gamma^{\Omega(d_{\min})} / d_{\min}\right)$. With our asymptotic parameters, we obtain $R = \exp(-\Omega(\lambda)) / \lambda^2$.

For a more precise bound we shall use

$$R = \max_{\substack{w \in [0, d_{\max}] \\ N \geq 1}} \frac{\gamma^w / \sqrt{2\pi}}{w\sqrt{N} + \frac{1}{\sqrt{N}} \left(\frac{\ell}{d_{\min}}\right)^{w-1} \times \frac{2^{d_{\min}}}{\binom{\ell}{w}}}. \tag{3}$$

Experience shows this is reached for $N = 1$. Intuitively, this means that using a single multiple polynomial which is essentially easy to get is the best strategy because the advantage benefit is not worth working hard on lowering w.

As an example, the parameter vector I_{65} (as well as II_{65}) in Table 1 gives $R \leq 2^{-65}$ for the optimal $w = 1936$ and $N = 1$. (Actually, all other parameter vectors satisfy $R \leq 2^{-80}$.) Note that in the worst case where $d_P = d_{\min}$, "random multiples" of P with degree close to $d_{\min}$ have random weights with expected value $d_{\min}/2 = 2900$ and standard deviation $\sqrt{d_{\min}}/2 = 38$. So, a weight of 1936 is within 25 standard deviations, which is pretty large. With higher degrees, the distance is more important. As our computation assumes that getting a bit of bias γ^w is easy, our analysis may still be pessimistic. So, those parameters may be more secure than what this $R \leq 2^{-65}$ bound suggests.

Assumption 3. *Suppose $d_{\min} \geq 2\lambda$ and $\gamma \leq 2^{1-\lambda/d_{\min}} - 1$ and the conditions of Assumption 1 are met. Then, for any ℓ, on average over P generated by* Gen *as defined in Assumption 1, a distinguisher between $S_{\mathcal{L}_P}^\ell + S_\gamma^\ell$ and S_0^ℓ has an advantage/complexity ratio lower than R as defined by Eq. (3).*

This leads to the following result.

Theorem 4. *Under Assumptions 1 and 3, there exists ν such that for any λ and t and any* TCHo *parameters satisfying the conditions in Assumptions 1 and 3,* TCHo *is $(t - \nu \cdot \ell, R \cdot t)$-IND-CPA secure.*

Security Level Assessment. The above parameters provide semantic security against adversaries with an advantage/complexity ratio upper bounded by R as given by Eq. (3). More precisely, to compare this with a security level of an exhaustive key search for an s-bit key, we should set $R = 2^{-s}$ in Eq. (3). Asymptotically, we have $s = \Theta(\lambda)$. For the parameter vectors I_{65} and II_{65} we have $s \geq 65$. For all others we have $s \geq 80$.

5   Construction of an **IND-CCA** Secure Scheme

We propose a generic hybrid construction by using the (revisited) Fujisaki-Okamoto paradigm based on tag-KEM [1,2,15]. The encryption scheme obtained offers IND-CCA security when the public encryption scheme is OW-CPA and Γ-uniform, and the symmetric cipher one-time secure. For instance, one can simply choose $\mathsf{Sym}_{\mathsf{enc}(\psi)}(x) = x + F(\psi)$ for some random oracle F. The construction requires two random oracles H and G. The IND-CPA security of TCHo implies OW-CPA security, and the proof of Γ-uniformity of TCHo1 [14] applies to TCHo as well. So the following hybrid encryption scheme is IND-CCA secure.

Encryption. Given a message x:

1. Choose a random σ uniformly in $\{0,1\}^k$
2. Compute the symmetric key: $\psi \leftarrow G(\sigma)$
3. Encrypt the message x: $y \leftarrow \mathsf{Sym}_{\mathsf{enc}(\psi)}(x)$
4. Encapsulate the key: $\chi \leftarrow \mathsf{TCHo}_{\mathsf{enc}}(\sigma, H(\sigma||y))$
5. Output the ciphertext (χ, y).

Decryption. Given a ciphertext (χ, y):

1. Compute the encapsulated key: $\psi \leftarrow G(\mathsf{TCHo}_{\mathsf{dec}}(\chi))$
2. Decrypt the message: $x \leftarrow \mathsf{Sym}_{\mathsf{dec}(\psi)}(y)$
3. Output the plaintext x.

Table 1 shows examples of parameters for a symmetric encryption key of typical length 128 bits. So the construction encrypts a message with an overhead of ℓ bits (the length of a ciphertext in TCHo).

6   Implementation of TCHo

TCHo was implemented in C++, using the NTL library [26] for arithmetic over $\mathbb{F}_2[X]$, including GCD and factorization algorithms. All performances were measured on 1.5 GHz Pentium 4 computer.

6.1   Choice of Parameters

Here we summarize the inequalities that must hold to get IND-CPA and $2^{\Theta(\lambda)}$ security, deduced from Assumptions 1 and 3, when using block repetition codes.

- To correctly decrypt, ρ, given by Eq. (2), must be small.
- K must be impossible to recover from P:

$$\binom{d_K}{w_K-1} \leq 2^{d_{\min}} \text{ and } w_K \log_2 \frac{d_K}{d_{\max}} \geq \lambda.$$

- Semantic security is assumed to hold when

$$d_{\min} \geq 2\lambda, \gamma \leq 2^{1-\lambda/d_{\min}} - 1 \text{ and } R \leq 2^{-\lambda},$$

where R is given by Eq. (3).

In practice, one may fix a block size k, a security level λ, and a ciphertext length ℓ, then deduce the degree and weight of K, an interval for the degree of a public key P, and a bias γ for the pseudo-random bits. But there is no strict rule to choose parameters $(k, d_{\min}, d_{\max}, d_K, w_K, \gamma, \ell)$, indeed TCHo is very flexible, and one may adapt them to its requirements, e.g. by allowing an average failure probability so as to reduce the expansion, or by setting a high degree d for the private key K and a high expansion in order to get a negligible error probability ρ, at the price of a very long key generation. Experiments in Section 6.3 will give concrete examples of these trade-offs.

6.2   Chosen Algorithms

Our LFSR implementation uses a variant of the block-oriented algorithm introduced in [9,10]. In software, LFSR's are slower than in hardware; for a random polynomial of degree 6 000, our implementation could only reach a rate of 150 Kb/s. The number of bitwise operations required to compute a bitstream of length ℓ is roughly $\frac{1}{16}\ell d_P$. Our generator for $\mathcal{S}_\gamma$ uses a source of uniform pseudo-random bits to produce blocks of n bits in two steps:

1. pick a weight $q \in [0, n]$ (with suitable probability distribution),
2. pick a word of weight q (uniformly).

The first step is accomplished by partitioning the interval $[0, 1] \subset \mathbb{Q}$ into n intervals with respect to the weight distribution induced by the bias, and then picking a random, uniform rational number in this interval with high enough precision. For blocks of 32 bits and precision 2^{-64}, the statistical distance to the ideal generator is negligible. The pseudo-random generator ISAAC [19] is used as a source of random bits[4]. Compared to the LFSR, our generator is quite efficient: more than 28 Mb of biased random bits are produced per second.

6.3   Software Implementation Results

Table 2 shows performances for the repetition codes scenarios described in Table 1. Encryption time is roughly equal to the time needed to compute $\mathcal{S}^{\ell}_{\mathcal{L}_P(r_1)}$ (in all scenarios $\mathcal{S}^{\ell}_{\gamma}$ is computed in less than 1 ms), while for decryption the most expensive operation is the multiplication by K (majority decoding and product by the precomputed matrix require less than 1 ms).

Table 2. Performances of TCHo with repetition codes

	enc. (ms)	dec. (ms)	kgen. (s)	unreliability	sec. key (bit)	pub. key (bit)	plaintext (bit)	ciphertext (bit)
I_{65}	38.7	47.4	1 180	$2^{-26.5}$	455	7 000	128	50 000
II_{65}	148.0	115.4	361	$2^{-48.5}$	507	12 470	128	68 000
III	75.5	49.0	2 290	$2^{-22.4}$	281	4 433	128	90 000
IV	90.1	65.1	1 970	$2^{-22.9}$	506	8 000	128	56 000
V	228.4	423.7	200	$2^{-13.0}$	726	8 795	128	150 000
VI	232.5	178.7	870	$2^{-54.7}$	652	13 200	128	100 000

Using precomputed look-up tables could speed up encryption: given a P, we can compute a table of $d_P \times \ell$ bits, containing the bitstreams produced by each initial state of $\mathcal{L}_P$ of weight 1. Computing such a table takes less than a second using optimized algorithms, then the generation of a bitstream requires roughly $\frac{\ell}{32} \times \frac{d_P}{2}$ XOR operations (in our implementation, with a 32 bits processor). Experimentally the time gain is not significant, since memory access takes a non-negligible time (about 70 megabytes are precomputed for common parameters).

Results in Table 2 show that a trade-off must be made between key generation time, encryption and decryption time, ciphertext expansion, and reliability. The parameter sets proposed all tend to optimize one of these points while keeping the others at a reasonable level. Depending on the application, users should choose one set or an other.

- I_{65}: Fast encryption/decryption for low security requirements of 2^{65}.
- II_{65}: Well balanced parameters for low security requirements.
- III: Fast encryption/decryption. This also implies smaller key sizes.
- IV: Smaller message expansion and reasonably fast encryption/decryption.
- V: "Fast" key generation.
- VI: Negligible unreliability is reached.

---

[4] Some weaknesses on ISAAC were reported in [3]. So the question whether ISAAC is still appropriate for our design is left open.

One can note that, even though it is possible to improve them a little, the ciphertext expansion and the key generation time will always remain very high. Concerning ciphertext expansion it is possible to improve it significantly by encrypting larger blocks. For a standard 128 bit key exchange, it seems impossible to go below blocks of 50 000 bits (for a security of 2^{80} operations), but if more data needs to be exchanged, using larger blocks (while adjusting ℓ so as to keep the same unreliability) can decrease expansion to a factor of about 100.

In contrast, not much can be done concerning the prohibitive key generation time. Given the values of $d_{\min}$ and w_K, while keeping the security constant, it is possible to choose optimal values for $d_{\max}$ and d_K. These values will always correspond to $d_{\max} \approx 1.5 \, d_{\min}$ (it would be an equality if factorization was done in quadratic time). However, factoring a polynomial of degree over 20 000 is a costly operation which is difficult to speed-up.

6.4 Hardware Implementation

Encryption requires the computation of ℓ bits from a large LFSR, as many bits with bias γ, and the repetition of the plaintext $\lfloor \ell/k \rfloor$ times. Let's examine those three operations.

- LFSR's can be very fast in integrated circuits: the number of gates required is roughly equal to the length of the register, and it outputs one bit per clock cycle. We assume that the over-cost induced by our large registers does not dramatically slow down the computation, and remains feasible in spite of the unusual size.
- To compute the non-uniform random bitstream, one may use a specially tuned generator fed with physical entropy; otherwise, a solution is to use an algorithm producing non-uniform random sequence from a uniform one. For instance, to generate words of given length, one may use a binary search tree (precomputed) where each leaf is labeled with a word, and go through the tree by successive coin flips in order to simulate the bias. Such a construction roughly requires as many uniform bits as biased bits produced (in comparison, our software generator needs about three uniform bits to compute a biased one).
- Repetition of a word is straightforward.

Note that, since the operations are independent, parallelization is possible.

Decryption looks more complicated to implement, but it only consists of linear operations over $\mathbb{F}_2$, usually easily implemented. For instance, there exists [29] a library for FPGA devices performing matrix-vector product and dot product efficiently (note that the product $K \otimes S$ is simply a sequence of dot products). It also requires a small amount of additional memory to perform the majority decoding (namely $k \log_2 \frac{\ell - d_K}{k}$ bits to count the number of occurrences of each bit of $\tilde{m}$).

It thus appears that TCHo's encryption and decryption only need hardware-friendly operations (no integer multiplication or addition, no modular arithmetic). However, the implementation should be flexible, so as to be adaptable to any public key – that is, tune the LFSR taps. Unfortunately, we could not implement TCHo in a hardware environment, but we can estimate requirements and performances: looking at the parameters in Table 1, a 128-bit key can be encrypted with a circuit of about 10 000 gates (for the LFSR and the repetition), with an external source of randomness. With an ASIC running at 4 MHz (0.25 μs cycle time), we roughly estimate encryption time to 15 ms. The power consumption is estimated to be of at most 20-100μW, which is suitable for RFID.

7   Comparison with Other Cryptosystems

The security of TCHo relies mostly on results from coding theory and it is thus tempting to compare it to the famous code based cryptosystem of McEliece [23]. The two cryptosystems function in a similar way: first the message is encoded using a public code, then some random noise is added to it. However, the two constructions are quite different in the way noise is added: in McEliece's cryptosystem, a small amount of completely random noise is added to the codeword, whereas in TCHo a huge amount of structured noise is added. In TCHo, this noise should even be indistinguishable from an unbiased random binary sequence: decoding is only possible because this noise has a hidden structure. In McEliece, it is the code which contains a hidden structure which make decoding possible.

To measure the efficiency of TCHo, we need to compare both the timing we obtained for practical parameters and the asymptotic complexities of TCHo with those of other ciphers. For practical comparisons we used the benchmark feature of the `Crypto++` library [11] running on the same 1.5 GHz Pentium 4 as our tests. We then use RSA 1024/2048 as a reference for comparison with other systems. Results are presented in Table 3. The key generation time of TCHo is of course way higher than for any other public key cryptosystem, however, encryption and decryption speed are close to those of RSA or elliptic curve cryptosystems [20]. NTRU [17] is however much faster. Anyway, we believe that for a hardware oriented cryptosystem these performances are not bad.

From an asymptotic point of view, things are a little different. We need to compare parameters yielding an equivalent asymptotic security of 2^λ. For RSA this means that we use a modulus of size $\mathcal{O}\left(\lambda^3\right)$ and for EC a group of order

Table 3. Comparison of TCHo with other public-key cryptosystems

	security	enc. (ms)	dec. (ms)	kgen. (s)	sk/pk (bit)	pt (bit)	ct (bit)
TCHo I_{65}	2^{65}	38.7	47.4	1 180	455/7 000	128	50 000
TCHo IV	2^{80}	90.1	65.1	1 970	506/8 000	128	56 000
RSA 1024	2^{72}	0.4	12.8	0.3	2 048/1 024	1 024	1 024
RSA 2048	2^{102}	1.0	75.0	1.8	4 096/2 048	2 048	2 048
EC on $GF(2^{163})$	2^{78}	16.9	10.2	–	160/326	160	326
NTRU `ees251ep4`	2^{80}	~ 0.1	~ 0.2	~ 0.003	502/2 008	251	2 008

Table 4. Asymptotic comparison of TCHo with other cryptosystems (the $\mathcal{O}$ ()'s have been omitted)

	security	enc.	dec.	kgen.	sk/pk	pt	ct
TCHo	2^λ	λ^5	λ^4	$\lambda^6 \cdot \log\lambda \cdot \log\log\lambda$	$\lambda \cdot \log\lambda / \lambda^2$	λ	λ^3
RSA	2^λ	λ^6	λ^9	λ^{12}	λ^3 / λ^3	λ^3	λ^3
EC	2^λ	λ^3	λ^3	λ^3	λ / λ	λ	λ
NTRU	2^λ	λ^2	λ^2	λ^2	λ / λ	λ	λ
McEliece	2^λ	λ^2	$\lambda^2 \cdot \log\lambda$	λ^3	λ^2 / λ^2	λ	λ

$2^{\mathcal{O}(\lambda)}$. For NTRU, the asymptotic complexity is not explicitly known, but it is assumed that a length of $\mathcal{O}(\lambda)$ can achieve a security of 2^λ. The results obtained are reported in Table 4, where we also added the McEliece cryptosystem[5] [23]. It appears that TCHo is better than RSA on all points, including the key generation complexity. However, some alternate public-key cryptosystems remain better asymptotically.

8   Conclusion

Our TCHo cryptosystem is much more efficient than TCHo1: encryption and decryption algorithms are faster, larger blocks can be encrypted, a precise estimate of the decryption failure probability can be given, and experimental results are much better than for TCHo1. Meanwhile, TCHo performs pretty well asymptotically. It is semantically secure, which makes it possible to use it to build an IND-CCA secure hybrid encryption scheme using the KEM/DEM framework. However, it inherits some undesirable properties of the original scheme: first the key generation is still heavy and the expansion rate remains huge.

As TCHo seems well suited for tiny hardware we may consider using it for ensuring strong privacy in RFID as suggested in [27].

Finally, as TCHo security only relies on heuristic assumptions, further work could be devoted to giving concrete elements of proof or attack.

References

1. Abe, M., Gennaro, R., Kurosawa, K.: Tag-KEM/DEM: A new framework for hybrid encryption. IACR ePrint archive 2005/027 (2005) Available at http://eprint.iacr.org/2005/027 Newer version in [2]
2. Abe, M., Gennaro, R., Kurosawa, K., Shoup, V.: Tag-KEM/DEM: A new framework for hybrid encryption and a new analysis of Kurosawa-Desmedt KEM. In: Cramer, R.J.F. (ed.) EUROCRYPT 2005. LNCS, vol. 3494, pp. 128–146. Springer, Heidelberg (2005) Older version in [1]

---

[5] We could not find any practical timings to include in Table 3. For asymptotic behavior we use a code of length 2^m correcting t errors, with $t = \mathcal{O}(\frac{\lambda}{\log\lambda})$ and $m = \mathcal{O}(\log t + \log\log t)$.

3. Aumasson, J.-P.: On the pseudo-random generator ISAAC. IACR ePrint archive 2006/438 (2006). Available at http://eprint.iacr.org/2006/438

4. Baignères, T., Junod, P., Vaudenay, S.: How far can we go beyond linear cryptanalysis? In: Lee, P.J. (ed.) ASIACRYPT 2004. LNCS, vol. 3329, pp. 432–450. Springer, Heidelberg (2004)

5. Bellare, M., Desai, A., Jokipii, E., Rogaway, P.: A concrete security treatment of symmetric encryption. In: Proceedings of the 38th Annual Symposium on Foundations of Computer Science (FOCS'97), p. 394. IEEE Computer Society, Los Alamitos (1997)

6. Canteaut, A., Chabaud, F.: A new algorithm for finding minimum-weight words in a linear code: Application to McEliece's cryptosystem and to narrow-sense BCH codes of length 511. IEEE Transactions on Information Theory 44(1), 367–378 (1998)

7. Canteaut, A., Trabbia, M.: Improved fast correlation attacks using parity check equations of weight 4 and 5. In: Preneel, B. (ed.) EUROCRYPT 2000. LNCS, vol. 1807, pp. 573–588. Springer, Heidelberg (2000)

8. Cantor, D.G., Zassenhaus, H.: A new algorithm for factoring polynomials over finite fields. Mathematics of Computation 36(154), 587–592 (1981)

9. Chowdhury, S., Maitra, S.: Efficient software implementation of linear feedback shift registers. In: Pandu Rangan, C., Ding, C. (eds.) INDOCRYPT 2001. LNCS, vol. 2247, pp. 297–307. Springer, Heidelberg (2001)

10. Chowdhury, S., Maitra, S.: Efficient software implementation of LFSR and boolean function and its application in nonlinear combiner model. In: Zhou, J., Yung, M., Han, Y. (eds.) ACNS 2003. LNCS, vol. 2846, pp. 387–402. Springer, Heidelberg (2003)

11. Dai, W.: Crypto++ library. http://www.eskimo.com/~weidai/

12. Diffie, W., Hellman, M.E.: New directions in cryptography. IEEE Transactions on Information Theory 22(6), 644–654 (1976)

13. Ellis, J.H.: The possibility of secure non-secret digital encryption. GCHQ-CESG publication (1970)

14. Finiasz, M., Vaudenay, S.: When stream cipher analysis meets public-key cryptography (invited talk). In: the Proceedings of SAC 2006, Lecture Notes in Computer Science (to appear)

15. Fujisaki, E., Okamoto, T.: Secure integration of asymmetric and symmetric encryption schemes. In: Wiener, M.J. (ed.) CRYPTO 1999. LNCS, vol. 1666, pp. 537–554. Springer, Heidelberg (1999)

16. Gupta, K.C., Maitra, S.: Multiples of primitive polynomials over GF(2). In: Pandu Rangan, C., Ding, C. (eds.) INDOCRYPT 2001. LNCS, vol. 2247, pp. 62–72. Springer, Heidelberg (2001)

17. Hoffstein, J., Pipher, J., Silverman, J.H.: NTRU: A ring-based public key cryptosystem. In: Buhler, J.P. (ed.) Algorithmic Number Theory. LNCS, vol. 1423, pp. 267–288. Springer, Heidelberg (1998)

18. Jambunathan, K.: On choice of connection-polynominals for LFSR-based stream ciphers. In: Roy, B., Okamoto, E. (eds.) INDOCRYPT 2000. LNCS, vol. 1977, pp. 9–18. Springer, Heidelberg (2000)

19. Jenkins Jr., R.J.: ISAAC. In: Gollmann, D. (ed.) Fast Software Encryption. LNCS, vol. 1039, pp. 41–49. Springer, Heidelberg (1996)

20. Koblitz, N.: Elliptic curve cryptosystems. Mathematics of Computation 48(177), 203–209 (1987)

21. Lee, P.J., Brickell, E.F.: An observation on the security of McEliece's public-key cryptosystem. In: Günther, C.G. (ed.) EUROCRYPT 1988. LNCS, vol. 330, pp. 275–280. Springer, Heidelberg (1988)

22. Maitra, S., Gupta, K.C., Venkateswarlu, A.: Results on multiples of primitive polynomials and their products over GF(2). Theoretical Computer Science 341(1-3), 311–343 (2005)

23. McEliece, R.J.: A public-key cryptosystem based on algebraic coding theory. DSN Prog. Rep. Jet Prop. Lab. California Inst. Technol. Pasadena, CA, pp. 114–116 (January 1978)

24. Meier, W., Staffelbach, O.: Fast correlation attacks on stream ciphers. In: Günther, C.G. (ed.) EUROCRYPT 1988. LNCS, vol. 330, pp. 301–314. Springer, Heidelberg (1988)

25. Shor, P.W.: Polynomial-time algorithms for prime factorization and discrete logarithms on a quantum computer. SIAM Journal on Computing 26(5), 1484–1509 (1997)

26. Shoup, V.: NTL: A library for doing number theory. http://shoup.net/ntl/

27. Vaudenay, S.: RFID privacy based on public-key cryptography (invited talk). In: Rhee, M.S., Lee, B. (eds.) ICISC 2006. LNCS, vol. 4296, pp. 1–6. Springer, Heidelberg (2006)

28. Wagner, D.: A generalized birthday problem. In: Yung, M. (ed.) CRYPTO 2002. LNCS, vol. 2442, pp. 288–304. Springer, Heidelberg (2002)

29. Zhuo, L., Prasanna, V.K.: High performance linear algebra operations on reconfigurable systems. In: Gschwind, T., Aßmann, U., Nierstrasz, O. (eds.) SC 2005. LNCS, vol. 3628, Springer, Heidelberg (2005)

A   On the Choice of the Code

TCHo1 uses a code C generated by $\mathcal{L}_Q^\ell$ with a primitive polynomial Q of degree k. The drawback of this code is that decoding requires $\mathcal{O}\left(k2^k\right)$.

Note that if Q is a trinomial, decoding algorithms more efficient than MLD exist; the Algorithm B in [24] or Gallager decoding as used, *e.g.*, in [7] for fast correlation attacks can be applied. The success probability of these algorithms depends on the weight of the feedback polynomial of the LFSR, the bias γ^{w_K}, and the ratio between the length of known output and the size of the LFSR for which the initial state is searched for. Again, concerning the reliability of these iterative algorithms, only experimental results seem to be available. For trinomials it can be seen from Table 3 in [24] that, for example, correct decoding is expected if the known output has length 100 times the LFSR-length, and $\frac{1}{2}(1 + \gamma^{w_K})$ is 0.6 or larger.

We rather use block repetition codes which is equivalent to setting $Q = X^k + 1$ in TCHo1 although this would be illegal in TCHo1 since $X^k + 1$ is not primitive.

Anonymity on Paillier's Trap-Door Permutation

Ryotaro Hayashi[1,*] and Keisuke Tanaka[2]

[1] TOSHIBA Corporation
1 Komukai Toshiba-cho, Saiwai-ku, Kawasaki-shi, Kanagawa 212-8582, Japan
[2] Dept. of Mathematical and Computing Sciences, Tokyo Institute of Technology
W8-55, 2-12-1 Ookayama, Meguro-ku, Tokyo 152-8552, Japan
keisuke@is.titech.ac.jp

Abstract. It is said that an encryption scheme provides anonymity when it is infeasible for the adversary to determine under which key the ciphertext was created. (i.e. the receiver of the ciphertext is anonymous from the point of view of the adversary.) From the previous results, we can find four techniques, repeating, expanding, RSACD, and sampling twice, for achieving the anonymity property of the encryption schemes based on RSA.

In this paper, we focus on the four techniques described above in the case using Paillier's bijective function instead of the RSA function. We slightly modify his function and construct a family of Paillier's trap-door permutations, and a family of Paillier's trap-door permutations with a common domain. We also apply our proposed families of Paillier's trap-door permutations to encryption with the above four techniques, and prove their security.

Keywords: Paillier's function, Paillier's trap-door permutation, key-privacy, anonymity, encryption.

1 Introduction

1.1 Background

It is said that an encryption scheme provides anonymity when it is infeasible for the adversary to determine under which key the ciphertext was created. (i.e. the receiver of the ciphertext is anonymous from the point of view of the adversary.) Similarly, it is said that a signature scheme provides anonymity when it is infeasible to determine which user generated the signature. A simple observation that seems to be folklore is that standard RSA encryption, namely, a ciphertext is $x^e \bmod N$ where x is a plaintext and (N, e) is a public key, does not provide anonymity, even when all moduli in the system have the same length. Suppose an adversary knows that the ciphertext y is created under one of two keys (N_0, e_0) or (N_1, e_1), and suppose $N_0 \leq N_1$. If $y \geq N_0$ then the adversary bets it was created under (N_1, e_1), else the adversary bets it was created under (N_0, e_0). It

---

* Work done while at the Dept. of Mathematical and Computing Sciences, Tokyo Institute of Technology.

J. Pieprzyk, H. Ghodosi, and E. Dawson (Eds.): ACISP 2007, LNCS 4586, pp. 200–214, 2007.

is not hard to see that this attack has non-negligible advantage. To construct the schemes with anonymity, it is necessary that the space of ciphertexts is common to each user. We can say the same thing about RSA-based signature schemes.

From the previous results, we can find four techniques, repeating, expanding, RSACD, and sampling twice, for achieving the anonymity property of cryptosystems based on RSA.

Repeating. Repeating the evaluation of the encryption (respectively the signing) with plaintext x (resp. message m), random r, and the RSA function, each time using different r until the resulting value is smaller than any public key N of each user. In [1], Bellare, Boldyreva, Desai, and Pointcheval used this technique for the encryption scheme.

Expanding. Doing the evaluation of the encryption (respectively the signing) with plaintext x (resp. message m), random r, and the RSA function, and expanding it to the common domain. This technique was proposed by Desmedt [4]. In [6], Galbraith and Mao used this technique for the undeniable signature scheme. In [12], Rivest, Shamir, and Tauman also used this technique for the ring signature scheme.

RSACD. Doing the evaluation of the encryption (respectively the signing) with plaintext x (resp. message m), random r, and the RSACD (RSA with a Common Domain) function. For any N where $|N| = k$, the domain and the range of the RSACD function with N are $[0, 2^k)$. This function was proposed by Hayashi, Okamoto, and Tanaka [7].

Sampling Twice. Doing the evaluation of the encryption (respectively the signing) twice with plaintext x (resp. message m), random r_1 and r_2, and the RSA function, and applying the algorithm `ChooseAndShift` for the two resulting values. Then, the output of this algorithm is uniformly distributed over $[0, 2^k)$ for any $|N| = k$. This technique was proposed by Hayashi and Tanaka [8].

The RSA-based anonymous encryption schemes with the above four techniques were proposed, and these schemes are variants of RSA-OAEP (Bellare and Rogaway [2], Fujisaki, Okamoto, Pointcheval, and Stern [5]). Bellare, Boldyreva, Desai, and Pointcheval [1] proposed the scheme with the repeating technique, which is called RSA-RAEP. Hayashi, Okamoto, and Tanaka [7] constructed the scheme with the RSACD function. Hayashi and Tanaka [8] proposed the scheme by using the sampling twice technique. In [8], they also mentioned the scheme with the expanding technique for comparison, and they proved the security of the scheme in [10].

In the security proofs, the anonymity (and the indistinguishability) of the scheme with repeating [1], that with expanding [8,10], and that with sampling twice [8] are reduced directly to the θ-partial one-wayness of the RSA function. (Roughly speaking, given a function f and an element $y = f(x)$, it is hard to compute a θ fraction of the most significant bits of x.) Since the θ-partial one-wayness of RSA is equivalent to the one-wayness of RSA for $\theta > 0.5$ (Fujisaki, Okamoto, Pointcheval, and Stern [5]), the schemes with repeating, expanding, and sampling twice are secure assuming that RSA is one-way.

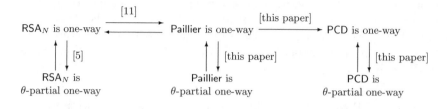

Fig. 1. Relationships between RSA_N, Paillier, and PCD for $\theta > 0.5$

In contrast, in the security proof, the anonymity (and the indistinguishability) of the scheme with RSACD is reduced directly to the θ-partial one-wayness of the RSACD function. Hayashi, Okamoto, and Tanaka [7] showed that the θ-partial one-wayness of RSACD is reduced to the one-wayness of RSA for $\theta > 0.5$. Therefore, the scheme with RSACD is secure assuming that RSA is one-way.

1.2 Our Contribution

In [11], Paillier provided a trap-door one-way bijective function, and proved that the function is one-way if and only if the problem of extracting N-th roots modulo N is hard.

In this paper, we focus on the four techniques described above in the case using Paillier's bijective function instead of the RSA function. We slightly modify his function and construct a family of Paillier's trap-door permutations denoted by Paillier. We also construct a family of Paillier's trap-door permutations with a common domain denoted by PCD, and prove the relations in Figure 1 for $\theta > 0.5$. Here, RSA_N denotes an RSA family of trap-door permutations with the fixed exponent N.

We prove that the one-wayness of Paillier is reduced to that of PCD. In [7], Hayashi, Okamoto, and Tanaka proved that the one-wayness of RSA is reduced to that of RSACD. Our proof is similar to theirs. However, we cannot prove the partial one-wayness of Paillier by directly applying a similar argument for that of RSA in [5]. Furthermore, although the construction of PCD is similar to that of RSACD, we cannot prove the partial one-wayness of PCD by directly applying a similar argument for that of RSACD in [7].

We also apply Paillier and PCD to encryption, and obtain Paillier-OAEP (OAEP with Paillier's trap-door permutation) with repeating, that with expanding, that with sampling twice, and PCD-OAEP (OAEP with Paillier's trap-door permutation with a common domain). We prove that the anonymity and the indistinguishability of Paillier-OAEP with repeating, that with expanding, and that with sampling twice can be reduced directly to the θ-partial one-wayness of Paillier. We also prove that the anonymity and the indistinguishability of PCD-OAEP is reduced directly to the θ-partial one-wayness of PCD. From the relations in Figure 1, our proposed schemes provide the anonymity and the indistinguishability assuming that RSA_N is one-way.

The organization of this paper is as follows. In Section 2, we review some definitions. In Section 3, after reviewing Paillier's bijective function [11], we propose a family of Paillier's trap-door permutations denoted by Paillier and a family of Paillier's trap-door permutations with a common domain denoted by PCD. We also show the relationships between Paillier, PCD, and RSA_N. In Section 4, we propose applications of Paillier and PCD to encryption and prove that our schemes provide the anonymity and the indistinguishability in the random oracle model assuming that RSA_N is one-way.

Due to lack of space, all of the proofs have been omitted from this paper. See the full version.

2   Preliminaries

In this section, we review some definitions.

First, we describe the definitions of families of functions, families of trap-door permutations, and θ-partial one-wayness. We employ the definitions described in [1].

Definition 1 (families of functions, families of trap-door permutations).
A family of functions $F = (K, S, E)$ is specified by three algorithms.

- *The randomized key-generation algorithm K takes as input a security parameter k and returns a pair (pk, sk) where pk is a public key and sk is an associated secret key (In cases where the family is not trap-door, the secret key is simply the empty string.).*
- *The randomized sampling algorithm S takes pk and returns a random point in a set that we call the domain of the function and denote by $\mathrm{Dom}_F(pk)$.*
- *The deterministic evaluation algorithm E takes pk and $x \in \mathrm{Dom}_F(pk)$ and returns an output we denote by $E_{pk}(x)$. We let $\mathrm{Rng}_F(pk) = \{E_{pk}(x) \mid x \in \mathrm{Dom}_F(pk)\}$ denote the range of the function.*

We say that F is a family of trap-door permutations if $\mathrm{Dom}_F(pk) = \mathrm{Rng}_F(pk)$, E_{pk} is a bijection on this set, and there exists a deterministic inversion algorithm I that takes sk and $y \in \mathrm{Rng}_F(pk)$ and returns $x \in \mathrm{Dom}_F(pk)$ such that $E_{pk}(x) = y$.

Definition 2 (θ-partial one-wayness). *Let $F = (K, S, E)$ be a family of functions. Let $b \in \{0, 1\}$ and $k \in \mathbb{N}$. Let $0 < \theta \leq 1$ be a constant. Let A be an adversary. We consider the following experiments:*

$$\text{Experiment } \mathbf{Exp}_{F,A}^{\theta\text{-pow-fnc}}(k)$$
$$(pk, sk) \leftarrow K(k); \ x \xleftarrow{R} \mathrm{Dom}_F(pk); \ y \leftarrow E_{pk}(x)$$
$$x_1 \leftarrow A(pk, y) \text{ where } |x_1| = \lceil \theta \cdot |x| \rceil$$
$$\text{if } \big(E_{pk}(x_1 \| x_2) = y \text{ for some } x_2\big) \text{ return } 1 \text{ else return } 0$$

We define the advantages of the adversary via

$$\mathbf{Adv}_{F,A}^{\theta\text{-pow-fnc}}(k) = \Pr[\mathbf{Exp}_{F,A}^{\theta\text{-pow-fnc}}(k) = 1].$$

We say that the family F is θ-partial one-way if the function $\mathbf{Adv}_{F,A}^{\theta\text{-pow-fnc}}(\cdot)$ is negligible for any adversary A whose running time is polynomial in k.

Note that when $\theta = 1$ the notion of θ-partial one-wayness coincides with the standard notion of one-wayness. We say that the family F is one-way when F is 1-partial one-way.

Next, we describe the RSA family of trap-door permutations with the fixed exponent N denoted by RSA_N. In [11], Paillier provided the trap-door one-way bijective function whose one-wayness is equivalent to that of RSA_N.

Definition 3 (the RSA family of trap-door permutations with the fixed exponent N). *The RSA family $\mathsf{RSA}_N = (K, S, E)$ of trap-door permutations with the fixed exponent N is as follows. The key generation algorithm K takes a security parameter k and picks random, distinct primes p, q such that $2^{\lceil k/2 \rceil - 1} < p, q < 2^{\lceil k/2 \rceil}$ and $|p^2 q^2| = 2k$. It sets $N = pq$ (i.e. $2^{2k-1} < N^2 < 2^{2k}$.) and $\lambda = \lambda(N) = \mathrm{lcm}(p-1, q-1)$. It returns a public key $pk = (N, k)$ and a secret key $sk = (N, k, \lambda)$. $\mathrm{Dom}_{\mathsf{RSA}_N}(N, k)$ and $\mathrm{Rng}_{\mathsf{RSA}_N}(N, k)$ are both equal to $\mathbb{Z}_N^*$. The sampling algorithm returns a random point in $\mathbb{Z}_N^*$. The evaluation algorithm $E_{N,k}(x) = x^N \bmod N$ and the inversion algorithm $I_{N,k,\lambda}(y) = y^{N^{-1} \bmod \lambda} \bmod N$.*

3 A Family of Paillier's Trap-Door Permutations and That with a Common Domain

In this section, we propose a family of Paillier's trap-door permutations and that with a common domain.

3.1 Paillier's Bijective Functions

In [11], Paillier provided the bijective function $g_N : \{x_1 + x_2 \cdot N | x_1 \in \mathbb{Z}_N, x_2 \in \mathbb{Z}_N^*\} \to \mathbb{Z}_{N^2}^*$. The public key and the secret key are those for RSA_N, respectively. The function g_N is defined as $g_N(x) = (1 + N x_1) x_2^N \bmod N^2$ where $x_1 = x \bmod N$ and $x_2 = x \ \mathrm{div} \ N$. By using the trap-door $\lambda = \mathrm{lcm}(p-1, q-1)$, we can invert g_N by computing $g_N^{-1}(y) = x_1 + x_2 \cdot N$, where $x_1 \leftarrow \frac{L(y^\lambda \bmod N^2)}{\lambda} \bmod N$, $x_2 \leftarrow (y \cdot (1 - N x_1))^{N^{-1} \bmod \lambda} \bmod N$, and $L(u) = (u-1)/N$. He proved the following proposition.

Proposition 1 ([11]). *The family of Paillier's bijective functions is one-way if and only if RSA_N is one-way.*

3.2 A Family of Paillier's Trap-Door Permutations

In this section, we propose a family of Paillier's trap-door permutations denoted by Paillier and prove that the θ-partial one-wayness of Paillier is equivalent to the one-wayness of Paillier for $\theta > 0.5$.

The domain and the range of Paillier's bijective function are different. In order to construct a *permutation* based on Paillier's bijective function, we consider a function $h_N : \mathbb{Z}_{N^2}^* \to \{x_1 + x_2 \cdot N | x_1 \in \mathbb{Z}_N, x_2 \in \mathbb{Z}_N^*\}$ such that $h_N(x) = (x \text{ div } N) + (x \bmod N) \cdot N$. It is clear that h_N is bijective and $h_N^{-1}(y) = (y \text{ div } N) + (y \bmod N) \cdot N$. Therefore, $h_N \circ g_N$ is a trap-door permutation over $\{x_1 + x_2 \cdot N | x_1 \in \mathbb{Z}_N, x_2 \in \mathbb{Z}_N^*\}$.

We now propose a family of Paillier's trap-door permutations denoted by Paillier.

Definition 4 (the family of Paillier's trap-door permutations). *The specifications of the family of Paillier's trap-door permutations* Paillier $= (K, S, E)$ *are as follows. The key generation algorithm K takes as input a security parameter k, runs the key generation algorithm for* RSA$_N$, *and returns a public key $pk = (N, k)$ and a secret key $sk = (N, k, \lambda)$.* Dom$_{\mathsf{Paillier}}(N, k)$ *and* Rng$_{\mathsf{Paillier}}(N, k)$ *are both equal to $\{x_1 + x_2 \cdot N | x_1 \in \mathbb{Z}_N, x_2 \in \mathbb{Z}_N^*\}$. The sampling algorithm returns a random point in* Dom$_{\mathsf{Paillier}}(N, k)$. *The evaluation algorithm $E_{N,k}(x) = F_N^{\mathsf{P}}(x)$, and the inversion algorithm $I_{N,k,\lambda}(y) = G_{N,\lambda}^{\mathsf{P}}(y)$ are as follows. Note that $F_N^{\mathsf{P}} = h_N \circ g_N$ and $G_{N,\lambda}^{\mathsf{P}} = g_N^{-1} \circ h_N^{-1}$.*

Function $F_N^{\mathsf{P}}(x)$
$x_1 \leftarrow x \bmod N; \quad x_2 \leftarrow x \text{ div } N$
$Y \leftarrow (1 + Nx_1)x_2^N \bmod N^2$
$y_1 \leftarrow Y \text{ div } N; \quad y_2 \leftarrow Y \bmod N$
$y \leftarrow y_1 + y_2 \cdot N$
return y

Function $G_{N,\lambda}^{\mathsf{P}}(y)$
$y_1 \leftarrow y \bmod N; \quad y_2 \leftarrow y \text{ div } N$
$Y \leftarrow y_1 \cdot N + y_2$
$x_1 \leftarrow \frac{L(Y^\lambda \bmod N^2)}{\lambda} \bmod N$
$x_2 \leftarrow (Y \cdot (1 - Nx_1))^{N^{-1} \bmod \lambda} \bmod N$
$x \leftarrow x_1 + x_2 \cdot N$
return x

From Proposition 1, we can easily see the following lemma.

Lemma 1. Paillier *is one-way if and only if* RSA$_N$ *is one-way.*

We can prove the following theorem. Note that we cannot prove the following theorem by directly applying a similar argument for RSA in [5].

Theorem 1. *The θ-partial one-wayness of* Paillier *is equivalent to the one-wayness of* Paillier *for $\theta > 0.5$.*

Fujisaki, Okamoto, Pointcheval, and Stern [5] showed that the θ-partial one-wayness of RSA is equivalent to the one-wayness of RSA for $\theta > 0.5$. In their reduction, they assume the θ-partial inverting algorithm A for RSA with advantage ϵ, and construct the inverting algorithm B for RSA by running A twice. Then, the success probability of B is approximately $\sqrt{\epsilon}$. Furthermore, their reduction can be extended to the case that θ is a constant fraction less than 0.5. That is, B runs A $1/\theta$ times, and the success probability decreases to approximately $\epsilon^{1/\theta}$.

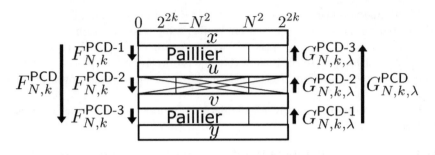

Fig. 2. The functions $F_{N,k}^{\mathsf{PCD}}$ and $G_{N,k,\lambda}^{\mathsf{PCD}}$

Our reduction for Paillier is tighter than that for RSA in [5] with respect to both the success probability and the running time. However, our reduction cannot be extended to the case that θ is a constant fraction less than 0.5.

3.3   A Family of Paillier's Trap-Door Permutations with a Common Domain

In this section, we construct a family of Paillier's trap-door permutations with a common domain denoted by PCD and prove that the θ-partial one-wayness of PCD is equivalent to the one-wayness of Paillier for $\theta > 0.5$.

The construction of PCD. The construction of PCD is similar to that of RSACD in [7].

Definition 5 (the family of Paillier's trap-door permutations with a common domain). *The family of Paillier's trap-door permutations with a common domain* $\mathsf{PCD} = (K, S, E)$ *is as follows. The key generation algorithm is the same as that of Paillier.* $\mathrm{Dom}_{\mathsf{PCD}}(N, k)$ *and* $\mathrm{Rng}_{\mathsf{PCD}}(N, k)$ *are both equal to* $\{x_1 + x_2 \cdot N | (x_1 + x_2 \cdot N) \in [0, 2^{2k}),\ x_1 \in \mathbb{Z}_N,\ (x_2 \bmod N) \in \mathbb{Z}_N^*\}$. *The sampling algorithm returns a random point in* $\mathrm{Dom}_{\mathsf{PCD}}(N, k)$. *The evaluation algorithm* $E_{N,k}(x) = F_{N,k}^{\mathsf{PCD}}(x)$, *and the inversion algorithm* $I_{N,k,\lambda}(y) = G_{N,k,\lambda}^{\mathsf{PCD}}(y)$ *are as follows. (See also Figure 2.)*

Function $F_{N,k}^{\mathsf{PCD}}(x)$	Function $F_{N,k}^{\mathsf{PCD}\text{-}1}(x)$
$\quad u \leftarrow F_{N,k}^{\mathsf{PCD}\text{-}1}(x);\ v \leftarrow F_{N,k}^{\mathsf{PCD}\text{-}2}(u)$	$\quad$ if $(x < N^2)\ u \leftarrow F_N^{\mathsf{P}}(x)$
$\quad y \leftarrow F_{N,k}^{\mathsf{PCD}\text{-}3}(v)$	$\quad$ else $u \leftarrow x$
$\quad$ return y	$\quad$ return u
Function $F_{N,k}^{\mathsf{PCD}\text{-}2}(u)$	Function $F_{N,k}^{\mathsf{PCD}\text{-}3}(v)$
$\quad$ if $(u < 2^{2k} - N^2)\ v \leftarrow u + N^2$	$\quad$ if $(v < N^2)\ y \leftarrow F_N^{\mathsf{P}}(v)$
$\quad$ elseif $(2^{2k} - N^2 \le u < N^2)\ v \leftarrow u$	$\quad$ else $y \leftarrow v$
$\quad$ else $v \leftarrow u - N^2$	$\quad$ return y
$\quad$ return v	

Function $G_{N,k,\lambda}^{\mathrm{PCD}}(y)$ $\quad v \leftarrow G_{N,k,\lambda}^{\mathrm{PCD\text{-}1}}(y); \ u \leftarrow G_{N,k,\lambda}^{\mathrm{PCD\text{-}2}}(v)$ $\quad x \leftarrow G_{N,k,\lambda}^{\mathrm{PCD\text{-}3}}(u)$ $\quad$ return x	Function $G_{N,k,\lambda}^{\mathrm{PCD\text{-}1}}(y)$ $\quad$ if $(y < N^2) \ v \leftarrow G_{N,\lambda}^{\mathrm{P}}(y)$ else $v \leftarrow y$ $\quad$ return v
Function $G_{N,k,\lambda}^{\mathrm{PCD\text{-}2}}(v)$ $\quad$ if $(v < 2^{2k} - N^2) \ u \leftarrow v + N^2$ $\quad$ elseif $(2^{2k} - N^2 \leq v < N^2) \ u \leftarrow v$ $\quad$ else $u \leftarrow v - N^2$ $\quad$ return u	Function $G_{N,k,\lambda}^{\mathrm{PCD\text{-}3}}(u)$ $\quad$ if $(u < N^2) \ x \leftarrow G_{N,\lambda}^{\mathrm{P}}(u)$ $\quad$ else $x \leftarrow u$ $\quad$ return x

The choice of N^2 from $(2^{2k-1}, 2^{2k})$ ensures that all elements in $\mathrm{Dom}_{\mathsf{PCD}}(N, k)$ are permuted by F_N^P at least once. Since F_N^P is a permutation over $\mathrm{Dom}_{\mathsf{Paillier}}(N, k)$, both $F_{N,k}^{\mathsf{PCD\text{-}1}}$ and $F_{N,k}^{\mathsf{PCD\text{-}3}}$ are permutations over $\mathrm{Dom}_{\mathsf{PCD}}(N, k)$. Since it is clear that $F_{N,k}^{\mathsf{PCD\text{-}2}}$ is a permutation over $\mathrm{Dom}_{\mathsf{PCD}}(N, k)$, we have that $F_{N,k}^{\mathsf{PCD}}$ is a permutation over $\mathrm{Dom}_{\mathsf{PCD}}(N, k)$.

The Properties of PCD. We show the θ-partial one-wayness of PCD is equivalent to the one-wayness of PCD for $\theta > 0.5$, and that the one-wayness of PCD is equivalent to the one-wayness of Paillier.

We can prove the following theorem. Note that we cannot prove this by directly applying a similar argument for that of RSACD in [7].

Theorem 2. *The θ-partial one-wayness of* PCD *is equivalent to the one-wayness of* PCD *for $\theta > 0.5$.*

We can prove the following theorem in a similar way as that of the relationship between RSA and RSACD in [7].

Theorem 3. *If* Paillier *is one-way then* PCD *is one-way.*

Fujisaki, Okamoto, Pointcheval, and Stern [5] proved that the one-wayness of RSA_N is equivalent to the θ-partial one-wayness of RSA_N for $\theta > 0.5$. Therefore, the relations in Figure 1 are satisfied for $\theta > 0.5$.

4 Applications to Public-Key Encryption with Anonymity

4.1 Anonymity for Public-Key Encryption

The classical security requirements of public-key encryption schemes, for example the indistinguishability under the adaptive chosen-ciphertext attack (IND-CCA2), provide privacy of the encryption data. In [1], Bellare, Boldyreva, Desai, and Pointcheval proposed a new security requirement of encryption schemes called "key-privacy" or "anonymity." It asks that the encryption provides (in addition to privacy of the data being encrypted) privacy of the key under which the encryption was performed. They formalized the property of "anonymity" as IK-CPA and IK-CCA (IK means "indistinguishability of keys.").

In a heterogeneous public-key environment, encryption will probably fail to be anonymous for trivial reasons. For example, different users might be using different cryptosystems, or, if the same cryptosystem, have keys of different lengths. In [1], a public-key encryption scheme with common-key generation is described as follows.

Definition 6. *A public-key encryption scheme with common-key generation* $\mathcal{PE} = (\mathcal{G}, \mathcal{K}, \mathcal{E}, \mathcal{D})$ *consists of four algorithms.*

- *The common-key generation algorithm $\mathcal{G}$ takes as input some security parameter k and returns some common key I.*
- *The key generation algorithm $\mathcal{K}$ is a randomized algorithm that takes as input the common key I and returns a pair (pk, sk) of keys, the public key and a matching secret key.*
- *The encryption algorithm $\mathcal{E}$ is a randomized algorithm that takes the public key pk and a plaintext x to return a ciphertext y.*
- *The decryption algorithm $\mathcal{D}$ is a deterministic algorithm that takes the secret key sk and a ciphertext y to return the corresponding plaintext x or a special symbol $\perp$ to indicate that the ciphertext was invalid.*

We describe their definition of IK-CCA (the indistinguishability of keys against the adaptive chosen-ciphertext attack).

Definition 7 (IK-CCA [1]). *Let $\mathcal{PE} = (\mathcal{G}, \mathcal{K}, \mathcal{E}, \mathcal{D})$ be an encryption scheme. Let $b \in \{0, 1\}$ and $k \in \mathbb{N}$. Let $A = (A_1, A_2)$ be the adversary which runs in two stages and has access to the oracles $\mathcal{D}_{sk_0}(\cdot)$ and $\mathcal{D}_{sk_1}(\cdot)$. Note that si is the state information. By using this, A_1 passes some information, for example pk_0, pk_1, to A_2. We consider the following experiment. Note that in this experiment A_2 cannot ask the challenge ciphertext y to either $\mathcal{D}_{sk_0}(\cdot)$ or $\mathcal{D}_{sk_1}(\cdot)$.*

$$\textbf{Experiment } \mathbf{Exp}_{\mathcal{PE},A}^{\text{ik-cca-}b}(k)$$
$$I \leftarrow \mathcal{G}(k); \ (pk_0, sk_0), (pk_1, sk_1) \leftarrow \mathcal{K}(I)$$
$$(m, \mathsf{si}) \leftarrow A_1(pk_0, pk_1); \ y \leftarrow \mathcal{E}_{pk_b}(m); \ d \leftarrow A_2(y, \mathsf{si}); \ \textbf{return } d$$

The scheme $\mathcal{PE}$ is said to be IK-CCA secure if the advantage defined by

$$\mathbf{Adv}_{\mathcal{PE},A}^{\text{ik-cca}}(k) = \left| \Pr[\mathbf{Exp}_{\mathcal{PE},A}^{\text{ik-cca-}1}(k) = 1] - \Pr[\mathbf{Exp}_{\mathcal{PE},A}^{\text{ik-cca-}0}(k) = 1] \right|$$

is negligible for any polynomial-time adversary A.

In the following, we propose encryption schemes with anonymity by using Paillier, PCD, and the four techniques described in Section 1.

4.2 Our Proposed Schemes

In this section, we propose Paillier-OAEP with repeating, that with expanding, that with sampling twice, and PCD-OAEP.

Definition 8 (Paillier-OAEP with repeating). *Paillier-OAEP* $\mathcal{PE} = (\mathcal{G}, \mathcal{K}, \mathcal{E}, \mathcal{D})$ *with repeating is as follows. The common-key generation algorithm* $\mathcal{G}$ *takes a security parameter* k *and returns parameters* k, k_0, *and* k_1 *such that* $k_0 + k_1 < 2k$ *for all* $k > 1$. *This defines an associated plaintext-length function* $n = 2k - k_0 - k_1$. *The key generation algorithm* $\mathcal{K}$ *takes* k, k_0, k_1, *runs the key-generation algorithm of* Paillier, *and gets* N, k, λ. *The public key pk is* N, k, k_0, k_1 *and the secret key sk is* $(N, \lambda), k, k_0, k_1$. *The other algorithms are depicted below. Let* $G : \{0,1\}^{k_0} \to \{0,1\}^{n+k_1}$ *and* $H : \{0,1\}^{n+k_1} \to \{0,1\}^{k_0}$ *be hash functions. Note that* $[x]^{\ell}$ *denotes the* ℓ *most significant bits of* x *and* $[x]_{\ell}$ *denotes the* ℓ *least significant bits of* x.

```
Algorithm E_pk(x)                    Algorithm D_sk(y)
  ctr ← −1                             b ← [y]¹;  v ← [y]_{k_0+k_1+n}
  repeat                               if (b = 1)
    ctr ← ctr + 1;  r ← {0,1}^{k_0}      w ← [v]^{k_0+k_1};  x ← [v]_n
    u ← OAEP(x,r);  v ← F^P_N(u)         if (w = 0^{k_0+k_1}) z ← x else z ←⊥
  until((v < 2^{2k−1}) ∨ (ctr = k_1))  else
  if (ctr = k_1) y ← 1||0^{k_0+k_1}||x   u ← G^P_{N,λ}(v);  z ← OAEP^{−1}(u)
  else y ← 0||v                        return z
  return y
```

where

```
Algorithm OAEP(x;r)      Algorithm OAEP^{−1}(u)
  s ← (x||0^{k_1}) ⊕ G(r)   s ← [u]^{n+k_1};  t ← [u]_{k_0};  r ← t ⊕ H(s)
  t ← r ⊕ H(s)             x ← [s ⊕ G(r)]^n;  p ← [s ⊕ G(r)]_{k_1}
  return s||t              if (p = 0^{k_1}) z ← x else z ←⊥;  return z
```

Definition 9 (Paillier-OAEP with expanding). *Paillier-OAEP* $\mathcal{PE} = (\mathcal{G}, \mathcal{K}, \mathcal{E}, \mathcal{D})$ *with expanding is as follows. The common-key generation algorithm* $\mathcal{G}$, *the key generation algorithm* $\mathcal{K}$, *and the hash functions* G, H *are the same as those of Paillier-OAEP with repeating. The other algorithms are depicted below. Note that the valid ciphertext* y *satisfies* $y \in [0, 2^{2k+160})$ *and* $(y \bmod N^2) \in \mathrm{Rng}_{\mathsf{Paillier}}(N, k)$.

```
Algorithm E_pk(x)                              Algorithm D_sk(y)
  r ← {0,1}^{k_0};  u ← OAEP(x,r);  v ← F^P_N(u)   v ← y mod N²
  α ←^R {0,1,2,⋯,⌊(2^{2k+160} − v)/N²⌋}           u ← G^P_{N,λ}(v)
  y ← v + αN²                                      z ← OAEP^{−1}(u)
  return y                                         return z
```

Definition 10 (PCD-OAEP). *PCD-OAEP* $\mathcal{PE} = (\mathcal{G}, \mathcal{K}, \mathcal{E}, \mathcal{D})$ *is as follows. The common-key generation algorithm* $\mathcal{G}$, *the key generation algorithm* $\mathcal{K}$, *and the hash functions* G, H *are the same as those of Paillier-OAEP with repeating.*

	Repeating	Expanding	PCD	Sampling Twice
# of mod. exp. to encrypt (average / worst)	$1.5 / k_1$	$1 / 1$	$1.5 / 2$	$2 / 2$
# of mod. exp. to decrypt (average / worst)	$1 / 1$	$1 / 1$	$1.5 / 2$	$1 / 1$
size of ciphertexts	$2k + 1$	$2k + 160$	$2k$	$2k$
# of random bits to encrypt (average / worst)	$1.5k_0 / k_1 k_0$	$k_0 + 160$ / $k_0 + 160$	k_0 / k_0	$2k_0 + 2k + 3$ / $2k_0 + 2k + 3$

Fig. 3. The costs of the encryption schemes

The other algorithms are depicted below. Note that the valid ciphertext y satisfies $y \in \mathrm{Rng}_{\mathsf{PCD}}(N, k)$.

Algorithm $\mathcal{E}_{pk}(m)$
  $r \overset{R}{\leftarrow} \{0,1\}^{k_0}$; $u \leftarrow \mathsf{OAEP}(x, r)$
  $y \leftarrow F^{\mathsf{PCD}}_{N,k}(u)$; return y

Algorithm $\mathcal{D}_{sk}(y)$
  $u \leftarrow G^{\mathsf{PCD}}_{N,k,\lambda}(y)$; $z \leftarrow \mathsf{OAEP}^{-1}(u)$
  return z

Definition 11 (Paillier-OAEP with sampling twice). *Paillier-OAEP $\mathcal{PE} = (\mathcal{G}, \mathcal{K}, \mathcal{E}, \mathcal{D})$ with sampling twice is as follows. The common-key generation algorithm $\mathcal{G}$, the key generation algorithm $\mathcal{K}$, and the hash functions G, H are the same as those of Paillier-OAEP with repeating. The other algorithms are depicted below. Note that the valid ciphertext y satisfies $y \in [0, 2^{2k})$ and $(y \bmod N^2) \in \mathrm{Rng}_{\mathsf{Paillier}}(N, k)$.*

Algorithm $\mathcal{E}_{pk}(x)$
  $r_1 \leftarrow \{0,1\}^{k_0}$; $u_1 \leftarrow \mathsf{OAEP}(x, r_1)$; $v_1 \leftarrow F^{\mathsf{P}}_N(u_1)$
  $r_2 \leftarrow \{0,1\}^{k_0}$; $u_2 \leftarrow \mathsf{OAEP}(x, r_2)$; $v_2 \leftarrow F^{\mathsf{P}}_N(u_2)$
  $y \leftarrow \mathsf{ChooseAndShift}_{N^2, 2k}(v_1, v_2)$
  return y

Algorithm $\mathcal{D}_{sk}(y)$
  $v \leftarrow y \bmod N^2$
  $u \leftarrow G^{\mathsf{P}}_{N,\lambda}(v)$
  $z \leftarrow \mathsf{OAEP}^{-1}(u)$
  return z

where

Algorithm $\mathsf{ChooseAndShift}_{N,k}(x_1, x_2)$

  if $(0 \le x_1, x_2 < 2^k - N)$ return $\begin{cases} x_1 & \text{with probability } \frac{1}{2} \\ x_1 + N & \text{with probability } \frac{1}{2} \end{cases}$
  elseif $(2^k - N \le x_1, x_2 < N)$ return x_1
  else
    $y_1 \leftarrow \min\{x_1, x_2\}$; $y_2 \leftarrow \max\{x_1, x_2\}$
    return $\begin{cases} y_1 & \text{with probability } (\frac{1}{2} + \frac{N}{2^{k+1}}) \times \frac{1}{2} \\ y_1 + N^2 & \text{with probability } (\frac{1}{2} + \frac{N}{2^{k+1}}) \times \frac{1}{2} \\ y_2 & \text{with probability } \frac{1}{2} - \frac{N}{2^{k+1}} \end{cases}$

We show the costs of our schemes in Figure 3. We show the number of modular exponentiations to encrypt, the number of modular exponentiations to decrypt, the size of ciphertexts, and the number of random bits to encrypt. We assume that N is uniformly distributed in $(2^{2k-1}, 2^{2k})$.

4.3   Security

PCD-OAEP. Fujisaki, Okamoto, Pointcheval, and Stern [5] proved OAEP with any partial one-way permutation is secure in the sense of IND-CCA2 in the random oracle model. Thus, PCD-OAEP is secure in the sense of IND-CCA2 in the random oracle model assuming PCD is partial one-way.

We can also prove PCD-OAEP is secure in the sense of IK-CCA in the random oracle model assuming PCD is partial one-way. More precisely, we can prove the following lemma.

Lemma 2. *For any adversary A attacking the anonymity of PCD-OAEP $\mathcal{PE}$ under the adaptive chosen ciphertext attack, and making at most q_{dec} decryption oracle queries, q_{gen} G-oracle queries, and q_{hash} H-oracle queries, there exists a θ-partial inverting adversary B for the PCD family, such that for any k, k_0, k_1, and $\theta = \frac{2k-k_0}{2k}$,*

$$\mathbf{Adv}_{\mathcal{PE},A}^{\text{ik-cca}}(k) \leq 8q_{\text{hash}}((1-\epsilon_1)(1-\epsilon_2))^{-1} \cdot \mathbf{Adv}_{\text{PCD},B}^{\theta\text{-pow-fnc}}(k) + q_{\text{gen}} \cdot (1-\epsilon_2)^{-1} \cdot 2^{-k+2}$$

where $\epsilon_1 = \frac{4}{2^{k/2-3}-1}, \epsilon_2 = \frac{2q_{\text{gen}}+q_{\text{dec}}+2q_{\text{gen}}q_{\text{dec}}}{2^{k_0}} + \frac{2q_{\text{dec}}}{2^{k_1}} + \frac{2q_{\text{hash}}}{2^{2k-k_0}}$, and the running time of B is that of A plus $q_{\text{gen}} \cdot q_{\text{hash}} \cdot O(k^3)$.

Since if RSA_N is one-way then PCD is θ-partial one-way for $\theta > 0.5$ (See Figure 1.), PCD-OAEP is secure in the sense of IND-CCA2 and IK-CCA in the random oracle model assuming RSA_N is one-way.

Paillier-OAEP with Repeating. Fujisaki, Okamoto, Pointcheval, and Stern [5] proved OAEP with any partial one-way permutation is secure in the sense of IND-CCA2 in the random oracle model. Thus, Paillier-OAEP (OAEP with Paillier's trap-door permutation) is secure in the sense of IND-CCA2 in the random oracle model assuming Paillier is partial one-way.

We can prove that if Paillier-OAEP provides the indistinguishability then that with repeating also provides the indistinguishability. More precisely, if there exists a CCA2-adversary $A = (A_1, A_2)$ attacking the indistinguishability of Paillier-OAEP with repeating with advantage ϵ, then there exists a CCA2-adversary $B = (B_1, B_2)$ attacking the indistinguishability of Paillier-OAEP with advantage $\epsilon/2$. We construct B as follows.

1. B_1 gets pk and passes it to A_1. B_1 gets (m_0, m_1, si) which is an output of A_1, and B_1 outputs it.
2. B_2 gets a challenge ciphertext y. If $y \geq 2^{2k-1}$ then B_2 outputs Fail and halts; otherwise B_2 passes (y', si) to A_2 where $y' \leftarrow 0||y$. B_2 gets $d \in \{0,1\}$ which is an output of A_2, and B_2 outputs it.

If B does not output Fail, A outputs correctly with advantage ϵ. Since $\Pr[B$ outputs Fail$] < 1/2$, the advantage of B is greater than $\epsilon/2$.

Furthermore, we can prove that Paillier-OAEP with repeating is secure in the sense of IK-CCA in the random oracle model assuming Paillier is partial one-way. Noticing that the functions $F_{N,k}^{\text{PCD}}$ and $G_{N,k,\lambda}^{\text{PCD}}$ are replaced by F_N^{P} and $G_{N,\lambda}^{\text{P}}$, respectively, and the domain of valid ciphertexts changes, we can prove the following lemma in a similar way as that for PCD-OAEP.

Lemma 3. *For any adversary A attacking the anonymity of Paillier-OAEP $\mathcal{PE}$ with repeating under the adaptive chosen ciphertext attack, and making at most q_{dec} decryption oracle queries, q_{gen} G-oracle queries, and q_{hash} H-oracle queries, there exists a θ-partial inverting adversary B for the* Paillier *family, such that for any k, k_0, k_1, and $\theta = \frac{2k - k_0}{2k}$,*

$$\mathbf{Adv}_{\mathcal{PE},A}^{\text{ik-cca}}(k) \le 16 q_{\text{hash}}((1-\epsilon_1)(1-\epsilon_2))^{-1} \cdot \mathbf{Adv}_{\text{Paillier},B}^{\theta\text{-pow-fnc}}(k) + q_{\text{gen}} \cdot (1-\epsilon_2)^{-1} \cdot 2^{-k+2}$$

where $\epsilon_1 = \frac{1}{2^{k/2-3}-1}, \epsilon_2 = \frac{2q_{\text{gen}} + q_{\text{dec}} + 2q_{\text{gen}}q_{\text{dec}}}{2^{k_0}} + \frac{2q_{\text{dec}}}{2^{k_1}} + \frac{2q_{\text{hash}}}{2^{2k-k_0}}$, and the running time of B is that of A plus $q_{\text{gen}} \cdot q_{\text{hash}} \cdot O(k^3)$.

Since the θ-partial one-wayness of Paillier is equivalent to the one-wayness of RSA_N for $\theta > 0.5$, Paillier-OAEP with repeating is secure in the sense of IND-CCA2 and IK-CCA in the random oracle model assuming RSA_N is one-way.

Paillier-OAEP with Sampling Twice. In order to prove that Paillier-OAEP with sampling twice is secure in the sense of IND-CCA2, we need the restriction as follows.

Since if c is a ciphertext of m for $pk = (N, k)$ and $c < 2^{2k} - N^2$ then $c + N^2$ is also a ciphertext of m. Thus, the adversary can ask $c + N^2$ to decryption oracle $\mathcal{D}_{sk}$ where c is a challenge ciphertext such that $c < 2^{2k} - N^2$ and $pk = (N, k)$, and if the answer of $\mathcal{D}_{sk}$ is m, then the adversary knows that c is a ciphertext of m for the key pk.

To prevent this attack, we add some natural restriction to the adversary in the definition of IND-CCA2. That is, in the definition of IND-CCA2, it is mandated that the adversary never queries D_{sk} on $(c \bmod N^2) + \gamma N^2$ where $\gamma \in \lfloor (2^{2k} - (c \bmod N^2))/N^2 \rfloor$.

We think this restriction is natural and reasonable. Actually, in the case of undeniable and confirmer signature schemes, Galbraith and Mao [6] defined the anonymity on undeniable signature schemes with the above restriction. Hayashi and Tanaka [8,9,10] also proved the anonymity of their schemes with the above restriction.

If we add this restriction then we can prove that Paillier-OAEP with sampling twice is secure in the sense of IND-CCA2 in the random oracle model assuming Paillier is partial one-way. Noticing that the domain of valid ciphertexts changes, we can prove this in a similar way as that for Paillier-OAEP with repeating.

Similarly, in order to prove that Paillier-OAEP with sampling twice is secure in the sense of IK-CCA, we need the same kind of restriction. That is, it is mandated that the adversary never queries D_{sk_0} on $(c \bmod N_0^2) + \beta_0 N_0^2$ where $\beta_0 \in \lfloor (2^{2k} - (c \bmod N_0^2))/N_0^2 \rfloor$, and D_{sk_1} on $(c \bmod N_1^2) + \beta_1 N_1^2$ where $\beta_1 \in \lfloor (2^{2k} - (c \bmod N_1^2))/N_1^2 \rfloor$.

If we add this restriction then we can prove that Paillier-OAEP with sampling twice is secure in the sense of IK-CCA in the random oracle model assuming Paillier is partial one-way. More precisely, we can prove the following lemma, and the proof is similar to that for PCD-OAEP.

Lemma 4. *For any adversary A attacking the anonymity of Paillier-OAEP $\mathcal{PE}$ with sampling twice under the adaptive chosen ciphertext attack, and making at most q_{dec} decryption oracle queries, q_{gen} G-oracle queries, and q_{hash} H-oracle queries, there exists a θ-partial inverting adversary B for the* Paillier *family, such that for any k, k_0, k_1, and $\theta = \frac{2k-k_0}{2k}$,*

$$\mathbf{Adv}_{\mathcal{PE},A}^{\text{ik-cca}}(k) \leq 16 q_{hash}((1-\epsilon_1)(1-\epsilon_2))^{-1} \cdot \mathbf{Adv}_{\text{Paillier},B}^{\theta\text{-pow-fnc}}(k) + q_{gen} \cdot (1-\epsilon_2)^{-1} \cdot 2^{-k+2}$$

where $\epsilon_1 = \frac{4}{2^{k/2-3}-1}, \epsilon_2 = \frac{2q_{gen}+q_{dec}+2q_{gen}q_{dec}}{2^{k_0}} + \frac{2q_{dec}}{2^{k_1}} + \frac{2q_{hash}}{2^{2k-k_0}},$ and the running time of B is that of A plus $q_{gen} \cdot q_{hash} \cdot O(k^3)$.

Since the θ-partial one-wayness of Paillier is equivalent to the one-wayness of RSA_N for $\theta > 0.5$, Paillier-OAEP with sampling twice is secure in the sense of IND-CCA2 and IK-CCA in the random oracle model assuming RSA_N is one-way.

Paillier-OAEP with Expanding. In order to prove that Paillier-OAEP with expanding is secure in the sense of IND-CCA2 and IK-CCA, we need a similar restriction as that for Paillier-OAEP with sampling twice. That is, in the definition of IND-CCA2, it is mandated that the adversary never queries D_{sk} on $(c \bmod N^2) + \gamma N^2$ where $\gamma \in \lfloor (2^{2k+160} - (c \bmod N^2))/N^2 \rfloor$. Similarly, in the definition of IK-CCA, it is mandated that the adversary never queries D_{sk_0} on $(c \bmod N_0^2) + \beta_0 N_0^2$ where $\beta_0 \in \lfloor (2^{2k+160} - (c \bmod N_0^2))/N_0^2 \rfloor$, and D_{sk_1} on $(c \bmod N_1^2) + \beta_1 N_1^2$ where $\beta_1 \in \lfloor (2^{2k+160} - (c \bmod N_1^2))/N_1^2 \rfloor$.

If we add these restrictions then we can prove that Paillier-OAEP with expanding is secure in the sense of IND-CCA2 and IK-CCA in the random oracle model assuming Paillier is partial one-way. Noticing that the domain of valid ciphertexts changes, we can prove them in a similar way as those for Paillier-OAEP with repeating. In particular, we can prove the following lemma for the anonymity property.

Lemma 5. *For any adversary A attacking the anonymity of Paillier-OAEP $\mathcal{PE}$ with expanding under the adaptive chosen ciphertext attack, and making at most q_{dec} decryption oracle queries, q_{gen} G-oracle queries, and q_{hash} H-oracle queries, there exists a θ-partial inverting adversary B for the* Paillier *family such that for any k, k_0, k_1, and $\theta = \frac{2k-k_0}{2k}$,*

$$\mathbf{Adv}_{\mathcal{PE},A}^{\text{ik-cca}}(k) \leq 8 q_{hash}((1-\epsilon_1)(1-\epsilon_2))^{-1} \cdot \mathbf{Adv}_{\text{Paillier},B}^{\theta\text{-pow-fnc}}(k) + q_{gen} \cdot (1-\epsilon_2)^{-1} \cdot 2^{-k+2}$$

where $\epsilon_1 = \frac{4}{2^{k/2-3}-1} + \frac{1}{2^{159}}, \epsilon_2 = \frac{2q_{gen}+q_{dec}+2q_{gen}q_{dec}}{2^{k_0}} + \frac{2q_{dec}}{2^{k_1}} + \frac{2q_{hash}}{2^{2k-k_0}},$ and the running time of B is that of A plus $q_{gen} \cdot q_{hash} \cdot O(k^3)$.

Since the θ-partial one-wayness of Paillier is equivalent to the one-wayness of RSA_N for $\theta > 0.5$, Paillier-OAEP with expanding is secure in the sense of IND-CCA2 and IK-CCA in the random oracle model assuming RSA_N is one-way.

References

1. Bellare, M., Boldyreva, A., Desai, A., Pointcheval, D.: Key-Privacy in Public-Key Encryption. In: Boyd, C. (ed.) ASIACRYPT 2001. LNCS, vol. 2248, pp. 566–582. Springer, Heidelberg (2001) http://www-cse.ucsd.edu/users/mihir/
2. Bellare, M., Rogaway, P.: Optimal Asymmetric Encryption – How to Encrypt with RSA. In: De Santis, A. (ed.) EUROCRYPT 1994. LNCS, vol. 950, pp. 92–111. Springer, Heidelberg (1995)
3. Boyd, C. (ed.): ASIACRYPT 2001. LNCS, vol. 2248. Springer, Heidelberg (2001)
4. Desmedt, Y.: Securing traceability of ciphertexts: Towards a secure software escrow scheme. In: Guillou, L.C., Quisquater, J.-J. (eds.) EUROCRYPT 1995. LNCS, vol. 921, pp. 147–157. Springer, Heidelberg (1995)
5. Fujisaki, E., Okamoto, T., Pointcheval, D., Stern, J.: RSA-OAEP is Secure under the RSA Assumption. In: Kilian, J. (ed.) CRYPTO 2001. LNCS, vol. 2139, pp. 260–274. Springer, Heidelberg (2001)
6. Galbraith, S.D., Mao, W.: Invisibility and Anonymity of Undeniable and Confirmer Signatures. In: Joye, M. (ed.) CT-RSA 2003. LNCS, vol. 2612, pp. 80–97. Springer, Heidelberg (2003)
7. Hayashi, R., Okamoto, T., Tanaka, K.: An RSA Family of Trap-door Permutations with a Common Domain and its Applications. In: Bao, F., Deng, R., Zhou, J. (eds.) PKC 2004. LNCS, vol. 2947, pp. 291–304. Springer, Heidelberg (2004)
8. Hayashi, R., Tanaka, K.: The Sampling Twice Technique for the RSA-based Cryptosystems with Anonymity. In: Vaudenay, S. (ed.) PKC 2005. LNCS, vol. 3386, pp. 216–233. Springer, Heidelberg (2005)
9. Hayashi, R., Tanaka, K.: Universally Anonymizable Public-Key Encryption. In: Roy, B. (ed.) ASIACRYPT 2005. LNCS, vol. 3788, pp. 293–312. Springer, Heidelberg (2005)
10. Hayashi, R., Tanaka, K.: Schemes for Encryption with Anonymity and Ring Signature. IEICE Transactions on Fundamentals of Electronics, Communications and Computer Sciences, Special Section on Cryptography and Information Security E89-A 1, 66–73 (2006)
11. Paillier, P.: Public-Key Cryptosystems Based on Composite Degree Residuosity Classes. In: Stern, J. (ed.) EUROCRYPT 1999. LNCS, vol. 1592, pp. 223–238. Springer, Heidelberg (1999)
12. Rivest, R.L., Shamir, A., Tauman, Y.: How to Leak a Secret. In: Boyd [3], pp. 552–565

Generic Certificateless Key Encapsulation Mechanism*

Qiong Huang and Duncan S. Wong

Department of Computer Science,
City University of Hong Kong,
Hong Kong, China

Abstract. We propose the *first generic* construction of certificateless key encapsulation mechanism (CL-KEM) in the standard model, which is also secure against malicious-but-passive KGC attacks. It is based on an ID-based KEM, a public key encryption and a message authentication code. The high efficiency of our construction is due to the efficient implementations of these underlying building blocks, and is comparable to Bentahar et al.'s CL-KEMs, which are only proven secure under the random oracle model with no consideration of the malicious-but-passive KGC attacks. The second contribution of our work is that we introduce the notion of certificateless tag-based KEM (CL-TKEM), which is an extension of Abe et al.'s work in the certificateless setting. We show that an efficient CL-TKEM can be constructed by modifying our CL-KEM. We also show that with a CL-TKEM and a one-time data encapsulation mechanism (DEM), an efficient hybrid certificateless encryption can be constructed by applying Abe et al.'s transformation in the certificateless setting.

1 Introduction

In Asiacrypt 2003, Al-Riyami and Paterson introduced the concept of *certificateless cryptography* [3], which aims to solve the inherent key escrow problem of identity-based cryptography [21]. Compared with identity-based cryptography, certificateless cryptography requires less extent of users' trust in the KGC (Key Generation Center). Besides a unique identity ID, a user also independently generates a key pair (upk_{ID}, usk_{ID}). The complete public key of the user will consist of both ID and upk_{ID}, and the corresponding private key will consist of usk_{ID} and a partial key psk_{ID}, which is generated by the KGC according to the value of ID. To encrypt a message, both ID and upk_{ID} are used; to decrypt a ciphertext, both usk_{ID} and psk_{ID} are required. Without any of these two keys, decryption cannot be performed properly.

Since the introduction of certificateless cryptography, there have been quite a number of schemes proposed [29,13,17,12,4,18]. The original definition of certificateless cryptography [3] has seven algorithms, which were later simplified to

---

* The authors are supported by a grant from CityU (Project No. 7001959).

J. Pieprzyk, H. Ghodosi, and E. Dawson (Eds.): ACISP 2007, LNCS 4586, pp. 215–229, 2007.

five algorithms by Hu et al. in [12] and shown to be more versatile than the original one. In this paper, we also use the five-algorithm variant to define a certificateless cryptosystem.

Yum and Lee proposed a generic certificateless encryption scheme in [28] which has later been shown to be insecure under the model of [3] by Libert and Quisquater [17]. In [17], the authors also proposed a generic certificateless encryption scheme. However, their scheme is only proven secure in the random oracle model, which is a heuristic method for showing the security of cryptographic schemes. The security may not preserve when the random oracle is replaced by a hash function, even if the scheme is reduced to some complexity (or number-theoretic) assumption. Recently, Liu et al. [18] proposed a certificateless encryption scheme which, to the best of our knowledge, is the first one in the standard model. In [4], Au et al. considered another strong security model for certificateless cryptography, in which users' trust in the KGC is further relaxed. By using the term introduced in [4], the KGC of a certificateless cryptosystem can be *malicious-but-passive*. This means the KGC can be malicious so that it may not follow the scheme specification for generating system parameters and master key, while it does not actively replace a user's public key or corrupt the user's secret key. The purpose of such a malicious-but-passive KGC is to compromise a user's secret key without being detected. Since the KGC does not need to replace the user's public key or compromise the user's machine for corrupting the user's secret key, in practice, it is very difficult to detect the occurrence of this attack. Under the *malicious-but-passive* KGC attacking model, certificateless cryptosystems proposed in [3,13,16] have been shown to be insecure. We can see that the newly proposed certificateless encryption scheme in [18] is also insecure under this model. The only provably secure certificateless encryption scheme against malicious-but-passive KGC attack currently available is due to Libert and Quisquater [17], as showed in [4]. However, the security is only proven in the random oracle model.

On the other side, most of the (public key) encryption schemes in the literature have limited message spaces. That is, a message to be encrypted is assumed to have a limited length or belong to a specific group. However, this is often not the case in practice. It is inconvenient and expensive for people to transmit arbitrary messages securely by using purely public key encryption schemes. To encrypt large messages, symmetric encryption schemes are usually used as they enjoy high efficiency. However, they also suffer from the key distribution problem. To achieve high efficiency while getting rid of key distribution problem, in practice, we adopt the *hybrid encryption* [8,23] mechanism, which encrypts bulk messages using a symmetric encryption scheme and encrypts a symmetric key using a public key encryption scheme. A *hybrid encryption* consists of two components: *key encapsulation mechanism* (KEM, which is the asymmetric part) and *data encapsulation mechanism* (DEM, which is the symmetric part). KEM encrypts the symmetric encryption key while DEM encrypts the actual message. The KEM/DEM framework was first formalized by Shoup in [22]. It is very attractive and has been received a lot of attention in recent years [2,8,9,22,23,6,5,1].

To achieve the CCA2 security of the *hybrid encryption*, it is very natural and reasonable for us to require both the KEM part and DEM part to be CCA2 secure. However, Kurosawa and Desmedt's hybrid encryption scheme [15] is an exception. Their scheme, which is a variant of Cramer and Shoup's scheme [8], has the encryption scheme being CCA2 secure, but the KEM part is not [11]. Dent proposed a number of efficient constructions of CCA2 secure KEMs based on some weakly secure public key encryption schemes. Bentahar et al's [5] extended Dent's work into identity-based setting and certificateless setting, and also proposed several efficient constructions of ID-based KEMs and certificateless KEMs. Later, Chen et al. [6] considered KEM/DEM framework for ID-based encryption and proposed an efficient construction of ID-based KEM, which is based on Sakai et al.'s key construction [20]. However, both Dent's schemes and Bentahar et al.'s schemes are only proven in the random oracle model. Besides, the security of Bentahar et al's certificateless KEM schemes does not consider the malicious-but-passive KGC attack. Recently, Abe et al. [1] showed how to transform weakly secure (i.e., selective-ID CPA, or adaptive-ID CPA) identity-based KEMs to fully secure public key encryption schemes. But their transformation only applies to a specific class of IB-KEMs, named *partitioned* IB-KEM. An IB-KEM is partitioned if the encapsulated key K and the first part c_1 of the ciphertext does not depend on ID, and given c_1 and ID, the second part of the ciphertext c_2 is uniquely determined.

(*Tag-KEM.*) Abe et al. introduced in [2] a strengthened variant of KEM, called Tag-KEM, which is essentially a KEM but with a tag. It can be viewed as an analogue of tag-based public key encryption [23,24,19,14]. Several methods for constructing Tag-KEMs were given in [2]. Interestingly, they also showed that a one-time secure DEM is enough for transforming a CCA2 secure Tag-KEM to a CCA2 secure public key encryption. This is one of the most useful applications of Tag-KEM.

Our Work. We propose the *first generic* construction of certificateless key encapsulation mechanism (CL-KEM) in the standard model, which is also secure against malicious-but-passive KGC attacks. The construction is based on an ID-based KEM IB-KEM, a public key encryption PKE and a message authentication code MAC. The high efficiency of our construction is due to the efficient implementations of these underlying building blocks, and is comparable to Bentahar et al.'s CL-KEMs [5], which are only proven secure under the random oracle model with no consideration of the malicious-but-passive KGC attacks.

The idea of constructing a CL-KEM is as follows: first IB-KEM is invoked to generate a key K along with its encapsulation; then PKE is invoked to hide the encapsulation; at last, the final symmetric encryption key dk and a message authentication key mk are generated from K, where mk is used by MAC for ensuring the integrity of the ciphertext.

The second contribution of our work is that we introduce the notion of certificateless tag-based KEM (CL-TKEM), which is an extension of Abe et al.'s work [2] from the conventional setting to the certificateless setting. We show that an efficient CL-TKEM can be constructed by modifying our CL-KEM. We also show that with a CL-TKEM and a data encapsulation mechanism (DEM) secure under our proposed notions, an efficient hybrid certificateless encryption can be constructed by applying Abe et al.'s transformation in the certificateless setting.

Paper Organization. We review the definition and adversarial model of certificateless encryption in Sec. 2. In Sec. 3, we consider the certificateless KEM (CL-KEM), describe some building blocks for constructing a CL-KEM, and then show how to construct a CL-KEM in the standard model, which is also secure against the malicious-but-passive KGC attack. In Sec. 4, we extend the work of Abe et al. to the certificateless setting and give the construction of CL-TKEM as well as a certificateless hybrid encryption scheme (CL-HE). The paper is concluded in Sec. 5.

2   Definition and Adversarial Model

A certificateless encryption scheme [3,4] consists of five (probabilistic) polynomial-time (PPT) algorithms:

- MasterKeyGen: On input 1^k where $k \in \mathbb{N}$ is a security parameter, it generates a master public/private key pair (mpk, msk).
- PartialKeyGen: On input msk and a user identity $\mathsf{ID} \in \{0, 1\}^*$, it generates a user partial key psk_{ID}.
- UserKeyGen: On input mpk and a user identity ID, it generates a user public/private key pair $(upk_{\mathsf{ID}}, usk_{\mathsf{ID}})$.
- Enc: On input mpk, a user identity ID, a user public key upk_{ID} and a message m, it returns a ciphertext c.
- Dec: On input a user partial key psk_{ID}, a user private key usk_{ID}, and a ciphertext c, it returns the plaintext m or $\perp$ indicating the failure of decryption.

In practice, the KGC (Key Generation Center) performs the first two algorithms: MasterKeyGen and PartialKeyGen. The master public key mpk is then published and it is assumed that everyone in the system can get a legitimate copy of mpk. It is also assumed that the partial key is issued to the corresponding user via a secure channel so that no one except the intended user can get it. Every user in the system also performs UserKeyGen for generating its own public/private key pair and publishes the public key. The correctness requirement is defined in the conventional way. We refer readers to [3,4] for details.

Adversarial Model. We consider two security types: Type-I and Type-II, along with two adversaries, $\mathcal{A}_1$ and $\mathcal{A}_2$, respectively. Adversary $\mathcal{A}_1$ can compromise user private key usk_{ID} or replace user public key upk_{ID}, but can neither compromise master private key msk nor get access to user partial key psk_{ID}. Adversary $\mathcal{A}_2$ models a malicious-but-passive KGC [4] which controls the generation of the master public/private key pair, and that of any user partial key psk_{ID}. The following are five oracles which can be accessed by the adversaries.

- CreateUser: On input an identity $\mathsf{ID} \in \{0, 1\}^*$, if ID has not been created, the oracle runs $psk_{\mathsf{ID}} \leftarrow$ PartialKeyGen(msk, ID) and $(upk_{\mathsf{ID}}, usk_{\mathsf{ID}}) \leftarrow$

UserKeyGen(mpk, ID). It then stores (ID, psk_{ID}, upk_{ID}, usk_{ID}) into List[1] and ID is said to be *created*. upk_{ID} is returned.

- RevealPartialKey: On input an identity ID, the oracle searches List for an entry corresponding to ID. If it is not found, $\perp$ is returned; otherwise, the corresponding psk_{ID} is returned.
- RevealSecretKey: On input an identity ID, the oracle searches List for the entry of ID. If it is not found, $\perp$ is returned; otherwise, the corresponding usk_{ID} is returned.
- ReplaceKey: On input ID along with a user public/private key pair (upk', usk'), the oracle searches List for the entry of ID. If it is not found, nothing will be carried out. If $usk' = \perp$, the oracle sets $usk' = usk_{ID}$. Then, it replaces (ID, psk_{ID}, upk_{ID}, usk_{ID}) in List with (ID, psk_{ID}, upk', usk').
- Decryption: On input an identity ID and a ciphertext c, the oracle searches List for the entry of ID. If it is not found, $\perp$ is returned. Otherwise, it runs $m \leftarrow$ Dec(psk_{ID}, usk_{ID}, c) and returns m. Note that the original upk_{ID} (which is returned by CreateUser oracle) may have been replaced by the adversary.

Remark: In the original adversarial model of certificateless encryption [3,17], it is required that the Decryption oracle should provide correct decryptions even after the user public key has been replaced by the adversary while the corresponding user secret key is not known. We believe that the model is hardly realistic. In this paper, we only require the Decryption oracle to perform the decryption task by using the current user keys. This also captures the case in which the user public key is replaced by the adversary, but the user secret key remains the same. It is possible that the message m recovered from the ciphertext by using the current usk_{ID} is $\perp$.

We now specify the two security types using the following games. For simplicity, we denote by $\mathcal{C}$ the challenger/simulator (instead of $\mathcal{C}_1$ or $\mathcal{C}_2$), and by $\mathcal{A}$ the adversary in the game (instead of $\mathcal{A}_1$ in **Game-I** or $\mathcal{A}_2$ in **Game-II**).

Game-I (Game-II): Let $k \in \mathbb{N}$ be the security parameter.
   1. If this is **Game-I**, $\mathcal{C}$ runs $(mpk, msk) \leftarrow$ MasterKeyGen(1^k), and then invokes $\mathcal{A}$ on input 1^k and mpk. If this is **Game-II**, $\mathcal{C}$ runs $\mathcal{A}$ on input 1^k, which returns a master public key mpk to $\mathcal{C}$.
   2. In the game, $\mathcal{A}$ can query CreateUser, RevealPartialKey, RevealSecretKey, ReplaceKey and Decryption. Note that in **Game-II**, the oracle Reveal-PartialKey is not needed by $\mathcal{A}$ since it has the knowledge of the master private key, and when $\mathcal{A}$ issues a query to oracle CreateUser, it has to additionally provide user partial private key psk_{ID}.
   3. $\mathcal{A}$ submits two equal-length messages (m_0, m_1) along with a target identity ID*.
   4. $\mathcal{C}$ selects a random bit $b \in \{0, 1\}$, computes a challenge ciphertext c^* by running $c^* \leftarrow$ Enc(mpk, ID*, upk_{ID^*}, m_b), and returns c^* to $\mathcal{A}$, where upk_{ID^*} is the user public key currently in List for ID*.
   5. $\mathcal{A}$ continues to issue queries as in step 2. Finally it outputs a bit b'.

---

[1] Note that the list List is shared among all the oracles.

$\mathcal{A}$ is said to win the game if $b' = b$, and (1) $\mathcal{A}$ did not query Decryption on (ID^*, c^*), (2) $\mathcal{A}$ did not query RevealPartialKey on ID^* (if this is **Game-I**), (3) $\mathcal{A}$ did not query RevealSecretKey on ID^*, nor query ReplaceKey on $(\mathsf{ID}^*, \cdot, \cdot)$ (if this is **Game-II**). We denote by $Pr[\mathcal{A}\ \mathsf{Succ}]$ the probability that $\mathcal{A}$ wins the game, and define the *advantage* of $\mathcal{A}$ in **Game-I** (or **Game-II**) to be $\mathsf{Adv}_{\mathcal{A}} = |Pr[\mathcal{A}\ \mathsf{Succ}] - \frac{1}{2}|$.

Definition 1. *A certificateless encryption scheme* CLE *is said to be* Type-I ID-CCA2 *secure (resp.* Type-II ID-CCA2 *secure) if there is no probabilistic polynomial-time adversary* $\mathcal{A}_1$ *(resp.* $\mathcal{A}_2$*) which wins* **Game-I** *(resp.* **Game-II***) with non-negligible advantage.* CLE *is said to be* ID-CCA2 *secure if it is both* Type-I ID-CCA2 *secure and* Type-II ID-CCA2 *secure.*

3   Certificateless KEM

In this section, we first define a certificateless KEM (CL-KEM) and specify its security requirements. Then we describe two of the building blocks used in our CL-KEM construction. The building blocks are a *strong one-time unforgeable* message authentication code and a key derivation function. Finally, we propose a CL-KEM (Sec. 3.3) and show its security in the standard model.

A standard KEM (in the public key setting) is defined by the following three PPT algorithms (KG, Encap, Decap):

- KG is a key generation algorithm, which takes 1^k as input and outputs a public/private key pair (pk, sk).
- Encap is a key encapsulation algorithm, which takes as input pk and outputs an encapsulation key pair $(K, e) \in \mathcal{K}_{pk} \times \mathcal{E}_{pk}$, where e is called the *encapsulation* of key K, and K is considered to be distributed uniformly in the key space $\mathcal{K}_{pk}$.
- Decap is a decapsulation algorithm, which takes as input (sk, e) and outputs the corresponding key K, or an invalid encapsulation symbol $\perp$.

Now we extend the standard KEM to the certificateless setting, and obtain the definition of a *certificateless* KEM (CL-KEM).

A CL-KEM is defined by the following quintuple of PPT algorithms (Master KeyGen, PartialKeyGen, UserKeyGen, Encap, Decap), the first three of which are defined in the same way as that for a certificateless encryption scheme (Sec. 2):

- Encap takes as input $(mpk, upk_{\mathsf{ID}}, \mathsf{ID})$ and outputs an encapsulation key pair $(K, e) \in \mathcal{K}^K_{mpk, upk_{\mathsf{ID}}, \mathsf{ID}} \times \mathcal{E}_{mpk, upk_{\mathsf{ID}}, \mathsf{ID}}$, where e is called the encapsulation of key K and K is considered to be uniformly distributed in $\mathcal{K}^K_{mpk, upk_{\mathsf{ID}}, \mathsf{ID}}$.
- Decap takes as input $((psk_{\mathsf{ID}}, usk_{\mathsf{ID}}), \mathsf{ID}, e)$ and outputs the corresponding key K, or a special symbol $\perp$ indicating invalid encapsulation.

On the security requirements of a CL-KEM scheme, we consider two security types: Type-I and Type-II, as we do for a certificateless encryption scheme (Sec. 2). Similarly, adversaries in the corresponding games will have access to the same oracles as that in the security models of a certificateless encryption scheme (Sec. 2), except that oracle Decryption is replaced with Decapsulation, which is defined as follows:

Decapsulation: On input an identity ID and an encapsulation e, the oracle searches List for the entry of ID. If it is not found, $\perp$ is returned. Otherwise, it returns $K \leftarrow \mathsf{Decap}(psk_{\mathsf{ID}}, usk_{\mathsf{ID}}, \mathsf{ID}, e)$.

The security games for Type-I and Type-II security are described as follows:

Game-I' (Game-II'). The game descriptions are almost the same as those of a certificateless encryption scheme, except that the Decryption oracle is replaced with the Decapsulation oracle, and Step 3 and 4 are replaced with the following:

    3. $\mathcal{A}$ submits a target identity $\mathsf{ID}^* \in \{0,1\}^*$.
    4. $\mathcal{C}$ runs $(K_1, e^*) \leftarrow \mathsf{Encap}(mpk, upk_{\mathsf{ID}^*}, \mathsf{ID}^*)$ and randomly selects $K_0 \leftarrow \mathcal{K}^K_{mpk, upk_{\mathsf{ID}^*}, \mathsf{ID}^*}$. A coin b is then flipped, and (K_b, e^*) is returned to $\mathcal{A}$.

$\mathcal{A}$ wins the game if $b' = b$ and (1) it did not query Decapsulation on (ID^*, e^*), (2) it did not query RevealPartialKey on ID^* (if this is **Game-I'**), and (3) it did not query ReplaceKey on $(\mathsf{ID}^*, \cdot, \cdot)$ nor query RevealSecretKey on ID^* (if this is **Game-II'**). We denote by $Pr[\mathcal{A} \text{ Succ}]$ the probability that $\mathcal{A}$ wins the game and define the advantage of $\mathcal{A}$ in the game to be $\mathsf{Adv}_{\mathcal{A}} = \left| Pr[\mathcal{A} \text{ Succ}] - \frac{1}{2} \right|$.

Definition 2. *A certificateless key encapsulation mechanism CL-KEM is said to be* Type-I ID-CCA2 *secure (resp.* Type-II ID-CCA2 *secure) if there is no probabilistic polynomial-time adversary $\mathcal{A}_1$ (resp. $\mathcal{A}_2$) which wins* **Game-I'** *(resp.* **Game-II'***) with non-negligible advantage. CL-KEM is said to be* ID-CCA2 *secure if it is both* Type-I ID-CCA2 *secure and* Type-II ID-CCA2 *secure.*

3.1   Message Authentication Code

A *message authentication code* MAC is a pair of polynomial-time algorithms (Mac, Vrfy) such that:

- Mac takes as input a key $mk \in \mathcal{K}_M$ and a message m, and outputs a tag σ, where m is in some implicit message space. We denote this by $\sigma \leftarrow \mathsf{Mac}_{mk}(m)$. Without loss of generality, we assume that the key space $\mathcal{K}_M$ of MAC is $\{0,1\}^k$ where k is a security parameter.
- Vrfy takes as input a key mk, a message m and a tag σ and outputs a bit $b \in \{0,1\}$ where the 1-value of b indicates 'accept' and 0-value indicates 'reject'. We denote this by $b \leftarrow \mathsf{Vrfy}_{mk}(m, \sigma)$.

For the security of MAC, we consider the following game:

1. A random key $mk \in \{0,1\}^k$ is chosen;
2. Adversary $\mathcal{A}_M(1^k)$ is allowed to submit one message m and get $\sigma \leftarrow \mathsf{Mac}_{mk}(m)$.
3. Finally, $\mathcal{A}_M$ outputs (m^*, σ^*).

We say that $\mathcal{A}_M$ wins if $1 \leftarrow \mathsf{Vrfy}_{mk}(m^*, \sigma^*)$ and $(m^*, \sigma^*) \neq (m, \sigma)$ (assuming that $\mathcal{A}_M$ did issue a query for a tag on input m in step 2).

Definition 3. *A message authentication code* MAC *is said to be* strong one-time unforgeable, *if for any PPT adversary* $\mathcal{A}_M$, *the probability that* $\mathcal{A}_M$ *wins the game above is* negligible *in* k.

3.2   Key Derivation Function (KDF)

As in [2,8], our proposed construction of CL-KEM (Sec. 3.3) also uses a key derivation function, KDF_2, that maps a key K generated by KEM into a pair of keys (dk, mk) for data encapsulation mechanism DEM [2,8] and message authentication code MAC. We require the output distribution (dk, mk) of KDF_2 to be (computationally) indistinguishable from uniform, when the input K is uniformly distributed.

Let $KDF_2 : \mathcal{K}_K \to \mathcal{K}_D \times \mathcal{K}_M$ and $\{KDF_2\}_k$ be a family of functions indexed by the key-spaces associated to the same security parameter k. In our case, $\mathcal{K}_K$ is the union of all $\mathcal{K}^K_{mpk,upk_{ID},ID}$. We require that the distribution of KDF_2 is indistinguishable from uniform over $\mathcal{K}_D \times \mathcal{K}_M$. Formally, let

$$D_1 = \{(dk, mk)|K \leftarrow \mathcal{K}_K, (dk, mk) \leftarrow KDF_2(K)\}, \text{ and}$$
$$D_0 = \{(dk, mk)|(dk, mk) \leftarrow \mathcal{K}_D \times \mathcal{K}_M\}$$

We say that KDF_2 is *secure* if for any probability polynomial time algorithm $\mathcal{A}_{KDF}$, the following probability

$$\left| Pr\left[b \leftarrow \{0,1\}, (dk, mk) \leftarrow D_b, b' \leftarrow \mathcal{A}_{KDF}((mpk, upk_{ID}, ID), KDF_2, (dk, mk)); b' = b\right] - \frac{1}{2} \right|$$

is *negligible* in k, where the probability is taken over the choice of KDF_2 which includes the coins of CL-KEM.MasterKeyGen and CL-KEM.UserKeyGen that determine $\mathcal{K}_K$, and the choice of (dk, mk), b and the coins of $\mathcal{A}_{KDF}$. In our construction of certificateless KEM, we need to consider the following two distributions:

$$U_1 = D_1, \text{ and } U_0 = \{(dk, mk)|K \leftarrow \mathcal{K}_K, (dk, *) \leftarrow KDF_2(K), mk \leftarrow \mathcal{K}_M\}$$

It is easy to obtain the following lemma:

Lemma 1. *If* KDF_2 *is secure, then for any PPT adversary* $\mathcal{A}$,

$$|Pr[1 \leftarrow \mathcal{A}(dk, mk)|(dk, mk) \leftarrow U_0] - Pr[1 \leftarrow \mathcal{A}(dk, mk)|(dk, mk) \leftarrow U_1]|$$

is negligible in k.

3.3   A Generic Construction of CL-KEM

Let IB-KEM = (KG, Extract, Encap, Decap) be an ID-CCA2 secure identity-based key encapsulation mechanism [6], PKE = (KG, Enc, Dec) be an CCA2 secure public key encryption scheme, KDF_2 be a secure key derivation function, and MAC = (Mac, Vrfy) be a strong one-time message authentication code. The certificateless KEM CL-KEM is constructed as in Fig. 1.

- **MasterKeyGen:** On input 1^k, the KGC runs $(mpk, msk) \leftarrow$ IB-KEM.KG(1^k) and returns mpk.
- **PartialKeyGen:** On input an identity ID, the KGC runs $psk_{\text{ID}} \leftarrow$ IB-KEM.Extract(msk, ID) and returns psk_{ID}.
- **UserKeyGen:** On input 1^k and mpk, the user ID runs $(upk_{\text{ID}}, usk_{\text{ID}}) \leftarrow$ PKE.KG(1^k), and returns upk_{ID}.

$-\ (dk, e) \leftarrow$ Encap$(mpk, upk_{\text{ID}}, \text{ID})$:	$-\ dk \leftarrow$ Decap$(psk_{\text{ID}}, usk_{\text{ID}}, \text{ID}, e)$:
$(K, \psi) \leftarrow$ IB-KEM.Encap(mpk, ID)	$(\varphi, \sigma) \leftarrow e$
$\varphi \leftarrow$ PKE.Enc(upk_{ID}, ψ)	$\psi \leftarrow$ PKE.Dec$(usk_{\text{ID}}, \varphi)$
$(dk, mk) \leftarrow$ KDF$_2(K)$	$K \leftarrow$ IB-KEM.Decap$(psk_{\text{ID}}, \text{ID}, \psi)$
$\sigma \leftarrow$ MAC.Mac$_{mk}(\varphi)$	$(dk, mk) \leftarrow$ KDF$_2(K)$
$e \leftarrow (\varphi, \sigma)$	If $0 \leftarrow$ MAC.Vrfy$_{mk}(\sigma, \varphi)$, $dk \leftarrow \perp$.

Fig. 1. CL-KEM

Note that in CL-KEM.Decap, if either of PKE.Dec and IB-KEM.Decap outputs $\perp$, then $\perp$ is returned. For the security of the above construction of CL-KEM, intuitively, the strong one-time unforgeability of MAC prevents the adversary from gaining any advantage by manipulating the MAC; the ID-CCA2 security of IB-KEM prevents the Type-I adversary from gaining advantage by manipulating ψ; and the CCA2 security of PKE prevents the Type-II adversary from gaining any advantage by manipulating φ. Also we should note that the *malicious-but-passive* KGC attack is avoided since each user uses its own independently generated parameters for PKE. Then we have the following two theorems:

Theorem 1. *The* CL-KEM *proposed above is* Type-I ID-CCA2 *secure.*

Theorem 2. *The* CL-KEM *proposed above is* Type-II ID-CCA2 *secure.*

Proof (Sketch). We consider Theorem 1 here. Below is the attacking game:

1. $(mpk, msk) \leftarrow$ CL-KEM.MasterKeyGen(1^k);
2. $(\text{ID}^*, st) \leftarrow \mathcal{A}^{\mathcal{O}}(1^k, mpk)$;
3. $(K_1, \psi^*) \leftarrow$ IB-KEM.Encap(mpk, ID^*), $\varphi^* \leftarrow$ PKE.Enc$(upk_{\text{ID}^*}, \psi^*)$, $(dk_1, mk) \leftarrow$ KDF$_2(K_1)$, $\sigma^* \leftarrow$ MAC.Mac$_{mk}(\varphi^*)$; $dk_0 \leftarrow \mathcal{K}_D$; $b \leftarrow \{0, 1\}$;
4. $b' \leftarrow \mathcal{A}^{\mathcal{O}}(st, (mpk, \text{ID}^*), (dk_b, \varphi^*, \sigma^*))$.

Note that in step 2 and step 4, we denote by $\mathcal{O}$ the oracles that $\mathcal{A}$ has access to in the game. We first modify the attacking game of the adversary in such a way that the key of MAC, mk, is randomly selected at the beginning of the game, which causes only negligible difference in the probability that the adversary wins the game. This is guaranteed by Lemma 1.

Then modify the game in a way that dk_0 is generated by first randomly select another key K_0 and then run $(dk_0, *) \leftarrow$ KDF$_2(K_0)$. Note that in the game dk_1 is still generated according to the scheme specification. Again, guaranteed by the security of KDF$_2$, the adversary's advantage remains almost the same.

Let $(\mathsf{ID}^*, (dk_b, (\varphi^*, \sigma^*)))$ be the challenge encapsulation of $\mathcal{A}$, and $(\mathsf{ID}, (\varphi, \sigma))$ be a Decapsulation query issued by it. We say (φ, σ) is a valid encapsulation with respect to ID if the Decapsulation oracle would not output $\perp$ on input $(\mathsf{ID}, (\varphi, \sigma))$, and we denote by $\mathsf{Forge_I}$ the event that (φ, σ) is valid and σ is a valid MAC on φ with respect to mk (i.e., $1 \leftarrow \mathsf{MAC.Vrfy}_{mk}(\varphi, \sigma)$).

Next, we further modify G_2 in such a way that if event $\mathsf{Forge_I}$ occurs, we simply halt the game. Guaranteed by the strong one-time unforgeability of MAC, this modification results in only negligible difference in $\mathcal{A}$'s advantage.

Finally, in the resulting game we can reduce the Type-I ID-CCA2 security of CL-KEM to the ID-CCA2 security of IB-KEM. Given $\mathcal{A}$, we construct a PPT algorithm $\mathcal{B}$ to break the ID-CCA2 security of IB-KEM. On input the master public key mpk, an Extrac oracle $\mathcal{O}_E$ and a Decapsulation oracle $\mathcal{O}_D$, $\mathcal{B}$ runs $\mathcal{A}$ on input mpk and a randomly selected MAC key $mk \in \mathcal{K}_M$, and uses its own oracles to simulate oracles for $\mathcal{A}$. $\mathcal{B}$ forwards $\mathcal{A}$'s target identity ID^* to its own challenger. After receiving the challenge encapsulation (K_b, ψ^*), it computes $\varphi^* \leftarrow \mathsf{PKE.Enc}(usk_{\mathsf{ID}^*}, \psi^*)$, $\sigma^* \leftarrow \mathsf{MAC.Mac}_{mk}(\varphi^*)$ and $(dk_b^*, *) \leftarrow \mathsf{KDF}_2(K_b)$, and returns $(dk_b, (\varphi^*, \sigma^*))$ to $\mathcal{A}$. Finally, it outputs the bit output by $\mathcal{A}$. It's readily to see that $\mathcal{B}$'s advantage is no less than $\mathcal{A}$'s. Guaranteed by the ID-CCA2 security, we get that the advantage of $\mathcal{A}$ in the resulting game is negligible, and thus so is $\mathcal{A}$'s advantage in the original attacking game.

As for Theorem 2, the Type-II ID-CCA2 security of CL-KEM can be proved in a similar way with above. It is guaranteed by the security of KDF_2, the strong one-time unforgeability of MAC and the CCA2 security of PKE.   □

The detailed proofs will be included in the full version of this paper. From the theorems we immediately get the following corollary:

Corollary 1. CL-KEM *is an* ID-CCA2 *secure certificateless KEM scheme.*

Discussions: Since any ID-CCA2 secure identity-based encryption is trivially an ID-CCA2 secure ID-based KEM, it is optional for us to instantiate IB-KEM with such an IBE scheme, such as the schemes in [26,10]. As for PKE, we can instantiate it with Cramer and Shoup's scheme [7] or Kurosawa and Desmedt's scheme [15]. Besides these two, there are still many efficient public key encryption schemes for us to choose.

There are a number of efficient strong one-time message authentication code in the literature. For our case, we may use CBC-MAC with 128-bit AES as the underlying block cipher. However, it is still a good choice for us to use strong one-time MACs with information-theoretic security [25,27].

4   Hybrid Certificateless Encryption

In this section we show how to construct a *hybrid certificateless encryption* scheme to encrypt messages of unbounded length, by using the certificateless KEM CL-KEM and a one-time DEM scheme. (Readers can refer to [2] for a formal definition of DEM.) We show that this can be achieved by extending the idea of Abe et al. [2] to our certificateless setting. In short, their result shows that a combination of a strengthened variant of (CCA2 secure) KEM, Tag-KEM, and a one-time DEM leads to a CCA2 hybrid public key encryption. We show a similar result detailed below but under the certificateless setting.

4.1   Our Certificateless Tag-KEM (CL-TKEM)

Essentially, a Tag-KEM is a KEM with a tag. The Encap algorithm of a KEM is splitted into two in a Tag-KEM, Key and Encap. KG remains the same in a Tag-KEM and Decap is modified to take a tag as an additional input. Similar to the extension from KEM to Tag-KEM in the public key setting in [2], we now extend CL-KEM to certificateless Tag-KEM (CL-TKEM):

- MasterKeyGen, PartialKeyGen, UserKeyGen are the same as those of a CL-KEM.
- Key takes as input mpk, ID and upk_{ID}, and outputs a key dk and some internal state information w. We denote it by $(dk, w) \leftarrow \text{Key}(mpk, \text{ID}, upk_{\text{ID}})$.
- Encap takes as input w and a $tag \ \tau \in \{0,1\}^*$, and outputs the corresponding encapsulation e. We denote it by $e \leftarrow \text{Encap}(w, \tau)$.
- Decap takes as input psk_{ID}, usk_{ID}, ID, a tag τ and a purported encapsulation e, and outputs the corresponding key dk, or a special symbol $\perp$ indicating invalid encapsulation. We denote it by $dk \leftarrow \text{Decap}(psk_{\text{ID}}, usk_{\text{ID}}, \text{ID}, \tau, e)$.

Analogously, we can define the security of CL-TKEM. In a CL-TKEM, an adversary has access to the same five oracles as in a CL-KEM, with the only exception that the Decapsulation oracle has a tag τ as an additional input. The security of a CL-TKEM requires the adversary could not distinguish whether a given dk is the one embeded in the encapsulation or not, with adaptive access to these oracles, even though the tag is selected by itself. We also consider two types of security of a CL-TKEM, and described the two games together as follows:

Game-I″ (Game-II″) : The first two steps of the games are the same as those of a certificateless KEM.

3. $\mathcal{A}$ submits a target identity ID^* to $\mathcal{C}$, which then computes $(dk_1, w) \leftarrow \text{Key}(mpk, upk_{\text{ID}^*}, \text{ID})$, randomly selects $dk_0 \leftarrow \mathcal{K}_D$, flips a coin $b \in \{0, 1\}$ and returns dk_b back to $\mathcal{A}$.

4. $\mathcal{A}$ continues to issue queries to its oracles. At some point it submits a target tag τ^* to $\mathcal{C}$, which then computes $e^* \leftarrow \text{Encap}(w, \tau^*)$ and returns e^* back to $\mathcal{A}$.

5. $\mathcal{A}$ continues to issue queries again. Finally it outputs a bit b' as its guess for whether e^* is an encapsulation of dk_b.

The conditions on which $\mathcal{A}$ wins the game are the same as those of a CL-KEM, except that condition '(1)' is replaced with that $\mathcal{A}$ did not issue a Decapsulation query on $(\text{ID}^*, \tau^*, e^*)$.

Definition 4. *A certificateless Tag-KEM* CL-TKEM *is said to be* Type-I Tag-ID-CCA2 *secure (resp.* Type-II Tag-ID-CCA2 *secure) if there is no PPT adversary* $\mathcal{A}_I$ *(resp.* $\mathcal{A}_{II}$*) which wins* **Game-I″** *(resp.* **Game-II″**) *with non-negligible advantage.* CL-TKEM *is said to be* Tag-ID-CCA2 *secure if it is both* Type-I Tag-ID-CCA2 *secure and* Type-II Tag-ID-CCA2 *secure.*

Now we show how to modify the above construction of CL-KEM to a certificateless Tag-KEM CL-TKEM, as shown in Fig. 2.

– MasterKeyGen, PartialKeyGen and UserKeyGen are the same as those of CL-KEM.
– $(dk, w) \leftarrow$ Key(mpk, upk_{ID}, ID):

$$(K, \psi) \leftarrow \text{IB-KEM.Encap}(mpk, ID)$$
$$(dk, mk) \leftarrow \text{KDF}_2(K)$$
$$w \leftarrow (upk_{ID}, mk, \psi)$$

– $e \leftarrow$ Encap(w, τ):	– $dk \leftarrow$ Decap($psk_{ID}, usk_{ID}, ID, \tau, e$):
$(upk_{ID}, mk, \psi) \leftarrow w$	$(\varphi, \sigma) \leftarrow e$
$\varphi \leftarrow \text{PKE.Enc}(upk_{ID}, \psi)$	$\psi \leftarrow \text{PKE.Dec}(usk_{ID}, \varphi)$
$\sigma \leftarrow \text{MAC.Mac}_{mk}(\varphi \| \tau)$	$K \leftarrow \text{IB-KEM.Decap}(psk_{ID}, ID, \psi)$
$e \leftarrow (\varphi, \sigma)$	$(dk, mk) \leftarrow \text{KDF}_2(K)$
	If $0 \leftarrow \text{MAC.Vrfy}_{mk}(\sigma, \varphi \| \tau)$, $dk \leftarrow \bot$.

Fig. 2. CL-TKEM

As we can see from the above construction, CL-TKEM differs from CL-KEM in the generation of σ, and the tag τ merely appears in the MAC during the generation of an encapsulation. By the ID-CCA2 security of CL-KEM and the strong one-time unforgeability of MAC, the adversary would not gain any advantage by manipulating (φ, σ). Thus, we have the following theorem:

Theorem 3. CL-TKEM *is a* Tag-ID-CCA2 *secure certificateless Tag-KEM.*

The security proof is quite similar with those of Theorem 1 and 2. Due to the page limitation, the complete proof has been skipped. It will be included in the full version of this paper.

Discussion: The construction of Tag-KEM in [2] combines a KEM and a message authentication code MAC. Since a MAC is already used in our construction of CL-KEM, there is no need for us to add a new MAC into the construction of CL-TKEM as in [2]. Thus, our construction of CL-TKEM is essentially the same as that of CL-KEM, with only a difference in the generation of σ. The computation cost of CL-TKEM is merely slightly more than that of CL-KEM, due to the larger input to MAC.

4.2 Our Hybrid Certificateless Encryption

As shown in [2], a one-time secure data encapsulation mechanism DEM is enough for constructing a CCA2 public key encryption scheme, by integrating with a CCA2 secure Tag-KEM. Roughly speaking, at first a symmetric key is generated, and the message is encrypted under DEM by using this key, then the resulting symmetric ciphertext is used as a tag to encrypt the key under the Tag-KEM. Based on this idea, we can also construct a hybrid certificateless encryption scheme CL-HE from a certificateless Tag-KEM CL-TKEM and a DEM. The scheme is described as in Fig. 3.

– MasterKeyGen, PartialKeyGen and UserKeyGen are the same as those of CL-TKEM.	
– $c \leftarrow \mathsf{Enc}(mpk, upk_{\mathsf{ID}}, \mathsf{ID}, m)$:	– $m \leftarrow \mathsf{Dec}(psk_{\mathsf{ID}}, usk_{\mathsf{ID}}, \mathsf{ID}, c)$:
$(w, dk) \leftarrow \mathsf{CL\text{-}TKEM.Key}(mpk, \mathsf{ID})$	$(e, \chi) \leftarrow c$
$\chi \leftarrow \mathsf{DEM.Enc}_{dk}(m)$	$dk \leftarrow \mathsf{CL\text{-}TKEM.Decap}(psk_{\mathsf{ID}}, usk_{\mathsf{ID}}, \mathsf{ID}, \chi, e)$
$e \leftarrow \mathsf{CL\text{-}TKEM.Encap}(w, \chi)$	$m \leftarrow \mathsf{DEM.Dec}_{dk}(\chi)$
$c \leftarrow (e, \chi)$	If $dk = \bot$, then $\bot$ is returned.

Fig. 3. CL-HE

Analogously to Theorem 3.1 in [2], we have the following theorem:

Theorem 4. *The hybrid certificateless encryption scheme* CL-HE *proposed above is* ID-CCA2 *secure, provided that the underlying certificateless Tag KEM* CL-TKEM *is* Tag-ID-CCA2 *secure and* DEM *is one-time secure.*

Again, due to the page limitation, the complete proof has been skipped. It will be included in the full version of this paper.

5 Conclusion

We proposed the *first generic* construction of CL-KEM in the standard model, which is also secure against malicious-but-passive KGC attacks. Our construction can be instantiated efficiently and is comparable to Bentahar et al.'s CL-KEMs [5], which have only been proven secure under the random oracle model with no consideration of the malicious-but-passive KGC attacks.

We also introduced notion of certificateless tag-based KEM (CL-TKEM), which is an extension of Abe et al.'s work [2] from the standard setting to the certificateless setting. We showed that an efficient CL-TKEM can be constructed by modifying our CL-KEM. We also showed that with a CL-TKEM and a data encapsulation mechanism (DEM) secure under our proposed notions, an efficient hybrid certificateless encryption can be constructed by applying Abe et al.'s transformation in the certificateless setting.

References

1. Abe, M., Cui, Y., Imai, H., Kiltz, E.: Efficient hybrid encryption from ID-based encryption. Cryptology ePrint Archive, Report 2007/023 (2007) http://eprint.iacr.org/2007/023
2. Abe, M., Gennaro, R., Kurosawa, K., Shoup, V.: Tag-KEM/DEM: A new framework for hybrid encryption and a new analysis of Kurosawa-Desmedt KEM. In: Cramer, R.J.F. (ed.) EUROCRYPT 2005. LNCS, vol. 3494, pp. 128–146. Springer, Heidelberg (2005) Full paper can be found at http://eprint.iacr.org/2005/027
3. Al-Riyami, S.S., Paterson, K.G.: Certificateless public key cryptography. In: Laih, C.-S. (ed.) ASIACRYPT 2003. LNCS, vol. 2894, pp. 452–473. Springer, Heidelberg (2003)
4. Au, M.H., Chen, J., Liu, J.K., Mu, Y., Wong, D.S., Yang, G.: Malicious KGC attacks in certificateless cryptography. To appear in ACM ASIACCS 2007, also at http://eprint.iacr.org/2006/255
5. Bentahar, K., Farshim, P., Malone-Lee, J., Smart, N.: Generic constructions of identity-based and certificateless KEMs. Cryptology ePrint Archive, Report 2005/058 (2005) Also to appear in Journal of Cryptology, http://eprint.iacr.org/2005/012
6. Chen, L., Cheng, Z., Malone-Lee, J., Smart, N.: Efficient ID-KEM based on the Sakai-Kasahara key construction. IEE Proceedings - Information Security 153(1), 19–26 (2006)
7. Cramer, R., Shoup, V.: A practical public key cryptosystem provably secure against adaptive chosen ciphertext attack. In: Krawczyk, H. (ed.) CRYPTO 1998. LNCS, vol. 1462, pp. 13–25. Springer, Heidelberg (1998)
8. Cramer, R., Shoup, V.: Design and analysis of practical public-key encryption schemes secure against adaptive chosen ciphertext attack. SIAM J. Computing 33(1), 167–226 (2003)
9. Dent, A.: A designer's guide to kems. In: Paterson, K.G. (ed.) Cryptography and Coding. LNCS, vol. 2898, pp. 133–151. Springer, Heidelberg (2003)
10. Gentry, C.: Practical identity-based encryption without random oracles. In: Vaudenay, S. (ed.) EUROCRYPT 2006. LNCS, vol. 4004, pp. 445–464. Springer, Heidelberg (2006)
11. Herranz, J., Hofheinz, D., Kiltz, E.: The Kurosawa-Desmedt key encapsulation is not chosen-ciphertext secure. Cryptology ePrint Archive, Report 2005/207 (2005) http://eprint.iacr.org/2005/207
12. Hu, B.C., Wong, D.S., Zhang, Z., Deng, X.: Key replacement attack against a generic construction of certificateless signature. In: Batten, L.M., Safavi-Naini, R. (eds.) ACISP 2006. LNCS, vol. 4058, pp. 235–246. Springer, Heidelberg (2006)
13. Huang, X., Susilo, W., Mu, Y., Zhang, F.: On the security of certificateless signature schemes from Asiacrypt 2003. In: Desmedt, Y.G., Wang, H., Mu, Y., Li, Y. (eds.) CANS 2005. LNCS, vol. 3810, pp. 13–25. Springer, Heidelberg (2005)
14. Kiltz, E.: Chosen-ciphertext security from tag-based encryption. In: Halevi, S., Rabin, T. (eds.) TCC 2006. LNCS, vol. 3876, pp. 581–600. Springer, Heidelberg (2006)
15. Kurosawa, K., Desmedt, Y.: A new paradigm of hybrid encryption scheme. In: Franklin, M. (ed.) CRYPTO 2004. LNCS, vol. 3152, pp. 426–442. Springer, Heidelberg (2004)
16. Li, X., Chen, K., Sun, L.: Certificateless signature and proxy signature schemes from bilinear pairings. Lithuanian Mathematical Journal 45(1), 76–83 (2005)

17. Libert, B., Quisquater, J.-J.: On constructing certificateless cryptosystems from identity based encryption. In: Yung, M., Dodis, Y., Kiayias, A., Malkin, T.G. (eds.) PKC 2006. LNCS, vol. 3958, pp. 474–490. Springer, Heidelberg (2006)
18. Liu, J.K., Au, M.H., Susilo, W.: Self-generated-certificate public key cryptography and certificateless signature/encryption scheme in the standard model. To appear in ACM ASIACCS 2007. Full paper http://eprint.iacr.org/2006/373
19. MacKenzie, P., Reiter, M.K., Yang, K.: Alternatives to non-malleability: Definitions, constructions, and applications. In: Naor, M. (ed.) TCC 2004. LNCS, vol. 2951, pp. 171–190. Springer, Heidelberg (2004)
20. Sakai, R., Kasahara, M.: Id based cryptosystems with pairing on elliptic curve. Cryptology ePrint Archive, Report 2003/054 (2003) http://eprint.iacr.org/2003/054
21. Shamir, A.: Identity-based cryptosystems and signature schemes. In: Blakely, G.R., Chaum, D. (eds.) CRYPTO 1984. LNCS, vol. 196, pp. 47–53. Springer, Heidelberg (1985)
22. Shoup, V.: Using hash functions as a hedge against chosen ciphertext attack. In: Preneel, B. (ed.) EUROCRYPT 2000. LNCS, vol. 1807, pp. 275–288. Springer, Heidelberg (2000)
23. Shoup, V.: ISO 18033-2: an emerging standard for public-key encryption (committee draft) (June 2004) Available at http://shoup.net/iso/
24. Shoup, V., Gennaro, R.: Secure threshold cryptosystems against chosen ciphertext attack. Journal of Cryptology 15(2), 75–96 (2002)
25. Stinson, D.R.: Universal hashing and authentication codes. Designs, Codes, and Cryptography 4(4), 369–380 (1994)
26. Waters, B.: Efficient identity-based encryption without random oracles. In: Cramer, R.J.F. (ed.) EUROCRYPT 2005. LNCS, vol. 3494, pp. 114–127. Springer, Heidelberg (2005)
27. Wegman, M.N., Carter, J.L.: New hash functions and their use in authentication and set equality. Journal of Computer and System Sciences 22(3), 265–279 (1981)
28. Yum, D.H., Lee, P.J.: Generic construction of certificateless encryption. In: Laganà, A., Gavrilova, M., Kumar, V., Mun, Y., Tan, C.J.K., Gervasi, O. (eds.) ICCSA 2004. LNCS, vol. 3043, pp. 802–811. Springer, Heidelberg (2004)
29. Yum, D.H., Lee, P.J.: Generic construction of certificateless signature. In: Wang, H., Pieprzyk, J., Varadharajan, V. (eds.) ACISP 2004. LNCS, vol. 3108, pp. 200–211. Springer, Heidelberg (2004)

Double-Size Bipartite Modular Multiplication

Masayuki Yoshino, Katsuyuki Okeya, and Camille Vuillaume

Hitachi, Ltd., Systems Development Laboratory, Kawasaki, Japan
{masayuki.yoshino.aa,katsuyuki.okeya.ue,camille.vuillaume.ch}@hitachi.com

Abstract. This paper proposes new techniques of double-size *bipartite* multiplications with single-size *bipartite* modular multiplication units. Smartcards are usually equipped with crypto-coprocessors for accelerating the computation of modular multiplications, however, their operand size is limited. Security institutes such as NIST and standards such as EMV have recommended or forced to increase the bit-length of RSA cryptography over years. Therefore, techniques to compute double-size modular multiplications with single-size modular multiplication units has been studied this decade to extend the life expectancy of the low-end devices. We propose new double-size techniques based on multipliers implementing either *classical* or *Montgomery* modular multiplications, or even both simultaneously (*bipartite* modular multiplication), in which case one can potentially compute modular multiplications twice faster.

Keywords: bipartite modular multiplication, double-size technique, RSA, crypto-coprocessor, smartcard.

1 Introduction

The algorithm proposed by Kaihara et al. [KT05] called "bipartite modular multiplication" efficiently computes modular multiplications, which are time-critical operations in public-key cryptosystems such as RSA [RSA78], ElGamal, DSA and others. The *bipartite* modular multiplication utilizes both of the major approaches for computing modular multiplications: *classical* modular multiplications [MOV96] and *Montgomery* multiplications [Mon85], which run in parallel during the bipartite computations. Furthermore, thanks to this combination of two different approaches, the bipartite technique can not only potentially double the speed of modular multiplications, but also remove costly precomputations which are necessary for Montgomery multiplications, that is, the modular square of the Montgomery constant.

The well-known RSA algorithm is the de facto standard for public-key cryptography. However, the bit-length of RSA must be increased regularly because of progresses in integer factorization techniques [RSA]. Many security institutes have been increasing their recommended key-length for public-key cryptography over years [EMV, ?, NIST]. Smartcards typically are not powerful enough to compute modular multiplications with long bit-length in software, and need the assistance of a crypto-coprocessor in hardware [NM96]. However, such crypto-coprocessors suffer from an important restriction: their operand size is limited

J. Pieprzyk, H. Ghodosi, and E. Dawson (Eds.): ACISP 2007, LNCS 4586, pp. 230–244, 2007.
© Springer-Verlag Berlin Heidelberg

[Pai99]. On the one hand, thanks to the Chinese Remainder Theorem, *private* computations require only single-size multiplications for computing a double-size decryption or signature generation [QC82]. On the other hand, in the case of *public* computations, the Chinese Remainder Theorem is of no help, and techniques requiring public information only are necessary.

Double-size modular multiplication techniques have been studied for about one decade. Residue Number Systems are combined with classical multiplications [PP95] and Montgomery multiplications [BDK97]. These works motivated the seminal paper for multi-size techniques, where Paillier showed how to efficiently compute a kn-bit classical modular multiplication with n-bit classical modular multiplication units [Pai99]. Later, Fischer et al. optimized the scheme for the $2n$-bit case [FS03] and Chevallier-Mames et al. showed further improvements [CJP03]. Furthermore, Yoshino et al. extended the double-size techniques to Montgomery multiplications [YOV06].

Unfortunately, the double-size technique is much slower than the techniques of the Chinese Remainder Theorem. For example, double-size techniques of Chevallier-Mames et al. need 12 calculations of single-size classical multiplication. Therefore, in order to reduce computation time of double-size multiplication, high performance of single-size modular multiplication unit is necessary. However, all of the previous techniques cannot be applied in the case where the underlying multipliers are equipped with latest modular multiplication algorithm, that is, bipartite multiplication. They cannot take advantage of the attractive features of bipartite multiplications, such as greater speed and the absence of precomputations.

This paper proposes a technique for computing $2n$-bit bipartite modular multiplications with n-bit bipartite multiplication units, that can potentially double processing speed when the gate size of the multiplier is doubled. In double-size techniques, the performance has been evaluated by the number of calls to multipliers, and the proposal is the same as the best known method for classical multiplications and better than for Montgomery multiplications. Therefore, the proposal double-size techniques can get benefit from the greater speed of bipartite modular multiplication units, and be applied to modular exponentiation with not only small exponent such as *public* computations, but also big exponent such as *private* computations. From the viewpoint of system vendors such as smartcard makers, when an algorithm of modular multiplication is selected for a new coprocessor, the double-size technique should be ready for the new coprocessor, and keep compatibility for the current coprocessor, to enlarge key-length according to recommendations of security standards. In fact, our double-size technique is based on bipartite multiplications, will work with classical or Montgomery multipliers, and even both of them running in parallel. Thanks to our techniques, new coprocessors can be equipped with hardware implementation of bipartite modular multiplication for high-speed computation and software implementation of our scheme for enlargement of bit-length.

The rest of this paper is organized as follows. Section 2 introduces the bipartite modular multiplications, and Section 3 reviews previous double-size techniques and states problems for applying them to the bipartite multiplications. Section 4 explains our idea for computing $2n$-bit bipartite multiplications. Our technique requires the n-bit quotients of the bipartite multiplications, thus, in Section 5 we describe approaches to compute such quotients. Section 6 gives features of our proposal and shows results to compare the proposal to others. Finally, we conclude with Section 7.

Notation. We let "n" denote the operand size of modular multiplication units, the capital letters A, B and N denote $2n$-bit integers, where N means modulus, and is odd and greater than 2^n because of $2n$-bit public-key cryptosystems such as RSA. We also let small letters denote the other integers, such as n-bit quotients "q" and remainders "r".

2   Modular Multiplications

The bipartite modular multiplication proposed by Kaihara et al. [KT05] is a new technique which combines and unifies two major approaches: classical and Montgomery multiplications. In hardware, Montgomery multiplications are often preferred to classical modular multiplications due to the fact that they eliminate the need to wait for carries and therefore reduce delays. On the other hand, Montgomery multiplications use a different representation of integers, and in order to convert integers to this representation, a precomputed modulus-dependent value is required. In the case of public computations (for example signature verifications), the modulus is not known in advance, and the precomputations must be performed online. In addition to potentially doubling the computation speed, bipartite modular multiplications can decrease the precomputation effort, and even eliminate it in some settings.

2.1   Bipartite Modular Multiplication

For n-bit integers x, y, w, the bipartite modular multiplication algorithm[1] computes a remainder r: $r \equiv xy2^{-m} \pmod{w}$, where $0 \leq x, y < w$, $0 \leq m \leq n$, w is coprime to 2^m and 2^{-m} is the inverse of 2^m modulo w. The basic idea of bipartite modular multiplications is to combine two major approaches: classical modular multiplications and Montgomery multiplications. In the computational process, two multiplications can be executed in parallel. More precisely, by splitting the multiplier y into two integers y_h and y_l such that $y = y_h 2^m + y_l$ where $0 \leq y_h < 2^{n-m}$ and $0 \leq y_l < 2^m$, the bipartite modular multiplication algorithm executes one classical and one Montgomery multiplication according to the following equation:

$$xy2^{-m} \equiv x(y_h 2^m + y_l)2^{-m} \pmod{w} \equiv xy_h + xy_l 2^{-m} \pmod{w}.$$

---

[1] The paper assumes that the bipartite modular multiplication includes classical modular multiplication ($m = 0$) and Montgomery multiplication ($m = n$) for simplicity, although it is different from the original proposed by Kaihara [KT05], which defined a range of m; $0 < m < n$.

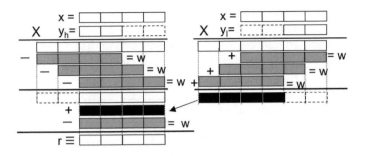

Fig. 1. Basic idea of bipartite modular multiplications

Figure 1 illustrates the principle of bipartite multiplications. In the left side, the classical multiplier subtracts the modulus w from the most significant bit of the product xy_h and save the remainder r_C in the least significant side. In the right side, unlike classical multiplications, the Montgomery multiplier adds the modulus w and save the remainder r_M in the most significant side. Finally, both remainders are added, and, if necessary, the modulus w is subtracted.

3   Double-Size Techniques

The bit-length of RSA must be increased regularly because of progresses in integer factorization techniques [RSA]. Many security institutes have been increasing their recommended key-length over years. For example, EMV, which is a standard specification for payment systems of smartcards, defined deadlines for using some bit-lengths in the framework of RSA. For instance, 1024-bit RSA keys will expire in 2009, and 1984-bit keys in 2016 [EMV]. In the US, the National Institute of Standards and Technology (NIST) has recommended to use 1024-bit RSA until 2010, 2048-bit RSA until 2030 and 3072 bits beyond 2030. One approach to extend the key-length is to implement double-size techniques; it allows a hardware-software co-design without any necessity to change the hardware.

3.1   Previous Double-Size Modular Multiplications

Recently, Chevallier-Mames et al. [CJP03] optimized double-size techniques in the case of *classical* modular multiplications and Yoshino et al. introduced double-size *Montgomery* multiplications [YOV06]. Chevallier-Mames et al. proposed Algorithm 1 to compute the $2n$-bit classical modular multiplications (AB mod N), given $2n$-bit integers A, B and $2n$-bit modulus N with MultModDiv instructions which output the quotients q_C and the remainders r_C of n-bit classical modular multiplications: $(q_C, r_C) = $ MultModDiv (x, y, w), where $0 \le x$, $y < w$, $q_C = \lfloor (xy)/w \rfloor$ and $r_C \equiv xy \pmod{w}$. The MultModDiv instruction can be emulated with two calls to the multiplier outputting only the remainder r_C or small changes of the hardware multiplier itself to output the quotient q_C.

Yoshino et al. proposed Algorithm 2 to compute $2n$-bit Montgomery multiplications ($AB2^{-2n} \mod N$), where $0 \leq A, B < N < 2^{2n}$. They assumed another instructions which compute quotients $q_{\mathcal{M}}$ and remainders $r_{\mathcal{M}}$ of n-bit Montgomery multiplications satisfying the following equation: $xy = q_{\mathcal{M}}w + r_{\mathcal{M}}2^n$, where $0 \leq x, y, r_{\mathcal{M}} < w$ and $-2^n < q_{\mathcal{M}} < 2^n$.

Algorithm 1. $2n$-bit *classical* modular multiplication [CJP03]

INPUT: $A = a_1 2^n + a_0$, $B = b_1 2^n + b_0$, $N = n_1 2^n + n_0$, where $0 \leq A, B < N < 2^{2n}$, $0 \leq a_1, a_0, b_1, b_0, n_0 < 2^n$ and $2^{n-1} \leq n_1 < 2^n$;
OUTPUT: $AB \pmod{N}$;

---

1. $(q_1, r_1) \leftarrow \mathsf{MultModDiv}(a_1, b_1, n_1)$
2. $(q_2, r_2) \leftarrow \mathsf{MultModDiv}(q_1, n_0, 2^n)$
3. $(q_3, r_3) \leftarrow \mathsf{MultModDiv}(a_0 + a_1, b_0 + b_1, 2^n - 1)$
4. $(q_4, r_4) \leftarrow \mathsf{MultModDiv}(a_0, b_0, 2^n)$
5. $(q_5, r_5) \leftarrow \mathsf{MultModDiv}(2^n - 1, -q_2 + q_3 - q_4 + r_1, n_1)$
6. $(q_6, r_6) \leftarrow \mathsf{MultModDiv}(q_5, n_0, 2^n)$
7. **Return** $(-q_6 - r_2 + r_3 - r_4 + r_5)2^n + (r_2 + r_4 - r_6)$

Algorithm 2. $2n$-bit *Montgomery* multiplication [YOV06]

INPUT: $A = a_1 z + a_0 2^n$, $B = b_1 z + b_0 2^n$, $N = n_1 z + n_0 2^n$, where $0 \leq A, B < N < 2^{2n}$, $-2^n < a_0, b_0, n_0 < 2^n$, $0 \leq a_1, b_1 < 2^n$, $0 < n_1 < 2^n$, $1 \leq z < 2^n$ and n_1 and z are odd;
OUTPUT: $AB2^{-2n} \pmod{N}$;

---

1. $(q_1, r_1) \leftarrow \mathsf{MultMonDiv}(b_1, z, n_1)$
2. $(q_2, r_2) \leftarrow \mathsf{MultMonDiv}(q_1, n_0, z)$
3. $(q_3, r_3) \leftarrow \mathsf{MultMonDiv}(a_1, b_0 - q_2 - r_1, n_1)$
4. $(q_4, r_4) \leftarrow \mathsf{MultMonDiv}(a_0, b_1, n_1)$
5. $(q_5, r_5) \leftarrow \mathsf{MultMonDiv}(q_3 + q_4, n_0, z)$
6. $(q_6, r_6) \leftarrow \mathsf{MultMonDiv}(a_1, r_2, z)$
7. $(q_7, r_7) \leftarrow \mathsf{MultMonDiv}(a_0, b_0, z)$
8. **Return** $(-q_5 - q_6 + q_7 + r_3 + r_4)z + (-r_5 - r_6 + r_7)2^n$

3.2   Double-Size Bipartite Modular Multiplication

Unfortunately, previous double-size techniques cannot be applied straightforwardly to the case of bipartite modular multiplications for the following reasons.

Notion of Quotient. In double-size techniques, not only the remainders but also the quotients of single-size modular multiplications are necessary. The notion of quotient depends on the type of the multiplication: the quotients are in the most significant side in the framework of the classical modular multiplications, but in the least significant side in the framework of the Montgomery multiplications. The bipartite modular multiplication combines remainders of the classical multiplications and the Montgomery multiplications, but has no definition of a quotient.

Integer Representation. In the framework of double-size techniques, $2n$-bit integers are decomposed into n-bit integers. Double-size classical modular multiplications simply divide a $2n$-bit integer X into x_1 and x_0 as follows: x_1 consists of the upper n bits of X and x_0 of the lower n bits; then $X = x_1 2^n + x_0$. Since x_0 is derived from the remainder $(X \bmod 2^n)$ and x_1 is residual information, that is, the quotient. In the case of Montgomery multiplications, x_0 consists of the upper n bits and x_1 of the lower n bits of X, which is the opposite of the classical multiplication; then $X = x_1 + x_0 2^n$. Both cases can clearly divide $2n$-bit integer X into x_0 and x_1 using the lower and upper n bits of X.

The bipartite modular multiplications outputs a remainder $(X2^{-m} \bmod 2^n)$ with parameter 2^m where $0 \leq m \leq n$. One could be tempted to consider the following representation derived from the bipartite remainder by applying an idea inspired by the cases of classical and Montgomery multiplications: $X = x_1 2^{n-m} + x_0 2^m$. However, this approach fails since the equation cannot represent integers close to 0 and 2^{2n}.

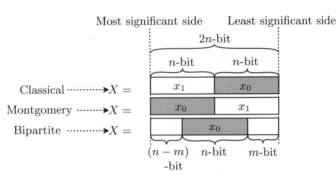

Fig. 2. $2n$-bit representation for each modular multiplication

4   New Double-Size Techniques

This section explains our idea to compute $2n$-bit bipartite modular multiplications using n-bit bipartite multipliers. Since we assume that there is an instruction implementing n-bit bipartite modular multiplications, such as a coprocessor in a smartcard, Section 4.1 explains how to implement the instruction in practice. Our double-size techniques need quotients of modular multiplications, therefore, Section 4.2 shows another instruction to output the quotient, which is based on the instruction in Section 4.1. Note that the bit-length of the instruction is limited to n bits; thus we show how to split $2n$-bit integers into small integers in Section 4.3. Finally, Section 4.4 shows an algorithm to perform $2n$-bit bipartite multiplications with n-bit remainders and quotients.

4.1   Bipartite Modular Multiplication Units

First, we define the instruction of the bipartite modular multiplications in Definition 1.

Definition 1. *For integers x, y, w, the* BIP *instruction is defined as r=BIP(x, y, w) with $r = xy2^{-m}$ (mod w) where $0 \le x, y < w$, $0 \le m \le n$ and $\gcd(w, 2^m)=1$.*

The BIP instruction covers classical multiplications when $m = 0$ and Montgomery multiplications when $m = n$.

4.2   Quotients of Bipartite Modular Multiplication

Similarly to previous double-size techniques, which make use of the quotients of their respective multiplication algorithm, our scheme requires the quotient of n-bit bipartite modular multiplications to construct the $2n$-bit remainder. We extend the notion of quotient to the case of bipartite modular multiplications. Indeed, from Definition 1, the following equation holds: $xy \equiv r2^m$ (mod w). This equation means that there is some integer q satisfying: $xy = qw + r2^m$. We call the integer q *quotient* of the bipartite modular multiplications. Now, we define the instruction to output the quotient q in Definition 2.

Definition 2. *For integers x, y, w, the* XBIP *instruction is defined as $(q, r) =$ XBIP(x, y, w) with $r \equiv xy2^{-m}$ (mod w) and q satisfying the equation: $xy = qw + r2^m$ where $0 \le x, y < w$, $0 \le m \le n$ and $\gcd(w, 2^m) = 1$.*

Section 5 will show two different algorithms to build the XBIP instruction on the BIP instruction.

4.3 $2n$-Bit Integer Representations

In double-size techniques, $2n$-bit integer should be decomposed on two n-bit integers, later processed by n-bit bipartite multipliers. The decomposition utilizes both quotients and remainders of the bipartite multiplication. Definition 3 and Algorithm 3 show how to divide a $2n$-bit integer into two integers.

Definition 3. *$2n$-bit integers X are represented as follows: $X = x_1 z + x_0 2^m$, where $0 \le X < 2^{2n}$, $-2^m < x_1 \le (2^{n-m} - 1)2^m$, $0 \le x_0 \le 2z$, $z = 2^n - 1$ and $0 \le m \le n$.*

Algorithm 3 shows how to represent the $2n$-bit integers with n-bit integers.

Algorithm 3. $2n$-bit integer representation for bipartite modular multiplication

---

INPUT: X where $0 \le X < 2^{2n}$;
OUTPUT: x_1, x_0 such that $X = x_1 z + x_0 2^m$ where $-2^m < x_1 \le (2^{n-m} - 1)2^m$, $0 \le x_0 \le 2z$, $z = 2^n - 1$, and $0 \le m \le n$. ;

---

1. $t_2 \leftarrow X/(2^{m+n})$
2. $t_1 \leftarrow \{X \pmod{2^{m+n}}\}/2^m$
3. $t_0 \leftarrow X \pmod{2^m}$
4. $x_1 \leftarrow t_2 2^m - t_0$
5. $x_0 \leftarrow (t_0 2^{n-m} + t_2) + t_1$
6. **Return** (x_1, x_0)

Proposition 1. *Algorithm 3 outputs integers x_1 and x_0 satisfying the equation $X = x_1 z + x_0 2^m$ where $0 \leq X < 2^{2n}$, $-2^m < x_1 \leq (2^{n-m} - 1)2^m$, $0 \leq x_0 \leq 2z$, $z = 2^n - 1$ and $0 \leq m \leq n$.*

We show the proof of Proposition 1 in Appendix A.

Since RSA requires $2n$-bit odd modulus, Algorithm 3 can output odd x_1 in the case of $2n$-bit modulus. This x_1 can be modulus for the XBIP instruction, because it is satisfied with the assumption of Definition 2; $\gcd(x_1, 2^m) = 1$ where $0 \leq m \leq n$.

There are many values acceptable for z, for instance, $z = 2^n + 1$. We choose $z = 2^n - 1$, because it is easy to be satisfied with the assumption of XBIP instruction; $0 \leq x, y < z$, where x and y are n-bit integers and z is n-bit modulus. x_0 and x_1 may cause problems to break the assumption of XBIP instruction, such as x_0, $x_1 < 0$ or $x_0 > 2^n$, but there is a way to avoid these problems which will be introduced at the end of this section.

4.4   Double-Size Bipartite Modular Multiplications

Our new algorithm for double-size *bipartite* modular multiplications is derived from Algorithm 1 which only requires the moduli n_1 and z, and Algorithm 3 which set n_1 as odd and $z = 2^n - 1$. n-bit bipartite modular multiplications output the n-bit remainder $xy2^{-m} \pmod{w}$, where $0 \leq x, y < w$ and $0 \leq m \leq n$, therefore, our algorithm outputs the $2n$-bit remainder of the bipartite modular multiplication $AB2^{-2m} \pmod{N}$ where $0 \leq A, B < N < 2^{2n}$ and $0 \leq m \leq n$.

Algorithm 4. $2n$-bit bipartite modular multiplication

INPUT: $A = a_1 z + a_0 2^m$, $B = b_1 z + b_0 2^m$, $N = n_1 z + n_0 2^m$, where $0 \leq A, B < N < 2^{2n}$, $-2^m < a_1, b_1, n_1 \leq (2^{n-m} - 1)2^m$, $0 \leq a_0, b_0, n_0 \leq 2z$, $z = 2^n - 1$ and $0 \leq m \leq n$;
OUTPUT: $AB2^{-2m} \pmod{N}$;

---

1. $(q_1, r_1) \leftarrow \mathsf{XBIP}(a_1, b_1, n_1)$
2. $(q_2, r_2) \leftarrow \mathsf{XBIP}(q_1, n_0, z)$
3. $(q_3, r_3) \leftarrow \mathsf{XBIP}(a_0 + a_1, b_0 + b_1, z)$
4. $(q_4, r_4) \leftarrow \mathsf{XBIP}(a_0, b_0, z)$
5. $(q_5, r_5) \leftarrow \mathsf{XBIP}(z, -q_2 + q_3 - q_4 + r_1, n_1)$
6. $(q_6, r_6) \leftarrow \mathsf{XBIP}(q_5, n_0, z)$
7. **Return** $(q_2 + q_4 - q_6 - r_1 - r_2 + r_3 - r_4 + r_5)z + (r_2 + r_4 - r_6)2^m$

Theorem 1. *Algorithm 4 computes $AB2^{-2m} \pmod{N}$ calling the XBIP instruction, provided that $0 \leq A, B < N < 2^{2n}$ and $0 \leq m \leq n$.*

We show the proof of Theorem 1 in Appendix B.

Practical Implementation Issues

In order not to break the assumption of XBIP instruction, that is, $0 \leq x, y < w$, Algorithm 4 needs to adjust values of intermediate data. There are two strategies:

the first one is to change a value of modulus: Specially when modulus is small, it requires little additional work. The second strategy is to change values of multiplier x or/and multiplicand y; the work is more costly.

1. Modification of modulus

   The modulus w must be greater than multiplier x and multiplicand y, however, step1 and step5 of Algorithm 4 use n_1 as modulus, which is the output of Algorithm 3 and can be smaller than or equal to x or y. In order to solve the problem, when $n_1 \leq \max(x, y)$, we use $(n_1 + i2^m)$ such that $n_1 + i2^m > \max(x, y)$ instead of n_1 itself where $0 \leq m \leq n$ and i is some positive integer. This is based on the following fact: if $xy = qn_1 + r2^m$, then $xy = q(n_1 + i2^m) + (-iq + r)2^m$ holds.

2. Modification of multiplier or/and multiplicand

   The intermediate value of multiplier x or multiplicand y can break the assumption, such that $x, y < 0$. The problem is solved using the following fact: if $xy2^{-m} \pmod{w} \equiv r$, then $(x + i2^m)(y + j2^m)2^{-m} \pmod{w} \equiv r + jx + iy + ij2^m$ holds, such that $0 \leq x + i2^m$, $y + j2^m < w$, where $0 \leq m \leq n$, and i and j are some integers.

5   How to Compute Quotients of Bipartite Multiplications

In Section 4, we have defined the quotient of bipartite modular multiplications; in fact, this quotient is necessary to compute the $2n$-bit bipartite modular multiplications. We consider two types of settings, and in each case, show efficient algorithms to calculate the quotients. In the first settings, we assume a pure software implementation, based on normal n-bit multipliers implementing bipartite modular multiplications such as the BIP instruction. Section 5.1 shows how to compute the quotient with two calls to the n-bit multiplier. In the second settings, modifications of the hardware multiplier are allowed, but still restricted to n-bit operands. Section 5.2 shows how to modify the multipliers with minimal changes.

5.1   Software Approach

Algorithm 5 is based on bipartite modular multipliers, and as such, will work with classical or Montgomery multipliers, and even both of them running in parallel. Algorithm 5 emulates the computation of the quotients with two calls to the n-bit multipliers.

Theorem 2. *Algorithm 5 computes the* XBIP(x, y, w) *instruction calling the* BIP *instruction twice, provided that $0 \leq x, y < w$, $0 \leq m \leq n$ and $gcd(w, 2^m) = 1$.*

We show the proof of Theorem 2 in Appendix C.

Algorithm 5. XBIP instruction calling BIP instruction

INPUT: x, y, w with $0 \leq x, y < w$, $0 \leq m \leq n$ and $\gcd(w, 2^m) = 1$;
OUTPUT: q, r;

---

1. $r \leftarrow \mathsf{BIP}(x, y, w)$
2. $r' \leftarrow \mathsf{BIP}(x, y, w + 2^m)$
3. $q \leftarrow r - r'$
4. If $q \leq -2^m$, $q \leftarrow q + w + 2^m$.
5. **Return** (q, r)

5.2   Hardware Approach

Alternatively, the algorithm of bipartite modular multiplications itself can be changed to keep intermediate data and output the quotient required by double-size techniques. This subsection shows an algorithm implementing the XBIP instruction, which is essentially the same as the BIP instruction, but in addition, computes the quotients of n-bit bipartite multiplications. It is necessary to build or change the multipliers itself, however, the hardware cost of XBIP instruction is almost same as the BIP instruction. In Algorithm 6, the representation of the integers x, y, u and r are stored in array of n-bit elements, where $i = 0$ is the least significant bit and there are underlines under instructions inserted to compute quotients.

Algorithm 6. XBIP instruction based on a modified BIP

INPUT: x, y, w where $0 \leq x, y < w$, $w' = 1(-w^{-1} \mod 2)$, $0 \leq m \leq n$ and $\gcd(w, 2^m) = 1$;
OUTPUT: q, r;

---

1 $\underline{q_C \leftarrow 0}$, $r_C \leftarrow 0$, $\underline{q_\mathcal{M} \leftarrow 0}$ and $r_\mathcal{M} \leftarrow 0$
2 $\underline{y_h \leftarrow y/2^m}$ and $\underline{y_l \leftarrow y} \pmod{2^m}$
3 If $m = 0$, do the the classical multiplication steps.
   Else if $m = n$, do the Montgomery multiplication steps.
   Else do the the Montgomery steps and the classical multiplication steps in parallel.

(Montgomery multiplication steps)	(Classical multiplication steps)
M1. For i from 0 to $(m-1)$, do the following steps (a)–(c): (a) $u_i \leftarrow (r_0 + x_0 y_i) w' \mod 2$ (b) $\underline{q_\mathcal{M} \leftarrow q_\mathcal{M} - u_i 2^i}$ (c) $r_\mathcal{M} \leftarrow (r_\mathcal{M} + x y_i + u_i w)/2$ M2. If $r_\mathcal{M} \geq w$, do the following steps (a) and (b): (a) $r_\mathcal{M} \leftarrow r_\mathcal{M} - w$ (b) $\underline{q_\mathcal{M} \leftarrow q_\mathcal{M} - 2^m}$	C1. For i from $(n-1)$ down to m do the following steps (a)–(d): (a) $r_C \leftarrow 2 r_C + x y_i$ (b) $u_i \leftarrow r_C/w$ (c) $\underline{q_C \leftarrow 2 q_C + u_i}$ (d) $r_C \leftarrow r_C - u_i w$

4 . $r \leftarrow r_C + r_\mathcal{M}$ and $\underline{q \leftarrow q_C + q_\mathcal{M}}$
5 . If $r \geq w$ do $r \leftarrow r - w$ and $\underline{q \leftarrow q + 2^m}$
6 . **Return** $(\underline{q}, r)$

---

6   Remarkable Features

Design of Crypto-coprocessors. Due to progresses of mathematical crypt-analysis techniques, the size of the key-length of most public-key cryptosystems is growing rapidly. Hardware designers are often confronted with the following dilemma: having an efficient hardware multiplier, typically with a limited operand size, and being able to keep pace with new specifications and larger key sizes. The latter feature is usually achieved using a hardware-software co-design, for example with a double-size technique. Our scheme allows the crypto-coprocessor to have such co-design, with a unique and fast hardware implementation, as well as extensions supported in software.

Performance. Despite their limited computational power, low-end devices such as smartcards can achieve high performance thanks to hardware accelerators. in the framework of high-performance implementations, one should not only consider the type of multiplier, but also the number of calls to the multiplier, which should be kept as small as possible. In the case of a pure software approach, our $2n$-bit bipartite modular multiplication requires only 12 calls to the multipliers, which is the same calls as the best $2n$-bit *classical* modular multiplications proposed by Chevallier-Mames et al. [CJP03] and less calls than $2n$-bit *Montgomery* multiplications proposed by Yoshino et al. [YOV06]. The hardware approach for computing the quotient results in half the number of calls compared to the software approach in similar conditions.

In addition, in the case where the classical multiplier has the same or a greater bit-length than the Montgomery unit, our technique virtually eliminates the need for precomputations for the Montgomery unit. In an RSA encryption/signature verification with a small exponent, these precomputations require a computational effort on the same order as the encryption/verification, and since they are modulus-dependent, they must be performed in the runtime. Therefore, the use of bipartite multiplications results in significant improvements in speed.

Compatibility. Recently, even low-devices such as smartcards are equipped with virtual machine such as Java Card and MULTOS which can actualize same environments on different hardware. Therefore, the software on such environments should be supported even in different system environments. Unfortunately, so far, the proposed double-size techniques only fit in the particular platform they were designed for. From the viewpoint of software designers, a common method for every hardware multiplier is desirable. Unlike the previous schemes, our scheme accepts different types of n-bit multiplications.

Table 1 compares our techniques with the others. Our scheme supports not only bipartite modular multiplications, but also classical and Montgomery multiplications. Furthermore, in double-size techniques, the performance is essentially determined by the number of calls to the multiplier, and ours is the same calls as the most optimized case of the classical multiplication proposed by Chevallier-Mames et al.

Table 1. Comparison of double-size techniques

Scheme	Montgomery constants	Multipliers	Calls	
			Software approach	Hardware approach
Fischer et al. [FS03]	1(fixed)	Classical	14	7
Chevallier-Mames et al. [CJP03]	1(fixed)	Classical	12	6
Yoshino et al. [YOV06]	2^n(fixed)	Montgomery	14	7
This paper	1	Classical	12	6
	2^n	Montgomery		
	$0 < 2^m < 2^n$	Bipartite		

7   Conclusion

We proposed a novel technique for $2n$-bit *bipartite* modular multiplications based on n-bit multiplication units. Our scheme works with not only Montgomery multipliers, but also classical multipliers, or even both of them running in parallel to achieve even greater speed in bipartite modular multiplication settings. Thanks to our techniques, hardware designers can design and modify coprocessors, take advantage of the fast bipartite modular multiplication algorithm, and extend their bit-length without changing the hardware of the coprocessor according to future specifications of the key sizes. Furthermore, our scheme offers compatibility with different hardware multipliers, which is desirable for virtual environments, and achieves high performance: it needs the same number of calls to the multiplier as the fastest known double-size technique for classical multiplications but less number of calls than the best technique for Montgomery multiplications.

References

[BDK97] Bajard, J.-C., Didier, L.-S., Kornerup, P.: An RNS Montgomery Modular Multiplication Algorithm. In: Proceedings of ARITH13, pp. 234–239. IEEE Computer Society, Los Alamitos (1997)

[CJP03] Chevallier-Mames, B., Joye, M., Paillier, P.: Faster Double-Size Modular Multiplication From Euclidean Multipliers. In: D.Walter, C., Koç, Ç.K., Paar, C. (eds.) CHES 2003. LNCS, vol. 2779, pp. 214–227. Springer, Heidelberg (2003)

[EMV] EMVco. EMV Issuer and Application Security Guidelines, Version 1.3 (2005) http://www.emvco.com/specifications.asp?show=4

[FS03] Fischer, W., Seifert, J.-P.: Increasing the bitlength of crypto-coprocessors. In: Kaliski Jr., B.S., Koç, Ç.K., Paar, C. (eds.) CHES 2002. LNCS, vol. 2523, pp. 71–81. Springer, Heidelberg (2003)

[HP98] Handschuh, H., Paillier, P.: Smart card crypto-coprocessors for public-key cryptography. In: Schneier, B., Quisquater, J.-J. (eds.) CARDIS 1998. LNCS, vol. 1820, pp. 372–379. Springer, Heidelberg (2000)

[KT05] Kaihara, M.E., Takagi, N.: Bipartite modular multiplication. In: Rao, J.R., Sunar, B. (eds.) CHES 2005. LNCS, vol. 3659, pp. 201–210. Springer, Heidelberg (2005)

[LV01]   Lenstra, A.K., Verheul, E.R.: Selecting Cryptographic Key Sizes. J. Cryptology 14(4), 255–293 (2001)

[Mon85]   Montgomery, P.L.: Modular multiplication without trial division. Mathematics of Computation 44(170), 519–521 (1985)

[MOV96]   Menezes, A.J., van Oorschot, P.C., Vanstone, S.A.: Handbook of Applied Cryptography. CRC Press, Boca Raton (1996)

[NIST]   National Institute of Standards ant Technology, NIST Special Publication 800-57 DRAFT, Recommendation for KeyManagement Part 1: General (2006) http://csrc.nist.gov/CryptoToolkit/tkkeymgmt.html

[NM96]   Naccache, D., M'Raïhi, D.: Arithmetic co-processors for public-key cryptography: The state of the art. In: CARDIS, pp. 18–20 (1996)

[Pai99]   Paillier, P.: Low-cost double-size modular exponentiation or how to stretch your cryptoprocessor. In: Imai, H., Zheng, Y. (eds.) PKC 1999. LNCS, vol. 1560, pp. 223–234. Springer, Heidelberg (1999)

[PP95]   Posch, K.C., Posch, R.: Modulo reduction in Residue Number Systems. IEEE Transactions on Parallel and Distributed Systems 6(5), 449–454 (1995)

[QC82]   Quisquater, J.-J., Couvreur, C.: Fast decipherment algorithm for rsa public-key cryptosystem. Electronics Letters 18(21), 905–907 (1982)

[RSA]   RSA Laboratories, RSA challenges, http://www.rsa.com/rsalabs

[RSA78]   Rivest, R.L., Shamir, A., Adelman, L.M.: A method for obtaining digital signatures and public-key cryptosystems. Communications of the ACM 21(2), 120–126 (1978)

[YOV06]   Yoshino, M., Okeya, K., Vuillaume, C.: Unbridle the Bit-Length of a Crypto-Coprocessor with Montgomery Multiplication. In: Preproceedings of the 13th Annual Workshop on Selected Areas in Cryptography (SAC'06), pp. 184–198 (2006)

A   Proof of Proposition 1

Algorithm 3 outputs two n-bit integers x_1 and x_0 satisfying the equation $X = x_1 z + x_0 2^m$ where $0 \leq X < 2^{2n}$, $-2^m < x_1 \leq (2^{n-m} - 1)2^m$, $0 \leq x_0 \leq 2z$, $z = 2^n - 1$ and $0 \leq m \leq n$.

Proof. $2n$-bit integer X can be decomposed on the following equation;

$$X = t_2 2^{m+n} + t_1 2^m + t_0$$

where $0 \leq m \leq n$, $0 \leq t_2 < 2^{n-m}$, $0 \leq t_1 < 2^n$ and $0 \leq t_0 < 2^m$. Then,

$$\begin{aligned} X &= t_2 2^{m+n} + t_1 2^m + t_0 \\ &= (t_2 2^m - t_0)(2^n - 1) + (t_2 + t_1 + t_0 2^{n-m})2^m. \end{aligned}$$

The part of second term, $(t_2 + t_1 + t_0 2^{n-m})$, is evaluated as follows.

$$\begin{aligned} t_2 + t_1 + t_0 2^{n-m} &\leq (2^{n-m} - 1) + (2^n - 1) + (2^m - 1) \\ &= 2^n + (2^{n-m} + 2^m) - 3 \\ &\leq 2^n + (2^n + 1) - 3 \\ &= 2(2^n - 1) \end{aligned}$$

Since $-2^m < t_2 2^m - t_0 \leq (2^{n-m} - 1)2^m$ and $0 \leq t_2 + t_1 + t_0 2^{n-m} \leq 2(2^n - 1)$, then $X = x_1(2^n - 1) + x_0 2^m$, where $x_1 = t_2 2^m - t_0$ and $x_0 = t_2 + t_1 + t_0 2^{n-m}$. □

B   Proof of Theorem 1

Algorithm 4 computes $AB2^{-2m} \pmod{N}$ calling the XBIP instruction, provided that $0 \le A, B < N < 2^{2n}$ and $0 \le m \le n$.

Proof. Firstly, $2n$-bit integers A, B, N are decomposed on the following equation;

$$A = a_1 z + a_0 2^m,\ B = b_1 z + b_0 2^m,\ N = n_1 z + n_0 2^m$$

where $\gcd(z, 2^m) = 1$ and $0 \le m \le n$. Then, we continue to be the following.
The following equation holds by Karatsuba.

$$
\begin{aligned}
AB &= (a_1 z + a_0 2^m)(b_1 z + b_0 2^m) \\
&= a_1 b_1 z(z - 2^m) + (a_1 + a_0)(b_1 + b_0)z 2^m - a_0 b_0 (z - 2^m)2^m
\end{aligned}
\tag{1}
$$

First term of equation(1) is represented in the following equation. There is <u>underline</u> related to computation with multipliers for easy reference.

$$
\begin{aligned}
\underline{a_1 b_1} z(z - 2^m) &= (q_1 n_1 + r_1 2^m)z(z - 2^m) \\
&= (q_1 n_1 z + r_1 z 2^m)(z - 2^m) \\
&\equiv (-q_1 n_0 2^m + r_1 z 2^m)(z - 2^m) \\
&= (-q_1 n_0 + r_1 z)(z - 2^m)2^m \\
&= (-q_2 z - r_2 2^m + r_1 z)(z - 2^m)2^m \\
&= (-q_2 + r_1)z^2 2^m + (q_2 - r_1 - r_2)z 2^{2m} + r_2 2^{3m}
\end{aligned}
$$

Similarly, second term of equation(1) is represented in the following equation.

$$
\begin{aligned}
\underline{(a_1 + a_0)(b_1 + b_0)}z 2^m &= (q_3 z + r_3 2^m)z 2^m \\
&= q_3 z^2 2^m + r_3 z 2^{2m}
\end{aligned}
$$

Similarly, third term of equation(1) is represented in the following equation.

$$
\begin{aligned}
\underline{a_0 b_0}(z - 2^m)2^m &= (q_4 z + r_4 2^m)(z - 2^m)2^m \\
&= q_4 z^2 2^m + (-q_4 + r_4)z 2^{2m} - r_4 2^{3m}
\end{aligned}
$$

Then, whole equation(1) is represented in the following equation.

$$
\begin{aligned}
AB &= \underline{(-q_2 + q_3 - q_4 + r_1)}z^2 2^m \\
&\quad + (q_2 + q_4 - r_1 - r_2 + r_3 - r_4)z 2^{2m} + (r_2 + r_4)2^{3m} \\
&= (q_5 n_1 + r_5 2^m)z 2^m \\
&\quad + (q_2 + q_4 - r_1 - r_2 + r_3 - r_4)z 2^{2m} + (r_2 + r_4)2^{3m}
\end{aligned}
$$

$$= (q_5 n_1 z + r_5 z 2^m) 2^m$$
$$+ (q_2 + q_4 - r_1 - r_2 + r_3 - r_4) z 2^{2m} + (r_2 + r_4) 2^{3m}$$
$$\equiv (-q_5 n_0 2^m + r_5 z 2^m) 2^m$$
$$+ (q_2 + q_4 - r_1 - r_2 + r_3 - r_4) z 2^{2m} + (r_2 + r_4) 2^{3m}$$
$$= (-q_6 z - r_6 2^m + r_5 z) 2^{2m}$$
$$+ (q_2 + q_4 - r_1 - r_2 + r_3 - r_4) z 2^{2m} + (r_2 + r_4) 2^{3m}$$
$$= \{(q_2 + q_4 - q_6 - r_1 - r_2 + r_3 - r_4 + r_5) z + (r_2 + r_4 - r_6) 2^m\} 2^{2m}$$

As a result, the following equation; $AB 2^{-2m} = qz + r 2^m$ where $q = (q_2 + q_4 - q_6 - r_1 - r_2 + r_3 - r_4 + r_5)$ and $r = (r_2 + r_4 - r_6)$, proofs that algorithm 4 computes the remainder of $2n$-bit bipartite modular multiplications. □

C   Proof of Theorem 2

Algorithm 5 computes the $\mathsf{XBIP}(x, y, w)$ instruction calling the BIP instruction twice; $r = \mathsf{BIP}(x, y, w)$ with $r \equiv xy 2^{-m} \pmod{w}$ and $r' = \mathsf{BIP}(x, y, w + 2^m)$ with $r' \equiv xy 2^{-m} \pmod{(w + 2^m)}$, provided that $0 \le x, y < w$, $0 \le m \le n$ and $\gcd(w, 2^m) = 1$.

Proof. Since $w > 0$ and $-w 2^m < xy - r 2^m < w^2$,

$$-2^m < q < w \tag{2}$$

holds. From the equation: $qw + r 2^m = q'(w + 2^m) + r' 2^m$, we have:

$$q 2^m = (q - q')(w + 2^m) + (r - r') 2^m. \tag{3}$$

Since $(w + 2^m)$ is coprime to 2^m, $q - q' = \delta 2^m$ holds, where δ is some integer. The equation (3) is divided by 2^m,

$$q = \delta(w + 2^m) + r - r'.$$

$(w + 2m)$ is greater than the range of q by the equation (2), δ is uniquely defined. From $0 \le r < w$ and $0 \le r' < w + 2^m$, we have: $-w - 2^m < w < 2^m$. If $-2^m < r - r' < w$, then $\delta = 0$ and $q = r - r'$ holds. Else, in the case that $r - r' \le -2^m$, $\delta = 1$ and $q = w + 2^m + r - r'$ holds. □

Affine Precomputation with Sole Inversion in Elliptic Curve Cryptography

Erik Dahmen[1], Katsuyuki Okeya[2], and Daniel Schepers[1]

[1] Technische Universität Darmstadt, Fachbereich Informatik,
Hochschulstr.10, D-64289 Darmstadt, Germany
{dahmen,schepers}@cdc.informatik.tu-darmstadt.de
[2] Hitachi, Ltd., Systems Development Laboratory,
1099, Ohzenji, Asao-ku, Kawasaki-shi, Kanagawa-ken, 215-0013, Japan
katsuyuki.okeya.ue@hitachi.com

Abstract. This paper presents a new approach to precompute all odd points $[3]P, [5]P, \ldots, [2k-1]P$, $k \geq 2$ on an elliptic curve over $\mathbb{F}_p$. Those points are required for the efficient evaluation of a scalar multiplication, the most important operation in elliptic curve cryptography. The proposed method precomputes the points in affine coordinates and needs only one single field inversion for the computation. The new method is superior to all known methods that also use one field inversion. Compared to methods that require several field inversions for the precomputation, the proposed method is faster for a broad range of ratios of field inversions and field multiplications. The proposed method benefits especially from ratios as they occur on smart cards.

Keywords: affine coordinates, elliptic curve cryptosystem, precomputation, scalar multiplication.

1 Introduction

Koblitz [Kob87] and Miller [Mil86] independently proposed to use elliptic curves for cryptographic purposes. The main advantage of elliptic curves is, that high security can be achieved by using only small key sizes [BSS99].

One of the most time-consuming operation in cryptosystems based on elliptic curves is a scalar multiplication $[u]P$, where u is the scalar and P is a point on an elliptic curve over $\mathbb{F}_p$. Scalar multiplications are computed using the double-and-add algorithm. The number of point additions required by this algorithm can be reduced by representing the scalar in a signed representation that provides fewer non-zero digits [Ava04, Möl02, Möl04, MS04, OSST04, Sol00, SST04]. In this case, the double-and-add algorithm requires several precomputed points. For efficiency reasons, those points are usually represented in affine coordinates [CMO98]. If the point P is not fixed, the precomputation cannot be performed offline and requires a significant amount of time, since expensive field inversions are required to precompute points in affine coordinates. Scalar multiplications with non-fixed points for example occur in the Diffie-Hellman key exchange

J. Pieprzyk, H. Ghodosi, and E. Dawson (Eds.): ACISP 2007, LNCS 4586, pp. 245–258, 2007.
© Springer-Verlag Berlin Heidelberg 2007

[DH76] and the verification step of the elliptic curve digital signature algorithm [JM99]. One important research goal is to reduce the number of field inversions that are involved in the precomputation. In [CJLM06], a method to compute $[3]P$ with only one inversion was proposed.

This paper generalizes this method and presents a new approach to precompute points on an elliptic curve over $\mathbb{F}_p$. The proposed scheme computes all odd points $[3]P, \ldots, [2k-1]P$, $k \geq 2$ by using only one single field inversion, independent of the number of points to precompute. The main idea is to use a recursive strategy to express all values that have to be inverted using only known parameters. Then, all values are inverted simultaneously using the Montgomery trick, e.g. see [CF05] p. 209. Further, the proposed scheme does not require additional memory for temporary calculations.

Compared to previous approaches for the precomputation (e.g. [CMO98]), the proposed method benefits from a large ratio of inversions and multiplications (I/M). This ratio is especially large on smart cards that are equipped with a cryptographic coprocessor, which is usually the case [Infineon, Renesas]. In [Sey05], Seysen states that on such smart cards an I/M ratio of $I > 100M$ is realistic. In [CF05, ELM03, JP03], the authors state that on smart cards with a cryptographic coprocessor, the inversion is best computed using Fermat's little theorem. This approach requires about $\log_2 p$ field multiplications, where p is the prime that defines the field. Note that p must be at least 160 bit to guarantee security.

After introducing the proposed method, this paper states a thorough comparison with known methods for the precomputation. Rather than specifying the advantage of a certain method for a given I/M ratio, the I/M *break even points* of the different methods are estimated. The I/M break even points provide information about which method is the most efficient for a certain I/M ratio. As it will turn out, the proposed method is the most efficient for I/M ratios as they occur on smart cards.

The remainder of this paper is organized as follows: Section 2 introduces the basics of elliptic curves and scalar multiplications. Section 3 reviews known methods for the precomputation. Section 4 describes the proposed scheme. Section 5 compares the proposed scheme with known methods and Section 6 states the conclusion.

2   Scalar Multiplications in Elliptic Curve Cryptography

An elliptic curve over a prime field $\mathbb{F}_p$ is defined by the implicit equation $E : y^2 = x^3 + ax + b$, where $a, b \in \mathbb{F}_p$ and $p > 3$ prime. A further condition on a and b is, that the so-called discriminant $\Delta = 4a^3 + 27b^2$ is non-zero. The points on an elliptic curve can be used to construct an abelian group $E(\mathbb{F}_p)$ with identity element $\mathcal{O}$ called the "point at infinity" [BSS99]. Point additions $(P + Q)$ and doublings $(2P)$ are denoted by ECADD and ECDBL, respectively. Points on an elliptic curve can be represented in several coordinate systems, such as affine $(\mathcal{A})$, projective $(\mathcal{P})$, Jacobian $(\mathcal{J})$, modified Jacobian $(\mathcal{J}^m)$, and Chudnovsky

Jacobian ($\mathcal{J}^c$) coordinates [CMO98]. The number of field multiplications (M), squarings (S), and inversions (I) required for an ECADD or ECDBL operation depends on the coordinate system used to represent the points. See [CMO98] for an overview of the costs and explicit formulas.

A scalar multiplication $[u]P$ of a point $P \in E(\mathbb{F}_p)$ and a scalar $u > 0$ is defined by adding P to itself u times. An efficient method to compute a scalar multiplication is the *double-and-add algorithm* shown in Algorithm 1. This algorithm uses an n-bit *base-2 representation* $(u_{n-1}, \dots, u_0)$ of u, e.g. the binary representation or one of the representations proposed in [Ava04, Möl02, Möl04, MS04, OSST04, Sol00, SST04].

Algorithm 1. Double-and-Add Algorithm

Require: Point $P \in E(\mathbb{F}_p)$, n-bit scalar u.
Ensure: Scalar multiplication $[u]P$
 1: $X \leftarrow \mathcal{O}$
 2: **for** $i = n - 1$ down to 0 **do**
 3:     $X \leftarrow \text{ECDBL}(X)$
 4:         **if** $u_i \neq 0$ **then** $X \leftarrow \text{ECADD}(X, [u_i]P)$
 5: **end for**
 6: **return** X

Algorithm 1 performs a point doubling in each iteration (line 3) and a point addition each time the current digit u_i is non-zero (line 4). Hence a scalar multiplication needs $n \cdot$ AHD ECADD $+ n$ ECDBL, where AHD denotes the *average Hamming density*, i.e. the average density of non-zero digits in the base-2 representation of u. The points $[u_i]P$ required in line 4 are precomputed beforehand. Which and how many points must be precomputed depends on the base-2 representation used for u.

To reduce the required number of field operations in the different steps of Algorithm 1, the authors of [CMO98] represent the points using mixed coordinates. They use $\mathcal{J}^m$ coordinates for the result of a doubling followed by a doubling ($u_i = 0$) and $\mathcal{J}$ coordinates for the result of a doubling followed by an addition ($u_i \neq 0$). The costs for a doubling then are $4M + 4S$ and $3M + 4S$, respectively. The precomputed points $[u_i]P$ are represented either in $\mathcal{A}$ or $\mathcal{J}^c$ coordinates. The costs for an addition then are $9M + 5S$ or $12M + 5S$, respectively. Using mixed coordinates, a scalar multiplication with Algorithm 1 requires

$$\text{cs}_{\mathcal{A}} = n \cdot \text{AHD}(9M + 5S) + n\big(\text{AHD}(3M + 4S) + (1 - \text{AHD})(4M + 4S)\big) \quad (1)$$

$$\text{cs}_{\mathcal{J}^c} = n \cdot \text{AHD}(12M + 5S) + n\big(\text{AHD}(3M + 4S) + (1 - \text{AHD})(4M + 4S)\big) \quad (2)$$

with precomputed points in $\mathcal{A}$ and $\mathcal{J}^c$ coordinates, respectively.

A very flexible base-2 representation is the *fractional window recoding* method [Möl02, Möl04, SST04]. For an arbitrary $k \geq 1$, this representation uses the digits in the *digit set* $\mathcal{D}_k = \{0, \pm 1, \pm 3, \dots, \pm(2k - 1)\}$. When used with Algorithm 1, the $k - 1$ points $[3]P, [5]P, \dots, [2k - 1]P$ must be precomputed. Note, that only the positive points must be precomputed, since point inversions are virtually for free, e.g. if $[-3]P$ is required by Algorithm 1, it is obtained from $[3]P$ by an "on-the-fly" point inversion [BSS99]. The AHD of this representation is

$$\text{AHD}_k = \left(\frac{k}{2^{\lfloor \log_2 k \rfloor}} + \lfloor \log_2 k \rfloor + 2 \right)^{-1} \tag{3}$$

which is minimal among all base-2 representations that use this digit set [Möl04]. Note, that if $k = 2^{w-2}$ for some $w \geq 2$, the fractional window recoding method has the same AHD as the *width-w non adjacent form* [Sol00] and its analogs [Ava04, MS04, OSST04], i.e. $1/(w+1)$.

Increasing the parameter k on the one hand decreases the AHD and therefore the number of ECADD operations in Algorithm 1 and on the other hand increases the number of points that must be precomputed. Therefore, increasing k does not automatically yield a better total performance, since additional ECADD and ECDBL operations are required for the precomputation.

3   Precomputing the Required Points

In this section, several methods for the precomputation of the $k-1$ points $[3]P, [5]P, \ldots, [2k-1]P$ required by the fractional window recoding method are reviewed. Recall that according to [CMO98], the precomputed points should be represented in $\mathcal{A}$ or $\mathcal{J}^c$ coordinates. The most straightforward method is to compute each point separately using the chain $P \rightarrow [2]P \rightarrow [3]P \rightarrow [5]P \rightarrow \ldots \rightarrow [2k-1]P$. This method needs

$$\text{cp}_{\mathcal{A}} = 2kM + (k+1)S + kI \tag{4}$$

$$\text{cp}_{\mathcal{J}^c} = (11k - 6)M + (3k + 3)S \tag{5}$$

when using $\mathcal{A}$ or $\mathcal{J}^c$ coordinates for the precomputed points, respectively. Storing the points requires $2(k-1)$ registers for affine coordinates and $5(k-1)$ registers for Chudnovsky Jacobian coordinates.

The following methods compute the points in $\mathcal{A}$ coordinates and trade inversions for multiplications using the *Montgomery trick* for simultaneous inversions [CF05] p. 209. This algorithm computes n inverses using $3nM + I$.

Let $k = 2^{w-2}$ for some $w \geq 2$. In [CMO98] the authors compute the points using the chain $P \rightarrow 2P \rightarrow [3]P, [4]P \rightarrow [5]P, [7]P, [8]P \rightarrow \ldots \rightarrow [2^{w-3}+1]P, \ldots, [2^{w-2}-1]P, [2^{w-2}]P \rightarrow [2^{w-2}+1]P, \ldots, [2^{w-1}-1]P$. The inversions required in each of the $w - 1$ steps are computed simultaneously using the Montgomery trick. In terms of k, this method needs

$$\text{cp}_{\text{CMO}} = (5k + 2\lceil \log_2 k \rceil - 8)M + (k + 2\lceil \log_2 k \rceil - 1)S + (\lceil \log_2 k \rceil + 1)I. \tag{6}$$

The logarithm has to be rounded up to cover the case where k is chosen such that it is not a power of 2. Storing the points requires $2(k-1)$ registers.

The last method is a straightforward method that first computes the points separately in $\mathcal{P}, \mathcal{J}, \mathcal{J}^m$, or $\mathcal{J}^c$ coordinates. Then the points are converted to $\mathcal{A}$

coordinates. A conversion from $\mathcal{P}$ to $\mathcal{A}$ needs $2M + I$. A conversion from $\mathcal{J}$, $\mathcal{J}^c$, or $\mathcal{J}^m$ to $\mathcal{A}$ needs $3M + S + I$. The inversions required for the conversion are computed simultaneously using the Montgomery trick. These methods need

$$\text{cp}_{\mathcal{P} \to \mathcal{A}} = (17k - 10)M + (2k + 3)S + I \tag{7}$$

$$\text{cp}_{\mathcal{J} \to \mathcal{A}} = (18k - 14)M + (5k + 1)S + I \tag{8}$$

$$\text{cp}_{\mathcal{J}^c \to \mathcal{A}} = (17k - 12)M + (4k + 2)S + I \tag{9}$$

$$\text{cp}_{\mathcal{J}^m \to \mathcal{A}} = (19k - 15)M + (7k - 3)S + I \tag{10}$$

Storing the points in affine coordinates requires $2(k - 1)$ registers. However, it has to be considered that the points require more memory prior to conversion to affine coordinates. The required number of registers is $3(k - 1)$ for $\mathcal{P}$ and $\mathcal{J}$ coordinates, $5(k - 1)$ for $\mathcal{J}^c$ coordinates, and $4(k - 1)$ for $\mathcal{J}^m$ coordinates.

4   Proposed Scheme

This section describes the proposed scheme. The proposed scheme computes the required points $[3]P, [5]P, \ldots, [2k-1]P$, $k \geq 2$ directly in affine coordinates using only one field inversion. The proposed scheme needs $(10k - 11)M + (4k)S + I$ for the precomputation and $2(k - 1)$ registers to store the points.

The proposed scheme computes $[2i - 1]P = (x_{i+1}, y_{i+1})$ as $[2]P + [2i - 3]P$, $i = 2, \ldots, k$ and therefore the computation of $[2]P$ is also required. The formulas to compute the points in affine coordinates are

$$
\begin{aligned}
[2]P = (x_2, y_2): \quad & \lambda_1 = \frac{(3x_1^2 + a)}{(2y_1)} & & \begin{aligned} x_2 &= \lambda_1^2 - 2x_1 \\ y_2 &= \lambda_1(x_1 - x_2) - y_1 \end{aligned} \\[4pt]
[3]P = (x_3, y_3): \quad & \lambda_2 = \frac{(y_2 - y_1)}{(x_2 - x_1)} & & \begin{aligned} x_3 &= \lambda_2^2 - x_2 - x_1 \\ y_3 &= \lambda_2(x_2 - x_3) - y_2 \end{aligned} \\[4pt]
[2i - 1]P = (x_{i+1}, y_{i+1}): \quad & \lambda_i = \frac{(y_i - y_2)}{(x_i - x_2)} & & \begin{aligned} x_{i+1} &= \lambda_i^2 - x_2 - x_i \\ y_{i+1} &= \lambda_i(x_2 - x_{i+1}) - y_2 \end{aligned}
\end{aligned}
\tag{11}
$$

The most time consuming operation when computing points in affine coordinates is the field inversion required to invert the denominator of the λ_i. Call those denominators δ_i. According to the last section, it is possible to compute field inversions simultaneously using the Montgomery trick [CF05]. However to do so, *all values to invert must be known*. For the precomputation this is not the case, since each point depends on a previous computed point, e.g. $[7]P = [2]P + [5]P$.

The main idea of the proposed scheme is to write down all δ_i using only the base point $P = (x_1, y_1)$ and the elliptic curve parameters a and b. Then, all δ_i are known and can be inverted simultaneously using the Montgomery trick. The proposed strategy is divided into four steps. The pseudocode of those steps can be found in Appendix A.

Step 1: The first step computes $d_1, \ldots, d_k$, such that $d_i = d_1^2 \cdot \ldots \cdot d_{i-1}^2 \cdot \delta_i$ holds for $i = 1, \ldots, k$. This is done by the following recursive strategy which successively substitutes the formulas for x_i, y_i in the formulas for x_{i+1}, y_{i+1}.

$[2]P: \ d_1 = 2y_1$

$[3]P: \ d_2 = A_2^2 - B_2$
$A_2 = 3x_1^2 + a$
$B_2 = d_1^2 \cdot 3x_1$

$[5]P: \ d_3 = A_3^2 - 2D_3 - B_3$
$A_3 = -d_2 \cdot A_2 - C_3$
$B_3 = d_2^2 \cdot B_2$
$C_3 = d_1^4$
$D_3 = d_2^3$

$[7]P: \ d_4 = A_4^2 - D_4 - B_4$
$A_4 = -d_3 \cdot A_3 - C_4$
$B_4 = d_3^2 (B_3 + 3D_3)$
$C_4 = D_3 (2A_3 + C_3)$
$D_4 = d_3^3$

$[2i-1]P: \ d_i = A_i^2 - D_i - B_i$
$i > 4 \quad A_i = -d_{i-1} \cdot A_{i-1} - C_i$
$B_i = d_{i-1}^2 \cdot B_{i-1}$
$C_i = D_{i-1} \cdot C_{i-1}$
$D_i = d_{i-1}^3$

For example, $d_1 = 2y_1 = \delta_1$ and

$$
\begin{aligned}
d_2 &= A_2^2 - B_2 \\
&= (3x_1^2 + a)^2 - (2y_1)^2 \cdot 3x_1 \\
&= (2y_1)^2 \left(\left(\frac{3x_1^2 + a}{2y_1} \right)^2 - 2x_1 - x_1 \right) \\
&= (2y_1)^2 \left((\lambda_1^2 - 2x_1) - x_1 \right) \\
&= (2y_1)^2 (x_2 - x_1) = d_1^2 \cdot \delta_2.
\end{aligned}
$$

Step 2: The second step computes the inverses of $d_1, \ldots, d_k$ using the Montgomery Trick [CF05]. At first, the values $e_i = \prod_{j=1}^{i} d_j$ are computed for $i = 1, \ldots, k$. Next, the inverse of e_k,

$$
e_k^{-1} = (d_1 \cdot \ldots \cdot d_k)^{-1} = d_1^{-1} \cdot \ldots \cdot d_k^{-1}
$$

is computed. Then, the inverses of $d_1, \ldots, d_k$ are obtained as

$$
\begin{aligned}
d_k^{-1} &= e_{k-1} \cdot (d_1 \cdot \ldots \cdot d_k)^{-1} \\
d_i^{-1} &= e_{i-1} \cdot (d_1 \cdot \ldots \cdot d_k)^{-1} \cdot d_k \cdot \ldots \cdot d_{i+1}, \quad i = k-1, \ldots, 2 \\
d_1^{-1} &= (d_1 \cdot \ldots \cdot d_k)^{-1} \cdot d_k \cdot \ldots \cdot d_2
\end{aligned}
$$

Step 3. The third step recovers the inverses of the denominators $\delta_1^{-1}, \ldots, \delta_k^{-1}$ from $d_1^{-1}, \ldots, d_k^{-1}$ computed in Step 2. According to Step 1,

$$
d_i = d_1^2 \cdot \ldots \cdot d_{i-1}^2 \cdot \delta_i \iff \delta_i^{-1} = d_1^2 \cdot \ldots \cdot d_{i-1}^2 \cdot d_i^{-1}
$$

holds. Therefore, δ_i^{-1} can be recovered as

$$
\delta_i^{-1} = e_{i-1}^2 \cdot d_i^{-1}, \quad i = 1, \ldots, k
$$

using $e_1, \ldots, e_k$ computed in Step 2.

Step 4. The fourth step computes the points $[3]P, [5]P, \ldots, [2k-1]P$, using the inverses of the denominators $\delta_1^{-1}, \ldots, \delta_k^{-1}$ recovered in Step 3 and the formulas for point additions and doublings shown in Equation (11).

Theorem 1. *In total, the proposed scheme needs*

$$\mathrm{cp}_{\mathrm{Prop}} = (10k - 11)M + (4k)S + I \tag{12}$$

to compute the points $[3]P, [5]P, \ldots, [2k-1]P$. *Further, the proposed scheme requires* $2(k-1)$ *registers to store the points and no additional memory for temporary calculations.*

The proof of this theorem can be found in Appendix B.

5 Analysis

The proposed method as well as the methods reviewed in Section 3 trade field inversions for multiplications and squarings. Hence, the advantage of a respective method depends on the ratio of inversions and multiplications I/M and the ratio of squarings and multiplications S/M. In this analysis, the S/M ratio is set to $S = 0.8M$. For software implementations of an inversion in a prime field, the I/M ratios vary between $I = 4M$ [ELM03, BSS99] and $I = 80M$ [HMV04]. These ratios depend on many factors like the architecture, the methods used for multiplication, modular reduction, and inversion, and the size of the prime field. In software implementations, the inverse is usually computed using the binary GCD algorithm [HMV04]. However, this algorithm is hardly available in embedded devices like smart cards. On a smart card equipped with a cryptographic coprocessor it is faster to compute the inverse using Fermat's little theorem, i.e. $a^{-1} = a^{p-2} \bmod p$, since it uses only operations that are supported by hardware [CF05, ELM03, JP03]. When using Fermat's little theorem to compute an inversion in a prime field $\mathbb{F}_p$ the I/M ratio becomes very large, i.e. about $I = \log_2 p \; M$, since the inverse is computed using a modular exponentiation. According to [Sey05], I/M ratios of $I > 100M$ are realistic on smart cards equipped with a cryptographic coprocessor. In the following, the I/M break even points for the methods introduced in Section 3 and the proposed scheme are estimated.

I/M **Break Even Points for the Precomputation.** At first, the proposed scheme is compared to the last four methods introduced in Section 3. Note that all those methods require only one single inversion. If the S/M ratio $S = 0.8M$ is substituted in Equations (7)-(10) and (12) one gets

$$
\begin{aligned}
\mathrm{cp}_{\mathcal{P} \to \mathcal{A}} &= (17k - 10)M + (2k + 3)S + I = (18.6k - 7.6)M + I \\
\mathrm{cp}_{\mathcal{J} \to \mathcal{A}} &= (18k - 14)M + (5k + 1)S + I = (22.0k - 13.2)M + I \\
\mathrm{cp}_{\mathcal{J}^c \to \mathcal{A}} &= (17k - 12)M + (4k + 2)S + I = (20.2k - 10.4)M + I \\
\mathrm{cp}_{\mathcal{J}^m \to \mathcal{A}} &= (19k - 15)M + (7k - 3)S + I = (24.6k - 17.4)M + I \\
\mathrm{cp}_{\mathrm{Prop}} &= (10k - 11)M + (4k)S + I = (13.2k - 11.0)M + I
\end{aligned}
$$

This shows that, regardless of the I/M ratio, the proposed method is more efficient than precomputing the points in a different coordinate system and converting them to $\mathcal{A}$ coordinates using the Montgomery trick.

The next step is to estimate the I/M break even points of the proposed scheme, the precomputation proposed in [CMO98], and the straightforward precomputation in $\mathcal{A}$ coordinates. A comparison with the straightforward precomputation in $\mathcal{J}^c$ coordinates will be done only for a complete scalar multiplication. This is because the computation of a scalar multiplication is more expensive if the precomputed points are represented in $\mathcal{J}^c$ coordinates (see Equations (1) and (2)). Table 1 shows for different k, for which I/M ratios the proposed scheme and the affine precomputation are the most efficient. The method proposed in [CMO98] is the fastest for the values in between.

Table 1. I/M break even points for the precomputation

k	2	3	4	5	6	7	8	9	10
Proposed	$\geqslant 9.0$	$\geqslant 9.7$	$\geqslant 9.9$	$\geqslant 10.0$	$\geqslant 10.5$	$\geqslant 12.9$	$\geqslant 15.4$	$\geqslant 12.5$	$\geqslant 14.4$
Affine	$\leqslant 9.0$	$\leqslant 9.7$	$\leqslant 9.9$	$\leqslant 10.0$	$\leqslant 9.6$	$\leqslant 7.4$	$\leqslant 6.3$	$\leqslant 8.0$	$\leqslant 7.0$

k	11	12	13	14	15	16	17	18	19
Proposed	$\geqslant 16.2$	$\geqslant 18.0$	$\geqslant 19.9$	$\geqslant 21.8$	$\geqslant 23.6$	$\geqslant 25.5$	$\geqslant 21.1$	$\geqslant 22.6$	$\geqslant 24.0$
Affine	$\leqslant 6.3$	$\leqslant 5.8$	$\leqslant 5.5$	$\leqslant 5.2$	$\leqslant 5.0$	$\leqslant 4.8$	$\leqslant 5.4$	$\leqslant 5.2$	$\leqslant 5.0$

For example if $k = 8$, the most efficient method is: the proposed method if $I/M \geq 15.4$, the [CMO98] method if $6.3 \leq I/M \leq 15.4$, and the affine method if $I/M \leq 6.3$. This table is visualized in Figure 1. Obviously, the advantage of one method is small if the I/M ratio is close to the break even point and large if the I/M ratio is far away from the break even point. Also, the I/M break even points shown in Table 1 are independent of the bit length of the scalar or the size of the prime field, whereas the actual I/M ratio on a certain platform is not. This comparison shows, that the affine and the [CMO98] method perform worse than the proposed method on devices with a large I/M ratio such as smart cards [Sey05].

I/M Break Even Points for a Scalar Multiplication.

In section 2 it was shown that a scalar multiplication requires three additional field multiplications for each point addition if the precomputed points are represented in $\mathcal{J}^c$ coordinates instead of $\mathcal{A}$ coordinates. In order to compare the proposed scheme with the straightforward precomputation in $\mathcal{J}^c$ coordinates (from now on called $\mathcal{J}^c$ method), the total costs for a scalar multiplication must be considered. In this case, the size of the prime field and the bit length n of the scalar is also important. It is assumed that the scalar is *recoded* using the fractional window recoding method and therefore has an AHD as shown in Equation (3). Using

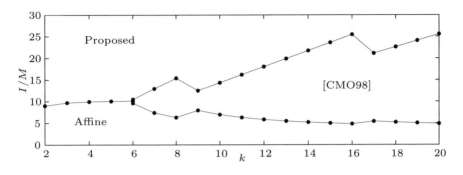

Fig. 1. I/M break even points for the precomputation

Equations (1),(2),(5), and (12) one obtains that the proposed method is more efficient than the $\mathcal{J}^c$ method if

$$I/M < 0.2k + 7.4 + 3n \cdot \text{AHD}_k.$$

Table 2 shows the I/M break even points corresponding to a complete scalar multiplication for different prime fields $\mathbb{F}_{p_n}$, where p_n is an n bit prime. Smaller I/M ratios benefit the proposed method.

Table 2. I/M break even points for the proposed and $\mathcal{J}^c$ method

k	2	3	4	5	6	7	8	9	10
p_{192}	151.8	136.0	123.4	118.1	113.3	109.0	105.0	103.2	101.6
p_{224}	175.8	157.3	142.6	136.4	130.8	125.7	121.0	118.9	116.9
p_{256}	199.8	178.7	161.8	154.7	148.2	142.4	137.0	134.6	132.3

The I/M break even point gets smaller if k grows. However, the total costs for a scalar multiplication are minimal if $k = 8$. This can be determined by comparing the total costs of the proposed method ((1)+(12)) and the $\mathcal{J}^c$ method ((2)+(5)) for different k. The optimal value for k is independent from the I/M ratio, since the proposed method requires only one inversion regardless of k. Note, that such large I/M ratios as shown in Table 2 actually do occur, especially on smart cards where the field inversion is computed using Fermat's little theorem [CF05, ELM03, JP03, Sey05].

The above comparison has one flaw, it does not consider the memory requirement of the precomputed points. Note, that the $\mathcal{J}^c$ method requires 2.5 times the memory of the proposed method for the same k. This is due to the fact that a point in $\mathcal{J}^c$ coordinates consists of five coordinates, whereas a point in $\mathcal{A}$ coordinates consists of only two coordinates [CMO98]. Let r denote the maximum number of registers that can be used for the precomputed points. Then $k_p = \lfloor (r + 2)/2 \rfloor$ and $k_c = \lfloor (r + 5)/5 \rfloor$ denote the maximum value of k that can be used for the proposed method and the $\mathcal{J}^c$ method, respectively. For example, if $r = 15$ then $k_p = 8$ and $k_c = 4$. The proposed method with $k = 8$ needs $1861M + I$ and the $\mathcal{J}^c$ method with $k = 4$ needs $2008.4M$ for a scalar multiplication with a 192 bit scalar. This means, that the proposed method is more efficient as long as $I/M \leq 147.4$. Table 3 shows the I/M break even point corresponding to a complete scalar multiplication for different limitations on the number of registers r and different prime fields $\mathbb{F}_{p_n}$, where p_n is an n bit prime. Again, smaller I/M ratios benefit the proposed method.

Table 3. I/M break even points for fixed registers

r	5	6,7	8,9	10,11	12,13	14	15-19	20-24	25-29	30-34	≥ 35
k_p	3	4	5	6	7	8	8	8	8	8	8
k_c	2	2	2	3	3	3	4	5	6	7	8
p_{192}	202.6	240.6	249.3	189.5	194.5	198.0	147.4	133.4	121.8	112.5	105.0
p_{224}	237.3	283.8	296.2	226.3	234.4	240.7	179.4	160.8	145.1	131.9	121.0
p_{256}	271.9	327.0	343.1	263.2	274.3	283.3	211.4	188.2	168.4	151.4	137.0

If less than five registers are available, the only option is to use the proposed method. If more than 14 registers are available, the proposed method still uses $k = 8$ since using a larger value would decrease the total performance. The same argument holds for the $\mathcal{J}^c$ method if more than 35 registers are available. Table 3 shows, that including the number of registers in the comparison increases the I/M break even point of the proposed method and the $\mathcal{J}^c$ method compared to Table 2. The I/M break even points of the CMO method, the $\mathcal{A}$ method, and the proposed method shown in Table 1 still hold, since all three methods require the same number of registers for storing the precomputed points.

To summarize, the proposed method provides the most efficient precomputation for I/M ratios as they occur on smart cards [Sey05]. Another advantage of the proposed method is, that it precomputes the points in affine coordinates which require less storage space than $\mathcal{J}^c$ coordinates. If the memory for the precomputed points is limited, it is possible to choose larger values of k which further improves a scalar multiplication compared to the $\mathcal{J}^c$ method.

6   Conclusion

This paper presented a new method to precompute all odd points $[3]P, \ldots, [2k-1]P$, $k \geq 2$ on an elliptic curve defined over a prime field $\mathbb{F}_p$ in affine coordinates. The proposed method requires only one field inversion regardless of the number of points to precompute. In total, the proposed scheme requires $(10k - 11)M + (4k)S + I$ field operations for the precomputation and no additional memory for temporary calculations. The proposed method is the most efficient for a large range of I/M ratios, especially for ratios as they occur on smart cards. Further research includes an implementation of the proposed scheme on a smart card.

References

[Ava04]   Avanzi, R.: A Note on the Signed Sliding Window Integer Recoding and a
           Left-to-Right Analogue. In: Handschuh, H., Hasan, M.A. (eds.) SAC 2004.
           LNCS, vol. 3357, pp. 130–143. Springer, Heidelberg (2004)
[BSS99]   Blake, I., Seroussi, G., Smart, N.: Elliptic Curves in Cryptography (London
           Mathematical Society). Lecture Note Series, vol. 265. Cambridge University
           Press, Cambridge (1999)
[CF05]   Cohen, H., Frey, G.: Handbook of elliptic and hyperelliptic curve cryptog-
           raphy. CRC Press, Boca Raton (2005)
[CJLM06]   Ciet, M., Joye, M., Lauter, K., Montgomery, P.: Trading Inversions for
           Multiplications in Elliptic Curve Cryptography. Designs, Codes and Cryp-
           tography 39(2), 189–206 (2006)
[CMO98]   Cohen, H., Miyaji, A., Ono, T.: Efficient Elliptic Curve Exponentiation
           Using Mixed Coordinates. In: Ohta, K., Pei, D. (eds.) ASIACRYPT 1998.
           LNCS, vol. 1514, pp. 51–65. Springer, Heidelberg (1998)
[DH76]   Diffie, W., Hellman, M.: New directions in cryptography. IEEE Transac-
           tions on Information Theory IT-22(6), 644–654 (1976)
[ELM03]   Eisenträger, K., Lauter, K., Montgomery, P.: Fast elliptic curve arithmetic
           and improved Weil pairing evaluation. In: Joye, M. (ed.) CT-RSA 2003.
           LNCS, vol. 2612, pp. 343–354. Springer, Heidelberg (2003)
[HMV04]   Hankerson, D., Menezes, A., Vanstone, S.: Guide to Elliptic Curve Cryp-
           tography. Springer, Heidelberg (2004)
[Infineon] Infineon Technologies, http://www.infineon.com/
[JM99]   Johnson, D., Menezes, A.: The Elliptic Curve Digital Signature Algorithm
           (ECDSA) University of Waterloo, Technical Report CORR 99-34 (1999),
           available at http://www.cacr.math.uwaterloo.ca
[JP03]   Joye, P., Paillier, P.: GCD-Free Algorithms for Computing Modular In-
           verses. In: D.Walter, C., Koç, Ç.K., Paar, C. (eds.) CHES 2003. LNCS,
           vol. 2779, pp. 243–253. Springer, Heidelberg (2003)
[Kob87]   Koblitz, N.: Elliptic Curve Cryptosystems. Mathematics of Computa-
           tion 48(177), 203–209 (1987)
[Mil86]   Miller, V.S.: Use of Elliptic Curves in Cryptography. In: Williams, H.C.
           (ed.) CRYPTO 1985. LNCS, vol. 218, pp. 417–426. Springer, Heidelberg
           (1986)
[Möl02]   Möller, B.: Improved Techniques for Fast Exponentiation. In: Lee, P.J., Lim,
           C.H. (eds.) ICISC 2002. LNCS, vol. 2587, pp. 298–312. Springer, Heidelberg
           (2003)
[Möl04]   Möller, B.: Fractional Windows Revisited: Improved Signed-Digit Repre-
           sentations for Efficient Exponentiation. In: Park, C.-s., Chee, S. (eds.)
           ICISC 2004. LNCS, vol. 3506, pp. 137–153. Springer, Heidelberg (2005)
[MS04]   Muir, J., Stinson, D.: New Minimal Weight Representations for Left-to-
           Right Window Methods. In: Menezes, A.J. (ed.) CT-RSA 2005. LNCS,
           vol. 3376, pp. 366–383. Springer, Heidelberg (2005)
[OSST04]   Okeya, K., Schmidt-Samoa, K., Spahn, C., Takagi, T.: Signed Binary
           Representations Revisited. In: Franklin, M. (ed.) CRYPTO 2004. LNCS,
           vol. 3152, pp. 123–139. Springer, Heidelberg (2004)
[Renesas] Renesas Technologies, http://www.renesas.com/homepage.jsp/
[Sey05]   Seysen, M.: Using an RSA Accelerator for Modular Inversion. In: Rao,
           J.R., Sunar, B. (eds.) CHES 2005. LNCS, vol. 3659, pp. 226–236. Springer,
           Heidelberg (2005)

[Sol00]   Solinas, J.A.: Efficient Arithmetic on Koblitz Curves. Design, Codes and Cryptography 19, 195–249 (2000)

[SST04]   Schmidt-Samoa, K., Semay, O., Takagi, T.: Analysis of Some Fractional Window Recoding Methods and their Application to Elliptic Curve Cryptosystems. IEEE Transactions on Computers 55(1), 1–10 (2006)

A   Pseudocode of the Proposed Scheme

This section contains the pseudocode of the four steps of the proposed scheme.

Algorithm 2. Step 1: Computation of $d_1, \ldots, d_k$

Require: $P = (x_1, y_1), k, a$
Ensure: $d_1, \ldots, d_k$

1: $d_1 \leftarrow 2y_1$

2: $C \leftarrow d_1^2$
3: $A \leftarrow 3x_1^2 + a$
4: $B \leftarrow C \cdot 3x_1$
5: $d_2 \leftarrow A^2 - B$

6: $E \leftarrow d_2^2$
7: $B \leftarrow E \cdot B$
8: $C \leftarrow C^2$
9: $D \leftarrow E \cdot d_2$
10: $A \leftarrow -d_2 \cdot A - C$
11: $d_3 \leftarrow A^2 - 2D - B$

12: $E \leftarrow d_3^2$
13: $B \leftarrow E(B + 3D)$
14: $C \leftarrow D(2A + C)$
15: $D \leftarrow E \cdot d_3$
16: $A \leftarrow -d_3 \cdot A - C$
17: $d_4 \leftarrow A^2 - D - B$

18: **for** $i = 5$ to k **do**
19:        $E \leftarrow d_{i-1}^2$
20:        $B \leftarrow E \cdot B$
21:        $C \leftarrow D \cdot C$
22:        $D \leftarrow E \cdot d_{i-1}$
23:        $A \leftarrow -d_{i-1} \cdot A - C$
24:        $d_i \leftarrow A^2 - D - B$
25: **end for**
26: **return** $d_1, \ldots, d_k$.

Algorithm 3. Step 2: Simultaneous inversion of $d_1, \ldots, d_k$

Require: $d_i, i = 1, \ldots, k$
Ensure: $f_i = d_i^{-1}, e_i = \prod_{j=1}^{i} d_i, i = 1, \ldots, k$
1: $e_1 \leftarrow d_1$
2: **for** $i = 2$ to k **do**
3:     $e_i \leftarrow e_{i-1} \cdot d_i$
4: **end for**
5: $T_1 \leftarrow e_k^{-1}$
6: **for** $i = k$ down to 2 **do**
7:     $T_2 \leftarrow d_i$
8:     $f_i \leftarrow e_{i-1} \cdot T_1$
9:     $T_1 \leftarrow T_1 \cdot T_2$
10: **end for**
11: $f_1 \leftarrow T_1$
12: **return** $e_1, \ldots, e_k, f_1, \ldots, f_k$

Algorithm 4. Step 3: Retrieval of the inverses of the $\delta_1, \ldots, \delta_k$

Require: f_i and $e_i, i = 1, \ldots, k$
Ensure: Inverse of denominators $l_i = \delta_i^{-1}, i = 1, \ldots, k$
1: $l_1 \leftarrow f_1$
2: **for** $i = 2$ to k **do**
3:     $l_i \leftarrow e_{i-1}^2 \cdot f_i$
4: **end for**
5: **return** $l_1, \ldots, l_k$

Algorithm 5. Step 4: Computation of the required points

Require: $P = (x_1, y_1), k, a$ and $l_i, i = 1, \ldots, k$
Ensure: $3P = (x_3, y_3), 5P = (x_4, y_4), \ldots, (2k - 1)P = (x_{k+1}, y_{k+1})$
1: $T \leftarrow (3x_1^2 + a) \cdot l_1$
2: $x_2 \leftarrow T^2 - 2x_1$
3: $y_2 \leftarrow T(x_1 - x_2) - y_1$
4: $T \leftarrow (y_2 - y_1) \cdot l_2$
5: $x_3 \leftarrow T^2 - x_2 - x_1$
6: $y_3 \leftarrow T(x_2 - x_3) - y_2$
7: **for** $i = 3$ to k **do**
8:     $T \leftarrow (y_i - y_2) \cdot l_i$
9:     $x_{i+1} \leftarrow T^2 - x_2 - x_i$
10:     $y_{i+1} \leftarrow T(x_2 - x_{i+1}) - y_2$
11: **end for**
12: **return** $x_3, \ldots, x_{k+1}, y_3, \ldots, y_{k+1}$

B   Proof of Theorem 1

This section states the proof of the Theorem 1 of Section 4.

Theorem 1. *In total, the proposed scheme requires*

$$(10k - 11)M + (4k)S + I$$

field operations to compute the points $3P, 5P, \ldots, (2k-1)P$. Further, the proposed scheme requires $2(k - 1)$ registers to store the points and no additional memory for temporary calculations.

Proof. The costs of each algorithm are calculated separately and summed up. Additions and multiplications with small numbers are neglected since they can be computed very fast. Algorithm 2 requires $8M + 8S + (k-4)(4M+2S) = (4k-8)M + (2k)S$ to compute the d_i. Algorithm 3 requires $3(k-1)M + I$ to invert the d_i and compute the e_i. Algorithm 4 requires $(k-1)(S+M) = (k-1)M + (k-1)S$ to recover the l_i. Algorithm 5 requires $(4M + 3S) + (k - 2)(2M + S) = (2k)M + (k+1)S$ to compute the points $[3]P, [5]P, \ldots, [2k - 1]P$. The sum of the costs of all four steps is given as $(10k - 11)M + (4k)S + I$.

To store the points $[3]P, [5]P, \ldots, [2k - 1]P$, $2(k - 1)$ registers are required. Note, that since the double-and-add algorithm stores the intermediate results in modified Jacobian coordinates, which are represented using four coordinates, 4 additional registers are required for the evaluation of a scalar multiplication. Hence, $2k + 2$ registers are available in total. Algorithm 2 requires $k + 5$ registers to hold d_i and the temporary variables A, B, C, D, E. Algorithm 3 requires $2k + 2$ registers to hold e_i, f_i and the temporary variables T_1, T_2. The f_i can use the same registers as the d_i which explains the necessity of line 7. Algorithm 4 requires k registers to hold l_i. The l_i can use the same registers as the f_i. Algorithm 5 requires $2k + 1$ registers to hold x_i, y_i and one temporary variable T. The x_i and y_i can use the same registers as the e_i and l_i. In total, $2k + 2$ registers are required and therefore no additional memory has to be allocated.

□

Construction of Threshold (Hybrid) Encryption in the Random Oracle Model: How to Construct Secure Threshold Tag-KEM from Weakly Secure Threshold KEM

Takeru Ishihara[1], Hiroshi Aono[1], Sadayuki Hongo[1], and Junji Shikata[2]

[1] NTT DoCoMo, Inc., 3-5 Hikari-no-oka, Yokosuka, Kanagawa, Japan
ishiharat@nttdocomo.co.jp
[2] Yokohama National University, 79-7 Tokiwadai, Hodogaya-ku, Yokohama, Japan
shikata@ynu.ac.jp

Abstract. The security of a public key cryptosystem can be enhanced by distributing secret keys among a number of decryption servers: the threshold encryption approach. In EUROCRYPT 2005, Abe et al. showed that the secure threshold key encapsulation mechanism with a tag (threshold Tag-KEM) immediately yields secure threshold encryption; we only have to construct threshold Tag-KEM to construct threshold encryption. In this paper, we propose a construction of CCA-secure threshold Tag-KEM from threshold KEM (without a tag) that achieves one-wayness by utilizing a signature scheme with tight security reduction. Through our construction, we show *the first* instantiation of CCA-secure threshold encryption whose ciphertext-size and encryption-cost are independent of the number of servers under the RSA assumption in the random oracle model.

1 Introduction

1.1 Background

The threshold encryption scheme distributes the decryption function among a number of decryption servers. Such a cryptosystem is especially useful in applications where it is dangerous to give the power of decryption to just one server. In this paper, we focus on (γ, n)-threshold encryption (for simplicity, we refer to threshold encryption in the sequel), where any γ out of n servers can decrypt ciphertexts, while any combination of corrupted servers less than γ cannot.

The key encapsulation mechanism in the threshold settings (threshold KEM, for short) and that with a tag (threshold Tag-KEM, for short) are used to encrypt a key instead of a message. These schemes distribute the decryption function among a number of decryption servers as in threshold encryption. Hereafter, we refer to threshold (Tag-)KEM instead of (γ, n)-threshold (Tag-)KEM.

The security notions of threshold encryption are very similar to those of public-key encryption: the notion of *indistinguishability against chosen plaintext*

J. Pieprzyk, H. Ghodosi, and E. Dawson (Eds.): ACISP 2007, LNCS 4586, pp. 259–273, 2007.
© Springer-Verlag Berlin Heidelberg 2007

attacks (IND-CPA) in public key encryption corresponds to the notion of *indistinguishability against chosen plaintext attacks in the threshold setting (IND-TCPA)*, and the strongest security notion of threshold encryption corresponds to the notion of *indistinguishability against chosen ciphertext attacks (IND-CCA)* in public-key encryption, and hence is called *indistinguishability against chosen ciphertext attacks in the threshold setting (IND-TCCA)* (See [13]).

The security notions of threshold (Tag-)KEM are similar to those of threshold encryption; the strongest security notion of threshold (Tag-)KEM is *IND-TCCA*, *indistinguishability against chosen ciphertext attacks in the threshold setting.*

The adversary, who is assumed to corrupt some servers and has access to their internal data for threshold encryption, is classified as follows (See [13]).

- The adversary is said to be *active* if the adversary can modify its behavior. Otherwise, the adversary is called *passive*.
- The adversary is said to be *non-adaptive* or *static* if the adversary is restricted to choosing which servers to corrupt before any execution, while the *adaptive* adversary can choose the servers to corrupt during the attack.

The above classification can also be applied to threshold (Tag-)KEM.

1.2   Related Works and Motivation

Many papers have dealt with threshold cryptosystem in the public key encryption setting (i.e. threshold encryption) and various threshold encryption and construction methods have been proposed. In particular, if we pay attention to the underlying computational assumption, threshold encryption falls into two categories: those based on the discrete logarithm problem [5,6,10,20,23,24]; and those based on the integer factoring problem [13,14,18,21]. Of particular note, the scheme in [18] is constructed based on the GM-encryption scheme [15] and has been shown to be secure under the Quadratic Residuosity Assumption (QRA). Note that QRA is not proven to be equivalent to the integer factoring problem itself. Also, the scheme in [13] has been proven to be secure under the Decisional Composite Residuosity Assumption, which is thought to be stronger than QRA, however, the ciphertext-size is shorter than that in [18]. Note that [5,6] achieve IND-TCCA in the standard model.

A generic construction to obtain strong (i.e. IND-TCCA secure) threshold encryption from weak (i.e. IND-TCPA) schemes was proposed in [13], and it uses the zero-knowledge proof system. There are other approaches to obtaining strong threshold encryption. In fact, methods that use signature schemes to realize secure threshold encryption are proposed in [11,20,24]. However, these methods [20,24] require strong assumptions: [20] assumes the generic model; and [24] assumes the existence of a knowledge extractor that magically obtains the knowledge without rewinding the prover. On the other hand, in the context of multiple encryption, we note that Dodis and Katz [11] propose a composition method that does not require such strong assumptions and can also be used for constructing threshold encryption. If all components are secure in the standard model, the resulting threshold encryption is also secure in the standard model.

However, unfortunately, the ciphertext-size and encryption-cost depend on the number of servers in [11]. In prior works, these are constant with regard to the number of servers. This dependence stems from their construction. Prior other works require to share the decryption key, however, [11] requires to share a message, to encrypt all shared messages in respective servers' public keys, and to sign a set of all ciphertexts. Our approach requires to share decryption key and aims to construct secure threshold encryption without strong assumptions such as the generic model or the existence of a magical knowledge extractor (in the random oracle model).

In the context of key encapsulation mechanism and data encryption mechanism (KEM/DEM), Abe et al. showed a new framework, named Tag-KEM/DEM in EUROCRYPT 2005. They pointed out that (CCA-)secure threshold Tag-KEM immediately yields secure threshold encryption by combining it with DEM which is secure only against passive attacks; we only have to construct secure threshold Tag-KEM. Motivated by this work, this paper proposes how to obtain secure threshold Tag-KEM. Recall that secure threshold encryption can generally be converted into secure encryption but not vice versa.

To the best of our knowledge, no threshold encryption uses the padding technique to enhance security. One reason is that the validity check must be done before making the decryption shares to prevent the adversary from acquiring any information other than invalid symbol in the threshold settings. Threshold encryption based on the RSA assumption (in the random oracle model) is only described in [11], however, [11] has a disadvantage as described above.

1.3 Our Contributions

In this paper, we propose a generic method to obtain IND-TCCA secure threshold Tag-KEM from weakly secure threshold KEM by in the random oracle model using signature schemes with tight security reduction. Note that Abe et al. pointed out that it is easy to construct threshold Tag-KEM that meets IND-TCCA if threshold encryption that meets IND-TCCA or threshold KEM that meets IND-TCCA exists, whereas our starting point is threshold KEM (without a tag) that meets much weaker security, one-wayness.

Also, we provide four instantiations: Scheme A (RSA based construction) and Scheme B (CDH based construction) are new. The other two mirror schemes in [23], which shows the relationship between [23] and signature schemes in [17,19,8]; our generic construction can also be viewed as a generalization of Shoup and Gennaro's schemes [23]. Our construction provides IND-TCCA secure threshold encryption against both active and adaptive adversary if threshold KEM is one-way for both active and adaptive adversary; our concrete instantiations can be converted into IND-TCCA secure threshold encryption against both active and adaptive adversary by using the single-inconsistent-player (SIP) technique [7].

In summary, in this paper,

- We propose a *generic construction method for IND-TCCA secure threshold Tag-KEM* from weakly secure threshold KEM.

- We propose the *first RSA-based threshold encryption* that meets IND-TCCA in which ciphertext-size and encryption-cost are independent of the number of servers.
- We revisit Shoup-Gennaro's schemes (and give a slight improvement) through our generic construction method.

The rest of this paper is organized as follows. Section 2 describes threshold encryption, threshold Tag-KEM, and signature schemes. Section 3 shows our main result, a generic conversion from threshold KEM that meets one-wayness against passive attacks into threshold Tag-KEM that meets IND-TCCA. Finally, section 4 shows some examples of how our conversion can be implemented.

2 Preliminaries

This section is devoted to definitions of threshold encryption, threshold Tag-KEM and signature schemes with tight security reduction.

2.1 Threshold Encryption

In this section we briefly explain the model of threshold encryption. In threshold encryption, there are n decryption servers (simply called servers in the sequel), a trusted dealer, a sender, and a combiner. All servers are assumed to be connected by a complete network of private channels. In addition, all servers have access to an authenticated broadcast channel so that the sender of a message can always be correctly recognized. For simplicity, the servers are numbered $1, 2, \ldots, n$, and the set of servers is denoted by $\mathcal{P} = \{1, 2, \ldots, n\}$. We assume that public-key ek contains the verification key of partial decryption results and that server i has secret key sk_i. The set of secret keys is denoted by $SK = \{sk_i\}_{i \in \mathcal{P}}$.

In place of describing the formal model of the threshold encryption, we describe here the difference between public-key encryption and threshold encryption. In threshold encryption, decryption function is realized by using a partial decryption algorithm and a combining algorithm. The partial decryption algorithm takes as input a ciphertext and outputs a partial decryption result (or the invalid symbol). The combining algorithm takes as input a ciphertext and γ partial decryption results and outputs a plaintext (or the invalid symbol). For more details, see [13].

Threshold encryption is executed as follows. The trusted dealer runs the key generation algorithm. The trusted dealer publishes a public-key and sends secret-key sk_i to the server i over a secret channel. The sender creates a ciphertext by encrypting a plaintext and broadcasts the ciphertext to all servers. After that, γ servers can individually calculate partial decryption results by running the partial decryption algorithm with their own secret keys, and they send the results to the combiner. The adversary may change the partial decryption results issued by the corrupted servers. By using the combining algorithm, the combiner first checks the validity of the partial decryption results. If some of them are invalid, the combiner returns an invalid symbol. If all are valid, it returns a plaintext m.

2.2   Threshold (Tag-)KEM

In this section we explain the formal model of the key encapsulation mechanism in the threshold settings with a tag (threshold Tag-KEM, for short). Threshold Tag-KEM is executed in a similar way to threshold encryption. In threshold Tag-KEM, encapsulation is the same as in ordinary Tag-KEM, while decapsulation is done by some servers and a combiner as in threshold encryption.

We give some definitions of threshold Tag-KEM below. They are obtained by combining the definitions of threshold encryption in [13] with those of Tag-KEM in [3]. From the definition of threshold Tag-KEM, we can obtain a definition of threshold KEM (without a tag) by fixing a tag and a definition of (non-threshold) Tag-KEM by replacing the partial decryption algorithm and the combining algorithm with the decryption algorithm.

Definition 1. (Threshold Tag-KEM) *A (γ, n)-threshold KEM with tags (threshold Tag-KEM, for short)* $\mathbf{E}^{\mathrm{kem_T}} = (\mathcal{G}^{\mathrm{tkem_T}}, \mathcal{K}^{\mathrm{tkem_T}}, \mathcal{E}^{\mathrm{tkem_T}}, \mathcal{PD}^{\mathrm{tkem_T}}, \mathcal{U}^{\mathrm{tkem_T}})$ *is composed of the following algorithms:*

- The key generation algorithm $\mathcal{G}^{\mathrm{tkem_T}}$ is a probabilistic algorithm that takes as input a security parameter 1^Λ, and outputs public key ek and a set of secret keys $SK = \{sk_i\}_{i \in \mathcal{P}}$. It also determines space for tags $\mathcal{T}$. We write $(ek, SK) \leftarrow \mathcal{G}^{\mathrm{tkem_T}}(1^\Lambda)$ for this processing.
- The key generation algorithm $\mathcal{K}^{\mathrm{tkem_T}}$ is a probabilistic algorithm that generates a one-time key $z \in \mathcal{K}^{\mathrm{dem}}$ and internal state information s (a key z is embedded in s). $\mathcal{K}^{\mathrm{dem}}$ is a key space of DEM with regard to encapsulation-key ek. We write $(s, z) \leftarrow \mathcal{K}^{\mathrm{tkem_T}}(ek)$ for this processing.
- The encryption algorithm $\mathcal{E}^{\mathrm{tkem_T}}$ is a probabilistic algorithm that takes as input internal state information s , tag τ, and encapsulation key ek, and outputs a ciphertext h. We write $h \leftarrow \mathcal{E}^{\mathrm{tkem_T}}_{ek}(s, \tau)$ for this processing.
- The partial decryption algorithm $\mathcal{PD}^{\mathrm{tkem_T}}$ is a deterministic algorithm that takes a ciphertext h, tag τ, and user i's secret key sk_i, and outputs a partial decryption result δ_i or an invalid symbol $\bot$ which implies that the ciphertext is invalid. We write $\delta_i (\mathrm{or}\ \bot) = \mathcal{PD}^{\mathrm{tkem_T}}_{sk_i}(h, \tau)$ for this processing.
- The combining algorithm $\mathcal{U}^{\mathrm{tkem_T}}$ is a deterministic algorithm that takes as input a public key ek, ciphertext h, partial decryption results $\mathrm{PDR}^{\mathrm{tkem_T}}_\Gamma(h, \tau)$ for user set Γ, and tag τ, and outputs key z or an invalid symbol $\bot$ which implies that the input is invalid, where $\Gamma \in \{\Gamma \subset \mathcal{P} || \Gamma |= \gamma\}$ and $\mathrm{PDR}^{\mathrm{tkem_T}}_\Gamma(h, \tau) = \{\delta_{i_1}, \delta_{i_2}, \ldots, \delta_{i_\gamma}\}_{i_1, i_2, \ldots, i_\gamma \in \Gamma}$. We write $z (\mathrm{or}\ \bot) = \mathcal{U}^{\mathrm{tkem_T}}(h, \mathrm{PDR}^{\mathrm{tkem_T}}_\Gamma(h, \tau), \tau)$ for this processing. Here, for any ek, z, and Γ, we require that z be embedded in s and $\mathcal{U}^{\mathrm{tkem_T}}_{ek}(\mathcal{E}^{\mathrm{tkem_T}}_{ek}(s, \tau), \mathrm{PDR}^{\mathrm{tkem_T}}_\Gamma(\mathcal{E}^{\mathrm{tkem_T}}_{ek}(s, \tau), \tau), \tau) = z$.

We define the strongest security of threshold Tag-KEM, i.e., IND-TCCA, which is only a combination of IND-TCCA in threshold encryption and that in Tag-KEM. From the following definition, we obtain a definition of IND-TCCA in Tag-KEM by replacing the partial decryption oracles and a combining algorithm in the definition of threshold Tag-KEM with a decryption oracle.

Definition 2. (IND-TCCA) Let $\mathbf{E}^{\text{tkem}_T}$ be a threshold Tag-KEM. Suppose that A is an adversary that plays the following game for $\mathbf{E}^{\text{tkem}_T}$.

1 The adversary A chooses $\gamma - 1$ servers to corrupt.

2 The key generation algorithm $\mathcal{G}^{\text{tkem}_T}$ is run. The secret keys of the corrupted servers, a public key, and verification keys are given to A. The other secret keys are kept secret and sent to the uncorrupted servers, respectively.

3 The adversary A gives arbitrary ciphertext to the set of the partial decryption oracles and obtains partial decryption results. This step is repeated as polynomially many times as A wishes.

4 The key generation algorithm $\mathcal{K}^{\text{tkem}_T}$ is run and the challenger obtains s, k_1. The challenger also selects $k_0 \leftarrow \mathcal{K}^{\text{dem}}, b \leftarrow \{0,1\}$ uniformly at random.

5 The adversary obtains k_b and repeats Step 3.

6 The adversary A chooses arbitrary tag τ and gives it to the challenger.

7 The challenger produces a target ciphertext by encrypting s with the tag τ that A gives and sends back the target ciphertext.

8 The adversary A repeats Step 3, where there is the restriction that A cannot give the target ciphertext to the partial decryption oracles.

9 The adversary A outputs b'.

If $b' = b$, A wins. The advantage of A over $\mathbf{E}^{\text{tkem}_T}$ is defined by $2 \Pr[b' = b] - 1$, where the probability is taken over the coin flips of A, $\mathcal{G}^{\text{tkem}_T}$, $\mathcal{E}^{\text{tkem}_T}$, and the choice of b. The adversary A (t, ϵ, q_H, q_D)-*breaks* $\mathbf{E}^{\text{tkem}_T}$ *under chosen ciphertext attacks in the threshold setting* if A can win by making at most q_H queries to random oracle $\mathcal{H}$ and at most q_D queries to the set of the partial decryption oracle $\{\mathcal{PD}^{\text{tkem}_T}_{sk_i}(\cdot)\}_{i \in \mathcal{P}}$, within running time t, with advantage ϵ. $\mathbf{E}^{\text{tkem}_T}$ is called *indistinguishable against chosen ciphertext attacks in the threshold setting (IND-TCCA)* if any polynomial-time Turing machine A wins under chosen ciphertext attacks with the advantage that is negligible with respect to the security parameter.

We define a notion of a threshold version of one-wayness (OW) in threshold KEM.

Definition 3. (One-wayness) Let $\mathbf{E}^{\text{kem}_T} = (\mathcal{G}^{\text{kem}_T}, \mathcal{K}^{\text{kem}_T}, \mathcal{E}^{\text{kem}_T}, \mathcal{PD}^{\text{kem}_T}, \mathcal{U}^{\text{kem}_T})$ be a threshold KEM. Suppose that A is an adversary that plays the following game for $\mathbf{E}^{\text{kem}_T}$.

1 The adversary A chooses $\gamma - 1$ servers to corrupt.

2 The key generation algorithm $\mathcal{G}^{\text{kem}_T}$ is run. The secret keys of the corrupted servers, a public key, and verification keys are given to A. The other secret keys are kept secret and sent to the respective uncorrupted servers.

3 The key generation algorithm $\mathcal{K}^{\text{kem}_T}$ is run. The challenger obtains s, z and produces a target ciphertext by encrypting s. The challenger sends the target ciphertext to the adversary.

4 The adversary A outputs z'.

If $z' = z$ holds, A wins. The adversary A $(t_{\text{kem}_T}, \epsilon_{\text{kem}_T})$-*breaks* $\mathbf{E}^{\text{kem}_T}$ if A can win within running time t_{kem_T}, with probability ϵ_{kem_T}. $\mathbf{E}^{\text{kem}_T}$ is said to be *one-way (OW)* if any polynomial-time Turing machine A wins with the advantage that is negligible with respect to the security parameter.

2.3   Signature Scheme with Tight Security Reduction

In this section, we describe the definition of signature schemes.

Definition 4. *A signature scheme* $\mathbf{S}^{\mathsf{sig}} = (\mathcal{G}^{\mathsf{sig}}, \mathcal{S}^{\mathsf{sig}}, \mathcal{V}^{\mathsf{sig}})$ *consists of the following algorithms:*

- The key generation algorithm $\mathcal{G}^{\mathsf{sig}}$ is a probabilistic algorithm that takes a security parameter 1^{Λ} as input and outputs a pair of signing key sgk and verification-key vk. We write $(sgk, vk) \leftarrow \mathcal{G}^{\mathsf{sig}}(1^{\Lambda})$ for this processing.
- The signing algorithm $\mathcal{S}^{\mathsf{sig}}$ is a (probabilistic) algorithm that takes a message m and a signing key sgk, and outputs a signature σ for the message m. We write $\sigma \leftarrow \mathcal{S}^{\mathsf{sig}}_{sgk}(m)$ for this processing.
- The verification algorithm $\mathcal{V}^{\mathsf{sig}}$ is an algorithm that takes a pair of message m and its signature σ and a verification-key vk as input, and outputs 1 or 0, where it outputs 1 if the signature σ is valid and 0 otherwise. We write $1/0 = \mathcal{V}^{\mathsf{sig}}_{vk}(m, \sigma)$ for this processing. Here, we require that $\mathcal{V}^{\mathsf{sig}}_{vk}(m, \mathcal{S}^{\mathsf{sig}}_{sgk}(m)) = 1$ for any m and (sgk, vk) generated by $\mathcal{G}^{\mathsf{sig}}$.

If we clarify hash functions H used in the signature scheme, we denote the signature scheme by $\mathbf{S}^{\mathsf{sig}}_H = (\mathcal{G}^{\mathsf{sig}}_H, \mathcal{S}^{\mathsf{sig}}_H, \mathcal{V}^{\mathsf{sig}}_H)$.

We now give a one-time version of the strongest security notion in the signature scheme.

Definition 5. (sEUF-OCMA) *Let* A *be an adversary that plays the following game for* $\mathbf{S}^{\mathsf{sig}}$.

1 The key generation algorithm $\mathcal{G}^{\mathsf{sig}}$ is run. A obtains a verification key vk.
2 The adversary A outputs (m, σ) after making at most one query to the signing oracle.

If $\mathcal{V}^{\mathsf{sig}}_{vk}(m, \sigma) = 1$ holds, A wins. There is an obvious restriction that (m, σ) is not the answer of the query from the signing oracle. The adversary A (t, ϵ, q_H)-*breaks* $\mathbf{S}^{\mathsf{sig}}$ *under one-time chosen message attacks* if A can win by making at most q_H queries to $\mathcal{H}$, within running time t, with success probability of ϵ. $\mathbf{S}^{\mathsf{sig}}$ is said to be *strongly existentially unforgeable against one-time chosen message attacks (sEUF-OCMA)* if any polynomial-time Turing machine A wins with probability that is negligible with respect to the security parameter.

Moreover, suppose that the security of $\mathbf{S}^{\mathsf{sig}}$ depends on the problem X. Namely, suppose that there is a probabilistic polynomial-time algorithm that solves X with probability of at most ϵ_X within running time t_X using the adversary that $(t_{\mathsf{sig}}, \epsilon_{\mathsf{sig}}, q_H)$-breaks $\mathbf{S}^{\mathsf{sig}}$ under OCMA. If $\epsilon_{\mathsf{sig}} - \epsilon_X$ is negligible and $t_X - t_{\mathsf{sig}} = o(1)$, then $\mathbf{S}^{\mathsf{sig}}$ achieves *tight security reduction*.

3   Construction of Secure Threshold Tag-KEM

In this section, we propose a generic conversion from threshold KEM that meets OW into threshold Tag-KEM that meets IND-TCCA using signature schemes with tight security reduction. First, we introduce polynomial-time computable functions to combine threshold KEM and signature schemes seamlessly. These functions closely resemble those introduced in [1,2]. Intuitively, if the adversary knows internal state information s whose encrypted form is a ciphertext h, the decrypted result of the ciphertext h is useless. (In fact, internal state information s contains the decrypted result of the ciphertext h.) To show the knowledge of internal state information, we use signature schemes, where the ciphertext h is treated as a verification key and internal state information s is treated as a signing key. These functions describe how a ciphertext h and internal state information s are transformed into a verification key and a signing key, respectively.

Definition 6. (Joint functions) Let $\mathbf{S}^{\mathsf{sig}} = (\mathcal{G}^{\mathsf{sig}}, \mathcal{S}^{\mathsf{sig}}, \mathcal{V}^{\mathsf{sig}})$ be a signature scheme and $\mathbf{E}^{\mathsf{kem}_\mathsf{T}} = (\mathcal{G}^{\mathsf{kem}_\mathsf{T}}, \mathcal{K}^{\mathsf{kem}_\mathsf{T}}, \mathcal{E}^{\mathsf{kem}_\mathsf{T}}, \mathcal{PD}^{\mathsf{kem}_\mathsf{T}}, \mathcal{U}^{\mathsf{kem}_\mathsf{T}})$ a threshold KEM. Joint functions for these schemes, $DeriveSgk$, and $DeriveVk$, are defined as follows.

- The signing key derivation function $DeriveSgk$ is a function that returns a signing key sgk of $\mathbf{S}^{\mathsf{sig}}$ from input internal state information s and encapsulation key ek used in $\mathcal{E}_{ek}^{\mathsf{kem}_\mathsf{T}}(s)$, denoted by $DeriveSgk(s, ek) = sgk$.
- The verification-key derivation function $DeriveVk$ is a function that, given encapsulated form $h = \mathcal{E}_{ek}^{\mathsf{kem}_\mathsf{T}}(s)$ and encapsulation key ek, returns a verification key vk that corresponds to signing key sgk generated by $DeriveSgk(s, ek)$. We denote $DeriveVk(h, ek) = vk$. Here, it is required that the distribution of the resulting key pair (sgk, vk) created by $DeriveSgk$ and $DeriveVk$ is the same as that of pairs of signing keys and verification-keys generated by $\mathcal{G}^{\mathsf{sig}}$, if s and ek are chosen uniformly at random.

Here, we note the possibility of the existence of the joint functions. We can construct a signature scheme with tight security reduction if Fiat-Shamir proof of knowledge exists for relation W with one-way instance generator $\mathcal{I}$ by using Construction 4 in [12]. Therefore, if the encryption algorithm is deterministic, the case of $DeriveSgk(s, ek) = s$ and $DeriveVk(h, ek) = h$ is one candidate for constructing our scheme.

We now provide a construction of the threshold Tag-KEM. The basic idea lies in using non-interactive proof of knowledge to guarantee integrity; we use a signature scheme in which one, who produces a new signature, knows the answer to the problem X on which security of the signature depends, whereas the notion of plaintext-awareness means that one, who produces a new ciphertext, knows the plaintext. Intuitively, this basic idea seems to be secure. However, as noted in [23], security proofs would be difficult since rewinding causes another rewinding and the proof does not end in polynomial time. Therefore, we use a signature scheme with tight security reduction as a non-interactive proof of knowledge to simulate partial decryption oracle which avoids such avalanches. In addition, to ensure the integrity of the verification key, we put the verification key into hash functions that are used in a signature scheme. Recall that the verification key in a signature scheme is utilized in a non-malleable way assuming the existence of CA (certification authority), whereas verification keys included in ciphertexts may be malleable. Therefore, we put it into hash functions to ensure non-malleability. From the viewpoints, our construction is provided as follows.

Scheme 1. Given a threshold KEM $\mathbf{E}^{\mathsf{kem_T}}=(\mathcal{G}^{\mathsf{kem_T}}, \mathcal{K}^{\mathsf{kem_T}}, \mathcal{E}^{\mathsf{kem_T}}, \mathcal{PD}^{\mathsf{kem_T}}, \mathcal{U}^{\mathsf{kem_T}})$ and a signature scheme $\mathbf{S}_H^{\mathsf{sig}} = (\mathcal{G}_H^{\mathsf{sig}}, \mathcal{S}_H^{\mathsf{sig}}, \mathcal{V}_H^{\mathsf{sig}})$, where H is a hash function used in the signature scheme, converted threshold Tag-KEM $\mathbf{E}^{\mathsf{tkem_T}} = (\mathcal{G}^{\mathsf{tkem_T}}, \mathcal{K}^{\mathsf{tkem_T}}, \mathcal{E}^{\mathsf{tkem_T}}, \mathcal{PD}^{\mathsf{tkem_T}}, \mathcal{U}^{\mathsf{tkem_T}})$ is constructed as follows: Let $\mathbf{S}_{H'}^{\mathsf{sig}} = (\mathcal{G}_{H'}^{\mathsf{sig}}, \mathcal{S}_{H'}^{\mathsf{sig}}, \mathcal{V}_{H'}^{\mathsf{sig}})$ be a signature scheme obtained from $\mathbf{S}_H^{\mathsf{sig}}$ by replacing the hash function H with the modified hash function $H'(\cdot) = H(vk, \cdot)$, where vk is the verification-key. Also, let $G : \{0,1\}^* \to \{0,1\}^{\Lambda}$ be a hash function. The key generation algorithm $\mathcal{G}^{\mathsf{tkem_T}}$ is the same as $\mathcal{G}^{\mathsf{kem_T}}$ of $\mathbf{E}^{\mathsf{kem_T}}$.

$(s, k) \leftarrow \mathcal{K}^{\mathsf{tkem_T}}(ek)$
    1. $(s, z) \leftarrow \mathcal{K}^{\mathsf{kem_T}}(ek)$ (z is embedded in s)
    2. $k = G(z)$ (generation of session-key k)
$C \leftarrow \mathcal{E}_{ek}^{\mathsf{tkem_T}}(s, \tau)$, where $C = (h, \sigma)$
    1. $h = \mathcal{E}_{ek}^{\mathsf{kem_T}}(s)$ (key-encapsulation)
    2. $sgk = DeriveSgk(s, ek)$ (signing-key derivation)
    3. $vk = DeriveVk(h, ek)$ (verification-key derivation)
    4. $\sigma = \mathcal{S}_{sgk,H'}^{\mathsf{sig}}(\tau)$ (signature generation by sgk and vk)
$\delta_i / \perp = \mathcal{PD}_{sk_i}^{\mathsf{tkem_T}}(C, \tau)$ for $sk_i \in SK$, where $C = (h, \sigma)$
    1. $vk = DeriveVk(h, ek)$ (verification-key derivation)
    2. Output invalid symbol $\perp$ if $\mathcal{V}_{vk,H'}^{\mathsf{sig}}(\tau, \sigma) = 0$ (checking validity of the signature)
    3. $\delta_i = \mathcal{PD}_{sk_i}^{\mathsf{kem_T}}(h)$ for $sk_i \in SK$.
$k / \perp = \mathcal{U}_{ek}^{\mathsf{tkem_T}}(C, \mathrm{PDR}_{\Gamma}^{\mathsf{tkem_T}}(C, \tau), \tau)$
    1. Output the invalid symbol $\perp$, if h is invalid or there are some invalid partial decryption results (verification of partial decryption results)
    2. $z = \mathcal{U}_{ek}^{\mathsf{kem_T}}(h, \mathrm{PDR}_{\Gamma}^{\mathsf{kem_T}}(h))$, $k = G(z)$ (extraction of session-key k)

The security of Scheme 1 is shown as follows. The proof of Lemma 1 will be given in the full version of this paper.

Lemma 1. Let X be the computational problem (e.g. RSA or CDH). Suppose there exists adversary A_{X_1} that $(t_{X_1}, \epsilon_{X_1})$-solves the problem X, which means A_{X_1} solves X within time t_{X_1} with probability ϵ_{X_1}, if there is an adversary A_{sig} that $(t_{\mathsf{sig}}, \epsilon_{\mathsf{sig}}, q_{H''})$-breaks $\mathbf{S}_H^{\mathsf{sig}}$ under one-time chosen message attacks, where $t_{\mathsf{sig}} \approx t_{X_1}$ and $\epsilon_{\mathsf{sig}} \approx \epsilon_{X_1}$. Also, suppose there exists an adversary A_{X_2} that $(t_{X_2}, \epsilon_{X_2})$-solves the problem X if there is an adversary $A_{\mathsf{kem_T}}$ that $(t_{\mathsf{kem_T}}, \epsilon_{\mathsf{kem_T}})$-breaks $\mathbf{E}^{\mathsf{kem_T}}$. Then, if there is an adversary B that can (t, ϵ, q_H, q_D)-break Scheme 1 under chosen ciphertext attacks in the threshold setting, there exists an adversary B_X that can (t_X, ϵ_X)-solve the problem X with $q_{H''} + q_G \le q_H$,

$$\epsilon_X \ge \frac{\epsilon \cdot (\epsilon_{X_1}/\epsilon_{\mathsf{sig}})^{q_D + q_H + 1} \cdot \epsilon_{X_2}}{q_H \cdot \epsilon_{\mathsf{kem_T}}}, \tag{1}$$

$$t_X \le t + (q_D + q_H + 1)(t_{\mathsf{sig}} - t_{X_1}) + (q_D + 1)(t_{\mathsf{kem_T}} - t_{X_2}) + q_H t_G,$$

where A makes at most q_G queries to hash function G with maximum running time t_G for simulating the random oracle of G.

If ϵ is not negligible under the condition where $\epsilon_{\mathsf{kem_T}}/\epsilon_{\mathsf{X}_2}$ and q_H are polynomially bounded in Λ, ϵ_{X} is also not negligible. Therefore, if we suppose ϵ_{X} is negligible, ϵ must also be negligible and $\mathbf{E}^{\mathsf{tkem_T}}$ is IND-TCCA. Here, we say X is hard if there is no probabilistic polynomial-time algorithm that can solve the problem X. Consequently, the above lemma induces the following theorem.

Theorem 1. Let X be a computational problem. If $\mathbf{E}^{\mathsf{kem_T}}$ is a threshold KEM that meets OW under the assumption of the hardness of the problem X, and $\mathbf{S}_H^{\mathsf{sig}}$ is a signature scheme that meets sEUF-OCMA with tight security reduction under the assumption of hardness of the problem X, then Scheme 1 results in the threshold Tag-KEM that meets IND-TCCA under the same assumption.

Remarks . This remark explains why we consider the situation where the security of threshold KEM and that of signature scheme depend on the same assumption using Fig.1. Fig. 1 shows the relationship between threshold KEM,

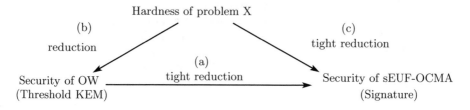

Fig. 1. Relationships among threshold KEM, signature scheme, and the base of security

signature, and the problem X in Scheme 1: if threshold KEM or the signature scheme is broken, the problem X is solved by reduction. Arrow (a) in Fig.1 means that there is an extractor that extracts z in $\mathbf{E}^{\mathsf{kem_T}}$ from h in $\mathbf{E}^{\mathsf{kem_T}}$ without rewinding if there is a forger that can forge valid a signature σ for some m with fixed vk. This means that we do not need a magical extractor unlike [24]. In instantiations in Sect.4, to construct a signature based on (a), we construct a signature based on (c) with tight reduction. Since the opposite of (b) is tight reduction, the composition of (c) and the opposite of (b) leads to (a) with tight reduction, which is needed in our scheme.

Notes: It is shown that Lemma 1 and Theorem 1 hold true even if we relax the condition of security proof of signature scheme S_H^{sig}: the simulation of the signing oracle is not necessarily shown tightly under the hardness of X but it is enough to be shown loosely under the hardness of X. For example, Scheme 1 is applicable to the case where succeeding in a simulation of the signing oracle depends on DDH whereas the security of threshold KEM depends on CDH. The proof of the above case is done in a very similar way to that of Lemma 1.

4   Instantiations

In this section, we consider four instantiations. These are threshold encryption by combining threshold Tag-KEM and a one-time pad, in which threshold Tag-KEM is constructed by using Scheme 1 in Section 3. Of these, we actually describe new two instantiations: one is the first provably secure scheme under the RSA assumption in the random oracle model where ciphertext-size and encryption-cost are independent of the number of servers; and the other is provably secure under the CDH assumption in the random oracle model, which is slightly more efficient than [23]. Two others of the four mirrors TDH1 and TDH2 in [23]. We summarize four instantiations in Table 1, where Assumption means the hardness of a problem (e.g., RSA or CDH). It should be noted that DEM parts can be replaced by any symmetric-key scheme that is one-time secure against passive attacks if we are interested in threshold hybrid encryption.

Table 1. Constructions of instantiations: threshold Tag-KEM that meets IND-TCCA is composed of threshold KEM that meets OW and signature scheme that meets sEUF-OCMA through our construction method; threshold hybrid encryption is a combination of threshold Tag-KEM that meets IND-TCCA and weakly secure DEM (one-time pad)

IND-TCCA threshold Tag-KEM		DEM	IND-TCCA Hybrid threshold encryption	Assumption
OW threshold KEM	sEUF-OCMA signature scheme			
Scheme in [21]	GQ Identification and Fischlin's transformation [12]		Scheme A in this paper (see Theorem 1)	RSA
Scheme in [10]	Scheme in Chapter 4 of [8]	one-time pad	Scheme B in this paper (see Theorem 1)	CDH
Scheme in [10]	Scheme in Appendix B of [8]		Scheme TDH1 in [23] (see Theorem 1)	CDH
Scheme in [10]	Scheme in [19]		Scheme TDH2 in [23] (see Notes in Sect.3)	DDH

We describe the first threshold encryption based on the RSA assumption in the random oracle model where ciphertext-size and encryption-cost are independent of the number of servers. Note that the scheme in [18] is secure under Quadratic Residuosity Assumption (QRA), not the RSA assumption. In the proposed instantiation, we use the scheme in [21] as threshold KEM. Note that the paper [21] originally deals with a threshold signature scheme, however, we can easily convert it into threshold KEM in the same way as [14]. In addition, we use a signature scheme whose security depends on the RSA assumption with tight security reduction obtained by combining the GQ Identification scheme and Fischlin's transformation [12]. A threshold encryption secure under RSA assumption is described as follows.

Scheme A . A threshold encryption $\mathbf{E}^{\mathsf{pub}_T} = (\mathcal{G}^{\mathsf{pub}_T}, \mathcal{E}^{\mathsf{pub}_T}, \mathcal{PD}^{\mathsf{pub}_T}, \mathcal{U}^{\mathsf{pub}_T})$ is as follows.

Key generation: $(ek, SK) \leftarrow \mathcal{K}(1^\Lambda)$, where $ek = (e, N, v, h_1, \ldots, h_n)$:

$\mathcal{G}^{\mathsf{pub}_T}$ takes inputs $\Lambda, \omega, \eta, b, l, A$ as security parameters and selects strong $\frac{\Lambda}{2}$-bit primes p, q and calculates $N = pq$. Define p', q', and W as $p = 2p'+1, q = 2q'+1$, and $W = p'q'$, resp., where we require A to be sufficiently larger than $l \times W$. Select $e(> n)$ s.t. $\gcd(e, \phi(N)) = 1$ and compute d that satisfies $ed = 1 \bmod W$. Define $\Delta = n!$ and $f_0 = d$. Secret keys are generated as follows. Choose random elements $f_1, \ldots, f_{\gamma-1} \in \mathbf{Z}_W$, and then define a polynomial $F(X) = \sum_{j=0}^{\gamma-1} f_j X^j \in \mathbf{Z}_W[X]$. For $0 \le i \le n$, set $sk_i = F(i) \bmod W \in \mathbf{Z}_W$ as the secret key for the i-th server. A generator, v, of $\mathbf{Q}_N$ is selected uniformly and $h_i = v^{\Delta sk_i} \bmod N (i = 1, 2, \ldots, n)$ is a verification key for the partial decryption result from the i-th server. Hash functions are defined as $G : \mathbf{Z}_N \to \mathbf{Z}_{2^l}, H : \mathbf{Z}_N \times \mathbf{Z}_{2^l} \times \mathbf{Z}_N \times \mathbf{Z}_{2^\omega} \times \mathbf{Z}_{2^\eta} \times \mathbf{Z}_N \to \mathbf{Z}_{2^b}, \Theta : \mathbf{Z}_N^6 \to \mathbf{Z}_{2^l}$.

Encryption: $C \leftarrow \mathcal{E}^{\mathsf{pub}_T}(m; s)$:

1 $h = s^e \bmod N, k = G(s), c = k \oplus m (m \in \{0, 1\}^l)$

2 Select $r_j \in \mathbf{Z}_N (j = 1, 2, \ldots, \omega)$ and set $\mathbf{r} = \{r_j^e\}_{j=1,2,\ldots,\omega}$.

3 For $j = 1, 2, \ldots, \omega$, repeat the following calculations. Set ch_j as the value that ensures that $H(h, c, r_j^e, j, \mathsf{ch}_j, r_j s^{\mathsf{ch}_j})$ equals 0 where $\mathsf{ch}_j \in \mathbf{Z}_{2^\eta}$ (if no such value exists, set ch_j such that $H(h, c, r_j^e, j, \mathsf{ch}_j, r_j s^{\mathsf{ch}_j})$ is minimum for $\mathsf{ch}_j = 0, 1, 2, \ldots, 2^\eta - 1$.) and calculate $v_j = r_j s^{\mathsf{ch}_j} \bmod N$.

4 Set $\mathsf{ch} = \{\mathsf{ch}_j\}_{j=1,2,\ldots,\omega}, \mathbf{v} = \{v_j\}_{j=1,2,\ldots,\omega}$, and $C = (h, c, \mathbf{r}, \mathsf{ch}, \mathbf{v})$.

Partial decryption: $\{\delta_i, e_i, y_i\} / \perp \leftarrow \mathcal{PD}_{sk_i}^{\mathsf{pub}_T}(C)$:

1 If $\sum_{j=1}^\omega H(h, c, r_j^e, j, \mathsf{ch}_j, v_j) \le \omega$ does not hold, output $\perp$ and abort.

2 If $r_j^e = v_j^e h^{-\mathsf{ch}_j} \bmod N (j = 1, 2, \ldots, \omega)$ does not hold, output $\perp$ and abort.

3 Calculate $\delta_i \equiv h^{2\Delta s_i} \bmod N$. Select $r \xleftarrow{R} \mathbf{Z}_A$ and $x_i = v^r, x_i' = h^r$. $e_i = \Theta(v, h, h_i^2, \delta_i, x_i, x_i'), y_i = r + e_i \times 2\Delta sk_i$.

Combining: $m / \perp = \mathcal{U}_{ek}^{\mathsf{pub}_T}(C, \mathcal{PDR}_\Gamma^{\mathsf{pub}_T}(h))$

1 For each server $i (\in \Gamma = \{i_1, \ldots, i_\gamma\})$ that sends δ_i , check if $\Theta(v, h, h_i^2, \delta_i, v^{y_i}/h_i^{2e_i}, h^y/\delta_i^{e_i}) = e_i$ holds. If it does not hold, output $\perp$ and abort.

2 $\prod_{i \in \Gamma} \delta_i^{2\lambda_{0,j}^\Gamma} \bmod N = s^{4\Delta^2} \bmod N$

3 From h and $s^{4\Delta^2}$, calculate s. $k = G(s), m = c \oplus k$

Here, we define $\lambda_{0,j}^\Gamma = \Delta \times \frac{\prod_{j' \in \Gamma \setminus \{j\}}(-j')}{\prod_{j' \in \Gamma \setminus \{j\}}(j-j')} \in \mathbf{Z}$ in the same way as [21]. s is obtained from h and $s^{4\Delta^2}$, using the technique in [14] as follows. e and $4\Delta^2$ are co-prime from the property of e; integers X, Y that satisfy $X \times 4\Delta^2 + Y \times e = 1$ can be calculated in polynomial-time by using the extended Euclidean algorithm. It holds that $(s^{4\Delta^2})^X \times (h \bmod N)^Y = s^{X \times 4\Delta^2 + Y \times e} = s \bmod N$.

Here, $DeriveVk(h, ek) = h, DeriveSgk(s, ek) = s$, a tag of the threshold Tag-KEM is c, and the answer to h is s. A more efficient scheme, RSA-PSS [9], that has tight security reduction seems to be possible with our construction, however, it seems to be difficult to use since function $DeriveSgk$ is not efficiently computable, that is, obtaining a signing key would cover the process of factoring integers.

Next, we describe three instantiations based on DLP. Two schemes mirror TDH1 and TDH2 in [23]. Interestingly, we can observe a relationship among threshold encryption in [23], the scheme in Appendix B of [8] and the scheme in [19] through our generic construction. In fact, Goh and Jarecki [17] already mentioned the technique of replacing the proof of knowledge with the proof of knowledge of equality as in [23]. Also, [17,8,19] use the same technique. Our construction makes it easier to understand why [17,8,19] use the same technique as [23]. This fact also means that our generic construction can be regarded as *a generalization* of Shoup and Gennaro's schemes [23]. Surprisingly, to the best of our knowledge, no scheme based on the CDH or DDH assumption that is more efficient than the schemes in [23] has been proposed since 1998, which implies that Shoup and Gennaro's threshold encryption schemes in [23] are quite efficient. Table 1 shows that our construction involves such efficient schemes.

We describe the last one, a new scheme called Scheme B in Table 1. In Scheme B, we use the threshold KEM that is similar to the scheme in [10], in which $ek = (g, \bar{g}), \bar{g} = g^x, z = \bar{g}^s, h = g^s$, and SK is a set of shares obtained by the Shamir's secret sharing scheme to share x. Also, we use the signature scheme in [8]. A threshold encryption scheme secure under the CDH assumption is formally described as follows.

Scheme B . A threshold encryption $\mathbf{E}^{\mathsf{pub}_T} = (\mathcal{G}^{\mathsf{pub}_T}, \mathcal{E}^{\mathsf{pub}_T}, \mathcal{PD}^{\mathsf{pub}_T}, \mathcal{U}^{\mathsf{pub}_T})$ is constructed as follows.

Key generation: $(ek, SK) \leftarrow \mathcal{G}(1^{\Lambda})$, $ek = (g, y, p, q, G_q, y_1, \ldots, y_n)$: Details are as follows. Choose security parameter Λ, l, and (G_q, g), where G_q is a finite cyclic group of prime order q and g is a generator of G_q. We assume that G_q is a multiplicative subgroup of $\mathbf{Z}_p^*$ with prime p, where $q|(p-1)$; all arithmetic operations are done in modulo p unless otherwise noted. Select $x(\in_R \mathbf{Z}_q)$ and publish $y = g^x$. Publish hash functions $G : G_q \to \{0,1\}^l$, $H_1 : G_q^2 \to G_q$, $H_2 : G_q \times \{0,1\}^l \times \{0,1\}^l \times G_q^3 \to \mathbf{Z}_q$, and $\Theta : G_q^3 \to \mathbf{Z}_q$. Random elements $f_1, \ldots, f_{\gamma-1} \in \mathbf{Z}_q$ are chosen, and $f_0 = x$. Define a polynomial $F(X) = \sum_{j=0}^{\gamma-1} f_j X^j$. For $0 \le i \le n$, set $sk_i = F(i) \bmod q$ as a secret key for the i-th server. $y_i = g^{sk_i}$ is a verification key for the partial decryption result from the i-th server.

Encryption: Select plaintext $m \in \{0,1\}^l$, a label L, and $r, s \in_R \mathbf{Z}_q$. The ciphertext is $C = (c, L, u, \bar{u}, e, f)$, where $c = G(y^s) \oplus m, u = g^s, w = g^r, \bar{g} = H_1(u, w), \bar{u} = \bar{g}^s, \bar{w} = \bar{g}^r, e = H_2(u, c, L, \bar{g}, \bar{u}, \bar{w}), f = r + se \bmod q$.

Partial decryption: First, check if $e = H_2(u, c, L, \bar{g}, \bar{u}, \bar{g}^f/\bar{u}^e)$ holds after computing $\bar{g} = H_1(u, g^f/u^e)$. If this condition does not hold, output $(i, \perp)$. Otherwise, choose $s_i \in \mathbf{Z}_q$ uniformly at random and compute $u_i = u^{sk_i}, \hat{u}_i = u^{s_i}, \hat{y}_i = g^{s_i}, e_i = \Theta(u_i, \hat{u}_i, \hat{y}_i), f_i = s_i + sk_i e_i$. The output is (i, u_i, e_i, f_i).

Combining: First, check if $e = H_2(u, c, L, \bar{g}, \bar{u}, \bar{g}^f/\bar{u}^e)$ holds. Second, check if $e_i = \Theta(u_i, u^{f_i}/u_i^{e_i}, g^{f_i}/y_i^{e_i})$ for $i \in \Gamma$, where Γ is a set of γ servers. If they hold, compute $m = G(\prod_{i \in \Gamma} u_i^{\lambda_{0,i}^{\Gamma}}) \oplus c$, where $\lambda_{0,j}^{\Gamma} = \frac{\prod_{j' \in \Gamma \setminus \{j\}}(-j')}{\prod_{j' \in \Gamma \setminus \{j\}}(j-j')} \in \mathbf{Z}$.

Here, $DeriveVk(h, ek) = h, DeriveSgk(s, ek) = s$, and the answer to h is z. If we use the Diffie-Hellman self-corrector [22], the reduction-cost in Scheme B decreases as described in [23]. We note that Scheme 1 is pre-computable if the used signature scheme is pre-computable. Therefore, Scheme B is also pre-computable (see [8]). Also, note that we added u as input to $\mathcal{H}_1$ and $\mathcal{H}_2$, whereas u can be removed as input of $\mathcal{H}_2$. Intuitively, this is because the role of $\bar{u}$ is the same as that of u in the viewpoint of a label. Furthermore, the parameters g, h, y in [8] were removed from the input to the hash functions since this does not influence the security of the signature scheme.

Acknowledgments. We would like to thank Masayuki Terada (NTT DoCoMo, Inc.) for some discussions on improving this paper. We would also like to thank anonymous referees for their valuable comments.

References

1. Abe, M.: Securing Encryption + Proof of Knowledge in the Random Oracle Model. In: Preneel, B. (ed.) CT-RSA 2002. LNCS, vol. 2271, pp. 277–289. Springer, Heidelberg (2002)
2. Abe, M.: Combining Encryption and Proof of Knowledge in the Random Oracle Model. The Computer Journal 47(1), 58–70 (2004)
3. Abe, M., Gennaro, R., Kurosawa, K., Shoup, V.: Tag-KEM/DEM: A New Framework for Hybrid Encryption and A New Analysis of Kurosawa-Desmedt KEM. In: Cramer, R.J.F. (ed.) EUROCRYPT 2005. LNCS, vol. 3494, pp. 128–146. Springer, Heidelberg (2005)
4. Bellare, M., Rogaway, P.: Optimal Asymmetric Encryption. In: De Santis, A. (ed.) EUROCRYPT 1994. LNCS, vol. 950, pp. 92–111. Springer, Heidelberg (1995)
5. Boneh, D., Boyen, X., Halevi, S.: Chosen Ciphertext Secure Public Key Threshold Encryption Without Random Oracles. In: Pointcheval, D. (ed.) CT-RSA 2006. LNCS, vol. 3860, pp. 226–243. Springer, Heidelberg (2006)
6. Boyen, X., Mei, Q., Waters, B.: Direct chosen ciphertext security from identity-based techniques. In: CCS 2005, pp. 320–329. ACM Press, New York (2005)
7. Canetti, R., Gennaro, R., Jarecki, S., Krawczyk, H., Rabin, T.: Adaptive security for threshold cryptosystems. In: Wiener, M.J. (ed.) CRYPTO 1999. LNCS, vol. 1666, pp. 98–115. Springer, Heidelberg (1999)
8. Chevallier-Mames, B.: An Efficient CDH-based Signature Scheme with a Tight Security Reduction. In: Shoup, V. (ed.) CRYPTO 2005. LNCS, vol. 3621, pp. 511–526. Springer, Heidelberg (2005)
9. Coron, J.-S.: Optimal Security Proofs for PSS and Other Signature Schemes. In: Knudsen, L.R. (ed.) EUROCRYPT 2002. LNCS, vol. 2332, pp. 272–287. Springer, Heidelberg (2002)
10. Desmedt, Y., Frankel, Y.: Threshold Cryptosystems. In: Brassard, G. (ed.) CRYPTO 1989. LNCS, vol. 435, pp. 307–315. Springer, Heidelberg (1990)

11. Dodis, Y., Katz, J.: Chosen-Ciphertext Security of Multiple Encryption. In: Kilian, J. (ed.) TCC 2005. LNCS, vol. 3378, pp. 188–209. Springer, Heidelberg (2005)
12. Fischlin, M.: Communication-Efficient Non-Interactive Proofs of Knowledge with Online Extractors. In: Shoup, V. (ed.) CRYPTO 2005. LNCS, vol. 3621, pp. 152–168. Springer, Heidelberg (2005)
13. Fouque, P.-A., Pointcheval, D.: Threshold Cryptosystems Secure against Chosen-Ciphertext Attacks. In: Boyd, C. (ed.) ASIACRYPT 2001. LNCS, vol. 2248, pp. 351–368. Springer, Heidelberg (2001)
14. Fouque, P.-A., Pointcheval, D., Stern, J.: Sharing Decryption in the Context of Voting or Lotteries. In: Frankel, Y. (ed.) FC 2000. LNCS, vol. 1962, pp. 90–104. Springer, Heidelberg (2001)
15. Goldwasser, S., Micali, S.: Probabilistic Encryption. Journal of Computer and System Sciences 28(2), 270–299 (1984)
16. Guillou, L.C., Quisquater, J.-J.: A Practical Zero-Knowledge Protocol Fitted to Security Microprocessor Minimizing Both Transmission and Memory. In: Günther, C.G. (ed.) EUROCRYPT 1988. LNCS, vol. 330, pp. 123–128. Springer, Heidelberg (1988)
17. Goh, E., Jarecki, S.: A Signature Scheme as Secure as the Diffie-Hellman Problem. In: Biham, E. (ed.) Advances in Cryptology – EUROCRPYT 2003. LNCS, vol. 2656, pp. 401–415. Springer, Heidelberg (2003)
18. Katz, J., Yung, M.: Threshold Cryptosystems Based on Factoring. In: Zheng, Y. (ed.) ASIACRYPT 2002. LNCS, vol. 2501, pp. 192–205. Springer, Heidelberg (2002)
19. Katz, J., Wang, N.: Efficiency Improvements for Signature Schemes with Tight Security Reductions. In: CCS 2003, pp. 155–164. ACM Press, New York (2003)
20. Schnorr, C.-P., Jakobsson, M.: Security of Signed ElGamal Encryption. In: Okamoto, T. (ed.) ASIACRYPT 2000. LNCS, vol. 1976, pp. 73–89. Springer, Heidelberg (2000)
21. Shoup, V.: Practical Threshold Signatures. In: Preneel, B. (ed.) EUROCRYPT 2000. LNCS, vol. 1807, pp. 207–220. Springer, Heidelberg (2000)
22. Shoup, V.: Lower Bounds for Discrete Logarithms and Related Problems. In: Fumy, W. (ed.) EUROCRYPT 1997. LNCS, vol. 1233, pp. 256–266. Springer, Heidelberg (1997)
23. Shoup, V., Gennaro, R.: Securing Threshold Cryptosystems against Chosen Ciphertext Attack. In: Nyberg, K. (ed.) EUROCRYPT 1998. LNCS, vol. 1403, Springer, Heidelberg (1998) Journal of Cryptology 15(2), 75–96 (2002)
24. Tsiounis, Y., Yung, M.: On the Security of ElGamal Based Encryption. In: Imai, H., Zheng, Y. (eds.) PKC 1998. LNCS, vol. 1431, pp. 117–134. Springer, Heidelberg (1998)

Efficient Chosen-Ciphertext Secure Identity-Based Encryption with Wildcards

James Birkett[1], Alexander W. Dent[1], Gregory Neven[2],
and Jacob C.N. Schuldt[1,3]

[1] Information Security Group,
Royal Holloway, University of London,
Egham, TW20 0EX, UK
{j.m.birkett,a.dent}@rhul.ac.uk

[2] Department of Electrical Engineering, Katholieke Universiteit Leuven,
Kasteelpark Arenberg 10, 3001 Heverlee, Belgium;
and Département d'Informatique, Ecole normale supériure,
45 Rue d'Ulm, 75005 Paris, France
Gregory.Neven@esat.kuleuven.be

[3] Institute of Industrial Science, University of Tokyo,
4-6-1 Komaba, Meguro-ku, Tokyo 153-8505, Japan
schuldt@iis.u-tokyo.ac

Abstract. We propose new instantiations of chosen-ciphertext secure of identity-based encryption schemes with wildcards (WIBE). Our schemes outperform all existing alternatives in terms of efficiency as well as security. We achieve these results by extending the hybrid encryption (KEM–DEM) framework to the case of WIBE schemes. We propose and prove secure one generic construction in the random oracle model, and one direct construction in the standard model.

1 Introduction

One of the major obstacles for the deployment of public-key cryptography in the real world is the secure linking of users to their public keys. While typically solved through public-key infrastructures (PKI), identity-based encryption [19,18,10,8] can avoid some of the costs related to PKIs because it simply uses the identity of a user (e.g., her email address) as her public key. This way, Bob can for example send an encrypted email to Alice by encrypting it under her identity alice@cs.univ.edu, which only Alice can decrypt using the private key that only she can obtain from a trusted key distribution centre.

Abdalla *et al.* [1] recently proposed a very intuitive extension to this idea by allowing the recipient identity to contain *wildcards*. A ciphertext can then be decrypted by multiple recipients with related identities. For example, Bob can send an encrypted email to the entire computer science department by encrypting under identity *@cs.univ.edu, or to all system administrators in the university by encrypting under identity sysadmin@*.univ.edu. This extension therefore provides a very intuitive interface for identity-based mailing lists.

J. Pieprzyk, H. Ghodosi, and E. Dawson (Eds.): ACISP 2007, LNCS 4586, pp. 274–292, 2007.

ARBITRARY-LENGTH PLAINTEXTS. As is the case for most public-key and identity-based encryption schemes, the identity-based encryption with wildcards (WIBE) schemes of [1] can only be used to encrypt relatively short messages, typically about 160 bits. To encrypt longer messages, one will have to resort to *hybrid* techniques: the sender uses the WIBE to encrypt a fresh symmetric key K and encrypts the actual message under the key K. The basic construction has been used within the cryptographic community for years, dating back to the work of Blum and Goldwasser in 1984 [4], but its security for the case of public-key encryption was not properly analysed until the work of Cramer and Shoup [11]. One would intuitively expect these results to extend to the case of WIBEs, but this was never formally shown to be the case.

CHOSEN-CIPHERTEXT SECURITY. The basic schemes of [1] are proved secure under an appropriate adaptation of indistinguishability (IND) under chosen-plaintext attack (CPA) [13], where the adversary is given access to a key derivation oracle and has to distinguish between encryptions of two messages of its choice. This security notion is often not considered sufficient for practise though. Rather, the community seems to have settled with the stronger notion of indistinguishability under chosen-ciphertext attack (CCA) [16] as the "right" security notion for practical use.

A GENERIC CONSTRUCTION. Canetti *et al.* [9] proposed a generic construction of a CCA-secure hierarchical identity-based encryption (HIBE) scheme with up to L hierarchy levels from any $(L + 1)$-level CPA-secure HIBE scheme and any one-time signature scheme. Abdalla *et al.* adapted their techniques to the WIBE setting, but their construction requires a $(2L+2)$-level CPA-secure WIBE scheme to obtain an L-level CCA-secure one. (The reason is that the construction of [9] prefixes a bit to identity strings indicating whether it is a real identity or a public key of the one-time signature scheme. In the case of WIBE schemes, these bits must be put on separate levels, because if not the simulator may need to make illegal key derivation queries to answer the adversary's decryption queries.)

Doubling the hierarchy depth has a dramatic impact on efficiency and security of the schemes. First, the efficiency of all known WIBE schemes (in terms of computation, key length, and ciphertext length) is linear in the hierarchy depth, so the switch to CCA-security essentially doubles most associated costs. Second, the security of all known WIBE schemes degrades exponentially with the maximal hierarchy depth L. If the value of L is doubled, then either the scheme is restricted to half the (already limited) number of "useful" hierarchy levels, or that the security parameter must be increased to restore security. The first measure seriously limits the functionality of the scheme, the second increases costs even further.

For example, the WIBE scheme from [1] based on Waters' HIBE scheme [20] loses a factor of $(2nq_K)^L$ in the reduction to the BDDH problem, where n is the bit length of an identity string at each level of the hierarchy and q_K is the number of adversarial key derivation queries. Assume for simplicity that the advantage of solving the BDDH problem in a group of order $p > 2^k$ is $2^{-k/2}$. If $n = 128$ and $q_K = 2^{20}$, then to limit an adversary's advantage to 2^{-80} in a WIBE scheme with $L = 5$ levels, one should use a group order of at least $160 + 56L = 440$ bits. In the CCA-secure construction however, one needs a group order of $160 + 56(2L + 2) = 832$ bits, almost doubling the size of the representation of a group element, and multiplying by eight the cost of most (cubic-time) algorithms! Furthermore, since there are twice as many levels, the ciphertext must contain twice as many group elements, so overall, ciphertexts are four times as large and the cost of encryption and decryption is multiplied by sixteen!

OUR CONTRIBUTIONS. In this paper, we provide formal support for the use of hybrid encryption with WIBE schemes, and we present CCA-secure schemes that are more efficient and secure than those obtained through the generic construction of [1]. We achieve these results by considering WIBE schemes as consisting of separate key and data encapsulation mechanisms (KEM–DEM) [11], leading to the definition of identity-based key encapsulation mechanisms with wildcards (WIB-KEM). Here, the WIB-KEM encrypts a random key under a (wildcarded) identity, while the DEM encrypts the actual data under this random key.

We first show that the combination of a CPA-secure (resp. CCA-secure) WIB-KEM with a CPA-secure (resp. CCA-secure) DEM indeed yields a CPA-secure (resp. CCA-secure) WIBE scheme. This result may be rather unsurprising, but needed proof: it is necessary to validate the use of hybrid techniques for the case of WIBEs, in the same way that it was necessary for the public-key [11] and identity-based [3] cases. Furthermore, it should be noted that subtleties can arise in the proving of such results, for example in the case of certificateless KEMs [3].

Obviously, any secure WIBE scheme can be used to instantiate the WIB-KEM in the hybrid construction. (If the WIBE securely encrypts arbitrary messages, it also securely encrypts random keys.) This solves the problem of encrypting arbitrary-length messages, but still requires a CCA-secure WIBE scheme to achieve chosen-ciphertext security. As we argued above, all known instantiations of such schemes suffer from efficiency problems due to the doubling of the number of levels.

We therefore present a generic construction of L-level CCA-secure WIB-KEMs in the random oracle model [2] along the lines of Dent [12] from any L-level WIBE scheme that is one-way (OW) secure under chosen-plaintext attack. One-wayness is a much weaker security requirement than CCA-security, allowing much more efficient instantiations. In particular, one-wayness is implied by indistinguishability (for sufficiently large message spaces), so we can use any of the IND-CPA secure constructions of [1]. We also note that this construction can also be used to build CCA-secure HIBE schemes.

The resulting efficiency gains are summarised in Fig. 1. Abdalla *et al.* present two efficient schemes in the random oracle model based on the HIBE schemes of [5,7]. One can see that our schemes perform significantly better in terms of key sizes, ciphertext length, and encapsulation and decapsulation times. When

Scheme	$|mpk|$	$|d|$	$|C|$	Encap	Decap	Security loss
2-$L(\mathcal{BB})$	$4L+7$	$2L+1$	$3L+2$	$3L+2$	$2L+1$	q_{H}^{2L+2}
$\mathcal{OW}(\mathcal{BB})$	$2L+3$	$L+1$	$2L+2$	$2L+2$	$L+1$	q_{H}^{L}
2-$L(\mathcal{BBG})$	$2L+6$	$2L$	$L+3$	$L+3$	2	q_{H}^{2L+2}
$\mathcal{OW}(\mathcal{BBG})$	$L+4$	$L+1$	$L+3$	$L+3$	2	q_{H}^{L}
2-$L(\mathcal{Wa})$	$(n+3)L+3$	$2L+1$	$(n+2)L+2$	$(n+2)L+2$	$2L+1$	$(2nq_{\mathrm{K}})^{2L+2}$
$no\text{-}\mathcal{RO}$	$(n+1)L+3$	$L+1$	$(n+1)L+2$	$(n+1)L+2$	$L+3$	$L(20(n+1)q_{\mathrm{K}})^{L}$

Fig. 1. Efficiency comparison between our CCA-secure schemes and those of [1]. The $\mathcal{BB}$, $\mathcal{BBG}$ and $\mathcal{Wa}$ schemes are the WIBE schemes based on [5,7,20] presented in [1]. The $no\text{-}\mathcal{RO}$ scheme is our direct construction without random oracles. The 2-$L(\cdot)$ transformation refers to the generic CCA-secure construction of [1]; the $\mathcal{OW}(\cdot)$ transformation is our random-oracle based construction. We compare the schemes in terms of master public key size ($|mpk|$), user secret key size ($|d|$), ciphertext size ($|C|$), key encapsulation time (Encap), key decapsulation time (Decap), and the factor lost in the security reduction to the underlying assumption. The given values refer to the number of group elements for $|mpk|$, $|d|$, $|C|$; to the number of exponentiations for Encap; and to the number of pairing computations for Decap. L is the maximal hierarchy depth and n is the bit length of (a collision-resistant hash of) an identity string. The values q_{H}, q_{K} and q_{D} refer to the number of queries of an adversary to the random oracle, key derivation oracle and decryption oracle, respectively.

taking into account the security loss, one either has to conclude that our scheme supports twice the hierarchy depth, or that the inefficiency of the existing schemes in terms of memory size and computation time is blown up by a factor of at least two and eight, respectively.

Finally, we present a direct construction of a WIB-KEM scheme in the standard (i.e., non-random-oracle) model based on the HIB-KEM scheme by Kiltz and Galindo [15], which on its turn is based on Waters' HIBE scheme [20]. Note that the original version of the Kiltz-Galindo HIB-KEM scheme [14] is insecure, a fact which was noticed in [17], but the updated scheme in [15] does not suffer from the same weakness. We compare our scheme's efficiency to that of the only standard-model CCA-secure scheme in [1], namely the scheme obtained by applying their generic CCA transformation to the WIBE scheme based on Waters' HIBE. For fair comparison, we consider the optimised variant suggested in the full version of [1] that takes advantage of the fact that intermediate levels only contain one-bit identities. Our scheme is twice as efficient as the non-random-oracle scheme of [1] in terms of secret key size and pairing computations during decapsulation. The difference with regard to ciphertext size and encapsulation time is less pronounced, but this is disregarding the difference in security loss. As argued above, taking the security loss into account significantly blows up the costs of the scheme of [1]. For completeness, we should add that Fig. 1 hides the fact that our scheme relies on a hash function with a slightly stronger security assumption than the standard notion of second-preimage resistance.

2   Definitions

2.1   Notation

We first introduce some notation that we will use throughout the paper. We let $\{0,1\}^n$ denotes the set of bitstrings of length n, $\{0,1\}^{\leq n}$ denote the set of bitstrings of length at most n, and $\{0,1\}^*$ denote the set of bitstrings of arbitrary length. The notation $x \xleftarrow{\$} S$ denotes that x is assigned the value of an element selected uniformly at random from the set S. If A is an algorithm, then $x \leftarrow \mathsf{A}^{\mathcal{O}}(y, z)$ assigns to x the output of running A on inputs y and z, with access to oracle $\mathcal{O}$. A may be deterministic or probabilistic.

2.2   Syntax of WIBE Schemes, WIB-KEMs and DEMs

SYNTAX OF WIBE SCHEMES. A pattern P is a tuple $(P_1, \ldots, P_l) \in (\{0,1\}^* \cup \{*\})^l$, for some $l \leq L$, where L is the maximum number of levels. An identity $ID = (ID_1, \ldots, ID_{l'})$ "matches" the pattern P if $l' \leq l$ and for all $1 \leq i \leq l'$, $ID_i = P_i$ or $P_i = *$. We write this as $ID \in_* P$. A WIBE scheme of depth L consists of the following algorithms:

- Setup generates a master key pair (mpk, msk).
- KeyDer(d_{ID}, ID_{l+1}) takes the secret key d_{ID} for $ID = (ID_1, \ldots, ID_l)$, generates a secret key $d_{ID'}$ for the identity $ID' = (ID_1, \ldots, ID_{l+1})$. The root user, who has identity $\varepsilon = ()$, uses $d_\varepsilon = msk$ as his private key. This will be used to derive keys for single level identities.
- Encrypt(mpk, P, m) encrypts a message $m \in \{0,1\}^*$ intended for all identities matching a pattern P, and returns a ciphertext C.
- Decrypt(d_{ID}, C) decrypts ciphertext C using the secret key d_{ID} for an identity $ID \in_* P$ and returns the corresponding message m. If the encryption is invalid, the Decrypt algorithm "rejects" by outputting $\perp$.

We will overload the notation for key derivation, writing KeyDer(msk, ID) to mean repeated application of the key derivation function in the obvious way. Soundness requires that for all key pairs (mpk, msk) output by Setup, all $0 \leq l \leq L$, all patterns $P \in (\{0,1\}^* \cup \{*\})^l$, all identities ID such that $ID \in_* P$, and all messages $m \in \{0,1\}^*$:

$$\Pr\left[\mathsf{Decrypt}(\mathsf{KeyDer}(msk, ID), \mathsf{Encrypt}(mpk, P, m)) = m\right] = 1.$$

SYNTAX OF WIB-KEMs. We will now define an Identity-Based Key Encapsulation Mechanism with Wildcards (WIB-KEM). A WIB-KEM consists of the following algorithms:

- Setup and KeyDer algorithms are defined as in the WIBE case.
- Encap(mpk, P) takes the master public key mpk of the system and a pattern P, and returns (K, C), where $K \in \{0,1\}^\lambda$ is a one-time symmetric key and C is an encapsulation of the key K.

IND-WID security game for WIBEs:

1. $(mpk, msk) \leftarrow \mathsf{Setup}$
2. $(P^*, m_0, m_1, s) \leftarrow \mathcal{A}_1^{\mathcal{O}}(mpk)$
3. $b \xleftarrow{\$} \{0, 1\}$
4. $C^* \leftarrow \mathsf{Encrypt}(mpk, P^*, m_b)$
5. $b' \leftarrow \mathcal{A}_2^{\mathcal{O}}(C^*, s)$

OW-WID security game for WIBEs:

1. $(mpk, msk) \leftarrow \mathsf{Setup}$
2. $(P^*, s) \leftarrow \mathcal{A}_1^{\mathcal{O}}(mpk)$
3. $m \xleftarrow{\$} \mathcal{M}$
4. $C^* \leftarrow \mathsf{Encrypt}(mpk, P^*, m)$
5. $m' \leftarrow \mathcal{A}_2^{\mathcal{O}}(C^*, s)$

IND-WID security game for WIB-KEMs:

1. $(mpk, msk) \leftarrow \mathsf{Setup}$
2. $(P^*, s) \leftarrow \mathcal{A}_1^{\mathcal{O}}(mpk)$
3. $(K_0, C^*) \leftarrow \mathsf{Encap}(mpk, P^*)$
4. $K_1 \xleftarrow{\$} \{0, 1\}^\lambda$
5. $b \xleftarrow{\$} \{0, 1\}$
6. $b' \leftarrow \mathcal{A}_2^{\mathcal{O}}(K_b, C^*, s)$

IND security game for DEMs:

1. $(m_0, m_1, s) \leftarrow \mathcal{A}_1()$
2. $K \xleftarrow{\$} \{0, 1\}^\lambda$
3. $b \xleftarrow{\$} \{0, 1\}$
4. $C^* \leftarrow \mathsf{Encrypt}(K, m_b)$
5. $b' \leftarrow \mathcal{A}_2^{\mathcal{O}}(C^*, s)$

Fig. 2. Security games for WIBEs, WIB-KEMs and DEMs

- $\mathsf{Decap}(mpk, d_{ID}, C)$ takes a private key d_{ID} for an identity $ID \in_* P$ and an encapsulation C, and returns the corresponding secret key K. If the encapsulation is invalid, the Decap algorithm "rejects" by outputting $\perp$.

A WIB-KEM must satisfy the following soundness property: for all pairs (mpk, msk) output by Setup, all $0 \le l \le L$, all patterns $P \in (\{0, 1\}^* \cup \{*\})^l$, and all identities $ID \in_* P$,

$$\Pr[K' = K : (K, C) \leftarrow \mathsf{Encap}(mpk, P); K' \leftarrow \mathsf{Decap}(\mathsf{KeyDer}(msk, ID), C)] = 1.$$

HIBE schemes and HIB-KEMs can be thought of as special cases WIBEs and WIB-KEMs restricted to patterns without wildcards.

SYNTAX OF DEMs. A DEM consists of a pair of deterministic algorithms:

- $\mathsf{Encrypt}(K, m)$ takes a key $K \in \{0, 1\}^\lambda$, and a message m of arbitrary length and outputs a ciphertext C.
- $\mathsf{Decrypt}(K, C)$ takes a key $K \in \{0, 1\}^\lambda$ and a ciphertext C and outputs either the corresponding message m or the "reject" symbol $\perp$.

The DEM must satisfy the following soundness property: for all $K \in \{0, 1\}^\lambda$, for all $m \in \{0, 1\}^*$, $\mathsf{Decrypt}(K, \mathsf{Encrypt}(K, m)) = m$.

2.3 Security Notions

Security games for WIBEs, WIB-KEMs and DEMs are presented in Figure 2. In all four games, s is some state information and $\mathcal{O}$ denotes the oracles the adversary has access to. In the OW-WID game, $\mathcal{M}$ denotes the message space of the WIBE. This will depend on the system parameters.

SECURITY OF WIBE SCHEMES. We use the security definitions of indistinguishability under chosen-plaintext and chosen-ciphertext as per [1]. In both WIBE
security games shown in Figure 2, $\mathcal{A}$ has access to a private key extraction oracle, which given an identity ID outputs $d_{ID} \leftarrow$ KeyDer(msk, ID). In the CCA
model only, $\mathcal{A}$ also has access to a decryption oracle, which on input (C, ID),
returns $m \leftarrow$ Decrypt(KeyDer$(msk, ID), C)$.

The adversary wins the IND-WID game (as shown in Figure 2) if $b' = b$ and it
never queried the key derivation oracle on any identity matching the pattern P^*.
Furthermore, in the CCA model, the adversary must never query the decryption
oracle on (ID, C^*), for any ID matching the pattern P^*. We define the advantage
of the adversary as $\epsilon = |2 \Pr[b' = b] - 1|$.

The adversary wins the OW-WID-CPA game if $m' = m$ and it never queried
the key derivation oracle on any identity matching the pattern P^*. We define
the advantage of the adversary to be $\epsilon = \Pr[m' = m]$.

SECURITY OF WIB-KEMS. In the IND-WID game for WIB-KEMs (also shown
in Figure 2) $\mathcal{A}$ has access to a private key extraction oracle, which given an
identity ID outputs $d_{ID} \leftarrow$ KeyDer(msk, ID). In the CCA model only, $\mathcal{A}$ additionally has access to a decapsulation oracle, which on input (ID, C), returns
$K \leftarrow$ Decap(KeyDer$(msk, ID), C)$.

Again, the adversary wins the IND-WID game if $b' = b$ and it never queried
the key derivation oracle on any identity matching the pattern P^*. Furthermore,
in the CCA model, the adversary must never query the decapsulation oracle on
(C^*, ID), for any ID matching the pattern P^*. We define the advantage of the
adversary as $\epsilon = |2 \Pr[b' = b] - 1|$.

SECURITY OF DEMS. In the IND-CPA game for DEMs, the adversary has access
to no oracles. In the IND-CCA model, $\mathcal{A}_2$ may call a decryption oracle, which on
input $C \neq C^*$ returns $m \leftarrow$ Decrypt(K, C). Note that this oracle is only available
in the second phase of the attack. The adversary wins if $b' = b$. We define the
advantage of the adversary as $\epsilon = |2 \Pr[b' = b] - 1|$.

Definition 1. *A WIBE scheme (resp. WIB-KEM) is (t, q_K, ϵ) IND-WID-CPA
secure if all time t adversaries making at most q_K queries to the key derivation
oracle have advantage at most ϵ in winning the IND-WID-CPA game described
above.*

Definition 2. *A WIBE scheme (resp. WIB-KEM) is (t, q_K, q_D, ϵ) IND-WID-
CCA secure if all time t adversaries making at most q_K queries to the key derivation oracle and at most q_D queries to the decryption (resp. decapsulation) oracle
have advantage at most ϵ in winning the IND-WID-CCA game described above.*

The (t, q_K, ϵ) IND-HID-CPA and (t, q_K, q_D, ϵ) IND-HID-CCA security of a HIBE
scheme and HIB-KEM are defined analogously.

Definition 3. *A WIBE scheme is (t, q_K, ϵ) OW-WID-CPA secure if all time t
adversaries making at most q_K queries to the key derivation oracle have advantage at most ϵ in winning the OW-WID-CPA game described above.*

Definition 4. *A DEM is (t, q_D, ϵ) IND-CCA secure if all time t adversaries making at most q_D decryption queries in the the IND-CCA game described above has advantage at most ϵ.*

When working in the random oracle model, we add the number of queries made to the oracle as a parameter, so for example we would say a WIBE is $(t, q_K, q_D, q_H, \epsilon)$ IND-WID-CCA secure, where q_H is the total number of hash queries. The other definitions may be adapted in a similar manner.

3   Security of the Hybrid Construction

Suppose we are given an IND-WID-CCA secure WIB-KEM scheme $\mathcal{WIB\text{-}KEM} =$ (Setup, KeyDer, Encap, Decap) and an IND-CCA secure data encapsulation method $\mathcal{DEM} =$ (Encrypt, Decrypt). Let us also suppose that the length λ of keys generated by the WIB-KEM is the same as the length of keys used by the DEM. Then, following the method of [11], we can combine them to form a WIBE scheme $\mathcal{WIBE} =$ (Setup, KeyDer, Encrypt$'$, Decrypt$'$) as follows:

- Encrypt$'(mpk, P, m)$: Compute $(K, C_1) \leftarrow$ Encap(mpk, P), $C_2 \leftarrow$ Encrypt (K, m). Return $C = (C_1, C_2)$.
- Decrypt$'(d_{ID}, C)$: Parse C as (C_1, C_2). If the parsing fails, return $\perp$. Otherwise, compute $K \leftarrow$ Decap(d_{ID}, C_1). If Decap rejects, return $\perp$. Finally, compute $m \leftarrow$ Decrypt(K, C_2), and return m.

Theorem 5. *Suppose there is a (t, q_K, q_D, ϵ)-adversary $\mathcal{A} = (\mathcal{A}_1, \mathcal{A}_2)$ against IND-WID-CCA security of the hybrid WIBE. Then there is a $(t_\mathcal{B}, q_K, q_D, \epsilon_\mathcal{B})$-adversary $\mathcal{B} = (\mathcal{B}_1, \mathcal{B}_2)$ against the IND-WID-CCA security of the WIB-KEM and a $(t_\mathcal{C}, q_D, \epsilon_\mathcal{C})$-adversary $\mathcal{C} = (\mathcal{C}_1, \mathcal{C}_2)$ against the IND-CCA security of the DEM such that:*

$$t_\mathcal{B} \leq t + q_D t_{\mathsf{Dec}} + t_{\mathsf{Enc}}$$
$$t_\mathcal{C} \leq t + q_D(t_{\mathsf{Dec}} + t_{\mathsf{Decap}} + t_{\mathsf{KeyDer}}) + q_K t_{\mathsf{KeyDer}} + t_{\mathsf{Encap}} + t_{\mathsf{Setup}}$$
$$\epsilon = \epsilon_\mathcal{B} + \epsilon_\mathcal{C}$$

where t_{Enc} is the time to run the DEM's Encrypt algorithm, t_{Dec} is the time to run the DEM's Decrypt algorithm, t_{Setup} is the time to run Setup, t_{Decap} is the time to run Decap and t_{KeyDer} is the time to run KeyDer.

The theorem and proof are straightforward generalisations to the WIBE case of those in [11]. The proof is given in the full version of the paper. Intuitively, the construction is secure as the KEM generates a one time symmetric key K, which "looks" random to the adversary, (i.e. is computationally indistinguishable from random) and this is enough for the DEM to be secure.

4   A Generic Construction in the Random Oracle Model

One approach to building systems secure against adaptive chosen ciphertext attacks is to first construct a primitive that is secure against passive attacks, and use some generic transformation to produce a system secure against the stronger adaptive attacks. We will apply a method proposed by Dent in [12] which converts an OW-CPA secure probabilistic encryption scheme into an IND-CCA KEM. We will use the same idea to convert an OW-WID-CPA secure WIBE scheme into an IND-WID-CCA secure WIB-KEM. Suppose we have an OW-WID-CPA secure probabilistic WIBE scheme $\mathcal{WIBE} = $ (Setup, KeyDer, Encrypt, Decrypt) with message space $\mathcal{M}$. We will write Encrypt($mpk, P^*, m; r$) to mean running the encryption algorithm with inputs (mpk, P^*, m) using a ρ-bit string of randomness r. We require that for all master keys mpk generated by Setup, all patterns P, all messages $m \in \mathcal{M}$ and all ciphertexts C:

$$\Pr\left[\mathsf{Encrypt}(mpk, P, m; r) = C \; : \; r \xleftarrow{\$} \{0,1\}^\rho\right] \leq \gamma$$

where γ is a parameter of the scheme.

The only difficulty in applying the method of Dent [12] is that we must re-encrypt the recovered message as an integrity check. In the WIBE setting, this means we must know the pattern under which the message was originally encrypted. We assume that the set $W = \{i \in \mathbb{Z} : P_i = *\}$ is easily derived from the ciphertext. This is certainly possible with the Waters and BBG based WIBEs presented in [1]. If a scheme does not already have this property, it could be modified so that the set W is included explicitly as a ciphertext component. W can then be used to give an algorithm P, which on input (ID, C), where C is a ciphertext and $ID = (ID_1, \ldots, ID_l)$ is an identity, returns the pattern $P = (P_1, \ldots, P_l)$ given by $P_i = *$ for $i \in \mathsf{W}(C)$ and $P_i = ID_i$ otherwise.

We will use $\mathcal{WIBE}$ to construct an IND-WID-CCA secure WIB-KEM

$$\mathcal{WIB\text{-}KEM} = (\mathsf{Setup}, \mathsf{KeyDer}, \mathsf{Encap}, \mathsf{Decap})$$

using two hash functions $H_1 : \{0,1\}^* \times (\{0,1\}^n \cup \{*\}) \rightarrow \{0,1\}^\rho$ and $H_2 : \{0,1\}^* \rightarrow \{0,1\}^\lambda$, where λ is the length of keys output by the WIB-KEM. The algorithms of the WIB-KEM are given by:

- Setup and KeyDer are exactly as in $\mathcal{WIBE}$.
- Encap(mpk, P): Choose a random message $m \xleftarrow{\$} \mathcal{M}$. Compute $r \leftarrow H_1(m, P)$, $K \leftarrow H_2(m)$ and compute $C \leftarrow \mathsf{Encrypt}(mpk, P, m; r)$. Return (K, C)
- Decap(d_{ID}, C): Compute $m \leftarrow \mathsf{Decrypt}(d_{ID}, C)$. If $m = \bot$, return $\bot$. Compute $r \leftarrow H_1(m, \mathsf{P}(ID, C))$ and check that $C = \mathsf{Encrypt}(mpk, \mathsf{P}(ID, C), m; r)$. If so, return $K \leftarrow H_2(m)$; otherwise return $\bot$.

Theorem 6. *Suppose there is a $(t, q_K, q_D, q_H, \epsilon)$ adversary $\mathcal{A}$ against the IND-WID-CCA security of the WIB-KEM in the random oracle model. Then there is a (t', q_K, ϵ') adversary $\mathcal{B}$ against the OW-WID-CPA security of the WIBE, where:*

$$\epsilon' \geq \left(\epsilon - q_D\left(\frac{1}{|\mathcal{M}|} + \gamma\right)\right)/(q_D + q_H)$$

$$t' \leq t + q_H t_H + q_D q_H t_{Enc}$$

where t_{Enc} is the time taken to do an encryption, and t_H is the time needed to look up a hash value in a list.

This proof of this theorem is a straightforward generalisation of the result of Dent [12]. The proof is given in the full version of the paper.

5   A Direct Construction without Random Oracles

5.1   The Kiltz-Galindo HIB-KEM

We present a construction for a WIB-KEM based on the Kiltz-Galindo HIB-KEM [15]. This construction is based on the Waters HIBE [20] and belongs to the Boneh-Boyen family of identity-based encryption schemes [6]. Before presenting our construction, we briefly recall the definitions for bilinear maps and second-preimage resistant hash functions:

Definition 7 (Bilinear map). *Let $\mathbb{G} = \langle g \rangle$ and $\mathbb{G}_T$ be multiplicative groups of prime order p. We say that $e : \mathbb{G} \times \mathbb{G} \to \mathbb{G}_T$ is an admissible bilinear map if the following hold true:*

- *For all $a, b \in \mathbb{Z}_p$ we have $e(g^a, g^b) = e(g, g)^{ab}$.*
- *$e(g, g)$ is not the identity element of $\mathbb{G}_T$.*
- *e is efficiently computable.*

Definition 8 (BDDH problem). *We say that the BDDH problem in $\mathbb{G}$ is (t, ϵ)-hard if*

$$\left| \Pr\left[\mathcal{A}(g^a, g^b, g^c, e(g,g)^{abc}) = 1 \; : \; a, b, c \xleftarrow{\$} \mathbb{Z}_p \right] \right.$$
$$\left. - \Pr\left[\mathcal{A}(g^a, g^b, g^c, e(g,g)^d) = 1 \; : \; a, b, c, d \xleftarrow{\$} \mathbb{Z}_p \right] \right| \leq \epsilon$$

for any algorithm $\mathcal{A}$ running in time at most t.

Definition 9 (Second-preimage resistant hash function). *A family $F_{\{k \in \mathcal{K}\}} : \mathbb{G} \to \mathbb{Z}_p$ of hash functions with key space $\mathcal{K}$ is called (t, ϵ) second-preimage resistant if all time t algorithms $\mathcal{A}$ have advantage at most ϵ, where the advantage of $\mathcal{A}$ is defined by:*

$$\Pr[x \neq y \wedge F_k(x) = F_k(y) : x \xleftarrow{\$} \mathbb{G}; k \xleftarrow{\$} \mathcal{K}; y \leftarrow \mathcal{A}(k, x)].$$

In principle, a key k for the hash function should be included as part of the public parameters, but to simplify the description of the scheme, we will treat the family of hash functions as if it were a fixed function.

We recall the Kiltz-Galindo HIB-KEM [15] in Figure 3. Note that the identities at each level are assumed to be n bits long i.e., $ID_i \in \{0,1\}^n$, and we set

$$[ID_i] = \{1 \leq j \leq n : \text{ the } j^{th} \text{ bit of } ID_i \text{ is one}\} .$$

We assume the function $h_1 : \mathbb{G} \to \mathbb{Z}_p^*$ is a second-preimage resistant hash function. The security of the Kiltz-Galindo scheme rests on the bilinear decisional Diffie-Hellman (BDDH) problem. Kiltz and Galindo proved the following security result of their scheme.

Theorem 10. *If there exists a* (t, q_K, q_D, ϵ) *attacker for the Kiltz-Galindo HIB-KEM in the IND-HID-CCA model, then there exists a* (t', ϵ') *algorithm which solves the BDDH problem in* $\mathbb{G}$ *and a* (t_h, ϵ_h) *attacker against the second pre-image resistance property of* h_1 *such that* $t' \leq t + O(\epsilon^{-2} \cdot \ln(\epsilon^{-1}))$, $t_h \leq O(t)$ *and*

$$\epsilon' \geq \frac{\epsilon - \epsilon_h}{(10(n+1)q)^L} - q/p ,$$

where $q = q_K + q_D$ *and* p *is the order of* $\mathbb{G}$.

Algorithm Setup:
  $v_1, v_2, v_3, \alpha \xleftarrow{\$} \mathbb{G}$; $z \leftarrow e(g, \alpha)$
  $u_{i,j} \xleftarrow{\$} \mathbb{G}$ for $i = 1 \ldots L, j = 0 \ldots n$
  $mpk \leftarrow (v_1, v_2, v_3, u_{1,0}, \ldots, u_{L,n}, z)$
  $msk \leftarrow \alpha$
  Return (mpk, msk)

Algorithm KeyDer$(d_{(ID_1,\ldots,ID_l)}, ID_{l+1})$:
  Parse $d_{(ID_1,\ldots,ID_l)}$ as $(d_0, \ldots, d_l)$
  $s_{l+1} \xleftarrow{\$} \mathbb{Z}_p^*$; $d'_{l+1} \leftarrow g^{s_{l+1}}$
  $d'_0 \leftarrow d_0 \cdot \left(u_{l+1,0} \prod_{j \in ID_{l+1}} u_{l+1,j} \right)^{s_{l+1}}$
  Return $(d'_0, d_1, \ldots, d_l, d'_{l+1})$

Algorithm Encap(mpk, ID):
  Parse ID as $(ID_1, \ldots, ID_l)$
  $r \xleftarrow{\$} \mathbb{Z}_p^*$; $C_0 \leftarrow g^r$; $t \leftarrow h_1(C_0)$
  For $i = 1 \ldots l$ do
    $C_i \leftarrow \left(u_{i,0} \prod_{j \in [ID_i]} u_{i,j} \right)^r$
  $C_{l+1} \leftarrow (v_1^t v_2^l v_3)^r$
  $K \leftarrow z^r$
  Return $(K, (C_0, \ldots, C_{l+1}))$

Algorithm Decap$(d_{(ID_1,\ldots,ID_l)}, C)$:
  Parse $d_{(ID_1,\ldots,ID_l)}$ as $(d_0, \ldots, d_l)$
  Parse C as $(C_0, \ldots, C_{l+1})$
  $t \leftarrow h_1(C_0)$
  If any of $(g, C_0, v_1^t v_2^l v_3, C_{l+1})$
    or $(g, C_0, u_{i,0} \prod_{j \in [ID_i]} u_{i,j}, C_i)$,
    for $i = 1 \ldots l$ is not a DH tuple
    then $K \leftarrow \bot$
    else $K \leftarrow e(C_0, d_0) / \prod_{i=1}^l e(C_i, d_i)$
  Return K

Fig. 3. The Kiltz-Galindo HIB-KEM scheme

Note that the Kiltz-Galindo scheme generates keys which are elements of the group $\mathbb{G}_T$, and we will follow this practise in our construction of the WIB-KEM. However, our definition of a WIB-KEM requires that the keys it generates are bitstrings. This discrepancy can be overcome by hashing the group element used as the key using a smooth hash function. A hash function $h : \mathbb{G}_T \to \{0,1\}^\lambda$ is ϵ-smooth if for all $K \in \{0,1\}^\lambda$ and for all $z \in \mathbb{G}_T^*$, the probability

$$\Pr[h(z^r) = K : r \xleftarrow{\$} \mathbb{Z}_p] = 1/2^\lambda + \epsilon .$$

5.2   The Kiltz-Galindo WIB-KEM

We attempt to build a WIB-KEM using a similar approach to that of Kiltz-Galindo [15] using the techniques of Abdalla *et al.* [1]. A naive implementation might try to construct an encapsulation algorithm as follows:

- Encap(mpk, P) : Parse the pattern P as $(P_1, \ldots, P_l) \in (\{0,1\}^n \cup \{*\})^l$. Pick $r \xleftarrow{\$} \mathbb{Z}_p^*$, set $C_0 \leftarrow g^r$, and for $1 \leq i \leq l$ compute C_i as

$$C_i \leftarrow \begin{cases} \left(u_{i,0} \prod_{j \in [P_i]} u_{i,j}\right)^r & \text{if } P_i \neq * \\ \left(u_{i,0}^r, \ldots, u_{i,n}^r\right) & \text{if } P_i = * \,. \end{cases}$$

Finally, compute $t \leftarrow h_1(C_0)$, and $C_{l+1} \leftarrow (v_1^t v_2^l v_3)^r$.
The ciphertext $C = (C_0, \ldots, C_{l+1})$ is the encapsulation of key $K = z^r$.

However, such an implementation would be insecure in the IND-WID-CCA model. An attacker could output a challenge pattern $P^* = (*)$ and would receive a key K and an encapsulation (C_0, C_1, C_2) where $C_0 = g^{r^*}$ and $C_1 = (u_0^{r^*}, \ldots, u_n^{r^*})$. It would be simple for the attacker then to construct a valid encapsulation of the same key for a particular identity ID by setting $C_1' \leftarrow u_0^{r^*} \prod_{j \in [ID]} u_i^{r^*}$. Thus, submitting the identity ID and the ciphertext (C_0, C_1', C_2) to the decryption oracle will return the correct decapsulation of the challenge.

This attack demonstrates the importance of knowing the location of the wildcards that were used to create an encapsulation. We solve this problem by increasing the scope of the hash function h_1. In the original proof of security, the hash function prevents an attacker from submitting a valid ciphertext C to the decapsulation oracle where C has the same decapsulation as C^* but $C_0 \neq C_0^*$. We extend this to prevent an attacker from submitting a valid ciphertext C to the decapsulation oracle where C has the same decapsulation but either $C_0 \neq C_0^*$ or C and C^* have wildcards in different positions. To do this we make use of a function h_2, which on input of a pattern $P = (P_1, \ldots, P_l)$, returns a bitstring $b_1 b_2 \ldots b_l$, where $b_i = 1$ if P_i is a wildcard, otherwise $b_i = 0$. Note that two patterns P_1, P_2 have wildcards in the same location if and only if $h_2(P_1) = h_2(P_2)$.

However, since an attacker can submit ciphertexts to the decapsulation oracle with patterns of his own choice, the increased scope of the hash function means that we have to rely on a slightly stronger assumption than standard second-preimage resistance. Informally, we will require the hash function to be second-preimage resistant, even when the attacker is allowed to choose the first L bits (corresponding to $h_2(P)$) of the challenge input for which he tries to find a collision. We formally define this property as follows:

Definition 11 (Extended second-preimage resistant hash function). *A family* $F_{\{k \in \mathcal{K}\}} : \{0,1\}^{\leq L} \times \mathbb{G} \rightarrow \mathbb{Z}_p$ *of hash functions with key space* $\mathcal{K}$ *is called* (t, ϵ) *extended second-preimage resistant if all time* t *algorithms* $\mathcal{A}$ *have advantage at most* ϵ, *where the advantage of* $\mathcal{A}$ *is defined by*

$$\Pr[(l_x, x) \neq (l_y, y) \wedge F_k(l_x, x) = F_k(l_y, y) : x \xleftarrow{\$} \mathbb{G}; k \xleftarrow{\$} \mathcal{K}; (l_x, l_y, y) \leftarrow \mathcal{A}(k, x)].$$

As in the description of the Kiltz-Galindo HIB-KEM, we will treat the family of hash functions as a fixed function to simplify the description of our scheme.

- Setup : Pick random elements $v_1, v_2, \alpha \stackrel{\$}{\leftarrow} \mathbb{G}$ and compute $z \leftarrow e(\alpha, g)$ where g is the generator of $\mathbb{G}$. Furthermore, pick elements $u_{i,j} \stackrel{\$}{\leftarrow} \mathbb{G}$ for $1 \leq i \leq L$ and $0 \leq j \leq n$. The master public key is $mpk = (v_1, v_2, u_{1,0}, \ldots, u_{L,n}, z)$ and the master secret is $msk = \alpha$.
- KeyDer(msk, ID_1) : Pick $s_1 \stackrel{\$}{\leftarrow} \mathbb{Z}_p$. Compute $d_0 \leftarrow \alpha(u_{1,0} \prod_{j \in [ID_1]} u_{1,j})^{s_1}$ and $d_1 \leftarrow g^{s_1}$. The private key for ID_1 is (d_0, d_1). This can be thought of as an example of the next algorithm where the decryption key for the null identity is $d_0 \leftarrow \alpha$.
- KeyDer(d_{ID}, ID_{l+1}) : Parse the private key d_{ID} for $ID = (ID_1, \ldots, ID_l)$ as $(d_0, \ldots, d_l)$. Pick $s_{l+1} \stackrel{\$}{\leftarrow} \mathbb{Z}_p$ and compute $d'_{l+1} \leftarrow g^{s_{l+1}}$. Lastly, compute

$$d'_0 \leftarrow d_0 \cdot \left(u_{l+1,0} \prod_{j \in [ID_{l+1}]} u_{l+1,j} \right)^{s_{l+1}}.$$

The private key for $ID' = (ID_1, \ldots, ID_l, ID_{l+1})$ is $d_{ID'} = (d'_0, d_1, \ldots, d_l, d'_{l+1})$.
- Encap(mpk, P) : Parse the pattern P as $(P_1, \ldots, P_l) \in (\{0,1\}^n \cup \{*\})^l$. Pick $r \stackrel{\$}{\leftarrow} \mathbb{Z}_p^*$, set $C_0 \leftarrow g^r$, and for $1 \leq i \leq l$ compute C_i as

$$C_i \leftarrow \begin{cases} \left(u_{i,0} \prod_{j \in [P_i]} u_{i,j} \right)^r & \text{if } P_i \neq * \\ (u_{i,0}^r, \ldots, u_{i,n}^r) & \text{if } P_i = * . \end{cases}$$

If $P_i = *$ we will use the notation $C_{i,j}$ to mean the jth component of C_i i.e. $u_{i,j}^r$. Finally, compute $t \leftarrow h_1(h_2(P), C_0)$, and $C_{l+1} \leftarrow (v_1^t v_2)^r$. The ciphertext $C = (C_0, \ldots, C_{l+1})$ is the encapsulation of key $K = z^r$.
- Decap(d_{ID}, C) : Parse d_{ID} as $(d_0, \ldots, d_{l'})$ and C as $(C_0, \ldots, C_{l+1})$. First compute $t \leftarrow h_1(h_2(P), C_0)$ where P is the pattern under which C was encrypted. Note that $h_2(P)$ is implicitly given by C, even though P is not. Test whether

$$(g, C_0, v_1^t v_2, C_{l+1})$$
$$(g, C_0, u_{i,0} \prod_{j \in [ID_i]} u_{i,j}, C_i) \quad \text{for } 1 \leq i \leq l, P_i \neq *$$
$$(g, C_0, u_{i,j}, C_{i,j}) \quad \text{for } 1 \leq i \leq l, P_i = *, 0 \leq j \leq n$$

are all Diffie-Hellman tuples. If not, return $\perp$. Rather than doing this test in the naive way by performing two pairing computations for each tuple, they can be aggregated in a single test as follows. Choose random exponents $r \stackrel{\$}{\leftarrow} \mathbb{Z}_p$, $r_i \stackrel{\$}{\leftarrow} \mathbb{Z}_p$ for $P_i \neq *$ and $r_{i,j} \stackrel{\$}{\leftarrow} \mathbb{Z}_p$ for $P_i = *, 0 \leq j \leq n$, compute

$$A \leftarrow (v_1^t v_2)^r \cdot \prod_{P_i \neq *} \left(u_{i,0} \prod_{j \in [ID_i]} u_{i,j} \right)^{r_i} \cdot \prod_{P_i = *} \prod_{j=0}^{n} u_{i,j}^{r_{i,j}}$$

$$B \leftarrow C_{l+1}^r \cdot \prod_{P_i \neq *} C_i^{r_i} \cdot \prod_{P_i = *} \prod_{j=0}^{n} C_{i,j}^{r_{i,j}}$$

and check whether $e(g, B) = e(C_0, A)$. If one or more of the tuples are not Diffie-Hellman tuples, this test fails with probability $1 - 1/p$. If it succeeds, decapsulate the key by first setting

$$C_i' \leftarrow \begin{cases} C_i & \text{if } P_i \neq * \\ C_{i,0} \prod_{j \in [ID_i]} C_{i,j} & \text{if } P_i = * \end{cases} \quad \text{for } 1 \leq i \leq l'$$

and then computing $K \leftarrow e(C_0, d_0) / \prod_{i=1}^{l'} e(C_i', d_i)$.

Soundness. Given a correctly formed encapsulation $C = (C_0, \ldots, C_{l+1})$ of a key $K = z^r$ for a pattern P, it can be verified that decapsulation of C with a private key $d_{ID} = (d_0, \ldots, d_{l'})$ for $ID \in_* P$ yields the correct key since

$$\frac{e(C_0, d_0)}{\prod_{i=1}^{l'} e(C_i', d_i)} = \frac{e\left(g^r, \alpha \prod_{i=1}^{l'} \left(u_{i,0} \prod_{j \in [ID_i]} u_{i,j}\right)^{s_i}\right)}{\prod_{i=1}^{l'} e\left(\left(u_{i,0} \prod_{j \in [ID_i]} u_{i,j}\right)^r, g^{s_i}\right)}$$

$$= \frac{e(g^r, \alpha) \prod_{i=1}^{l'} e\left(g^r, \left(u_{i,0} \prod_{j \in [ID_i]} u_{i,j}\right)^{s_i}\right)}{\prod_{i=1}^{l'} e\left(\left(u_{i,0} \prod_{j \in [ID_i]} u_{i,j}\right)^r, g^{s_i}\right)}$$

$$= e(g, \alpha)^r$$

$$= z^r.$$

Thus the scheme is sound.

Theorem 12. *If there exists a (t, q_K, q_D, ϵ) attacker for the Kiltz-Galindo WIB-KEM in the IND-WID-CCA model, then there exists a (t', ϵ') algorithm which solves the BDDH problem in $\mathbb{G}$ and a (t_h, ϵ_h) attacker against the extended second pre-image resistance property of h_1 such that $t' \leq t + O(\epsilon^{-2} \cdot \ln(\epsilon^{-1}))$, $t_h \leq O(t)$ and*

$$\epsilon' \geq \frac{\epsilon - \epsilon_h - q_D/p}{L(20(n+1)q_K)^L},$$

where p is the order of $\mathbb{G}$.

The proof is given in Appendix A.

Note that, as is the case for all known HIBE and WIBE schemes, the security of our WIB-KEM degrades exponentially with the maximal hierarchy depth L. The scheme can therefore only be used for relatively small (logarithmic) values of L. We leave the construction of a WIB-KEM with polynomial efficiency and security in all parameters as an open problem. Any solution to this problem would directly imply a WIBE and a HIBE scheme with polynomial security as well, the latter of which has been an open problem for quite a while now.

We also note that the security proof for our construction can be completed, even if the used hash function is only assumed to be standard second-preimage resistant. However, this will add an additional security loss of $L2^L$ with respect to the hash function. Considering that security already degrades exponentially with L, this will not be a significant addition to the existing security loss and might be preferred instead of introducing a stronger assumption about the hash function.

6 Conclusion

We have proposed new chosen-ciphertext secure instantiations of WIBE schemes that improve on the existing schemes in both efficiency and security. To this end, we extended the KEM–DEM framework to the case of WIBE schemes. We proposed a generic construction in the random oracle model that transforms any one-way secure WIBE into a chosen-ciphertext secure WIB-KEM. We also proposed a direct construction of a WIB-KEM that is secure in the standard model. Our schemes overall gain at least a factor two in efficiency, especially when taking into account (as one should) the loose security bounds of all previously existing constructions.

Acknowledgements

The work described in this paper has been supported in part by the European Commission through the IST Programme under Contract IST-2002-507932 ECRYPT. The information in this document reflects only the authors' views, is provided as is and no guarantee or warranty is given that the information is fit for any particular purpose. The user thereof uses the information at its sole risk and liability. The first author was also funded in part by the EPSRC. The third author is a Postdoctoral Fellow of the Research Foundation – Flanders (FWO), and was supported in part by the Concerted Research Action (GOA) Ambiorics 2005/11 of the Flemish Government and by the IAP Programme P6/26 BCRYPT of the Belgian State (Belgian Science Policy).

References

1. Abdalla, M., Catalano, D., Dent, A.W., Malone-Lee, J., Neven, G., Smart, N.P.: Identity-based encryption gone wild. In: Bugliesi, M., Preneel, B., Sassone, V., Wegener, I. (eds.) ICALP 2006. LNCS, vol. 4052, pp. 300–311. Springer, Heidelberg (2006)
2. Bellare, M., Rogaway, P.: Random oracles are practical: A paradigm for designing efficient protocols. In: ACM CCS 93, pp. 62–73. ACM Press, New York (1993)
3. Bentahar, K., Farshim, P., Malone-Lee, J., Smart, N.P.: Generic constructions of identity-based and certificateless KEMs. Cryptology ePrint Archive, Report 2005/058, (2005) http://eprint.iacr.org/
4. Blum, M., Goldwasser, S.: An efficient probabilistic public-key encryption scheme which hides all partial information. In: Blakely, G.R., Chaum, D. (eds.) CRYPTO 1984. LNCS, vol. 196, pp. 289–299. Springer, Heidelberg (1985)
5. Boneh, D., Boyen, X.: Efficient selective-ID secure identity based encryption without random oracles. In: Cachin, C., Camenisch, J.L. (eds.) EUROCRYPT 2004. LNCS, vol. 3027, pp. 223–238. Springer, Heidelberg (2004)
6. Boneh, D., Boyen, X.: Secure identity based encryption without random oracles. In: Franklin, M. (ed.) CRYPTO 2004. LNCS, vol. 3152, pp. 443–459. Springer, Heidelberg (2004)

7. Boneh, D., Boyen, X., Goh, E.-J.: Hierarchical identity based encryption with constant size ciphertext. In: Cramer, R.J.F. (ed.) EUROCRYPT 2005. LNCS, vol. 3494, pp. 440–456. Springer, Heidelberg (2005)

8. Boneh, D., Franklin, M.K.: Identity-based encryption from the Weil pairing. In: Kilian, J. (ed.) CRYPTO 2001. LNCS, vol. 2139, pp. 213–229. Springer, Heidelberg (2001)

9. Canetti, R., Halevi, S., Katz, J.: Chosen-ciphertext security from identity-based encryption. In: Cachin, C., Camenisch, J.L. (eds.) EUROCRYPT 2004. LNCS, vol. 3027, pp. 207–222. Springer, Heidelberg (2004)

10. Cocks, C.: An identity based encryption scheme based on quadratic residues. In: Honary, B. (ed.) Cryptography and Coding. LNCS, vol. 2260, pp. 360–363. Springer, Heidelberg (2001)

11. Cramer, R., Shoup, V.: Design and analysis of practical public-key encryption schemes secure against adaptive chosen ciphertext attack. SIAM Journal of Computing 33, 167–226 (2004)

12. Dent, A.W.: A designer's guide to KEMs. In: Paterson, K.G. (ed.) Cryptography and Coding. LNCS, vol. 2898, pp. 133–151. Springer, Heidelberg (2003)

13. Goldwasser, S., Micali, S.: Probabilistic encryption. Journal of Computer and System Sciences 28(2), 270–299 (1984)

14. Kiltz, E., Galindo, D.: Direct chosen-ciphertext secure identity-based key encapsulation without random oracles. In: Batten, L.M., Safavi-Naini, R. (eds.) ACISP 2006. LNCS, vol. 4058, pp. 336–347. Springer, Heidelberg (2006)

15. Kiltz, E., Galindo, D.: Direct chosen-ciphertext secure identity-based key encapsulation without random oracles. Unpublished manuscript (2007)

16. Rackoff, C., Simon, D.R.: Non-interactive zero-knowledge proof of knowledge and chosen ciphertext attack. In: Feigenbaum, J. (ed.) CRYPTO 1991. LNCS, vol. 576, pp. 433–444. Springer, Heidelberg (1992)

17. Sarkar, P., Chatterjee, S.: Transforming a CPA-secure HIBE protocol into a CCA-secure HIBE protocol without loss of security. Cryptology ePrint Archive, Report 2006/362 (2006) http://eprint.iacr.org/

18. Sakai, R., Ohgishi, K., Kasahara, M.: Cryptosystems based on pairing. In: Proc. of SCIS 2000, Okinawa, Japan (January 2000)

19. Shamir, A.: Identity-based cryptosystems and signature schemes. In: Blakely, G.R., Chaum, D. (eds.) CRYPTO 1984. LNCS, vol. 196, Springer, Heidelberg (1985)

20. Waters, B.: Efficient identity-based encryption without random oracles. In: Cramer, R.J.F. (ed.) EUROCRYPT 2005. LNCS, vol. 3494, pp. 114–127. Springer, Heidelberg (2005)

A   Proof of security for Kiltz-Galindo WIB-KEM

Proof (Sketch). We combine the ideas of Abdalla *et al.* [1] and Kiltz-Galindo [15]. We will assume that starred variables correspond to the challenge ciphertext. For example, P^* is the challenge pattern. Consider a polynomial-time attacker $\mathcal{A}$. We begin the proof by changing the conditions in which $\mathcal{A}$ is said to win the game so that $\mathcal{A}$ wins the game if $b = b'$ and it never submitted a ciphertext C to the decapsulation oracle with $t = t^*$. Since $t = h_1(h_2(P), C_0)$ and the pair (C_0, P) uniquely defines the entire ciphertext, this collision can only occur if $\mathcal{A}$

submits the ciphertext C^* to the decapsulation oracle before the challenge phase (which can occur with probability at most q_D/p since r is chosen at random) or if there is an extended second pre-image collision in the hash function (which occurs with probability at most ϵ_h).

We now show that we can reduce the security of the scheme in this game to the DBDH problem. We begin by guessing the length of the challenge pattern and the position of the wildcards within the pattern. We guess this correctly with probability at least $1/(L2^L)$ and we abort if the attacker outputs a challenge pattern that differs from our guess or if the attacker makes an oracle query in the first stage that implies that our guess is incorrect. Let $W \subseteq \{1, 2, \ldots, L\}$ be the set of integers corresponding to the levels at which the wildcards appear in the challenge pattern.

The basic principle of the proof is to handle levels $i \notin W$ in exactly the same way as in the Kiltz-Galindo proof and to handle levels $i \in W$ in a naive way. We may extract private keys for identities in the same way as in the Waters HIBE. If we guess the position of the wildcards in the challenge pattern correctly, then this will mean we can extract private keys for all valid queries made by the attacker.

Note that since we have guessed the length and the location of the wildcards in the challenge pattern, we may immediately compute $h_2(P^*)$ even though we do not know the value of P^*.

Setup. Our simulator takes as input a BDDH instance (g^a, g^b, g^c, Z). We will use g^c as C_0^* in the challenge ciphertext. Hence, we can immediately compute $t^* \leftarrow h_1(h_2(P^*), C_0^*)$. We use this to construct the public parameters for the encryption scheme as follows:

$$v_1 \leftarrow g^a \qquad d \xleftarrow{\$} \mathbb{Z}_p \qquad v_2 \leftarrow (g^a)^{-t^*} g^d \qquad z \leftarrow e(g^a, g^b) \qquad m \leftarrow 2q$$

Note that this implicitly defines $\alpha = g^{ab}$. For each level $i \notin W$ we compute

$$k_i \leftarrow \{1, \ldots, n\} \quad x_{i,0}, x_{i,1}, \ldots, x_{i,n} \xleftarrow{\$} \mathbb{Z}_p \qquad y_{i,0}, y_{i,1}, \ldots, y_{i,n} \xleftarrow{\$} \{0, \ldots, m-1\}$$
$$u_{i,0} \leftarrow g^{x_{i,0}} v_1^{y_{i,0}-km} \qquad u_{i,j} \leftarrow g^{x_{i,j}} v_1^{y_{i,j}} \text{ for } 1 \leq j \leq n$$

For each level $i \in W$ we compute

$$x_{i,0}, x_{i,1}, \ldots, x_{i,n} \xleftarrow{\$} \mathbb{Z}_p \qquad u_{i,j} \leftarrow g^{x_{i,j}} \text{ for } 0 \leq j \leq n$$

We define the functions

$$F_i(ID_i) \leftarrow -mk_i + y_{i,0} + \sum_{j \in [ID_i]} y_{i,j}$$

$$J_i(ID_i) \leftarrow x_{i,0} + \sum_{j \in [ID_i]} x_{i,j}$$

$$K_i(ID_i) \leftarrow \begin{cases} 0 & \text{if } y_{i,0} + \sum_{j \in [ID_i]} y_{i,j} \equiv 0 \mod m \\ 1 & \text{otherwise} \end{cases}$$

Note that $F_i(ID_i) \equiv 0 \mod q$ if and only if $F_i(ID_i) = 0$, and so we have that $F_i(ID_i) \equiv 0 \mod q$ implies $K_i(ID_i) = 0$. Therefore, if $K_i(ID_i) = 1$ then $F_i(ID_i)$ can be inverted modulo q.

Key extraction oracle queries. Suppose an attacker makes a key extraction oracle query on the identity $ID = (ID_1, \ldots, ID_l)$. If this query is legal, then $ID \notin_* P^*$, which means that there must exists an integer i' such that $ID_{i'} \neq P_{i'} \neq *$. We demand that $K_{i'}(ID_{i'}) = 1$. This will occur with probability at least $1 - 1/m$. To extract the private key for ID we randomly choose $r_1, r_2, \ldots, r_l \xleftarrow{\$} \mathbb{Z}_p$ and compute

$$d_0 \leftarrow v_1^{-\frac{J_{i'}(ID_{i'})}{F_{i'}(ID_{i'})}} \prod_{i=1}^{l} \left(u_{i,0} \prod_{j \in [ID_i]} u_{i,j}\right)^{r_i}$$
$$d_{i'} \leftarrow v_1^{-\frac{1}{F_{i'}(ID_{i'})}} g^{r_{i'}} \qquad d_i \leftarrow g^{r_i} \text{ for all } i \neq i'.$$

A simple computation can verify that $(d_0, \ldots, d_l)$ is a valid private key for ID. The probability that such a private key can be computed for every key extraction oracle query is at least $(1 - 1/m)^{q_K} \geq 1 - q_K/m$. At this stage, the probability that the key extraction simulator fails may not be independent of the value of the message; hence, we use artificial aborts to ensure that we abort with the same probability regardless of the message value. By answering key extraction oracle queries in this way, we fail to accurately simulate the key extraction oracle with probability at most q_K/m.

Decryption oracle queries. Suppose an attacker makes a decryption oracle query for a ciphertext $C = (C_0, \ldots, C_{l+1})$ and an identity $ID = (ID_1, \ldots, ID_l)$. We first check that the ciphertext is consistent, i.e. that

$$(g, C_0, v_1^t v_2, C_{l+1})$$
$$(g, C_0, u_{i,0} \prod_{j \in [ID_i]} u_{i,j}, C_i) \quad \text{for } 1 \leq i \leq l, P_i \neq *$$
$$(g, C_0, u_{i,j}, C_{i,j}) \quad \text{for } 1 \leq i \leq l, P_i = *, 0 \leq j \leq n$$

are all Diffie-Hellman tuples, where $t = h_1(h_2(P), C_0)$ and P is the pattern under which the ciphertext was encrypted. If these tests fail, then the decryption oracle (correctly) outputs $\bot$. If the tests succeed and $t \neq t^*$ then we may decrypt the ciphertext by computing $K \leftarrow e\left(C_{l+1}/C_0^d, g^b\right)^{1/(t-t^*)}$.

The challenge ciphertext. We assume that we correctly guessed the location of the wildcards in the challenge pattern $P^* = (P_1^*, \ldots, P_l^*)$. For every $i \notin W$ we require that $F_i(ID_i) = 0$. This will occur with probability at least $1/(nm)^L$ (as we require $K_i(ID_i) = 0$ and the correct value k_i to have been chosen). The challenge ciphertext is then built as follows. We set

$$K^* \leftarrow Z \qquad C_0^* \leftarrow g^c \qquad C_{l+1}^* \leftarrow (g^c)^d.$$

For each $i \notin W$, we set

$$C_i^* \leftarrow (g^c)^{J_i(ID_i)}.$$

For each $i \in W$, we set

$$C_{i,j}^* \leftarrow (g^c)^{x_{i,j}} \text{ for all } 1 \leq j \leq n.$$

It is clear to see that if the attacker can distinguish a valid key K from a randomly generated key K, then they will have distinguished a random value Z from the value $Z = e(g,g)^{abc}$. Hence, providing our simulation is correct, the simulator solves the BDDH problem whenever the attacker breaks the WIB-KEM.   □

Combining Prediction Hashing and MDS Codes for Efficient Multicast Stream Authentication

Christophe Tartary[1] and Huaxiong Wang[1,2]

[1] Centre for Advanced Computing, Algorithms and Cryptography
Department of Computing
Macquarie University
NSW 2109 Australia
[2] Division of Mathematical Sciences
School of Physical and Mathematical Sciences
Nanyang Technological University
Singapore
ctartary@ics.mq.edu.au,
HXWang@ntu.edu.sg

Abstract. We study the multicast stream authentication problem when the communication channel is under control of an opponent who can drop, reorder and inject data packets. In this work, we consider that the stream to be authenticated is divided into block of n packets and we assume that the sender can memorize λ such blocks. Two important parameters for stream authentication protocols are packet overhead and computing efficiency. Our construction will exhibit the following advantages. First, our packet overhead will be a few hashes long. Second, the number of signature verifications per family of λ blocks will be $O(1)$ as a function of both λ and n. Third, hash chains will enable the receiver to check the validity of received elements upon reception. As a consequence he will only buffer those consistent with the original data packets. Fourth, the receiver will be able to recover all the data packets emitted by the sender despite erasures and injections by running the decoding algorithm of the maximal distance separable code onto the elements which have passed the previous filtering process.

Keywords: Stream Authentication, Polynomial Reconstruction, Adversarial Network, Erasure Codes, Prediction Hashing, Hash Chains.

1 Introduction

Multicast communication enables a single sender to distribute digital content to a large audience via a public channel such as the Internet. It has applications in sensor networks, pay-TV, air traffic control, stock quotes and military defense systems for instance. Nevertheless large-scale broadcasts prevent lost content from being redistributed since the lost of any piece of data could generate a prohibitive number of redistribution requests at the sender. Furthermore, the channel can be under the control of adversaries performing malicious actions on the data stream[1]. Thus the security of multicast

---

[1] In broadcasting, the sequence of information sent into the network is called *stream*.

J. Pieprzyk, H. Ghodosi, and E. Dawson (Eds.): ACISP 2007, LNCS 4586, pp. 293–307, 2007.
© Springer-Verlag Berlin Heidelberg 2007

protocols relies on two aspects: the opponents' computational powers and the network properties. Several unconditionally secure schemes were designed in [3, 9, 38]. Unfortunately their optimal security is at the cost of a large storage requirement or a single-time use which makes these constructions unsuitable for practical applications. In this paper, we will assume that the adversaries have bounded computational powers.

In recent years, many protocols were designed to deal with the multicast authentication problem [4]. An application such as a TV channel broadcasting 24 hours a day implies that the size of the stream can be infinite. On the other hand, the receivers must be able to authenticate data within a short period of delay upon reception. Since many protocols will distribute private or sensitive content, non-repudiation of the sender is required for most of them as using data from an incorrect origin can have disastrous consequences during military operations for instance. As a consequence, schemes like TESLA [31, 33] and its variations [20, 21, 32, 44] are not suitable since data authenticity is guaranteed using message authentication codes whose keys are disclosed after some period of time. Notice that the assumptions made by Perrig et al. to guarantee the security of TESLA were proved to be insufficient by Jakimoski [16]. Thus, constructions for multicast distribution rely on digital signatures to provide non-repudiation. Nevertheless signing each data packet[2] is not a practical solution as digital signatures are generally too expensive to generate and/or verify. In addition, bandwidth limitations prevent one-time and k-time signatures [12, 37] from being used due to their size. That is why a general approach consists of generating a single signature and amortizing its computational cost and overhead over several data packets using hash functions for instance.

In order to deal with erasures, Perrig et al. [31, 33], Challal et al. [5], Golle and Modadugu [13] and Miner and Staddon [26] appended the hash of each packet to several followers according to specific patterns. In these papers, packet loss was modeled by k-state Markov chains [11] and bounds on the packet authentication probability were computed. Nevertheless the drawback of these schemes is that they rely on the reception of signed packets which cannot be guaranteed over networks such as the Internet since they only provide a best effort delivery. This problem restricts the range of applications for the previous protocols.

An approach to overcome this problem is to split the signature into k smaller parts where only ℓ of them $(\ell < k)$ are sufficient for recovery. Different techniques were employed to obtain the dispersion of the signature: Perrig et al. [28, 29] and Park and Cho [30] used the Information Dispersal Algorithm [35], Al-Ibrahim and Pieprzyk [1] combined linear equations and polynomial interpolation whereas Pannetrat and Molva [27] utilized erasure codes. Unfortunately none of these constructions tolerates a single packet injection which is a major drawback since it is unlikely to have only reliable network nodes between the sender and each receiver if you consider, in particular, the Internet.

In 2003, Lysyanskaya et al. [22] used Reed-Solomon codes [36] to design a protocol resistant to packet loss and data injections. Their augmented packets[3] are $O(1)$ bits long

---

[2] Since the data stream is large, it is divided into fixed-size chunks called *packets*.

[3] We call *augmented packets* the elements sent into the network. They generally consist of the original data packets with some redundancy used to prove the authenticity of the element.

while the number of signature verifications per block[4] turns out to be $O(1)$ as functions of the block length n. In 2004, Karlof et al. designed a scheme called PRABS [17] combining an erasure code (to recover lost content) and a one-way accumulator [2] based on a Merkle hash tree [25] (to deal with injections). This approach is similar to Wong and Lam's scheme [45] but the number of signature verifications for PRABS is $O(1)$ even in the worst case. The bound on the number of signature verifications for PRABS is much smaller than in [22] (see [42]) but this is at the expense of having $\Theta(\log_2(n))$-bit augmented packets since each of them has to carry $\lceil \log_2(n) \rceil$ hashes.

In order to reduce this overhead, Di Pietro et al. proposed a modified distribution of hashes so that the Merkle hash tree can still be reconstructed [10]. Another benefit of their scheme is to decrease the number of decoding operations to be performed at the receiver. Nevertheless this approach has two drawbacks. First, some augmented packets still carry $\lceil \log_2(n) \rceil$ hashes while others only have a few digests. This results in important variations in packet sizes leading to irregular throughput of information in the channel and can cause data congestion in the network. Second, the number of signature verifications to be performed by the receiver is equal to the number of injections in the worst case which creates a potential weakness against Denial-of-Service (DoS) attacks. In [6], Choi used PRABS as a subroutine to ensure the security of his prediction hashing-based construction. Nevertheless this scheme exhibits the same logarithmic overhead as PRABS. Recently, Tartary and Wang proposed a construction based on [22] and Maximal Distance Separable (MDS) codes [23] (denoted TWMDS in this paper) which is resistant against packet loss and data injections and requires $O(1)$ signature verifications like PRABS but only has a $O(1)$-bit packet overhead and allows recovery of all data packets [42].

As the number of signature verifications for TWMDS is higher than PRABS (see Table 2), we propose a multiple block construction similar to the approach by Tartary and Wang [41] (denoted TWMB in this article). As TWMB, we will generate a single signature per family of λ blocks where each of them consists of n packets. The receivers will still be able to authenticate data per block and it is possible to join the communication group at any block boundary as in [41]. The number of signature verifications per family of λ block will be identical to the number of verifications for a single block of TWMDS. As for TWMDS, we will use MDS codes to provide full recovery of data packets. The security of schemes in [22, 41, 42] relies on the use of a polynomial time algorithm by Guruswami and Sudan called Poly-Reconstruct [15]. The idea of prediction hashing (PH) is that each block of n packets conveys information which will be used to authenticate (or predict) the following block of packets. Using PH, our construction will enable to filter elements upon reception and thus the receiver will exclusively buffer elements consistent with the original data stream. The first advantage is that memory is not wasted by storing irrelevant pieces of data contrary to [6, 17, 22, 41, 42]. The second benefit is that the previous filtering process will also reduce the number of queries to Poly-Reconstruct to 2 per family of λ blocks which will speed up the authentication process at the receiver considerably. The authenticated packets of our construction will still be $O(1)$ bits long as for TWMB and TWMDS.

---

[4] In order to be processed, packets are gathered into fixed-size sets called *blocks*.

This paper is organized as follows. In the next section, we will present our network model as well as an algorithm from [42] to be used as a subroutine in our construction. In Sect. 3 we will describe our authentication scheme. Its security and recovery property will be studied in Sect. 4. In Sect. 5, we will compare our scheme to PRABS, TWMB and TWMDS as our work can be seen as their extension. Finally we will summarize our contribution to the multicast authentication problem.

2   Preliminaries

In this section, we introduce the assumptions and constructions to be used as subroutines for our scheme. First, we present our network model. Second, we justify our choice of erasure codes. Finally we recall a modified version of the algorithm Poly-Reconstruct by Guruswami and Sudan since it will play a key role to deal with packet injections as in [22, 41, 42].

Network Model. We consider that the communication channel is unsecured. This means that it is under the control of an opponent $\mathcal{O}$ who can drop and rearrange packets of his choice as well as inject bogus data into the network [24]. Our area of investigation is the multicast stream authentication problem. Thus we can assume that a reasonable number of original augmented packets reaches the receivers and not too many incorrect elements are injected by $\mathcal{O}$. Indeed if too many original packets are dropped then data transmission becomes the main problem to treat since the small number of received elements would be probably useless even authenticated. On this other hand, if $\mathcal{O}$ injects a large number of forged packets then the main problem to be solved becomes increasing the resistance against DoS attacks. In order to build our signature amortization scheme, we need to split the data stream into blocks of n packets: $P_1, \ldots, P_n$. We define two parameters: $\alpha\,(0 < \alpha \leq 1)$ (the *survival* rate) and $\beta\,(\beta \geq 1)$ (the *flood* rate). It is assumed that at least a fraction α and no more than a multiple β of the number of augmented packets are received. This means that at least $\lceil \alpha n \rceil$ original augmented packets are received amongst a total which does not exceed $\lfloor \beta n \rfloor$ elements.

We would like to point out that we are not interested in the cases $(\alpha = 1)$ and $(\beta = 1)$. Indeed, in the first case, all original data packets are received. Thus we only need to distinguish correct elements from bogus ones which can be achieved using Wong and Lam's technique [45]. In the second case, there are no packet injections from $\mathcal{O}$. Thus using an erasure code (see [8] as an example) is sufficient to recover $P_1, \ldots, P_n$. Therefore in this work we will only study the case: $0 < \alpha < 1 < \beta$. Notice, however, that our construction also works when $\alpha = 1$ and $\beta = 1$.

Code Construction. In this paper we consider linear codes. A linear code of length N, dimension K and minimum distance D is denoted $[N, K, D]$. The Singleton bound states that any $[N, K, D]$ code satisfies: $D - 1 \leq N - K$[23]. It is known that any $[N, K, D]$ code can correct up to $D - 1$ erasures [46]. Thus a $[N, K, D]$ code cannot correct more than $N - K$ erasures. In order to maximize the efficiency of our construction, we are interested in codes correcting exactly $N - K$ erasures. These codes are called *Maximum Distance Separable* (MDS) codes [23]. Even if the scheme we propose works with any MDS code, we suggest to use the construction by Lacan and Fimes [18] for better practical efficiency (see [42] for details). Note that any linear code can be represented by a *generator matrix G*. *Encoding* a message m (represented as a row vector) means computing the corresponding codeword c as: $c := m\, G$ [23].

Polynomial Reconstruction Algorithm. In [15], Guruswami and Sudan developed an algorithm Poly-Reconstruct to solve the polynomial reconstruction problem. They proved that if T points were given as input then their algorithm output the list of all polynomials of degree at most K passing through at least N of the T points provided: $T > \sqrt{KN}$. We will use the same modified version of Poly-Reconstruct as in [42] where it was named MPR. Denote $\mathbb{F}_{2^q}$ the field representing the coefficients of the polynomial. Every element of $\mathbb{F}_{2^q}$ can be represented as a polynomial of degree at most $q - 1$ over $\mathbb{F}_2$ [19]. Operations in $\mathbb{F}_{2^q}$ are performed modulo a polynomial $\mathcal{Q}(X)$ of degree q which is irreducible over $\mathbb{F}_2$.

MPR

Input: The maximal degree of the polynomial K, the minimal number of agreeable points N, T points $\{(x_i, y_i), 1 \le i \le T\}$ and the polynomial $\mathcal{Q}(X)$ of degree q.
1. If there are no more than $\sqrt{KN}$ distinct points then the algorithm stops.
2. Using $\mathcal{Q}(X)$, run Poly-Reconstruct on the T points to get the list of all polynomials of degree at most K over $\mathbb{F}_{2^q}$ passing through at least N of the previous points.
3. Write the list $\{L_1(X), \ldots, L_\mu(X)\}$ and each element: $L_i(X) := \mathcal{L}_{i,0} + \ldots + \mathcal{L}_{i,K} X^K$ where $\forall i \in \{0, \ldots, K\} \mathcal{L}_{i,j} \in \mathbb{F}_{2^q}$. Form the elements: $\mathcal{L}_i := \mathcal{L}_{i,0} \| \cdots \| \mathcal{L}_{i,K}$.
Output: $\{\mathcal{L}_1, \ldots, \mathcal{L}_\mu\}$: list of candidates

Note that Poly-Reconstruct runs in time quadratic in N and outputs a list of size at most quadratic in N as well (see Theorem 6.12 and Lemma 6.13 from [14]).

3 Our Construction

We need a collision resistant hash function h [34] and an unforgeable signature scheme (Sign$_{SK}$, Verify$_{PK}$) [40] the key pair of which (SK,PK) is created by a generator KeyGen as in [17, 22, 41, 42].

Scheme Overview. We have λ blocks of packets $\{P_{i,1}, \ldots, P_{i,n}\}_{i=1,\ldots,\lambda}$. In order to use PH, we proceed backwards. We encode the last block using the $[n, \lceil \alpha n \rceil, n - \lceil \alpha n \rceil + 1]$ code into the codeword $(C_{\lambda,1}, \ldots, C_{\lambda,n})$. Then we append the hashes $h(C_{\lambda,1}), \ldots, h(C_{\lambda,n})$ to the packets of block $\lambda - 1$ and encode the resulting n elements into $(C_{\lambda-1,1}, \ldots, C_{\lambda-1,n})$. We repeat this process to the first block of packets. We generate the family signature as in [41]. That is, we compute the λ block hashes $h_i := h(h(C_{i,1}) \| \cdots \| h(C_{i,n}))$ and sign $h(h_1 \| \cdots \| h_\lambda)$ into σ. We build the family polynomial $\mathcal{F}(X)$ of degree at most ρn (for some constant ρ) the coefficients of which represent $h_1 \| \cdots \| h_n \| \sigma$. In order to allow new members to join the communication group at block boundaries, we build λ block polynomials $\mathcal{B}_1(X), \ldots, \mathcal{B}_\lambda(X)$ of degree at most $\rho\,n$ such as the coefficients of each $\mathcal{B}_i(X)$ represent $h(C_{i,1})\|\cdots\|h(C_{i,n})$. The augmented packets of the family of λ blocks are such as:

$$\forall i \in \{1,\ldots,\lambda\}\,\forall j \in \{1,\ldots,n\}\ \mathrm{AP}_{i,j} := \mathrm{FID}\|i\|j\|C_{i,j}\|\mathcal{B}_i(j)\|\mathcal{F}(j)$$

where FID represents the position of the family $P_{1,1},\ldots,P_{\lambda,n}$ within the whole stream.

Upon reception of data for the ith block, the receiver adapts his reaction whether or not he knows its digests.

- If the hashes are known (via PH) then he only needs to filter the received elements and drop those which are inconsistent with those digests. Finally he corrects erasures using the MDS code to recover the n data packets $\{P_{i,1},\ldots,P_{i,n}\}$ as well as the n hashes corresponding to block $i+1$ which updates the values for PH.

- If the hashes are unknown then he proceeds as in [41]. That is, he first checks whether the family signature corresponding to data he obtained is valid by reconstructing $\mathcal{F}(X)$. If so, he checks whether the block information is consistent with the previous signature by reconstructing $\mathcal{B}_i(X)$. Then he sorts the received pieces of data and drops those which are inconsistent with $\mathcal{B}_i(X)$. Finally he corrects erasures using the MDS code to recover the n data packets $\{P_{i,1},\ldots,P_{i,n}\}$ as well as the n hashes corresponding to block $i+1$ which updates the values for PH.

Formal Scheme Construction. We assume that α and β are rational numbers so that we can represent them over a finite number of bits using their numerator and denominator. In order to run Poly-Reconstruct as a part of MPR, we have to choose $\rho \in (0, \frac{\alpha^2}{\beta})$. Remark that it is suggested in [42] to choose $\rho = \frac{\alpha^2}{2\beta}$ to get a small list returned by Poly-Reconstruct. Notice that ρ has to be rational since ρn is an integer. We also consider that the $[n, \lceil\alpha\,n\rceil, n - \lceil\alpha\,n\rceil + 1]$ code is uniquely determined (i.e. its generator matrix G is known) when n, α, β and ρ are known. Denote $\mathbb{F}_{2^{\tilde{q}}}$ the field of this MDS code. The values of $q, \tilde{q}$ as well as the length of the different pads used by our scheme have been omitted due to space limitations and can be found in the extended version of this paper. Table 1 summarizes the scheme parameters which are assumed to be publicly known.

Table 1. Public parameters for our authentication scheme

n: Block length	$\tilde{\mathcal{Q}}(X)$: Polynomial representing the field for the MDS code
λ: Family length	$\mathcal{P}$: bit size of data packets
α, β: Network rates	G: Generating matrix of the MDS code
ρ: Ratio	$\mathcal{Q}(X)$: Polynomial representing the field for polynomial interpolation

The hash function h as well as Verify and PK are also assumed to be publicly known. We did not include them in Table 1 since they can be considered as general parameters. For instance h can be SHA-256 while the digital signature is a 1024-bit RSA signature. We denote $\mathcal{H}$ the digest bit length and s the bit length of a signature. Since h and the digital signature are publicly known, so are $\mathcal{H}$ and s.

Authenticator

Input: The family number FID, the secret key SK, the parameters of Table 1 and data packets $P_{1,1}, \ldots, P_{\lambda,n}$.

/* Packet Encoding */

1. Parse $P_{\lambda,1} \| \cdots \| P_{\lambda,n}$ as $M_{\lambda,1} \| \cdots \| M_{\lambda,\lceil \alpha n \rceil}$ after padding. Encode the message $(M_{\lambda,1}, \ldots, M_{\lambda,\lceil \alpha n \rceil})$ into the codeword $(C_{\lambda,1}, \ldots, C_{\lambda,n})$ using the MDS code.

2. For i from $\lambda - 1$ to 1 do

    2.1. Compute the hashes $h(C_{i+1,j})$ for $j \in \{1, \ldots, n\}$ and append them to packets of block i as: $\widetilde{P}_{i,j} := P_{i,j} \| h(C_{i+1,j})$

    2.2. Parse $\widetilde{P}_{i,1} \| \cdots \| \widetilde{P}_{i,n}$ as $M_{i,1} \| \cdots \| M_{i,\lceil \alpha n \rceil}$ after padding. Encode the message $(M_{i,1}, \ldots, M_{i,\lceil \alpha n \rceil})$ into the codeword $(C_{i,1}, \ldots, C_{i,n})$ using the MDS code.

/* Block Identification */

3. For i from 1 to λ do

    3.1. Parse $h(C_{1,1}) \| \cdots \| h(C_{1,n})$ as $b_{i,0} \| \cdots \| b_{i,\rho n}$ where each $b_i \in \mathbb{F}_{2^q}$ after padding and compute the block hash h_i as $h_i := h(h(C_{1,1}) \| \cdots \| h(C_{1,n}))$.

    3.2. Construct the block polynomial $\mathcal{B}_i(X) := b_{i,0} + b_{i,1} X + \cdots + b_{i,\rho n} X^{\rho n}$ and evaluate it at the first n points[5] of $\mathbb{F}_{2^q}$.

/* Signature Generation */

4. Write h_f as $h_f := h_1 \| \cdots \| h_\lambda$. Compute the family signature σ as $\sigma := \text{Sign}_{SK}(h(\text{FID} \| \lambda \| n \| \alpha \| \beta \| \rho \| h_f))$. Parse $h_f \| \sigma$ as $f_0 \| \cdots \| f_{\rho n}$ where each $f_i \in \mathbb{F}_{2^q}$ after padding.

5. Construct the family polynomial $\mathcal{F}(X) := f_0 + f_1 X + \cdots + f_{\rho n} X^{\rho n}$ and evaluate it at the first n points of $\mathbb{F}_{2^q}$.

/* Construction of Augmented Packets */

6. Build the augmented packet $\text{AP}_{i,j}$ as $\text{AP}_{i,j} := \text{FID} \| i \| j \| C_{i,j} \| \mathcal{B}_i(j) \| \mathcal{F}(j)$ for $i \in \{1, \ldots \lambda\}$ and for $j \in \{1, \ldots, n\}$.

Output: The λn augmented packets $\{\text{AP}_{1,1}, \ldots, \text{AP}_{\lambda,n}\}$ which are sent to the network per block of n elements $\{\text{AP}_{i,1}, \ldots, \text{AP}_{i,n}\}_{i=1,\ldots,\lambda}$.

In order to verify the correctness of the family signature, the receiver will use the same algorithm VerifySignatureFamily as TWMD [41].

VerifySignatureFamily

Input: The family number FID, the public key PK, the elements of Table 1 and a set of pairs of field elements $\{(x_i, y_i), 1 \leq i \leq m\}$.

1. Run MPR on $\{(x_i, y_i), 1 \leq i \leq m\}$ to get a list $\mathcal{L}$ of candidates for the family signature verification. If MPR rejects this input then the algorithm stops.

2. While the signature has not been verified and the list $\mathcal{L}$ has not been exhausted, pick a new candidate $\tilde{h}_1 \| \cdots \| \tilde{h}_\lambda \| \tilde{\sigma}$. If $\text{Verify}_{PK}(h(\text{FID} \| \lambda \| n \| \alpha \| \beta \| \rho \| \tilde{h}_1 \| \cdots \| \tilde{h}_\lambda), \tilde{\sigma})$

---

[5] Any element of $\mathbb{F}_{2^q}$ can be represented as $\lambda_0 Y^0 + \lambda_1 Y^1 + \ldots + \lambda_{q-1} Y^{q-1}$ where each λ_i belongs to $\mathbb{F}_2$. We define the first n elements as $(0, \ldots, 0)$, $(1, 0, \ldots, 0)$, $(0, 1, 0, \ldots, 0)$, $(1, 1, 0, \ldots, 0)$ and so on until the binary decomposition of $n - 1$.

= TRUE then $\tilde{\sigma}$ is considered as the authentic family signature σ and the $\tilde{h}_i$'s are memorized within the table HashBlock as the authentic block digests h_i's.

3. If the signature has not been verified then our algorithm stops.
Output: $(\sigma, \text{HashBlock})$: family signature and hashes of the λ blocks

Our scheme embeds the digests of the codeword related to block $i + 1$ into block i. This will enable each receiver to filter data in order to speed up the authentication scheme and reduce the number of elements to be buffered. We now present FilterElements which provides on-the-fly verification of received elements.

FilterElements
Input: The family number FID, the block number BID, the elements of Table 1, a table HashCodeword and a flow of packets.
1. Set $T(i) := 0$ for $i \in \{1, \ldots, n\}$, set $\mathcal{C}' := (\emptyset, \ldots, \emptyset)$ and KnownHashes = FALSE.
2. Upon reception of a new data packet do
   2.1. Write it as $\text{FID}_i \| \text{BID}_i \| j_i \| C'_{\text{BID}_i, j_i} \| \mathcal{B}_{\text{BID}_i, j_i} \| \mathcal{F}_{\text{BID}_i, j_i}$. If $\text{FID}_i \neq \text{FID}$ or $\text{BID}_i \neq \text{BID}$ or $j_i \notin \{1, \ldots, n\}$ or $T(j_i) = 1$ then discard the packet.
   2.2 If $h(C'_{\text{BID}, j_i}) = \text{HashCodeword}(j_i)$ then set $T(j_i) = 1$ and set the j_i^{th} coordinate of $\mathcal{C}'$ to C'_{BID, j_i}.
/* After Reception of all Packets for Values (FID, BID) */
3. If $\mathcal{C}'$ has less than $\lceil \alpha n \rceil$ non-erased coordinates then the algorithm stops.
   Else
   3.1. Correct the erasures of $\mathcal{C}'$ using the MDS decoding process and denote $(M'_{\text{BID}, 1}, \ldots, M'_{\text{BID}, \lceil \alpha n \rceil})$ the corresponding message.
   3.2. Remove the pad from $M'_{\text{BID}, 1} \| \cdots \| M'_{\text{BID}, \lceil \alpha n \rceil}$ and write the resulting string as

$$\begin{cases} P'_{\text{BID}, 1} \| h'_{\text{BID}, 1} \| \cdots \| P'_{\text{BID}, n} \| h'_{\text{BID}, n} & \text{if BID} \neq \lambda \\ P'_{\text{BID}, 1} \| \cdots \| P'_{\text{BID}, n} & \text{otherwise} \end{cases}$$

   3.3. If BID $\neq \lambda$ then set $\text{HashCodeword}(i) = h'_{\text{BID}, i}$ for $i \in \{1, \ldots, n\}$ and set KnownHashes = TRUE.
Output: The set of identified packets $\{P'_{\text{BID}, 1}, \ldots, P'_{\text{BID}, n}\}$, the boolean value KnownHashes and HashCodeword containing the digests of the next block.

It should be noticed that the boolean value KnownHashes indicates if the table of digests HashCodeword has been updated. This enables the receiver to switch between buffering all incoming data elements and on-the-fly validation of data.

The reader may notice that we only verified the consistency of the substring $\text{FID}_i \| \text{BID}_i \| j_i \| C'_{\text{BID}_i, j_i}$ to our parameters FID, BID, n and HashCodeword. Since we did not check any condition on $\mathcal{B}_{\text{BID}_i, j_i} \| \mathcal{F}_{\text{BID}_i, j_i}$, one may think that an opponent can submit an incorrect element making our decoding process fail. We would like to emphasize that it is not the case. As just noticed, the elements going successfully through this process are written as $\text{FID} \| \text{BID} \| \theta \| C_{\text{BID}, \theta} \| x \| y$ for some $\theta \in \{1, \ldots, n\}$. Nevertheless the substring $x \| y$ does not play any role in our algorithm since we only use

$C_{\text{BID},\theta}$ to recover the original data packets. Therefore even if $x\|y$ is a bogus string (i.e. $x\|y \neq \mathcal{B}_{\text{BID}}(\theta)\|\mathcal{F}(\theta)$) then it has no influence whatsoever on the output of FilterElements which makes the attack by the adversary pointless.

The array T is used to dodge duplication attacks by an opponent who would submit several strings $\text{FID}\|\text{BID}\|\theta\|C_{\text{BID},\theta}\|x\|y$ (for different values of $x\|y$) in order to exhaust the receiver computational power by recomputing $h(C_{\text{BID},\theta})$ whereas the original coordinate $C_{\text{BID},\theta}$ has already been recovered.

We now introduce DecoderBlock used for the first block of the family. Notice that DecoderBlock is a modification of $\text{DecoderBlock}_\epsilon$ from [41].

DecoderBlock

Input: The family number FID, the block number BID, the elements of Table 1, a set of received packets RP.

/* Signature Verification */

1. Write the packets as $\text{FID}_i\|\text{BID}_i\|j_i\|C'_{\text{BID}_i,j_i}\|\mathcal{B}_{\text{BID}_i,j_i}\|\mathcal{F}_{\text{BID}_i,j_i}$ and discard those having $\text{FID}_i \neq \text{FID}$, $\text{BID}_i \neq \text{BID}$ or $j_i \notin \{1,\ldots,n\}$. Denote m' the number of remaining packets. If $m' < \lceil \alpha\,n \rceil$ or $m' > \lfloor \beta\,n \rfloor$ then the algorithm stops.
2. Run VerifySignatureFamily on the m' remaining points $\{(j_i, \mathcal{F}_{\text{BID},j_i}), 1 \leq i \leq m'\}$. If it rejects the input then the algorithm stops.

/* Block Hashes Verification */

3. Run MPR on the set $\{(j_i, \mathcal{B}_{\text{BID},j_i}), 1 \leq i \leq m'\}$ and get a list L of candidates for block tag verification. If MPR rejects that set then the algorithm stops.
4. While the hash for block BID has not been verified and the list L has not been exhausted, we pick a new candidate $\tilde{c} := \tilde{h}^1_{\text{BID}}\|\cdots\|\tilde{h}^n_{\text{BID}}$. If $(h(\tilde{c}) = \text{HashBlock}(\text{BID}))$ then the tag of block BID is verified and we set $h^j_{\text{BID}} = \tilde{h}^j_{\text{BID}}$ for $j \in \{1,\ldots,n\}$. If L is exhausted without a successful block tag verification then the algorithm stops.

/* Packet Decoding */

5. Set $\mathcal{C}' := (\emptyset,\ldots,\emptyset)$ and KnownHashes $:=$ FALSE. For each of the m' remaining packets, $\text{FID}\|\text{BID}\|j_i\|C'_{\text{BID},j_i}\|\mathcal{B}_{\text{BID},j_i}\|\mathcal{F}_{\text{BID},j_i}$, if $h(C'_{\text{BID},j_i}) = h^t_{\text{BID}}$ for some $t \in \{1,\ldots,n\}$ then set the tth coordinate of $\mathcal{C}'$ to C'_{BID,j_i}.
6. Perform Step 3 of FilterElements to recover the data packets as well as the digests of the next block to be stored into HashCodeword.

Output: The set of identified packets $\{P'_{\text{BID},1},\ldots,P'_{\text{BID},n}\}$, the boolean value Known-Hashes and HashCodeword containing the digests of the next block.

Finally we build our dynamic decoder run by the receivers to authenticate data. We assume that the boolean value KnownHashes is set to FALSE when a receiver joins the communication group and re-initialized to FALSE when the receiver processes the first received block of a new family $\text{FID}'\ (> \text{FID})$.

DynamicDecoder

Input: The family number FID, the block number BID, the public key PK, the elements of Table 1, a boolean KnownHashes, a table HashCodeword and a set of received packets RP.

If KnownHashes = FALSE then
    Query DecoderBlock on input $(\mathrm{PK}, \mathrm{FID}, \mathrm{BID}, \lambda, n, \alpha, \beta, \rho, \mathcal{Q}(X), \mathrm{RP})$
Else
    Query FilterElements on input $(\mathrm{FID}, \mathrm{BID}, \lambda, n, \alpha, \beta, \rho, \mathrm{HashCodeword}, \mathrm{RP})$
Output: The set of identified packets $\{P'_{\mathrm{BID},1}, \ldots, P'_{\mathrm{BID},n}\}$, the updated boolean value
KnownHashes and the updated table HashCodeword as output of either DecoderBlock
or FilterElements.

Note that when DynamicDecoder stops then the whole content of block BID is lost.
Nevertheless the definitions of α and β ensure that this will never happen (see Theorem 2). In a practical point of view, one can choose α small and β large enough so that
the real threat of the opponent is bounded by those values. Nevertheless inaccurate values, such as $\alpha = 10^{-10}$ and $\beta = 10^{10}$ for instance, will lead to excessive overhead and
computation. So the values α and β set by the sender should accurately reflect the opponent actual ability. Developing techniques allowing the determination of such values
are beyond the scope of this paper.

4 Security and Recovery Analysis

Security of the Scheme. We adopt the same security definition as in [41]. It can be seen
as an extension to the notion of "family of blocks" of the definitions from [22, 42]. The
definition is as follows:

Definition 1. (KeyGen,Authenticator,DynamicDecoder) *is a secure and* (α, β)*-correct
multicast authentication scheme if no probabilistic polynomial-time opponent* $\mathcal{O}$ *can
win with a non-negligible probability to the following game:*
    i) *A key pair* $(\mathrm{SK}, \mathrm{PK})$ *is generated by* KeyGen
    ii) $\mathcal{O}$ *is given:* (a) *The public key* PK *and* (b) *Oracle access to* Authenticator *(but* $\mathcal{O}$
can only issue at most one query with the same family identification tag FID*)*
    iii) $\mathcal{O}$ *outputs* $(\mathrm{FID}, \mathrm{BID}, \lambda, n, \alpha, \beta, \rho, \mathcal{Q}(X), \mathrm{RP})$

$\mathcal{O}$ *wins if one of the following happens:*
    a) *(correctness violation)* $\mathcal{O}$ *succeeds to output* RP *such that even if it contains* $\lceil \alpha n \rceil$
packets (amongst a total number of elements which does not exceed $\lfloor \beta n \rfloor$*) of some
authenticated packets set* AP *for some family identification tag* FID *and block identification tag* BID*, the decoder still fails at identifying some of the correct packets.*
    b) *(security violation)* $\mathcal{O}$ *succeeds to output* RP *such that the decoder returns*
$\{P'_{\mathrm{BID},1}, \ldots, P'_{\mathrm{BID},n}\}$ *(for some* BID $\in \{1, \ldots, \lambda\}$*) that was never authenticated by*
Authenticator *(as the* BIDth *block of a family of* λ *blocks) for the family tag* BID *and
parameters* $(\lambda, n, \alpha, \beta, \rho, \mathcal{Q}(X))$*.*

As in [22, 41, 42], we have the following result regarding the security and correctness
of our construction whose proof has been omitted due to space limitations.

Theorem 1. *Our scheme* (KeyGen,Authenticator,DynamicDecoder) *is secure and*
(α, β)*-correct.*

Recovery Property. We now prove that our scheme enables any receiver to recover the n data packets for any of the λ blocks and the number of signature verifications to be performed per family is $O(1)$ as a function of both n and λ. As in [41, 42], we introduce the following definition:

Definition 2. *We say that the survival and flood rates (α, β) are* accurate *to the network for a flow of n symbols if: (1) data are sent per block of n elements through the network and (2) for any block of n elements $\{E_1, \cdots, E_n\}$ emitted by the sender, if we denote $\{\tilde{E}_1, \ldots, \tilde{E}_\mu\}$ the set of received packets then $\mu \leq \lfloor \beta n \rfloor$ and at least $\lceil \alpha n \rceil$ elements of $\{E_1, \cdots, E_n\}$ belong to $\{\tilde{E}_1, \ldots, \tilde{E}_\mu\}$. Condition (2) must be true for each receiver belonging to the communication group.*

We now assume that (α, β) is accurate for our network flow n in the remaining of this paper. As shown in [42], it is a realistic assumption to consider the accuracy of (α, β) for PRABS as well. We have the following result whose proof has been omitted due to space limitations.

Theorem 2. *For any FID, for any BID, each receiver recovers the n original data packets $P_{BID,1}, \ldots, P_{BID,n}$. In addition the number of signature verifications to be performed for the whole family of λ blocks is upper bounded by $U(n) := \min(\lfloor U_1(n) \rfloor, \lfloor U_2(n) \rfloor)$ where:*

$$
\begin{cases}
U_1(n) = \dfrac{1}{\rho n} \left(\dfrac{1}{\sqrt{\alpha^2 - \beta \rho}} - 1 \right) + \dfrac{\beta}{\alpha^2 - \beta \rho} + \dfrac{1}{\rho} \\[4mm]
U_2(n) = \dfrac{\beta}{2(\alpha^2 - \beta \rho)} + \dfrac{1}{\rho} + \dfrac{\sqrt{\beta^2 + \frac{4}{\rho^2 n^2}(1 - \rho\alpha)}}{2(\alpha^2 - \beta \rho)} - \dfrac{1}{\rho n}
\end{cases}
$$

which is $O(1)$ as a function of the block length n and the family length λ.

5 Comparison of Authentication Protocols

In this section, we will compare our construction to PRABS, TWMB and TWMDS as our approach can be seen as their extension. As underlined in Sect. 1, the computing efficiency and the packet overhead are two important factors to determine the practicality of a stream authentication protocol. Our comparison focuses on these two factors.

Computing Efficiency. In the proof of Theorem 2 (see the extended version of the article for details), it is shown that DecoderBlock is queried only once for the whole family of λ blocks. Thus Poly-Reconstruct is run only twice per family (once within VerifySignatureFamily and once at Step 3 of DecoderBlock). At the same time, the receiver can filter elements for the remaining $\lambda - 1$ blocks. Using PH, our filtering process allows efficient buffering and faster authentication as the receiver treats elements upon reception (on-the-fly verification) and memorizes only the correct code coordinates.

Table 2 summarizes the benefits provided by the different authentication schemes. In order to have a fair comparison, we assumed that PRABS and TWMDS were iterated λ

Table 2. Efficiency comparison for multicast stream protocols

	Signature Verification	Complexity	Calls to Poly-Reconstruct	Filtering	Total Recovery
Our Scheme	$U(n)$	$O(1)$	2	Yes	Yes
PRABS	$\lambda V(n)$	$O(\lambda)$	N/A	No	No
TWMB	$U(n)$	$O(1)$	$\lambda + 1$	No	No
TWMDS	$\lambda U(n)$	$O(\lambda)$	λ	No	Yes

times. Notice that the value $V(n)$ can be found in [17] and is equal to $\left\lfloor \frac{\lfloor \beta n \rfloor}{\lceil \alpha n \rceil} \right\rfloor$. Remark that a comparison between $U(n)$ and $V(n)$ (when $n = 1000$) for different pairs (α, β) can be found in [42].

Packet Overhead. In our scheme, augmented packets sent through the network are written as: $\text{FID}\|i\|j\|C_{i,j}\|\mathcal{B}_i(j)\|\mathcal{F}(j)$. The packet overhead is the length of the extra tag of information used to provide authentication. Notice that an augmented packet without a tag is assumed to be written as: $\text{FID}\|i\|j\|P_{i,j}$. Remember that the bit size of packets $P_{i,j}$ is $\mathcal{P}$. Our overhead is: $\text{length}(C_{i,j}) + \text{length}(\mathcal{B}_i(j)) + \text{length}(\mathcal{F}(j)) - \mathcal{P}$. The element $C_{i,j}$ belongs to the field used for the MDS code. Thus it is $\tilde{q}$ bits long. In addition $\mathcal{B}_i(j)$ and $\mathcal{F}(j)$ are q bits long. Using the values q and $\tilde{q}$ (see the extended version of this paper), we deduce that our packet overhead is:

$$\left\lceil \frac{n(\mathcal{P} + \mathcal{H})}{\lceil \alpha n \rceil} \right\rceil + 2 \left\lceil \frac{\max(n\mathcal{H}, \lambda\mathcal{H} + s)}{\rho n + 1} \right\rceil - \mathcal{P}$$

which is $O(1)$ as a function of the block length n. Notice that when n is large the previous value can be approximated by $\left(\frac{1}{\alpha} - 1\right) \mathcal{P} + \left(\frac{1}{\alpha} + \frac{2}{\rho}\right) \mathcal{H}$. Table 3 summarizes the overhead comparison of the different authentication schemes.

Notice that the values $\left(\left\lceil \frac{n(\mathcal{P}+\mathcal{H})}{\lceil \alpha n \rceil} \right\rceil - \mathcal{P}\right)$ and $\left(\left\lceil \frac{n\mathcal{P}}{\lceil \alpha n \rceil} \right\rceil - \mathcal{P}\right)$ correspond to a stretching coefficient roughly equal to $\frac{1}{\alpha} - 1$. This is the price to pay in order to use the MDS code which guarantees total recovery of all data packets. The apparent low overhead of TWMB comes from the fact that scheme does not provide recovery of lost content (see Table 2). Remark that when the survival rate α is close to 1 (i.e. the channel has a good delivery rate), the previous values get close to $\mathcal{H}$ and 0 respectively. Thus the packet overhead of our construction is asymptotically $\left(1 + \frac{2}{\rho}\right)$ hashes long.

Table 3. Overhead comparison for multicast stream protocols

	Bit Size	Complexity
Our Scheme	$\left(\left\lceil \frac{n(\mathcal{P}+\mathcal{H})}{\lceil \alpha n \rceil} \right\rceil - \mathcal{P}\right) + 2q$	$O(1)$
PRABS	$\left\lceil \frac{n\mathcal{H}+s}{\lceil \alpha n \rceil} \right\rceil + \log_2(n)\,\mathcal{H}$	$\Theta(\log_2(n))$
TWMB	$2q$	$O(1)$
TWMDS	$\left(\left\lceil \frac{n\mathcal{P}}{\lceil \alpha n \rceil} \right\rceil - \mathcal{P}\right) + \left\lceil \frac{n\mathcal{H}+s}{\rho n+1} \right\rceil$	$O(1)$

If we compare our construction to TWMDS then our packet overhead is one field element plus, roughly, $\frac{\mathcal{H}}{\alpha}$ bits longer. Notice, however, that our field elements are smaller than those in TWMDS. Indeed λ can be seen as small in comparison to the block length n and thus $q < \left\lceil \frac{n\,\mathcal{H}+s}{\rho\,n+1} \right\rceil$.

6   Conclusion

In this paper, we presented a stream authentication protocol which can be considered as an extension of PRABS, TWMB and TWMDS presented in [17, 41, 42]. Our construction only requires the generation of a single signature for every family of λ blocks of n packets and allows any group member to join the communication group at any block boundary as TWMB. The number of signature verifications to be performed at the receiver and the bit size of our packet overhead are $O(1)$ as functions of n and λ, contrary to PRABS, where they are linear in λ and logarithmic in n respectively. These two advantages already existed for TWMB but our construction also allows total recovery of the data packets which is not provided by either TWMB or PRABS. This feature is beneficial when the packets represent audio or video information as our approach prevent audio gaps and frozen images for instance. Furthermore, using PH, we are able to save memory at the receiver as those hash chains enable him to decide whether or not dropping data packets upon reception which is not possible for any of PRABS, TWMB and TWMDS. As a consequence, the running time at the receiver is decreased since he only needs to use the erasure code to recover the data packets contrary to PRABS, TWMB and TWMDS where he must first build Merkle hash trees (for PRABS) or query Poly-Reconstruct (for TWMB and TWMDS) before using the erasure code.

It should be noticed that we can improve the running time at the receiver even further by using a trapdoor hash function [39] (such as Very Smooth Hash [7] for instance) instead of a digital signature as in [43].

Acknowledgment

The authors would like to thank Professor Josef Pieprzyk for his valuable comments on this work. The authors are also grateful to the anonymous reviewers for their feedback to improve the quality of this paper. This work was supported by the Australian Research Council under ARC Discovery Projects DP0558773 and DP0665035. The first author's work was also funded by an iMURS scholarship supported by Macquarie University.

References

[1] Al-Ibrahim, M., Pieprzyk, J.: Authenticating multicast streams in lossy channels using threshold techniques. In: Lorenz, P. (ed.) ICN 2001. LNCS, vol. 2094, pp. 239–249. Springer, Heidelberg (2001)

[2] Benaloh, J., de Mare, M.: One-way accumulators: A decentralized alternative to digital signatures. In: Helleseth, T. (ed.) EUROCRYPT 1993. LNCS, vol. 765, pp. 274–285. Springer, Heidelberg (1993)

[3] Blundo, C., De Santis, A., Herzberg, A., Kutten, S., Vaccaro, U., Yung, M.: Perfectly-secure key distribution for dynamic conferences. In: Brickell, E.F. (ed.) CRYPTO 1992. LNCS, vol. 740, pp. 471–486. Springer, Heidelberg (1992)

[4] Challal, Y., Bettahar, H., Bouabdallah, A.: A taxonomy of multicast data origin authentication: Issues and solutions. IEEE Communications Surveys and Tutorials 6(3), 34–57 (2004)

[5] Challal, Y., Bouabdallah, A., Bettahar, H.: H_2A: Hybrid hash-chaining scheme for adaptive multicast source authentication of media-streaming. Computer & Security 24(1), 57–68 (2005)

[6] Choi, S.: Denial of service resistant multicast authentication protocol with prediction hashing and one-way key chain. In: ISM 2005, pp. 701–706. IEEE Press, New York (2005)

[7] Contini, S., Lenstra, A.K., Steinfeld, R.: VSH: an efficient and provable collision resistant hash collision. In: Vaudenay, S. (ed.) EUROCRYPT 2006. LNCS, vol. 4004, pp. 165–182. Springer, Heidelberg (2006)

[8] Dana, A.F., Gowaikar, R., Palanki, R., Hassibi, B., Effros, M.: Capacity of wireless erasure networks. IEEE Transactions on Information Theory 52(3), 789–804 (2006)

[9] Desmedt, Y., Frankel, Y., Yung, M.: Multi-receiver/multi-sender network security: Efficient authenticated multicast/feedback. In: IEEE INFOCOM 1992, vol. 3, pp. 2045–2054. IEEE Press, New York (1992)

[10] Di Pietro, R., Chessa, S., Maestrini, P.: Computation memory and bandwidth efficient distillation codes to mitigate DoS in multicast. In: SecureComm 2005, pp. 13–22. IEEE Press, New York (2005)

[11] Fu, J.C., Lou, W.Y.W.: Distribution Theory of Runs and Patterns and its Applications. World Scientific Publishing (2003)

[12] Gennaro, R., Rohatgi, P.: How to sign digital streams. In: Kaliski Jr., B.S. (ed.) CRYPTO 1997. LNCS, vol. 1294, pp. 180–197. Springer, Heidelberg (1997)

[13] Golle, P., Modadugu, N.: Authenticating streamed data in the presence of random packet loss. In: NDSS 2001, pp. 13–22. Internet Society (2001)

[14] Guruswami, V.: List Decoding of Error-Correcting Codes. Springer, Heidelberg (2004)

[15] Guruswami, V., Sudan, M.: Improved decoding of Reed-Solomon and algebraic-geometric codes. IEEE Transactions on Information Theory 45(6), 1757–1767 (1999)

[16] Jakimoski, G.: Primitives and Schemes for Non-Atomic Information Authentication. PhD thesis, The Florida State University College of Arts and Sciences, Spring Semester (2006)

[17] Karlof, C., Sastry, N., Li, Y., Perrig, A., Tygar, J.D.: Distillation codes and applications to DoS resistant multicast authentication. In: NDSS 2004 (2004)

[18] Lacan, J., Fimes, J.: Systematic MDS erasure codes based on Vandermonde matrices. IEEE Communications Letters 8(9), 570–572 (2004)

[19] Lidl, R., Niederreiter, H.: Introduction to Finite Fields and their Applications - Revised Edition. Cambridge University Press, Cambridge (2000)

[20] Liu, D., Ning, P.: Multi-level μTESLA: Broadcast authentication for distributed sensor networks. ACM Transactions in Embedded Computing Systems 3(4), 800–836 (2004)

[21] Liu, D., Ning, P., Zhu, S., Jajodia, S.: Practical broadcast authentication in sensor networks. In: MobiQuitous 2005, pp. 118–129. IEEE Press, New York (2005)

[22] Lysyanskaya, A., Tamassia, R., Triandopoulos, N.: Multicast authentication in fully adversarial networks. In: IEEE Symposium on Security and Privacy, pp. 241–253. IEEE Computer Society Press, New York (2003)

[23] MacWilliams, F.J., Sloane, N.J.A.: The Theory of Error-Correcting Codes. North-Holland (1977)

[24] Menezes, A.J., van Oorschot, P.C., Vanstone, S.A.: Handbook of Applied Cryptography. CRC Press, Boca Raton (1996)

[25] Merkle, R.: A certified digital signature. In: Brassard, G. (ed.) CRYPTO 1989. LNCS, vol. 435, pp. 218–238. Springer, Heidelberg (1989)

[26] Miner, S., Staddon, J.: Graph-based authentication of digital streams. In: IEEE Symposium on Security and Privacy, pp. 232–246. IEEE Press, New York (2001)

[27] Pannetrat, A., Molva, R.: Authenticating real time packet streams and multicasts. In: ISCC 2002, IEEE Computer Society Press, Los Alamitos (2002)

[28] Park, J.M., Chong, E.K.P., Siegel, H.J.: Efficient multicast packet authentication using signature amortization. In: IEEE Symposium on Security and Privacy, pp. 227–240. IEEE Press, New York (2002)

[29] Park, J.M., Chong, E.K.P., Siegel, H.J.: Efficient multicast stream authentication using erasure codes. ACM Transactions on Information and System Security 6(2), 258–285 (2003)

[30] Park, Y., Cho, Y.: The eSAIDA stream authentication scheme. In: Laganà, A., Gavrilova, M., Kumar, V., Mun, Y., Tan, C.J.K., Gervasi, O. (eds.) ICCSA 2004. LNCS, vol. 3046, pp. 799–807. Springer, Heidelberg (2004)

[31] Perrig, A., Canetti, R., Tygar, J., Song, D.: Efficient authentication and signing of multicast streams over lossy channels. In: IEEE Symposium on Security and Privacy, pp. 56–73. IEEE Press, New York (2000)

[32] Perrig, A., Szewczyk, R., Tygar, J.D., Wen, V., Culler, D.E.: SPINS: Security protocols for sensor networks. Wireless Networks 8(5), 521–534 (2002)

[33] Perrig, A., Tygar, J.D.: Secure Broadcast Communication in Wired and Wireless Networks. Kluwer Academic Publishers, Boston (2003)

[34] Pieprzyk, J., Hardjono, T., Seberry, J.: Fundamentals of Computer Security. Springer, Heidelberg (2003)

[35] Rabin, M.O.: Efficient dispersal of information for security, load balancing, and fault tolerance. Journal of the Association for Computing Machinery 36(2), 335–348 (1989)

[36] Reed, I.S., Solomon, G.: Polynomial codes over certain finite fields. Journal of Society for Industrial and Applied Mathematics 8(2), 300–304 (1960)

[37] Rohatgi, P.: A compact and fast hybrid signature scheme for multicast packet authentication. In: ACM CCS'99, pp. 93–100. ACM Press, New York (1999)

[38] Safavi-Naini, R., Wang, H.: New results on multi-receiver authentication code. In: Nyberg, K. (ed.) EUROCRYPT 1998. LNCS, vol. 1403, pp. 527–541. Springer, Heidelberg (1998)

[39] Shamir, A., Tauman, Y.: Improved online/offline signature schemes. In: Kilian, J. (ed.) CRYPTO 2001. LNCS, vol. 2139, pp. 355–367. Springer, Heidelberg (2001)

[40] Stinson, D.R.: Cryptography: Theory and Practice, 3rd edn. Chapman & Hall/CRC (2006)

[41] Tartary, C., Wang, H.: Efficient multicast stream authentication for the fully adversarial network. In: Song, J., Kwon, T., Yung, M. (eds.) WISA 2005. LNCS, vol. 3786, pp. 108–125. Springer, Heidelberg (2006)

[42] Tartary, C., Wang, H.: Achieving multicast stream authentication using MDS codes. In: Pointcheval, D., Mu, Y., Chen, K. (eds.) CANS 2006. LNCS, vol. 4301, pp. 108–125. Springer, Heidelberg (2006)

[43] Tartary, C., Wang, H.: Efficient multicast stream authentication for the fully adversarial network. International Journal of Security and Network (Special Issue on Cryptography in Networks) 2(3/4), 175–191 (2007)

[44] Wong, C.K., Chan, A.: Immediate data authentication for multicast resource constrained networks. In: Boyd, C., González Nieto, J.M. (eds.) ACISP 2005. LNCS, vol. 3574, pp. 113–121. Springer, Heidelberg (2005)

[45] Wong, C.K., Lam, S.S.: Digital signatures for flows and multicasts. IEEE/ACM Transactions on Networking 7(4), 502–513 (1999)

[46] Zanotti, J.-P.: Le code correcteur C.I.R.C. Available online at:
http://zanotti.univ-tln.fr/enseignement/divers/chapter3.html

Certificateless Signature Revisited[*]

Xinyi Huang[1], Yi Mu[1], Willy Susilo[1], Duncan S. Wong[2], and Wei Wu[1]

[1] Centre for Computer and Information Security Research
School of Computer Science & Software Engineering
University of Wollongong, Australia
{xh068,ymu,wsusilo}@uow.edu.au,weiwu81@gmail.com
[2] Dept. of Computer Science, City University of Hong Kong, Hong Kong, China
duncan@cityu.edu.hk

Abstract. In this paper we revisit the security models of certificateless signatures and propose two new constructions which are provably secure in the random oracle model. We divide the potential adversaries according to their attack power, and for the first time, three new kinds of adversaries are introduced into certificateless signatures. They are Normal Adversary, Strong Adversary and Super Adversary (ordered by their attack power). Combined with the known Type I Adversary and Type II Adversary in certificateless system, we then define the security of certificateless signatures in different attack scenarios. Our new models, together with the others in the literature, will enable us to better understand the security of certificateless signatures. Two concrete schemes with different security levels are also proposed in this paper. The first scheme, which is proved secure against Normal Type I and Super Type II Adversary, enjoys the shortest signature length among all the known certificateless signature schemes. The second scheme is secure against Super Type I and Type II adversary. Compared with the scheme in ACNS 2006 which has a similar security level, our second scheme requires lower operation cost but a little longer signature length.

Keywords: Certificateless cryptology, Random oracle, Security model, Signature.

1 Introduction

In secret-key or symmetric-key cryptography, the sender and receiver share a secret key. The sender uses the secret key to encrypt the message, and the receiver uses the same secret key to decrypt the message. One drawback of a symmetric system is that it requires the distribution of the secret key. They must use a secure channel to transmit this secret key since anyone who overhears or intercepts the key can later read, modify, and forge all encrypted messages. If the sender and receiver are in separate geographical locations, key distribution then becomes problematic.

[*] Supported by National Science Foundation of China (NSFC 60673070) and ARC Discovery Grant DP0557493 and DP0663306.

J. Pieprzyk, H. Ghodosi, and E. Dawson (Eds.): ACISP 2007, LNCS 4586, pp. 308–322, 2007.

In order to solve this problem, Diffie and Hellman [7] introduced the concept of public-key cryptography in 1976. In this system, each person has a pair of keys: public key and private key. The public key is published, while the private key is kept secret. All communications involve only public keys, and no private key is ever transmitted or shared. Therefore, the need for the sender and receiver to share secret information is eliminated. A central problem for public key cryptography is: proving that a user's public key is authentic, and has not been tampered with or replaced by a malicious third party. The usual approach to solve this problem is to use a public key infrastructure (PKI), in which one or more third parties, known as certificate authorities, issue certificates to bind a user with his public key. Public key system which uses certificates is called as *traditional* public key system. History has shown that the certificates in traditional PKI is generally considered to be costly to use and manage.

Identity-based (or ID-based) cryptography, as proposed by Shamir in [16], was introduced to solve the above problem. In the new setting, the user's public key is some unique information about the identity of the user (e.g., a user's email address) which is assumed to be publicly known. Therefore, the need of certification can be eliminated. In ID-based system, a trusted third party, called the Key Generation Center (KGC), generates users' private keys. The KGC first publishes a "master" public key, and retains the corresponding master secret key. To obtain a private key, one should contact KGC, which uses the master secret key to generate the corresponding private key. However, this approach creates a new inherent problem, namely the *key escrow* of a user's private key, since (KGC) must be *completely trusted*. This is due to the knowledge of the KGC on the user's private key. Hence, KGC can always *impersonate* any user of his choice, and therefore, the essential assumption is a complete trust on the KGC.

In 2003, Al-Riyami and Paterson [2] proposed a new type of public key system that avoids the above mentioned drawbacks. They termed it as *Certificateless* public key system. In contrast to the traditional public key system cryptography, certificateless cryptography does *not* require any certificates to ensure the authenticity of public keys. Certificateless cryptography relies on the existence of a semi-trusted third party KGC who has the master secret key. In this sense, it is similar to identity-based cryptography. Nevertheless, certificateless cryptography *does not* suffer from the key escrow property that seems to be inherent in the identity-based cryptography. In a certificateless system, KGC only supplies a user with a *partial private key* D_{ID_i}, which is computed from an identity ID_i. The user also holds a secret value which is chosen by himself. Then, the user combines his partial private key with his secret value to generate his actual private key. This private key is *not* available to the KGC. The user also combines his secret value with system's public parameters to generate his public key PK_{ID_i}. The public key PK_{ID_i} needs to be made available to the other participants (e.g. transmit it along with messages, in the case of message signing). Hence, it is no longer an identity-based cryptography, since the public key needs to be provided (but in contrast to the traditional cryptography, the public key does not require any certificate).

Due to the lack of public key authentication, it is important to assume that an adversary in the certificateless system can replace the user's public key with a false key of its choice, which is also known as **Type I Adversary** [2]. In order to provide a secure certificateless signature scheme, this type of attacks must not be able to produce signatures that can get through the verification algorithm with the false public key. An assumption that must be made is that KGC does not mount a public key replacement attack to a target user since he is armed with this user's partial private key. However, KGC might engage in other adversarial activities: eavesdropping on signatures and making signing queries, which is also known as **Type II Adversary**. In this way, the level of trust is similar to the trust in a CA in a traditional PKI. However, there is a debate on how to define these two types of attacks in the literature.

Related Work. The first concrete construction of the certificateless signature (**CLS**) scheme was proposed in [2]. Recently, Huang, Susilo, Mu and Zhang [10] pointed out a security weakness of this signature scheme. A generic construction of CLS was proposed by Yum and Lee [17] in ACISP 2004. However, Hu, Wong, Zhang and Deng [11] showed that the Yum-Lee construction is insecure and proposed a fix in the standard model. In ACNS 2006, Zhang, Wong, Xu and Feng [19] presented an efficient CLS scheme from pairings. Gorantla and Saxena [9] introduced a new construction of CLS without providing formal proofs. Their scheme has been shown to be insecure by Cao, Paterson and Kou [5]. Park [14] showed that a similar problem also exists in the scheme proposed by Yap, Heng and Goi [18]. The first concrete CLS scheme in the standard model was proposed by Liu, Au and Susilo [12]. Au *et al.* [1] proposed a new model of Type II adversary for certificateless systems and presented that several schemes using the same key structure as [2] are vulnerable to this kind of attacks. According to the conclusion given in [1], the scheme in [12] is not secure against the new adversary defined in [1]. Similarly, this new kind of adversary can also break Li, Chen and Sun's scheme [13].

Motivations. In the security model of a signature scheme, the adversary is allowed to access the sign oracle, which enables him to obtain some valid signatures. This is for simulating the fact that the adversary may be able to gain some signatures from the signer, eavesdropping, or a legitimate receiver. It is well acceptable that the adversary should be provided with such kind of sign oracle and obtain some "valid" signatures of messages that are adaptively chosen by the adversary. But "valid" in certificateless system could have *different* meanings, considering the fact that the adversary has the ability to replace any user's public key. Namely, signatures could be valid under the user's original public key chosen by this user himself or the false public key chosen by the attacker.

When the first CLS scheme was proposed in [2], there was no formal security definition for CLS. The adversaries defined in CLE were used to analyze its security. There have been some good works [1,11,12,19] on this topic and some security models of CLS have been well-defined. Although these models are different from each other, almost all argue that the adversary should be allowed to obtain signatures that can be verified with the false public key chosen by the adversary himself. However, in the real world, the signatures that a *realistic* adversary can obtain are usually generated by the signer himself and valid under this signer's original public key. So, the adversary defined in the known CLS security models seems to enjoy more power than it could have in the real world.

If a CLS scheme is secure against the attacker defined in [1,11,12,19], then it enjoys a higher security level. In this sense, the above security models are reasonable and acceptable. Stronger models can ensure a CLS scheme with a higher security level, but realistic models can lead to more efficient schemes. Therefore, it is still worthwhile to define the adversary against CLS in the real world, which can be regarded as the complementary to the known models. The new models will enable us to better understand the security of CLS. Motivated by the method in the survey of CLE given by Dent [6], we will define different sign oracles to different adversaries and divide them by their attack power.

Our Contributions. In this paper, we revisit the security models of CLS and propose two concrete certificateless signature schemes. First, we divide the potential adversaries against certificateless signatures according to their attack power. Three kinds of attackers are introduced to CLS for the first time: Normal Adversary, Strong Adversary and Super Adversary (ordered by their attack power). Combined with the known Type I Adversary and Type II Adversary, we can obtain Normal Type I Adversary, Strong Type I Adversary and etc. The security models of CLS against these kinds of adversaries are also formulated. We believe the new models, together with other known CLS models, will enable us to better understand the security of CLS. Second, two concrete schemes are proposed. The first scheme is provably secure against Normal Type I adversary and Super Type II adversary which are defined in this paper. The signature length of this scheme is the *shortest* compared to any existing CLS scheme in the literature (as short as the BLS [4] signature). The second scheme is provably secure against Super Type I and Type II Adversary. Compared with another concrete scheme in ACNS 2006 [19] which has the similar security level, our second scheme has lower operation cost but a little longer signature length.

Organization. In the next section, we will present the outline of CLS. In Section 3, new types of adversaries in CLS are introduced and the security of certificateless signatures against different attackers are also defined. We then propose our first construction of the certificateless signature in the Section 4.2. Its security analysis is also given in this section. The second certificateless signature scheme is proposed in Section 4.3, together with the formal security proof. We compare our two schemes with other schemes in Section 5. Finally, Section 6 concludes the paper.

2   Certificateless Signature

In this section, we firstly review the outline of CLS. Then we describe the basic types of adversaries in CLS.

2.1   Outline of the Certificateless Signature Schemes

A certificateless signature scheme is defined by six algorithms: Setup, Partial-Private-Key-Extract, Set-Secret-Value, Set-Public-Key, Sign and Verify. The description of each algorithm is as follows.

- Setup: This algorithm takes as input a security parameter 1^k and returns the master secret key msk and master public key mpk. It also outputs a parameter param which is shared in the system.
- Partial-Private-Key-Extract: This algorithm takes as input the master secret key msk, the master public key mpk, system parameter param and an identity ID. It outputs a partial private key D_{ID}.
- Set-Secret-Value: This algorithm takes as input the master public key mpk and system parameter param. It outputs a secret value $x_{ID} \in S$. Here S denotes the set of the valid secret values.
- Set-Public-Key: This algorithm takes as input the master public key mpk, system parameter param, an identity ID and this identity's secret value $x_{ID} \in S$. It outputs the public key $PK_{ID} \in \mathcal{PK}$. Here $\mathcal{PK}$ denotes the set of the valid public key values.
- Sign: This algorithm takes as input the master public key mpk, system parameter param, an identity ID, this identity's secret value $x_{ID} \in S$, partial private key D_{ID} and a message M. It outputs a certificateless signature σ.
- Verify: This algorithm takes as input the the master public key mpk, system parameter param, an identity ID, this identity's public key PK_{ID} and a message/signature pair (M, σ). It outputs $true$ if the signature is correct, or $false$ otherwise.

In general, KGC (Key Generation Center) performs the algorithms Setup and Partial-Private-Key-Extract.

2.2   Adversaries and Oracles

Similarly to the adversaries against CLE defined in [2], there are basically two types of adversaries in CLS: $\mathcal{A}_I$ and $\mathcal{A}_{II}$. $\mathcal{A}_I$ simulates attacks when the adversary (anyone except the KGC) replaces the user public key PK_{ID}. However, $\mathcal{A}_I$ is not given this user's partial private key D_{ID}. Adversary $\mathcal{A}_{II}$ simulates attacks when the adversary knows the master secret key but cannot replace the target user's public key. We will give a more detailed description of these two kinds of adversaries in Section 3. Generally, there are three oracles which can be accessed by both $\mathcal{A}_I$ and $\mathcal{A}_{II}$:

1. **Create-User:** This oracle takes as input a query ID $\in \{0,1\}^*$, if ID has already been created, nothing is to be carried out by the oracle. Otherwise, the oracle runs the algorithms Partial-Private-Key-Extract, Set-Secret-Value, Set-Public-Key to obtain the partial private key D_{ID}, secret value x_{ID} and public key PK_{ID}. Then it adds $(ID, D_{ID}, x_{ID}, PK_{ID})$ to the list L. In this case, ID is said to be *created*. In both cases, PK_{ID} is returned.

2. **Public-Key-Replace:** This oracle takes as input a query $(\mathsf{ID}, PK'_{\mathsf{ID}})$, where ID denotes the identity which has been created and PK'_{ID} is a public key value in the public key space $\mathcal{PK}$. This oracle replaces user ID's public key with PK'_{ID} and updates the corresponding information in the list L. Note that the adversary is not required to provide the secret value x'_{ID} which is used to generate $PK'_{\mathsf{ID}}{}^1$.

3. **Secret-Value-Extract:** This oracle takes as input a query ID, where ID is the identity which has been created. It browses the list L and returns the secret value x_{ID}. Note that, the secret-value output by this oracle is the one which is used to generate ID's original public key PK_{ID}. The Secret-Value-Extract oracle does not output the secret value associated with the replaced public key PK'_{ID}.

3   Security Models

In this section, we discuss the definition of the security for a certificateless signature scheme.

3.1   Security Against a Normal Type I Adversary

In this section, we will consider the first kind of Type I adversary $\mathcal{A}_I$: Normal Type I adversary. Informally, we want to capture the attack scenarios as follows:

1. $\mathcal{A}_I$ can obtain some message/signature pairs (m_i, σ_i) which are generated by the target user ID using this ID's secret value x_{ID} and partial private key D_{ID}.
2. The target user ID will keep x_{ID} and D_{ID} as secret.
3. $\mathcal{A}_I$ can replace the target user ID's public key with PK'_{ID} which is chosen by himself. He can also dupe any other third party to verify user ID's signatures using the replaced public key PK'_{ID}.

In the real world, the adversary may be able to gain ID's some valid signatures from eavesdropping or the intended receivers. These signatures are generated by ID using his own secret value and partial private key. Although $\mathcal{A}_I$ can replace ID's public key with PK'_{ID} which is chosen by himself, we assume that, in most cases, it is hard for a realistic $\mathcal{A}_I$ to get any signature that is valid under PK'_{ID}. On the other hand, we also assume that user ID will keep $(x_{\mathsf{ID}}, D_{\mathsf{ID}})$ as secret and $\mathcal{A}_I$ can not obtain either of these two secrets. The existential unforgeability of a certificateless signature scheme against a Normal Type I adaptively chosen message and chosen identity adversary $\mathcal{A}_I$ is defined as the following games:

---

[1] In the security model defined in [10,18], adversary is required to issue a query $(\mathsf{ID}, PK'_{\mathsf{ID}}, x'_{\mathsf{ID}})$ to the oracle **Public-Key-Replace**, where x'_{ID} is the secret value which is used to generate PK'_{ID}. It is not reasonable since an adversary could pick a random element in the public key place $\mathcal{PK}$ and even himself does not know what is the corresponding secret value.

Phase 1: The challenger runs the algorithm Setup and returns the system parameters param and the system master pubic key mpk to $\mathcal{A}_I$.

Phase 2: In this phase, $\mathcal{A}_I$ can adaptively access all the oracles defined in Section 2.2. In addition, $\mathcal{A}_I$ can also access the **Partial-Private-Key-Extract** oracle and **Normal Sign** oracle which are defined as:

Partial-Private-Key-Extract: This oracle takes as input a query ID, where ID is the identity which has been created. It browses the list L and returns the partial private key D_{ID}.

Normal-Sign: This oracle takes as input a query (ID, m), where ID denotes the identity which has been created and m denotes the message to be signed. It outputs a signature σ such that $\texttt{true} \leftarrow \textsf{Verify}(m, \sigma, \textsf{params}, ID, PK_{ID})$. Here PK_{ID} is the public key returned from the oracle **Create-User**.

Phase 3: After all the queries, $\mathcal{A}_I$ outputs a forgery (m^*, σ^*, ID^*). Let $\mathcal{PK}_{ID^*}$ be the current public key of the user ID^* in the list L. We say $\mathcal{A}_I$ wins the game if the forgery satisfies the following requirements:

1. $\mathcal{A}_I$ has never submitted (ID^*, m^*) to the oracle **Normal-Sign**.
2. $\mathcal{A}_I$ has never submitted ID^* to **Partial-Private-Key-Extract** oracle or **Secret-Value-Extract** oracle.
3. $true \leftarrow \textsf{Verify}(m, \sigma, \textsf{params}, ID, \mathcal{PK}_{ID^*})$.

The success probability of a Normal Type I adaptively chosen message and chosen identity adversary $\mathcal{A}_I$ wins the above games is defined as $Succ^{cma,cida}_{\mathcal{A}_I,normal}$.

Definition 1. *We say a certificateless signature scheme is secure against a $(t, q_{CU}, q_{PPK}, q_{PKR}, q_{SV}, q_{NS})$ Normal Type I adaptively chosen message and chosen identity adversary $\mathcal{A}_I$, if $\mathcal{A}_I$ runs in polynomial time t, makes at most q_{CU} queries to the oracle* **Create-User**, q_{PPK} *queries to the oracle* **Partial-Private-Key-Extract**, q_{PKR} *queries to the oracle* **Public-Key-Replace**, q_{SV} *queries to the oracle* **Secret-Value-Extract**, q_{NS} *queries to the oracle* **Normal-Sign** *and $Succ^{cma,cida}_{\mathcal{A}_I,normal}$ is negligible.*

3.2 Security Against a Strong Type I Adversary

In this section, we will boost the attack capabilities of the adversary $\mathcal{A}_I$ and define the second type of $\mathcal{A}_I$ which is called "Strong Type I adversary". We want to capture the attack scenario that $\mathcal{A}_I$ can see some message/signature pairs (m_i, σ_i) which are generated by algorithm Sign using the secret value sv and the user ID's partial-private key D_{ID}. Here the secret value sv can be the original secret value x_{ID} chosen by the user ID, or, the secret value supplied by the adversary $\mathcal{A}_I$. Similar models were also proposed in [11,19]. If a scheme is secure against this Strong Type I adversary, it is also secure against a Normal Type I adversary. On the other hand, more operation cost or longer signature length are therefore needed to construct a CLS scheme that is secure under this stronger model. If we put this kind of attack in the real world, it means that the target user ID will use his own partial private key and the secret value supplied by $\mathcal{A}_I$ to sign messages. It considers the scenario where the user ID will intentionally help $\mathcal{A}_I$ to attack himself. This assumption might stand in some particular situations, but might be stronger for most other situations. The existential unforgeability of a certificateless signature scheme against a Strong Type I adaptively chosen message and chosen public key adversary $\mathcal{A}_I$ is defined by the similar games as defined in Section 3.1, with the only difference that the strong Type I adversary $\mathcal{A}_I$ can query a different sign oracle **Strong-Sign** which will be defined later.

Phase 1: The challenger runs the algorithm Setup and returns the system parameters param and the system master public key mpk to $\mathcal{A}_I$.

Phase 2: In this phase, $\mathcal{A}_I$ can adaptively access all the oracles defined in Section 2.2. In addition, he can also access the **Partial-Private-Key-Extract** oracle and **Strong-Sign** oracle which are defined as:

Partial-Private-Key-Extract: Same as defined in Section 3.1.

Strong-Sign: This oracle takes as input a query (ID, m, sv), where ID denotes the identity which has been created, m denotes the message to be signed and sv is some information $sv \in \{nil\} \cup \mathcal{S}$.

- If $sv = nil$, this oracle uses ID's original secret value x_{ID} and partial private key D_{ID} to generate the signature σ for this message. It outputs σ as the answer.
- Otherwise, $sv \in \mathcal{S}$, this oracle uses sv and ID's partial private key D_{ID} to generate the signature σ for this message. It outputs σ as the answer.

Phase 3: After all the queries, $\mathcal{A}_I$ outputs a forgery (m^*, σ^*, ID^*). Let $\mathcal{PK}_{ID^*}$ be the current public key of the user ID^* in the list L. We say a strong $\mathcal{A}_I$ wins the game if the forgery satisfies the following requirements:

1. $\mathcal{A}_I$ has never submitted (ID^*, m^*, sv) $(sv \in \{nil\} \cup \mathcal{S})$ to the oracle **Strong-Sign**.
2. $\mathcal{A}_I$ has never submitted ID^* to the oracle **Partial-Private-Key-Extract**.
3. $true \leftarrow \text{Verify}(m, \sigma, \text{params}, ID, \mathcal{PK}_{ID^*})$.

The success probability of a Strong Type I adaptively chosen message and chosen identity adversary $\mathcal{A}_I$ wins the above game is defined as $Succ_{\mathcal{A}_I, strong}^{cma, cida}$.

Definition 2. *We say a certificateless signature scheme is secure against a* $(t, q_{CU}, q_{PPK}, q_{PKR}, q_{SV}, q_{SS})$ *Strong Type I adaptively chosen message and chosen identity adversary* $\mathcal{A}_I$, *if* $\mathcal{A}_I$ *runs in polynomial time* t, *makes at most* q_{CU} *queries to the oracle* **Create-User**, q_{PPK} *queries to the oracle* **Partial-Private-Key-Extract**, q_{PKR} *queries to the oracle* **Public-Key-Replace**, q_{SV} *queries to the oracle* **Secret-Value-Extract**, q_{SS} *queries to the oracle* **Strong-Sign** *and* $Succ_{\mathcal{A}_I, strong}^{cma, cida}$ *is negligible.*

3.3 Security Against a Super Type I Adversary

In this section, we will define the third type of $\mathcal{A}_I$: Super Type I adversary. We want to capture the following attack scenario: $\mathcal{A}_I$ can obtain some message/signature pairs (m_i, σ_i) such that $true \leftarrow \text{Verify}(m_i, \sigma_i, \text{params}, ID, \mathcal{PK}_{ID})$.

Here $\mathcal{PK}_{\mathsf{ID}}$ is chosen by $\mathcal{A}_I$, and it could be the user ID's original public key, or any valid public key value in the public key space. In the latter case, the Super Type I adversary $\mathcal{A}_I$ is not required to supply the corresponding secret value which is used to generate the pubic key chosen by himself.

In the above scenario, we give $\mathcal{A}_I$ as much power as possible. Namely, $\mathcal{A}_I$ can obtain some message/signature pairs which are valid under the public key chosen by himself. Meanwhile, he dose not need to supply the secret value sv of the public key chosen by himself. This accounts for the name "Super Adversary". It implies that there exists a black-box knowledge exactor which can extract the secret value from the public key chosen by $\mathcal{A}_I$ and then signs messages using ID's partial private key and this secret value. This is the strongest attacker compared with other two attackers defined in Section 3.1 and Section 3.2. It is still unclear whether it represents a realistic attack scenario. The existential unforgeability of a certificateless signature scheme against a Super Type I adaptively chosen message and chosen identity adversary $\mathcal{A}_I$ is defined by the similar games as defined in Section 3.1, with the only difference that $\mathcal{A}_I$ can have access to the oracle **Super-Sign** which will be defined later.

Phase 1: The challenger runs the algorithm Setup and returns the system parameters param and the system master public key mpk to $\mathcal{A}_I$.

Phase 2: In this phase, $\mathcal{A}_I$ can adaptively access all the above oracles defined in Section 2.2. In addition, he can also access the **Partial-Private-Key-Extract** oracle and **Super-Sign** oracle which are defined as:

Partial-Private-Key-Extract: Same as defined in Section 3.1.

Super-Sign: This oracle takes as input a query (ID, m), where ID denotes the identity which has been created and m denotes the message to be signed. This oracle outputs a signature σ such that $true \leftarrow$ Verify$(m, \sigma, \mathsf{params}, \mathsf{ID}, \mathcal{PK}_{\mathsf{ID}})$. Here $\mathcal{PK}_{\mathsf{ID}}$ denotes the user ID's current public key in the list L. If this user's public key has not been replaced, $\mathcal{PK}_{\mathsf{ID}} = PK_{\mathsf{ID}}$ where PK_{ID} is the public key returned from the oracle **Create-User**. Otherwise, $\mathcal{PK}_{\mathsf{ID}} = PK'_{\mathsf{ID}}$ where PK'_{ID} is the latest public key value submitted to the oracle **Public-Key-Replace**.

Phase 3: After all the queries, $\mathcal{A}_I$ outputs a forgery $(m^*, \sigma^*, \mathsf{ID}^*)$. Let $\mathcal{PK}_{\mathsf{ID}^*}$ be the current public key of the user ID in the list L. We say a Super $\mathcal{A}_I$ wins the game if the forgery satisfies the following requirements:

1. $\mathcal{A}_I$ has never submitted (ID^*, m^*) to the oracle **Super-Sign**.
2. $\mathcal{A}_I$ has never submitted ID^* to the oracle **Partial-Private-Key-Extract**.
3. $true \leftarrow$ Verify$(m, \sigma, \mathsf{params}, \mathsf{ID}, \mathcal{PK}_{\mathsf{ID}^*})$.

The success probability of a Super Type I adaptively chosen message and chosen identity adversary $\mathcal{A}_I$ wins the above game is defined as $Succ^{cma,cida}_{\mathcal{A}_I,super}$.

Definition 3. [2] *We say a certificateless signature scheme is secure against a $(t, q_{CU}, q_{PPK}, q_{PKR}, q_{SV}, q_{SS})$ Super Type I adaptively chosen message and chosen identity adversary $\mathcal{A}_I$, if $\mathcal{A}_I$ runs in polynomial time t, makes at most*

---

[2] This definition is similar the one given in [1,12].

q_{CU} queries to the oracle **Create-User**, q_{PPK} queries to the oracle **Partial-Private-Key-Extract**, q_{PKR} queries to the oracle **Public-Key-Replace**, q_{SV} queries to the oracle **Secret-Value-Extract**, q_{SS} queries to the oracle **Super-Sign** and $Succ_{A_I, super}^{cma, cida}$ is negligible.

3.4   Type II Adversaries

The Type II adversary A_{II} simulates the KGC who holds the master secret key and might engage in other adversarial activities, such as eavesdropping on signatures and making signing queries. According to the different sign oracles A_{II} can access, it can be further divided into: Normal A_{II} (access the oracle **Normal-Sign**), Strong A_{II} (access the oracle **Strong-Sign**) and Super A_{II} (access the oracle **Super-Sign**). The existential unforgeability of a certificateless signature scheme against a Type II adaptively chosen message and chosen identity adversary A_{II} is defined by the following games:

Phase 1: The challenger runs the algorithm Setup and returns the system parameters param, the system master public key mpk and the master secret key s to A_{II}.

Phase 2: In this phase, A_{II} can adaptively access all the oracles defined in Section 2.2. In addition, he can also access only one of the following oracle: **Normal-Sign**, **Strong-Sign** or **Super-Sign**.

Phase 3: After all the queries, A_{II} outputs a forgery $(m^*, \sigma^*, \mathsf{ID}^*)$. We say A_{II} wins the game if the forgery satisfies the following requirements:

1. A_{II} has never submitted (ID^*, m^*) to the sign oracle.
2. A_I has never submitted ID^* to the oracle **Secret-Value-Extract**.
3. $\mathsf{true} \leftarrow \mathsf{Verify}(m, \sigma, \mathsf{params}, \mathsf{ID}^*, PK_{\mathsf{ID}^*})$. Here PK_{ID^*} is the original public key returned from the oracle **Create-User**.

The success probability of a Type II adaptively chosen message and chosen identity adversary A_{II} wins the above game is defined as $Succ_{A_{II}}^{cma, cida}$.

Definition 4. [3] *We say a certificateless signature scheme is secure against a* $(t, q_{CU}, q_{PKR}, q_{SV}, q_S)$ *Type II adaptively chosen message and chosen identity adversary* A_{II}, *if* A_{II} *runs in polynomial time* t, *makes at most* q_{CU} *queries to the oracle* **Create-User**, q_{PKR} *queries to the oracle* **Public-Key-Replace**, q_{SV} *queries to the oracle* **Secret-Value-Extract**, q_S *queries to the oracle* **Sign** *and* $Succ_{A_{II}}^{cma, cida}$ *is negligible. Here the oracle* **Sign** *can be one of the following oracles:* **Normal-Sign**, **Strong-Sign** *or* **Super-Sign**.

3.5   Malicious but Passive KGC Attack

Very recently, a new kind of Type II attack-*Malicious* but *Passive* KGC attack is introduced in [1]. In the new attack, the KGC that holds the master secret key is assumed malicious at the very beginning of the Setup stage of the system.

---

[3] Similar definitions are also give in [11,12,19].

KGC may generate his master public/secret key pair maliciously so that it can launch a Type II attack more easily in the later stage of the system. Combined with different **Sign** oracles, the security of the certificateless signature schemes against malicious but passive KGC attack can be defined by the similar games in [1]. Due to page limitation, we will describe it in the full version.

4   Our Proposed Schemes

4.1   Bilinear Groups and Security Assumptions

Let $\mathbb{G}_1$ denote an additive group of prime order p and $\mathbb{G}_T$ be a multiplicative group of the same order. Let P denote a generator in $\mathbb{G}_1$. Let $e : \mathbb{G}_1 \times \mathbb{G}_1 \to \mathbb{G}_T$ be a bilinear pairing with the properties defined in [4].

Discrete Logarithm Problem: Given $(P, aP) \in \mathbb{G}_1$, find a.
Computational Diffie-Hellman Problem: Given a triple $\mathbb{G}_1$ elements (P, aP, bP), find the element abP.

4.2   Scheme I

In this section, we propose our first certificateless signature scheme which is secure against a Normal Type I adversary and Super Type II adversary. It consists of the following algorithms:

- Setup: Let $(\mathbb{G}_1, \mathbb{G}_T)$ be bilinear groups where $|\mathbb{G}_1| = |\mathbb{G}_T| = p$, for some prime number $p \geq 2^k$, k be the system security number. e denotes the bilinear pairing $\mathbb{G}_1 \times \mathbb{G}_1 \to \mathbb{G}_T$. Let $H_0, H_1 : \{0,1\}^* \to \mathbb{G}_1^*$ be two secure cryptographic hash functions. KGC chooses a random number $s \in \mathbb{Z}_p^*$ and a random element $P \in \mathbb{G}_1^*$. It sets system's master public key $P_{pub} = sP$, master secret key as s and publishes $\{\mathbb{G}_1, \mathbb{G}_T, p, e, P, H_0, H_1, P_{pub}\}$.
- Partial-Private-Key-Extract: Given a user's identity ID, KGC first computes $Q_{\mathsf{ID}} = H_0(\mathsf{ID})$. It then sets this user's partial private key $D_{\mathsf{ID}} = sQ_{\mathsf{ID}}$ and transmits it to ID secretly.
- Set-Secret-Value: The user ID chooses a random number $x_{\mathsf{ID}} \in \mathbb{Z}_p^*$ and sets x_{ID} as his secret value. Here the valid secret key value space is $\mathcal{S} = \mathbb{Z}_p^*$.
- Set-Public-Key: Given the secret value x_{ID}, User ID can compute his public key $PK_{\mathsf{ID}} = x_{\mathsf{ID}}P$. Here the valid public key space is $\mathcal{PK} = \mathbb{G}_1^*$.
- Sign: For a message m, the user ID computes the signature $\sigma = D_{\mathsf{ID}} + x_{\mathsf{ID}}H_1(m\|\mathsf{ID}\|PK_{\mathsf{ID}})$.
- Verify: Given a pair (m, σ) and user ID's public key PK_{ID}, anyone can check whether $e(\sigma, P) \stackrel{?}{=} e(Q_{\mathsf{ID}}, P_{pub})e(PK_{\mathsf{ID}}, H_1(m\|\mathsf{ID}\|PK_{\mathsf{ID}}))$. If the equality holds, outputs $true$. Otherwise, $false$.

Security Analysis of Scheme I

Theorem 1. *If there is a* $(t, q_{CU}, q_{PPK}, q_{PKR}, q_{SV}, q_{NS})$ *Normal Type I adaptively chosen message and chosen identity adversary* $\mathcal{A}_I$ *which can submit additional* q_R *queries to random oracles and win the game defined in Section 3.1* with probability $Succ_{A_I,normal}^{cma,cida}$, then there exists another algorithm $\mathcal{B}$ which can solve a random instance of Computational Diffie-Hellman problem in polynomial time with success probability

$$Succ_{\mathcal{B},\mathbb{G}_1}^{CDH} \geq (1 - \frac{1}{q_{CU}})^{q_{PPK}+q_{SV}}(1 - \frac{1}{q_{NS}+1})^{q_{NS}}\frac{1}{q_{CU}(q_{NS}+1)}Succ_{A_I,normal}^{cma,cida}.$$

Theorem 2. *If there is a* $(t, q_{CU}, q_{PKR}, q_{SV}, q_{SS})$ *Super Type II adaptively chosen message and chosen identity adversary* A_{II} *which can submit additional* q_R *queries to random oracles and win the game defined in Section 3.4 with probability* $Succ_{A_{II},super}^{cma,cida}$, *then there exists another algorithm* $\mathcal{B}$ *which can solve a random instance of Computational Diffie-Hellman problem in polynomial time with success probability* $Succ_{\mathcal{B},\mathbb{G}_1}^{CDH} \geq (1 - \frac{1}{q_{CU}})^{q_{SV}}(1 - \frac{1}{q_{SS}+1})^{q_{SS}}\frac{1}{q_{CU}(q_{SS}+1)}Succ_{A_{II},super}^{cma,cida}.$

Due to page limitation, the proofs will be presented in the full version of this paper.

4.3 Scheme II

In this section, we propose our second certificateless signature scheme which is secure against a Super Type I and Type II adversary. The first four algorithms are the same as those defined in the first scheme, with the only exception that H_1 is defined as $\{0,1\}^* \rightarrow \mathbb{Z}_p$. The Sign and Verify algorithms are defined as:

- Sign: For a message m, the user ID computes the signature $\sigma = (u, v, W)$ where
  - $u = H_1(m\|ID\|PK_{ID}\|r_1 P\|e(P,P)^{r_2})$ for random numbers $r_1, r_2 \in \mathbb{Z}_p$ which are chosen by user ID.
  - $v = r_1 - ux_{ID} \pmod{p}$, $W = r_2 P - uD_{ID}$.
- Verify: Given a message/signature pair $(m, \sigma = (u, v, W))$ and user ID's public key PK_{ID}, anyone can check whether $u \stackrel{?}{=} H_1(m\|ID\|PK_{ID}\|vP + uPK_{ID}\|e(W,P)e(Q_{ID}, P_{pub})^u)$. If the equality holds, outputs *true*. Otherwise, *false*.

Security Analysis of Scheme II

Theorem 3. *If there is a* $(t, q_{CU}, q_{PPK}, q_{PKR}, q_{SV}, q_{SS})$ *Super Type I adaptively chosen message and chosen identity adversary* A_I *which can submit additional* q_R *queries to random oracles and win the game defined in Section 3.3 with probability* $Succ_{A_I,super}^{cma,cida}$, *then there exists another algorithm* $\mathcal{B}$ *which can solve a random instance of Computational Diffie-Hellman problem in polynomial time with success probability* $Succ_{\mathcal{B},\mathbb{G}_1}^{CDH} \geq \frac{1}{q_{CU}}(1 - \frac{1}{q_{CU}})^{q_{PPK}}Succ_{A_I,super}^{cma,cida}.$

Theorem 4. *If there is a* $(t, q_{CU}, q_{PKR}, q_{SV}, q_{SS})$ *Super Type II adaptively chosen message and chosen identity adversary* A_{II} *which can submit additional* q_R *queries to random oracles and win the game defined in Section 3.4 with probability* $Succ_{A_{II},super}^{cma,cida}$, *then there exists another algorithm* $\mathcal{B}$ *which can solve a random instance of Discrete Logarithm problem in polynomial time with success probability* $Succ_{\mathcal{B},\mathbb{G}_1}^{DL} \geq \frac{1}{q_{CU}}(1 - \frac{1}{q_{CU}})^{q_{SV}}Succ_{A_{II},super}^{cma,cida}.$

Due to page limitation, the proof will be presented in the full version of this paper.

5   Comparison

In this section, we first compare our schemes with other known CLS schemes from the aspect of security level.

Security Levels of Known CLS Schemes

Scheme	Security against $\mathcal{A}_I$	Security against $\mathcal{A}_{II}$
Al-Riyami and Paterson's [2]	insecure against $\mathcal{A}_{I,normal}$[10]	insecure against $\mathcal{A}_{II,M-A}$[1]
Gorantla and Saxena's [9]	insecure against $\mathcal{A}_{I,normal}$ [5]	no formal proof provided
Huang et al.'s [10]		insecure against $\mathcal{A}_{II,M-A}$[1]
Hu et al.'s [11]	super $\mathcal{A}_I$	strong $\mathcal{A}_{II,M-A}$ [1]
Liu-Au-Susilo's[12]	super $\mathcal{A}_I$	insecure against $\mathcal{A}_{II,M-A}$[1]
Li-Chen-Sun [13]	no formal proof provided	insecure against $\mathcal{A}_{II,M-A}$[1]
Yum-Lee's [17]	insecure against $\mathcal{A}_{I,normal}$ [11]	normal $\mathcal{A}_{II}$
Yap-Heng-Goi [18]	insecure against $\mathcal{A}_{I,normal}$ [14,20]	
Zhang et al.'s [19]	super $\mathcal{A}_I$	super $\mathcal{A}_{II}$
Our Scheme I	normal $\mathcal{A}_I$	super $\mathcal{A}_{II}$
Our Scheme II	super $\mathcal{A}_I$	super $\mathcal{A}_{II}$

According to the comparison given in the above table, the only known CLS scheme which can be proved secure against malicious but passive Type II adversary is the generic scheme in [11] (its proof was given in [1]). Most other schemes are insecure under this attack. Except our scheme II, Zhang et al.'s [19] scheme[4] in ACNS 2006 is the only concrete secure scheme with formal security proofs against super adversaries. As we have explained in Section 2.2, the **Public-Key-Replace** oracle defined in [10] is not reasonable, and therefore the security of Huang et al.'s scheme against Type I adversary remains unknown. Similarly, the security of Yap-Heng-Goi's scheme [18] against Type II adversary is also unknown.

We further compare our schemes with Zhang-Wong-Xu-Feng's scheme [19] in detail. The following notations will be used in the comparison.

Notations:	$\|\mathbb{G}_1\|$: bit length of a point in $\mathbb{G}_1$	$\|p\|$: bit length in $\mathbb{Z}_p$
	BP: bilinear pairing	**PA**: point addition in $\mathbb{G}_1$
	$\mathbf{E}_{\mathbb{G}_1}$: exponentiation in $\mathbb{G}_1$	$\mathbf{E}_{\mathbb{G}_2}$: exponentiation in $\mathbb{G}_2$

We omit other operations which are trivial when compared with the above operations. In the comparison, we also assume that $e(P, P)$ and $e(P_{pub}, Q_{\mathsf{ID}})$ can be pre-computed and therefore they are not counted into the operation cost in this table.

Further Comparison with Zhang-Wong-Xu-Feng's scheme[19]

Scheme	Signature Length	Operation Cost	Security
Our Scheme I	$\|\mathbb{G}_1\|$	$2\mathbf{BP}+ \mathbf{E}_{\mathbb{G}_1} + \mathbf{PA}$	Normal $\mathcal{A}_I$ and Super $\mathcal{A}_{II}$
Scheme in [19]	$2\|\mathbb{G}_1\|$	$3\mathbf{BP}+ 3\mathbf{E}_{\mathbb{G}_1} +2\mathbf{PA}$	Super $\mathcal{A}_I$ and $\mathcal{A}_{II}$
Our Scheme II	$\|\mathbb{G}_1\| + 2\|p\|$	$1\mathbf{BP}+ 4\mathbf{E}_{\mathbb{G}_1} + 2\mathbf{E}_{\mathbb{G}_2} +2\mathbf{PA}$	Super $\mathcal{A}_I$ and $\mathcal{A}_{II}$

---

[4] The Adversary models given in [19] are similar to the Strong Type I and II adversary defined in our paper, however, it is claimed in [19] that their scheme is also secure against the Super adversary.

From the above table, one can see that our scheme I enjoys the *shortest* signature length, but the others have a higher security level. The signature length of our scheme II is a little longer than Zhang-Wong-Xu-Feng's scheme [19]. For the operation cost, our scheme II requires 1 bilinear pairing, 4 exponentiations in $\mathbb{G}_1$, 2 exponentiations in $\mathbb{G}_2$ and 2 point additions. Zhang-Wong-Xu-Feng's scheme requires 3 bilinear pairing, 3 exponentiations in $\mathbb{G}_1$ and 2 point additions. Since pairing operations cost much more than other operations, our scheme II has lower operation cost than the scheme in [19].

6   Conclusion

In this paper, we first revisited the security models of certificateless signature schemes and proposed three new types of adversaries. The security of certificateless signatures against these adversaries is formulated. We then proposed two concrete certificateless signature schemes and proved their security in the random oracle model. Our first scheme has the shortest signature length compared to any existing CLS schemes in the literature. The second scheme has lower operation cost but a little longer signature length, compared with another concrete scheme in ACNS 2006 which has the similar security level.

References

1. Au, M.H., Chen, J., Liu, J.K., Mu, Y., Wong, D.S., Yang, G.: Malicious KGC Attacks in Certificateless Cryptography. In: ASIACCS (2007), also available at http://eprint.iacr.org/2006/255
2. Al-Riyami, S.S., Paterson, K.G.: Certificateless Public Key Cryptography. In: Laih, C.-S. (ed.) ASIACRYPT 2003. LNCS, vol. 2894, pp. 452–473. Springer, Heidelberg (2003)
3. Al-Riyami, S.S., Paterson, K.G.: Certificateless Public Key Cryptography. Available online http://eprint.iacr.org/2003/126
4. Boneh, D., Lynn, B., Shacham, H.: Short Signatures from the Weil Pairing. Journal of Cryptology 17, 297–319 (2004)
5. Cao, X., Paterson, K.G., Kou, W.: An Attack on a Certificateless Signature Scheme. In: Cryptology ePrint Archive. Available online http://eprint.iacr.org/2006/367
6. Dent, A.W.: A Survey of Certificateless Encryption Schemes and Security Models. In: Cryptology ePrint Archive. Available online: http://eprint.iacr.org/2006/211
7. Diffie, W., Hellman, M.E.: New Directions in Cryptography. IEEE Transactions on Information Theory 22, 644–654 (1976)
8. Goldwasser, S., Micali, S., Rivest, R.: A Secure Digital Signature Scheme. SIAM Journal on Computing 17, 281–308 (1988)
9. Gorantla, M.C., Saxena, A.: An Efficient Certificateless Signature Scheme. In: Hao, Y., Liu, J., Wang, Y.-P., Cheung, Y.-m., Yin, H., Jiao, L., Ma, J., Jiao, Y.-C. (eds.) CIS 2005. LNCS (LNAI), vol. 3802, pp. 110–116. Springer, Heidelberg (2005)
10. Huang, X., Susilo, W., Mu, Y., Zhang, F.: On the Security of Certificateless Signature Schemes from Asiacrypt 2003. In: Desmedt, Y.G., Wang, H., Mu, Y., Li, Y. (eds.) CANS 2005. LNCS, vol. 3810, pp. 13–25. Springer, Heidelberg (2005)

11. Hu, B.C., Wong, D.S., Zhang, Z., Deng, X.: Key Replacement Attack Against a Generic Construction of Certificateless Signature. In: Batten, L.M., Safavi-Naini, R. (eds.) ACISP 2006. LNCS, vol. 4058, pp. 235–246. Springer, Heidelberg (2006)

12. Liu, J.K., Au, M.H., Susilo, W.: Self-Generated-Certificate Public Key Cryptography and Certificateless Signature/Encryption Scheme in the Standard Model. In: 2007 ACM Symposium on InformAtion, Computer and Communications Security - ASIACCS'07 (2007)

13. Li, X., Chen, K., Sun, L.: Certificateless Signature and Proxy Signature Schemes from Bilinear Pairings. Lithuanian Mathematical Journal 45, 76–83 (2005)

14. Park, Je. H.: An Attack on the Certificateless Signature Scheme from EUC Workshops 2006. In: Cryptology ePrint Archive. Available online:
http://eprint.iacr.org/2006/442

15. Pointcheval, D., Stern, J.: Security Arguments for Digital Signatures and Blind Signatures. Journal of Cryptology 13(3), 361–396 (2000)

16. Shamir, A.: Identity-based Cryptosystems and Signature Schemes. In: Blakely, G.R., Chaum, D. (eds.) CRYPTO 1984. LNCS, vol. 196, pp. 47–53. Springer, Heidelberg (1985)

17. Yum, D.H., Lee, P.J.: Generic Construction of Certificateless Signature. In: Wang, H., Pieprzyk, J., Varadharajan, V. (eds.) ACISP 2004. LNCS, vol. 3108, pp. 200–211. Springer, Heidelberg (2004)

18. Yap, W.-S., Heng, S.-H., Goi, B.-M.: An Efficient Certificateless Signature Scheme. In: Zhou, X., Sokolsky, O., Yan, L., Jung, E.-S., Shao, Z., Mu, Y., Lee, D.C., Kim, D., Jeong, Y.-S., Xu, C.-Z. (eds.) Emerging Directions in Embedded and Ubiquitous Computing. LNCS, vol. 4097, pp. 322–331. Springer, Heidelberg (2006)

19. Zhang, Z., Wong, D.: Certificateless Public-Key Signature: Security Model and Efficient Construction. In: Zhou, J., Yung, M., Bao, F. (eds.) ACNS 2006. LNCS, vol. 3989, pp. 293–308. Springer, Heidelberg (2006)

20. Zhang, Z., Feng, D.: Key Replacement Attack on a Certificateless Signature Scheme. In: Cryptology ePrint Archive. Available online
http://eprint.iacr.org/2006/453

Identity-Committable Signatures and Their Extension to Group-Oriented Ring Signatures*

Cheng-Kang Chu and Wen-Guey Tzeng

Department of Computer Science, National Chiao Tung University,
Hsinchu, Taiwan 30050
{ckchu,wgtzeng}@cs.nctu.edu.tw

Abstract. The identity of "Deep Throat", a pseudonym of the information source in the Watergate scandal, remained mysterious for more than three decades. In 2005, an ex-FBI official claimed that he was the anonymous source. Nevertheless, some are still inconvinced.

In this paper, we introduce a new notion of identity-committable signatures (ICS) to ensure the anonymity of "Deep Throat" inside a group. A member of an organization can sign a message on behalf of himself (regular signature) or the organization (identity-committed signature). In the latter case, the signer's identity is hidden from anyone, and can be opened by himself only. We describe the requirements of ICS and give the formal definition of it. Then we extend the notion of ICS to *group-oriented ring signatures* (GRS) which further allow the signer to hide his identity behind multiple groups. We believe a GRS scheme is more efficient and practical than a ring signature scheme for leaking secrets. Finally, we provide concrete constructions of ICS and GRS with *information-theoretic* anonymity, that is, the identity of the signer is fully-protected.

Keywords: group signatures, ring signatures, anonymous signatures.

1 Introduction

In the early of 1970s, Woodward and Bernstein, two reporters of Washington Post, broke many stories that eventually led to the resignation of President Richard M. Nixon. This is the famous Watergate scandal in the history of the United States. The information source, assumed the pseudonym "Deep Throat", remained confidential for more than three decades. Woodward and Bernstein guaranteed that they would not reveal Deep Throat's identity unless he is willing to or he died. It is not till 2005 that, Felt, the ex-FBI No. 2, claimed that he was the anonymous source for Watergate affairs.

From this story, we learn some characteristics of being a "Deep Throat":

- **Full-Anonymity.** Keeping identity anonymous is the most important thing for Deep Throat. Even the president can not trace the information source. Felt

---

* Research supported in part by National Science Council grant 95-2221-E-009-031, Taiwan and Taiwan Information Security Center at NCTU (TWISC@NCTU).

J. Pieprzyk, H. Ghodosi, and E. Dawson (Eds.): ACISP 2007, LNCS 4586, pp. 323–337, 2007.
© Springer-Verlag Berlin Heidelberg 2007

is fortunate that the reporters are dependable. If they were threatened or bribed, the identity of Deep Throat may be exposed much early.

– **Group Authenticity.** Although we can not learn the identity of Deep Throat, we should be able to verify that the information comes from a specific organization for these inside stories. The two reporters described above knew that the information from Felt is trustworthy because Felt was working in FBI at that time.

– **Self-Identifiability.** After the event, in order to benefit from the identity or witness in the court, Deep Throat should be able to prove that he was the information source. In fact, although the Washington Post confirmed that Felt was Deep Throat, some people still question that.

Based on these characteristics, we try to construct a signature scheme in the following scenario.

> David, an employee of a government organization, owns a personal signing key issued by the organization. He uses this key to sign official documents. One day, he discovers a startling scandal inside the organization. He decides to be a "Deep Throat", i.e. anonymously expose it to people. So he uses his signing key to generate a signature on a report of the scandal on behalf of the organization rather than his personal identity, and sends it to a journalist. The journalist first verifies that the information indeed comes from someone inside the organization, and then publishes it. No one, including the chief of the organization who owns the master secret key, can determine the identity of Deep Throat. After that, David continues his work in that organization as usual. Someday, if David wishes to, he can exhibit a witness identifying himself as Deep Throat.

Consider the existent signature schemes which may achieve this objective. For group signatures, there is a group manager with identifiability. David will be afraid to expose the scandal. For ring signatures, David needs to collect all public keys (or identities) of the staff in the organization to form the ring. The computation and communication costs are too large to be practical. Besides, in some secret agency, the identities of its staff are classified. David may not be able to get the public keys of other secret agents.

In this paper, we propose a new notion of identity-committable signatures (ICS) which fits for the above scenario. A member of an organization can sign a message on behalf of himself (regular signature) or the organization (identity-committed signature). In the latter case, the signer's identity is hidden from anyone, and can be opened by himself only. We describe the requirements of ICS and give the formal definition of it. Then we extend the notion of ICS to *group-oriented ring signatures* (GRS) which further allow the signer to hide his identity behind multiple groups. Deep Throat who works in FBI can sign secrets on behalf of numerous related organizations such as FBI, CIA, NSA, etc. The size of the signature is only linear to the number of included organizations. Since the signer can include the whole members of a group at a time, a GRS scheme is more efficient and practical than general ring signature schemes.

Related Works. In fact, ICS are intermediate between group signatures and ring signatures. We consider some concrete constructions of these two signature schemes:

- Group signatures: The notion of group signatures was introduced by Chaum and Van Heyst [17]. Since then, many other schemes were proposed [18, 15, 12, 13, 3, 6, 4, 9, 25, 11]. Some works mentioned separability [26, 14], where the identifying ability can be designated to a revocation manager. It is possible to use such separable group signature to construct ICS, but we try to find more direct and more efficient solutions. Some group signature schemes with traceability [24, 31] give the signer self-identifiability, but there is still a group manager identifying the signer.
- Ring signatures: Rivest, Shamir, and Tauman [33, 34] first introduced the notion of ring signatures. Subsequently, many constructions were proposed under various settings of signing keys [36, 1, 21, 20, 8]. Some works also mentioned the self-identifiability [33, 29]. But in their constructions, this property either needs to store witnesses with size linear to the number of non-signers in the ring, or only guarantees the computational anonymity. Linkable ring signatures [35, 27, 28] stress the ability of checking whether two ring signatures are signed by the same signer. There are some ID-based constructions [36, 22, 19, 30, 5] and constant-size constructions [20, 30, 5]. All these schemes need a private key generator (PKG) with a master secret. In fact, we can regard signers under the same PKG as the members of a group. So signing on behalf of the whole group is a better idea than signing on behalf of a list of group members. Even for constant-size schemes, the computation cost of the signing and verifying procedures are linear to the number of ring members.

2 Definition of ICS

In this section we give the formal definition of identity-committable signatures.

2.1 Components

An identity-committable signature scheme consists of the following algorithms.

- **Setup**(1^λ): For the security parameter in unary, 1^λ, the algorithm chooses a master secret key K and outputs the corresponding public parameter μ.
- **Extract**(μ, ID, K): Output the private key SK for the identity ID.
- **Sign**(μ, m, SK): Output the regular signature σ on message m.
- **Verify**(μ, ID, m, σ): If σ is signed by ID's private key on m, output 'accept'; otherwise, output 'reject'.
- **IC-Sign**(μ, m, SK): Output an identity-committed signature σ_{IC} on message m and a witness ω for identifying.
- **IC-Verify**(μ, m, σ_{IC}): If σ_{IC} is signed by a private key of the organization on m, output 'accept'; otherwise output 'reject'.

– **Identify**$(\mu, ID, \omega, \sigma_{IC})$: If σ_{IC} is a valid identity-committed signature and ω opens σ_{IC} to ID, output 'valid'; otherwise output 'invalid'.

Let PKG be the private key generator of an organization. PKG first runs **Setup**, and publishes the public parameters. Then it issues the private key for each organization member by performing **Extract**. Each member uses **Sign** and **Verify** algorithms for regular signing and verification. When a member tries to anonymously sign a message, he performs **IC-Sign** to get the identity-committed signature and a witness. He outputs the signature to the verifier such that the verifier can verify it via the **IC-Verify** algorithm. The signer holds the witness secretly for later revealing his identity if he wants. Someday, he can execute **Identify** by using the witness to prove that he is the original signer.

2.2   Security Definition

Bellare et al. [7] characterize the fundamental properties of group signatures in terms of two crucial security requirements. But the two requirements are not sufficient for ICS. Informally speaking, an identity-committable signature scheme should satisfy the following properties.

1. Completeness: With the private key issued by the PKG of an organization, one can sign messages on behalf of himself or the organization. In the latter case, he can prove that he is the original signer.
2. Unforgeability: The scheme should be secure against existential forgery of regular signature under adaptively chosen message and identity attack.
3. ICS-Unforgeability: For someone outside the organization, the scheme should be secure against existential forgery of identity-committed signature under adaptively chosen message attack.
4. ICS-Anonymity: No one but the signer himself can identify the signer of an identity-committed signature.
5. ICS-Binding: The identity-committed signature can only be opened to the original signer.

Formally, we have the following definition for an identity-committable signature scheme.

Definition 1 (Identity-Committable Signatures). *Define the following oracles which can be queried adaptively by any probabilistic polynomial-time algorithm (PPTA) $\mathcal{A}$ against the challenger $\mathcal{C}$.*

– *$Extract^{\mathcal{A}}(ID)$: $\mathcal{C}$ returns the private key for identity ID.*
– *$Sign^{\mathcal{A}}(ID, m)$: $\mathcal{C}$ returns a regular signature of identity ID on message m.*
– *$IC\text{-}Sign^{\mathcal{A}}(ID, m)$: $\mathcal{C}$ returns an identity-committed signature on m along with a witness which identifies ID as the signer.*

An identity-committable signature scheme is secure if it meets the following requirements.

– **Completeness.** *For any* m *and* ID, *it holds that*

$$\Pr[\textbf{\textit{Verify}}(\mu, ID, m, \sigma) = accept : \sigma \leftarrow \textbf{\textit{Sign}}(\mu, m, SK);$$
$$SK \leftarrow \textbf{\textit{Extract}}(\mu, ID, K); (\mu, K) \leftarrow \textbf{\textit{Setup}}(1^\lambda)] = 1$$

and

$$\Pr[\textbf{\textit{IC-Verify}}(\mu, m, \sigma_{IC}) = accept, \textbf{\textit{Identify}}(\mu, ID, \omega, \sigma_{IC}) = valid :$$
$$(\sigma_{IC}, \omega) \leftarrow \textbf{\textit{IC-Sign}}(\mu, m, SK); SK \leftarrow \textbf{\textit{Extract}}(\mu, ID, K);$$
$$(\mu, K) \leftarrow \textbf{\textit{Setup}}(1^\lambda)] = 1.$$

– **Unforgeability.** *Given the public parameters and access of all oracles, no PPTA $\mathcal{A}$ can output a valid regular signature* (ID, m, σ) *with non-negligible probability if* $Extract^{\mathcal{A}}(ID)$ *and* $Sign^{\mathcal{A}}(ID, m)$ *are never queried.*
– **ICS-Unforgeability.** *Given the public parameters and access of Sign and IC-Sign oracles, no PPTA $\mathcal{A}$ can output a valid identity-committed signature* (m, σ_{IC}) *with non-negligible probability if* $Sign^{\mathcal{A}}(ID^*, m)$ *and IC-Sign$^{\mathcal{A}}(ID^*, m)$ are never queried for any* ID^*.
– **ICS-Anonymity.** *Given the public parameters and access of all oracles, no PPTA $\mathcal{A}$ has a non-negligible advantage against a challenger $\mathcal{C}$ in the following game:*
  1. *$\mathcal{A}$ chooses two identities ID_0, ID_1 and a message m, and sends them to $\mathcal{C}$.*
  2. *$\mathcal{C}$ chooses $b \in_R \{0, 1\}$, and computes an identity-committed signature σ_{IC} on m by ID_b's private key. Then $\mathcal{C}$ sends σ_{IC} to $\mathcal{A}$.*
  3. *$\mathcal{A}$ outputs the guess b'. If $b' = b$, $\mathcal{A}$ wins the game.*
– **ICS-Binding.** *Given the public parameters and access of all oracles, no PPTA $\mathcal{A}$ can output a valid identity-committed signature (m, σ_{IC}) and two witnesses (ID, ω) and (ID', ω') with non-negligible probability.*

3   Definition of GRS

In this section we give the formal definition of group-oriented ring signatures.

3.1   Components

A group-oriented ring signature scheme consists of the following algorithms.

– **Setup**(1^λ): For the security parameter 1^λ, the algorithm chooses a master secret key K and outputs the corresponding public parameter μ.
– **Extract**(μ, ID, K): Output the private key SK for the identity ID.
– **GR-Sign**(L, m, SK): For the list L of public parameters of all groups, output a group-oriented ring signature σ_{GR} on message m.
– **GR-Verify**(L, m, σ_{GR}): If σ_{GR} is signed by a private key of a group in the list L, output 'accept'; otherwise output 'reject'.

Each PKG of groups first performs **Setup**, and publish the public parameters. It also issues the private key for each group member by performing **Extract**. When a signer wants to sign messages on behalf of some groups, he takes the public parameters of these groups to form the list L. Then the signer executes **GR-Sign** to generate the group-oriented ring signature. The verifier also takes the list L, and executes **GR-Verify** to confirm that σ_{GR} is signed by a member of one group in L.

3.2   Security Definition

We have the following definition for a group-oriented ring signature scheme.

Definition 2 (Group-Oriented Ring Signatures). *Define the following oracles which can be queried adaptively by any PPTA $\mathcal{A}$ against the challenger $\mathcal{C}$ with a list L of public parameters.*

- *$Extract^{\mathcal{A}}(i, ID)$: $\mathcal{C}$ returns the private key for identity ID of the i-th group in L.*
- *$GR\text{-}Sign^{\mathcal{A}}(i, L', ID, m)$: $\mathcal{C}$ returns a group-oriented ring signature, signed by identity ID of the i-th group in L, on m for the list L'. Note that L' must contain the i-th parameter of L, but the other parameters of L' need not be in the list L.*

A group-oriented ring signature scheme is secure if it meets the following requirements.

- **Completeness.** *For any m, ID and L, it holds that*

$$\Pr[\textbf{GR-Verify}(L, m, \sigma_{GR}) = accept : \sigma_{GR} \leftarrow \textbf{GR-Sign}(L, m, SK);$$
$$SK \leftarrow \textbf{Extract}(\mu, ID, K); (\mu, K) \leftarrow \textbf{Setup}(1^{\lambda}); \mu \in L] = 1.$$

- **Unforgeability.** *Given a list of public parameters $L = (\mu_1, \ldots, \mu_l)$ and access of all oracles, let C be the set of $\mu_i \in L$ where $Extract^{\mathcal{A}}(i, ID^*)$ is queried for any ID^*. No PPTA $\mathcal{A}$ can output a valid group-oriented ring signature (L^*, m, σ_{GR}) with non-negligible probability if $L^* \subseteq L \backslash C$ and $GR\text{-}Sign^{\mathcal{A}}(i^*, L^*, ID^*, m)$ is never queried for any i^* and ID^*.*
- **Anonymity.** *Given a list of public parameters $L = (\mu_1, \ldots, \mu_l)$ and access of all oracles, no PPTA $\mathcal{A}$ has a non-negligible advantage against a challenger $\mathcal{C}$ in the following game:*
  1. *$\mathcal{A}$ chooses two identities $(i_0, ID_0), (i_1, ID_1)$, a list L^* and a message m, where $\mu_{i_0}, \mu_{i_1} \in L^*$, and sends them to $\mathcal{C}$.*
  2. *$\mathcal{C}$ chooses $b \in_R \{0, 1\}$, and computes a group-oriented ring signature σ_{GR} on m for L^* by the private key of ID_b of the i_b-th group in L. Then $\mathcal{C}$ sends σ_{GR} to $\mathcal{A}$.*
  3. *$\mathcal{A}$ outputs the guess b'. If $b' = b$, $\mathcal{A}$ wins the game.*

4   Concrete Constructions

In this section we first think of a generic construction of ICS and then propose specific constructions of ICS and GRS.

4.1   Generic ICS Construction

We first provide a generic ICS scheme from an ID-based signature scheme $\Sigma = (\mathsf{Setup}_\Sigma, \mathsf{Extract}_\Sigma, \mathsf{Sign}_\Sigma, \mathsf{Verify}_\Sigma)$ and a commitment scheme $\Gamma = (\mathsf{Commit}_\Gamma, \mathsf{Reveal}_\Gamma)$. The organization designates a special ID_G as the group identity, and issues the corresponding private key SK_G along with personal private keys to all members. When a member wants to generate an identity-committed signature, he uses the key SK_G to sign the message and commits the regular signature on that message. In the **Identify** process, the signer just reveals the regular signature from the commitment. The detail is given as follows.

- **Setup**(1^λ): Perform $\mathsf{Setup}_\Sigma(1^\lambda)$ to get the public parameters μ and master secret key K. Define a group identity ID_G which differs from all members. Output (μ, ID_G, K).
- **Extract**(μ, ID, K): Perform $\mathsf{Extract}_\Sigma(\mu, ID_G, K)$ and $\mathsf{Extract}_\Sigma(\mu, ID, K)$ to get SK_G and SK_{ID}, respectively. Output (SK_G, SK_{ID}) as the private key for identity ID.
- **Sign**(μ, m, SK_{ID}): Output the regular signature $\sigma = \mathsf{Sign}_\Sigma(\mu, m, SK_{ID})$.
- **Verify**(μ, ID, m, σ): Output the result of $\mathsf{Verify}_\Sigma(\mu, ID, m, \sigma)$.
- **IC-Sign**(μ, m, SK_G, SK_{ID}): Perform $\mathsf{Commit}_\Gamma(\sigma)$ to get a committed value γ and a witness ω, where $\sigma = \mathsf{Sign}_\Sigma(\mu, m, SK_{ID})$. Then compute $\sigma_G = \mathsf{Sign}_\Sigma(\mu, m\|\gamma, SK_G)$. Output the identity-committed signature $\sigma_{IC} = (\sigma_G, \gamma)$ and the witness ω.
- **IC-Verify**(μ, m, σ_{IC}): Parse the identity-committed signature σ_{IC} as (σ_G, γ). Output the result of $\mathsf{Verify}_\Sigma(\mu, ID_G, m\|\gamma, \sigma_G)$.
- **Identify**($\mu, ID, \omega, \sigma_{IC}$): If $\sigma_{IC} = (\sigma_G, \gamma)$ is a valid identity-committed signature on m, then output the result of $\mathsf{Verify}_\Sigma(\mu, ID, m, \sigma)$, where $\sigma = \mathsf{Reveal}_\Gamma(\gamma, \omega)$.

The security of this scheme directly comes from the security of Σ and Γ. Note that if Γ has *perfect hiding* property, the scheme is information-theoretically anonymous.

   Although the generic scheme meets the security requirements of ICS, it is weak in some scenario while all group members use the same private key to generate identity-committed signatures. For example, if Alice signs a personal message in the private communication with Bob, Bob may use Alice's signature to generate an identity-committed signature, and then frame Alice as Deep Throat. Moreover, the generic scheme loses some additional properties such as *chosen-linkability* and *private-communicability* introduced later.

4.2   The ICS Scheme Based on Pairings

Let $\mathbb{G}$ and $\mathbb{G}_1$ be two cyclic groups of prime order p. We write $\mathbb{G}$ additively and $\mathbb{G}_1$ multiplicatively. Let $e : \mathbb{G} \times \mathbb{G} \rightarrow \mathbb{G}_1$ is a map with the following properties:

- Bilinear: for all $P, Q \in \mathbb{G}$ and $a, b \in \mathbb{Z}$, $e(aP, bQ) = e(P, Q)^{ab}$.
- Non-degenerate: for some $P \in \mathbb{G}$, $e(P, P) \neq 1$.

We say that $\mathbb{G}$ is a bilinear group [23] if the group operations in $\mathbb{G}$ and $\mathbb{G}_1$, and the bilinear map are efficiently computable.

Our scheme needs three following complexity assumptions. The first two are the discrete logarithm problem and the computational Diffie-Hellman problem in bilinear group $\mathbb{G}$. The third one is the Diffie-Hellman problem with chosen bases.

Discrete Logarithm Problem (DLP). The discrete logarithm problem in an (additive) cyclic group $\mathbb{G}$ is, given $P, aP \in \mathbb{G}$, to output $a \in \mathbb{Z}_p$. We say that a PPTA algorithm $\mathcal{A}$ has advantage ϵ in solving DLP in $\mathbb{G}$ if

$$\Pr[\mathcal{A}(P, aP) = a : P, aP \in_R \mathbb{G}] \geq \epsilon.$$

The DL assumption in $\mathbb{G}$ holds if no PPTA $\mathcal{A}$ has non-negligible advantage ϵ in solving DL problem in $\mathbb{G}$.

Computational Diffie-Hellman Problem (CDHP). The computational Diffie-Hellman problem in an (additive) cyclic group $\mathbb{G}$ is, given $P, aP, bP \in \mathbb{G}$, to output $abP \in \mathbb{G}$. We say that a PPTA algorithm $\mathcal{A}$ has advantage ϵ in solving CDHP in $\mathbb{G}$ if

$$\Pr[\mathcal{A}(P, aP, bP) = abP : P, aP, bP \in_R \mathbb{G}] \geq \epsilon.$$

The CDH assumption in $\mathbb{G}$ holds if no PPTA $\mathcal{A}$ has non-negligible advantage ϵ in solving CDH problem in $\mathbb{G}$.

Chosen-Base CDH Problem (CB-CDHP). The chosen-base CDH problem in an (additive) cyclic group $\mathbb{G}$ is, given $P, aP, bP \in \mathbb{G}$, to output $Q, abQ \in \mathbb{G} \backslash \{e_{\mathbb{G}}\}$, where $e_{\mathbb{G}}$ is the identity of $\mathbb{G}$. We say that a PPTA algorithm $\mathcal{A}$ has advantage ϵ in solving CB-CDHP in $\mathbb{G}$ if

$$\Pr[\mathcal{A}(P, aP, bP) = (Q, abQ), Q \in \mathbb{G} \backslash \{e_{\mathbb{G}}\} : P, aP, bP \in_R \mathbb{G}] \geq \epsilon.$$

The CB-CDH assumption in $\mathbb{G}$ holds if no PPTA $\mathcal{A}$ has non-negligible advantage ϵ in solving CB-CDH problem in $\mathbb{G}$.

The ICS Scheme. The algorithms of our construction are described as follows. The construction is based on the ID-based signature scheme proposed by Cha and Cheon [16], which can be proved secure in the random oracle model.

- **Setup**(1^λ): On input security parameter 1^λ, randomly choose two groups $\mathbb{G}$ and $\mathbb{G}_1$, a bilinear map e and a generator P defined above. Choose two random values $x, y \in \mathbb{Z}_p$, compute

$$P_X = xP \qquad \text{and} \qquad P_Y = yP.$$

Choose two cryptographically secure hash functions $H_1 : \{0,1\}^* \to \mathbb{G}$ and $H_2 : \{0,1\}^* \times \mathbb{G} \to \mathbb{Z}_p$. Output (x, y) as the master secret key and $\mu = (\mathbb{G}, \mathbb{G}_1, e, P, P_X, P_Y, H_1, H_2)$ as the public parameters.

- **Extract**(μ, ID, x, y): Let $Q_{ID} = H_1(ID)$, compute

$$Q'_{ID} = xQ_{ID} \quad \text{and} \quad S_{ID} = xyQ_{ID}.$$

Output (Q'_{ID}, S_{ID}) as the private key for identity ID.

- **Sign**$(\mu, m, Q'_{ID}, S_{ID})$: Compute

$$U = rQ'_{ID} \quad \text{and} \quad V = (r + h)S_{ID},$$

where $r \in_R \mathbb{Z}_p$ and $h = H_2(m, U)$. Output the regular signature $\sigma = (Q'_{ID}, U, V)$.

- **Verify**(μ, ID, m, σ): Parse the regular signature σ as (Q'_{ID}, U, V). Compute $Q_{ID} = H_1(ID)$ and $h = H_2(m, U)$. Check that

$$e(Q_{ID}, P_X) \stackrel{?}{=} e(Q'_{ID}, P) \quad \text{and} \quad e(U, P_Y) \stackrel{?}{=} e(V, P)e(Q'_{ID}, -P_Y)^h.$$

If both equations hold, output 'accept'; otherwise output 'reject'.

- **IC-Sign**$(\mu, m, Q'_{ID}, S_{ID})$: Randomly choose a value $w \in \mathbb{Z}_p^*\backslash\{1\}$, compute

$$Q = wQ_{ID}, \quad Q' = wQ'_{ID}, \quad U = rQ' \quad \text{and} \quad V = (r + h)S,$$

where $S = wS_{ID}, r \in_R \mathbb{Z}_p$ and $h = H_2(m, U)$. Output the identity-committed signature $\sigma_{IC} = (Q, Q', U, V)$ and the witness w.

- **IC-Verify**(μ, m, σ_{IC}): Parse the identity-committed signature σ_{IC} as (Q, Q', U, V). Compute $h = H_2(m, U)$. Check that

$$e(Q, P_X) \stackrel{?}{=} e(Q', P) \quad \text{and} \quad e(U, P_Y) \stackrel{?}{=} e(V, P)e(Q', -P_Y)^h.$$

If both equations hold, output 'accept'; otherwise output 'reject'.

- **Identify**$(\mu, ID, w, \sigma_{IC})$: Compute $Q_{ID} = H_1(ID)$. If $\sigma_{IC} = (Q, Q', U, V)$ is a valid identity-committed signature and $Q_{ID} = w^{-1}Q$, output 'valid'; otherwise output 'invalid'.

Note that we cannot verify whether $w = 1$ in the **IC-Verify** algorithm. One may directly use a standard signature for some ID as an identity-committed signature. However, this is reasonable because ICS is designed for exposing messages. If someone already signed a message m, then the identity-committed signature for the same m is meaningless.

The security argument of this construction can be found in Appendix A.

Additional Properties. In addition to the properties of ICS we defined, our construction provides two characteristics.

- Chosen-Linkability. The signer can decide the linkability of his identity-committed signatures. If a signer wants to show that some identity-committed signatures are signed by him, he can use the same witness w to mask his identity. The verifier knows that the signatures with the same Q come from the same signer.

– Private-Communicability. One can privately communicate with the signer of an identity-committed signature without revealing the signer's identity. For an identity-committed signature (Q, Q', U, V), one can treat Q as the public key of the signer, and encrypt messages using Boneh and Franklin's IBE scheme [10] (let Q be the hashed value of H_1). The ciphertext can be posted onto some bulletin board, and only the original signer[1] can decrypt the message.

4.3   Group-Oriented Ring Signatures

Abe et al. [1] proposed a ring signature scheme that allows mixed use of different flavors of keys at the same time. All participants can choose their keys with different parameter domains. By applying their construction to our ICS scheme, we get an efficient GRS scheme. A signer can sign messages on behalf of the organization which he belongs to, and then take the public parameters of other organizations to form a ring signature. These groups have their own public parameters, respectively.

First, we slightly modify **IC-Sign** and **IC-Verify** of our ICS scheme to be a three-move type signature scheme.

– **IC-Sign'**$(\mu, m, Q'_{ID}, S_{ID})$: Randomly choose a value $w \in \mathbb{Z}_p^* \backslash \{1\}$, compute

$$Q = wQ_{ID}, \quad Q' = wQ'_{ID}, \quad U = rQ' \quad \text{and} \quad V = (r + h)S,$$

where $S = wS_{ID}$, $r \in_R \mathbb{Z}_p$ and $h = H'_2(m, e(U, P_Y))$. Output the identity-committed signature $\sigma_{IC} = (Q, Q', h, V)$ and the witness w.

– **IC-Verify'**(μ, m, σ_{IC}): Parse the identity-committed signature σ_{IC} as (Q, Q', h, V). Compute $U' = e(V, P)e(Q', -P_Y)^h$. Check that

$$e(Q, P_X) \stackrel{?}{=} e(Q', P) \quad \text{and} \quad h \stackrel{?}{=} H'_2(m, U').$$

If both equations hold, output 'accept'; otherwise output 'reject'.

The security proof is similar to the proof of the original scheme. We omit it here.

Let $L = \{\mu^{(i)} = (\mathbb{G}^{(i)}, \mathbb{G}_1^{(i)}, e^{(i)}, P^{(i)}, P_X^{(i)}, P_Y^{(i)}, H_1^{(i)}, H_2^{(i)}) | 1 \le i \le n\}$ be the list of public parameters of the n groups that the signer wants to form the ring. Assume that the signer belongs to the s-th group. The GRS scheme is as follows.

– **Setup** and **Extract:** The same as the algorithms of the ICS scheme.
– **GR-Sign**(L, m, Q'_{ID}, S_{ID})
  • For $i = s$: Perform **IC-Sign'**$(\mu^{(s)}, m, Q'_{ID}, S_{ID})$ to get the identity-committed signature $(Q^{(s)}, Q'^{(s)}, h^{(s)}, V^{(s)})$ and set

$$U'^{(s)} = e^{(s)}(V^{(s)}, P^{(s)})e^{(s)}(Q'^{(s)}, -P_Y^{(s)})^{h^{(s)}}.$$

---

[1] The PKG also can decrypt the message, but we can use the certificateless encryption scheme [2] to eliminate the trust of PKG.

- For $i = s+1, \ldots, n, 1, \ldots, s-1$: Randomly choose $z^{(i)} \in \mathbb{Z}$ and $V^{(i)} \in \mathbb{G}^{(i)}$. Compute

$$Q^{(i)} = z^{(i)} P^{(i)}, \quad Q'^{(i)} = z^{(i)} P_X^{(i)}, \quad \text{and} \quad h^{(i)} = H_2^{(i)}(L, m, U'^{(i-1)})$$

and set $U'^{(i)} = e^{(i)}(V^{(i)}, P^{(i)})e^{(i)}(Q'^{(i)}, -P_Y^{(i)})^{h^{(i)}}$.
Output $\sigma_{GR} = (h^{(1)}, (Q^{(1)}, Q'^{(1)}, V^{(1)}), \ldots, (Q^{(n)}, Q'^{(n)}, V^{(n)}))$.
- **GR-Verify**(L, m, σ_{GR})
  For $i = 1, \ldots, n$, compute

$$U'^{(i)} = e^{(i)}(V^{(i)}, P^{(i)})e^{(i)}(Q'^{(i)}, -P_Y^{(i)})^{h^{(i)}},$$

where $h^{(i)} = H_2^{(i)}(L, m, U'^{(i-1)})$ if $i \neq 1$. Check that

$$e^{(i)}(Q^{(i)}, P_X^{(i)}) \stackrel{?}{=} e^{(i)}(Q'^{(i)}, P^{(i)}) \quad \text{and} \quad h^{(1)} \stackrel{?}{=} H_2'^{(1)}(m, U'^{(n)}).$$

If both equations hold, output 'accept'; otherwise output 'reject'.

Certainly, the signer can also add some single persons to the list of the ring. By the generic construction of [1], these individual public keys can be "three-move type" or "trapdoor-one-way type". Therefore, this extension improves the efficiency of ring signatures without loss of generality.

The security proofs of this construction is based on the proofs of the ICS scheme. The detail will be provided in the full version of this work.

5   Conclusions

In this paper we introduce the new notion of identity-committable signatures that allow the signer to "commit" his identity on the signature generated on behalf of the signer's group. Later, the signer can open the identity and prove that he is the original signer. Furthermore, we also introduce the extension of ICS, group-oriented ring signatures, which can be regarded as a very efficient and practical ring signature scheme. We give the definitions of ICS and GRS schemes. Finally, we provide the implementations providing unconditional anonymity, chosen-linkability and private-communicability.

References

1. Abe, M., Ohkubo, M., Suzuki, K.: 1-out-of-n signatures from a variety of keys. In: Zheng, Y. (ed.) ASIACRYPT 2002. LNCS, vol. 2501, pp. 415–432. Springer, Heidelberg (2002)
2. Al-Riyami, S.S., Paterson, K.G.: Certificateless public key cryptography. In: Laih, C.-S. (ed.) ASIACRYPT 2003. LNCS, vol. 2894, pp. 452–473. Springer, Heidelberg (2003)
3. Ateniese, G., Camenisch, J., Joye, M., Tsudik, G.: A practical and provably secure coalition-resistant group signature scheme. In: Bellare, M. (ed.) CRYPTO 2000. LNCS, vol. 1880, pp. 255–270. Springer, Heidelberg (2000)

4. Ateniese, G., de Medeiros, B.: Efficient group signatures without trapdoors. In: Laih, C.-S. (ed.) ASIACRYPT 2003. LNCS, vol. 2894, pp. 246–268. Springer, Heidelberg (2003)

5. Au, M.H., Liu, J.K., Yuen, Y.H., Wong, D.S.: Id-based ring signature scheme secure in the standard model. Cryptology ePrint Archive, Report 2006/205 (2006)

6. Baudron, O., Stern, J.: Non-interactive private auctions. In: Syverson, P.F. (ed.) FC 2001. LNCS, vol. 2339, pp. 364–378. Springer, Heidelberg (2002)

7. Bellare, M., Micciancio, D., Warinschi, B.: Foundations of group signatures: Formal definitions, simplified requirements, and a construction based on general assumptions. In: Biham, E. (ed.) Advances in Cryptology – EUROCRPYT 2003. LNCS, vol. 2656, pp. 614–629. Springer, Heidelberg (2003)

8. Bender, A., Katz, J., Morselli, R.: Ring signatures: Stronger definitions, and constructions without random oracles. In: Halevi, S., Rabin, T. (eds.) TCC 2006. LNCS, vol. 3876, pp. 60–79. Springer, Heidelberg (2006)

9. Boneh, D., Boyen, X., Shacham, H.: Short group signatures. In: Franklin, M. (ed.) CRYPTO 2004. LNCS, vol. 3152, pp. 41–55. Springer, Heidelberg (2004)

10. Boneh, D., Franklin, M.K.: Identity-based encryption from the weil pairing. In: Kilian, J. (ed.) CRYPTO 2001. LNCS, vol. 2139, pp. 213–229. Springer, Heidelberg (2001)

11. Boyen, X., Waters, B.: Compact group signatures without random oracles. In: Vaudenay, S. (ed.) EUROCRYPT 2006. LNCS, vol. 4004, pp. 427–444. Springer, Heidelberg (2006)

12. Camenisch, J.: Efficient and generalized group signatures. In: Fumy, W. (ed.) EUROCRYPT 1997. LNCS, vol. 1233, pp. 465–479. Springer, Heidelberg (1997)

13. Camenisch, J., Michels, M.: A group signature scheme with improved efficiency. In: Ohta, K., Pei, D. (eds.) ASIACRYPT 1998. LNCS, vol. 1514, pp. 160–174. Springer, Heidelberg (1998)

14. Camenisch, J., Michels, M.: Separability and efficiency for generic group signature schemes. In: Wiener, M.J. (ed.) CRYPTO 1999. LNCS, vol. 1666, pp. 413–430. Springer, Heidelberg (1999)

15. Camenisch, J., Stadler, M.: Proof systems for general statements about discrete logarithms. Technical Report 260, Institute for Theoretical Computer Science, ETH Zurich (March 1997)

16. Cha, J.C., Cheon, J.H.: An identity-based signature from gap diffie-hellman groups. In: Desmedt, Y.G. (ed.) PKC 2003. LNCS, vol. 2567, pp. 18–30. Springer, Heidelberg (2002)

17. Chaum, D., van Heyst, E.: Group signatures. In: Davies, D.W. (ed.) EUROCRYPT 1991. LNCS, vol. 547, pp. 257–265. Springer, Heidelberg (1991)

18. Chen, L., Pedersen, T.P.: New group signature schemes. In: De Santis, A. (ed.) EUROCRYPT 1994. LNCS, vol. 950, pp. 171–181. Springer, Heidelberg (1995)

19. Chow, S.S.M., Yiu, S.-M., Hui, L.C.K.: Efficient identity based ring signature. In: Ioannidis, J., Keromytis, A.D., Yung, M. (eds.) ACNS 2005. LNCS, vol. 3531, pp. 499–512. Springer, Heidelberg (2005)

20. Dodis, Y., Kiayias, A., Nicolosi, A., Shoup, V.: Anonymous identification in ad hoc groups. In: Cachin, C., Camenisch, J.L. (eds.) EUROCRYPT 2004. LNCS, vol. 3027, pp. 609–626. Springer, Heidelberg (2004)

21. Herranz, J., Sáez, G.: Forking lemmas for ring signature schemes. In: Johansson, T., Maitra, S. (eds.) INDOCRYPT 2003. LNCS, vol. 2904, pp. 266–279. Springer, Heidelberg (2003)

22. Herranz, J., Sáez, G.: New identity-based ring signature schemes. In: Lopez, J., Qing, S., Okamoto, E. (eds.) ICICS 2004. LNCS, vol. 3269, pp. 27–39. Springer, Heidelberg (2004)
23. Joux, A.: A one round protocol for tripartite diffie-hellman. Journal of Cryptology 17(4), 263–276 (2004)
24. Kiayias, A., Tsiounis, Y., Yung, M.: Traceable signatures. In: Cachin, C., Camenisch, J.L. (eds.) EUROCRYPT 2004. LNCS, vol. 3027, pp. 571–589. Springer, Heidelberg (2004)
25. Kiayias, A., Yung, M.: Group signatures with efficient concurrent join. In: Cramer, R.J.F. (ed.) EUROCRYPT 2005. LNCS, vol. 3494, pp. 198–214. Springer, Heidelberg (2005)
26. Kilian, J., Petrank, E.: Identity escrow. In: Krawczyk, H. (ed.) CRYPTO 1998. LNCS, vol. 1462, pp. 169–185. Springer, Heidelberg (1998)
27. Liu, J.K., Wei, V.K., Wong, D.S.: Linkable spontaneous anonymous group signature for ad hoc groups. In: Wang, H., Pieprzyk, J., Varadharajan, V. (eds.) ACISP 2004. LNCS, vol. 3108, pp. 325–335. Springer, Heidelberg (2004)
28. Liu, J.K., Wong, D.S.: Linkable ring signatures: Security models and new schemes. In: Gervasi, O., Gavrilova, M., Kumar, V., Laganà, A., Lee, H.P., Mun, Y., Taniar, D., Tan, C.J.K. (eds.) Computational Science and Its Applications – ICCSA 2005. LNCS, vol. 3481, pp. 614–623. Springer, Heidelberg (2005)
29. Lv, J., Wang, X.: Verifiable ring signature. In: Proceedings of The 3rd International Workshop on Cryptology and Network Security (CANS '03, in conjunction with DMS '03), pp. 663–667 (2003)
30. Nguyen, L.: Accumulators from bilinear pairings and applications. In: Menezes, A.J. (ed.) CT-RSA 2005. LNCS, vol. 3376, pp. 275–292. Springer, Heidelberg (2005)
31. Nguyen, L., Safavi-Naini, R.: Efficient and provably secure trapdoor-free group signature schemes from bilinear pairings. In: Cachin, C., Camenisch, J.L. (eds.) EUROCRYPT 2004. LNCS, vol. 3027, pp. 372–386. Springer, Heidelberg (2004)
32. Pointcheval, D., Stern, J.: Security arguments for digital signatures and blind signatures. Journal of Cryptology 13(3), 361–396 (2000)
33. Rivest, R.L., Shamir, A., Tauman, Y.: How to leak a secret. In: Boyd, C. (ed.) ASIACRYPT 2001. LNCS, vol. 2248, pp. 552–565. Springer, Heidelberg (2001)
34. Rivest, R.L., Shamir, A., Tauman, Y.: How to leak a secret: Theory and applications of ring signatures. In: Goldreich, O., Rosenberg, A.L., Selman, A.L. (eds.) Theoretical Computer Science. LNCS, vol. 3895, pp. 164–186. Springer, Heidelberg (2006)
35. Tsang, P.P., Wei, V.K., Chan, T.K., Au, M.H., Liu, J.K., Wong, D.S.: Separable linkable threshold ring signatures. In: Canteaut, A., Viswanathan, K. (eds.) INDOCRYPT 2004. LNCS, vol. 3348, pp. 384–398. Springer, Heidelberg (2004)
36. Zhang, F., Kim, K.: Id-based blind signature and ring signature from pairings. In: Zheng, Y. (ed.) ASIACRYPT 2002. LNCS, vol. 2501, pp. 533–547. Springer, Heidelberg (2002)

A Security Proofs of The ICS Scheme Based on Pairings

Since the completeness requirement can be checked straightforward, we provide the other security arguments as follows. The proof techniques of unforgeability and ICS-unforgeability are similar to that of the underlying signature scheme [16]. We omit the detail proofs of them because of the lack of space.

Lemma 1. *[16, Lemma 1] If there is an algorithm $\mathcal{A}$ that forges a regular signature of our scheme under adaptively chosen message and identity attack with advantage ϵ in time t, then there is an algorithm $\mathcal{A}_1$ which can forge a signature under chosen message and given identity attack with advantage $\epsilon_1 \geq \epsilon(1 - \frac{1}{p})\frac{1}{q_{H_1}}$ in time $t_1 \leq t$, where q_{H_1} is the maximum number of queries to H_1 made by $\mathcal{A}$.*

Lemma 2. *If there is an algorithm $\mathcal{A}_1$ that forges a regular signature of our scheme under adaptively chosen message and given identity attack with advantage $\epsilon_1 \geq 10(q_S + 1)(q_S + q_{H_2})/p$ in time t_1, then there is an algorithm $\mathcal{B}$ which can solve CDHP with advantage $\epsilon' \geq 1/9$ in time $t' \leq 23q_{H_2}t_1/\epsilon_1$, where q_{H_2} and q_S are the maximum number of queries to H_2 and Sign, respectively.*

Theorem 1 (Unforgeability). *If there is an algorithm $\mathcal{A}$ that forges a regular signature of our scheme under adaptively chosen message and identity attack with advantage $\epsilon \geq 10(q_S + 1)(q_S + q_{H_2})q_{H_1}/(p - 1)$ in time t, then there is an algorithm $\mathcal{B}$ which can solve CDHP with advantage $\epsilon' \geq 1/9$ in time $t' \leq \frac{23q_{H_1}q_{H_2}t}{\epsilon(1-\frac{1}{p})}$, where q_{H_1}, q_{H_2} and q_S are the maximum number of queries to H_1, H_2 and Sign, respectively.*

Proof. By the above two lemmas, the theorem holds.

Theorem 2 (ICS-Unforgeability). *If there is an algorithm $\mathcal{A}$ that forges an identity-committed signature of our scheme under adaptively chosen message attack with advantage $\epsilon \geq 10(q_{S_{IC}} + 1)(q_{S_{IC}} + q_{H_2})/p$ in time t, then there is an algorithm $\mathcal{B}$ which can solve CB-CDHP with advantage $\epsilon' \geq 1/9$ in time $t' \leq 23q_{H_2}t/\epsilon$, where q_{H_1}, q_{H_2} and $q_{S_{IC}}$ are the maximum number of queries to H_1, H_2 and IC-Sign, respectively.*

Theorem 3 (ICS-Anonymity). *Our scheme has the information-theoretic ICS-Anonymity property.*

Proof. For a valid identity-committed signature $\sigma_{IC} = (Q, Q', U, V)$, it can be opened to any identity ID^* because there is a w^* such that

$$Q = w^* Q_{ID^*},$$

where $Q_{ID^*} = H_1(ID^*)$. Therefore, the signature has information-theoretic ICS-Anonymity.

Theorem 4 (ICS-Binding). *If there is an algorithm $\mathcal{A}$ that breaks ICS-Binding property with advantage ϵ in time t, then there is an algorithm $\mathcal{B}$ which can solve DLP with advantage $\epsilon' \geq \epsilon(1 - \frac{1}{p^2})\frac{1}{q_{H_1}^2}$ in time $t' \leq t$, where q_{H_1} is the maximum number of queries to H_1.*

Proof. On input $(\tilde{P}, a\tilde{P})$, $\mathcal{B}$ computes a as follows.

1. Run **Setup** and execute $\mathcal{A}$ on the output system parameters.
2. Answer the oracle queries as the real scheme except that when $\mathcal{A}$ queries $H_1^{\mathcal{A}}(ID_j)$ and $H_1^{\mathcal{A}}(ID_{j'})$ for two randomly chosen $j, j' \in \{1, 2, \ldots, q_{H_1}\}$, return $\tilde{P}$ and $a\tilde{P}$ respectively.
3. $\mathcal{A}$ outputs an identity-committed signature (Q, Q', U, V) on m, and two witnesses (w, ID) and (w', ID'). If $ID \neq ID_j$ or $ID' \neq ID_{j'}$, output fail and abort. Otherwise, output $a = w/w'$.

We can see that since $Q = wQ_{ID} = w\tilde{P}$ and $Q = w'Q_{ID'} = w'a\tilde{P}$, the value a is properly computed. Moreover, since H_1 is modeled as a random oracle, the output distribution of all oracles queried by $\mathcal{A}$ are indistinguishable from the distribution of the real scheme. By the assumption of $\mathcal{A}$, we have

$$\Pr[w \text{ and } w' \text{ are witnesses for } ID \text{ and } ID'] \geq \epsilon.$$

For the same reason, the probability that $\mathcal{A}$ outputs valid witnesses (w, ID) and (w', ID') without queries to $H_1(ID)$ and $H_1(ID')$ is negligible. That is,

$$\Pr[ID = ID_i, ID' = ID_{i'}, i, i' \in \{1, 2, \ldots, q_{H_1}\}|$$
$$w \text{ and } w' \text{ are witnesses for } ID \text{ and } ID'] \geq 1 - \frac{1}{p^2}.$$

Moreover, since j and j' are randomly chosen, we have

$$\Pr[ID = ID_j = \tilde{P}, ID' = ID_{j'} = a\tilde{P}|$$
$$ID = ID_i, ID' = ID_{i'} i, i' \in \{1, 2, \ldots, q_{H_1}\}] \geq \frac{1}{q_{H_1}^2}.$$

By combining these equations, we have

$$\Pr[\mathcal{B} \text{ outputs the correct answer } a \text{ for DLP }] \geq \epsilon \cdot (1 - \frac{1}{p^2}) \cdot \frac{1}{q_{H_1}^2}.$$

Hash-and-Sign with Weak Hashing Made Secure

Sylvain Pasini and Serge Vaudenay

EPFL
CH-1015 Lausanne, Switzerland
http://lasecwww.epfl.ch

Abstract. Digital signatures are often proven to be secure in the random oracle model while hash functions deviate more and more from this idealization. Liskov proposed to model a weak hash function by a random oracle together with another oracle allowing to break some properties of the hash function, e.g. a preimage oracle. To avoid the need for collision-resistance, Bellare and Rogaway proposed to use target collision resistant (TCR) randomized pre-hashing. Later, Halevi and Krawczyk suggested to use enhanced TCR (eTCR) hashing to avoid signing the random seed. To avoid the increase in signature length in the TCR construction, Mironov suggested to recycle some signing coins in the message preprocessing. In this paper, we develop and apply all those techniques. In particular, we obtain a generic preprocessing which allows to build strongly secure signature schemes when hashing is weak and the internal (textbook) signature is weakly secure. We model weak hashing by a preimage-tractable random oracle.

1 Introduction

A textbook signature scheme usually does a poor job because it restricts to input messages of fixed length and is often weakly secure. In order to sign messages of arbitrary length, hash functions [17,15,19,20] and the so-called *hash-and-sign paradigm* appeared. Clearly, the hash function must be collision resistant but they are threaten species these days [23,22,24]. In this paper we wonder how to recycle signature schemes that are currently implemented and based on (now) weak hash functions. To do so, we consider *generic* transform using preprocessing based on [4,9,13].

One crucial task is to find a model which fits to the current security of hash functions. A solution is to use the Liskov [12] idea. It consists of a random oracle that are provided together with another oracle that "breaks" the hash function, e.g. a first preimage oracle. We apply the preimage-tractable random oracle model (PT-ROM) to model weak hashing in digital signatures.

A natural solution to avoid the collision-resistance assumption is to add randomness in hashing. Bellare and Rogaway [4] proposed to sign $(K, H_K(m))$ with a random salt K where H is a Target Collision Resistant (TCR) hash function (also known as universal one-way hash function). More recently, Halevi and Krawczyk [9] proposed the concept of enhanced TCR (eTCR) hash function,

J. Pieprzyk, H. Ghodosi, and E. Dawson (Eds.): ACISP 2007, LNCS 4586, pp. 338–354, 2007.
© Springer-Verlag Berlin Heidelberg 2007

some eTCR construction techniques, and the RMX construction based on current hash functions. This latter scheme only adds a randomized preprocessing on the input message and thus standard implementations can be used as-is. As an application to their eTCR constructions, they suggest to use it as preprocessing for signatures and thus the salt K needs not to be signed. Here, we prove in our PT-ROM that this construction is *strongly* secure based on any textbook signature scheme which is *weakly* secure.

The disadvantage of the methods using a random seed K is that K must be appended to the signature. To avoid the increase in signature length, Mironov [13] proposed for DSA [7,6], RSA-PSS [3], and the Cramer-Shoup [5] schemes to re-use the randomness from the signature scheme instead of adding a new one. Finally, we generalize this construction and propose a *generic* transform that applies to special signature schemes. Indeed, we define special signature scheme for which we can split the sign algorithm in two parts: first, there is a randomized algorithm independent from the input message, then there is a deterministic algorithm which outputs the signature. We call these schemes Signatures with Randomized Precomputation (SRP). This makes the preprocessing transform less generic because we must assume that the signature generates some random coins which are available before the message is processed and which are extractable from the signature.

In this paper, we start with some preliminaries and then we present the hash-and-sign paradigm with many existing hashing methods. In particular, we present the TCR-based from Bellare-Rogaway [4] and eTCR-based signature from Halevi-Krawczyk [9] constructions. In Section 4, we give a formal proof of the Halevi-Krawczyk construction using weak hashing. In the subsequent section, we generalize the technique by Mironov [13] and we give a formal security proof. Finally, we present a direct application to DSA and validate the Halevi-Krawczyk construction with RMX preprocessing.

2 Preliminaries

Given a security parameter λ, we say that $f(\lambda)$ is polynomially bounded and we write $f(\lambda) = \mathsf{poly}(\lambda)$ if there exists n such that $f(\lambda) = \mathcal{O}(\lambda^n)$ when $\lambda \to +\infty$. We say that $f(\lambda)$ is negligible and we .write $f(\lambda) = \mathsf{negl}(\lambda)$ if there exists $x > 0$ such that $f(\lambda) = \mathcal{O}(x^{-\lambda})$ when $\lambda \to +\infty$. For the sake of readability, our theorems are stated in terms of asymptotic complexity although they are proven by using exact complexities in some real-life computational model. The security parameter λ is almost always hidden in notations.

2.1 Digital Signature Schemes

Let $\mathcal{M}$ be the set of possible input messages, i.e. the *domain*. We define *fixed message-length digital signature* schemes (FML-DS) any signature scheme which applies only to a restricted message space $\mathcal{M} = \{0,1\}^{r(\lambda)}$ and *arbitrary message-length digital signature* (AML-DS) schemes the schemes when $\mathcal{M} = \{0,1\}^*$.

We formalize a *digital signature scheme* S by three algorithms: The setup algorithm $(K_p, K_s) \leftarrow S.\mathsf{setup}(1^\lambda)$ generates a key pair depending on a security parameter λ. The sign algorithm $\sigma \leftarrow S.\mathsf{sign}(K_s, m)$ outputs a signature $\sigma \in S$ of a message $m \in \mathcal{M}$. The verify algorithm $b \leftarrow S.\mathsf{verify}(K_p, m, \sigma)$ tells whether the pair (m, σ) is valid or not. It returns 1 if and only if the signature is valid and 0 otherwise.

An FML-DS can be transformed into AML-DS following the hash-and-sign paradigm. Here, hashing is used as a *domain extender*. For instance, DSA [7,6] is based on SHA-1 [20] while RSA [16] uses MD5 [15] in the standard PKCS #1 v1.5 that is used in X.509 [11].

Consider an adversary $\mathcal{A}$ against S. $\mathcal{A}$ plays a game against a challenger $\mathcal{C}$ who can sign messages. The goal of $\mathcal{A}$ is to yield a valid pair $(\widehat{m}, \widehat{\sigma})$ which was not produced by $\mathcal{C}$. Textbook signature schemes such as ElGamal [8] or plain RSA [16] signatures are often existentially forgeable. We consider the *strong* security model EF-CMA and the *weak* security model UF-KMA.

UF-KMA and EF-CMA Games. The signature scheme is said (T, ℓ, ε)-UF-KMA (resp. EF-CMA) resistant if any adversary $\mathcal{A}$ bounded by a complexity T and ℓ valid signatures on known (resp. chosen) messages cannot win the game of Fig. 1 (resp. Fig. 2) with probability higher than ε^1. The scheme is said UF-KMA secure (resp. EF-CMA-secure) if for any $T = \mathsf{poly}$ and $\ell = \mathsf{poly}$ there exists $\varepsilon = \mathsf{negl}$ such that the scheme is (T, ℓ, ε)-UF-KMA (resp. EF-CMA) resistant.

Fig. 1. UF-KMA game   **Fig. 2.** EF-CMA game

2.2 Hash Functions

Collision Resistant Hash Functions. (CRHF) are hash functions in which we cannot construct two inputs x and y such that $H(x) = H(y)$ and $x \neq y^2$. We say H depending on a security parameter λ is CRHF if any polynomially bounded adversary finds collisions with negligible probability.

Target Collision Resistant (TCR) Hash Functions. was introduced by Naor and Yung [14] and then renammed in [4]. A (T, ε)-TCR is a keyed function H : $\{0,1\}^k \times \{0,1\}^* \mapsto \{0,1\}^n$ such that any adversary bounded by a complexity

---

[1] Our results holds even if the winning conditions are replaced by $(\widehat{m}, \widehat{\sigma}) \neq (m_i, \sigma_i)$.

[2] Note that this definition is not so formal as discussed in Rogaway [18].

T cannot win the game of Fig. 3 with probability higher than ε. For H^λ : $\{0,1\}^{k(\lambda)} \times \{0,1\}^* \mapsto \{0,1\}^{n(\lambda)}$, we say H is TCR if any polynomially bounded adversary wins with negligible probability.

Enhanced Target Collision Resistant (eTCR) hash function. was introduced by Halevi and Krawczyk [9]. A (T, ε)-eTCR is a stronger TCR function such that any adversary bounded by a complexity T cannot win the game of Fig. 4 with probability higher than ε. We say H is eTCR if any polynomially bounded adversary wins with negligible probability. A OW-eTCR hash function is an eTCR hash function for which $(\kappa, m) \mapsto H_\kappa(m)$ is also OW.

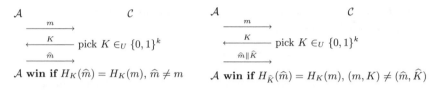

Fig. 3. TCR game   **Fig. 4.** eTCR game

Random Oracle Hashing. A *Random Oracle* $\mathsf{R} : \{0,1\}^* \mapsto \{0,1\}^n$ often represents a uniformly distributed random hash function [2]. It is simulated by an oracle managing a table that is initially empty. When R receives a query with input m and there is an (m, r) entry in the table, it simply returns r. Otherwise, it picks a random value $r \in \{0,1\}^n$, returns it, and inserts a new entry (m, r) in the table.

Preimage-Tractable Random Oracle Hashing. *Preimage-Tractable Random Oracles* were introduced by Liskov [12]. It is used to idealize some weak hash function for which preimages are computable, i.e. the one-wayness is not guaranteed. It consists of two oracles:

- the first oracle G can be used to compute images like a random oracle, i.e. $r = \mathsf{G}(m)$,
- the second oracle $\mathsf{preimageG}$ can be used to find a preimage of a hashed value. When $\mathsf{preimageG}$ is queried with input r, it picks uniformly at random an element within the set of all its preimages, i.e. it outputs $m \in_u \mathsf{G}^{-1}(r)$.

The simulation of G is done as for random oracle hashing with a table $\mathbb{T}$. To simulate $\mathsf{preimageG}$, upon a new query r we first compute the probability q to answer an m that is not new, i.e. $q = \Pr\left[(\mathsf{G}^{-1}(r), r) \in \mathbb{T} \mid \bigwedge_{(m',r') \in \mathbb{T}} \mathsf{G}(m') = r'\right]$. Then flip a biased coin b with $\Pr[b = 0] = q$ and if $b = 0$ we pick uniformly one (m, r) in $\mathbb{T}$ otherwise we pick uniformly one m such that $(m, r) \notin \mathbb{T}$, insert (m, r) in $\mathbb{T}$. Finally, answer by m. Note that this oracle can be used to find collisions as well.

From a theoretical viewpoint, the preimage-tractable random oracle is as powerful as the random oracle since $\mathsf{preimageG}(0\|\alpha) \oplus \mathsf{preimageG}(1\|\alpha)$ is indifferentiable from a random oracle even when $(\mathsf{G}, \mathsf{preimageG})$ is a preimage-tractable random oracle. Our motivation is to model weak hash functions which are in place without changing the algorithm implementations.

3   Domain Extension

3.1   Deterministic Hash-and-Sign

Given a hash function $H : \{0,1\}^* \rightarrow \{0,1\}^k$ and an FML-DS S_0 on domain $\{0,1\}^k$, we construct S' on domain $\{0,1\}^*$ by $S'.\text{sign}(K_s, m) = S_0.\text{sign}(K_s, H(m))$.

Theorem 1. *If H is a collision resistant hash function and S_0 is EF-CMA-secure, then S' is EF-CMA-secure.*

This folklore result is nicely treated in [18].

Theorem 2. *If H is a random oracle and S_0 is UF-KMA-secure, then S' is EF-CMA-secure.*

The proof of this folklore result is rather straightforward. Indeed, H brings *collision resistance* in domain extension as well as *unpredictability*.

3.2   Randomized Hash-and-Sign

The idea of using a TCR comes from Bellare and Rogaway [4] and was also reused recently by Mironov [13]. The constructed signature consists of the pair $(\kappa, S.\text{sign}(K_s, \kappa \| H_\kappa(M)))$ where $H_\kappa(\cdot)$ is a TCR hash function. The following result is a straightforward generalization of Mironov [13].

Theorem 3. *Consider an FML-DS S_0 with domain $\{0,1\}^r$ and a function $G_0 : \{0,1\}^* \mapsto \{0,1\}^r$. We assume that $G_0(X)$ is indistinguishable from $Y \in_u \{0,1\}^r$ when $X \in_u \{0,1\}^{2r}$. Let $H : \{0,1\}^k \times \{0,1\}^* \mapsto \{0,1\}^n$ be a TCR hash function and $\mathsf{R} : \{0,1\}^{k+n} \mapsto \{0,1\}^r$ be a random oracle. We construct two AML-DS S and S' by*

$$S.\text{sign}(K_s, m) = S_0.\text{sign}(K_s, G_0(m))$$
$$S'.\text{sign}(K_s, m) = (\kappa \ \| \ S_0.\text{sign}(K_s, \mathsf{R}(\kappa \| H_\kappa(m)))) \qquad \text{with } \kappa \in_u \{0,1\}^k$$

Assuming that S is EF-CMA-secure, then S' is also EF-CMA-secure.

This means that if there exists a domain extender G_0 that makes S secure, then S' is secure.

Proof. Consider $H : \{0,1\}^k \times \{0,1\}^* \mapsto \{0,1\}^n$ is a $(T + \mu_H, \varepsilon_H)$-TCR hash function for μ_H to be defined later, $\mathsf{R} : \{0,1\}^{k+n} \mapsto \{0,1\}^r$ is a random oracle bounded to q queries, and S_0 an FML-DS scheme with r-bit input messages. We assume that the construction S is $(T + \mu_S, \ell, \varepsilon_S)$-EF-CMA secure for μ_S to be defined later. We assume that G_0 is $(T + \mu_G, q + \ell + 1, \varepsilon_d)$-PRG when restricted to

$(2r)$-bit inputs. We will prove that the construction S' is $(T, \ell, \varepsilon_S + \ell\varepsilon_H + \varepsilon_c + \varepsilon_d)$-EF-CMA secure where ε_c represents a probability of collision on the outputs of the random oracle.

We consider an adversary $\mathcal{A}$ playing the EF-CMA game against S'. We assume without loss of generality that $\mathcal{A}$ queries R with $H_{\widehat{\kappa}}(\widehat{m})$ before releasing the final forgery $(\widehat{m}, \widehat{\kappa}, \widehat{\sigma})$ (so we have up to $q + 1$ queries to R). By using an algorithm $\mathcal{B}$, we prove that we can reduce $\mathcal{A}$ to an adversary against either the signature construction S or the TCR hash function H.

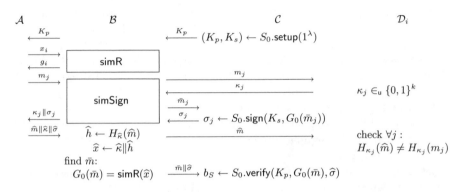

Fig. 5. Reduction to EF-CMA or TCR games (from EF-CMA)

The reduction is depicted on Fig. 5. Clearly, $\mathcal{B}$ has to simulate the random oracle R and the signing oracle that we refer to simR and simSign respectively. The simulations work as follows:

simR: $\mathcal{B}$ manages a table $\mathbb{T}$ initially empty. For each R-query with input x:
  - if $\mathsf{simR}(x)$ is not defined in $\mathbb{T}$, $\mathcal{B}$ picks a random $\bar{m}$ uniformly in $\{0,1\}^{2r}$ and answers $g \leftarrow G_0(\bar{m})$. Hence, a new entry $(x, g, \bar{m})$ is inserted in $\mathbb{T}$, meaning $\mathsf{simR}(x) = g = G_0(\bar{m})$. Note that the third entry $\bar{m}$ will be used by simSign only.
  - otherwise, $\mathcal{B}$ answers $\mathsf{simR}(x)$ as defined in $\mathbb{T}$.

simSign: For each sign-query with input m:
  1. $\mathcal{B}$ computes $h \leftarrow H_\kappa(m)$, $x \leftarrow \kappa \| h$ where κ is returned by $\mathcal{D}_i$ on query m,
  2. $\mathcal{B}$ queries $\mathsf{simR}(x)$. Let $\bar{m}$ be such that $\mathsf{simR}(x) = G_0(\bar{m})$ from $\mathbb{T}$,
  3. $\mathcal{B}$ queries $\mathcal{C}$ with $\bar{m}$ to obtain its signature σ,
  4. finally, $\mathcal{B}$ returns $\kappa \| \sigma$ to $\mathcal{A}$.

$\mathcal{B}$ is allowed to ℓ queries to the S_0.sign oracle, so $\mathcal{A}$ is also allowed to ℓ queries to simSign. Note that the simSign simulation is perfect but the simR simulation is not. At the end, if $\mathcal{A}$ succeeds, he returns a forged pair $(\widehat{m}, \widehat{\kappa}, \widehat{\sigma})$ to $\mathcal{B}$. We use the proof methodology of Shoup [21]:

- Let game_0 be the EF-CMA game against S' depicted on Fig. 2.
- Let E_1 be the event that there were no collision on the output of R. Let game_1 be game_0 in which E_1 occurred.

  Clearly, when E_1 does not occur, there is a collision on the R outputs. Since there is at most $q + \ell + 1$ elements in the simR table, this probability is bounded by $\varepsilon_c \leq \frac{(q+\ell+1)^2}{2} 2^{-r}$. So, $\Pr[\mathcal{A} \text{ wins } \mathsf{game}_0] - \Pr[\mathcal{A} \text{ wins } \mathsf{game}_1] \leq \varepsilon_c$.
- Let game_2 be game_1 where the R oracle was replaced by the simR simulator. Let $\mathcal{A}'$ simulate $\mathcal{A}$ and simR in which picking a random $\bar{m}$, computing $g \leftarrow G_0(\bar{m})$, and inserting $(x, g, \bar{m})$ in the table is replaced by getting a random g^* from a source Σ and storing (x, g^*) in the table. We consider the two following sources: Σ_0 picks g^* with uniform distribution and Σ_1 picks $\bar{m}$ and output $g^* \leftarrow G_0(\bar{m})$. Note that using Σ_0 perfectly simulates game_1 while using Σ_1 perfectly simulates game_2. At the end, $\mathcal{A}'$ checks whether the EF-CMA game succeeded. Clearly, this is a distinguisher of some complexity $T + \mu_G$ between Σ_0 and Σ_1 by using $q + \ell + 1$ samples. So, $|\Pr[\mathcal{A} \text{ wins } \mathsf{game}_1] - \Pr[\mathcal{A} \text{ wins } \mathsf{game}_2]| \leq \varepsilon_d$.
- Let game_3 be the simulated EF-CMA game of Fig. 5. Since the simulation simSign of the signing oracle is perfect, we have $\Pr[\mathcal{A} \text{ wins } \mathsf{game}_3] = \Pr[\mathcal{A} \text{ wins } \mathsf{game}_2]$.
- Let E_4 be the event that the final $\bar{m}$ was not queried to $\mathcal{C}$. Let game_4 be the game_3 in which E_4 occurred. In that case, $\mathcal{A}$ can be perfectly reduced to an EF-CMA adversary of complexity $T + \mu_s$ against $\mathcal{C}$. So, $\Pr[\mathcal{A} \text{ wins } \mathsf{game}_4] \leq \varepsilon_S$.

  Clearly, if E_4 did not occur, $\bar{m}$ was previously queried to $\mathcal{C}$. Let $\bar{m} = \bar{m}_j$, i.e. $\bar{m}$ was queried by $\mathcal{B}$ to $\mathcal{C}$ at the jth sign-query. Thus, $\mathcal{B}$ queried simR with an input x_j and obtained $(x_j, G_0(\bar{m}_j), \bar{m}_j)$. Since there were no collision on simR, $\bar{m} = \bar{m}_j$ implies that $\hat{x} = x_j$ thus $\hat{\kappa} = \kappa_j$ and $\hat{h} = h_j$. We have $H_{\hat{\kappa}}(\hat{m}) = H_{\hat{\kappa}}(m_j)$. $\hat{m}$ is different from all m_i since $\mathcal{A}$ won his attack against S'. Hence, $\mathcal{A}$ can be perfectly reduced to a TCR adversary against $\mathcal{D}_j$ and $\Pr[\mathcal{A} \text{ wins } \mathsf{game}_3] - \Pr[\mathcal{A} \text{ wins } \mathsf{game}_4] \leq \ell \varepsilon_H$.

We conclude by considering the above reductions that μ_H and μ_S are within the order of magnitude of the simulation cost which is polynomial. $\square$

The problems of such constructions are that (1.) we do not have a full reduction to the weak security of S_0; (2.) the signature enlarges; (3.) κ must be signed; (4.) we still need a random oracle R (implicitly meaning collision-resistant hashing) so the role of R is to concentrate on unpredictability and nevertheless, R is now restricted to $\{0, 1\}^{k+m}$.

Halevi and Krawczyk [9] also use a randomized hashing but avoid signing the κ salt. Indeed, they use an eTCR hash function. In [9], they proposed a construction technique for eTCR based on weak hashing and suggested to use it as preprocessing for signature schemes. The signature consists of the pair (κ, σ) where σ is $S.\mathsf{sign}(K_s, H_\kappa(m))$. One problem is that they do no provide any proof of security for the signature so far. Indeed, they only focus on the problem for constructing an eTCR hash function based on weak hashing.

4 Strong Signature Schemes with Weak Hashing

We consider a deterministic hash-and-sign signature S put together with the Halevi and Krawczyk [9] message processing. Namely, given a weakly-secure FML-DS S_0 we construct a strongly-secure AML-DS S' as follows:

$\sigma' \leftarrow S'.\text{sign}(K_s, m):$

- pick $\kappa \in_u \{0,1\}^k$
- $s \leftarrow H_\kappa(m)$
- $h \leftarrow G(s)$
- $\sigma' \leftarrow (\kappa \| S_0.\text{sign}(K_s, h))$

$b \leftarrow S'.\text{verify}(K_p, m, \sigma'): \quad (\sigma' = \kappa \| \sigma)$

- $s \leftarrow H_\kappa(m)$
- $h \leftarrow G(s)$
- $b \leftarrow S_0.\text{verify}(K_p, h, \sigma)$

where $H : \{0,1\}^k \times \{0,1\}^* $ to $ \{0,1\}^n$ is an eTCR hash function family, $G : \{0,1\}^n \rightarrow \{0,1\}^r$ a (weak) hash function, and S_0 is an UF-KMA secure FML-DS on domain $\{0,1\}^r$. Clearly, for S defined by $S.\text{sign}(K_s, m) = S_0.\text{sign}(K_s, G(m))$, our construction can be seen as a regular AML-DS based on hash-and-sign with an extra randomized preprocessing $H_\kappa(\cdot)$.

Theorem 4. *Consider H is an OW-eTCR hash function family, and G is a preimage-tractable random oracle. If S_0 is an UF-KMA-secure FML-DS, then S' in the above AML-DS construction is EF-CMA-secure.*

Clearly, we can build strong signature schemes for arbitrary messages based on any weak signature scheme restricted to fixed-length input messages *without* collision-resistance and *without* a full random oracle. The remaining drawback is that the signature enlarges.

Note that the OW assumption on H is necessary since G is assumed to be preimage-tractable (otherwise, existential forgeries on S_0 would translate in existential forgeries on S'). and eTCR hash functions may be not OW. Indeed, if H is eTCR, then H' defined by

$$H'_\kappa(m) = \begin{cases} 0\|m & \text{if } \kappa = 0\ldots 0 \text{ and } |m| = n-1, \\ 1\|H_\kappa(m) & \text{otherwise.} \end{cases}$$

is eTCR as well but not OW. However, when there exists a set of messages $\mathcal{M}$ such that H is a PRG when restricted to $\{0,1\}^{k \times \mathcal{M}}$, then eTCR implies OW-eTCR.

Proof. Let us assume that S_0 is $(T + \mu, \ell, \varepsilon_S)$-UF-KMA-secure, H is $(T + \mu, \varepsilon_H)$-eTCR and $(T + \mu, \varepsilon_w)$-OW, and G is a random oracle limited to $q < \ell$ queries where μ is some polynomially bounded complexity (namely, the overhead of some simulations). We will show that S' is $(T, \ell - q, \varepsilon_f + q_p \cdot \varepsilon_w + (\ell - q) \cdot \varepsilon_H + q \cdot \varepsilon_S)$-EF-CMA-secure where ε_f represents a probability of failure during the reduction.

We start by considering an EF-CMA adversary $\mathcal{A}$ against our constructed scheme S'. We assume that $\mathcal{A}$ is bounded by complexity T. By using an algorithm $\mathcal{B}$, we transform $\mathcal{A}$ into either an UF-KMA adversary against S_0 or into an eTCR adversary against H as depicted on Fig. 6. Here, $\mathcal{C}$ plays the role of the challenger

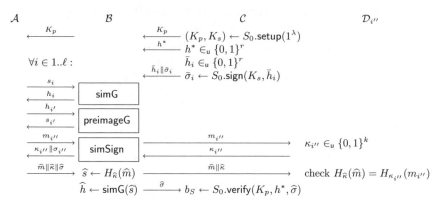

Fig. 6. Reduction to the UF-KMA or eTCR games (from EF-CMA)

in the UF-KMA game of Fig. 1 while each $\mathcal{D}_{i''}$ plays the role of the i''th challenger in the eTCR game of Fig. 4.

Clearly, algorithm $\mathcal{B}$ has to simulates for $\mathcal{A}$ the signing oracle and the two oracles that model the preimage-tractable hash function that we refer by simSign, simG, and preimageG respectively. To simulate G and preimageG, we use another existing preimage-tractable random oracle G_0 and preimageG$_0$ and we construct a random permutation φ such that $G = \varphi \circ G_0$. We consider a growing pool of values of s. The pool is initially empty. A new s is put in the pool if it is queried to simG or returned by preimageG. Without loss of generality, we assume that $\mathcal{A}$ makes no trivial queries to simG. Namely, he does not query simG with an s already in the pool. Similarly, we assume that if $\widehat{s} = H_{\widehat{\kappa}}(\widehat{m})$ is not in the pool, $\mathcal{A}$ queries simG$(\widehat{s})$ before releasing $\widehat{m}\|\widehat{\kappa}\|\widehat{\sigma}$ to make sure that $\widehat{s}$ is in the pool. (So we may have $q + 1$ queries to simG.) The simulations work as follows:

simG: At the beginning of the game, $\mathcal{B}$ picks a random $t \in_u \{1..q\}$. When $\mathcal{A}$ submits a G-query with input s:
 – if $\varphi(G_0(s))$ is undefined, it answers the next $\bar{h}_i$ in the sequence except that for the tth query it answers h^*. Hence, there is a new entry $\varphi(G_0(s)) = h$ in the φ table.
 – If $\varphi(G_0(s))$ is already defined, $\mathcal{B}$ aborts.
preimageG: When $\mathcal{A}$ submits a preimageG query with input h, if $x = \varphi^{-1}(h)$ is not defined, it picks a random x on which $\varphi(x)$ is not defined and define $\varphi(x) = h$. Then, it queries preimageG$_0(x)$ and answers s.
simSign: When $\mathcal{A}$ submits a sign-query with input m, $\mathcal{B}$ queries a new $\mathcal{D}_{i''}$ with input m, gets κ, and computes $s = H_\kappa(m)$. If s is in the pool, $\mathcal{B}$ abort. Otherwise, $\mathcal{B}$ runs $h \leftarrow$ simG(s) without counting this query (that is, use the next $\bar{h}_i$ in the sequence and not h^*). Thus, simG(s) is equal to one of the $\bar{h}_i$ and $\mathcal{B}$ uses the corresponding signature $\bar{\sigma}_i$ to answer $\kappa\|\bar{\sigma}_i$.

Note that $\mathcal{B}$ has ℓ signed samples from $\mathcal{C}$, thus $\mathcal{A}$ is limited to ℓ queries to simG and simSign. So, $q + q_s \leq \ell$. At the end, if $\mathcal{A}$ succeeds his EF-CMA game, he will send a tuple $(\widehat{m}, \widehat{\kappa}, \widehat{\sigma})$ to $\mathcal{B}$.

We use the proof methodology of Shoup [21]:

- Let game_0 be the EF-CMA game against S' of Fig. 2.
- Let game_1 be the simulated EF-CMA game against S' depicted on Fig. 6. Clearly, the simulations fails when a $\varphi(\mathsf{G}_0(s))$ is already defined while querying simG with s or when $s = H_\kappa(m)$ was already in the pool while querying $\mathsf{simSign}$. Let ε_f the bound on this failure probability. By using the difference lemma [21] we obtain $\Pr[\mathcal{A}$ wins $\mathsf{game}_0] - \Pr[\mathcal{A}$ wins $\mathsf{game}_1] \le \varepsilon_f$. Note that $\varepsilon_f \le \Pr[\mathcal{B}$ fails on a simG query$] + \Pr[\mathcal{B}$ fails on a $\mathsf{simSign}$ query$]$. We consider $\mathcal{A}$ is bounded by q, q_p and q_s queries to simG, $\mathsf{preimageG}$, and $\mathsf{simSign}$ respectively, and a space of 2^r elements. First, we compute the probability that $\mathcal{B}$ fails on a simG query, i.e. there were a collision of $\mathsf{G}_0(s)$ for one s queried to simG with one $\mathsf{G}_0(s')$ for s' in the pool. By considering the queries from $\mathcal{A}$ and from $\mathsf{simSign}$, there are at most $q + q_s + 1$ queries to simG and at most $q + q_s + q_p + 1$ elements still defined in the pool. Since they are uniformly distributed, the probability that two elements collide is 2^{-r}. So, $\Pr[\mathcal{B}$ fails on a simG query$] \le (q + q_s + 1)(q + q_s + q_p + 1) \cdot 2^{-r}$.

Now, we compute the probability that $\mathcal{B}$ fails on a $\mathsf{simSign}$ query, i.e. s was already in the pool. There are at most q_s queries to $\mathsf{simSign}$ and at most $q + q_s + q_p + 1$ elements s in the pool. For each query-s pair, we have the following scenario: $\mathcal{A}$ queries $\mathsf{simSign}$ with m, $\mathcal{B}$ queries $\mathcal{D}$ with m, gets κ, computes $H_\kappa(m)$, and looks if it is s. Clearly, this scenario can be described as game (a) of Fig.7. Let p the maximal success probability among all random coins of the adversary $\mathcal{A}$ in the game (a).

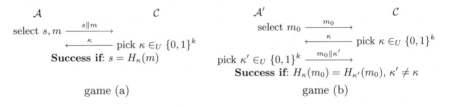

game (a)   game (b)

Fig. 7. Reduction to the eTCR Game

Now, consider game (b) depicted on Fig.7. Clearly, this game is harder than the eTCR game since $\mathcal{A}'$ has no control on the second message returned to $\mathcal{C}$, i.e. it is m_0. We know that ε_H is a bound on the success probability of A' in the eTCR game. Thus, we have:

$$\varepsilon_H \ge \Pr[s_0 = H_\kappa(m_0) = H_{\kappa'}(m_0) \text{ and } \kappa' \ne \kappa]$$
$$\ge \Pr[s_0 = H_\kappa(m_0) = H_{\kappa'}(m_0)] - \Pr[\kappa' = \kappa]$$
$$= p^2 - 2^{-k}.$$

We conclude that $p \le \sqrt{\varepsilon_H + 2^{-k}}$ and so, $\varepsilon_f \le (q + q_s + 1)(q + q_s + q_p + 1) \cdot 2^{-r} + q_s(q + q_s + q_p + 1) \cdot \sqrt{\varepsilon_H + 2^{-k}}$ is negligible.

- Let E_2 be the event that the forgery $\widehat{m}\|\widehat{\kappa}\|\widehat{\sigma}$ is such that $\widehat{s} \leftarrow H_{\widehat{\kappa}}(\widehat{m})$ was queried to simG. Let game_2 be game_1 in which E_2 occurred.

  Since we made sure that $\widehat{s}$ is in the pool, if E_2 does not occur, the $\widehat{s}$ was returned by some preimageG(h) for the first time once. Note that when preimageG returns an unused value, it is uniformly distributed among all unused values. Clearly, $\mathcal{A}$ has to find a pair $(\widehat{m}, \widehat{\kappa})$ with $H_{\widehat{\kappa}}(\widehat{m}) = \widehat{s}$ which breaks the one-wayness of H. So, $\Pr[\mathcal{A} \text{ wins } \mathsf{game}_1] - \Pr[\mathcal{A} \text{ wins } \mathsf{game}_2] \leq q_p \cdot \varepsilon_w$.

- Let E_3 be the event that $\widehat{s}$ is different from all $s_{i''} \leftarrow H_{\kappa_{i''}}(m_{i''})$. Let game_3 be game_2 in which E_3 occurred.

  Clearly, if E_3 did not occur, $\widehat{s}$ is equal to $s_{i''}$ for a certain i''. Recall that since $\mathcal{A}$ won his game $\widehat{m}$ is different from all $m_{i''}$. So, $\mathcal{A}$ found $\widehat{m}$ and $\widehat{\kappa}$ such that $H_{\widehat{\kappa}}(\widehat{m}) = H_{\kappa_{i''}}(m_{i''})$. Here, $\mathcal{A}$ can perfectly be reduced to an eTCR adversary against all $\mathcal{D}_{i''}$. So, $\Pr[\mathcal{A} \text{ wins } \mathsf{game}_2] - \Pr[\mathcal{A} \text{ wins } \mathsf{game}_3] \leq q_s \cdot \varepsilon_H \leq (\ell - q) \cdot \varepsilon_H$.

- Let E_4 be the event that $\widehat{h} = h^*$. In other words the forged value $\widehat{h}$ is equal to the expected value h^*. Let game_4 be game_3 in which E_4 occurred. Here, $\mathcal{A}$ can perfectly be reduced to an UF-KMA adversary against S_0. Clearly, $\Pr[\mathcal{A} \text{ wins } \mathsf{game}_4] \leq \varepsilon_S$.

  Finally $\Pr[\mathcal{A} \text{ wins } \mathsf{game}_3] \leq q \cdot \varepsilon_S$ since E_4 occurred with probability $1/q$ and so $\Pr[\mathcal{A} \text{ wins } \mathsf{game}_4]/\Pr[\mathcal{A} \text{ wins } \mathsf{game}_3] = 1/q$.

$\square$

5   The Entropy Recycling Technique

To keep the same signature length, we have to avoid to append κ in the signature. The idea from [13] is to use the randomness computed in the signature scheme instead of introducing a new random parameter. Mironov [13] present specific modifications for the DSA [7,6], RSA-PSS [3], and Cramer-Shoup [5] signature schemes. In this section, we generalize the construction from Mironov. For that, we introduce a special sort of signature schemes: Signature with Randomized Precomputation.

A *Signature with Randomized Precomputation* (SRP) is any signature scheme for which the signature algorithm can be separated in two parts:

- first, a *probabilistic* precomputation algorithm generates the randomness without the message to be signed,
- then, a signature algorithm signs the message using the previous randomness.

Note that the randomness must be recoverable from the signature itself, which requires another algorithm extract. We can formalize any SRP scheme by the following five algorithms:

$$(K_p, K_s) \leftarrow S.\mathsf{setup}(1^\lambda)$$
$$(\xi, r) \leftarrow S.\mathsf{presign}(K_s) \qquad\qquad r \leftarrow S.\mathsf{extract}(K_p, \sigma)$$
$$\sigma \leftarrow S.\mathsf{postsign}(K_s, m, \xi) \qquad\qquad b \leftarrow S.\mathsf{verify}(K_p, m, \sigma)$$

Actually, all digital signature schemes can be written this way (e.g. with r void), but we need r to have a large enough entropy. We provide the necessary quantitative definitions for that in Appendix. When talking about the entropy of a SRP scheme, we implicitly mean the entropy of r generated by $S.\mathsf{presign}(K_s)$ given a key K_s.

Theorem 5. *Consider H is an eTCR hash function with t-bit keys and S_0 is a FML-SRP. We assume that the signature construction S based on S_0 defined by*

$\sigma' \leftarrow S.\mathsf{sign}(K_s, m)$:

- *pick $\kappa \in_\mathsf{u} \{0,1\}^t$*
- *$(\xi, r) \leftarrow S_0.\mathsf{presign}(K_s)$*
- *$\sigma \leftarrow S_0.\mathsf{postsign}(K_s, H_\kappa(m), \xi)$*
- *output $\kappa \| \sigma$*

$b \leftarrow S.\mathsf{verify}(K_p, m, \kappa \| \sigma)$:

- *$b \leftarrow S_0.\mathsf{verify}(K_p, H_\kappa(m), \sigma)$*
- *output b*

is an EF-CMA secure AML-SRP requiring an additional randomness κ. We assume that the SRP produces t-bit strings that are indistinguishable from uniformly distributed ones.

Consider R is a random oracle with k-bit output strings limited to q queries. The signature construction S' defined by

$\sigma' \leftarrow S'.\mathsf{sign}(K_s, m)$:

- *$(\xi, r) \leftarrow S_0.\mathsf{presign}(K_s)$*
- *$\sigma \leftarrow S_0.\mathsf{postsign}(K_s, H_{\mathsf{R}(r)}(m), \xi)$*
- *output σ*

$b \leftarrow S'.\mathsf{verify}(K_p, m, \sigma')$: $(\sigma' = \sigma)$

- *$r \leftarrow S_0.\mathsf{extract}(K_p, \sigma)$*
- *$b \leftarrow S_0.\mathsf{verify}(K_p, H_{\mathsf{R}(r)}(m), \sigma)$*
- *output b*

is also EF-CMA-secure even by re-using the randomness from the SRP.

Proof. Assume that the AML-SRP construction S is $(T + \mu, \ell, \varepsilon_S)$-EF-CMA secure and that r is $(T + \mu, \ell, \varepsilon_d)$-PR where μ is some polynomially bounded complexity due to the game reduction. In the following, we prove that the construction S' is $(T, \ell, \varepsilon_S + \varepsilon_c)$-EF-CMA secure where ε_c represents the probability of collision on the R outputs as defined in Lemma 3. We consider any EF-CMA adversary $\mathcal{A}$ against S'. As depicted on Fig. 8, we transform $\mathcal{A}$ into an EF-CMA adversary against the eTCR-based scheme S by using an algorithm $\mathcal{B}$ which simulates the random oracle R, the transform of $S'.\mathsf{sign}$ to $S.\mathsf{sign}$, and replaces the final $(\widehat{m}, \widehat{\sigma})$ by $(\widehat{m}, \widehat{\kappa}, \widehat{\sigma})$.

The simulations works as follows:

simR works as defined in Section 2.2.

simSign When $\mathcal{A}$ submits a sign-query with input m, $\mathcal{B}$ obtains (κ, σ) by querying $\mathcal{C}$ and deduces $r \leftarrow S.\mathsf{extract}(K_p, \sigma)$. If r is free in the simG table, it lets $\kappa = \mathsf{R}(r)$ and returns σ to $\mathcal{A}$, otherwise $\mathcal{B}$ fails.

$\mathcal{B}$ is allowed to ℓ queries to the $S_0.\mathsf{sign}$ oracle, so $\mathcal{A}$ is also allowed to ℓ queries to simSign. At the end, if $\mathcal{A}$ succeeds his EF-CMA game, he will send a tuple $(\widehat{m}, \widehat{\kappa}, \widehat{\sigma})$ to $\mathcal{B}$. We use one more time the proof methodology of Shoup [21]:

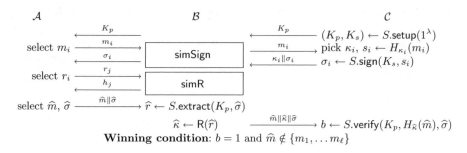

Fig. 8. Reduction to the EF-CMA game against the eTCR-based scheme S

- Let game_0 be the EF-CMA game against S' of Fig. 2.
- Let game_1 be the simulated EF-CMA game against S' depicted on Fig. 6.
  Clearly, the simulation fails if simSign fails, i.e. if an r_j in simSign is not free
  in the simR table. Let ε_c the bound on this probability of collision.
  Let E_1 the event that all r_j are free in the simR table. So, game_1 is game_0
  in which E_1 occurred. Here, $\mathcal{A}$ can perfectly be reduced to an EF-CMA
  adversary against S. So $\Pr[\mathcal{A}\text{ wins }\mathsf{game}_2] \le \varepsilon_S$.
  We obtain $\Pr[\mathcal{A}\text{ wins }\mathsf{game}_0] - \Pr[\mathcal{A}\text{ wins }\mathsf{game}_1] \le \varepsilon_c$ by using the difference
  lemma [21]. A detailed expression of ε_c is given on Lemma 3. It is clearly
  negligible.

$\square$

6   Application to DSA

We apply Theorem 4 and Theorem 5 to offer a quick fix to DSA in the case that
SHA-1 [20] became subject to preimage attacks. Here, standard implementations
of DSA could still be used: only a "message preprocessing" would be added.
First, note that DSA without hashing can be described using our SRP formalism
of Section 5. We denote by m the messages of arbitrary length (input of the
sign algorithm) and by h the digest in DSA, i.e. the 160-bit sting. The public
parameters are q a 160-bit prime, $p = a \cdot q + 1$ a 1024-bit prime, and $g \in \mathbb{Z}_p$ a
generator of order q.

The DSA construction is depicted on Fig. 9 where $f(m)$ describes some function mapping the arbitrary message length to a fixed length strings which represents the "message preprocessing".

DSA uses the (original) hash-and-sign paradigm. $f(m)$ is simply

$$h \leftarrow H^*(m)$$

where H^* is a collision resistant hash function.

Consider textbook DSA is an UF-$\emptyset$MA-secure FML-DS. Note that it is existentially forgeable. Theorem 4 says that the scheme of Fig. 9 where $f(m)$ is

$$h \leftarrow \mathsf{G}(H_\kappa(m)) \qquad \text{where } \kappa \in_{\mathsf{u}} \{0,1\}^k,$$

$$(K_s, K_p) \leftarrow S.\mathsf{setup}(1^\lambda): \quad \text{pick } K_s \in_u \mathbb{Z}_q$$
$$K_p \leftarrow g^{K_s} \bmod p$$

$$\sigma \leftarrow S.\mathsf{sign}(K_s, m, k, r): \quad \text{pick } k \in_u \mathbb{Z}_q^*$$
$$r \leftarrow (g^k \bmod p) \bmod q$$
$$h \leftarrow f(m)$$
$$s \leftarrow \frac{h + K_s \cdot r}{k} \bmod p$$
$$\sigma \leftarrow (r, s)$$

$$b \leftarrow S.\mathsf{verify}(K_p, m, \sigma): \quad h \leftarrow f(m)$$
$$\text{check } r = (g^{\frac{h}{s} \bmod q} y^{\frac{r}{s} \bmod q} \bmod p) \bmod q$$

Fig. 9. The DSA Construction

is EF-CMA-secure when G is a preimage-tractable random oracle (say SHA-1 in practice) and H is a one-way eTCR hash function. Thus, we build an EF-CMA-secure AML-DS based on DSA without collision-resistance. Assuming that $G(H_\kappa(m))$ can be instantiated by $\mathsf{SHA1}(\mathsf{RMX}(\kappa, m))$ where RMX denotes the implementation from Halevi-Krawczyk [10] of the message randomization, the Halevi-Krawczyk construction is secure. The drawback is that the signature enlarges sending κ.

Instead of picking some new randomness κ we re-use randomness from the presign algorithm if the implementation of DSA allows it, i.e. we use $\mathsf{R}(r)$ where R is a random oracle. Theorem 5 says that the scheme of Fig. 9 where $f(m)$ is

$$h \leftarrow \mathsf{G}(H_{\mathsf{R}(r)}(m))$$

is EF-CMA-secure as well.

From Theorem 4 and Theorem 5, we deduce that our construction is (T, Q, ε_s')-EF-CMA-secure where $\varepsilon_s' \leq \varepsilon_f + q_p \cdot \varepsilon_w + (\ell - q) \cdot \varepsilon_H + q \cdot \varepsilon_S + \varepsilon_c$. Assuming an adversary bounded by a time complexity T and an online complexity $Q \leq T$, considering that ε_H, ε_s and ε_w are all equals to $T \cdot 2^{-160}$, k is 160-bit long, q, q_s, and ℓ are bounded by Q, and q_p is bounded by T, we obtain $\varepsilon_f \leq 9 \cdot Q \cdot T \cdot 2^{-160}$, $\varepsilon_c \leq Q^2 \cdot 2^{-160}$ and so

$$\varepsilon_s' \leq \left(12 \cdot Q \cdot T + Q^2\right) \cdot 2^{-160}.$$

Clearly, $Q \cdot T$ must be bounded by 2^{160}. Since Q is often near 2^{30}, we deduce that T can be close to 2^{130} which is much better than actual implementations requiring a complexity T bounded by 2^{80} to avoid collision attacks.

In summary, by using Theorem 4 and Theorem 5, we build a DSA-based EF-CMA-secure scheme for input messages of arbitrary length and with signatures as long as the original DSA scheme.

7   Conclusion

Consider any signature implementation S based on a textbook signature scheme S_0 and using the original hash-and-sign paradigm with a hash function G, i.e.

$S.\mathsf{sign}(K_s, m) = S_0.\mathsf{sign}(K_s, G(m))$. Assume that S_0 is weakly secure and that some weakness on G was reported.

By using Theorem 4, we can build a strongly secure implementation by adding a preprocessing $H_\kappa(m)$ where H is an OW-eTCR hash function. Our new construction S' defined by $S'.\mathsf{sign}(K_s, m) = S.\mathsf{sign}(K_s, H_\kappa(m)) = S_0.\mathsf{sign}(K_s, G(H_\kappa(m)))$ is strongly secure and actual implementations can still be used, it simply needs to "preprocess" the input message. This assumes that G can be modeled as a preimage-tractable random oracle.

References

1. Shoup, V. (ed.): CRYPTO 2005. LNCS, vol. 3621. Springer, Heidelberg (2005)
2. Bellare, M., Rogaway, P.: Random oracles are practical: a paradigm for designing efficient protocols. In: Deza, M., Manoussakis, I., Euler, R. (eds.) CCS '93. LNCS, vol. 1120, pp. 62–73. ACM Press, New York (1996)
3. Bellare, M., Rogaway, P.: The exact security of digital signatures – how to sign with RSA and Rabin. In: Maurer, U.M. (ed.) EUROCRYPT 1996. LNCS, vol. 1070, pp. 399–416. Springer, Heidelberg (1996)
4. Bellare, M., Rogaway, P.: Towards Making UOWHFs Practical. In: Kaliski Jr., B.S. (ed.) CRYPTO 1997. LNCS, vol. 1294, pp. 470–484. Springer, Heidelberg (1997)
5. Cramer, R., Shoup, V.: Signature Schemes Based on the Strong RSA Assumption. ACM Transactions on Information and System Security 3(3), 161–185 (2000)
6. Digital signature standard (DSS). Federal Information Processing Standard, Publication 186-2, U.S. Department of Commerce, NIST (2000)
7. Digital signature standard (DSS). Federal Information Processing Standard, Publication 186, U.S. Department of Commerce, NIST (1994)
8. ElGamal, T.: A public key cryptosystem and a signature scheme based on discrete logarithms. IEEE Transactions on Information Theory 31(4), 469–472 (1985)
9. Halevi, S., Krawczyk, H.: Strengthening Digital Signatures via Randomized Hashing. In: Dwork, C. (ed.) CRYPTO 2006. LNCS, vol. 4117, pp. 41–59. Springer, Heidelberg (2006)
10. Halevi, S., Krawczyk, H.: The RMX Transform and Digital Signatures (2006) http://www.ee.technion.ac.il/$\sim$hugo/rhash/
11. Housley, R., Ford, W., Polk, W., Solo, D.: RFC 2459: Internet X.509 Public Key Infrastructure Certificate and CRL Profile. IETF RFC Publication (1999)
12. Liskov, M.: Constructing an Ideal Hash Function from Weak Ideal Compression Functions. In: SAC '06, pp. ???–?? (2006)
13. Mironov, I.: Collision-Resistant No More: Hash-and-Sign Paradigm Revisited. In: Yung, M., Dodis, Y., Kiayias, A., Malkin, T.G. (eds.) PKC 2006. LNCS, vol. 3958, pp. 140–156. Springer, Heidelberg (2006)
14. Naor, M., Yung, M.: Universal one-way hash functions and their cryptographic applications. In: ACM Symposium on Theory of Computing, pp. 33–43 (1989)
15. Rivest, R.L.: The MD5 message digest algorithm. Technical Report Internet RFC-1321,IETF (1992)
16. Rivest, R.L., Shamir, A., Adleman, L.M.: A Method for Obtaining Digital Signatures and Public-Key Cryptosystems. Communications of the ACM 21(2), 120–126 (1978)

17. Rivest, R.L.: The MD4 Message Digest Algorithm. In: Menezes, A.J., Vanstone, S.A. (eds.) CRYPTO 1990. LNCS, vol. 537, pp. 303–311. Springer, Heidelberg (1991)
18. Rogaway, P.: Formalizing Human Ignorance: Collision-Resistant Hashing without the Keys. In: Nguyen, P.Q. (ed.) VIETCRYPT 2006. LNCS, vol. 4341, pp. 221–228. Springer, Heidelberg (2006)
19. Secure hash standard. Federal Information Processing Standard, Publication 180, U.S. Department of Commerce, NIST (1993)
20. Secure hash standard. Federal Information Processing Standard, Publication 180-1, U.S. Department of Commerce, NIST (1995)
21. Shoup, V.: Sequences of Games: A Tool for Taming Complexity in Security Proofs. Cryptology ePrint Archive, Report 2004/332. http://eprint.iacr.org/
22. Wang, X., Yin, Y., Yu, H.: Finding collisions in the full SHA1. In: Shoup, V. (ed.) CRYPTO 2005. LNCS, vol. 3621, pp. 17–36. Springer, Heidelberg (2005)
23. Wang, X., Yu, H.: How to break MD5 and other hash functions. In: Cramer, R.J.F. (ed.) EUROCRYPT 2005. LNCS, vol. 3494, pp. 19–35. Springer, Heidelberg (2005)
24. Wang, X., Yu, X., Yin, L.Y.: Efficient collision search attacks on SHA-0. In: Shoup, V. (ed.) CRYPTO 2005. LNCS, vol. 3621, pp. 1–16. Springer, Heidelberg (2005)

A   Probability of Collisions

We provide the necessary quantitative definitions of the entropy of a random variable.

Definition 1. *Let X a random variable in a set $\mathcal{X}$ with distribution $\mathcal{D}$. We define:*
the min-entropy *of X by:* $\qquad\qquad H_\infty(\mathcal{D}) = -\log\max_{x\in\mathcal{D}\mathcal{X}}\Pr[X = x]$
the Renyi entropy *(of order 2) of X by:* $H_2(\mathcal{D}) = -\log\sum_{x\in\mathcal{D}\mathcal{X}}\Pr[X = x]^2$

Mironov [13] computed the probability of collision on the outputs of a random oracle R.

Lemma 1 ([13]). *Let $\mathcal{R}$ denotes a set of possible r_j values with cardinality q. We consider ℓ i.i.d. trials r_i with distribution $\mathcal{D}$. Let ε_c be the probability that at least one of the trials is in $\mathcal{R}$ or at least two of the trials are equal. We have*

$$\varepsilon_c \leq 2^{-2\cdot H_\infty(\mathcal{D})}\cdot\ell^2\cdot q + 2^{-H_\infty(\mathcal{D})}\cdot\ell^2 \tag{1}$$

Note that we can use another bound for ε_c in terms of Renyi entropy as described in Lemma 2 or as pseudo-randomness as described in Lemma 3.

Lemma 2. *Let $\mathcal{R}$ denotes a set of possible r_j values with cardinality q. We consider ℓ i.i.d. trials r_i with distribution $\mathcal{D}$. Let ε_c be the probability that at least one of the trials is in $\mathcal{R}$ or at least two of the trials are equal. We have*

$$\varepsilon_c \leq \frac{\ell^2}{2}\cdot 2^{-H_2(\mathcal{D})} + \ell\cdot\sqrt{q}\cdot 2^{-\frac{H_2(\mathcal{D})}{2}} \tag{2}$$

Proof. Let $p_x = \Pr[r = x]$. We have

$$\varepsilon_c = \Pr[\exists i, j : i \neq j, r_i = r_j \text{ or } r_i \in \mathcal{R}]$$

$$\leq \frac{\ell^2}{2} \sum_x p_x^2 + \ell \sum_{x \in \mathcal{R}} p_x \leq \frac{\ell^2}{2} \sum_x p_x^2 + \ell \sqrt{q} \sqrt{\sum_x p_x^2}$$

$\square$

Lemma 3. *Let $\mathcal{R}$ denotes a set of possible r_j values with cardinality q. We consider ℓ i.i.d. trials r_i with distribution $\mathcal{D}$. Let ε_c be the probability that at least one of the trials is in $\mathcal{R}$ or at least two of the trials are equal. Assuming that $\mathcal{D}$ is (ℓ, ε)-PR in $\{0,1\}^\rho$, we have*

$$\varepsilon_c \leq q \cdot 2^{-\rho} + \frac{\ell^2}{2} \cdot 2^{-\rho} + \varepsilon \tag{3}$$

"Sandwich" Is Indeed Secure: How to Authenticate a Message with Just One Hashing

Kan Yasuda

NTT Information Sharing Platform Laboratories, NTT Corporation
1-1 Hikarinooka Yokosuka-shi, Kanagawa-ken 239-0847 Japan
yasuda.kan@lab.ntt.co.jp

Abstract. This paper shows that the classical "Sandwich" method, which prepends and appends a key to a message and then hashes the data using Merkle-Damgård iteration, does indeed provide a secure Message Authentication Code (MAC). The Sandwich construction offers a single-key MAC which can use the existing Merkle-Damgård implementation of hash functions as is, without direct access to the compression function. Hence the Sandwich approach gives us an alternative for HMAC particularly in a situation where message size is small and high performance is required, because the Sandwich scheme is more efficient than HMAC: it consumes only two blocks of "waste" rather than three as in HMAC, and it calls the hash function only once, whereas HMAC requires two invocations of hash function. The security result of the Sandwich method is similar to that of HMAC; namely, we prove that the Sandwich construction yields a PRF(Pseudo-Random Functions)-based MAC, provided that the underlying compression function satisfies PRF properties. In theory, the security reduction of the Sandwich scheme is roughly equivalent to that of HMAC, but in practice the requirements on the underlying compression function look quite different. Also, the security of the Sandwich construction heavily relies on the filling and padding methods to the data, and we show several ways of optimizing them without losing a formal proof of security.

Keywords: Message Authentication Code, MAC, Hash Function, Compression Function, Merkle-Damgård, Envelope MAC, RFC1828, HMAC.

1 Introduction

A Message Authentication Code (MAC) is a symmetric-key cryptographic primitive that is widely used for ensuring authenticity and data integrity. It is an algorithm, usually deterministic, that takes as its input a message M (which may not be encrypted), processes it with a secret key K and then produces a fixed-length output τ called "tag". A secure MAC protects tags from being forged.

A MAC is commonly realized via a cryptographic hash function, like SHA-1 or SHA-256 [1], for its performance and availability in software libraries. A hash

J. Pieprzyk, H. Ghodosi, and E. Dawson (Eds.): ACISP 2007, LNCS 4586, pp. 355–369, 2007.
© Springer-Verlag Berlin Heidelberg 2007

function is usually constructed by a smaller primitive called "compression function." A compression function only processes messages of a fixed length. In order to create a hash function that accepts messages of variable lengths, the messages are padded and the compression function is iterated via a mode of operation. The most widespread mode is so called Merkle-Damgård strengthening (padding) and iteration. We are interested in hash functions that are implemented in this way.

The hash function, however, is keyless. In order to use it as a MAC, we must somehow make the hash function keyed. We briefly review four types of keying the hash function h, along the course of [2].

"PREFIX" METHOD. This faulty way prepends a key K to a message M and then lets the hash value $\tau = h(K\|M)$ be the tag. It is well known that this method is vulnerable against so called the "extension attack." Namely, an adversary asks its oracle the tag $\tau = h(K\|M)$ for a message M, computes a value $\tau' = h(\tau, M')$ where τ is used as the initial vector for h and M' an arbitrary message, and then succeeds in submitting the pair $(M\|M', \tau')$ as a forgery.

"SUFFIX" METHOD. An obvious way to avoid the extension attack is to append, rather than prepend, the key K to the message M and then obtain the tag $\tau = h(M\|K)$. This gets around the extension attack but suffers from the collision attack. Namely, let M, M' be two messages that produce a collision of the keyless hash function h, so that $h(M) = h(M')$. Then an adversary queries its oracle the tag $\tau = h(M\|K)$ and then submits a pair (M', τ) as a forgery. For more discussions on the notion of collision resistance for keyless hash functions, see [3].

"SANDWICH" METHOD. The combination of the above two approaches originates from the "hybrid method" in [4], where the tag τ is computed as $\tau = h(K\|p\|M\|K')$ with two independent keys K, K' and key filling (padding) p. A proof of security of the hybrid method is essentially given in [5]. The single-key version, in which the tag τ is computed as $\tau = h(K\|p\|M\|K)$, appears in the standardization of IPSec version 1 [2,6,7] and is known as the "envelope MAC." The envelope MAC, however, is shown to be vulnerable against key recovery attack [8] (which is more threatening than forgery attack.) We note that it is the lack of appropriate filling between the message M and the last key K, rather than the usage of a single key, that contributes to this key recovery attack.

Nowadays these hybrid/envelope techniques seem to attract little interest, mainly due to the above key recovery attack and the affirmative adoption of HMAC (described below) in IPSec version 2 ([7] is "obsoleted" by [9] which is also now "historic." [6] is still present only for the purpose of backward compatibility.) This paper calls attention back to this classical method. It is the contribution of this paper to show that the "Sandwich" scheme, which basically works as $\tau = h(K\|p\|M\|p'\|K)$, indeed yields a secure, single-key MAC, as long as the underlying compression function satisfies Pseudo-Random-Function (PRF) properties and appropriate fillings p, p' and padding methods are combined with. It should be remarked that as a byproduct the Sandwich scheme precludes the key recovery attack.

HMAC. HMAC is introduced in [10] with a (rather rough but formal) proof of security. Its new proof with complete reduction to the compression function is given in [11]. HMAC works as follows. It first computes the intermediate value $v = h\big((K \oplus IPAD)\|IPAD'\|M\big)$ and then computes the tag $\tau = h\big((K \oplus OPAD)\|OPAD'\|v\big)$, where $\oplus$ denotes bitwise exclusive-OR and $IPAD$, $IPAD'$, $OPAD$, $OPAD'$ are pre-defined constants. Note that unlike the other methods mentioned so far, HMAC requires two invocations of hash function h.

ORGANIZATION OF THIS PAPER. In Sect. 2 we identify the improvements in performance of the Sandwich scheme as compared to that of HMAC. In Sect. 3 we review some preliminaries of hash function, which are necessary in Sect. 4 to define the basic construction of the Sandwich scheme and to state its main security result. In Sect. 5 we compare this result to that of HMAC [11].

Section 7 is devoted for the security proof of the basic Sandwich construction, preceded by necessary definitions in Sect. 6. As to the reduction techniques in Sect. 7, we follow the line of [11], rather than that of [5] which essentially contains a proof of security for two-key hybrid method. Our approach enables us to prove the security of the single-key Sandwich scheme and also to compare our result directly with that of HMAC in [11].

It is also the contribution of this paper to introduce several variants of the basic Sandwich construction. Sections 8, 9 and 10 discuss these derivatives and show ways to modify the filling and padding methods in the basic construction, with improved efficiency and without loss of formal proofs of security. We emphasize the fact that although these improvements seem only subtle and minor, they become valuable in a situation with severe resource requirements and/or with short messages. The security results in Sect. 8 and 10 make use of the multi-oracle families introduced in [5].

2   Performance Comparison to HMAC

In Table 1 we summarize the performance comparison between the Sandwich method and HMAC. The Sandwich method consumes (at most) two blocks of "waste," corresponding to the very first and last blocks for the key. HMAC, on the other hand, consumes one more block for processing the intermediate value v, totaling three blocks (The "waste" is defined to be the number of invocations of compression function in the scheme minus that in the usual Merkle-Damgård.)

Also, the Sandwich method calls a hash function only once, as in $h(K\|M\|K)$, whereas HMAC requires two invocations of a hash function, one for producing the intermediate hash value $v = h\big((K \oplus IPAD)\|IPAD'\|M\big)$, and then another for processing the hash value v with the key K as in $h = \big((K \oplus OPAD)\|OPAD'\|v\big)$.

These problems of HMAC are discussed and improved in [12] (which appears in the standardization of CDMA2000 [13], where these drawbacks are critical.) Yet, the improved algorithm [12] still requires two invocations for long messages. The Sandwich scheme affords a way to authenticate any message with just one invocation.

Table 1. Numbers of waste blocks and hash function calls

	‖Waste blocks	Hash function calls
Sandwich‖	1-2	1
HMAC‖	3	2

3   Hash Function Basics

COMPRESSION FUNCTION. A compression function f is a keyless function $f : \{0,1\}^{n+d} \to \{0,1\}^n$. The first n bits of the input to f are referred to as a "chaining variable," where as the last d bits of the input are referred to as a "data input" or "message block." Typical values of n and d are $(n, d) = (160, 512)$ for SHA-1 and $(n, d) = (256, 512)$ for SHA-256. Hereafter in this section we fix our choice of compression function f.

MERKLE-DAMGÅRD ITERATION. The Merkle-Damgård iteration allows us to extend the domain of f from $\{0,1\}^{n+d}$ to $\{0,1\}^{d*}$, the set of bit strings whose lengths are multiples of d bits. Namely, the function $F_{IV} : \{0,1\}^{d*} \to \{0,1\}^n$ is constructed as follows: Let $M \in \{0,1\}^{d*}$ and divide M into message blocks as $M = m_1 \| \cdots \| m_\ell$, $m_i \in \{0,1\}^d$. Then the hash value $F_{IV}(M)$ is defined by:

$$v_1 \leftarrow f(IV\|m_1), \ v_i \leftarrow f(v_{i-1}\|m_i) \text{ for } i = 2, \ldots, \ell, \ F_{IV}(M) \overset{\text{def}}{=} v_\ell,$$

where the initial vector $IV \in \{0,1\}^n$ is a pre-defined constant.

PADDING. The current implementation of hash function is equipped with a padding so called the Merkle-Damgård strengthening. It is a padding method that takes the form of $M\|\pi(|M|) \in \{0,1\}^{d*}$ for messages $M \in \{0,1\}^{\leq \tilde{N}}$ whose lengths are at most $\tilde{N}$ bits (Note that the function π takes as its input the length $|M|$ in bits of the message M.) A typical value of $\tilde{N}$ is 2^{64}. The Merkle-Damgård iteration and strengthening are combined to yield the hash function $h : \{0,1\}^{\leq \tilde{N}} \to \{0,1\}^n$ by $h(M) \overset{\text{def}}{=} F_{IV}(M\|\pi(|M|))$.

DUAL FAMILIES. There are two ways of keying the compression function f. One is to key it via the first k bits of data input, yielding $f_K^\triangledown : \{0,1\}^{n+p} \to \{0,1\}^n$ with $K \in \{0,1\}^k$ and $p \overset{\text{def}}{=} d - k > 0$, precisely defined by $f_K^\triangledown(v\|z) \overset{\text{def}}{=} f(v\|K\|z)$ for $v \in \{0,1\}^n$, $z \in \{0,1\}^p$. The other way keys the chaining variable, yielding $f_{\check{K}}^\triangleright : \{0,1\}^d \to \{0,1\}^n$ with $\check{K} \in \{0,1\}^n$ defined by $f_{\check{K}}^\triangleright(m) \overset{\text{def}}{=} f(\check{K}\|m)$ for $m \in \{0,1\}^d$. If we are allowed to call only h (and not f), then we do not have direct access to the chaining variable. Hence $f^\triangledown$ appears explicitly whenever we try to key, whereas $f^\triangleright$ appears only implicitly for the purpose of security analysis.

OTHER KEYED FAMILIES. The Merkle-Damgård iteration F_{IV} can be also (implicitly) keyed, by replacing the initial vector IV with a key $\check{K} \in \{0,1\}^n$. This gives us a function family $\{F_{\check{K}} : \{0,1\}^{d*} \to \{0,1\}^n\}$. We then extend the domain

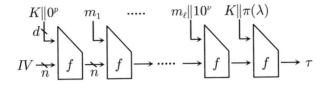

$$K\|0^p \quad m_1 \quad \cdots \quad m_\ell\|10^\nu \quad K\|\pi(\lambda)$$

Fig. 1. Sandwich scheme, basic version

$\{0,1\}^{d*}$ to $\{0,1\}^*$ via the trivial padding $M\|10^\nu$, where $\nu \overset{\text{def}}{=} d-(|M| \bmod d)-1$ (We view ν as a function of M and often write $\nu(M)$ to denote this quantity.) This defines another function family $\{\bar{F}_{\check{K}} : \{0,1\}^* \to \{0,1\}^n\}$ via $\bar{F}_{\check{K}}(M) \overset{\text{def}}{=} F_{\check{K}}(M\|10^\nu)$.

4 Our Contribution

Figure 1 depicts the basic construction of the Sandwich scheme (We call it "basic," because later in Sect. 8, 9 and 10 we introduce several derivatives with optimized filling or padding.) The basic Sandwich method S takes as its input a message M and a key $K \in \{0,1\}^k$ and lets the hash value $\tau = h(K\|0^p\|M\|10^\nu\|K)$ be the tag, with $\nu = \nu(M)$. The message M is divided into d-bit blocks as $M = m_1\|\ldots\|m_\ell$, where $\ell = \lceil(|M|+1)/d\rceil$ and m_ℓ is a bit string whose length varies from 0 (the null string) to $d-1$ bits. Note that the length of the data $K\|0^p\|M\|10^\nu\|K$ is $\tilde\lambda \overset{\text{def}}{=} d(\ell+1)+k$ bits, which is input to the padding function π, and we are assuming $|\pi(\lambda)| = p$. We view λ as a function of M and often write $\lambda(M)$ to denote this quantity. Now we have the basic Sandwich scheme $S_K : \{0,1\}^N \to \{0,1\}^n$, where $N = \tilde{N} - d - 1 - k$.

The main contribution of this paper is to show that the basic Sandwich approach S gives a secure, single-key MAC. More precisely, we prove that it yields a PRF-based MAC, under the conditions that $\pi(\lambda) \neq 0^p$ for any λ and that both $f^\triangledown$ and $f^\triangleright$ are PRFs.

5 Security Comparison to HMAC

The security of HMAC also relies on the pseudorandomness of $f^\triangledown$ and $f^\triangleright$ [11]. In order for these functions to be PRFs, they must resist adversary's queries to its oracles. In Table 2 we compare these numbers.

It should be noted that the two "2"s in Table 2 come from very different nature. The "2" in the Sandwich scheme has roots in collision resistance, whereas the "2" in HMAC originates from a key derivation. $f^\triangleright$ in the Sandwich method must resist two oracle queries m, m' of adversary's choice, while $f^\triangledown$ in HMAC only needs to resist constant queries $IV\|IPAD'$ and $IV\|OPAD'$. In this regard, HMAC is based on a weaker assumption.

Theoretically, there is no difference between the requirement that $f^\triangledown$ is a PRF and one that $f^\triangleright$ is a PRF, as long as $k = n$ (The difference is just which

Table 2. Numbers of oracle queries that compression function must resist

	$f^\triangledown$ (Keyed via message block)	$f^\triangleright$ (Keyed via chaining variable)
Sandwich	$q+1$	2
HMAC	2	q

bits of input are keyed). In practice, however, the nature of data input and that of chaining variable are quite dissimilar, for an adversary can directly access the former but not the latter. In fact, existing compression functions like SHA-1 and SHA-256 are designed so that data input and chaining variable are processed in completely separate procedures. It seems that we have to wait for further research [14,15] on existing compression functions to identify this difference in them.

Also, the coefficients in the security reduction of the Sandwich scheme are fundamentally the same as those in that of HMAC. The result given in Sect. 7 is essentially tight, due to the general "birthday attack" [16]. For more discussions on the exact tightness of this type of reduction, see [11].

6 Security Definitions

The notation $x \xleftarrow{\$} X$ denotes the operation of selecting an element x uniformly at random from a set X. An adversary is an algorithm A, possibly probabilistic, that may have access to a oracle. The notation $A^{\mathcal{O}} \Rightarrow x$ denotes the event that A with the indicated oracle outputs x. Oracles are often defined in a "game" style. We then write $A^{\mathcal{G}} \Rightarrow x$ to denote the event that A outputs x in the experiment of running A as specified in game $\mathcal{G}$.

PRFs. Any PRF is a secure MAC [17]. All the MACs that appear in this paper are PRF-based. Consider a function family $\{f_K : X \to Y\}_{K \in KEY}$. A prf-adversary A tries to distinguish between two oracles, one being $f_K(\cdot), K \xleftarrow{\$} KEY$ and the other being $f(\cdot), f \xleftarrow{\$} \{f : X \to Y\}$. Succinctly, define

$$\mathrm{Adv}_f^{\mathrm{prf}}(A) \overset{\mathrm{def}}{=} \Pr\left[A^{f_K, K \xleftarrow{\$}} \Rightarrow 1\right] - \Pr\left[A^{f \xleftarrow{\$}} \Rightarrow 1\right]$$

to be the prf-advantage of A against f.

cAU. The notion of "computationally Almost Universal (cAU)" measures a sort of collision resistance. An au-adversary A, given access to no oracle, just outputs a pair of messages $(M, M') \in X \times X$. Then define

$$\mathrm{Adv}_f^{\mathrm{au}}(A) \overset{\mathrm{def}}{=} \Pr\left[f_K(M) = f_K(M') \wedge M \neq M' \;\middle|\; A \Rightarrow (M, M'), K \xleftarrow{\$} KEY\right]$$

to be the au-advantage of A against f.

RESOURCES. An adversary A's resources are measured in terms of the time complexity t, the number q of oracle queries and the length μ in bits of each query. The time complexity t includes the total execution time of an overlying experiment (the maximum if more than one experiments are involved) plus the size of the code of A, in some fixed model of computation. We write $T_f(\mu)$ to denote the time needed for one computation of f on a input whose length is μ bits. For $* \in \{\mathrm{prf}, \mathrm{au}, \ldots\}$ we write

$$\mathrm{Adv}_f^*(t, q, \mu) \overset{\mathrm{def}}{=} \max \mathrm{Adv}_f^*(A),$$

where max is run over adversaries, each having time complexity at most t and making at most q oracle queries, each query of at most μ bits. One or more of the resources are often omitted from the notation if irrelevant in the context. In particular, we often omit the time complexity of an au-adversary A, due to the following lemma.

Lemma 1. *For any time complexity t, we have*

$$\mathrm{Adv}_f^{\mathrm{au}}(t, \mu) \leq \mathrm{Adv}_f^{\mathrm{au}}(2 \cdot T_f(\mu), \mu).$$

Proof. Let A be an au-adversary against f that has time complexity at most t and outputs messages of at most μ bits each. By definition we have

$$\mathrm{Adv}_f^{\mathrm{au}}(A) = \sum_{M, M'} \left(\Pr\left[\{M, M'\} = \{\bar{M}, \bar{M}'\} \,\middle|\, A \Rightarrow (\bar{M}, \bar{M}') \right] \right.$$
$$\left. \times \left[f_K(M) = f_K(M') \,\middle|\, K \overset{\$}{\leftarrow} KEY \right] \right),$$

where the summation is over all pairs $\{M, M'\}$ of two distinct messages whose lengths are at most μ bits each. Hence, there exists a pair (M, M') of distinct messages such that $\mathrm{Adv}_f^{\mathrm{au}}(A) \leq \Pr[f_K(M) = f_K(M')]$. Then we can create a new adversary B that has M, M' hardwired as a part of its code and simply outputs these messages. $\qquad\square$

7   Security Proof of the Basic Construction

The following theorem states the security result of the basic Sandwich scheme.

Theorem 1. *Let $f : \{0,1\}^{n+p} \to \{0,1\}^n$ be a compression function and $S_K : \{0,1\}^{\leq N} \to \{0,1\}^n$ the basic Sandwich scheme constructed from f, as described in Sect. 4. Then the basic Sandwich scheme S is a PRF, provided that both $f^\triangledown$ and $f^\triangleright$ are PRFs. More formally, we have*

$$\mathrm{Adv}_S^{\mathrm{prf}}(t, q, \mu) \leq \mathrm{Adv}_{f^\triangledown}^{\mathrm{prf}}(t, q+1) + \binom{q}{2} \cdot \left(\left(2 \cdot \left\lceil \frac{\mu}{d} \right\rceil + 1 \right) \cdot \mathrm{Adv}_{f^\triangleright}^{\mathrm{prf}}(t', 2) + \frac{1}{2^n} \right),$$

where $t' = 4 \cdot \lceil (\mu/d) + 1 \rceil \cdot T_f$.

The following three lemmas prove the above theorem.

Adversary B	Adversary C
Query $IV\|0^p$ to oracle f^∇	$s \leftarrow 0;\ \tau_1, \ldots, \tau_q \xleftarrow{\$} \{0,1\}^n$
and obtain $\check{K} = f^\nabla(IV\|0^p)$	$i \xleftarrow{\$} \{1, \ldots, q-1\};\ j \xleftarrow{\$} \{i+1, \ldots, q\}$
Run A; On A's query M do:	Run A; On A's query M do:
$\quad$ Compute $v \leftarrow \bar{F}_{\check{K}}(M)$	$\quad s \leftarrow s + 1$
$\quad$ Query $v\|\pi(\lambda(M))$ to oracle f^∇	$\quad M_s \leftarrow M$
$\quad$ and obtain $\tau = f^\nabla(v\|\pi(\lambda))$	$\quad$ Reply τ_s to A
$\quad$ Reply τ to A	Output (M_i, M_j)
Output whatever A outputs	

Fig. 2. Description of adversaries B and C

Game $\mathcal{G}$	Game $\mathcal{G}'$
$f^\nabla \xleftarrow{\$} \{f : \{0,1\}^{n+p} \to \{0,1\}^n\}$	$f^\nabla \xleftarrow{\$} \{f : \{0,1\}^{n+p} \to \{0,1\}^n\}$
$\check{K} \leftarrow f^\nabla(IV\|0^p)$	$\check{K} \xleftarrow{\$} \{0,1\}^n$
On query M	On query M
$\quad$ reply $f^\nabla(\bar{F}_{\check{K}}(M)\|\pi(\lambda(M)))$	$\quad$ reply $f^\nabla(\bar{F}_{\check{K}}(M)\|\pi(\lambda(M)))$

Fig. 3. Intermediate games $\mathcal{G}$ and $\mathcal{G}'$

Lemma 2. *If f^∇ is a PRF and $\bar{F}$ (constructed from f as in Sect. 3) is cAU, then the basic Sandwich scheme S is a PRF. More formally, we have*

$$\mathrm{Adv}_S^{\mathrm{prf}}(t, q, \mu) \leq \mathrm{Adv}_{f^\nabla}^{\mathrm{prf}}(t, q+1) + \binom{q}{2} \cdot \mathrm{Adv}_{\bar{F}}^{\mathrm{au}}(\mu).$$

Proof. Let A be a prf-adversary against S that has time complexity at most t and makes at most $q \geq 2$ oracle queries, each of at most μ bits. We shall construct a prf-adversary B against f^∇ and an au-adversary C against $\bar{F}$, each using A as a subroutine, as described in Fig. 2. Note that B has time complexity at most t and makes at most $q + 1$ oracle queries, and C outputs two messages, each of at most μ bits. We show that

$$\mathrm{Adv}_S^{\mathrm{prf}}(A) \leq \mathrm{Adv}_{f^\nabla}^{\mathrm{prf}}(B) + \binom{q}{2} \cdot \mathrm{Adv}_{\bar{F}}^{\mathrm{au}}(C).$$

Let $\mathcal{G}, \mathcal{G}'$ be two games defined in Fig. 3. These games define oracles for the adversary A.

Claim. We have

$$\mathrm{Adv}_{f^\nabla}^{\mathrm{prf}}(B) \overset{\mathrm{def}}{=} \Pr\left[B^{f_{\check{K}}^\nabla, K \xleftarrow{\$}} \Rightarrow 1\right] - \Pr\left[B^{f^\nabla \xleftarrow{\$}} \Rightarrow 1\right]$$

$$= \Pr\left[A^{S_K, K \xleftarrow{\$}} \Rightarrow 1\right] - \Pr\left[A^{\mathcal{G}} \Rightarrow 1\right].$$

Proof. If oracle $f^\triangledown$ to B is given by $f_K^\triangledown, K \xleftarrow{\$} \{0,1\}^k$, then observe that B correctly simulates the oracle $S_K, K \xleftarrow{\$} \{0,1\}^k$ for A. Hence $\Pr\left[B^{f_K^\triangledown, K \xleftarrow{\$}} \Rightarrow 1\right] = \Pr\left[A^{S_K, K \xleftarrow{\$}} \Rightarrow 1\right]$. On the other hand, if oracle $f^\triangledown$ to B is given by $f^\triangledown \xleftarrow{\$} \{f : \{0,1\}^{n+p} \to \{0,1\}^n\}$, then running B^A exactly corresponds to running $A^{\mathcal{G}}$. Thus $\Pr\left[B^{f^\triangledown \xleftarrow{\$}} \Rightarrow 1\right] = \Pr\left[A^{\mathcal{G}} \Rightarrow 1\right]$.

Claim. Game $\mathcal{G}$ is equivalent to Game $\mathcal{G}'$.

Proof. Recall that we assume the condition $\pi(\lambda(M)) \neq 0^p$ for every M. Hence in Game $\mathcal{G}$ we have $\bar{F}_{\check{K}}(M) \| \pi(\lambda(M)) \neq IV \| 0^p$ for every query M, and while replying to A's queries the random function $f^\triangledown$ is never invoked on the input value $IV \| 0^p$. This means that in Game $\mathcal{G}$ the key $\check{K} = f^\triangledown(IV \| 0^p)$ is a random value independent from A's queries, and the equivalence to Game $\mathcal{G}'$ follows.

Now we assume, without loss of generality, that the adversary A never repeats a query and that the total number of A's queries is always exactly q rather than at most q, no matter how replies to A's queries are made. Let $M_1, \ldots, M_q$ represent A's queries in order.

Let E be the event that $\bar{F}_{\check{K}}(M_i) \| \pi(\lambda(M_i)) = \bar{F}_{\check{K}}(M_j) \| \pi(\lambda(M_j))$ occurs for some $1 \leq i < j \leq q$. Observe that as long as E does not occur, Game $\mathcal{G}'$ for A and running A with the oracle $S \xleftarrow{\$} \{S : \{0,1\}^{\leq N} \to \{0,1\}^n\}$ proceed exactly the same. Therefore, by the Fundamental Lemma of Game Playing [18], we obtain

$$\Pr\left[A^{\mathcal{G}'} \Rightarrow 1\right] - \Pr\left[A^{S \xleftarrow{\$}} \Rightarrow 1\right] \leq \Pr[E].$$

Claim. We have

$$\Pr[E] \leq \binom{q}{2} \cdot \mathrm{Adv}_{\bar{F}}^{\mathrm{au}}(C).$$

Proof. Let E' denote the event that $\bar{F}_{\check{K}}(M_i) = \bar{F}_{\check{K}}(M_j)$ for some $1 \leq i < j \leq q$, so that $\Pr[E] \leq \Pr[E']$. For $1 \leq \alpha < \beta \leq q$ let $E'_{\alpha,\beta}$ denote the event that $\bar{F}_{\check{K}}(M_\alpha) = \bar{F}_{\check{K}}(M_\beta)$ occurs while $\bar{F}_{\check{K}}(M_{\bar{\alpha}}) \neq \bar{F}_{\check{K}}(M_{\bar{\beta}})$ for all $1 \leq \bar{\alpha} < \bar{\beta} < \beta$. Notice that the events $E'_{\alpha,\beta}$ for $1 \leq \alpha < \beta \leq q$ are disjoint and $E' = \bigvee_{1 \leq \alpha < \beta \leq q} E'_{\alpha,\beta}$. Then

$$\mathrm{Adv}_{\bar{F}}^{\mathrm{au}}(C) \geq \Pr\left[\bigvee_{1 \leq \alpha < \beta \leq q} E'_{\alpha,\beta} \wedge (i,j) = (\alpha, \beta)\right]$$

$$= \sum_{1 \leq \alpha < \beta \leq q} \Pr\left[E'_{\alpha,\beta} \wedge (i,j) = (\alpha, \beta)\right]$$

$$= \sum_{1 \leq \alpha < \beta \leq q} \Pr\left[E'_{\alpha,\beta}\right] \cdot \Pr\left[(i,j) = (\alpha, \beta)\right]$$

$$= \frac{1}{\binom{q}{2}} \sum_{1 \leq \alpha < \beta \leq q} \Pr\left[E'_{\alpha,\beta}\right] = \frac{1}{\binom{q}{2}} \Pr[E'] \geq \frac{1}{\binom{q}{2}} \Pr[E].$$

Now we see that

$$\mathrm{Adv}_S^{\mathrm{prf}}(A) \overset{\mathrm{def}}{=} \Pr\!\left[A^{S_K, K \overset{\$}{\leftarrow}} \Rightarrow 1\right] - \Pr\!\left[A^{S \overset{\$}{\leftarrow}} \Rightarrow 1\right]$$

$$= \Pr\!\left[A^{S_K, K \overset{\$}{\leftarrow}} \Rightarrow 1\right] - \Pr\!\left[A^{\mathcal{G}} \Rightarrow 1\right] + \Pr\!\left[A^{\mathcal{G}'} \Rightarrow 1\right] - \Pr\!\left[A^{S \overset{\$}{\leftarrow}} \Rightarrow 1\right]$$

$$\le \mathrm{Adv}_{f\triangledown}^{\mathrm{prf}}(B) + \binom{q}{2} \cdot \mathrm{Adv}_{\bar{F}}^{\mathrm{au}}(C).$$

$\square$

Lemma 3. *Let* $f : \{0,1\}^{n+d} \to \{0,1\}^n$ *be a compression function. If* F *(constructed from* f *as in Sect. 3) is cAU, then so is* $\bar{F}$. *More formally, we have*

$$\mathrm{Adv}_{\bar{F}}^{\mathrm{au}}(t, \mu) \le \mathrm{Adv}_F^{\mathrm{au}}(t, \mu + d).$$

Proof. Let A be an au-adversary against $\bar{F}$ that has time complexity at most t and outputs messages (M, M') of at most μ bits each. Then we can easily construct an au-adversary B against F, by letting B simply output the pair $(M \| 10^{\nu(M)}, M' \| 10^{\nu(M')})$. Note that $M \ne M'$ implies $M \| 10^{\nu(M)} \ne M' \| 10^{\nu(M')}$. $\square$

Lemma 4. *Let* $f : \{0,1\}^{n+d} \to \{0,1\}^n$ *be a compression function. If* $f^{\triangleright}$ *is a PRF, then* F *(constructed from* f *as in Sect. 3) is cAU. More formally, we have*

$$\mathrm{Adv}_F^{\mathrm{au}}(t, \mu) \le \left(2 \cdot \left\lceil \frac{\mu}{d} \right\rceil - 1\right) \cdot \mathrm{Adv}_{f^{\triangleright}}^{\mathrm{prf}}(t', 2) + \frac{1}{2^n},$$

where $t' = t + 2 \cdot \lceil \mu/d \rceil \cdot T_f$, T_f *being the time for one evaluation of* f.

Proof. This result is obtained in [11]. $\square$

Now from the above lemmas we have

$$\mathrm{Adv}_S^{\mathrm{prf}}(t, q, \mu) \le \mathrm{Adv}_{f\triangledown}^{\mathrm{prf}}(t, q+1) + \binom{q}{2} \cdot \mathrm{Adv}_{\bar{F}}^{\mathrm{au}}(\mu)$$

$$\le \mathrm{Adv}_{f\triangledown}^{\mathrm{prf}}(t, q+1) + \binom{q}{2} \cdot \mathrm{Adv}_F^{\mathrm{au}}(\mu + d)$$

$$\le \mathrm{Adv}_{f\triangledown}^{\mathrm{prf}}(t, q+1) + \binom{q}{2} \cdot \left(\left(2 \cdot \left\lceil \frac{\mu}{d} \right\rceil + 1\right) \cdot \mathrm{Adv}_{f^{\triangleright}}^{\mathrm{prf}}(t', 2) + \frac{1}{2^n}\right),$$

where $t' = 2 \cdot T_{\bar{F}}(\mu) + 2 \cdot \lceil (\mu/d) + 1 \rceil \cdot T_f \le 4 \cdot \lceil (\mu/d) + 1 \rceil \cdot T_f$. This proves Theorem 1.

8   Variant A: Reducing the First Filling 0^p

The filling 0^p after the first key K may be considered as consuming, particularly if p is large. Figure 4 describes a variant of the basic Sandwich scheme, which uses a one-bit filling 0 rather than 0^p. Note that in this variant a message M is now divided into blocks as $M = m_1\|m_2\| \ldots \|m_\ell$ with $|m_1| = p-1$, $|m_2| = \cdots = |m_{\ell-1}| = d$ and $0 \leq |m_\ell| \leq d-1$. In case $|M| \leq p-2$ the entire message $M = m_1$ is processed by the very first block (In this variant the condition $\pi(\mu) \neq 0^{p-1}$ is not required. Also, the functions ν and λ and the number N are re-defined accordingly.)

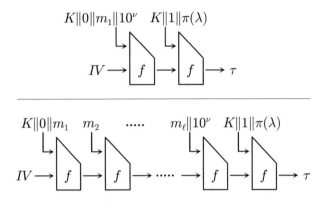

Fig. 4. Variant A: Reducing the filling 0^p to 0

This variant is secure. However, its analysis is more complex than that of the basic construction. The proof of security requires novel techniques that are not included in that of the basic version. Intuitively, this is because now an adversary can change the value of $\check{K}$ via querying different m_1. Owing to the pseudorandomness of $f^\triangledown$ (and appropriate fillings 0 and 1 after the key K), for different $m_1, m_1', m_1'', \ldots$ the adversary "sees" independently random keys $\check{K}, \check{K}', \check{K}'', \ldots$ (This, however, demands that $f^\triangledown$ be resistant against $2q$ oracle queries rather than $q+1$.) Now the difficulty lies in the treatment of the event that a "collision" is detected. Observe that there can be two different cases for a collision. One is with the same key as in $\bar{F}_{\check{K}}(M) = \bar{F}_{\check{K}}(M')$ with $M \neq M'$, and the other with different keys as in $\bar{F}_{\check{K}}(M) = \bar{F}_{\check{K}'}(M')$ (and not necessarily $M \neq M'$.) The first case can be handled in the same way as in the basic version. The problem is that we also have to bound the latter probability by the pseudorandomness of $f^\triangleright$.

We deal with this problem along the course of prefix-free PRFs and multi-oracle families [5]. Recall that F is a prefix-free PRF if $f^\triangleright$ is a PRF. Next we extend the result of multi-oracle families in [5] from PRFs to prefix-free PRFs. We can then bound the collision probability by the multi-oracle family of F. This does not affect the query number for $f^\triangleright$ (It still remains to be 2) but worsens the coefficient roughly by a factor of 2. We state the result concretely in the following theorem.

Theorem 2. *Let $f : \{0,1\}^{n+d} \to \{0,1\}^n$ be a compression function and $S_K :$ $\{0,1\}^{\leq N} \to \{0,1\}^n$ the Variant A constructed from f. Then we have*

$$\mathrm{Adv}_S^{\mathrm{prf}}(t,q,\mu) \leq \mathrm{Adv}_{f_\triangledown}^{\mathrm{prf}}(t,2q) + \binom{q}{2} \cdot \left(4 \cdot \left(\left\lceil \frac{\mu}{d} \right\rceil + 2\right) \cdot \mathrm{Adv}_{f_\triangleright}^{\mathrm{prf}}(t',2) + \frac{1}{2^n}\right),$$

where $t' = t + 2q \cdot \lceil \mu/d \rceil \cdot T_f$.

9   Variant B: Improving the Second Filling 10^ν

We go back to the basic Sandwich construction and discuss how to avoid the waste that occurs when the message size $|M|$ happens to be exactly equal to a multiple of d bits. Note that in such a case, the filling bits $1\|0^{d-1}$ is appended after the message M, producing an extra one block of compression function. We show a technique to get rid of this increase.

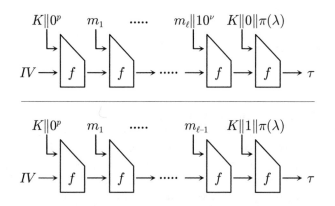

Fig. 5. Variant B: Case m_ℓ is not null (upper) and m_ℓ null (lower)

The technique works as follows: If the message size $|M|$ is not equal to a multiple of d, then the usual filling $1\|0^\nu$ is appended after the message M, and then the key K is appended, followed by $0\|\pi(\lambda)$. On the other hand, if the message size $|M|$ happens to be exactly a multiple of d, then *no* filling is appended after the message M; instead, we directly append the key K after the message M and then append the padding $1\|\pi(\lambda)$ (Again, the function λ and the number N are re-defined accordingly, and we assume $\pi(\lambda) \neq 0^{p-1}$ for all λ in this variant.)

This variant is also secure, and the proof of security does not require much modification to that of the basic version. So let us review the reduction proofs and see this new scheme actually preserves the security. First, the construction of adversary B naturally transforms into the new setting. The equivalence between Game $\mathcal{G}$ and Game $\mathcal{G}'$ still holds, for we assume $\pi(\lambda) \neq 0^{p-1}$, and hence $\check{K}$ is a random value independent from A's queries. A collision on the input value for $f^{\triangleright}$ can be divided into two cases in accordance with the padding $K\|0$ and $K\|1$, but both cases are bounded by $\mathrm{Adv}_F^{\mathrm{au}}$. So there is no degradation in the reduction:

Theorem 3. *Let $f : \{0,1\}^{n+d} \to \{0,1\}^n$ be a compression function and $S_K : \{0,1\}^{\leq N} \to \{0,1\}^n$ the Variant B constructed from f. Then*

$$\mathrm{Adv}_S^{\mathrm{prf}}(t, q, \mu) \leq \mathrm{Adv}_{f^{\triangledown}}^{\mathrm{prf}}(t, q+1) + \binom{q}{2} \cdot \left(\left(2 \cdot \left\lceil \frac{\mu}{d} \right\rceil + 1 \right) \cdot \mathrm{Adv}_{f^{\triangleright}}^{\mathrm{prf}}(t', 2) + \frac{1}{2^n} \right),$$

where $t' = 4 \cdot \lceil (\mu/d) + 1 \rceil \cdot T_f$.

We can extend this idea to gain further improvement, if there is enough "room" in the last block. Namely, let σ be the maximum number such that $K\|1\|m_\ell\|\pi(\lambda)$ fits in the last block with $m_\ell \in \{0,1\}^\sigma$ (Again, the number λ is re-defined accordingly.) For a message M with $|m_\ell| > \sigma$, we use the first case $m_\ell\|10^\nu\|K\|0\|\pi(\lambda)$ as is in the last two blocks. On the other hand, if $|m_\ell| \leq \sigma$ (including the case m_ℓ null), then we process the data $K\|1\|m_\ell\|\pi(\lambda)$ with only one computation in the very last block (and in the latter case note that for $m_\ell \neq m'_\ell$ we require $m_\ell\|\pi(\lambda) \neq m'_\ell\|\pi(\lambda')$.)

10   Variant C: Handling the Last Padding $\pi(\lambda)$

In this section we study the case where the block size d is too small to accommodate both the key K and padding $\pi(\lambda)$ in one block. The purpose of introducing this variant is twofold. One is to show the general applicability of the Sandwich approach with a low-ratio compression function. The other is to point out the powerfulness of the multi-oracle family techniques that we also used in Sect. 8.

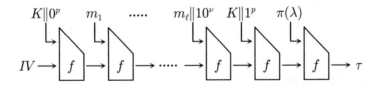

Fig. 6. Variant C: Padding with low-ratio compression function

The difference between this variant and the basic version is in the last padding. In this variant we use two blocks in order to process the second key K and the padding $\pi(\lambda)$ via $K\|1^p\|\pi(\lambda)$ (This, of course, does not provide any improvement in efficiency, and again, the function λ and the number N are re-defined.)

This variant is also secure, but the difficulty in analysis lies in the very last block. That is, we can "extract" a prf-adversary B against $f^{\triangledown}$ and an au-adversary C against $\bar{F}$ as in Sect. 7, but there still remains a "gap" (The gap arises from the very last block.) We have to fill in this gap somehow by the pseudorandomness of $f^{\triangleright}$. We do this via the multi-oracle family of $f^{\triangleright}$. This does not increase the query number "2," and the degradation in the reduction is only minor:

Theorem 4. *Let* $f : \{0,1\}^{n+d} \rightarrow \{0,1\}^n$ *be a compression function and* $S_K :$ $\{0,1\}^{\leq N} \rightarrow \{0,1\}^n$ *the Variant C constructed from* f. *Then*

$$\mathrm{Adv}_S^{\mathrm{prf}}(t,q,\mu) \leq \mathrm{Adv}_{f^{\triangledown}}^{\mathrm{prf}}(t,q+1)$$

$$+ \binom{q}{2} \cdot \left(\left(2 \cdot \left\lceil \frac{\mu}{d} \right\rceil + 1 \right) \cdot \mathrm{Adv}_{f^{\triangleright}}^{\mathrm{prf}}(t',2) + \frac{1}{2^n} \right) + q \cdot \mathrm{Adv}_{f^{\triangleright}}^{\mathrm{prf}}(t'',1),$$

where $t' = 4 \cdot \lceil (\mu/d) + 1 \rceil \cdot T_f$ *and* $t'' = t + 2q \cdot T_f$.

11   Concluding Remarks

The Sandwich approach offers a secure, single-key MAC which is more efficient than HMAC. The improvement in performance becomes beneficial especially for situations with severe resource requirements and/or with short messages. For short messages, the optimization techniques in variants A and B are quite effective. Any combination of the three variations A, B and C would work, provided that appropriate filling and padding methods are devised and used with.

The security reduction of the Sandwich scheme, in theory, is roughly equivalent to that of HMAC. They both rely on the pseudorandomness of $f^{\triangledown}$ and $f^{\triangleright}$. The difference between the requirement of $f^{\triangledown}$ being a PRF and that of $f^{\triangleright}$ a PRF would result in a difference between the security of the Sandwich scheme and that of HMAC. Thus in reality we have to wait for further research on existing hash functions like SHA-1 and SHA-256 in order to analyze how they satisfy the two requirements and to identify the differences.

Lastly, we remark that the key recovery attack known for previous hybrid and envelope MACs no longer applies to the Sandwich scheme presented here. A straight-forward observation tells us that a key recovery against the Sandwich scheme essentially amounts to the key recovery against $f^{\triangledown}$.

Acknowledgments

The author would like to thank ACISP2007 anonymous referees for their helpful comments, references to [4,8] and suggestions to improve notation and terminology. The final revision work of this paper has benefited greatly from advisory comments made by Kazumaro Aoki, including the reference to [2].

References

1. NIST: Secure hash standard, FIPS PUB 180-2 (2002)
2. Kaliski, B., Robshaw, M.: Message authentication with MD5. CryptoBytes (The Technical Newsletter of RSA Laboratories) 1(1), 5–8 (1995)

3. Rogaway, P.: Formalizing human ignorance: Collision-resistant hashing without the keys. In: Nguyen, P.Q. (ed.) VIETCRYPT 2006. LNCS, vol. 4341, pp. 211–228. Springer, Heidelberg (2006)
4. Tsudik, G.: Message authentication with one-way hash functions. ACM Computer Communication Review 22(5), 29–38 (1992)
5. Bellare, M., Canetti, R., Krawczyk, H.: Pseudorandom functions revisited: The cascade construction and its concrete security. IEEE Symposium on Foundations of Computer Science, 514–523 (1996)
6. Metzger, P., Simpson, W.A.: IP authentication using keyed MD5. IETF, RFC 1828 (1995)
7. Metzger, P., Simpson, W.A.: IP authentication using keyed SHA. IETF, RFC 1852 (1995)
8. Preneel, B., van Oorschot, P.C.: On the security of two MAC algorithms. In: Maurer, U.M. (ed.) EUROCRYPT 1996. LNCS, vol. 1070, pp. 19–32. Springer, Heidelberg (1996)
9. Metzger, P., Simpson, W.A.: IP authentication using keyed SHA1 with interleaved padding (IP-MAC). IETF, RFC 2841 (2000)
10. Bellare, M., Canetti, R., Krawczyk, H.: Keying hash functions for message authentication. In: Koblitz, N. (ed.) CRYPTO 1996. LNCS, vol. 1109, pp. 1–15. Springer, Heidelberg (1996)
11. Bellare, M.: New proofs for NMAC and HMAC: Security without collision-resistance. In: Dwork, C. (ed.) CRYPTO 2006. LNCS, vol. 4117, pp. 602–619. Springer, Heidelberg (2006)
12. Patel, S.: An efficient MAC for short messages. In: Nyberg, K., Heys, H.M. (eds.) SAC 2002. LNCS, vol. 2595, pp. 353–368. Springer, Heidelberg (2003)
13. TR45.AHAG: Enhanced cryptographic algorithms, revision B. TIA (2002)
14. Kim, J., Biryukov, A., Preneel, B., Hong, S.: On the security of HMAC and NMAC based on HAVAL, MD4, MD5, SHA-0 and SHA-1. In: De Prisco, R., Yung, M. (eds.) SCN 2006. LNCS, vol. 4116, pp. 242–256. Springer, Heidelberg (2006)
15. Contini, S., Yin, Y.L.: Forgery and partial key-recovery attacks on HMAC and NMAC using hash collisions. In: Lai, X., Chen, K. (eds.) ASIACRYPT 2006. LNCS, vol. 4284, pp. 37–53. Springer, Heidelberg (2006)
16. Preneel, B., van Oorschot, P.C.: On the security of iterated message authentication codes. IEEE Transactions on Information Theory 45(1), 188–199 (1999)
17. Bellare, M., Goldreich, O., Mityagin, A.: The power of verification queries in message authentication and authenticated encryption. Cryptology ePrint Archive: Report 2004/304 (2004)
18. Bellare, M., Rogaway, P.: The security of triple encryption and a framework for code-based game-playing proofs. In: Vaudenay, S. (ed.) EUROCRYPT 2006. LNCS, vol. 4004, pp. 409–426. Springer, Heidelberg (2006)

Threshold Anonymous Group Identification and Zero-Knowledge Proof

Akihiro Yamamura, Takashi Kurokawa, and Junji Nakazato

National Institute of Information and Communications Technology,
4-2-1, Nukui-Kitamachi, Koganei, Tokyo, 184-8795 Japan
{aki,blackriver,nakazato}@nict.go.jp
http://crypto.nict.go.jp/english/

Abstract. We show that the communication efficient t-out-of-m scheme proposed by De Santis, Di Crescenzo, and Persiano [Communication-efficient anonymous group identification, ACM Conference on Computer and Communications Security, (1998) 73–82] is incorrect; an authorized group may fail to prove the identity even though the verifier is honest. We rigorously discuss the condition where the scheme works correctly. In addition, we propose a new scheme attaining $\Theta(mn)$ communication complexity, where n is the security parameter. It improves the current best communication complexity $\Theta(mn \log m)$ of the t-out-of-m scheme, and it can be also considered as a zero-knowledge proof for t out of m secrets.

Keywords: t-out-of-m Anonymous Group Identification, Non-singular Matrix, Zero-Knowledge Proof.

1 Introduction

An identification scheme allows *users* to identify themselves to a *verifying authority* in a secure sense, that is, it does not reveal the secret information. An anonymous group identification scheme allows users to identify themselves as a member of a group of users in a secure and anonymous sense, that is, it does not reveal secret information or their identity. Such a scheme is called 1-out-of-m scheme. An anonymous group identification scheme is extended to a threshold scheme that allows at least t out of m users $(t < m)$ to identify themselves in a secure and anonymous way. Let us call it a t-out-of-m *scheme* in this paper.

A group identification scheme can be divided into two phrases: an *initialization phase* and an *identification phase*. The first phase is executed only once, at the start-up of the system, and consists of the following: the center and the users run a protocol such that at the end each user will be given a public and private key, to be used later, every time they need to run an identification phase. The second phase is run every time a group of users wish to identify themselves to the verifying authority run a protocol, in which usually such users try to convince the verifying authority of some statement which certifies their knowledge of private keys received in the initialization phase. It is required that qualified groups of

J. Pieprzyk, H. Ghodosi, and E. Dawson (Eds.): ACISP 2007, LNCS 4586, pp. 370–384, 2007.
© Springer-Verlag Berlin Heidelberg 2007

users can successfully identify themselves, while unauthorized groups of users cannot. A full and general account on anonymous group identification schemes is discussed in [2] based on the closure properties of statistical zero-knowledge languages under monotone logic formula composition.

The communication complexity of the scheme by De Santis, Di Crescenzo, Persiano and Yung[2] is $\Theta(mn)$ and $\Theta(mn \log m)$ for a 1-out-of-m scheme and a t-out-of-m scheme, respectively. In [1], De Santis, Di Crescenzo, and Persiano improved communication complexity to $\Theta(m+n)$ and $\Theta(tm+n)$ for a 1-out-of-m scheme and a t-out-of-m scheme, respectively, where n is the security parameter. In this paper, we shall point out that the t-out-of-m scheme in [1] is incorrect, that is, an authorized group may fail to identify themselves even though the verifier is honest. A small example where the scheme does not work will be shown in order to convince the readers. Then we briefly discuss the condition for the scheme to work correctly even though the condition is too restrictive. We also propose a new t-out-of-m scheme whose communication complexity is $\Theta(mn)$. Since the t-out-of-m scheme in [2] is $\Theta(mn \log m)$ and the t-out-of-m scheme in [1] is incorrect, the communication complexity of the proposed scheme is best ever as far as we know. The proposed scheme can be seen as a zero-knowledge proof in which a prover knowing t out of m secrets can convince the verifier. In such a scheme, a prover does not necessary to reveal which secret he actually knows in addition to that a prover does not have to reveal any secret. In addition, we briefly discuss how to extend the proposed t-out-of-m scheme to a t-out-of-m scheme in which every user can choose her own secret key as the 1-out-of-m scheme of Lee, Deng and Zhu [5] in which every user can choose her own secret key whereas the secret keys are provided by a *center* and distributed to the users in [2] and [1].

2 t-Out-of-m Scheme of De Santis, Di Crescenzo and Persiano

2.1 Description of the Scheme

Initialization: Suppose that there are m legitimate users U_i $(i = 1, 2, 3, \ldots, m)$. The center $\mathbf{C}$ generates a Blum integer x, where the size of x is n, and sends a quadratic residue y_i and its root w_i, that is $y_i = w_i^2 \bmod x$ to every user U_i $(i = 1, 2, 3, \ldots, m)$. The public key and the secret key of the user U_i are y_i and w_i, respectively.

Identification: Every group of at least t users should be able to identify themselves to the verifier $\mathbf{V}$ in a secure and anonymous way. Suppose that a subgroup $\mathbf{P}$ (called a *prover*) consisting of t users, $\mathbf{U}_{i_1}, \mathbf{U}_{i_2}, \ldots, \mathbf{U}_{i_t}$ $(2 \leq t \leq m)$, wishes to identify itself to the verifier $\mathbf{V}$. Then $\mathbf{P}$ computes an integer u as the product of a random subset of $\{y_1, y_2, \ldots, y_m\}$ times integer $r^2 \bmod x$, where r is randomly chosen from $\mathbb{Z}_x^*$. Then $\mathbf{P}$ sends u to $\mathbf{V}$. Now $\mathbf{V}$ sends t random bits $b_1, b_2, \ldots, b_t$ and t linearly independent vectors $\boldsymbol{h_1}, \boldsymbol{h_2}, \ldots, \boldsymbol{h_t} \in \{0, 1\}^m$ to $\mathbf{P}$ as a challenge.

Then $\mathbf{P}$ answers with an integer $s \in \mathbb{Z}_x^*$ and bits $d_1, d_2 \ldots, d_m$ satisfying

$$u = s^2 y_1^{d_1} y_2^{d_2} \cdots y_m^{d_m} \pmod{x} \tag{2.1}$$

and

$$\begin{pmatrix} h_{11} & h_{12} & \ldots & h_{1m} \\ h_{21} & h_{22} & \ldots & h_{2m} \\ & \ldots\ldots\ldots & \\ h_{t1} & h_{t2} & \ldots, & h_{tm} \end{pmatrix} \begin{pmatrix} d_1 \\ d_2 \\ \vdots \\ d_m \end{pmatrix} = \begin{pmatrix} b_1 \\ b_2 \\ \vdots \\ b_t \end{pmatrix} \pmod{2}, \tag{2.2}$$

where $\boldsymbol{h_1} = (h_{11}, h_{12}, \ldots, h_{1m})$, ..., $\boldsymbol{h_t} = (h_{t1}, h_{t2}, \ldots, h_{tm})$. Note that in [1] the matrix equation (2.2) is given by $\boldsymbol{h_j} \odot \boldsymbol{d} = b_j$ $(1 \le j \le t)$, where $\boldsymbol{d}$ denotes the vector $(d_1, d_2, \ldots, d_m)$. Then $\mathbf{P}$ solves the equation (2.2) for $d_{i_1}, d_{i_2}, \ldots d_{i_t}$.

In [1], $\mathbf{P}$ (consisting of $\mathbf{U}_{i_1}, \mathbf{U}_{i_2}, \ldots, \mathbf{U}_{i_t}$) sets d_j to be c_j for $j \in \{1, 2, \ldots, m\} \setminus \{i_1, i_2, \ldots, i_t\}$ and then solves the equation

$$\begin{pmatrix} h_{1i_1} & h_{1i_2} & \ldots & h_{1i_t} \\ h_{2i_1} & h_{2i_2} & \ldots & h_{2i_t} \\ & \ldots\ldots\ldots & \\ h_{ti_1} & h_{ti_2} & \ldots, & h_{ti_t} \end{pmatrix} \begin{pmatrix} d_{i_1} \\ d_{i_2} \\ \vdots \\ d_{i_t} \end{pmatrix} = \begin{pmatrix} b_1 - (\sum h_{1j} d_j) \\ b_2 - (\sum h_{2j} d_j) \\ \vdots \\ b_t - (\sum h_{tj} d_j) \end{pmatrix} \pmod{2}, \tag{2.3}$$

where j ranges over $\{1, \ldots, m\} \setminus \{i_1, \ldots, i_t\}$ in the sums in the right-hand side. Note that this is equivalent to the matrix equation (2.2). Then $\mathbf{P}$ computes s as $r w_{i1}^{c_{i1} \oplus d_{i1}} \cdots w_{it}^{c_{it} \oplus d_{it}} \bmod x$.

The verifier $\mathbf{V}$ checks whether or not both (2.1) and (2.2) are satisfied. If this is the case, $\mathbf{V}$ accepts, otherwise he rejects the protocol session. The protocol flow is illustrated in Fig. 1.

2.2   Flaw in the Scheme and How to Repair

The selection of a challenge in the t-out-of-m anonymous group identification scheme in [1] is not appropriate. The vectors $\boldsymbol{h_i}$ $(1 \le i \le t)$ are assumed to be linearly independent in [1], however, this does not guarantee the existence of the solution for (2.3) from the point of view of linear algebra. As a matter of fact, that the vectors $\boldsymbol{h_i}$ $(1 \le i \le t)$ are linearly independent does not imply the $t \times t$ submatrix

$$\begin{pmatrix} h_{1i_1} & h_{1i_2} & \ldots & h_{1i_t} \\ h_{2i_1} & h_{2i_2} & \ldots & h_{2i_t} \\ & \ldots\ldots\ldots & \\ h_{ti_1} & h_{ti_2} & \ldots, & h_{ti_t} \end{pmatrix}$$

is non-singular, and so (2.3) does not necessarily have a solution. We shall show an easy counterexample in Section 2.3. This must be fixed by changing the assumption on the matrix

$$H = \begin{pmatrix} \boldsymbol{h_1} \\ \boldsymbol{h_2} \\ \vdots \\ \boldsymbol{h_t} \end{pmatrix} = \begin{pmatrix} h_{11} & h_{12} & \ldots & h_{1m} \\ h_{21} & h_{22} & \ldots & h_{2m} \\ & \ldots\ldots\ldots & \\ h_{t1} & h_{t2} & \ldots, & h_{tm} \end{pmatrix}.$$

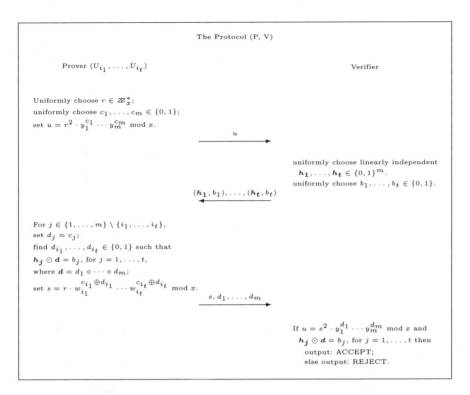

Fig. 1. De Santis etc. schemes (t-out-of-m)

A necessary and sufficient condition for every prover consisting of t users to have a solution of (2.3) for arbitrary $(b_1, b_2, \ldots, b_t)$ is that every $t \times t$ submatrix of H is non-singular. On the other hand, since each row vector $\boldsymbol{h_i}$ of the matrix H is chosen uniformly and randomly, every t minor ($t \times t$ submatrix) of the matrix H is not necessarily non-singular. In fact, we have the following lemma.

Lemma 1. *Suppose $2 \leq t \leq m - 2$. Every $t \times m$ matrix H over the finite field $\mathbb{Z}_2 = \{0, 1\}$ contains a singular $t \times t$ submatrix.*

Proof. Assume that every $t \times t$ submatrix of H is non-singular. In particular, the left most $t \times t$ submatrix is non-singular. Applying elementary column operations (multiplying H on the right by $m \times m$ elementary matrices properly), we can transform H to

$$
H' = \begin{array}{cc}
 & \begin{array}{ccccccc} 1 & \ldots & t & t+1 & \ldots & m \end{array} \\
\begin{array}{c} 1 \\ \vdots \\ t \end{array} &
\left(\begin{array}{ccccccc}
1 & \ldots & 0 & * & \ldots & * \\
\vdots & \ddots & \vdots & \vdots & \ddots & \vdots \\
0 & \ldots & 1 & * & \ldots & *
\end{array} \right).
\end{array}
$$

We may also assume that every $t \times t$ submatrix of H' is non-singular. Put $H' = (h'_{ij})$ and $\boldsymbol{h'_j} = (h'_{1j}, \ldots, h'_{tj})^T$ ($1 \leq j \leq m$), where $(h'_{1j}, \ldots, h'_{tj})^T$ is the transpose of $(h'_{1j}, \ldots, h'_{tj})$.

Now suppose that a certain k-th column vector $\boldsymbol{h}'_k$ $(t+1 \leq k \leq m)$ in H' has a 0 entry at a certain i-th row $(1 \leq i \leq t)$. Then t (≥ 2) column vectors $\boldsymbol{h}'_1, \ldots, \boldsymbol{h}'_{i-1}, \boldsymbol{h}'_{i+1}, \ldots, \boldsymbol{h}'_t, \boldsymbol{h}'_k$ are linearly dependent because all entries of them along the i-th row equal to 0:

$$
H' = \begin{matrix} \\ 1 \\ \vdots \\ i \\ \vdots \\ t \end{matrix}
\begin{array}{ccccccccccc}
1 & \ldots & i & \ldots & t & t+1 & \ldots & k & \ldots & m \\
\left(\begin{array}{ccccccccccc}
1 & \ldots & 0 & \ldots & 0 & * & \ldots & * & \ldots & * \\
\vdots & \ddots & \vdots & \ddots & \vdots & \vdots & \ddots & \vdots & \ddots & \vdots \\
0 & \ldots & 1 & \ldots & 0 & * & \ldots & 0 & \ldots & * \\
\vdots & \ddots & \vdots & \ddots & \vdots & \vdots & \ddots & \vdots & \ddots & \vdots \\
0 & \ldots & 0 & \ldots & 1 & * & \ldots & * & \ldots & *
\end{array}\right).
\end{array}
$$

Thus by the non-singularity of H', we can find that all entries of $\boldsymbol{h}'_k$ equal to 1. Because $2 \leq m - t$, there exits at least two column vectors $\boldsymbol{h}'_{k_1}$ and $\boldsymbol{h}'_{k_2}$ $(k_1 \neq k_2,\ t+1 \leq k_1, k_2)$ in H' whose entries of them equal to 1:

$$
H' = \begin{matrix} \\ 1 \\ \vdots \\ i \\ \vdots \\ t \end{matrix}
\begin{array}{ccccccccccc}
1 & \ldots & i & \ldots & t & t+1 & \ldots & k_1 & \ldots & k_2 & \ldots & m \\
\left(\begin{array}{ccccccccccc}
1 & \ldots & 0 & \ldots & 0 & * & \ldots & 1 & \ldots & 1 & \ldots & * \\
\vdots & \ddots & \vdots & \ddots & \vdots & \vdots & \ddots & 1 & \ddots & 1 & \ddots & \vdots \\
0 & \ldots & 1 & \ldots & 0 & * & \ldots & 1 & \ldots & 1 & \ldots & * \\
\vdots & \ddots & \vdots & \ddots & \vdots & \vdots & \ddots & 1 & \ddots & 1 & \ddots & \vdots \\
0 & \ldots & 0 & \ldots & 1 & * & \ldots & 1 & \ldots & 1 & \ldots & *
\end{array}\right).
\end{array}
$$

Therefore, t (≥ 2) column vectors containing $\boldsymbol{h}'_{k_1}$ and $\boldsymbol{h}'_{k_2}$ are linearly dependent. It contradicts the hypothesis.   □

We remark here the probability that a randomly chosen square matrix of size n over $\mathbb{Z}_2$ $(n \geq 2)$ is non-singular is at most 0.375. Because the order of $GL_n(\mathbb{F}_q)$ is $q^{n(n-1)/2} \prod_{i=1}^{n}(q^i - 1)$ [6] and the number of square matrices of size n over $\mathbb{F}_q$ is $q^{n \times n}$, the probability that a randomly chosen square matrix of size n over $\mathbb{F}_q$ is non-singular is

$$
\frac{q^{n(n-1)/2} \prod_{i=1}^{n}(q^i - 1)}{q^{n \times n}} = \frac{\prod_{i=0}^{n-1}(q^n - q^i)}{q^{n \times n}} = \prod_{i=0}^{n-1}\left(1 - \frac{q^i}{q^n}\right) = \prod_{i=1}^{n}\left(1 - \frac{1}{q^i}\right).
$$

Hence, the probability that a randomly chosen square matrix of size n over $\mathbb{Z}_2$ $(n \geq 2)$ is non-singular is bounded by $(1 - 1/2) \cdot (1 - 1/2^2) = 0.375$.

Lemma 1 implies (2.3) is not always solvable because the corresponding matrix may be singular. Therefore, $\mathbf{P}$ is not always able to find $d_1, d_2, \ldots, d_m$ satisfying (2.1) and (2.2). We can also conclude that the scheme works adequately only under the condition $m = t + 1$. Unfortunately, this condition is too restrictive and so the scheme is unsatisfactory. Under the condition the challenge, which is defined as a $(m-1) \times m$ matrix H, given by $\mathbf{V}$ must have the property that every $(m-1) \times (m-1)$ minor is non-singular. In addition, $\mathbf{P}$ also has to check whether or not the challenge received is adequate, that is, every $(m-1) \times (m-1)$ minor is non-singular. This imposes more computation task upon both $\mathbf{V}$ and $\mathbf{P}$.

2.3   Small Counterexample

We here exemplify the case that an authorized group cannot prove their identity.
Suppose that $m = 3$ and $t = 2$. So every group consisting of at least 2 users
must be able to prove the identity, but we shall show this is not true in general.
Let $\mathbf{P}$ consist of the user $\mathbf{U}_1$ and $\mathbf{U}_2$. Following the protocol, $\mathbf{P}$ chooses bits
$c_1, c_2, c_3, r \in \mathbb{Z}_x^*$ and computes $u = r^2 y_1^{c_1} y_2^{c_2} y_3^{c_3}$. Then u is sent to $\mathbf{V}$. Now
$\mathbf{V}$ chooses vectors $\mathbf{h}_1, \mathbf{h}_2$ from $\{0,1\}^3$ and bits b_1, b_2. Suppose that $\mathbf{V}$ chooses
$\mathbf{h}_1 = (010), \mathbf{h}_2 = (001)$. Note that $\mathbf{h}_1, \mathbf{h}_2$ are linearly independent as required.
There are only two possible cases, (1) $b_2 = c_3 \bmod 2$ and (2) $b_2 = 1 - c_3 \bmod 2$,
and these happen with the equal probability $\frac{1}{2}$. Here, we suppose $b_2 = 1 - c_3$
is chosen by $\mathbf{V}$. By the protocol, $\mathbf{P}$ sets $d_3 = c_3$ and tries to find d_1 and d_2
satisfying

$$\begin{pmatrix} 0 & 1 & 0 \\ 0 & 0 & 1 \end{pmatrix} \begin{pmatrix} d_1 \\ d_2 \\ d_3 \end{pmatrix} = \begin{pmatrix} b_1 \\ 1 - c_3 \end{pmatrix} \pmod 2. \tag{2.4}$$

The equation (2.4) turns out to be $d_2 = b_1 \bmod 2$ and $d_3 = 1 - c_3 \bmod 2$, which
contradicts to our assumption $d_3 = c_3$. Therefore, $\mathbf{P}$ is unable to find d_1, d_2, d_3
satisfying (2.4) and in fact fails to prove their identity.

We remark that the matrix $\begin{pmatrix} 0 & 1 & 0 \\ 0 & 0 & 1 \end{pmatrix}$ has a 2×2 submatrix which is singular,
therefore $\mathbf{P}$ is not always able to respond to the challenge. It is also easy to see
that if $\mathbf{h}_1 = (010), \mathbf{h}_2 = (101)$ then $\mathbf{P}$ can find the desired d_1, d_2, d_3 and in fact
every group consisting of at least 2 users can respond correctly. Unfortunately,
in the scheme of [1], the matrix is chosen by $\mathbf{V}$ and so not always $\mathbf{P}$ proves the
identity. In the next section, we fix this flaw.

3   Proposed t-Out-of-m Anonymous Group Identification

In this section, we construct t-out-of-m $(1 \leq t < m)$ anonymous group identification. The main idea in [1] is that the verifier gives a randomly chosen matrix
and bits as a challenge, and then the prover has to respond correctly to this
challenge using the secret information. However, the challenge given by the verifier is not always adequate for the prover to respond correctly as we saw in the
previous section. Our basic idea for constructing a t-out-of-m anonymous group
identification is similar to the idea but we give the matrix by another method
different from the one in [1]. In our construction, a matrix, which is a part of
a challenge in [1], is provided by the public keys and the matrix equation for
giving a correct response can be solved only by an authorized group of users.
The anonymity property is perfect zero-knowledge, and the communication complexity is $\Theta(mn)$ which improves $\Theta(mn \log m)$ of the previous construction [2].
The construction in [1] has $\Theta(tm + n)$, unfortunately, the scheme is incorrect.
Therefore, our construction achieves the best communication efficiency ever.

3.1 Proposed Scheme

Let $\mathbb{G}$ be a cyclic group of prime order p, and g a generator of $\mathbb{G}$. We assume that the size of p $(= \lceil p \rceil)$ is equal to the security parameter n. The generator g is a public information. We suppose the discrete logarithm problem of $\mathbb{G}$ is intractable. We divide a scheme into three phases: the *initialization*, the *challenge-and-response*, and the *verification*. In our scheme, there are three players; a *group of users*, a *verifier* and a *center* (or *trusted third party*). The center sets up the system parameters for each user and the verifier and thereafter will not participate in any session.

Initialization. The center chooses randomly and uniformly the secret keys $\{w_{j,i}\}$ $(1 \le j \le t$ and $1 \le i \le m)$ from $\mathbb{Z}_p$. Each user $\mathbf{U}_i$ $(1 \le i \le m)$ receives a secret key $(w_{1,i}, w_{2,i}, \ldots, w_{t,i})$. The corresponding public key for $\mathbf{U}_i$ is $(g^{w_{1,i}}, g^{w_{2,i}}, \ldots, g^{w_{t,i}})$ and these keys are publicized. We denote the group element $g^{w_{j,i}}$ by $y_{j,i}$ $(1 \le j \le t$ and $1 \le i \le m)$. Since the discrete logarithm problem for $\mathbb{G} = \langle g \rangle$ is intractable, it is impossible to obtain $w_{j,i}$ from $y_{j,i}$. Furthermore, the center checks whether or not the following condition holds.

Condition: For every $t \times t$ submatrix A of

$$\begin{pmatrix} w_{1,1} & w_{1,2} & \cdots & w_{1,t} & w_{1,t+1} & \cdots & w_{1,m} \\ w_{2,1} & w_{2,2} & \cdots & w_{2,t} & w_{2,t+1} & \cdots & w_{2,m} \\ \multicolumn{7}{c}{\dotfill} \\ w_{t,1} & w_{t,2} & \cdots & w_{t,t} & w_{t,t+1} & \cdots & w_{t,m} \end{pmatrix}, \tag{3.1}$$

the matrix $\begin{pmatrix} \mathbf{1}^T & A \\ \mathbf{0} & 1 \end{pmatrix}$ is non-singular, where $\mathbf{1}$ is the $1 \times t$ vector whose entries are 1 and $\mathbf{1}^T$ is its transpose, and $\mathbf{0}$ is the 1×1 vector whose entry is 0.

Lemma 2. *The matrix* $\begin{pmatrix} \mathbf{1}^T & A \\ \mathbf{0} & 1 \end{pmatrix}$ *is almost always non-singular for every* $t \times t$ *matrix A. In precise, if we choose uniformly and randomly $w_{i,j}$ from $\mathbb{Z}_p$, the probability that the matrix* $\begin{pmatrix} \mathbf{1}^T & A \\ \mathbf{0} & 1 \end{pmatrix}$ *is singular for a certain $t \times t$ submatrix of A is bounded above by* $\binom{m}{t}(t-1)/p$.

Proof. Counting the number of events that the matrix $\begin{pmatrix} \mathbf{1}^T & A \\ \mathbf{0} & 1 \end{pmatrix}$ is singular for a certain $t \times t$ submatrix A of (3.1), we investigate the number of solutions of the following equation in $t \times m$ unknowns $w_{i,j}$ $(1 \le i \le t, 1 \le j \le m)$

$$\prod_{\text{All } t \times t \text{ submatrix } A \text{ of (3.1)}} \begin{vmatrix} \mathbf{1}^T & A \\ \mathbf{0} & 1 \end{vmatrix} = 0$$

because we can consider the number of solutions as an upper bound of the number of events. We note the following fact. Let $\mathbb{F}_q$ be a finite field of order q

and $f \in \mathbb{F}_q[x_1, \ldots, x_n]$ with $deg(f) = d \neq 0$. Then the equation $f(x_1, \ldots, x_n) = 0$ has at most dq^{n-1} solutions in $\mathbb{F}_q^n$. The reader is referred to Theorem 6.13 in [6] for a proof.

Expanding each determinant by its first column cofactors, the degree of this equation is at most $\binom{m}{t}(t-1)$. By the fact mentioned above, we can obtain an upper bound of the number of solutions $\binom{m}{t}(t-1)p^{tm-1}$. So the probability of the event that for a certain $t \times t$ submatrix A the matrix $\begin{pmatrix} 1^T & A \\ 0 & 1 \end{pmatrix}$ is singular is bounded above by $\binom{m}{t}(t-1)p^{tm-1}/p^{tm} = \binom{m}{t}(t-1)/p$. $\square$

Challenge and Response. We may assume without loss of generality that the prover $\mathbf{P}$ consists of t users $\mathbf{U}_1, \mathbf{U}_2, \ldots, \mathbf{U}_t$ and wishes to identify itself to the verifier $\mathbf{V}$.

First, $\mathbf{P}$ chooses uniformly and randomly elements $c_0, c_1, c_2, \ldots, c_m$ from $\mathbb{Z}_p$ and computes $r_1, r_2, \ldots, r_t$ by

$$
\begin{cases}
r_1 & = g^{c_0} \prod_{i=1}^m (y_{1,i})^{c_i} \\
& = g^{c_0}(g^{w_{1,1}})^{c_1}(g^{w_{1,2}})^{c_2} \cdots (g^{w_{1,t}})^{c_t}(g^{w_{1,t+1}})^{c_{t+1}} \cdots (g^{w_{1,m}})^{c_m} \\
r_2 & = g^{c_0} \prod_{i=1}^m (y_{2,i})^{c_i} \\
& = g^{c_0}(g^{w_{2,1}})^{c_1}(g^{w_{2,2}})^{c_2} \cdots (g^{w_{2,t}})^{c_t}(g^{w_{2,t+1}})^{c_{t+1}} \cdots (g^{w_{2,m}})^{c_m} \\
& \vdots \\
r_t & = g^{c_0} \prod_{i=1}^m (y_{t,i})^{c_i} \\
& = g^{c_0}(g^{w_{t,1}})^{c_1}(g^{w_{t,2}})^{c_2} \cdots (g^{w_{t,t}})^{c_t}(g^{w_{t,t+1}})^{c_{t+1}} \cdots (g^{w_{t,m}})^{c_m}.
\end{cases}
\tag{3.2}
$$

Note that $y_{j,i}$ are public information and so it can be computed. Then $\mathbf{P}$ sends $(r_1, r_2, \ldots, r_t)$ to $\mathbf{V}$.

Second, $\mathbf{V}$ chooses uniformly and randomly an element b from $\mathbb{Z}_p$ and sends it to $\mathbf{P}$ as a challenge.

Third, $\mathbf{P}$ computes the response $d_0, d_1, d_2, \ldots, d_m$ as follows. Set

$$
\begin{cases}
f_1 = & c_0 + w_{1,1}c_1 + w_{1,2}c_2 + \cdots + w_{1,t}c_t \\
f_2 = & c_0 + w_{2,1}c_1 + w_{2,2}c_2 + \cdots + w_{2,t}c_t \\
& \vdots \qquad\qquad\qquad\qquad\qquad\qquad (\mathrm{mod}\ p) \\
f_t = & c_0 + w_{t,1}c_1 + w_{t,2}c_2 + \cdots + w_{t,t}c_t \\
f_{t+1} = & b - (c_{t+1} + c_{t+2} + \cdots + c_m).
\end{cases}
\tag{3.3}
$$

Note that $r_1 = g^{f_1 + w_{1,t+1}c_{t+1} + \cdots + w_{1,m}c_m}, r_2 = g^{f_2 + w_{2,t+1}c_{t+1} + \cdots + w_{2,m}c_m}, \ldots, r_t = g^{f_t + w_{t,t+1}c_{t+1} + \cdots + w_{t,m}c_m}$. Then $\mathbf{P}$ solves the following system of linear equations in the variables $X_0, X_1, \ldots, X_t$ over the field $\mathbb{Z}_p$.

$$\begin{pmatrix} 1 & w_{1,1} & w_{1,2} & \cdots & w_{1,t} \\ 1 & w_{2,1} & w_{2,2} & \cdots & w_{2,t} \\ & & \cdots\cdots\cdots & & \\ 1 & w_{t,1} & w_{t,2} & \cdots & w_{t,t} \\ 0 & 1 & 1 & \cdots & 1 \end{pmatrix} \begin{pmatrix} X_0 \\ X_1 \\ X_2 \\ \vdots \\ X_t \end{pmatrix} = \begin{pmatrix} f_1 \\ f_2 \\ \vdots \\ f_t \\ f_{t+1} \end{pmatrix}$$

$$= \begin{pmatrix} c_0 + w_{1,1}c_1 + w_{1,2}c_2 + \cdots + w_{1,t}c_t \\ c_0 + w_{2,1}c_1 + w_{2,2}c_2 + \cdots + w_{2,t}c_t \\ \vdots \\ c_0 + w_{t,1}c_1 + w_{t,2}c_2 + \cdots + w_{t,t}c_t \\ b - (c_{t+1} + c_{t+2} + \cdots + c_m) \end{pmatrix} \pmod{p} \tag{3.4}$$

The equation (3.4) has a unique solution by Lemma 2 because the matrix $\begin{pmatrix} \mathbf{1}^T & A \\ \mathbf{0} & 1 \end{pmatrix}$ is almost always non-singular for every $t \times t$ submatrix A of (3.1). We note that similarly every group consisting of at least t users can solve the equation (3.4) by Lemma 2. This is the missing point in [1] which suffers from a flaw because of lacking rigorous argument in linear algebra. Let $(d_0, d_1, \ldots, d_t)$ be the solution of (3.4). Then $\mathbf{P}$ defines

$$d_j = c_j \tag{3.5}$$

for every j $(t+1 \leq j \leq m)$. Then $\mathbf{P}$ sends $(d_0, d_1, \ldots, d_t, d_{t+1}, \ldots, d_m)$ to $\mathbf{V}$ as a response.

Verification. Receiving $(d_0, d_1, \ldots, d_t, d_{t+1}, \ldots, d_m)$, to verify the response $\mathbf{V}$ checks the validity of the following system of equations

$$\begin{cases} r_1 = g^{d_0}(y_{1,1})^{d_1}(y_{1,2})^{d_2} \cdots (y_{1,t})^{d_t}(y_{1,t+1})^{d_{t+1}} \cdots (y_{1,m})^{d_m} \\ r_2 = g^{d_0}(y_{2,1})^{d_1}(y_{2,2})^{d_2} \cdots (y_{2,t})^{d_t}(y_{2,t+1})^{d_{t+1}} \cdots (y_{2,m})^{d_m} \\ \qquad \vdots \\ r_t = g^{d_0}(y_{t,1})^{d_1}(y_{t,2})^{d_2} \cdots (y_{t,t})^{d_t}(y_{t,t+1})^{d_{t+1}} \cdots (y_{t,m})^{d_m} \end{cases} \tag{3.6}$$

and

$$b = d_1 + d_2 + \cdots + d_t + d_{t+1} + \cdots + d_m \pmod{p}. \tag{3.7}$$

Recall that g, $y_{i,j}$ $(1 \leq j \leq t, 1 \leq i \leq m)$ are public information and so $\mathbf{V}$ can verify (3.6) and (3.7). If all the equations hold then $\mathbf{V}$ accepts the response as correct, otherwise, rejects the protocol session. See Fig. 2 for the protocol flow when $\mathbf{V}$ consists of the users $\mathbf{U}_1, \mathbf{U}_2, \ldots, \mathbf{U}_t$. Clearly, the protocol can be similarly run by a more general prover consisting of $\mathbf{U}_{i_1}, \mathbf{U}_{i_2}, \ldots, \mathbf{U}_{i_t}$.

3.2 Algorithms

All the computation required to $\mathbf{P}$ and $\mathbf{V}$ can be performed in polynomial time in the security parameter n. We note that the system of linear equations (3.4) can be solved efficiently using the Gaussian elimination. Checking whether or not every t minor of the matrix (3.1) is non-singular may be omitted if the computation is a critical issue.

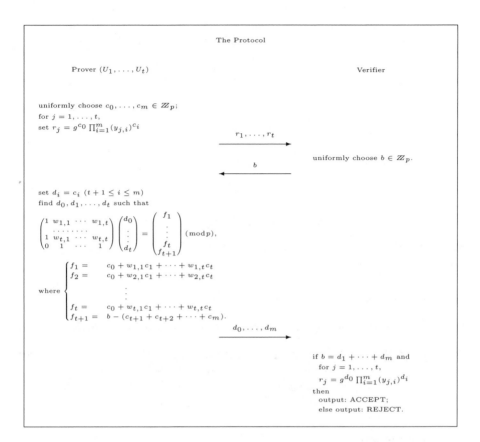

Fig. 2. Proposed protocol (in the case that $\mathbf{P}$ consists of $\mathbf{U}_1, \mathbf{U}_2, \ldots, \mathbf{U}_t$)

4   Properties of the Proposed Scheme

Security of an anonymous group identification scheme is evaluated from three aspects: *correctness*, *soundness* and *anonymity*. In this section we see the proposed scheme satisfies all these properties.

4.1   Correctness

We shall show that the prover $\mathbf{P}$ consisting of at least t members always succeeds in identifying itself to $\mathbf{V}$. As the previous section, we assume that $\mathbf{P}$ consists of $\mathbf{U}_1, \mathbf{U}_2, \ldots, \mathbf{U}_t$. Note that $\mathbf{P}$ can solve the equation (3.4) because the matrix

$$
\begin{pmatrix}
1 & w_{1,1} & w_{1,2} & \cdots & w_{1,t} \\
1 & w_{2,1} & w_{2,2} & \cdots & w_{2,t} \\
\multicolumn{5}{c}{\cdots\cdots\cdots\cdots\cdots} \\
1 & w_{t,1} & w_{t,2} & \cdots & w_{t,t} \\
0 & 1 & 1 & \cdots & 1
\end{pmatrix}
\tag{4.1}
$$

is almost always non-singular by Lemma 2. Let $(d_0, \ldots, d_m)$ be the solution of (3.4). We note that $f_1, f_2, \ldots, f_t, f_{t+1}$ are known only to $\mathbf{P}$. Then we have

$$
\begin{aligned}
r_j =& g^{c_0} \prod_{i=1}^{m} (y_{j,i})^{c_i} \\
=& g^{c_0} (g^{w_{j,1}})^{c_1} (g^{w_{j,2}})^{c_2} \cdots (g^{w_{j,t}})^{c_t} (g^{w_{j,t+1}})^{c_{t+1}} \cdots (g^{w_{j,m}})^{c_m} \\
=& g^{c_0 + w_{j,1} c_1 + w_{j,2} c_2 + \cdots + w_{j,t} c_t + w_{j,t+1} c_{t+1} + \cdots + w_{j,m} c_m} \\
=& g^{(c_0 + w_{j,1} c_1 + w_{j,2} c_2 + \cdots + w_{j,t} c_t) + w_{j,t+1} d_{t+1} + \cdots + w_{j,m} d_m} \\
=& g^{f_j + w_{j,t+1} d_{t+1} + \cdots + w_{j,m} d_m} \\
=& g^{(d_0 + w_{j,1} d_1 + w_{j,2} d_2 + \cdots + w_{j,t} d_t) + w_{j,t+1} d_{t+1} + \cdots + w_{j,m} d_m} \\
=& g^{d_0} (y_{j,1})^{d_1} (y_{j,2})^{d_2} \cdots (y_{j,t})^{d_t} (y_{j,t+1})^{d_{t+1}} \cdots (y_{j,m})^{d_m}
\end{aligned}
\tag{4.2}
$$

for every $1 \le j \le t$ by (3.2), (3.4) and (3.5). Therefore, (3.6) is satisfied. On the other hand, we have

$$
\begin{aligned}
b =& f_{t+1} + c_{t+1} + c_{t+2} + \cdots + c_m \\
=& f_{t+1} + d_{t+1} + d_{t+2} + \cdots + d_m \\
=& d_1 + d_2 + \cdots + d_t + d_{t+1} + d_{t+2} + \cdots + d_m \pmod{p}
\end{aligned}
\tag{4.3}
$$

by (3.3), (3.4) and (3.5). Thus, the equation (3.7) is also satisfied. It follows that every prover $\mathbf{P}$ consisting of at least t users always succeeds in providing a correct response $(d_0, d_1, \ldots, d_m)$ by solving the system of equations (3.4). Thus, $\mathbf{P}$ can always prove its identity to $\mathbf{V}$ and so the protocol is correct.

4.2   Soundness

We shall show that no prover $\mathbf{Q}$ consisting of less than t users succeeds in convincing $\mathbf{V}$. Suppose that a prover $\mathbf{Q}$ consists of $t-1$ users $\mathbf{U}_1, \mathbf{U}_2, \ldots, \mathbf{U}_{t-1}$. First, $\mathbf{Q}$ sends $r_1, r_2, \ldots, r_t$ possibly following (3.2). Then $\mathbf{Q}$ receives $b \in \mathbb{Z}_p$ uniformly and randomly chosen by $\mathbf{V}$. Now $\mathbf{Q}$ has to send $d_0, d_1, \ldots, d_m$ such that (3.6) and (3.7) are satisfied. The prover $\mathbf{Q}$ can control the information $c_0, c_1, \ldots, c_m$ and know their own secret keys: $w_{j,i}$ ($1 \le j \le t$ and $1 \le i \le t-1$). Suppose that $\mathbf{Q}$ can provide such $d_0, d_1, \ldots, d_m$. Then we have

$$
\begin{aligned}
& g^{c_0 - d_0 + w_{j,t}(c_t - d_t) + \cdots + w_{j,m}(c_m - d_m)} \\
&= g^{w_{j,1}(d_1 - c_1) + w_{j,2}(d_2 - c_2) + \cdots + w_{j,t-1}(d_{t-1} - c_{t-1})}
\end{aligned}
\tag{4.4}
$$

for every j ($1 \le j \le t$) by (3.2) and (3.6). If we set $z_j = c_0 - d_0 + w_{j,t}(c_t - d_t) + w_{j,t+1}(c_{t+1} - d_{t+1}) + \cdots + w_{j,m}(c_m - d_m)$ ($1 \le j \le t$), then we have

$$
g^{z_j} = g^{w_{j,1}(d_1 - c_1) + w_{j,2}(d_2 - c_2) + \cdots + w_{j,t-1}(d_{t-1} - c_{t-1})}
\tag{4.5}
$$

for every j ($1 \le j \le t$). Note that $z_1, z_2, \ldots, z_t$ are uniformly distributed over $\mathbb{Z}_p^t$ because $w_{j,t}, \ldots, w_{j,m}$ ($1 \le j \le t$) are chosen randomly and uniformly from $\mathbb{Z}_p^*$ and secret to $\mathbf{Q}$. The system of equations (4.5) is equivalent to

$$\begin{pmatrix} z_1 \\ z_2 \\ \vdots \\ z_t \end{pmatrix} = \begin{pmatrix} w_{1,1} & w_{1,2} & \cdots & w_{1,t-1} \\ w_{2,1} & w_{2,2} & \cdots & w_{2,t-1} \\ & \vdots & & \\ w_{t,1} & w_{t,2} & \cdots & w_{t,t-1} \end{pmatrix} \begin{pmatrix} d_1 - c_1 \\ d_2 - c_2 \\ \vdots \\ d_{t-1} - c_{t-1} \end{pmatrix} \pmod{p}. \qquad (4.6)$$

Let T be the linear transformation given by the matrix $(w_{j,i})_{1 \le j \le t, 1 \le i \le t-1}$. Then it maps $\mathbb{Z}_p^{t-1}$ into $\mathbb{Z}_p^t$. On the other hand, the vector $(z_1, z_2, \ldots, z_t)$ is uniformly distributed over $\mathbb{Z}_p^t$. Finding $c_0, c_1, \ldots, c_m, d_0, d_1, \ldots, d_m$ satisfying (4.6) is equivalent to the event that a randomly and uniformly chosen vector $(z_1, z_2, \ldots, z_t)$ belongs to the range $T(\mathbb{Z}_p^{t-1})$. The probability of such an event is is estimated as $\frac{|\mathbb{Z}_p^{t-1}|}{|\mathbb{Z}_p^t|} = \frac{1}{p}$, which is negligible. Consequently, the probability that $\mathbf{Q}$ provides $d_0, d_1, \ldots, d_m$ satisfying (3.6) and (3.7) is negligible.

Likewise we can show that every group of less than t members fails to identify itself to $\mathbf{V}$. Therefore, the proposed scheme satisfies the soundness; no group consisting of less than t users can identify itself.

4.3 Anonymity

In the protocol, the authorized group $\mathbf{P}$ provides $(d_0, d_1, \ldots, d_t, d_{t+1}, \ldots, d_m)$. Note that $(c_0, \ldots, c_m)$ is uniformly and randomly chosen from $\mathbb{Z}_p^{m+1}$ and we have $(d_{t+1}, \ldots, d_m) = (c_{t+1}, \ldots, c_m)$. Hence, $(d_{t+1}, \ldots, d_m)$ is uniformly distributed over $\mathbb{Z}_p^{m-t}$.

Next we shall show that $(d_0, \ldots, d_t)$ is also uniformly and randomly distributed over $\mathbb{Z}_p^{t+1}$. By (3.3) and (3.4), we have the following equation

$$\begin{pmatrix} 1 & w_{1,1} & w_{1,2} & \cdots & w_{1,t} \\ 1 & w_{2,1} & w_{2,2} & \cdots & w_{2,t} \\ & & \cdots\cdots\cdots & & \\ 1 & w_{t,1} & w_{t,2} & \cdots & w_{t,t} \end{pmatrix} \begin{pmatrix} d_0 \\ d_1 \\ d_2 \\ \vdots \\ d_t \end{pmatrix} = \begin{pmatrix} 1 & w_{1,1} & w_{1,2} & \cdots & w_{1,t} \\ 1 & w_{2,1} & w_{2,2} & \cdots & w_{2,t} \\ & & \cdots\cdots\cdots & & \\ 1 & w_{t,1} & w_{t,2} & \cdots & w_{t,t} \end{pmatrix} \begin{pmatrix} c_0 \\ c_1 \\ c_2 \\ \vdots \\ c_t \end{pmatrix} \pmod{p}.$$

Therefore, we have

$$(d_0, d_1, \ldots, d_t)^T = (c_0, c_1, \ldots, c_t)^T + (z_0, z_1, \ldots, z_t)^T,$$

where $(z_0, z_1, \ldots, z_t) \in \mathrm{Ker}(T)$, where T stands for the linear transformation $\mathbb{Z}_p^{t+1} \to \mathbb{Z}_p^t$ given by the matrix

$$\begin{pmatrix} 1 & w_{1,1} & w_{1,2} & \cdots & w_{1,t} \\ 1 & w_{2,1} & w_{2,2} & \cdots & w_{2,t} \\ & & \cdots\cdots\cdots & & \\ 1 & w_{t,1} & w_{t,2} & \cdots & w_{t,t} \end{pmatrix}.$$

Note that the vector subspace $\mathrm{Ker}(T)$ is one-dimensional and so $(z_0, z_1, \ldots, z_t) \in \mathrm{Ker}(T)$ gives the freeness to guarantee the equation (3.7). Thus, $(d_0, \ldots, d_m)$ is uniformly and randomly distributed over $\mathbb{Z}_p^{m+1}$. This implies that the scheme attains the perfect zero-knowledge, that is, the protocol does not reveal any knowledge on the secret keys and identity of the users in the information theoretical sense.

5   Communication Complexity

The messages transmitted between the group $\mathbf{U}$ of t members and the verifier $\mathbf{V}$ are $(r_1, r_2, \ldots, r_t)$, b, and $(d_0, d_1, \ldots, d_m)$, where $r_i \in \langle g \rangle$ $(1 \leq i \leq t)$ and $b, d_0, d_1, \ldots, d_m \in \mathbb{Z}_p$. Hence, the size of messages is $n(m + t + 2)$, where m is the number of users, n is the security parameter, that is, $\lceil \log p \rceil = n$ and t $(t \leq m)$ is the size for authorized groups. It follows that the proposed scheme attains $\Theta(nm)$ communication complexity.

In [1], De Santis, Di Crescenzo and Persiano claim that their t-out-of-m scheme would have $\Theta(tm + n)$ communication complexity, however, even an authorized group almost always fails to identify itself and so the scheme does not satisfy the necessary functionality. Only when $m = t + 1$ the scheme is correct and then the communication complexity is estimated as $\Theta(m^2 + n)$. Therefore, the best communication complexity has been $\Theta(mn \log m)$ by De Santis, Di Crescenzo, Persiano and Yung [2] up to date. The proposed scheme improves the communication complexity and is best ever as far as we know.

Table 1. Communication complexity

De Santis, Di Crescenzo Persiano and Yung [1]	De Santis, Di Crescenzo and Persiano [2]	Proposed scheme in this paper
$\Theta(mn \log m)$	$\Theta(tm + n)$ (protocol is incorrect) $\Theta(m^2 + n)$ if $m = t + 1$	$\Theta(mn)$

5.1   Issues on Public Keys

Our scheme improves the communication complexity, however, we sacrifices the size of both secret and public keys. A secret key of $\mathbf{U}_i$ is $(w_{1,i}, w_{2,i}, \ldots, w_{t,i})$ of t randomly chosen elements of $\mathbb{Z}_p^*$, and a public key is $(g^{w_{1,i}}, g^{w_{2,i}}, \ldots, g^{w_{t,i}})$ consisting of the elements of the group $\langle g \rangle$. Therefore their sizes are tn, respectively, and so these depend on the size of authorized groups.

It is also an issue on how to compute the answer $(d_0, d_1, \ldots, d_m)$ without revealing each user's secret keys each other. A similar problems occur in the scheme in [1] as well. When a prover $\mathbf{P}$ (consisting of $\mathbf{U}_{i_1}, \ldots, \mathbf{U}_{i_t}$) computes $s = r w_{i1}^{c_{i1} \oplus d_{i1}} \cdots w_{it}^{c_{it} \oplus d_{it}} \mod x$ in Section 2, each $\mathbf{U}_{i_j}$ has to provide the secret key w_{ij} if $c_{ij} \oplus d_{ij} = 1$. Therefore some of secret keys must be revealed.

An easy (but not realistic) solution is to use the public and secret keys for only one session unanimously; once a certain authorized group $\mathbf{U}$ establish a session with $\mathbf{V}$ then not only the members in $\mathbf{U}$ but every user gives away one of his secret and public keys. For this purpose, multiple key pairs for each users should be prepared and stored for the future use. It is desired to solve the equation (3.4) in a secret way, that is, each user $\mathbf{U}_i$ in $\mathbf{P}$ does not need to reveal his secret key $(w_{1,i}, \ldots, w_{t,i})$ to the other members of $\mathbf{P}$. We note that this cannot be done in a perfect zero-knowledge sense because a solution $(d_0, \ldots, d_m)$ together with $(c_0, \ldots, c_t)$ gives some information of the matrix (4.3) since we have $(d_0, d_1, \ldots, d_t)^T = (c_0, c_1, \ldots, c_t)^T + (z_0, z_1, \ldots, z_t)^T$, where $(z_0, z_1, \ldots, z_t) \in \mathrm{Ker}(\mathcal{T})$ and $\mathcal{T}$ is the linear transformation given by the matrix above as in Section 4.3.

As a referee points out that the proposed scheme (and in fact another t-out-of-m scheme) can be seen as a zero-knowledge proof in which a prover knows t out of m secrets and convinces the verifier. In such a scheme, a prover does not necessary to reveal which secret he actually knows in addition to that a prover does not have to reveal any secret. We also note that in the zero-knowledge proof a prover is required to know t out of m secrets to convince the verifier but not necessarily to have all m secrets.

6 Discussion

As the scheme of Lee, Deng and Zhu [5], it is possible to extend to a general case where each user makes his own secret key by himself because the secret keys are chosen randomly and uniformly from $\mathbb{Z}_p^*$ and then the public keys are announced by each user. There are a small issue of checking whether or not each $t \times t$ minor in the matrix (3.1) is non-singular. This is not an easy task and we leave it out for our future work.

Next let us discuss another plausible remedy of the scheme in [1]. One may suggest to repair the t-out-of-m scheme in [1] just by running it several times. Until the prover $\mathbf{P}$ obtains a matrix in which the corresponding $t \times t$ submatrix is non-singular, $\mathbf{P}$ does not go forward. When such a matrix is given to $\mathbf{P}$ as a challenge, $\mathbf{P}$ can compute a correct response and returns it to $\mathbf{V}$. So it seems the protocol could be repaired in this way. Unfortunately, the remedy by running several times causes another vulnerability; the anonymity of the prover is violated. An honest verifier $\mathbf{V}$ is able to obtain information on the prover's identity as we see below. So the remedy does not work.

Suppose that the prover $\mathbf{P}$ responds a correct answer to a challenge matrix H after several trials. Then H must contain a singular $t \times t$ submatrix by Lemma 1 unless $m = t + 1$. Let $\mathbf{P}_1$ be the prover corresponding to the $t \times t$ singular submatrix. Note that $\mathbf{P}_1$ is unlikely to be $\mathbf{P}$ because $\mathbf{P}_1$ may be unable to prepare a correct response because their corresponding matrix is singular and so the equation (2.2) may be unsolvable, on the other hand, $\mathbf{P}$ could do so. Although $\mathbf{V}$ generates randomly H, he knows which $t \times t$ submatrix of H is singular. Thus $\mathbf{V}$ can conclude the prover is not $\mathbf{P}_1$ with high probability. Likewise, $\mathbf{V}$ can obtain enormous information on the prover's identity just by eliminating provers corresponding to a singular submatrices. Moreover, if $\mathbf{V}$ is dishonest, he has much more chance to specify the prover by carefully selecting challenge matrices. For example, he could generate a challenge matrix whose specified $t \times t$ submatrices are singular, and then observes how the prover responds to this challenge. In this way, a dishonest verifier detects who the prover is.

Lastly, the authors would like to thank anonymous referees for their constructive comments and suggestions.

References

1. De Santis, A., Di Crescenzo, G., Persiano, G.: Communication-efficient anonymous group identification. In: CCS '98: Proceedings of the 5th ACM conference on Computer and communications security, pp. 73–82 (1998)
2. De Santis, A., Di Crescenzo, G., Persiano, G., Yung, M.: On monotone formula closure of SZK. In: FOCS'94: Proceedings of the 35th Annual Symposium on Foundations of Computer Science, pp. 454–465 (1994)
3. Feige, U., Fiat, A., Shamir, A.: Zero-knowledge proofs of identity. J. Cryptology 1, 77–94 (1988)
4. Goldwasser, S., Micali, S., Rackoff, C.: The knowledge complexity of interactive proof systems. SIAM J. Comp. 18, 186–208 (1989)
5. Lee, C.H., Deng, X., Zhu, H.: Design and security analysis of anonymou group identification protocols. In: Naccache, D., Paillier, P. (eds.) PKC 2002. LNCS, vol. 2274, pp. 188–198. Springer, Heidelberg (2002)
6. Lidl, R., Niderreiter, H.: Finite fields, 2nd edn. Cambridge University Press, Cambridge (1997)

Non-interactive Manual Channel Message Authentication Based on eTCR Hash Functions

Mohammad Reza Reyhanitabar, Shuhong Wang, and Reihaneh Safavi-Naini[*]

CCISR, SCSSE, Faculty of Informatics,
University of Wollongong,
NSW, Australia
{mrr790, shuhong, rei}@uow.edu.au
[*]Department of Computer Science, University of Calgary, 2500 University Drive NW,
Calgary Ab T2N 1N4
rei@cpsc.ucalgary.ca

Abstract. We present a new non-interactive message authentication protocol in manual channel model (NIMAP, for short) using the weakest assumption on the manual channel (i.e. assuming the strongest adversary). Our protocol uses enhanced target collision resistant (eTCR) hash family and is provably secure in the standard model. We compare our protocol with protocols with similar properties and show that the new NIMAP has the same security level as the best previously known NIMAP whilst it is more practical. In particular, to authenticate a message such as a 1024-bit public key, we require an eTCR hash family that can be constructed from any off-the-shelf Merkle-Damgård hash function using randomized hashing mode. The underlying compression function must be *evaluated second preimage resistant* (eSPR), which is a strictly weaker security property than collision resistance.

Keywords: Message authentication, manual channel, eTCR hash family, randomized hashing, hash function security.

1   Introduction

Message authentication protocols provide assurance that a received message is genuine and sent by the claimed sender. Authentication protocols have been studied in asymmetric (assuming PKI) and symmetric (assuming shared secret keys) settings. *Manual channel* (or two-channel) authentication model is a recently proposed model, motivated by security requirements of ad hoc networking applications. In this model a user wants to send an authenticated message to a receiver. There is neither a shared secret key between communicants nor there is a public key infrastructure. However the sender, in addition to an insecure broadband channel (e.g. a wireless channel) that is used to send the message, has access to a second narrow-band channel, referred to as *manual channel* that is authenticated in the sense that messages over this channel cannot be modified, although they can be delayed, replayed or removed. The channel is low capacity and can only transfer up to a few hundred bits. A manual channel models

J. Pieprzyk, H. Ghodosi, and E. Dawson (Eds.): ACISP 2007, LNCS 4586, pp. 385–399, 2007.
© Springer-Verlag Berlin Heidelberg 2007

human assisted channels such as face-to-face communication, telephone conversation between two parties, or communication between two devices facilitated by a human: a person reads a short number on a device display and inputs it into a second device using a keyboard. The *short authentication string* sent over the manual channel is called SAS [22]. A number of interactive and non-interactive protocols have been proposed in this model and their security has been proven in computational and unconditional security frameworks [8, 7, 1, 17, 12, 15]. In this paper we consider computationally secure non-interactive message authentication protocols (NIMAPs) in manual channel model and assume a *weak manual channel* as defined by Vaudenay [22] (see Sect. 2) which corresponds to the strongest adversary. We note that in NIMAP the scarce resource is the bandwidth of the manual channel.

Computationally Secure NIMAPs Using Manual Authentication. Balfanz, Smetters, Stewart, and Wong [1] (referred to as BSSW protocol) were the first to propose a manual channel NIMAP that was based on collision resistant hash functions. The basic idea is to send the massage m over the insecure channel, and send its hash value, computed using collision resistant hash function, over the manual channel. Vaudenay [22] proposed a formal security model for manual authentication protocols and gave a security reduction from the security of the protocol to collision resistance property of the hash function. He showed that to guarantee security against an adversary having time $T = 2^n$, the SAS length must be at least $2n$ bits.

Gehrmann, Mitchell, and Nyberg [7] proposed a number of protocols, MANA I, II and III, of which only MANA I is a NIMAP. MANA I requires low bandwidth for manual channel. For example to make the probability of a successful attack less than about 2^{-17}, one should use a SAS of length about 40 bits. The protocol requires manual channel to also provide confidentiality and Vaudenay in [22] pointed out that the manual channel must be at least stall-free. We will not include MANA I in our comparisons because of these extra requirements on manual channel.

Pasini-Vaudenay [17] presented a NIMAP (referred to as PV protocol) that requires, a hash function that is second preimage resistant, and a trapdoor commitment scheme in Common Reference String (CRS) model. Although compared with BSSW that uses collision resistant hash functions, PV protocol has weaker security requirements on hash functions (i.e. second preimage resistance), but it needs a secure trapdoor commitment scheme in CRS model which makes it a more demanding protocol.

Mashatan and Stinson [12] proposed a new property, *Hybrid Collision Resistance(HCR)* for hash functions and proposed a NIMAP (referred to as MS protocol) that is provably secure assuming the hash function is HCR. Mashatan et al use random oracle model to show that HCR is a weaker security property than CR for hash functions and so the protocol is of interest because it achieves the same level of security and efficiency as PV protocol without requiring a complex commitment scheme and the added assumption of CRS. In Section 3 we show that there is no clear method of instantiating the hash function used in this protocol to be used for arbitrary length messages. In particular, we point out that popular Merkle-Damgård construction cannot be used for domain extension of HCR functions. This leaves construction of efficient NIMAPs for arbitrary length messages in weak manual authentication model, an open problem.

Our Contributions. We propose a new NIMAP in weak manual channel model that uses a hash function family and is provably secure in standard model. The protocol is based on an *enhanced target collision resistant (eTCR)* hash function family and can be constructed using randomized hashing mode of a Merkle-Damgård hash function (Theorem 4 of [9]).

To evaluate our protocol we consider underlying security assumptions of existing NIMAP protocols that use weak manual channel model. This includes BSSW, PV and MS protocols. In all these cases, and also in the case of our protocol, the security relies on (in BSSW and our protocol reduces to) the required property of the hash function. We give a careful comparison of these properties (collision resistance, second-preimage-resistance, HCR and eTCR) from two view points. Firstly, in terms of implication or separation, i.e showing whether one property implies the other one, or there is a clear separation between them, and secondly, if the property can be guaranteed for arbitrary length messages. This latter requirement removes restriction on the message length sent over the manual channel. Our comparison also includes *evaluated second preimage resistance (eSPR)* property, a property of compression functions introduced to construct eTCR hash function families through Merkle-Damgård construction in the randomized hashing mode [9]. We show that eSPR notion is not strictly stronger than HCR notion, using previously known results [9] that eSPR is not strictly stronger than SPR notion.

The comparison is of of interest because of its direct application to NIMAP and also for grading properties of hash functions.

Paper Organization. In Section 2 we describe communication and security model for manual channel authentication. In Section 3 we give an overview of security notions for hash functions and describe the three security notions, eSPR, eTCR and HCR, that are directly related to our NIMAP and MS protocol. In Sect. 4 we present a new protocol and analyze its security. We also compare it with previous protocols and show its potential advantages. The paper is concluded in Sect. 5.

2   Communication and Security Model

Communication Model. We consider the problem of noninteractive authentication between a sender Alice and a verifier Bob: Alice wants to send a message, M, to Bob such that Bob can be assured that the message has come from Alice (entity authentication) and has not been modified by an adversary Eve (message authentication). It is assumed that Alice and Bob have access to two communication channels; a broadband insecure channel (denoted by $\longrightarrow$) and an authenticated narrow-band channel (denoted by $\Longrightarrow$). It is further assumed that the authenticated narrow-band channel is linked to the identity of the sender, i.e. Alice. In other words when Bob receives a message from this channel he is ensured that it is generated by Alice although the message can be a replay of a previous one. The most important restriction on the narrow-band channel is the limitation on the bandwidth: the channel can transmit messages of length at most n which in some applications n can be as small as 32 bits.

As a real world example of this scenario consider user-aided pairing of two wireless devices (e.g. Bluetooth) such as a mobile phone and a laptop. The user can read a message consisting of a number of characters on the screen of mobile phone and type them on laptop keyboard. In this case the user establishes the authenticated channel manually. These kinds of human controlled authenticated channel are also called *manual channels*.

Security Model. We assume *weak authenticated channel model* and the *strong adversary* described in Vaudney [22]. The adversary Eve has full control over the broadband channel, i.e. she can read, modify, delay, drop messages, or insert new ones. In the weak manual channel model, it is assumed that Eve can read, delay, replay and drop messages sent over manual channel, but she cannot modify or insert messages into this channel. In other words there is no extra security assumptions, like confidentiality or stall-freeness, on a weak manual channel. A manual channel with some additional security requirements on it is called a strong manual channel. It is also assumed that the adversary can employ adaptive chosen message attack: she can adaptively choose the input message to be sent by Alice and make Alice to produce messages of the protocol to be sent over the two channels. The number of such queries made by Eve is her *online complexity* and is denoted by Q. A second resource of Eve is her *offline complexity*, denoted by T, denoting the time spent on processing the messages in the attack. We assume that Eve has bounded computational resources.

A typical manual channel NIMAP works as follows. On input message M Alice uses (possibly randomized) algorithms to compute a tag x and a short authentication string (SAS) s. The message M together with the tag x are sent over insecure broadband channel and SAS is sent over the authenticated channel. Note that x may be a null string in which case no tag will be sent over the insecure channel. Figure 1 shows communication flows in such a protocol. We note that in PV protocol the message might not be explicitly sent over the insecure channel. However the message in their protocol can be transformed (i.e. re-coded) into our representation. The transformation is public and so will not affect security of the protocol. Received messages by Bob are denoted by M', x' and s' to show possible effects of an adversary. The verification process (accept or reject a received message) by Bob is abstractly denoted by a (publicly known) deterministic binary function $Verify(.)$. The function outputs 1 if the acceptance conditions (specified for the protocol) are satisfied by the received message, and 0 otherwise.

Definition 1 (Successful attack). *An adversary Eve, having resources Q (number of queries made from Alice) and T (time complexity), is successful if with probability at least ϵ, she can make Bob output (Alice , M') while M' has*

Alice	Bob
Alice	**Bob**
Input: M	
Compute x $\xrightarrow{M,\ x}$	M', x'
Compute s $\stackrel{s}{\Longrightarrow}$	s'
	output (Alice, M')
	if Verify(M', x',s')=1; else reject

Fig. 1. A typical manual channel NIMAP

never been an input of protocol on Alice side, i.e. it has never been authenticated by Alice. The protocol is called (T, Q, ϵ)-secure if there is no (T, Q, ϵ)-breaking adversary against it.

Note that to be considered a successful adversary, Eve should respect the communication and security model described above. For example she can only replay a previously obtained s from Alice but she cannot modify it or inject a new one. More specifically if Eve has made Q queries from Alice and has collected a data set $\{(M_i, x_i, s_i); 1 \leq i \leq Q\}$, then a successful attacker Eve should find an $M' \notin \{M_i; 1 \leq i \leq Q\}$, any x' and an $s' \in \{s_i; 1 \leq i \leq Q\}$ such that Verify(M', x', s')=1.

Proving security of a manual channel NIMAP consists of two steps. Firstly one should show that the protocol is $(T', 1, \epsilon')$-secure, i.e. secure against adversaries that can only make one query from Alice (called one-shot adversaries in [22]) and have time complexity T'. This is done by transforming such an adversary against the protocol into an adversary that can defeat security assumptions on the underlying building primitive(s) of protocol. The second step of proof (i.e., showing that protocol is (T, Q, ϵ)-secure) can be done (Lemma 6 in [22]) by transforming a (T, Q, ϵ)-breaking adversary to a $(T', 1, \epsilon')$-breaking adversary, where $\epsilon' = \frac{\epsilon}{Q}$.

3   Hash Functions and Security Notions

Cryptographic hash functions play an important role in design of NIMAPs as well as many other cryptographic protocols like MACs and digital signature schemes. There are numerous informal and formal definitions of security for hash functions. Definitions can be application specific. For example Brown [4] defined *Zero-Finder-Resistance* as the difficulty of finding a preimage for zero (i.e. finding a domain element that is hashed to 0) and showed it to be a necessary security assumption for the hash functions to prove security of DSA algorithm.

The most widely used security notions for hash functions are *Collision resistance(CR)*, *Second-preimage resistance(SPR)* and *Preimage resistance(PR)* and are required in applications such as digital signature, commitment and password protection. Informal definitions of these notions for *a fixed hash function* and formal definitions of CR notion and one of its weaker variants, UOWHF (Universal One Way Hash Function) for *a family of hash functions*, can be found in [5, 6, 13, 14, 16]. UOWHF notion (originally defined in asymptotic security framework in [14]) is also called *TCR (Target Collision Resistance)* (rephrased in concrete security framework in [3]).

Informally, for a fixed hash function H, CR means that it is computationally hard to find two distinct inputs $M' \neq M$ that collide under hash function, i.e. $H(M) = H(M')$. SPR means that for a given input M, it is computationally hard to find M' such that $M' \neq M$ and $H(M) = H(M')$. PR refers to one-wayness property and means that it is computationally hard to find a preimage (domain element x) for a given hash value (range element y), so that these constitute a valid (input, output) pair for the hash function (i.e. $H(x) = y$).

Regarding CR notion, there is a foundational problem, that is formal definition of CR security notion can only be given for a family of hash functions (also called keyed hash function) and not for a fixed hash function. There are also some other subtleties regarding formal definitions of security notions for hash functions and studying relationships (implications and separations) between different security notions. More details on CR definition dilemma and also a comprehensive formal treatment of security notions (including implications and separations between CR, SPR, PR and TCR notions), can be found in [18, 21, 19].

In comparing two security notions for hash functions, we say that *notion A is stronger than notion B* if A implies B; that is if a hash function H satisfies notion A then it also satisfies notion B. For instance, CR is a stronger security notion than SPR and the implication is shown in [18] and [21] for keyed and unkeyed settings, respectively.

3.1 Definitions for eSPR, eTCR and HCR Notions

We review in more details three security notions relevant to the discussion in the next section. First we recall Merkle-Damgård construction that provides a method of extending domain for hash functions.

Merkle-Damgård Construction. For a compression function $H : \{0,1\}^{n+b} \rightarrow \{0,1\}^n$, an L-round Merkle-Damgård construction is a method of constructing a hash function $MD_L[H] : \{0,1\}^{n+L.b} \rightarrow \{0,1\}^n$ with an extended domain. For an initial value $C_0 \in \{0,1\}^n$ and a message $M = M_1||M_2||\ldots||M_L$ consisting of L blocks each of size b bits, it outputs an n-bit hash value denoted by C_L as shown in Figure 2:

- The input message M is divided into L blocks $M_1, ..., M_L$, each block M_i of length b bits.
- The chaining variable C is initialized to C_0.
- For i=1 ... L :
  $C_i = H(C_{i-1}, M_i)$
- C_L is output as the hash value.

If the input message length is not a multiple of the block length b, proper padding can be used. For a fixed initial value C_0 we denote the transformation by $MD_L^{C_0}[H] : \{0,1\}^{Lb} \to \{0,1\}^n$.

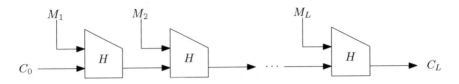

Fig. 2. L-round Merkle-Damgård construction

By *strengthened Merkle-Damgård* we mean Merkle-Damgård with a proper length indicating padding and some fixed initial value. Strengthened Merkle-Damgård's construction converts a compression function to a hash function for arbitrary length input while preserving CR property of the compression function.

In the sequel, we use $\overset{\$}{\leftarrow}$ and $\overset{R}{\leftarrow}$, to denote randomly selecting (computing) according to a specific distribution (output distribution of a probabilistic algorithm) and uniform distribution, respectively.

For the definition of HCR we follow [12] but parameterize the game explicitly with the length of the randomness (l_2). (As noted in [12], l_2 and n are security related parameters.) We use a state variable *State* to show the state information that the adversary A keeps between its attack phases.

Definition 2 (HCR notion). *A compression function* $H \colon \{0,1\}^{l_1+l_2} \to \{0,1\}^n$ *is* $(T,\epsilon) - HCR^{[l_2]}$ *if no adversary A, having time at most T, can win the following game with probability at least ϵ:*

$\begin{aligned}
&\textbf{\textit{Game(HCR}}^{[l_2]}, A)\\
&(M, State) \overset{\$}{\leftarrow} A() \quad //M \in \{0,1\}^{l_1}\\
&K \overset{R}{\leftarrow} \{0,1\}^{l_2}\\
&M' \overset{\$}{\leftarrow} A(K, State) \quad //M' \in \{0,1\}^{l_1+l_2}\\
\\
&A \text{ wins the game if } M' \neq M\|K \text{ and } H(M') = H(M\|K)
\end{aligned}$

Note that $HCR^{[l_2]}$ notion for an arbitrary-input-length hash function $H : \{0,1\}^* \to \{0,1\}^n$ can be defined by a game in which the adversary can output $M \in \{0,1\}^*$ and $M' \in \{0,1\}^*$, in the above game.

eSPR notion is defined for a compression function[9].

Definition 3 (eSPR notion). *A compression function* $H \colon \{0,1\}^{n+b} \to \{0,1\}^n$ *is* (T, L, ϵ)- *eSPR if no adversary, spending time at most T and using messages of length L (in b-bit blocks), can win the following game with probability at least ϵ. It is assumed that the adversary knows the initial value C_0 before starting the game, i.e. either C_0 is chosen at random and given to the adversary (uniform* *setting) or it is a parameter of the game that the adversary will receive as an 'advice' (non-uniform setting).*

Game(eSPR, A)

$\Delta_1, \ldots, \Delta_L \overset{\$}{\leftarrow} A()$ $//\Delta_i \in \{0,1\}^b$, $L \geq 2$

$r \overset{R}{\leftarrow} \{0,1\}^b$

$M = \Delta_L \oplus r;$ $C = MD_{L-1}^{C_0}[H](\Delta_1 \oplus r, \ldots, \Delta_{L-1} \oplus r)$

$(C', M') \overset{\$}{\leftarrow} A(C, M)$ $//C' \in \{0,1\}^n$, $M' \in \{0,1\}^b$

A wins the game if $C'\|M' \neq C\|M$ *and* $H(C'\|M') = H(C\|M)$

---

eTCR security notion is defined in [9] for arbitrary-input-length hash function *families*. Note that HCR and eSPR security notions were defined for a single hash function or a fixed compression function.

Definition 4 (eTCR notion). *An arbitrary-input-length hash function family,* $\mathcal{H} : \{0,1\}^k \times \{0,1\}^* \to \{0,1\}^n$, *is* (T, ϵ)- *eTCR*$^{[m]}$, *if no adversary spending time at most* T *can win the following game with probability at least* ϵ. *We use a state variable State to keep adversary state between its attack phases:*

Game(eTCR$^{[m]}$ **)**

$(M, State) \overset{\$}{\leftarrow} A()$ $//M \in \{0,1\}^m$

$K \overset{R}{\leftarrow} \{0,1\}^k$

$(K', M') \overset{\$}{\leftarrow} A(K, State)$ $//K' \in \{0,1\}^k$ *and* $M' \in \{0,1\}^*$

A wins the game if $(K, M) \neq (K', M')$ *and* $H_K(M) = H_{K'}(M')$

A method of constructing an eTCR hash function family is using an iterated hash method (e.g. Merkle-Damgård construction) with a compression function. Halevi et al's iterated construction [9] reduces eTCR notion to eSPR property for the compression function (Theorem 1). In [9], the length(in blocks) of the target message M, is denoted by L ($L = m/b$, where b denotes block length in bits) and is considered as another resource parameter of the adversary. So, alternatively the adversary can be denoted as a (T, L, ϵ) adversary and the notion can be defined as (T, L, ϵ)-eTCR, instead of specifying parameter m as a superscript.

3.2   Relations Among eSPR, eTCR and HCR Notions

In this section we study relationships between the three notions, eSPR, eTCR and HCR.

eSPR versus HCR.   We show that *eSPR notion is not stronger than HCR notion.* That is there exist compression functions that are eSPR but not HCR. This can be shown by considering the following two relations.

- R1. Halevi et al [9] pointed out a separation between eSPR and SPR and argued that (depending on the structure of the compression function) *there exist compression functions that are eSPR but not SPR.*

- R2. We show *if a compression function is not SPR then it is not HCR either* (i.e., HCR is stronger notion than SPR). This can be seen by noting that an adversary A against SPR property can be used to construct an adversary B against HCR property. To win in HCR game, B forwards $M \| K$ to A and outputs A's response (which is a second preimage of $H(M \| K)$) as M' in HCR game. Clearly B succeeds whenever A succeeds.

Now if eSPR is stronger than HCR, then combined with R2 we can conclude that eSPR is stronger that SPR. This contradicts R1 and so *eSPR is not a stronger notion than HCR* .

Relation Between HCR and eTCR.   We show (constructively) that *existence of a (T, ϵ)-HCR $^{[l_2]}$ compression function implies existence of a (T, ϵ)-eTCR compression function family.*

Assume that we have a (T, ϵ)-HCR$^{[l_2]}$ compression function $H : \{0,1\}^{l_1+l_2} \to \{0,1\}^n$. We construct a compression function family as follows: $\mathcal{H} = \{H_K\}_{K \in \{0,1\}^{l_2}}$, where $H_K : \{0,1\}^{l_1} \to \{0,1\}^n$ and $H_K(M) = H(M \| K)$. To show that the constructed family $\mathcal{H}$ is (T, ϵ)- eTCR, we note that an adversary A against eTCR property of the family $\mathcal{H}$ can be transformed into an adversary B against HCR property of H with the same advantage. Adversary B plays HCR game against H while accessing A. In the first move, B runs A to choose a message M. After receiving K, B forwards it to A who will generate (K', M') such that $H_K(M) = H_{K'}(M')$. Upon receiving (K', M') form A, adversary B outputs $M' \| K'$ in final move of its HCR game. Clearly B wins HCR game against H whenever A wins eTCR game against $\mathcal{H}$.

Using Merkle-Damgård Construction for HCR.   Let $MD_L[H]$ denote a L-round strengthened Merkle-Damgård construction. We show that a collision finding adversary A against $MD_L[H]$ can be used to construct an algorithm B that defeats $MD_{L+1}[H]$ in HCR$^{[l_2]}$ sense. We assume in HCR game $|K| = l_2 > 0$ (for $l_2 = 0$, HCR is the same as CR). B works as follows:

Algorithm B invokes A to obtain two colliding messages M and M' each of length L blocks. (Note that a successful adversary against strengthened Merkle-Damgård construction results in such a collision). In the first move of HCR game against $MD_{L+1}[H]$, algorithm B commits to M and when receives a random challenge $K \in \{0,1\}^{l_2}$, it outputs $M' \| K$ as colliding pair with $M \| K$. Clearly B succeeds whenever A succeeds.

In MS protocol, if the sum of the lengths of the message to be sent (i.e. l_1) and the security parameter l_2 (e.g. $l_2 = 70$ as in [12]) becomes more than one block, the hash function should be applied to a message with length more than one block and it should provide HCR property. In above, we showed that without CR assumption on one-round Merkle-Damgård version (i.e. compression function using specified initial value C_0 as part of input), the hash function cannot provide HCR property as needed in MS in such a case.

Reduction from eSPR to eTCR. The following theorem reproduced from [9] gives an explicit construction for eTCR hash function family.

Theorem 1. *[9] Assume that $h : \{0,1\}^{n+b} \rightarrow \{0,1\}^n$ is a $(T, L+1, \epsilon)$- eSPR compression function that is also (T', ϵ')-OWH. The $(L+1)$-round Merkle-Damgård construction based on h as compression function and used in randomized hashing mode, defines a family of hash functions $\widetilde{H}_r : \{0,1\}^b \times \{0,1\}^{Lb} \rightarrow \{0,1\}^n$ that is $(T-O(L), L, \epsilon'+(L+1)\epsilon)$- eTCR secure. This family is constructed as $\widetilde{H}_r(M) = \widetilde{H}(r,M) = MD_{L+1}^{C_0}[h](r, M_1 \oplus r \ldots M_L \oplus r)$, where $M = M_1||...||M_L$ and C_0 is a known initial value.*

As argued in [9], the second property in addition to eSPR, i.e., (T', ϵ')- OWH, is implied by eSPR assuming a mild structural property for the compression function and is redundant. We refer the reader to [9] for more discussion on this matter.

4 A NIMAP Based on eTCR Hash Function Families

4.1 Protocol Description and Security Reduction

Assume that we have a (T, ϵ)- eTCR hash function family $\mathcal{H}: \{0,1\}^k \times \{0,1\}^{<m} \rightarrow \{0,1\}^n$, where m is the maximum size of input length(e.g., $m = 2^{64}$). We construct a secure NIMAP between a claimant, Alice, and a verifier, Bob, in weak manual channel model. The NIMAP is as follows:

1. On input message M, Alice chooses uniformly at random a key $x \in \{0,1\}^k$ and computes $s = H_x(M)$;
2. Alice sends (M, x) to Bob over the insecure channel and sends $s = H_x(M)$ over the authenticated channel;
3. Bob receives (M', x') via insecure channel and s' via authenticated channel;
4. Bob outputs (Alice, M') if $s' = H_{x'}(M')$ and rejects M' otherwise.

The proposed protocol is illustrated in Figure 3.

Alice		Bob
Input: M		
$x \in_R \{0,1\}^k$	$\xrightarrow{\ M,\ x\ }$	M', x'
$s = H_x(M)$	$\overset{s}{\Longrightarrow}$	s'
		output (Alice, M')
	if $s' = H_{x'}(M')$; else reject	

Fig. 3. A new manual channel NIMAP based on eTCR hash family

The following Theorem guarantees security of the NIMAP.

Theorem 2. *Let* $\mathcal{H} : \{0,1\}^k \times \{0,1\}^{<m} \to \{0,1\}^n$ *be a* (T_H, ϵ_H)- *eTCR hash function family. The proposed NIMAP as in Fig. 3 is a* (T, Q, ϵ)-*secure NIMAP, where* $T = T_H - \mu Q - \sigma$, $\epsilon = Q\epsilon_H$. *Constants* μ *and* σ *represent the maximum time complexity of Alice over all* Q *queries and the time required for a single hash computation, respectively.*

Proof. First we show that any $(T', 1, \epsilon')$-breaking adversary $\widehat{A}$ against our NIMAP can be used to construct a $(T' + \sigma, \epsilon')$-breaking adversary B against eTCR hash family $\mathcal{H}$. Then we complete the proof by a general reduction from any (T, Q, ϵ)-breaking adversary A to a $(T', 1, \epsilon')$-breaking adversary $\widehat{A}$, where $T' = T + \mu Q$ and $\epsilon' \geq \frac{\epsilon}{Q}$.

To prove the first part, let $\widehat{A}$ be a $(T', 1, \epsilon')$-breaking adversary against the NIMAP. That is, the adversary makes a single query from Alice to obtain (M, x, s) and then spends time at most T' to mount a successful attack, i.e. produces (M', x') where $M' \neq M$ and $H_{x'}(M') = s$. Note that it is possible to have $x' = x$. Adversary B against H plays eTCR game using $\widehat{A}$ as follows. It runs $\widehat{A}$ and obtains the query M and commits to it in the first move of eTCR game. After receiving the hash function key, i.e. $x \in \{0,1\}^k$, B computes $s = H_x(M)$ in time σ, and forwards x and s to $\widehat{A}$. Adversary $\widehat{A}$ within time T' produce (M', x'). Adversary B outputs M' as the second message and x' as the second hash function key in eTCR game. This means that B succeeds in time $T' + \sigma$ and with the same success probability ϵ' as $\widehat{A}$.

The second part of the proof is a general transformation between a Q-query adversary and 1-query adversary [22]. For completeness of the proof, we have included the proof (i.e. two-party NIMAP). Let A be a (T, Q, ϵ)-breaking adversary against the NIMAP. We can construct a $(T', 1, \epsilon')$-breaking adversary $\widehat{A}$ as follows.

Adversary $\widehat{A}$ chooses uniformly at random $j \in \{1, 2, \ldots, Q\}$ and runs A. When A makes its $i - th$ query M^i, adversary $\widehat{A}$ selects at random an $x^i \in_R \{0,1\}^k$, computes $s^i = H_{x^i}(M^i)$ and provide A with x^i and s^i. This is done for every $i - th$ query except when $i = j$ in which case $\widehat{A}$ forwards the query ($j - th$ query of A) to Alice (in real protocol) and uses Alice's response to respond A. When A succeeds, it outputs (M', x', s') where $s' = H_{x'}(M')$, M', is different from all previously queried messages and s' is a replay of one of the previously obtained authenticated messages. With probability $\frac{1}{Q}$ we have $s' = s^j$ and so $\widehat{A}$ succeeds with probability $\epsilon' \geq \frac{\epsilon}{Q}$. Denote by μ the maximum overall time to run the protocol once, i.e., to compute x and s on an input M, where the maximum is over Q queries made by A. It is easy to see that time complexity of algorithm $\widehat{A}$ is $T' = T + \mu Q$. This completes the proof of the theorem. $\qquad\square$

4.2   Comparison with Previous Schemes

We compare our proposed NIMAP with the existing NIMAP protocols using weak manual channel, namely BSSW [1], PV [17] and MS [12]. The comparison is made for the same level of security, from following viewpoints:

1. Security assumptions required for the underlying primitives (commitment schemes and/or hash functions)
2. Required bandwidth for the manual channel (i.e., the SAS length).

Security Assumptions. We consider security assumptions required by BSSW, PV, MS and our protocol when there is no restriction on the length of the input message.

The BSSW protocol uses a fixed (unkeyed) hash function and requires it to be collision resistant (CR). CR is a strong security assumption for a hash function which cannot be formally defined for a single hash function [2, 18]. To obtain the property for arbitrary length messages Merkle-Damgård construction can be used [19].

The PV protocol uses SPR which is a weaker assumption than CR ([21, 18]). PV protocol also requires a secure trapdoor commitment scheme in CRS model. Furthermore, the commitment string c is taken as an input to the hash function ([17]) and so the hash domain needs to be of arbitrary size (if one uses an arbitrary commitment scheme); i.e., one needs an arbitrary-input-length hash function that provides security in SPR sense.

To compute SAS length, PV assumes that hash function provides ideal security in SPR sense, i.e., a hash function with security level of 2^{-n}, where n is the hash size. This assumption for the case of long messages is not satisfied by iterated Merkle-Damgård hash functions (like MD5, SHA1, RIPEMD-160, Whirlpool) as shown by recent analysis in [11].

MS protocol also uses a fixed hash function satisfying HCR property. The $HCR^{[l]}$ is a notion between CR and SPR, depending on the value of l. As shown in subsection 3.2, the commonly used Merkle-Damgård domain extension construction does not guarantee HCR (without CR assumption) and so it is not clear how to construct an arbitrary-input-length HCR hash functions from a fixed-input-length one.

Our NIMAP uses an eTCR hash *family* to hash arbitrary-length messages. Standard Merkle-Damgård iteration in randomized hashing mode can be used to construct such an eTCR hash family from an eSPR compression function (i.e. a fixed-input-length hash function) [9]. Hence *security of our protocol is reduced to eSPR property for a fixed-input-length hash function*. It has been argued [9] that eSPR notion is weaker than CR and also is not stronger than SPR. We also argued in subsection 3.2 that eSPR is not stronger than HCR. The above argument shows that our protocol, when used for arbitrary length messages, requires less demanding security assumption (namely, eSPR-ness of a fixed-input-length hash function) and benefits from provable security framework in constructing eTCR hash family for arbitrary length messages (Theorem 1).

Manual Channel Bandwidth. Assume an adversary with the same resources and required security level (denoted by ϵ) as in [12]. Namely, we require the NIMAP to be (T, Q, ϵ)-*secure* , where $T \leq 2^{70}$, $Q \leq 2^{10}$ and $\epsilon = 2^{-20}$.

In BSSW the SAS length must be at least 140 bits. In PV protocol a SAS of length 100 is required (, but as mentioned above for arbitrary long messages PV requires that the used hash function provides ideal SPR security for long messages which is not satisfied by Merkle-Damgård constructions due to recent attacks in [11]). MS can theoretically reach the same level of security using a SAS of 100 bits for $l_2 = 70$ bits (, but we are not aware of a practical hash function that provides HCR for arbitrary-length messages without need to a stronger than HCR assumption on the underlying compression function and as we showed Merkle-Damgård constructions cannot be used for this purpose).

Our NIMAP needs a SAS with length $n = 100 + \log_2(L + 2)$ bits, where L denotes the message length in blocks. (See more details and computation of SAS length below.) For a 1024-bit message using SHA1 in randomized hashing mode ($L = 2$), the required SAS length will be 102 bits. Our NIMAP can still use randomized hashing mode for messages up to about 2^{49} bits using a SAS of only 140 bits.

To calculate SAS length for our protocol to have a NIMAP that is (T, Q, ϵ)-secure (for $T = 2^{70}$, $Q = 2^{10}$, $\epsilon = 2^{-20}$), using Theorem 2, we need a hash function family that is 2^{-30} ($=2^{-20}/2^{10}$) secure in eTCR sense. Using Theorem 1, we can construct such an eTCR family assuming that the compression function is eSPR with $\epsilon = \frac{2^{-30}}{L+2}$ and L being the number of blocks in the input message of the eTCR function .(We assumed that $\epsilon' = \epsilon$ in Theorem 1). The length of SAS (i.e. required n) must be computed for each message length taking into account non-tightness of the reduction between eTCR and eSPR notions. One can use compression function of a standard hash function like SHA1 and truncate its output to n bits. Assuming that the *compression function* provides 2^{-n} security level *in eSPR sense*[1] , i.e. $\epsilon = T2^{-n}$, the SAS length of our NIMAP, i.e. n, for messages of length L blocks, is $n = 100 + log_2(L + 2)$ bits.

5   Conclusion

We proposed a new practical non-interactive message authentication protocol in manual channel model using a family of eTCR secure hash functions. For applications such as sending a public key where message length is small (e.g. 1024 bits), using randomized hashing mode one can construct an eTCR hash family using an off-the-shelf Merkle-Damgård hash function (e.g. SHA1). In this case security of the scheme will be based on eSPR property of the compression function which is strictly weaker than collision resistance property. For longer messages however, randomized hashing may not produce optimal result (shortest SAS) because of the non-tightness of reduction. Using randomized hashing for messages of up to 2^{49} bits results in SAS of around 140 bits. Other constructions of eTCR with tighter reduction can be directly used in the proposed NIMAP and could result in shorter SAS.

Acknowledgments. The authors would like to thank the anonymous reviewers for their insightful comments and suggestions. Mohammad Reza Reyhanitabar is fully supported by IPRS and UPA Scholarships from the University

---

[1] Note that this assumption is not the same as in PV, since here we require such a property from a compression function in eSPR sense (i.e., only for single-block inputs) and not for arbitrary-length messages as in PV in SPR sense.

of Wollongong. Shuhong Wang is fully supported by the ARC Discovery Grant DP0558490.

References

[1] Balfanz, D., Smetters, D.K., Stewart, P., Wong, H.C.: Talking to Strangers: Authentication in ad-hoc Wireless Networks. In: Network and Distributed Sytem Security Symposium, San Diego, California, U.S.A (February 2002)

[2] Bellare, M., Rogaway, P.: Introduction to Modern Cryptography (Page 3 of) Chapter 5: Hash Functions. Available at Bellare's homepage via: http://www-cse.ucsd.edu/users/mihir/cse207/index.html

[3] Bellare, M., Rogaway, P.: Collision-Resistant Hashing: Towards Making UOWHFs Practical. In: Kaliski Jr., B.S. (ed.) CRYPTO 1997. LNCS, vol. 1294, pp. 470–484. Springer, Heidelberg (1997)

[4] Brown, D.: Generic Groups, Collision Resistance and ECDSA. Journal of Designs, Codes and Cryptography 35, 119–152 (2005)

[5] Damgård, I.B.: Collision Free Hash Functions and Public Key Signature Schemes. In: Price, W.L., Chaum, D. (eds.) EUROCRYPT 1987. LNCS, vol. 304, pp. 203–216. Springer, Heidelberg (1988)

[6] Damgård, I.B.: A Design Principle for Hash Functions. In: Brassard, G. (ed.) CRYPTO 1989. LNCS, vol. 435, pp. 416–427. Springer, Heidelberg (1990)

[7] Gehrmann, C., Mitchell, C.J., Nyberg, K.: Manual Authentication for Wireless Devices. RSA Cryptobytes 7(1), 29–37 (2004)

[8] Gehrmann, C., Nyberg, K.: Security in Personal Area Networks. Security for Mobility, IEE, London, pp. 191–230 (2004)

[9] Halevi, S., Krawczyk, H.: Strengthening Digital Signatures Via Randomized Hashing. In: Dwork, C. (ed.) CRYPTO 2006. LNCS, vol. 4117, pp. 41–59. Springer, Heidelberg (2006)

[10] Hong, D., Preneel, B., Lee, S.: Higher Order Universal One-Way Hash Functions. In: Lee, P.J. (ed.) ASIACRYPT 2004. LNCS, vol. 3329, pp. 201–213. Springer, Heidelberg (2004)

[11] Kelsey, J., Schneier, B.: Second Preimages on n-Bit Hash Functions for Much Less than 2^n Work. In: Cramer, R.J.F. (ed.) EUROCRYPT 2005. LNCS, vol. 3494, pp. 474–490. Springer, Heidelberg (2005)

[12] Mashatan, A., Stinson, D.R.: Noninteractive Two-Channel Message Authentication Based on Hybrid-Collision Resistant Hash Functions. Cryptology ePrint Archive, Report 2006/302

[13] Merkle, R.: One Way Hash Functions and DES. In: Brassard, G. (ed.) CRYPTO 1989. LNCS, vol. 435, pp. 428–446. Springer, Heidelberg (1990)

[14] Naor, M., Yung, M.: Universal One-Way Hash Functions and Their Cryptographic Applications. In: Proc. of 21st ACM Symposium on the Theory of Computing, pp. 387–394 (1990)

[15] Naor, M., Segev, G., Smith, A.: Tight Bounds for Unconditional Authentication Protocols in the Manual Channel and Shared Key Models. In: Dwork, C. (ed.) CRYPTO 2006. LNCS, vol. 4117, pp. 214–231. Springer, Heidelberg (2006)

[16] Preneel, B.: Analysis and Design of Cryptographic Hash Functions. Doctoral dissertation, K.U.Leuven (1993)

[17] Pasini, S., Vaudenay, S.: An Optimal Non-interactive Message Authentication Protocol. In: Pointcheval, D. (ed.) CT-RSA 2006. LNCS, vol. 3860, pp. 280–294. Springer, Heidelberg (2006)

[18] Rogaway, P., Shrimpton, T.: Cryptographic Hash-Function Basics: Definitions, Implications, and Separations for Preimage Resistance, Second-Preimage Resistance, and Collision Resistance. In: Roy, B., Meier, W. (eds.) FSE 2004. LNCS, vol. 3017, pp. 371–388. Springer, Heidelberg (2004)

[19] Rogaway, P.: Formalizing Human Ignorance: Collision-Resistant Hashing without the Keys. In: Nguyen, P.Q. (ed.) VIETCRYPT 2006. LNCS, vol. 4341, pp. 221–228. Springer, Heidelberg (2006)

[20] Rivest, R.: Abelian Square-Free Dithering for Iterated Hash Functions. Presented at ECRYPT Hash Function Workshop, Cracow (June 21, 2005)

[21] Stinson, D.R.: Some Observation on the Theory of Cryptographic Hash Functions. Journal of *Design, Codes and Cryptography* 38, 259–277 (2006)

[22] Vaudenay, S.: Secure Communications over Insecure Channels Based on Short Authenticated Strings. In: Shoup, V. (ed.) CRYPTO 2005. LNCS, vol. 3621, pp. 309–326. Springer, Heidelberg (2005)

A Practical System for Globally Revoking the Unlinkable Pseudonyms of Unknown Users*

Stefan Brands[1], Liesje Demuynck[2], and Bart De Decker[2]

[1] Credentica & McGill School of Comp. Science
1010 Sherbrooke St. W., Suite 1800, Montreal, QC, Canada H3A 2R7
brands@{credentica.com,cs.mcgill.ca}
www.credentica.com
[2] K.U.Leuven, Department of Computer Science
Celestijnenlaan 200A, B-3001 Heverlee, Belgium
{Liesje.Demuynck,Bart.DeDecker}@cs.kuleuven.be
www.cs.kuleuven.be

Abstract. We propose the first single sign-on system in which a user can access services using unlinkable digital pseudonyms that can all be revoked in case she abuses any one service. Our solution does not rely on key escrow: a user needs to trust only her own computing device with following our protocols in order to be assured of the unconditional untraceability and unlinkability of her pseudonyms. Our solution involves two novel ingredients: a technique for invisibly chaining the user's pseudonyms such that all of them can be revoked on the basis of any one of them (without knowing the user's identity with the issuer) and a sublinear-time proof that a committed value is not on a list without revealing additional information about the value. Our solution is highly practical.

1 Introduction

Traditionally, most authenticated relations between users and online services are established on the basis of username and password. As users interact with more and more online services, however, passwords become increasingly vulnerable to phishing and to replay by dishonest service providers. In addition, users are struggling to remember usernames and passwords, which in turn poses a significant burden on the support systems of service providers. As a result, more and more organizations are migrating to secure *single sign-on* (SSO) systems for their users. SSO systems allow a user to access many services without having to manually authenticate more than once. In addition, SSO systems give organizations the ability to globally revoke all access privileges of users for any reason. This is desirable in intra-organizational settings where SSO is used for giving employees

---

* This research was performed under the auspices of McGill University (School of Comp. Science) from 07-2005 until 02-2006 when the second author was visiting the first author at Credentica. Liesje Demuynck is supported by a research assistantship and travel credit from the Fund for Scientific Research, Flanders (Belgium).

J. Pieprzyk, H. Ghodosi, and E. Dawson (Eds.): ACISP 2007, LNCS 4586, pp. 400–415, 2007.
© Springer-Verlag Berlin Heidelberg 2007

online access to corporate resources: when an employee leaves a company, for example, the organization can centrally revoke all her access privileges.

The demand for secure SSO systems goes beyond organizational boundaries. In the past years, industry efforts have resulted in a number of specifications and standards aimed at *cross-organizational* SSO. However, to date very few organizations have adopted cross-organizational SSO systems, especially in consumer-facing settings. A major reason for this lack of adoption is that the current generation of cross-organizational SSO systems create potential privacy and security problems for both users and service providers. These systems revolve around a central server (also known as an *identity provider*) that sees in real time which users interact with what service providers. The identity provider can arbitrarily deny access or revoke all access capabilities of any user at any time. Furthermore, the identity provider can impersonate users and can gain access to accounts they may have established with service providers. While these powers may be desirable in intra-organizational settings, they tend to be overly invasive to autonomous users and service providers.

The SSO system proposed in this paper overcomes these problems, while preserving the ability to globally deny access to any user who abuses a service.

Outline of our Solution. Our system also relies on a central identity provider, but any unwanted powers in that provider are eliminated. The identity provider is responsible for issuing to each user a number of *digital pseudonyms*, which are a special kind of authentication tokens. Users hook their pseudonyms up with service providers and authenticate in subsequent visits by proving knowledge of a secret pseudonym key. Digital pseudonyms are unconditionally unlinkable and untraceable, even vis-à-vis collusions of service providers and the identity provider; thus, by using a different pseudonym with each service provider, each user can ensure that her account information with different service providers cannot be compiled into a super-dossier. Replay attacks are prevented, because secret pseudonym keys are never disclosed when authenticating to service providers. Assuming user devices transparently manage pseudonyms on behalf of their users, users can be given an SSO experience; for instance, a single password could locally unlock all of a user's pseudonyms for the duration of a session.

To enable the global revocation of all of a user's pseudonyms in case the user abuses any one service, the identity provider invisibly chains all of these pseudonyms. Hereto, the identity provider invisibly encodes into all of a user's pseudonyms a set of random numbers that are unique to that user (without the identity provider knowing those numbers). For each pseudonym that a service provider associates with a user, the service provider requires its user to disclose one of these encoded random numbers. By disclosing a different random number for each pseudonym, users preserve the unconditional unlinkability of their pseudonyms. At the same time, service providers can blacklist disclosed numbers in such a manner that users can efficiently prove that their encoded numbers are not blacklisted without revealing any additional information about them.

This revocation technique does not impinge on user privacy, nor does it give covert powers to service providers and the identity provider. Firstly, the encoding of the invisible numbers into digital pseudonyms requires the cooperation of the user at issuing time. Secondly, in order to be able to blacklist a user, a service provider must ask *all* users who request access to prove that they are not on its blacklist. Thirdly, in order to compute a blacklist proof users require the blacklist as input, and so they can inspect the blacklist and sanction unreasonable requests for blacklist proofs. Fourthly, proving that one is not on the revocation list does *not* reveal any information about one's identity.

Comparison to Other Work. Blind signatures, invented in the eighties by Chaum [16,18], allow users to authenticate using unconditionally unlinkable pseudonyms. However, when using blind signatures as pseudonyms it is impossible to revoke the pseudonyms of a fraudulent user, whether on the basis of the user's identity with the issuer or on the basis of misuse of any one service. Thus, blind signatures provide privacy for users by trading away security for service providers.

Various adaptations of blind signatures have been proposed to enable global revocation in the context of electronic cash systems, to ensure either (1) that a designated party can identify all e-coin payments of a particular account holder or (2) that all of a payer's payments can be identified if that user engages in a fraudulent payment transaction. In the context of SSO systems, these two features correspond to the ability to revoke all of a user's pseudonyms for a known user (i.e., based on the user's identity with the issuer) and of an unknown user, respectively. Various proposals to extend electronic cash systems with one or both of these features have been presented. Unfortunately, in all of these proposals, the privacy of users is in fact illusional. Namely, most techniques [7,27,10,24,23] rely on key escrow: the bank encodes into each e-coin a tracing key that its user must disclose in encrypted form at payment time, so that it can be decrypted by a designated "escrow agent (or set of parties) if needed. In e-cash systems not requiring a trused escrow agent [12,28], users have to settle for computational unlinkability and untraceability only.

More recently, Camenisch et al. [8,13] and Nguyen [26] proposed credential revocation mechanisms based on *dynamic accumulators*. Dynamic accumulators enable individuals to prove list membership in constant time in the list size. The security of these accumulators relies on non-standard intractability assumptions, such as the strong RSA assumption and the q-strong Diffie-Hellman assumption. In addition, the schemes merely allow one to revoke the credentials of users on the basis of their identity with the issuer; it is not possible to revoke all of the pseudonyms of an unknown user. Finally, the proofs of knowledge in [13] are statistical zero-knowledge only and the set of accumulatable values is limited to prime numbers in a predefined interval.

An accumulator-based membership proof consists of two steps; the computation of the user's current "witness" (which is a secret value related to the user's accumulated value) and the execution of a zero-knowledge proof of knowledge. Although the latter can be executed in constant time, the former requires a time complexity which is at least linear in the number of elements deleted from the accumulator. Consider, for example, an accumulator to which no elements are added and of which n elements are removed, and assume that a small exponentiation has an exponent size equal to the maximal size of an accumulated value. In this setting, the recomputation of a witness may require n small exponentiations. (In [13], this corresponds to two exponentiations with very large exponents.) In addition, the final witness can only be computed when the final blacklist is known. Hence, not all of a user's exponentiations can be precomputed.

In the context of direct anonymous attestation, Brickell et al. [6] suggest a technique in which a user provides the service provider with a pseudonym $N_V = \zeta^f$ for f a user-specific secret value and ζ a random generator of a group in which the discrete logarithm (DL) problem is hard. The purpose of N_V is twofold: (1) providing the service provider with a pseudonym and (2) enabling revocation based either on the knowledge of f or on a list of other pseudonyms $\{(N_{V'}) = (\zeta')^{f'}, \ldots\}$. The latter can be achieved by proving in zero-knowledge the relation $(\log_{\zeta'} N_{V'} \neq \log_{\zeta} N_V)$ for all $N_{V'}$ in the list [15]. This solution has two major drawbacks. Firstly, the user's unlinkability is only computational. Second, the proof that a pseudonym is not revoked based on a list of pseudonyms requires a number of exponentiations linear in the length of the blacklist.

Brands [5] proposed a practical digital credential mechanism that allows an issuer to invisibly encode into all of a user's credentials a unique number that the issuer can blacklist in order to revoke that user's credentials. This mechanism does not rely on key escrow and preserves the unconditional untraceability and unlinkability of credentials; as such, it offers the same privacy strength as our proposal. Base credentials in the system are as efficient as standard DSA signatures, and the blacklist technique (which consists of repeating a NOT-proof for each blacklist element) is provably secure under the DL assumption. However, Brands' proposal does not allow the revocation of all of the pseudonyms of an unknown user. In addition, the complexity of the cryptographic proof for showing that one's invisibly encoded number is not contained in a blacklist grows linearly in the size of the blacklist. As such, the proposal is not practical for large blacklists.

Our proposal addresses both shortcomings by extending Brands' credentials system using two new techniques: a generalization of Brands' credentials so that multiple credentials can be revoked based on something unique to any one of them, and a sublinear-time cryptographic blacklist proof that is secure under the DL assumption.

Organization of the Paper. Section 2 provides a backgrounder on Brands' credential techniques and compares the system with other credential systems. Section 3 describe our cryptographic protocols in detail and analyzes their security and privacy properties. Finally, Sections 4 and 5 analyze the practicality of the proposal and outline various extensions and variations.

2 Digital Credentials

Our new system is based on Brands' credential techniques [5]. Section 2.1 provides a backgrounder on these techniques. To motivate the choice for Brands' system, Section 2.2 compares this system with other credential techniques.

2.1 Backgrounder of Brands' Digital Credentials

In the system of Brands [5], credentials are issued by a Credential Authority (CA) that has its own key pair for digitally signing messages. When issuing a credential to a user Alice, the CA through its digital signature binds one or more attributes to a digital credential public key, the secret key of which only Alice knows. The whole package that Alice receives is called a digital credential.

Alice can show her digital credential to Bob by providing him with her digital credential public key and the CA's signature. If desired, she selectively discloses a property of the attributes in her digital credential, while hiding any other information about these attributes. Finally, to prevent Bob from replaying the digital credential, Alice digitally signs a *nonce* using her secret key.

Since Alice reveals the digital credential public key and the CA's signature when showing a digital credential, these elements must be uncorrelated to the information that the CA sees when it issues the digital credential, even if the CA tries to cheat. At the same time, the CA must be able to encode the desired attributes into the digital credential, even if Alice tries to cheat. Here is how l attributes, $(x_1, \ldots, x_l)$, are encoded in a digital credential. The tuple $(x_1 s, \ldots, x_l s, s)$ is Alice's secret key for the digital credential. Alice generates s at random from $\mathbb{Z}_q$ in the issuing protocol. Even though Alice may disclose some attributes to Bob in the showing protocol, she keeps s secret at all times; this ensure that only she knows the entire secret key. The digital credential public key is the product $h = (g_1^{x_1} \cdots g_l^{x_l} h_0)^s$. Elements $g_1, \ldots, g_l, h_0$ are random generators of a group G_q of prime order q; they are part of the CA's public key. The digital credential public key reveals no information about $x_1, \ldots, x_l$: for any public key and for any tuple $(x_1, \ldots, x_l)$, there is exactly one $s \in \mathbb{Z}_q$ that would make the match. At the same time, regardless of the choice of l and under the DL assumption in G_q, Alice cannot compute a digital credential public key for which she knows more than one secret key [5, Proposition 2.3.3]. Hence, by signing the digital credential public key the CA indirectly binds a unique attribute tuple to Alice's digital credential: the CA's signature binds Alice's public key, which in turn binds her secret key containing the attributes.

To show a digital credential to Bob, Alice transmits to him the digital credential public key and the CA's digital signature. In addition, she selectively discloses a property of the attributes and digitally signs a nonce using her secret key. Alice's signature, which is derived from a *proof of knowledge*, proves not only that she knows a secret key but also that the attributes in her digital credential satisfy the particular attribute property she is disclosing to Bob. Under the DL assumption in G_q, Bob cannot compute any secret key when presented with Alice's digital credential public key, regardless of which property of $(x_1, \ldots, x_l)$ Alice discloses to him. Alice can demonstrate a wide spectrum of properties to Bob. Among others, using the notation $(x_1, \ldots, x_l) = \text{rep}_{(g_1, \ldots, g_l)} h$ to refer to a *representation* $(x_1, \ldots, x_l)$ such that $h = g_1^{x_1} \ldots g_l^{x_l}$, Alice can prove any of the following properties:

- *Knowledge of a representation containing known attribute values [5, Chapter 3]:* Alice can prove knowledge of a representation $(x_1, \ldots, x_l)$ of $h \in G_q$ with respect to any $(g_1, \ldots, g_l) \in G_q^l$, and in doing so she can disclose any subset $D \subset \{x_1, \ldots, x_l\}$. For an example subset $D = \{x_{j-1}, x_j\}$, we denote this protocol by $PK\{(\chi_1, \ldots, \chi_{j-2}, \chi_{j+1}, \ldots, \chi_l) : (\chi_1, \ldots, \chi_{j-2}, x_{j-1}, x_j, \chi_{j+1}, \ldots, \chi_l) = \mathrm{rep}_{(g_1, \ldots, g_l)} h\}$. (Greek letters represent the values that remain unknown to Bob.)

- *Knowledge and equality of discrete logarithms [17]:* Given values $h_1, h_2, g_1, g_2,$ g_3 and g_4 in G_q, Alice can demonstrate her knowledge of a tuple (x_1, x_2, x_3) such that $h_1 = g_1^{x_1} g_2^{x_2}$ and $h_2 = g_3^{x_1} g_4^{x_3}$. We denote this protocol by $PK\{(\chi_1, \chi_2, \chi_3) : (\chi_1, \chi_2) = \mathrm{rep}_{(g_1, g_2)} h_1 \wedge (\chi_1, \chi_3) = \mathrm{rep}_{(g_3, g_4)} h_2\}$. It can be extended towards a proof of equality of arbitrary exponents using arbitrary base tuples.

- *Knowledge of discrete logarithms constituting successive powers [11, Chapter 3]:* Let $h_1, \ldots, h_n, g_1$ and g_2 be values in G_q. Alice can prove knowledge of values $x, y_1, \ldots, y_n \in \mathbb{Z}_q$ such that $h_i = g_1^{x^i} g_2^{y_i}$ for $i \in \{1, \ldots, n\}$. We denote this protocol by $PK\{(\chi, \gamma_1, \ldots, \gamma_n) : (\chi, \gamma_1) = \mathrm{rep}_{(g_1, g_2)} h_1 \wedge (\chi^2, \gamma_1) = \mathrm{rep}_{(g_1, g_2)} h_2 \wedge \ldots \wedge (\chi^n, \gamma_n) = \mathrm{rep}_{(g_1, g_2)} h_n\}$.

- *Knowledge of a discrete logarithm unequal to zero [5, Chapter 3]:* Let h be a value in G_q. Alice can demonstrate to Bob that she knows a representation (x_1, x_2) of h w.r.t. base tuple $(g_1, g_2) \in (G_q)^2$, such that $x_1 \neq 0$. We denote this protocol by $PK\{(\chi_1, \chi_2) : (\chi_1, \chi_2) = \mathrm{rep}_{(g_1, g_2)} h \wedge \chi_1 \neq 0\}$. Brands calls this a NOT proof.

- *AND connections:* All previous formulae can be combined by "AND" connectives. Given formulae $F_1(x_{1,1}, \ldots, x_{1,l_1}), \ldots, F_n(x_{n,1}, \ldots, x_{n,l_n})$ about secrets $(x_{i,1}, \ldots, x_{i,l_i})$ $(i = 1, \ldots, n)$, we denote this protocol by $PK\{(\chi_{1,1}, \ldots, \chi_{n,l_n}) : F_1(\chi_{1,1}, \ldots, \chi_{1,l_1}) \wedge \ldots \wedge F_n(\chi_{n,1}, \ldots, \chi_{n,l_n})\}$.

Under the DL assumption, all protocols are perfect honest-verifier zero-knowledge. They can be made concurrent zero-knowledge at virtually no overhead by using techniques of Damgård [21].

We briefly review the most important properties of Brands' credential system based on the Chaum-Pedersen based issuing protocol [5, Section 4.5.2].

Proposition 1. *Brands' credential system [5] satisfies the following properties.*

1. *If an honest user Alice accepts the credential issuing protocol, she retrieves a credential secret key $(x_1, \ldots, x_l, s)$, a corresponding public key h and a signature $sign(h)$, such that $(h, sign(h))$ is uniformly distributed over the set $\{(h, sign(h)) | h \in G_q \setminus \{1\}\}$.*

2. *Assuming the Chaum-Pedersen protocol [17] is secure, it is infeasible to existentially forge a credential.*

3. *For any credential public key h and signature $sign(h)$, for any tuple $(x_1, \ldots, x_l)$, and for any view of CA on a credential issuing protocol in which $p = g_1^{x_1} \ldots g_l^{x_l}$ is used as initial input (with $(x_1, \ldots, x_l)$ known by CA), there is exactly one set of random choices that an honest user Alice could have made during the execution of this issuing protocol such that she would have output a credential containing both h and $sign(h)$.*

4. *Let h be a valid credential public key. Under the DL assumption and provided that $s \neq 0$, proving knowledge of a representation $(x_1^*, \ldots, x_l^*, s^*)$ of h_0^{-1}*

w.r.t. $(g_1, \ldots, g_l, h)$ is equivalent to proving knowledge of a valid secret key $(x_1^* s, \ldots, x_l^* s, s)$ corresponding to h. Moreover, the relation $s^* = -s^{-1}$ holds.

5. Consider any number of arbitrarily interleaved executions of a showing protocol with a computationally unbounded Bob in which Alice only discloses formulae about the attributes that do not contain s, and in which she uses only proofs of knowledge that are statistically witness-indistinguishable. Whatever information Bob can compute about the credential attributes, he can also compute using merely his a priori information (i.e., without engaging in showing protocol executions) and the status of the requested formulae.

Assumption 1. Under the DL assumption, if a computationally bounded attacker $\mathcal{A}$, after engaging in an execution of the issuing protocol with CA, in which $p = g_1^{x_1^*} \ldots g_l^{x_l^*}$ is used as input, outputs a valid credential containing a secret key $(x_1, \ldots, x_l, s)$, then $(x_1, \ldots, x_l, s) = (x_1^* s, \ldots, x_l^* s, s)$ with overwhelming probability. This assumption remains valid even when polynomially many executions of the issuing protocol are arbitrarily interleaved.

2.2 Comparison to Other Credential Systems

Before moving on to the new system, we compare Brands' system with the CL-based systems of Camenisch and Lysyanskaya [9,14]. The core of the CL-based systems is a signature scheme with additional protocols for the retrieval of a signature on committed values and for the demonstration of signature possession in zero knowledge. Consequently, a credential can be shown unlinkably multiple times and all pseudonyms based on the same credential can be revoked by simply revoking the credential.

We compare the complexity of Brands' scheme [5, Section 4.5.2] with the optimized CL-RSA scheme of [1] and the CL-DL system of [14]. The evaluation considers communication sizes and workloads in the number of exponentiations. Multiplications and additions are neglected, as their demand on computational resources is many orders of magnitude smaller. As for the schemes, we adopt Brands' scheme for a subgroup construction with $|p| = 1600$, $|q| = 256$ and $|s| = 160$ (see Brands [5, Section 4.5.2]), a CL-RSA scheme with parameters $\ell_m = 256$, $\ell_c = 160$, $\ell_s = 80$, $\ell_e = 259$ and $\ell_n = 1600$ (see Bangerter et al. [1]), and a CL-DL scheme based on a bilinear map over elliptic curves, with $|q| = 256$, $|\mathsf{G}| \approx 2^{1600}$ and a zero-knowledge challenge length of 160 bits (see Camenisch et al. [14]). Workloads are approximated by the number of small (256-bit) exponentiations that must be performed[1]. In addition, we assume the complexity of a bilinear pairing to be competitive to that of a small exponentiation. We evaluate an issuing protocol for a credential with l user-chosen attributes which are unknown to CA and a showing protocol in which no properties of the attributes are demonstrated. Table 1 summarizes the results.

Compared to the CL-RSA scheme, Brands' credentials are cheaper in all aspects. With respect to CL-DL, they are much cheaper to show and slightly more

---

[1] Larger exponentiations are reduced to small exponentiations using the guideline that an x-bit exponentiation roughly compares to x/y y-bit exponentiations.

Table 1. A comparison of complexity for different credential systems

size of credentials

Brands	$32l + 328$ bytes
CL-RSA	$32l + 473$ bytes
CL-DL	$96l + 128$ bytes

issuing protocol

	#expon. Alice		#expon. CA		comm.
	offline	online	offline	online	
Brands	$2l + 6$	3	2	$l + 3$	$32l + 1116$ bytes
CL-RSA	$3l + 14$	7	-	$2l + 21$	$62l + 1405$ bytes
CL-DL	$2l + 2$	-	$2l + 3$	$l + 3$	$96l + 213$ bytes

showing protocol

	#expon. Alice		#expon. Bob		comm.
	offline	online	offline	online	
Brands	$l + 2$	-	-	$l + 7$	$32l + 748$ bytes
CL-RSA	$2l + 18$	-	-	$2l + 9$	$62l + 785$ bytes
CL-DL	$4l + 8$	-	-	$6l + 8$	$96l + 380$ bytes

expensive to retrieve. Brands' credentials cannot be shown unlinkably. This property can however be simulated by using multiple copies of the same credential. One additional credential for identical attributes occupies 296 bytes and can be retrieved by 7 exponentiations from Alice. Hence, for l attributes, about $l/5$ Brands credentials occupy the same amount of space as one CL-DL credential. Additionally, the retrieval of $l/7 + 2$ of Brands credentials costs roughly as much for Alice as the retrieval of one CL-RSA credential.

The CL-DL scheme is based on elliptic curves and bilinear pairings. The adopted bilinear map must provide efficient computations as well as adequate security for the DL problem. Hence, the system's key setup must be chosen very carefully. In contrast, the CL-RSA scheme as well as Brands' system are very flexible in their choice of key setup.

Provided the issuer's key-setup is performed correctly, both Brands' system and the CL-DL scheme guarantee unconditional privacy for the user. In Brands' system, this key-setup can easily be checked by ensuring that p and q are prime and that $q|p - 1$. In contrast, the CL-RSA scheme provides statistical privacy only. Its procedure for checking the key-setup requires a signed proof of knowledge with binary challenges. In the setting described above, constructing the proof requires about $6(l + 1)\ell_c$ small exponentiations, while verifying it requires $7(l + 1)\ell_c$ small exponentiations.

Brands' credentials can easily be incorporated in wallets-with-observers [20,3,5] such that all inflow and outflow is prevented. The integration of trusted modules that can protect the security interests of the identity provider, relying parties, and/or third parties, is critical in many applications. It is not clear whether and how this can be achieved for the CL-based schemes.

Brands' system also offers other unique features, such as the ability to selectively censor user-disclosed attribute values from signed showing protocol transcripts, the ability to recertify previous issued credentials without knowing their attribute values and the ability to selectively update attribute values in previously issued credentials without knowing the values themselves. Note that the latter two properties could also be achieved using the CL-based schemes. In contrast to Brands' solution, however, their proposals are highly inefficient.

Brands' scheme does not provide multi-show unlinkability but achieves unconditional privacy and highly practical showing protocols. Because of the latter property and its richer feature set, we have opted for Brands' system.

3   The New System

The principal parties in our system are a user $\mathcal{U}$, an identity provider $\mathcal{IP}$ and l service providers $\mathcal{S}_i$ $(i = 1, \ldots, l)$. $\mathcal{U}$ retrieves her pseudonyms from $\mathcal{IP}$ and uses them to authenticate to service providers. In the remainder of the paper, $\mathcal{S}_i$ refers to the service provider as well as to the provided service.

In order to obtain her pseudonyms, $\mathcal{U}$ contacts $\mathcal{IP}$ and both parties engage into a pseudonym retrieval protocol. As private output of this protocol, $\mathcal{U}$ retrieves a set of l unlinkable pseudonyms, such that each of them encodes the same random tuple $(d_1, \ldots, d_l)$. To access service $\mathcal{S}_i$, $\mathcal{U}$ authenticates herself with her i-th pseudonym and additionally discloses d_i. She also proves, for each $j \in \{1, \ldots, l\}$, that value d_j encoded in her credential is not on a blacklist L_j. Blacklists are formed as follows: for any user $\mathcal{U}$, if $\mathcal{U}$ abuses service $\mathcal{S}_j$ then $\mathcal{U}$'s value d_j is added to a public blacklist L_j.

Next, we describe the system setup and the protocols for pseudonym retrieval, pseudonym registration and subsequent authentication to service providers.

3.1   System Setup

To set up the system, $\mathcal{IP}$ decides on a group G_q of prime order q in which the DL assumption is believed to hold. She generates a keypair (sk, pk) suitable for issuing digital credentials containing $l+1$ attributes. We assume $(g_1, \ldots, g_{l+1}, h_0) \in G_q$ to be part of $\mathcal{IP}$'s public key pk. Credential public keys are of the form $g_1^{x_1} \cdots g_l^{x_l} g_{l+1}^{t} h_0^{s}$, where $(x_1, \ldots, x_l, t, s)$ is the credential secret key.

Additionally, each service provider $\mathcal{S}_i$ sets up and publishes an empty list L_i that can only be modified by $\mathcal{S}_i$. $\mathcal{S}_i$ also publishes values $a_i, b_i \in_{\mathcal{R}} G_q$ where $z_i = \log_{a_i} b_i$ is privy to $\mathcal{S}_i$.

A pseudonym is a tuple $(P, sign(P))$. Here, $P \neq 1$ is a credential public key. User $\mathcal{U}$ is said to be the owner of $(P, sign(P))$ if she knows P's secret key $(x_1, \ldots, x_l, t, s)$.

3.2   Pseudonym Retrieval

Before retrieving a set of pseudonyms, $\mathcal{U}$ authenticates her identity to $\mathcal{IP}$. Assuming $\mathcal{U}$ meets the enrollment requirements of $\mathcal{IP}$, the following protocol is then executed:

1. User $\mathcal{U}$ generates random values $d_{(1,1)}, \ldots, d_{(1,l)}, e \in_{\mathcal{R}} \mathbb{Z}_q$ and sends $p_1 = (\prod_{i=1}^{l} g_i^{d_{(1,i)}}) g_{l+1}^e$ to $\mathcal{IP}$.
2. $\mathcal{IP}$ retrieves p_1, picks l random values $d_{(2,1)}, \ldots, d_{(2,l)} \in_{\mathcal{R}} \mathbb{Z}_q$ and computes $p = p_1 \prod_{i=1}^{l} g_i^{d_{(2,i)}}$. She sends $d_{(2,1)}, \ldots, d_{(2,l)}$ to $\mathcal{U}$.
3. $\mathcal{U}$ creates $d_i = d_{(1,i)} + d_{(2,i)}$ for $i = 1, \ldots, l$ and computes $p = (\prod_{i=1}^{l} g_i^{d_i}) g_{l+1}^e$.
4. $\mathcal{IP}$ and $\mathcal{U}$ perform l instances of the credential issuing protocol of Brands [5, Section 4.5.2], using p as initial input. As a result, user $\mathcal{U}$ obtains l tuples $(P_i, sign(P_i))$, and l values $s_i \in \mathbb{Z}_q$, such that $P_i = (ph_0)^{s_i}$ for $i = 1, \ldots l$. (All protocol executions may be done in parallel.)

During steps 1 to 3, a random tuple $(d_1, \ldots, d_l) \in_{\mathcal{R}} (\mathbb{Z}_q)^l$ is created such that neither $\mathcal{U}$ nor $\mathcal{IP}$ can control its final value. Note that, because of the random selection of e by $\mathcal{U}$, this tuple remains unconditionally hidden from $\mathcal{IP}$. Based on $(d_1, \ldots, d_l, e)$, a list of l pseudonyms $(P_i, sign(P_i))$ $(1 \leq i \leq l)$ is then created for $\mathcal{U}$ during step 4.

Provided $\mathcal{U}$ has followed the protocol, the resulting pseudonyms are unconditionally unlinkable and untraceable. $\mathcal{U}$ can also compute a secret key $(d_1 s_i, \ldots, d_l s_i, e s_i, s_i)$ for each pseudonym $(P_i, sign(P_i))$. As a result of Assumption 1, the same tuple $(d_1, \ldots, d_l, e)$ is encoded into all of these secret keys, even when $\mathcal{U}$ tries to cheat. We will refer to $(d_1, \ldots, d_l, e)$ as the tuple encoded into P_i, and to d_j $(j \in \{1, \ldots, l\})$ as the j-th value encoded into P_i.

The following result states the infeasibility to create a pseudonym encoding a value which is the same as the value encoded into another user's pseudonym.

Proposition 2. *Under the discrete logarithm assumption in G_q and for fixed values $d \in \mathbb{Z}_q$ and $i \in \{1, \ldots, l\}$. For any attacker $\mathcal{A}$ engaging into a pseudonym retrieval protocol with $\mathcal{IP}$ and as such retrieving a valid pseudonym $(P, sign(P))$. With negligible probability, value d is the i-th value encoded into P.*

3.3   Pseudonym Registration with the Service Provider

To register pseudonym $(P_i, sign(P_i))$ with service provider $\mathcal{S}_i$, user $\mathcal{U}$ shows $(P_i, sign(P_i))$ and discloses value d_i encoded into P_i. $\mathcal{U}$ and $\mathcal{S}_i$ then perform (possibly in signed proof mode)

$$PK\{(\delta_1, \ldots, \delta_{i-1}, \delta_{i+1}, \ldots, \delta_l, \epsilon, \varsigma) :$$
$$(\delta_1, \ldots, \delta_{i-1}, d, \delta_{i+1}, \ldots, \delta_l, \epsilon, \varsigma) = \text{rep}_{(g_1, \ldots, g_l, g_{l+1}, P_i)} h_0^{-1}\}$$

$\mathcal{S}_i$ accepts the protocol if and only if she accepts this proof and if $P_i \neq 1$ and if $(P_i, sign(P_i))$ constitutes a valid message/signature pair. $\mathcal{S}_i$ then stores

(P_i, d_i) and associates it with a new account or perhaps with a legacy account that it maintains on $\mathcal{U}$. (the latter requires a one-time legacy or out-of-band authentication step to ensure the right association is made).

As per Proposition 1 (property 4), this protocol proves Alice's ownership of $(P_i, sign(P_i))$ and proves that the disclosed value d_i is indeed the i-th value encoded into P_i. Furthermore, as a result of Proposition 1 (property 5), $\mathcal{S}_i$ cannot find out more information about the tuple $(d_1^*, \ldots, d_l^*, e^*)$ encoded into P_i, than what she can deduce from her previous knowledge and the fact that $d_i^* = d_i$.

3.4   Accessing a Service

Upon having registered her pseudonym with $\mathcal{S}_i$, $\mathcal{U}$ may either disconnect and return later on to access the service, or proceed immediately. In either case, to access the service of $\mathcal{S}_i$, $\mathcal{U}$ and $\mathcal{S}_i$ engage in the following protocol, for blacklists $\{L_1, \ldots, L_l\}$ as defined earlier. In step 1 of the following protocol, $\mathcal{S}_i$ checks whether d_i belongs to her own blacklist L_i; in step 2, $\mathcal{U}$ proves that each j-th value d_j $(j \in \{1, \ldots, l\} \setminus \{i\})$ encoded into P_i does not belong to blacklist L_j.

1. $\mathcal{S}_i$ verifies if $d_i \in L_i$. If so, she aborts the protocol and rejects $\mathcal{U}$'s request. If not, she proceeds to step 2.
2. If all of the blacklists L_j for $j \in \{1, \ldots, i-1, i+1, \ldots, l\}$ are empty, then $\mathcal{U}$ must prove knowledge to $\mathcal{S}_i$ of her pseudonym key (assuming she is not still in the pseudonym registration session with $\mathcal{S}_i$, in which case this step can be skipped); this can be done using the standard proof of knowledge of a representation, without disclosing any attributes (d_i has already been disclosed and proven to be correct). If not all of the blacklists are empty, then the following steps are executed for each $j \in \{1, \ldots, i-1, i+1, \ldots, l\}$ for which L_j is not empty:
   (a) Both $\mathcal{U}$ and $\mathcal{S}_i$ look up $L_j = \{y_1, \ldots, y_n\}$. They set $m = \lceil \sqrt{n} \, \rceil$ for $n = |L_j|$ and compute the coefficients $a_{i,j} \in \mathbb{Z}_q$ $(i \in \{1, \ldots, m\}, j \in \{0, \ldots, m\})$ of the following polynomials in $\mathbb{Z}_q$.
   $$p_1(x) = (x - y_1)(x - y_2) \ldots (x - y_m) = a_{1,m}x^m + a_{1,m-1}x^{m-1} + \ldots + a_{1,0}$$
   $$p_2(x) = (x - y_{m+1}) \ldots (x - y_{2m}) = a_{2,m}x^m + a_{2,m-1}x^{m-1} + \ldots + a_{2,0}$$
   $$\vdots$$
   $$p_m(x) = (x - y_{(m-1)m+1}) \ldots (x - y_n) = a_{m,m}x^m + a_{m,m-1}x^{m-1} + \ldots + a_{m,0}$$
   (b) $\mathcal{U}$ chooses random values $r_1, \ldots, r_m \in_R \mathbb{Z}_q$ and generates values $C_k = a_i^{d_j^k} b_i^{r_k}$ for all values $k \in \{1, \ldots, m\}$. She also computes $v_k = p_k(d_j)$, $w_k = a_{k,m}r_m + \ldots + a_{k,2}r_2 + a_{k,1}r_1$ and $C_{v_k} = a_i^{v_k} b_i^{w_k}$ for $k = 1, \ldots, m$. All values C_k, C_{v_k} $(k \in \{1, \ldots, m\})$ are sent to $\mathcal{S}_i$.
   (c) $\mathcal{S}_i$ receives C_k, C_{v_k} for all $k \in \{1, \ldots, m\}$ and checks for each $k \in \{1, \ldots, m\}$ if $C_{v_k} = (C_m)^{a_{k,m}}(C_{m-1})^{a_{k,m-1}} \ldots (C_1)^{a_{k,1}} a_i^{a_{k,0}}$. If this fails, $\mathcal{S}_i$ aborts and rejects $\mathcal{U}$'s request.
   (d) Next, the following proof of knowledge is executed. The proof makes use of the techniques described in Section 2. $\mathcal{S}_i$ accepts only if she accepts the proof.

$$PK\{(\delta_1, \ldots, \delta_l, \epsilon, \varsigma, \rho_1, \ldots, \rho_m, \upsilon_1, \ldots, \upsilon_m, \omega_1, \ldots, \omega_m):$$

$$(\delta_1, \ldots, \delta_j, \ldots, \delta_l, \epsilon, \varsigma) = \mathrm{rep}_{(g_1, \ldots, g_{l+1}, P_i)} h_0^{-1} \wedge \tag{1}$$

$$(\delta_j, \rho_1) = \mathrm{rep}_{(a_i, b_i)} C_1 \wedge \cdots \wedge (\delta_j^m, \rho_m) = \mathrm{rep}_{(a_i, b_i)} C_m \wedge \tag{2}$$

$$(\upsilon_1, \omega_1) = \mathrm{rep}_{(a_i, b_i)} C_{\upsilon_1} \wedge \upsilon_1 \neq 0 \wedge \cdots \wedge$$

$$(\upsilon_m, \omega_m) = \mathrm{rep}_{(a_i, b_i)} C_{\upsilon_m} \wedge \upsilon_m \neq 0\} \tag{3}$$

We now explain what happens in step 2. In step 2a, elements in L_j are divided into subsets $L_{j,k}$ of size $m = \lceil \sqrt{|L_j|} \rceil$. The polynomials $p_k(.)$ $(k = 1, \ldots, m)$ are then constructed such as to contain only the elements of $L_{j,k}$ as roots. For each k in $\{1, \ldots, m\}$, values C_k and C_{υ_k} are constructed in step 2b. C_k hides a power d_j^k of d_j, while C_{υ_k} hides the mapping $p_k(d_j)$ of d_j. Note that

$$(C_m)^{a_{k,m}} (C_{m-1})^{a_{k,m-1}} \cdots (C_1)^{a_{k,1}} a_i^{a_{k,0}}$$
$$= a_i^{a_{k,m} d_j^m + \ldots + a_{k,1} d_j + a_{k,0}} b_i^{a_{k,m} r_m + \ldots + a_{k,1} r_1}$$
$$= C_{\upsilon_k}.$$

In step 2d, $\mathcal{U}$ proves that the values hidden in $C_1, \ldots, C_k$ are consecutive powers of the same value d_j (equation 2), that this value d_j is also the j-th value encoded into P_i (equation 1), and that values $p_k(d_j)$ hidden in C_{υ_k} for $k = 1, \ldots, m$ differ from zero (equation 3). The latter proves that d_j is not a root of any of the polynomials p_k $(k \in \{1, \ldots, l\})$, and hence does not belong to L_j.

Proposition 3. *Under the discrete logarithm assumption, provided that $P_i \neq 1$, the subprotocol in step 2 is a perfect honest-verifier zero-knowledge proof that for all $j \in \{1, \ldots, l\} \setminus \{i\}$, the j-th value encoded into P_i does not belong to blacklist L_j.*

Proposition 4. *Consider a computationally unbounded service provider $\mathcal{S}_i$ and an honest user $\mathcal{U}$. Consider any number of arbitrary interleaved executions of step 2 for a pseudonym $(P, \mathrm{sign}(P))$ with $P \neq 1$ and for the same or different lists L_j $(j \in \{1, \ldots, l\} \setminus \{i\})$. Whatever information $\mathcal{S}_i$ can compute about $(d_1, \ldots, d_l)$ encoded into P, $\mathcal{S}_i$ can also compute it using merely her a-priori information and the shown formulae $d_j \notin L_j$ $(\forall j \in \{1, \ldots, l\} \setminus \{i\})$.*

For a detailed proof of Propositions 3 and 4, we refer to our technical report [4].

The following result can now easily be seen to hold, based on Propositions 1, 3 and 4.

Proposition 5. *Under the DL assumption, the following holds for any registered pseudonym $(P_i, \mathrm{sign}(P_i))$ and d_i that $\mathcal{S}_i$ has accepted, assuming $\mathcal{S}_i$ accepts $\mathcal{U}$'s blacklist proof. With overwhelming probability, $\mathcal{U}$ is the owner of a valid pseudonym $(P_i, \mathrm{sign}(P_i))$ which has not been revoked and for which d_i is the i-th value encoded into P_i. Furthermore, $\mathcal{S}_i$ cannot find out any more information about the values encoded into P_i than what she can deduce from her a-priori information, the fact that $(P_i, \mathrm{sign}(P_i))$ has not been revoked and the fact that d_i is the i-th value encoded into P_i.*

We also have the following result.

Proposition 6. *Given non-empty sets $D_1, \ldots, D_l \subset \mathbb{Z}_q$, for any pseudonym $(P, sign(P))$ such that P encodes a tuple $(d_1, \ldots, d_l) \in D_1 \times \ldots \times D_l$, for any view of $\mathcal{IP}$ in an execution of a retrieval protocol and for any $j \in \{1, \ldots, l\}$. There are exactly $(\prod_{i=1}^{l} |D_i|).(q-1)^{l-1}q^{2(l-1)} \neq 0$ sets of random choices that an honest user $\mathcal{U}$ could have made during the execution of this retrieval protocol, such that she would have output $(P, sign(P))$ as her j-th pseudonym.*

That is, a computationally unbounded $\mathcal{IP}$ cannot link a pseudonym $(P, sign(P))$ to its retrieval protocol, even if she would know the tuple $(d_1, \ldots, d_l)$ encoded into P. This is an immediate result of Proposition 1 (property 3) and the specifications of the credential issuing protocol ([5, Section 4.5.2]). Namely, there are exactly $\prod_{i=1}^{l}(|D_i|)$ tuples $(d_1, \ldots, d_l, e)$ such that p (and hence P) will be correctly formed. Furthermore, only 1 set of random choices remains during the j-th instance of the credential issuing protocol, and $q^2(q-1)$ sets of choices during each other instance $i \in \{1, \ldots, l\} \setminus \{j\}$.

4   Efficiency Analysis

The retrieval protocol is executed only once between $\mathcal{U}$ and $\mathcal{IP}$. It requires $\mathcal{U}$ to perform $9l + 1$ exponentiations in G_q, of which $3l + 1$ exponentiations can be precomputed. $\mathcal{IP}$ in turn performs $3l + 1$ exponentiations. A total of $2l + 2$ elements in G_q, and $3l$ elements in $\mathbb{Z}_q$ are communicated. By way of example, if we take $l = 100$, and if we set G_q to be the unique q-order subgroup of the multiplicative group $\mathbb{Z}_p^*$ for primes p and q of 1600 and 256 bits respectively, this amounts to 901 exponentiations for $\mathcal{U}$, 301 exponentiations for $\mathcal{IP}$, and 49kB of transferred data.

With regard to the service access protocol, we take into account the following optimizations:

1. The proofs of knowledge of step 2d, for all $j \in \{1, \ldots, l\} \setminus \{i\}$, can be collapsed into a single proof protocol. As a result, equation 1 has to be performed only once.
2. The check in step 2c can be sped up using the batch verification techniques [2]. S_i hereto chooses random values $o_1, \ldots, o_m$ in a set $V \subset \mathbb{Z}_q$, and checks the following equation: $\prod_{k=1}^{m} C_{v_k}^{o_k} \stackrel{?}{=} a_i^{\sum_{k=1}^{m} a_{k,0}o_k} \prod_{i=1}^{m} C_i^{\sum_{k=1}^{m} a_{k,i}o_k}$. If this check succeeds, the probability that S_i correctly accepts step 2c is at least $1 - 1/|V|$.
3. S_i can complement blacklists using whitelists. A whitelist $L_j' \subset L_j$ represents the set of values for which $\mathcal{U}$ has already passed the blacklist proof. A tuple $(L_1', \ldots, L_l')$ of whitelists is stored, both by $\mathcal{U}$ and by S_i, for each credential $(P, sign(P))$. Assuming the elements in L_j are ordered chronologically, it is sufficient for $\mathcal{U}$ and S_i to only store the last value that passed the proof. Whenever $\mathcal{U}$ requests access to S_i, she merely needs to perform a blacklist proof with respect to the "delta-blacklists" $L_j^* = L_j \setminus L_j'$ for $j = \{1, \ldots, l\}$.

4. All of $\mathcal{U}$'s exponentiations can be precomputed using a variation of Brands' error correction factors technique [5, Section 5.4.2]. A detailed description of this protocol can be found in our technical report [4]. Note that these precomputation can be performed even before the final blacklist is known. All that is needed is an upper bound on $\sqrt{n}$ for n the size of the blacklists.

5. By employing her private value z_i, $\mathcal{S}_i$ can collapse her multi-exponentiations $a_i^x b_i^y$ into one exponentiation of the form $a_i^{x+z_iy}$.

Using these optimizations, $\mathcal{U}$ performs $8 \sum_{j=1,j \neq i}^{l} (\lceil \sqrt{|L_j|} \rceil) + l + 2$ exponentiations in G_q and $\mathcal{S}_i$ performs $7 \sum_{j=1,j \neq i}^{l} (\lceil \sqrt{|L_j|} \rceil) + 2l + 6$ exponentiations. A total of $4 \sum_{j=1,j \neq i}^{l} (\lceil \sqrt{|L_j|} \rceil) + 3$ elements in G_q and $5 \sum_{j=1,j \neq i}^{l} (\lceil \sqrt{|L_j|} \rceil) + (l + 5)$ elements in $\mathbb{Z}_q$ are communicated. For an example value $l = 100$ and regardless of the construction of G_q. For blacklists $L_1, \ldots, L_l$ of more that 20 entries each, our blacklist technique is more efficient than the parallel execution of a NOT proof [5, Section 3.4.1] for each list entry.

5   Extensions and Variations

Abuse of any one service in practice may not necessitate banning the abuser from the entire system. In some cases, it may suffice to ban the abuser either from accessing just that service or from accessing a subset of all services. The former can be accommodated by blacklisting the user's public key, the latter by giving users different batches of pseudonyms for use at different service providers. Furthermore, users can be banned only temporarily by deleting their blacklisted numbers from the blacklists at a later stage.

By employing Brands' issuing protocol [5, Section 4.5.2], we enable the so-called refreshing of credentials [5, pp 190-191]. For example, if $\mathcal{U}$ loses the secret key of some of her pseudonyms, she could get a fresh set of pseudonyms with the same encoded values by refreshing one of her previous pseudonyms; in order to avoid linkability at this time, one of her old pseudonyms could be set aside to allow the bootstrapping of other pseudonyms with the same encoded values.

The complexity of steps 2a-2d of our blacklist protocol[2] is linear only in the number of multiplications for calculating the coefficients $a_{i,j}$. The number of exponentiations and the size of the communication are sublinear in the length of the blacklist. More precisely, $\mathcal{U}$ performs $8 \lceil \sqrt{|L_j|} \rceil$ exponentiations in G_q and $\mathcal{S}_i$ performs $7 \lceil \sqrt{|L_j|} \rceil + 3$ exponentiations. A total of $4 \lceil \sqrt{|L_j|} \rceil$ elements in G_q and $5 \lceil \sqrt{|L_j|} \rceil + 2$ elements in $\mathbb{Z}_q$ are communicated. On top, the protocol can be transformed in an equally efficient protocol for proving than an element is on a whitelist. For this, equation 3 of step 2d is replaced by the following equation:
$$((0, \omega_1) = \mathrm{rep}_{(a_i,b_i)} C_{v_1} \lor \ldots \lor (0, \omega_m) = \mathrm{rep}_{(a_i,b_i)} C_{v_m}).$$
Our blacklisting technique can be adapted to fit any homomorphic commitment scheme for which similar zero-knowledge proofs are available. Among others, it can be used with the RSAREP scheme of Brands [5, Section 2.3.3] and

---

[2] Equation 1 of step 2d can be omitted for a proof that $d \notin L$ without d having to be encoded into a credential.

the integer commitment scheme of Damgård and Fujisaki [22]. Note that the latter does not support Brands' NOT-proof. Instead, the NOT relation must be demonstrated by proving a statement $[(x \geq 1) \vee (x \leq -1)]$. This can be achieved in constant time using well-known techniques [25,19]. In both cases, the resulting zero-knowledge proof protocols require $O(|L|^{1/2})$ exponentiations from both parties and $O(|L|^{1/2})$ communicated values.

References

1. Bangerter, E., Camenisch, J., Lysyanskaya, A.: A cryptographic framework for the controlled release of certified data. In: IWSP (2004)
2. Bellare, M., Garay, J.A., Rabin, T.: Fast batch verification for modular exponentiation and digital signatures. In: Nyberg, K. (ed.) EUROCRYPT 1998. LNCS, vol. 1403, pp. 236–250. Springer, Heidelberg (1998)
3. Brands, S.: Untraceable off-line cash in wallets with observers. In: Stinson, D.R. (ed.) CRYPTO 1993. LNCS, vol. 773, Springer, Heidelberg (1994)
4. Brands, S., Demuynck, L., De Decker, B.: A pract. system for globally revoking the unlinkable pseudonyms of unknown users. Technical report, K.U.Leuven (2006)
5. Brands, S.A.: Rethinking Public Key Infrastructures and Digital Certificates: Building in Privacy. MIT Press, Cambridge (2000)
6. Brickell, E.F., Camenisch, J., Chen, L.: Direct anonymous attestation. In: ACM Conference on Computer and Communications Security, pp. 132–145 (2004)
7. Brickell, E.F., Gemmell, P., Kravitz, D.W.: Trustee-based tracing extensions to anonymous cash and the making of anonymous change. In: SODA (1995)
8. Camenisch, J., Lysyanskaya, A.: An efficient system for non-transferable anonymous credentials with optional anonymity revocation. In: Pfitzmann, B. (ed.) EUROCRYPT 2001. LNCS, vol. 2045, Springer, Heidelberg (2001)
9. Camenisch, J., Lysyanskaya, A.: A signature scheme with efficient protocols. In: Cimato, S., Galdi, C., Persiano, G. (eds.) SCN 2002. LNCS, vol. 2576, pp. 268–289. Springer, Heidelberg (2003)
10. Camenisch, J., Maurer, U.M., Stadler, M.: Digital payment systems with passive anonymity-revoking trustees. Journal of Computer Security 5(1), 69–90 (1997)
11. Camenisch, J.: Group Signature Schemes and Payment Systems Based on the Discrete Logarithm Problem. PhD thesis, ETH Zurich (1998)
12. Camenisch, J., Hohenberger, S., Lysyanskaya, A.: Compact e-cash. In: Cramer, R.J.F. (ed.) EUROCRYPT 2005. LNCS, vol. 3494, pp. 302–321. Springer, Heidelberg (2005)
13. Camenisch, J., Lysyanskaya, A.: Dynamic accumulators and application to efficient revocation of anonymous credentials. In: Yung, M. (ed.) CRYPTO 2002. LNCS, vol. 2442, pp. 61–76. Springer, Heidelberg (2002)
14. Camenisch, J., Lysyanskaya, A.: Signature schemes and anonymous credentials from bilinear maps. In: Franklin, M. (ed.) CRYPTO 2004. LNCS, vol. 3152, pp. 56–72. Springer, Heidelberg (2004)
15. Camenisch, J., Shoup, V.: Practical verifiable encryption and decryption of discrete logarithms. In: Boneh, D. (ed.) CRYPTO 2003. LNCS, vol. 2729, pp. 126–144. Springer, Heidelberg (2003)
16. Chaum, D.: Blind signatures for untraceable payments. In: McCurley, K.S., Ziegler, C.D. (eds.) Advances in Cryptology 1981 - 1997. LNCS, vol. 1440, Springer, Heidelberg (1999)

17. Chaum, D., Pedersen, T.: Wallet databases with observers. In: Brickell, E.F. (ed.) CRYPTO 1992. LNCS, vol. 740, Springer, Heidelberg (1993)
18. Chaum, D.: Blind signature system. In: McCurley, K.S., Ziegler, C.D. (eds.) Advances in Cryptology 1981 - 1997. LNCS, vol. 1440, p. 153. Springer, Heidelberg (1999)
19. Cramer, R., Damgård, I., Schoenmakers, B.: Proofs of partial knowledge and simplified design of witness hiding protocols. In: Desmedt, Y.G. (ed.) CRYPTO 1994. LNCS, vol. 839, pp. 174–187. Springer, Heidelberg (1994)
20. Cramer, R., Pedersen, T.P.: Improved privacy in wallets with observers (extended abstract). In: Helleseth, T. (ed.) EUROCRYPT 1993. LNCS, vol. 765, pp. 329–343. Springer, Heidelberg (1994)
21. Damgård, I.: Efficient concurrent zero-knowledge in the auxiliary string model. In: Preneel, B. (ed.) EUROCRYPT 2000. LNCS, vol. 1807, pp. 418–430. Springer, Heidelberg (2000)
22. Damgård, I., Fujisaki, E.: A statistically-hiding integer commitment scheme based on groups with hidden order. In: Zheng, Y. (ed.) ASIACRYPT 2002. LNCS, vol. 2501, pp. 125–142. Springer, Heidelberg (2002)
23. George, I.: Davida, Yair Frankel, Yiannis Tsiounis, and Moti Yung. Anonymity control in e-cash systems. In: Financial Cryptography, pp. 1–16 (1997)
24. Jakobsson, M., Yung, M.: Distributed "magic ink" signatures. In: Fumy, W. (ed.) EUROCRYPT 1997. LNCS, vol. 1233, pp. 450–464. Springer, Heidelberg (1997)
25. Lipmaa, H.: Statistical zero-knowledge proofs from diophantine equations
26. Nguyen, L.: Accumulators from bilin. pairings and applications. In: Menezes, A.J. (ed.) CT-RSA 2005. LNCS, vol. 3376, Springer, Heidelberg (2005)
27. Stadler, M., Piveteau, J.-M., Camenisch, J.: Fair blind signatures. In: Guillou, L.C., Quisquater, J.-J. (eds.) EUROCRYPT 1995. LNCS, vol. 921, pp. 209–219. Springer, Heidelberg (1995)
28. Wei, V.K.: More compact e-cash with efficient coin tracing. Cryptology ePrint Archive, Report 2005/411 (2005) http://eprint.iacr.org/

Efficient and Secure Comparison for On-Line Auctions

Ivan Damgård, Martin Geisler, and Mikkel Krøigaard

BRICS, Dept. of Computer Science, University of Aarhus

Abstract. We propose a protocol for secure comparison of integers based on homomorphic encryption. We also propose a homomorphic encryption scheme that can be used in our protocol and makes it more efficient than previous solutions. Our protocol is well-suited for application in on-line auctions, both with respect to functionality and performance. It minimizes the amount of information bidders need to send, and for comparison of 16 bit numbers with security based on 1024 bit RSA (executed by two parties), our implementation takes 0.28 seconds including all computation and communication. Using precomputation, one can save a factor of roughly 10.

1 Introduction

Secure comparison of integers is the problem of designing a two-party or multiparty protocol for deciding whether $n_A \geq n_B$ for given integers n_A, n_B, while keeping n_A, n_B secret. There exists many variants of this problem, depending on whether the comparison result is to be public or not, and whether n_A, n_B are known to particular players, or unknown to everyone. But usually, protocols can be easily adapted to fit any of the variants. Secure comparison protocols are very important ingredients in many potential applications of secure computation. Examples of this include auctions, benchmarking, and secure extraction of statistical data from databases.

As a concrete example to illustrate the application of the results from this paper, we take a closer look at on-line auctions: Many on-line auction systems offer as a service to their customers that one can submit a maximum bid to the system. It is then not necessary to be on-line permanently, the system will automatically bid for you, until you win the auction or your specified maximum is exceeded. We assume in the following what we believe is a realistic scenario, namely that the auction system needs to handle bidders that bid on-line manually, as well as others that use the option of submitting a maximum bid.

Clearly, such a maximum bid is confidential information: both the auction company and other participants in the auction have an interest in knowing such maximum bids in advance, and could exploit such knowledge to their advantage: The auction company could force higher prices (what is known as "shill bidding") and thereby increase its income and other bidders might learn how valuable a given item is to others and change their strategy accordingly.

J. Pieprzyk, H. Ghodosi, and E. Dawson (Eds.): ACISP 2007, LNCS 4586, pp. 416–430, 2007.
© Springer-Verlag Berlin Heidelberg 2007

In a situation where anyone can place a bid by just connecting to a web site, the security one can obtain by storing the maximum bids with a single trusted party is questionable, in particular if that trusted party is the auction company. Indeed, there are cases known from real auctions where an auction company has been accused of misusing its knowledge of maximum bids.

An obvious solution is to share the responsibility of storing the critical data among several parties, and do the required operations via secure multiparty computation. To keep the communication pattern simple and to minimize problems with maintenance and other logistical problems, it seems better to keep the number of involved players small. We therefore consider the following model:

An input client C supplies an ℓ bit integer m as private input to the computation, which is done by players A and B. Because of our motivating scenario, we require that the input is supplied by sending one message to A, respectively to B, and no further interaction with C is necessary. One may, for instance, think of A as the auction house and B as an accounting company. We will also refer to these as the *server* and *assisting server*.

An integer x (which we think of as the currently highest bid) is public input. As public output, we want to compute one bit that is 1 if $m > x$ and 0 otherwise, i.e., the output tells us if C is still in the game and wants to raise the bid, say by some fixed amount agreed in advance. Of course, we want to do the computation securely so that neither A nor B learns any information on m other than the comparison result.

We will assume that players are honest but curious. We believe this is quite a reasonable assumption in our scenario: C may submit incorrectly formed input, but since the protocol handles even malformed input deterministically, he cannot gain anything from this: any malformed bid will determine a number x_0 such that when the current price reaches x_0, the protocol output will cause C to leave the game. So this is equivalent to submitting x_0 in correct format. Moreover, the actions of A and B can be checked after the auction is over – if C notices that incorrect decisions were taken, he can prove that his bid was not correctly handled. Such "public disgrace" is likely to be enough to discourage cheating in our scenario. Nevertheless, we sketch later in the paper how to obtain active security at moderate extra cost.

1.1 Our Contribution

In this paper, we first propose a new homomorphic cryptosystem that is well suited for our application, this is the topic of Section 2. The cryptosystem is much more efficient than, e.g., Paillier-encryption [1] in terms of en- and decryption time. The efficiency is obtained partly by using a variant of Groth's [2] idea of exploiting subgroups of $\mathbb{Z}_n^*$ for an RSA modulus n, and partly by aiming for a rather small plaintext space, of size $\theta(\ell)$.

In Section 3 we propose a comparison protocol in our model described above, based on additive secret sharing and homomorphic encryption. The protocol is a new variant of an idea originating in a paper by Blake and Kolesnikov [3]. The original idea from [3] was also based on homomorphic encryption but required a plaintext space of size exponential in ℓ. Here, we present a new technique allowing us to make do with a smaller plaintext space. This means that the exponentiations we do will be with smaller exponents and this improves efficiency. Also, we save computing time by using additive secret sharing as much as possible instead of homomorphic encryption.

As mentioned, our encryption is based on a k bit RSA modulus. In addition there is an "information theoretic" security parameter t involved which is approximately the logarithm of the size of the subgroup of $\mathbb{Z}_n^*$ we use. Here, t needs to be large enough so that exhaustive search for the order of the subgroup and other generic attacks are not feasible. Section 4 contains more information about the security of the protocol.

In the protocol, C sends a single message to A and another to B, both of size $\mathcal{O}(\ell \log \ell + k)$ bits. To do the comparison, there is one message from A to B and one from B to A. The size of each of these messages is $\mathcal{O}(\ell k)$ bits. As for computational complexity, both A and B need to do $\mathcal{O}(\ell(t + \log \ell))$ multiplications mod n. Realistic values of the parameters might be $k = 1024$, $t = 160$, and $\ell = 16$. In this case, counting the actual number of multiplications works out to roughly 7 full scale exponentiations mod n, and takes 0.28 seconds in our implementation, including all computation and communication time. Moreover, most of the work can be done as preprocessing. Using this possibility in the concrete case above, the on-line work for B is about 0.6 exponentiations for A and 0.06 for B, so that we can expect to save a factor of at least 10 compared to the basic version. It is clear that the on-line performance of such a protocol is extremely important: auctions often run up a certain deadline, and bidders in practice sometimes play a strategy where they suddenly submit a much larger bid just before the deadline in the hope of taking other bidders by surprise. In such a scenario, one cannot wait a long time for a comparison protocol to finish.

We emphasize that, while it may seem easier to do secure comparison when one of the input numbers is public, we do this variant only because it comes up naturally in our example scenario. In fact, it is straightforward to modify our protocol to fit related scenarios. For instance, the case where A has a private integer a, B has a private integer b and we want to compare a and b, can be handled with essentially the same cost as in our model. Moreover, at the expense of a factor about 2 in the round, communication and computational complexities, our protocol generalizes to handle comparison of two integers that are shared between A and B, i.e., are unknown to both of them. It is also possible to keep the comparison result secret, i.e., produce it in encrypted form. More details on this are given in Section 5.

Finally, in Section 6 we describe our implementation and the results of a benchmark between our proposed protocol and the one from Fischlin [4].

1.2   Related Work

There is a very large amount of work on secure auctions, which we do not attempt to survey here, as our main concern is secure protocols for comparison, and the on-line auction is mainly a motivating scenario. One may of course do secure comparison of integers using generic multiparty computation techniques. For the two-party case, the most efficient generic solution is based on Yao-garbled circuits, which were proposed for use in auctions by Naor et al. [5]. Such methods are typically less efficient than ad hoc methods for comparison – although the difference is not very large when considering passive security. For instance, the Yao garbled circuit method requires – in addition to garbling the circuit – that we do an oblivious transfer of a secret key for every bit position of the numbers to compare. This last part is already comparable to the cost of the best known ad hoc methods.

There are several existing ad hoc techniques for comparison, we already mentioned the one from [3] above, a later variant appeared in [6], allowing comparison of two numbers that are unknown to the parties. A completely different technique was proposed earlier by Fischlin in [4].

It should be noted that previous protocols typically are for the model where A has a private number a, B has a number b, and we want to compare a and b. Our model is a bit different, as we have one public number that is to be compared to a number that should be known to neither party, and so has to be shared between them. However, the distinction is not very important: previous protocols can quite easily be transformed to our model, and as mentioned above, our protocol can also handle the other models at marginal extra cost. Therefore the comparison of our solution to previous work can safely ignore the choice of model.

Fischlin's protocol is based on the well-known idea of encrypting bits as quadratic residues and non-residues modulo an RSA modulus, and essentially simulates a Boolean formula that computes the result of the comparison. Compared to [3,6], this saves computing time, since creating such an encryption is much faster than creating a Paillier encryption. However, in order to handle the non-linear operations required in the formula, Fischlin extends the encryption of each bit into a sequence of λ numbers, where λ is a parameter controlling the probability that the protocol returns an incorrect answer. Since these encryptions have to be communicated, we get a communication complexity of $\Omega(\lambda\ell k)$ bits. The parameter λ should be chosen such that $5\ell \cdot 2^{-\lambda}$ is an acceptable (small enough) error probability, so this makes the communication complexity significantly larger than the $\mathcal{O}(\ell k)$ bits one gets in our protocol and the one from [6].

The computational complexity for Fischlin's protocol is $\mathcal{O}(\ell\lambda)$ modular multiplications, which for typical parameter values is much smaller than that of [3,6], namely $\mathcal{O}(\ell k)$ multiplications.[1] Fischlin's result is not directly comparable to ours, since our parameter t is of a different nature than Fischlin's λ: t controls the probability that the best known generic attack breaks our encryption scheme, while λ controls the probability that the protocol gives incorrect results. However, if we assume that parameters are chosen to make the two probabilities be roughly equal, then the two computational complexities are asymptotically the same.

---

[1] In [3,6] the emphasis is on using the comparison to transfer a piece of data, conditioned on the result of the comparison. For this application, their solution has advantages over Fischlin's, even though the comparison itself is slower.

Thus, in a nutshell, [3,6] has small communication and large computational complexity while [4] is the other way around. In comparison, our contribution allows us to get "the best of both worlds". In Section 6.3 we give results of a comparison between implementations of our own and Fischlin's protocols. Finally, note that our protocol always computes the correct result, whereas Fischlin's has a small error probability.

In concurrent independent work, Garay, Schoemakers and Villegas [7] propose protocols for comparison based on homomorphic encryption that are somewhat related to ours, although they focus on the model where the comparison result is to remain secret. They present a logarithmic round protocol based on emulating a new Boolean circuit for comparison, and they also have a constant round solution. In comparison, we do not consider the possibility of saving computation and communication in return for a larger number of rounds. On the other hand, their constant round solution is based directly on Blake and Kolesnikov's method, i.e., they do not have our optimization that allows us to make do with a smaller plaintext space for the encryption scheme, which means that our constant round protocol is more efficient.

2   Homomorphic Encryption

For our protocol we need a semantically secure and additively homomorphic cryptosystem which we will now describe.

To generate keys, we take as input parameters k, t, and ℓ, where $k > t > \ell$. We first generate a k bit RSA modulus $n = pq$ for primes p, q. This should be done in such a way that there exists another pair of primes u, v, both of which should divide $p - 1$ and $q - 1$. We will later be doing additions of small numbers in $\mathbb{Z}_u$ where we want to avoid reductions modulo u, but for efficiency we want u to be as small as possible. For these reasons we choose u as the minimal prime greater than $\ell + 2$. The only condition on v is that it is a random t bit prime.

Finally, we choose random elements $g, h \in \mathbb{Z}_n^*$ such that the multiplicative order of h is v modulo p and q, and g has order uv. The public key is now $pk = (n, g, h, u)$ and the secret key is $sk = (p, q, v)$. The plaintext space is $\mathbb{Z}_u$, while the ciphertext space is $\mathbb{Z}_n^*$.

To encrypt $m \in \mathbb{Z}_u$, we choose r as a random $2t$ bit integer, and let the ciphertext be

$$E_{pk}(m, r) = g^m h^r \bmod n.$$

We note that by choosing r as a much larger number than v, we make sure that h^r will be statistically indistinguishable from a uniformly random element in the group generated by h. The owner of the secret key (who knows v) can do it more efficiently by using a random $r \in \mathbb{Z}_v$.

For decryption of a ciphertext c, it turns out that for our main protocol, we will only need to decide whether c encrypts 0 or not. This is easy, since $c^v \bmod n = 1$ if and only if c encrypts 0. This follows from the fact that v is the order of h, uv is the order of g, and $m < u$. If the party doing the decryption has also stored the factors of n, one can optimize this by instead checking whether $c^v \bmod p = 1$, which will save a factor of 3–4 in practice.

It is also possible to do a "real" decryption by noting that

$$E_{pk}(m, r)^v = (g^v)^m \bmod n.$$

Clearly, g^v has order u, so there is a 1–1 correspondence between values of m and values of $(g^v)^m \bmod n$. Since u is very small, one can simply build a table containing values of $(g^v)^m \bmod n$ and corresponding values of m.

To evaluate the security, there are various attacks to consider: factoring n will be sufficient to break the scheme, so we must assume factoring is hard. Also note that it does not seem easy to compute elements with orders such as g, h unless you know the factors of n, so we implicitly assume here that knowledge of g, h does not help to factor. Note that it is very important that g, h both have the same order modulo both p and q. If g had order uv modulo p but was 1 modulo q, then g would have the correct order modulo n, but $\gcd(g-1, n)$ would immediately give a factor of n. One may also search for the secret key v, and so t needs to be large enough so that exhaustive search for v is not feasible. A more efficient generic attack (which is the best we know of) is to compute $h^R \bmod n$ for many large and random values of R. By the "birthday paradox", we are likely to find values R, R' where $h^R = h^{R'} \bmod n$ after about $2^{t/2}$ attempts. In this case v divides $R - R'$, so generating a few of these differences and computing the greatest common divisor will produce v. Thus, we need to choose t such that $2^{t/2}$ exponentiations is infeasible.

To say something more precise about the required assumption, let G be the group generated by g, and H the group generated by h. We have $H \leq G$ and that a random encryption is simply a uniformly random element in G. The assumption underlying security is now

Conjecture 1. For any constant ℓ and for appropriate choice of t as a function of the security parameter k, the tuple (n, g, h, u, x) is computationally indistinguishable from (n, g, h, u, y), where n, g, h, u are generated by the key generation algorithm sketched above, x is uniform in G and y is uniform in H.

Proposition 2. *Under the above conjecture, the cryptosystem is semantically secure.*

Proof. Consider any polynomial time adversary who sees the public key, chooses a message m and gets an encryption of m, which is of the form $g^m h^r \bmod n$, where g has order uv and h has order v modulo p and q. The conjecture now states that even given the public key, the adversary cannot distinguish between a uniformly random element from H and one from G. But h^r was already statistically indistinguishable from a random element in H, and so it must also be computationally indistinguishable from a random element in G. But this means that the adversary cannot distinguish the entire encryption from a random element of G, and this is equivalent to semantic security – recall that one of the equivalent definitions of semantic security requires that encryptions of m be computationally indistinguishable from random encryptions.

The only reason we set t to be a function of k is that the standard definition of semantic security talks about what happens asymptotically when a *single* security parameter goes to infinity. From the known attacks sketched above, we can choose t to be much smaller than k. Realistic values might be $k = 1024, t = 160$.

A central property of the encryption scheme is that it is homomorphic over u, i.e.,

$$E_{pk}(m, r) \cdot E_{pk}(m', r') \bmod n = E_{pk}(m + m' \bmod u, r + r').$$

The cryptosystem is related to that of Groth [2], in fact ciphertexts in his system also have the form $g^m h^r \bmod n$. The difference lies in the way n, g and h are chosen. In particular, our idea of letting h, g have the same order modulo p and q allows us to improve efficiency by using subgroups of Z_n^* that are even smaller than those from [2].

3   The Protocol

For the protocol, we assume that A has generated a key pair $sk = (p, q, v)$ and $pk = (n, u, g, h)$ for the homomorphic cryptosystem we described previously. The protocol proceeds in two phases: an input sharing phase in which the client must be on-line, and a computation phase where the server and assisting server determine the result while the client is offline.

In the input sharing phase C secret shares his input m between A and B:

- Let the binary representation of m be $m_\ell \ldots m_1$, where m_1 is the least significant bit. C chooses, for $i = 1, \ldots, \ell$, random pairs $a_i, b_i \in \mathbb{Z}_u$ subject to $m_i = a_i + b_i \bmod u$.
- C sends privately $a_1, \ldots, a_\ell$ to A and $b_1, \ldots, b_\ell$. This can be done using any secure public-key cryptosystem with security parameter k, and requires communicating $\mathcal{O}(\ell \log \ell + k)$ bits.[2] In practice, a standard SSL connection would probably be used.

In the second phase we wish to determine the result $m > x$ where x is the current public price (with binary representation $x_\ell \ldots x_1$).

Assuming a value $y \in \mathbb{Z}_u$ has been shared additively between A and B, as C did it in the first phase, we write $[y]$ for the pairs of shares involved, so $[y]$ stands for "a sharing of" y. Since the secret sharing scheme is linear over $\mathbb{Z}_u$, A and B can compute from $[y], [w]$ and a publicly known value α a sharing $[y + \alpha w \bmod u]$. Note that this does not require interaction but merely local computation. The protocol proceeds as follows:

- A and B compute, for $i = 1, \ldots, \ell$ sharings $[w_i]$ where

$$w_i = m_i + x_i - 2x_i m_i = m_i \oplus x_i.$$

---

[2] We need to send $\ell \log \ell$ bits, and public-key systems typically have $\theta(k)$-bit plaintexts and ciphertexts.

– A and B now compute, for $i = 1, \ldots, \ell$ sharings $[c_i]$ where

$$c_i = x_i - m_i + 1 + \sum_{j=i+1}^{\ell} w_j.$$

Note that if $m > x$, then there is exactly one position i where $c_i = 0$, otherwise no such position exists. Note also, that by the choice of u, it can be seen that no reductions modulo u take place in the above computations.

– Let α_i and β_i be the shares of c_i that A and B have now locally computed. A computes encryptions $E_{pk}(\alpha_i, r_i)$ and sends them all to B.

– B chooses at random $s_i \in \mathbb{Z}_u^*$ and s_i' as a $2t$ bit integer and computes a random encryption of the form

$$\gamma_i = (E_{pk}(\alpha_i, r_i) \cdot g^{\beta_i})^{s_i} \cdot h^{s_i'} \bmod n.$$

Note that, if $c_i = 0$, this will be an essentially random encryption of 0, otherwise it is an essentially random encryption of a random nonzero value. B sends these encryptions to A in randomly permuted order.

– A uses his secret key to decide, as described in the previous section, whether any of the received encryptions contain 0. If this is the case, he outputs "$m > x$", otherwise he outputs "$m \leq x$".

A note on preprocessing: one can observe that the protocol frequently instructs players to compute a number of form $h^r \bmod n$ where r is randomly chosen in some range, typically $[0 \ldots 2^{2t}[$. Since these numbers do not depend on the input, they can be precomputed and stored. As mentioned in the Introduction, this has a major effect on performance because all other exponentiations are done with very small exponents.

4 Security

In this section the protocol is proven secure against an honest but curious adversary corrupting a single player at the start of the protocol.

The client C has as input its maximum bid m and all players have as input the public bid x. The output given to A is the evaluation of $m > x$, and B and C get no output.

In the following we argue correctness and we argue privacy using a simulation argument. This immediately implies that our protocol is secure in Canetti's model for secure function evaluation [8] against a static and passive adversary.

4.1 Correctness

The protocol must terminate with the correct result: $m > x \iff \exists i : c_i = 0$. This follows easily by noting that both $x_i - m_i + 1$ and w_i is nonnegative so

$$c_i = x_i - m_i + 1 + \sum_{j=i+1}^{\ell} w_j = 0 \iff x_i - m_i + 1 = 0 \wedge \sum_{j=i+1}^{\ell} w_j = 0.$$

We can now conclude correctness of the protocol since $x_i - m_i + 1 = 0 \iff m_i > x_i$ and $\sum_{j=i+1}^{\ell} w_j = 0 \iff \forall j > i : m_j = x_j$, which together imply $m > x$. Note that since the sum of the w_j is positive after the first position in which $x_i \neq m_i$, there can be at most one zero among the c_i.

4.2   Privacy

Privacy in our setting means that A learns only the result of the comparison, and B learns nothing new. We can ignore the client as it has the only secret input and already knows the result based on its input.

First assume that A is corrupt, i.e, that A tries to deduce information about the maximum bid based on the messages it sees. From the client, A sees both his own shares $a_1, \ldots, a_\ell$, and the ones for B encrypted under some semantically secure cryptosystem, e.g., SSL. From B, A sees the message:

$$(E_{pk}(\alpha_i, r_i) \cdot g^{\beta_i})^{s_i} \cdot h^{s_i'} \bmod n.$$

By the homomorphic properties of our cryptosystem this can be rewritten as

$$E_{pk}(s_i \cdot \alpha_i, s_i \cdot r_i) \cdot E_{pk}(s_i \cdot \beta_i, s_i') = E_{pk}(s_i(\alpha_i + \beta_i), s_i \cdot r_i + s_i').$$

In order to prove that A learns no additional information, we can show that A could – given knowledge of the result, the publicly known number and nothing else – simulate the messages it would receive in a real run of the protocol.

The message received and seen from the client can trivially be simulated as it consists simply of ℓ random numbers modulo u and ℓ encrypted shares. The cryptosystem used for these messages is semantically secure, so the encrypted shares for B can be simulated with encryptions of random numbers.

To simulate the messages received from B, we use our knowledge of the result of the comparison. If the result is "$m > x$", we can construct the second message as $\ell - 1$ encryptions of a nonzero element of $\mathbb{Z}_u^*$ and one encryption of zero in a random place in the sequence. If the result is "$m \leq x$", we instead construct ℓ encryptions of nonzero elements in $\mathbb{Z}_u^*$.

If we look at the encryptions that B would send in a real run of the protocol, we see that the plaintexts are of form $(\alpha_i + \beta_i)s_i \bmod u$. Since s_i is uniformly chosen, these values are random in Z_u if $\alpha_i + \beta_i \neq 0$ and 0 otherwise. Thus the plaintexts are distributed identically to what was simulated above. Furthermore, the ciphertexts are formed by multiplying $g^{(\alpha_i + \beta_i)s_i}$ by

$$h^{s_i r_i + s_i'} = h^{s_i r_i} h^{s_i'}.$$

But h has order v which is t bits long, and therefore taking h to the power of the random $2t$ bit number s_i' will produce something which is statistically indistinguishable from the uniform distribution on the subgroup generated by h. But since $h^{s_i r_i} \in \langle h \rangle$, the product will indistinguishable from the uniform distribution on $\langle h \rangle$. So the s_i' effectively mask out $s_i r_i$ and makes the distribution of the encryption statistically indistinguishable from a random encryption of

$(\alpha_i + \beta_i)s_i$. Therefore, the simulation is statistically indistinguishable from the real protocol messages.

The analysis for the case where B is corrupt is similar. Again we will prove that we can simulate the messages of the protocol. The shares received from the client and the encryptions seen are again simply ℓ random numbers modulo u and ℓ random encryptions and are therefore easy to simulate. Also, B receives the following from A:

$$E_{pk}(\alpha_i, r_i).$$

But since the cryptosystem is semantically secure, we can make our own random encryptions instead and their distribution will be computationally indistinguishable from the one we would get by running the protocol normally.

5   Extensions

Although the protocol and underlying cryptosystem presented in this paper are specialized to one kind of comparison, both may be extended. In this section we will first consider how the protocol can be modified to handle more general comparisons where one input is not publically known, and we will also sketch how active security can be achieved. In the final version of this paper we will consider applications of the cryptosystem to general multiparty computation.

5.1   Both Inputs Are Private

Our protocol extends in straightforward way to the case where A and B have private inputs a, b and we want to compare them. In this case, A can send to B encryptions of the individual bits of a, using his own public key. Since the cryptosystem is homomorphic over u, B can now do the linear operations on the bits of a and b that in the original protocol were done on the additive shares of the bits. Note that B has his own input in cleartext, so the encryptions of the exclusive-or of bits in a and b can be computed without interaction, using the formula $x \oplus y = x + y - 2xy$ which is linear if one of x, y is a known constant. B can therefore produce, just as before, a set of encryptions of either random values or a set that contains a single 0. These are sent to A for decryption. The only extra cost of this protocol compared to the basic variant above is that B must do $\mathcal{O}(l)$ extra modular multiplications, and this is negligible compared to the rest of the protocol.

5.2   Both Inputs Are Shared, Shared Output

The case where both numbers a, b to compare are unknown to A and B can also be handled. Assume both numbers are shared between A and B using additive shares. The only difficulty compared to the original case is the computation of shares in the exclusive-or of bits in a and b. When all bits are unknown to both players, this is no longer a linear operation. But from the formula

$x \oplus y = x + y - 2xy$, it follows that it is sufficient to compute the product of two shared bits securely. Let x, y be bits that are shared so $x = x_a + x_b \bmod u$ and $y = y_a + y_b \bmod u$, where A knows x_a, y_a and B knows x_b, y_b. Now, $xy = x_a y_a + x_b y_b + x_b y_a + x_a y_b$. The two first summands can be computed locally, and for, e.g., $x_a y_b$, A can send to B an encryption $E_{pk}(x_a)$. B chooses $r \in Z_u$ at random and computes an encryption $E_{pk}(x_a y_b - r \bmod u)$ using the homomorphic property. This is sent to A, and after decryption $(x_a y_b - r \bmod u, r)$ forms a random sharing of $x_a y_b$. This allows us to compute a sharing of xy, and hence of $x \oplus y$. Putting this method for computing exclusive-ors together with the original protocol, we can do the comparison at cost roughly twice that of the original protocol.

It follows from an observation in [9] that a protocol comparing shared inputs that gives a public result can always be easily transformed to one that gives the result in shared form so it is unknown to both parties. The basic idea is to first generate a shared random bit $[B]$ where B is unknown to both parties. Then from (bit-wise) shared numbers a, b, we compute two new shared numbers $c = a + (b - a)B, d = b + (a - b)B$, this just requires a linear number of multiplications. Note that $(c, d) = (a, b)$ if $B = 0$ and $(c, d) = (b, a)$ otherwise. Finally, we compare c, d and get a public result B'. The actual result can then be computed in shared form as $[B \oplus B']$.

5.3   Active Security

Finally, we sketch how one could make the protocol secure against active cheating. For this, we equip both A and B with private/public key pairs (sk_A, pk_A) and (sk_B, pk_B) for our cryptosystem. It is important that both key pairs are constructed with the *same* value for u. The client C will now share its input as before, but will in addition send to both players encryptions of all of A's shares under pk_A and all of B's shares under pk_B. Both players are now committed to their shares, and can therefore prove in zero-knowledge during the protocol that they perform correctly. Since the cryptosystem is homomorphic and the secret is stored in the exponent, one can use standard protocols for proving relations among discrete logs, see for instance [10,11,12]. Note that since the two public keys use the same value of u, it is possible to prove relations involving both public keys, for instance, given $E_{pk_A}(x)$ and $E_{pk_B}(y)$, that $x = y$. In the final stage, B must show that a set of values encrypted under pk_A is a permutation of a set of committed values. This is known as the shuffle problem and many efficient solutions for this are known – see, e.g., [13]. Overall, the cost of adding active security will therefore be quite moderate, but the computing the exact cost requires further work: The type of protocol we would use to check players' behavior typically have error probability 1 divided by the smallest prime factor in the order of the group used. This would be $1/u$ in our case, and the protocols will have to be repeated if $1/u$ is not sufficiently small. This results in a tradeoff: we want a small u to make the original passively secure protocol more efficient, but a larger value of u makes the protocols we use for checking players' behavior more efficient. An exact analysis of this is outside the scope of this paper.

6   Complexity and Performance

In this section we measure the performance of our solution through practical tests. The protocol by Fischlin [4] provides a general solution to comparing two secret integers using fewer multiplications than the other known general solutions. We show that in the special case where one integer is publicly known and the other is additively shared between two parties, our solution provides for faster comparisons than our adaptation of [4].

6.1   Setup and Parameters

As described above, our special case consists of a server, an assisting server and a client. The client must be able to send his value and go offline, whereafter the other two parties should be able to do the computations together. In our protocol the client simply sends additive shares to each of the servers and goes offline. However, the protocol by Fischlin needs to be adapted to this scenario before we can make any reasonable comparisons. A very simple way to mimic the additive sharing is for the client to simply send his secret key used for the encoding of his value to the server while sending the actual encoding to the assisting server. Clearly the computations can now be done by the server and assisting server alone, where the server plays the role of the client.

Together, the key and encoding determine the client's secret value, but the key or the encoding alone do not. The key of course reveals no information about the value. Because of semantic security, the encryption alone does not reveal the secret to a computationally bounded adversary.

Another issue is to how to compare the two protocols in a fair way. Naturally, we want to choose the parameters such that the two protocols offer the same security level, but it is not clear what this should mean: some of the parameters in the protocols control events of very different nature. Below, we describe the choices we have made and the consequences of making different choices.

Both protocols use an RSA modulus for their encryption schemes, and it is certainly reasonable to use the same bit length of the modulus in both cases, say 1024 bits. Our encryption scheme also needs a parameter t which we propose to choose as $t = 160$. This is because the best known attack tries to have random results of exponentiations collide in the subgroup with about 2^{160} elements. Assuming the adversary cannot do much more than 2^{40} exponentiations, the collision probability is roughly $2^{2 \cdot 40}/2^{160} = 2^{-80}$.

We do not have this kind of attack against Fischlin, but we do have an error probability of $5\ell \cdot 2^{-\lambda}$ per comparison. If we choose the rationale that the probability of "something going wrong" should be the same in both protocols, we should choose λ such that Fischlin's protocol has an error probability of 2^{-80}. An easy computation shows that for $\ell = 16$, $\lambda = 86$ gives us the desired error probability, and it follows that $\lambda = 87$ works for $\ell = 32$.

We have chosen the parameter values as described above for our implementation, but it is also possible to argue for different choices. One could argue, for instance, that breaking our scheme should be as hard as factoring the (1024 bit) modulus using the best known algorithm, even when the generic attack is used. Based on this, t should probably be around 200. One could also argue that having one comparison fail is not as devastating as having the cryptosystem broken, so that one could perhaps live with a smaller value of λ than what we chose. Fischlin mentions an error probability of 2^{-40} as being acceptable. These questions are very subjective, but fortunately, the complexities of the protocols are linear in t and λ, so it is easy to predict how modified values would affect the performance data we give below. Since we find that our protocol is about 10 times faster, it remains competitive even with $t = 200, \lambda = 40$.

6.2   Implementation

To evaluate the performance of our proposed protocol we implemented it along with the modified version of the protocol by Fischlin [4] described above. The implementation was done in Java 1.5 using the standard BigInteger class for the algebraic calculations and Socket and ServerSocket classes for TCP communication. The result is two sets of programs, each containing a server, an assisting server, and a client. Both implementations weigh in at about 1,300 lines of code. We have naturally tried our best to give equal attention to optimizations in the two implementations.

We tested the implementations using keys of different sizes (k in the range of 512–2048 bits) and different parameters for the plaintext space ($\ell = 16$ and $\ell = 32$). We fixed the security parameters to $t = 160$ and $\lambda = 86$ which, as noted above, should give a comparable level of security.

The tests were conducted on six otherwise idle machines, each equipped with two 3 GHz Intel Xeon CPUs and 1 GiB of RAM. The machines were connected by a high-speed LAN. In a real application the parties would not be located on the same LAN: for credibility the server and assisting server would have to be placed in different locations and under the control of different organizations (e.g., the auction house and the accountant), and the client would connect via a typical Internet connection with a limited upstream bandwidth. Since the client is only involved in the initial sharing of his input, this should not pose a big problem – the majority of network traffic and computations are done between the server and assisting server, who, presumably, have better Internet connections and considerable computing power.

The time complexity is linear in ℓ, so using 16 bit numbers instead of 32 bit numbers cuts the times in half. In many scenarios one will find 16 bit to be enough, considering that most auctions have a minimum required increment for each bid, meaning that the entire range is never used. As an example, eBay require a minimum increment which grows with the size of the maximum bid meaning that there can only be about 450 different bids on items selling for less than \$5,000 [16]. The eBay system solves ties by extra small increments, but even when one accounts for them one sees that the 65,536 different prices offered by a 16 bit integer would be enough for the vast majority of cases.

6.3   Benchmark Results

The results of the benchmarks can be found in Tab. 1. From the table it is clear
to see that our protocol has performed significantly faster in the tests than the
modified Fischlin protocol. The results also substantiate our claim that the time
taken by an operation is proportional to the size of ℓ and that we do indeed
roughly halve the time taken by reducing the size of ℓ from 32 to 16 bits.

Table 1. Benchmark results. The first column denotes the key size k, the following
columns have the average time to a comparison. The average was taken over 500 rounds,
after an initial warm-up phase of 10 rounds. All times are in milliseconds. The abbre-
viation "DGK" refers to our protocol and "F" refers to the modified Fischlin protocol.
The subscripts refer to the ℓ parameter used in the timings.

k	DGK_{16}	F_{16}	DGK_{32}	F_{32}
512	82	844	193	1,743
768	168	1,563	331	3,113
1024	280	2,535	544	5,032
1536	564	4,978	1,134	10,135
2048	969	8,238	1,977	16,500

We should note that these results are from a fairly straight-forward implementation of both protocols. Further optimizations can likely be found, in both
protocols.

7   Conclusion

This paper has demonstrated a new protocol for comparing a public and a secret integer using only two parties, which among other things has applications
in on-line auctions. Our benchmarks suggest that our new protocol is highly
competitive and reaches an acceptably low time per comparison for real-world
application.

We have also shown how to extend the protocol to the more general case where
we have two secret integers and to the active security case. However, further work
is needed to evaluate the competitiveness of the extended protocols.

Acknowledgments

The authors would like to thank Tomas Toft, Rune Thorbek, Thomas Mølhave,
and the anonymous referees for their comments and suggestions.

References

1. Paillier, P.: Public-key cryptosystems based on composite degree residuosity
classes. In: Stern, J. (ed.) EUROCRYPT 1999. LNCS, vol. 1592, pp. 223–238.
Springer, Heidelberg (1999)

2. Groth, J.: Cryptography in subgroups of $\mathbb{Z}_n$. In: Kilian, J. (ed.) TCC 2005. LNCS, vol. 3378, pp. 50–65. Springer, Heidelberg (2005)
3. Blake, I.F., Kolesnikov, V.: Strong conditional oblivious transfer and computing on intervals. In: Lee, P.J. (ed.) ASIACRYPT 2004. LNCS, vol. 3329, pp. 515–529. Springer, Heidelberg (2004)
4. Fischlin, M.: A cost-effective pay-per-multiplication comparison method for millionaires. In: Naccache, D. (ed.) CT-RSA 2001. LNCS, vol. 2020, pp. 457–472. Springer, Heidelberg (2001)
5. Naor, M., Pinkas, B., Sumner, R.: Privacy preserving auctions and mechanism design. In: EC '99, pp. 129–139. ACM Press, New York (1999)
6. Blake, I.F., Kolesnikov, V.: Conditional encrypted mapping and comparing encrypted numbers. In: Di Crescenzo, G., Rubin, A. (eds.) FC 2006. LNCS, vol. 4107, Springer, Heidelberg (2006)
7. Garay, J., Schoenmakers, B., Villegas, J.: Practical and secure solutions for integer comparison. In: Okamoto, T., Wang, X. (eds.) PKC 2007. LNCS, vol. 4450, pp. 330–342. Springer, Heidelberg (2007)
8. Canetti, R.: Security and composition of multiparty cryptographic protocols. Journal of Cryptology 13(1), 143–202 (2000)
9. Toft, T.: Primitives and Applications for Multi-party Computation. PhD thesis, University of Aarhus, Aarhus, Denmark (2007)
10. Schnorr, C.P.: Efficient signature generation by smart cards. Journal of Cryptology 4(3), 161–174 (1991)
11. Fujisaki, E., Okamoto, T.: Statistical zero knowledge protocols to prove modular polynomial relations. In: Kaliski Jr., B.S. (ed.) CRYPTO 1997. LNCS, vol. 1294, pp. 16–30. Springer, Heidelberg (1997)
12. Brands, S.: Rapid demonstration of linear relations connected by boolean operators. In: Fumy, W. (ed.) EUROCRYPT 1997. LNCS, vol. 1233, pp. 318–333. Springer, Heidelberg (1997)
13. Groth, J.: A verifiable secret shuffle of homomorphic encryptions. In: Desmedt, Y.G. (ed.) PKC 2003. LNCS, vol. 2567, pp. 145–160. Springer, Heidelberg (2002)
14. Cramer, R., Damgård, I., Nielsen, J.B.: Multiparty computation from threshold homomorphic encryption. In: Pfitzmann, B. (ed.) EUROCRYPT 2001. LNCS, vol. 2045, pp. 280–299. Springer, Heidelberg (2001)
15. Pohlig, S.C., Hellman, M.E.: An improved algorithm for computing logarithms over GF(p) and its cryptographic significance. IEEE Transactions on Information Theory 24, 106–110 (1978)
16. eBay Inc.: Bid increments. Available online (2006) http://pages.ebay.com/help/buy/bid-increments.html

Practical Compact E-Cash

Man Ho Au, Willy Susilo, and Yi Mu

Centre for Computer and Information Security Research
School of Computer Science and Software Engineering
University of Wollongong, Australia
{mhaa456,wsusilo,ymu}@uow.edu.au

Abstract. Compact e-cash schemes allow a user to withdraw a wallet containing k coins in a single operation, each of which the user can spend unlinkably. One big open problem for compact e-cash is to allow multiple denominations of coins to be spent efficiently without executing the spend protocol a number of times. In this paper, we give a (*partial*) solution to this open problem by introducing two additional protocols, namely, compact spending and batch spending. Compact spending allows spending all the k coins in one operation while batch spending allows spending any number of coins in the wallet in a single execution. We modify the security model of compact e-cash to accommodate these added protocols and present a generic construction. While the spending and compact spending protocol are of constant time and space complexities, complexities of batch spending is linear in the number of coins to be spent together. Thus, we regard our solution to the open problem as *partial*. We provide two instantiations under the q-SDH assumption and the LRSW assumption respectively and present security arguments for both instantiations in the random oracle model.

Keywords: E-Cash, constant-size, compact, bilinear pairings.

1 Introduction

Electronic cash (e-cash) was invented by Chaum[12] in 1982. In its simplest form, an *e-cash* system consists of three parties (the bank $\mathcal{B}$, the user $\mathcal{U}$ and the shop $\mathcal{S}$) and four main procedures (account establishment, withdrawal, payment and deposit). The user $\mathcal{U}$ first performs an account establishment protocol with the bank $\mathcal{B}$. The currency circulating around is quantized as coins. $\mathcal{U}$ obtains a coin by performing a withdrawal protocol with $\mathcal{B}$ and spends the coin by participating in a spend protocol with $\mathcal{S}$. To deposit a coin, $\mathcal{S}$ performs a deposit protocol with $\mathcal{B}$.

Security of e-cash refers to the fact that only the bank $\mathcal{B}$ can produce a coin and for offline schemes, users who double-spent should be identified. The problem of double-spending only occurs in the electronic world due to easy duplication of digital coins. On the other hand, honest spenders cannot be slandered to have double spent (*exculpability*), and when the shops deposit the money from the payee, the bank should not be able to trace who the actual spender

J. Pieprzyk, H. Ghodosi, and E. Dawson (Eds.): ACISP 2007, LNCS 4586, pp. 431–445, 2007.

is (*anonymity*). Many e-cash systems that provide the function of identifying double-spenders have been proposed, but most of them rely on a trusted third party (TTP) to *revoke* the anonymity so as to identify the double-spenders [7,17,11]. While the TTP cannot slander an honest user, its existence in fact implies that even honest users are not anonymous.

High *efficiency* is also of key importance for practical *e-cash* systems. For efficiency, we look at: (1) the time and bandwidth needed for the withdrawal, payment and deposit protocols; (2) the size of an electronic coin; and (3) the size of the bank's database.

Camenisch, Hohenberger and Lysyanskaya [8] proposed a secure offline anonymous e-cash scheme (which we shall refer to as CHL scheme from now on) which is compact to address the efficiency issue. In their scheme, a wallet containing k coins can be withdrawn and stored in complexity $O(\lambda + \log(k))$ for a security parameter λ, where each coin can be spent unlinkably with complexity $O(\lambda + \log(k))$ as well. Au *et al.* [3] construct compact e-cash from another approach by using a bounded accumulator. However, both schemes involve extensive use of proof-of-knowledge and the exact cost of each operation is somehow hard to quantify. One big open problem of compact e-cash, as stated in the CHL paper, is how to spend several coins in the wallet together efficiently.

RELATED RESULTS. Compact e-cash scheme is closely related to k-TAA[20] and itself can be regarded as a multi-show credential system[13]. The main difference between a compact e-cash and a k-TAA is that in the former case, a token can only be used for a total of k times while in the latter, a token can be shown for k-times to each application provider where k is specified by each application provider independently. In some sense a k-TAA is more general. If the authentication of the k-TAA can be done non-interactively, that k-TAA scheme can be used as a compact e-cash system as follows. All shops play the role of a single application provider with k being specified by the bank, while the bank plays the role of a GM. A user withdraws a coin by obtaining a credential from the bank and spend the coin by authenticating himself to the shop non-interactively. The shop deposits by submitting the authentication transcript back to the bank.

Our Contributions. Specifically, we make the following contributions

- We solve an open problem stated in the CHL paper by introducing the idea of compact spending and batch spending into compact e-cash systems.
- We present generic construction of compact e-cash system with these two added protocols and propose two instantiations
- We formalize a model to accommodate batch spending and compact spending protocols into compact e-cash schemes and present security arguments for our schemes.
- We outline how size of the wallet can be chosen arbitrarily by users while preserving user privacy during spending.

Organization. We discuss related works and technical preliminaries in the next section. A security model is shown in Section 3. The construction is shown in Section 4, accompanied by security analysis. Finally we conclude in Section 5.

2 Preliminaries

2.1 Notations

Let $\hat{e}$ be a bilinear map such that $\hat{e} : \mathbb{G}_1 \times \mathbb{G}_2 \to \mathbb{G}_T$.

- $\mathbb{G}_1$ and $\mathbb{G}_2$ are cyclic multiplicative groups of prime order p.
- each element of $\mathbb{G}_1$, $\mathbb{G}_2$ and $\mathbb{G}_T$ has unique binary representation.
- g_0, h_0 are generators of $\mathbb{G}_1$ and $\mathbb{G}_2$ respectively.
- $\psi : \mathbb{G}_2 \to \mathbb{G}_1$ is a computable isomorphism from $\mathbb{G}_2$ to $\mathbb{G}_1$, with $\psi(h_0) = g_0$.
- (Bilinear) $\forall x \in \mathbb{G}_1$, $y \in \mathbb{G}_2$ and $a, b \in \mathbb{Z}_p$, $\hat{e}(x^a, y^b) = \hat{e}(x, y)^{ab}$.
- (Non-degenerate)$\hat{e}(g_0, h_0) \neq 1$.

$\mathbb{G}_1$ and $\mathbb{G}_2$ can be the same or different groups. We say that two groups ($\mathbb{G}_1$, $\mathbb{G}_2$) are a bilinear group pair if the group action in $\mathbb{G}_1$, $\mathbb{G}_2$, the isomorphism ψ and the bilinear mapping $\hat{e}$ are all efficiently computable.

2.2 Mathematical Assumptions

Definition 1 (Decisional Diffie-Hellman). *The Decisional Diffie-Hellman (DDH) problem in $\mathbb{G}$ is defined as follow: On input a quadruple $(g, g^a, g^b, g^c) \in \mathbb{G}^4$, output 1 if $c = ab$ and 0 otherwise. We say that the DDH assumption holds in $\mathbb{G}$ if no PPT algorithm has non-negligible advantage over random guessing in solving the DDH problem in $\mathbb{G}$.*

Definition 2 (q-Strong Diffie-Hellman[4]). *The q-Strong Diffie-Hellman (q-SDH) problem in $(\mathbb{G}_1, \mathbb{G}_2)$ is defined as follow: On input a $(q + 2)$-tuple $(g_0, h_0, h_0^x, h_0^{x^2}, \cdots, h_0^{x^q}) \in \mathbb{G}_1 \times \mathbb{G}_2^{q+1}$, output a pair (A, c) such that $A^{(x+c)} = g_0$ where $c \in \mathbb{Z}_p^*$. We say that the q-SDH assumption holds in $(\mathbb{G}_1, \mathbb{G}_2)$ if no PPT algorithm has non-negligible advantage in solving the q-SDH problem in $(\mathbb{G}_1, \mathbb{G}_2)$.*

Definition 3 (y-Decisional Diffie-Hellman Inversion Assumption[14,8]). *The y-Decisional Diffie-Hellman Inversion problem (y-DDHI) in prime order group $\mathbb{G}$ is defined as follow: On input a $(y + 2)$-tuple $(g, g^x, g^{x^2}, \cdots, g^{x^y}, g^c) \in \mathbb{G}^{y+2}$, output 1 if $c = 1/x$ and 0 otherwise. We say that the y-DDHI assumption holds in $\mathbb{G}$ if no PPT algorithm has non-negligible advantage over random guessing in solving the y-DDHI problem in $\mathbb{G}$.*

Definition 4 (LRSW Assumption[16]). *The LRSW problem in prime order group $\mathbb{G}$ is defined as follow: Let $\mathbb{G} = \langle g \rangle$ be a prime order cyclic group of order p and $u = g^x, v = g^y$. Define $O_{u,v}(\cdot)$ as an oracle such that on input a value $m \in \mathbb{Z}_p$, output (a, a^y, a^{x+mxy}) for a randomly chosen $a \in \mathbb{G}$. The problem is on input g, u, v, and the oracle $O_{u,v}(\cdot)$, output (m, a, b, c) such that*

$m \neq 0 \land a \in \mathbb{G} \land b = a^y \land c = a^{x+mxy}$ and m has not been input to $O_{u,v}(\cdot)$. We say that the LRSW assumption holds in $\mathbb{G}$ if no PPT algorithm has non-negligible advantage in solving the LRSW problem in $\mathbb{G}$.

Definition 5 (eXternal Diffie-Hellman). *The eXternal Diffie-Hellman (XDH) problem in $(\mathbb{G}_1, \mathbb{G}_2, \mathbb{G}_T)$ is defined as solving the DDH problem in $\mathbb{G}_1$ given the following three efficient oracles*

1. *solving DDH problem in $\mathbb{G}_2$,*
2. *computing the isomorphism from $\mathbb{G}_2$ to $\mathbb{G}_1$,*
3. *and computing the bilinear mapping of groups $\mathbb{G}_1 \times \mathbb{G}_2$ to $\mathbb{G}_T$.*

We say that the XDH assumption holds in $(\mathbb{G}_1, \mathbb{G}_2, \mathbb{G}_T)$ if no PPT algorithm has non-negligble advantage in solving the XDH problem in $(\mathbb{G}_1, \mathbb{G}_2, \mathbb{G}_T)$.

The above assumption implies that the isomorphism is computationally one-way, i.e. there does not efficient way to complete $\psi^{-1} : \mathbb{G}_1 \to \mathbb{G}_2$. This has proven to be false in supersingular curves while it is conjectured to hold over MNT curves. See [5] for a more throughout discussion.

2.3   Building Blocks

Verifiable Random Function. One of the building blocks of our e-cash system is the verifiable random function (VRF) from [14], which we shall refer to as DY VRF. The notion VRF was introduced in [18]. Roughly speaking, a VRF is a pseudo-random function with non-interactive proof of correctness of its output. The VRF defined in [14] is described as follow. The function f is defined by a tuple $(\mathbb{G}_p, p, g, s)$, where $\mathbb{G}_T$ is a cyclic group of prime order p, g a generator of $\mathbb{G}_p$ and s is a seed in $\mathbb{Z}_p$. On input x, $f_{\mathbb{G}_p,p,g,s}(x) = g^{\frac{1}{s+x+1}}$. Efficient proof such that the output is correctly formed (with respect to s and x in some commitment scheme such as Pedersen Commitment [19]) exists and the output of f is indistinguishable from random elements in $\mathbb{G}_p$ if the y-DDHI assumption in $\mathbb{G}_p$ holds.

Signature with Efficient Protocols. A signature scheme with efficient protocols refers to signature scheme with the following two protocols: (1) a protocol between a user and a signer with keys (pk, sk). Both the user and the signer agreed on a commitment scheme such as Pedersen commitment. The user input is a block of messages $(m_1, \cdots, m_L)$ and a random value r such that $C = \text{Commit}(m_1, \cdots, m_L, r)$. After executing the protocol, the user obtains a signature on $(m_1, \cdots, m_L)$ from the signer while the signer learns nothing about the block of messages; (2) a protocol to prove the knowledge of a signature. This allows the user to prove to a verifier that he is in possession of a signature. Examples include CL signature, CL+ signature [9,10] and a modification of the short group signature from Boneh *et al.*[5] that is called BBS+[1].

3   Security Model

3.1   Syntax

A compact e-cash system with compact spending and batch spending is a tuple (BankSetup, UserSetup, WithdrawalProtocol, SpendProtocol, BSpendProtocol, CSpendProtocol, DepositProtocol, RevokeDoubleSpender, VerifyGuilt) of nine polynomial time algorithms/protocols between three entities, namely Bank, Merchant and User. The following enumerates the syntax.

- BankSetup. On input an unary string 1^λ, where λ is the security parameter, the algorithm outputs the bank's master secret bsk and the public parameter bpk.
- UserSetup. On input bpk, outputs a key pair (pk, sk). Since merchants are a subset of users, they may use this algorithm to obtain keys as well.
- WithdrawalProtocol. The user with input (pk, sk) withdraws a wallet w of k coins from the bank. The bank's input is the master secret bsk. After executing the protocol, the user obtains a wallet w while the bank (possibly) retains certain information τ_w, called the trace information.
- SpendProtocol. This is the normal spend protocol when the user spends a single coin to a merchant. The user input is w and the merchant's identity. After the protocol, the merchant obtains a transcript including a proof of validity π of a coin from the wallet, and possibly some auxiliary information aux, and outputs $0/1$, depending whether the payment is accepted. The user's output is an updated wallet w'.
- BSpendProtocol. This is the batch spend protocol when the user spends n coins, $n < k$, together to a merchant. The user input is w and the merchant's identity. After the protocol, the merchant obtains a transcript including a proof of validity π of n coin from the wallet, and possibly some auxiliary information aux, and outputs $0/1$, depending whether the payment is accepted. The user's output is an updated wallet w'.
- CSpendProtocol. This is the compact spend protocol when the user spends all k coins in his wallet w together to a merchant. The user input is w and the merchant's identity. After the protocol, the merchant obtains a transcript including a proof of validity π of a wallet w, and possibly some auxiliary information aux, and outputs $0/1$, depending whether the payment is accepted.
- DepositProtocol. In a deposit protocol, the merchant submits (π, aux) to the bank for deposit. The bank outputs $0/1$, indicating whether the deposit is accepted. It is required whenever an honest merchant obtains (π, aux) by running any of the spend protocols with some user, there is a guarantee that this transaction will be accepted by the bank. The bank adds (π, aux) to the database of spent coins.
- RevokeDoubleSpender. Whenever a user double spends, this algorithm allows the bank to identify the double spender. Formally, on input two spending protocol transcripts involving the same coin, the algorithm outputs the public key pk of the double-spender. Intuitively, there are three possible cases

for a user to double-spend, namely, normal spend twice (or batch spend involving same coin), compact spend twice, or normal spend (or batch spend) and then compact spend or vice versa. The bank also output a proof π_D to prove that user pk indeed double-spends.

- VerifyGuilt This algorithm allows the public to verify that the user with public key pk is guilty of double-spending. In particular, when the bank uses RevokeDoubleSpender and output π_D and pk of the double-spender, everyone can check if the bank is honest.

SpendProtocol, BSpendProtocol and CSpendProtocol shall be collectively called spend protocols. In situations where ambiguity may arise, we shall refer to executing SpendProtocol as normal spending.

Remarks: We omit the Trace and VerifyOwnership algorithm defined in the CHL paper because our system does not support it, just as the first version in the CHL paper. We should remark, however, we can extend our system using the same technique as in the CHL paper to support these two algorithms. Details of extension can be found in the full version of the paper[2].

3.2   Security Notions

We first provide an informal description of the security requirements. A *secure* compact e-cash scheme should possess *correctness, balance, anonymity* and *exculpability*, introduced as follows.

- *Correctness.* If an honest user runs WithdrawalProtocol with an honest bank and runs any of the spend protocols with an honest merchant, the merchant accepts the payment. The merchant later runs Deposit with the bank, which will accept the transaction.
- *Balance.* This is the most important requirement from the bank's point of view. Roughly speaking, *balance* means that no collusion of users and merchants together can deposit more than they withdraw. More precisely, we require that collusion of users and merchants, having run the withdrawal protocol for n times, cannot deposit more than nk coins back to the bank. In case they do deposit $nk + 1$ coins, at least one of the colluders must be identified. A related notion is revocability, which means identity of the double-spender must be revoked. It is straight forward to see that revocability is implied by the definition of *balance*.
- *Anonymity.* It is required that no collusion of users, merchants and the bank can ever learn the spending habit of an honest user.
- *Exculpability.* It is required that an honest user cannot be accused of having double-spent, even all other users, merchants and the bank colludes.

From our definition, it can be seen that it is the bank's responsibility to identify the double-spender. The rationale behind this is that a user can always spend the same coin to different merchants in an offline e-cash system and the merchant has no way to detect such double-spending.

Next we are going to formally define the security model. While the model in CHL uses the UC framework, our model is game-based.

The capability of an adversary $\mathcal{A}$ is modeled as oracles.

- Withdrawal Oracle: $\mathcal{A}$ presents a public key pk and engages in the WithdrawalProtocol as user and obtains a wallet. The oracle stores pk in a set $\mathbb{X}_A$.
- Spend Oracle: $\mathcal{A}$ now acts as a merchant and request users to spend coins with it. It can request for CSpend, BSpend or normal Spend for any user of its choice.
- Hash Oracle: $\mathcal{A}$ can ask for the values of the hash functions for any input.

We require that the answers from the oracles are indistinguishable from the view as perceived by an adversary in real world attack.

Definition 6 (Game Balance)

- (Initialization Phase.) *The challenger $\mathcal{C}$ takes a sufficiently large security parameter λ and runs BankSetup to generate bpk and also a master secret key bsk. $\mathcal{C}$ keeps bsk to itself and sends bpk to $\mathcal{A}$.*
- (Probing Phase.) *The adversary $\mathcal{A}$ can perform a polynomially bounded number of queries to the oracles in an adaptive manner.*
- (End Game Phase.) *Let q_w be the number of queries to the Withdrawal Oracle and q_s be the number of queries to the Spend Oracle. Note that a compact spending query to the Spend Oracle is counted as k queries and a batch spending of n coins query is counted as n queries. $\mathcal{A}$ wins the game if it can run $kq_w + q_s + 1$ deposit to $\mathcal{C}$ such that $\mathcal{C}$ cannot point to any of the users during the Withdrawal Oracle query by running RevokeDoubleSpender.*

The advantage of $\mathcal{A}$ is defined as the probability that $\mathcal{A}$ wins.

Definition 7 (Game Anonymity)

- (Initialization Phase.) *The challenger $\mathcal{C}$ gives a sufficiently large security parameter λ to $\mathcal{A}$. $\mathcal{A}$ then generates bpk and bsk. $\mathcal{A}$ gives bpk to $\mathcal{C}$. Since $\mathcal{A}$ is in possession of bsk, only Hash oracle query is allowed in Game Anonymity.*
- (Challenge Phase.) *$\mathcal{C}$ then chooses two public keys PK and PK' and presents them to $\mathcal{A}$. $\mathcal{C}$ runs the WithdrawalProtocol with $\mathcal{A}$ acting as bank to obtain several wallets $w_0, \cdots, w_t$ and $w'_0, \cdots, w'_t$ on behalf of the two public keys, where t and t' are specified by $\mathcal{A}$. $\mathcal{A}$ then acts as merchant and ask for spending from $\mathcal{C}$. $\mathcal{A}$ is allowed to specify which wallet $\mathcal{C}$ uses, with the restriction that it cannot ask $\mathcal{C}$ to over-spend any of the wallets. Finally, $\mathcal{A}$ chooses a type of spending (normal spend, BSpend or CSpend) as challenge. $\mathcal{A}$ also chooses one wallet w from user PK and one wallet w' from user PK' from the set of wallets that are legal for the challenge (for example, if wallet w_0 has spent $k-1$ times already and BSepnd 2 coins is chosen as the challenge, $\mathcal{A}$ cannot specific wallet w_0). $\mathcal{C}$ then flips a fair coin to decide to use w or w' for the challenge spending.*

- (End Game Phase.) *The adversary $\mathcal{A}$ decides which public key $\mathcal{C}$ uses.*

$\mathcal{A}$ wins the above game if it guesses correctly. The advantage of $\mathcal{A}$ is defined as the probability that $\mathcal{A}$ wins minus $\frac{1}{2}$.

Definition 8 (Game Exculpability)

- (Initialization Phase.) *The challenger $\mathcal{C}$ gives a sufficiently large security parameter λ to $\mathcal{A}$. $\mathcal{A}$ then generates bpk and bsk. $\mathcal{A}$ gives bpk to $\mathcal{C}$. Since $\mathcal{A}$ is in possession of bsk, only Hash oracle query is allowed in Game Exculpability.*
- (Challenge Phase.) *$\mathcal{C}$ runs the WithdrawalProtocol for q_j times with $\mathcal{A}$ acting as bank to obtain wallets $w_1, \cdots, w_{q_j}$. $\mathcal{A}$ then act as merchant and ask for spending from $\mathcal{C}$. $\mathcal{A}$ is allowed to specific which wallet $\mathcal{C}$ uses, with the restriction that it cannot ask $\mathcal{C}$ to over-spend any of the wallets. $\mathcal{A}$ can also ask to corrupt any of the user in the above withdrawal protocol. A corrupted user needs to surrender its private key as well as the wallet to $\mathcal{A}$.*
- (End Game Phase.) *$\mathcal{A}$ runs two deposit protocol with $\mathcal{C}$. $\mathcal{A}$ wins the game if RevokeDoubleSpender on this two deposit protocol points to a user in any of the withdrawal protocol during initialization and that user has not been corrupted.*

The advantage of $\mathcal{A}$ is defined as the probability that $\mathcal{A}$ wins.

A compact e-cash scheme with compact spending is *secure* if no PPT adversary can win in Game Balance, Game Anonymity and Game Exculpability with non-negligible advantage.

4   Our Constructions

4.1   Generic Construction

BankSetup. Let (KeyGen, Sign, Verify) be a signature scheme with efficient protocols as discussed. Let $\mathrm{Vrf}(\cdot)$ be an verifiable random function as discussed. The bank generates the parameter of a signature scheme with efficient protocols using KeyGen and is in possession of the signing key. It also publishes, preferably using another key pair of the signature scheme, $\sigma_1 = \mathsf{Sign}(1), \cdots, \sigma_k = \mathsf{Sign}(k)$. Each user is in possession of a DL type key pair (x, u^x).

Withdrawal. To withdraw, the user obtains a signature $\sigma_x = \mathsf{Sign}(s,t,x,y,r)$ using the signature generation protocol. The banks learns nothing about the block of messages (s, t, x, y, r). The User keeps $(\sigma_x, s, t, x, y, r)$ as its wallet secret and sets the counter $J = 1$.

Spend Protocols. For payment, the user and the merchant with identity $I \in \{0,1\}^*$ first agree on the transaction information info. Then, they compute $R = H(\mathrm{info}, I)$ locally, for some cryptographic hash function H.

Spend. To spend a single coin, the user then sends to the merchant C which is a commitment of (s, t, x, y, r, J) and also $S = \mathsf{Vrf}(s, J)$, $T = PK\mathsf{Vrf}(t, J)^R$.

Note that $PK = u^x$ and $\mathsf{Vrf}(s, x)$ denotes the verifiable random function as discussed on input x with respect to seed s. It then sends the following signature of knowledge to the merchant.

$$\Pi_{\mathsf{Spend}} : SPK\Big\{(\sigma_x, s, t, x, y, r, \sigma_J, J) :$$

$$\mathsf{Verify}(\sigma_x, s, t, x, y, r) = 1 \wedge$$
$$\mathsf{Verify}(\sigma_J, J) = 1 \wedge \ S = \mathsf{Vrf}(s, J) \wedge$$
$$T = u^x \mathsf{Vrf}(t, J)^R \ \wedge \ C = \mathsf{Commit}(s, t, x, y, r, J)\Big\}(R)$$

If Π_{Spend} is a valid SPK, the merchant accepts the payment. Finally, the user increases the counter J of his wallet by 1. When J is bigger than k, the user can no longer spend his wallet unlinkably.

Compact Spend. To spend the whole wallet, the user then sends to the merchant C which is the commitment of (s, t, x, y, r) and also $T_c = PK\mathsf{Vrf}(y, 0)^R$. Then, it sends the following signature of knowledge to the merchant.

$$\Pi_{\mathsf{CSpend}} : SPK\Big\{(\sigma_x, s, t, x, y, r) :$$

$$\mathsf{Verify}(\sigma_x, s, t, x, y, r) = 1 \ \wedge \ T_c = u^x \mathsf{Vrf}(y, 0)^R$$
$$\wedge \ C = \mathsf{Commit}(s, t, x, y, r)\Big\}(R)$$

Finally, the user discloses s, t to the merchant. If Π_{CSpend} is valid and s, t is indeed the value in the commitment, the merchant accepts the whole payment.

Batch Spend. To spend n coins together, the user then sends to the merchant C which is the commitment of (s, t, x, y, r, J) and also $S_i = \mathsf{Vrf}(s, J + i)$, $T_i = PK\mathsf{Vrf}(t, J + i)^R$ for $i = 0, \cdots, n - 1$. Then, it sends the following signature of knowledge to the merchant.

$$\Pi_{\mathsf{BSpend}} : SPK\Big\{(\sigma_x, s, t, x, y, r, \sigma_J, J, \sigma_{J+n-1}) :$$

$$\mathsf{Verify}(\sigma_x, s, t, x, y, r) = 1 \ \wedge \ \mathsf{Verify}(\sigma_J, J) = 1 \wedge$$
$$S_0 = \mathsf{Vrf}(s, J) \ \wedge \ T_0 = u^x \mathsf{Vrf}(t, J)^R \ \wedge$$
$$\cdots \wedge \ S_i = \mathsf{Vrf}(s, J + i) \ \wedge \ T_i = u^x \mathsf{Vrf}(t, J + i)^R \ \wedge \ \cdots \wedge$$
$$S_{n-1} = \mathsf{Vrf}(s, J + n - 1) \ \wedge \ T_{n-1} = u^x \mathsf{Vrf}(t, J + n - 1)^R \ \wedge$$
$$\mathsf{Verify}(\sigma_{J+n-1}, J + n - 1) = 1 \ \wedge \ C = \mathsf{Commit}(s, t, x, y, r, J)\Big\}(R)$$

If Π_{BSpend} is a valid SPK, the merchant accepts the payment. Finally, the user increases the counter J of his wallet by n.

Remarks. S is called a serial number. For each wallet, only k valid serial numbers can be generated. Should a user attempt to double-spend, he must use a duplicated serial number. On the other hand, during CSpend, the user submits

s to the merchant and this is equivalent to submitting all k possible serial numbers. This is the main technique we used to achieve compact spending. Once double-spending is identified, T is the component used to revoke identity of double-spender, as shown in the RevokeDoubleSpender algorithm.

We achieve *constant-size compact e-cash*, due to the idea from [21], by having the bank publishes k signatures on 1 to k. User proving possession of these signatures on counter j indirectly proves counter j has not reached the limit k. Proving j is within 1 to k directly require a complexity of $O(logk)$ while with this technique, constant-size is achieved. The price is that public parameter size is increased to k. Note that if the bank is dishonest and gives signature on $k+1$ to a user, the user is able to spend the wallet for $k+1$ times without being noticed. However, this does not compromise the security since this only breaks the *balance* property which is exactly against the interest of the bank. Thus, it gives no incentive for the bank to behave dishonestly in this way.

Deposit. To deposit, the merchant simply gives the bank the whole communication transcript during the spend protocol. The bank verifies the transcript exactly as the merchant did. In addition, the bank has to verify that I is indeed the identity of the merchant and $R = H(\text{info}, I)$ is not used before by that merchant. This is to prevent colluding users and merchants from submitting a double spent coin (which have identical transcripts). It also prevents a malicious merchant from eavesdropping an honest transaction and depositing it (in that case, identity of the malicious merchant does not match with I). In case the check is successful, the bank stores S, T, R to the database. In case it is CSpend, the bank computes $S_i = \text{Vrf}(s, i)$ for $i = 1, \cdots, k$. The bank then stores all (S, T, R) $((S, T_c, s, t, R)$ in case it is CSpend) for each spending in the database.

RevokeDoubleSpender. When a new spending transcript is received, the bank checks if S exists in the database. If yes, then it is a double-spent coin. The bank identifies the double-spender as follows. There are three cases:

- (Double-spending of a single coin.) Let the entry in the database be (S, T', R') and the current transcript be (S, T, R). The bank computes PK as $(\frac{T^{R'}}{T'^R})^{1/(R'-R)}$.
- (CSpend and spend a single coin.) Suppose the entry in database is (S, T_c, s, t) and the current transcript is (S, T, R). The bank checks for an i such that $S = \text{Vrf}(s, i)$ and computes $PK = T/(\text{Vrf}(t, i)^R)$.
- (Double CSpend.) Suppose the two entries are (s, t, T_c, R) and (s, t, T_c', R'). The bank computes $PK = (\frac{T_c^{R'}}{T_c'^R})^{1/(R'-R)}$.

Remarks. Double spending can be falsely identified if there exists $J, J' \le k$ such that $J+s = J'+s'$ for two different wallets. However, the probability is negligible if k is much smaller than the security parameter. This applies to the CHL scheme too. The proof π_D such that bank is honest is the two double-spend transcripts.

VerifyGuilt. The bank outputs the double-spent transcripts as well as the public key of the double-spender. Everyone can check if the bank is honest by invoking the algorithm RevokeDoubleSpender on the two transcripts since it does not require any of the bank's secret.

4.2   Scheme 1 (Instantiation Using BBS+ Signature and DY VRF)

Following the generic construction, efficient compact e-cash can be constructed readily by choosing a suitable signature scheme with efficient protocols and VRF. One additional criterion is that $PK\{(t,x,j) : T = u^x \text{Vrf}(t,x,j)^R\}$ can be efficiently done since that may not be efficient for any VRF. Below we instantiate a q-SDH based compact e-cash using BBS+ signature and DY VRF.

BankSetup. Let λ be the security parameter. Let $(\mathbb{G}_1, \mathbb{G}_2)$ be a bilinear group pair with computable isomorphism ψ as discussed such that $|\mathbb{G}_1| = |\mathbb{G}_2| = p$ for some prime p of λ bits. Also assume $\mathbb{G}_p$ is a group of order p where DDH is intractable. Let $H : \{0,1\}^* \to \mathbb{Z}_p$ be a cryptographic hash function. Let $g_0, g_1, g_2, g_3, g_4, g_5$ be generators of $\mathbb{G}_1$, $h_0, h_1, h_2, h_3, h_4, h_5$ be generators of group $\mathbb{G}_2$ such that $\psi(h_i) = g_i$ and u_0, u_1, u_2, u_3 be generators of $\mathbb{G}_p$ such that related discrete logarithm of the generators are unknown. This can be done by setting the generators to be output by a hash function of some publicly known seed. The bank randomly selects $\gamma, \gamma_r \in_R \mathbb{Z}_p^*$ and computes $w = h_0{}^\gamma$, $w_r = h_0{}^{\gamma_r}$. The bank's public key is $bpk = (g_0, g_1, g_2, g_3, g_4, g_5, h_0, w, w_r, u_0, u_1, u_2, u_3, k)$ and the bank's secret key is $bsk = (\gamma, \gamma_r)$. It also publishes $\sigma_i = (B_i, d_i)$ s.t. $\hat{e}(B_i, w_r h_0^{d_i}) = \hat{e}(g_0, h_0)\hat{e}(g_1, h_0)^i$ for $i = 1, \cdots, k$. These are the BBS+ signature on i for $i = 1, \cdots, k$. k has to be much smaller than 2^λ. For efficiency consideration, it also publishes $E_j = \hat{e}(g_j, h_0)$ for $j = 0, \cdots, 5$ and $E_w = \hat{e}(g_2, w)$, $E_{wr} = \hat{e}(g_2, w_r)$ as part of the public key.

UserSetup. We assume PKI is implemented, that is, each user is equipped with a discrete logarithm type public and private key pair $(u_0{}^x, x) \in \mathbb{G}_p \times \mathbb{Z}_p^*$.

WithdrawalProtocol. A user randomly selects $s', t, y, r \in_R \mathbb{Z}_p^*$ and sends $C' = g_1^{s'} g_2^t g_3^x g_4^y g_5^r$, along with the proof $\Pi_0 = PK\{(s', t, x, y, r) : C' = g_1^{s'} g_2^t g_3^x g_4^y g_5^r \wedge PK = u_0^x\}$ to the bank. The bank verifies that Π_0 is valid and randomly selects $s'' \in_R \mathbb{Z}_p^*$. It computes $C = C' g_1^{s''}$ and selects $e \in_R \mathbb{Z}_p^*$. It then computes $A = (g_0 C)^{\frac{1}{e+\gamma}}$ and sends (A, e, s'') to the user. User computes $s = s' + s''$ and checks if $\hat{e}(A, w h_0^e) = \hat{e}(g_0 g_1^s g_2^t g_3^x g_4^y g_5^r, h_0)$. He then stores (A, e, s, t, x, y, r) as his wallet secret and sets counter $J = 1$.

Spend Protocols. Let the user wallet be (A, e, s, t, x, y, r, J) such that $J \le k$. The merchant with identity I and the user first agree on the transaction information info and compute $R = H(\text{info}, I)$ locally.

Single Coin Spend Protocol. The user computes $S = u_1^{\frac{1}{s+J+1}}$, $T = u_0^x u_1^{\frac{R}{t+J+1}}$. The user also computes the following quantities $A_1 = g_1^{r_1} g_2^{r_2}$, $A_2 = A g_2^{r_1}$, $A_3 = g_1^J g_2^t g_3^{r_3}$, $A_4 = g_1^{r_4} g_2^{r_5}$, $A_5 = B_J g_2^{r_4}$, for $r_1, r_2, r_3, r_4, r_5 \in_R \mathbb{Z}_p^*$, in $\mathbb{G}_1$. Recall that (B_J, d_J) is the BBS+ signature on J published by the bank. The following SPK Π_1 is then computed.

$$\Pi_1 : SPK\Big\{(r_1, r_2, r_3, r_4, r_5, \delta_1, \delta_2, \delta_3, \delta_4, \delta_5, \delta_J, \delta_t, e, d_J, s, t, x, y, r, J) :$$

$$A_1 = g_1^{r_1} g_2^{r_2} \ \wedge \ A_1^e = g_1^{\delta_1} g_2^{\delta_2} \ \wedge$$

$$\frac{\hat{e}(A_2, w)}{E_0} = E_1^s E_2^t E_3^x E_4^y E_5^r E_2^{\delta_1} E_w^{r_1} \hat{e}(A_2, h_0)^{-e} \ \wedge$$

$$\frac{u_1}{S} = S^J S^s \ \wedge \ A_3 = g_1^J g_2^t g_3^{r_3} \ \wedge \ A_3^x = g_1^{\delta_J} g_2^{\delta_t} g_3^{\delta_3} \ \wedge$$

$$\frac{u_1^R}{T} = T^J T^t u_0^{-\delta_J} u_0^{-\delta_t} u_0^{-x} \ \wedge \ A_4 = g_1^{r_4} g_2^{r_5} \ \wedge$$

$$A_4^{d_J} = g_1^{\delta_4} g_2^{\delta_5} \ \wedge \ \frac{\hat{e}(A_5, w_r)}{E_0} = E_1^J E_2^{\delta_4} E_{wr}^{r_4} \hat{e}(A_5, h_0)^{-d_J}\Big\}(R)$$

where $\delta_1 = r_1 e, \delta_2 = r_2 e, \delta_4 = r_4 d_J, \delta_5 = r_5 d_J, \delta_J = Jx, \delta_t = tx, \delta_3 = r_3 x$.

The user sends $S, T, A_1, A_2, A_3, A_4, A_5$ along with Π_1 to the merchant for payment. The merchant then verifies Π_1 and accepts the payment if it is valid.

CSpend Protocol. To spend the whole wallet, the user computes $T_c = u_0^x u_1^{\frac{R}{y+1}}$. He also computes the following quantities $A_1 = g_1^{r_1} g_2^{r_2}$, $A_2 = A g_2^{r_1}$, $A_3 = g_1^y g_2^{r_3}$ for $r_1, r_2, r_3 \in_R \mathbb{Z}_p^*$, in $\mathbb{G}_1$. The following SPK Π_2 is then computed.

$$\Pi_2 : SPK\Big\{(r_1, r_2, r_3, \delta_1, \delta_2, \delta_3, \delta_y, e, x, y, r) :$$

$$A_1 = g_1^{r_1} g_2^{r_2} \ \wedge \ A_1^e = g_1^{\delta_1} g_2^{\delta_2} \ \wedge$$

$$\frac{\hat{e}(A_2, w)}{E_0 E_1^s E_2^t} = E_3^x E_4^y E_5^r E_2^{\delta_1} E_w^{r_1} \hat{e}(A_2, h_0)^{-e} \ \wedge$$

$$A_3 = g_1^y g_2^{r_3} \ \wedge \ A_3^x = g_1^{\delta_y} g_2^{\delta_3} \ \wedge \ \frac{u_1^R}{T_c} = T_c^y u_0^{-\delta_y} u_0^{-x}\Big\}(R)$$

where $\delta_1 = r_1 e, \delta_2 = r_2 e, \delta_y = yx, \delta_3 = r_3 x$.

The user sends T_c, s, t, A_1, A_2, A_3, along with Π_2 to the merchant for payment. The merchant then verifies Π_2 and accepts the payment if it is valid.

BSpend Protocol. To spend n coins such that $J + n - 1 \le k$, the user computes $S_i = u_1^{\frac{1}{s+J+i}}$, $T_i = u_0^x u_1^{\frac{R}{t+J+i}}$ for $i = 1$ to n. Denotes $I = J + n - 1$. The user also computes the following quantities $A_1 = g_1^{r_1} g_2^{r_2}$, $A_2 = A g_2^{r_1}$, $A_3 = g_1^J g_2^t g_3^{r_3}$, $A_4 = g_1^{r_4} g_2^{r_5}$, $A_5 = B_J g_2^{r_6}$, $A_6 = g_1^{r_6} g_2^{r_7}$, $A_7 = B_I g_2^{r_6}$, for $r_1, r_2, r_3, r_4, r_5, r_6, r_7 \in_R \mathbb{Z}_p^*$, in $\mathbb{G}_1$. Recall that $(B_J, d_J), (B_I, d_I)$ are the BBS+ signatures published by the bank on J and I respectively. The following SPK Π_3 is then computed.

$$\Pi_3 : SPK\Big\{(r_1, r_2, r_3, r_4, r_5, r_6, r_7, \delta_1, \delta_2, \delta_3, \delta_4, \delta_5,$$
$$\delta_6, \delta_7, \delta_J, \delta_t, e, d_J, d_I, s, t, x, y, r, J) :$$

$$A_1 = g_1^{r_1} g_2^{r_2} \ \wedge \ A_1^e = g_1^{\delta_1} g_2^{\delta_2} \ \wedge \ \frac{\hat{e}(A_2, w)}{E_0} = E_1^s E_2^t E_3^x E_4^y E_5^r E_2^{\delta_1} E_w^{r_1} \hat{e}(A_2, h_0)^{-e} \ \wedge$$

$$\frac{u_1}{S_1^I} = S_1^J S_1^s \ \wedge \ \cdots \ \wedge \ \frac{u_1}{S_i^I} = S_i^J S_i^s \ \wedge \ \cdots \ \wedge \ \frac{u_1}{S_n^I} = S_n^J S_n^s \ \wedge$$

$$A_3 = g_1^J g_2^t g_3^{r_3} \ \wedge \ A_3^x = g_1^{\delta_J} g_2^{\delta_t} g_3^{\delta_3} \ \wedge$$

$$\frac{u_1^R}{T_1^I} = T_1^J T_1^t u_0^{-\delta_J} u_0^{-\delta_t} (u_0^1)^{-x} \ \wedge \ \cdots \ \wedge$$

$$\frac{u_1^R}{T_i^I} = T_i^J T_i^t u_0^{-\delta_J} u_0^{-\delta_t} (u_0^i)^{-x} \ \wedge \ \cdots \ \wedge$$

$$\frac{u_1^R}{T_n^I} = T_n^J T_n^t u_0^{-\delta_J} u_0^{-\delta_t} (u_0^n)^{-x} \ \wedge$$

$$A_4 = g_1^{r_4} g_2^{r_5} \ \wedge \ A_4^{d_J} = g_1^{\delta_4} g_2^{\delta_5} \ \wedge$$

$$\frac{\hat{e}(A_5, w_r)}{E_0} = E_1^J E_2^{\delta_4} E_{wr}^{r_4} \hat{e}(A_5, h_0)^{-d_J} \ \wedge \ A_6 = g_1^{r_6} g_2^{r_7} \ \wedge$$

$$A_6^{d_I} = g_1^{\delta_6} g_2^{\delta_7} \ \wedge \ \frac{\hat{e}(A_7, w_r)}{E_0 E_1^{n-1}} = E_1^J E_2^{\delta_6} E_{wr}^{r_6} \hat{e}(A_7, h_0)^{-d_I} \Bigg\} (R)$$

where $\delta_1 = r_1 e, \delta_2 = r_2 e, \delta_4 = r_4 d_J, \delta_5 = r_5 d_J, \delta_6 = r_5 d_I, \delta_7 = r_7 d_I, \delta_J = Jx, \delta_t = tx, \delta_3 = r_3 x$.

The user sends $S_1, T_1, \cdots, S_n, T_n, A_1, A_2, A_3, A_4, A_5, A_6, A_7$ along with Π_3 to the merchant for payment. The merchant then verifies Π_3 and accepts the payment if it is valid.

Deposit, RevokeDoubleSpender and VerifyGuilt have been described in the generic construction.

4.3   Scheme 2 (Instantiation Using CL+ Signature and DY VRF)

We can also build a compact e-cash system from CL+[10] Signature and DY VRF[14]. Due to space limitation, concrete instantiation of scheme 2 is shown in [2].

Following the parameters suggested by Boneh et al.[6,5], we can take $p = 170$ bits and each group element in $\mathbb{G}_1$, $\mathbb{G}_2$ can be represented by 171 bits. Assume elements in $\mathbb{G}_p$ are represented by 171 bits (using another elliptic curve group where pairing is not available[15]). We list the time and space complexity of our schemes and the CHL scheme in Fig.1. For the CHL scheme, we take the public modulus N to be 1024 bits.

	CHL	this paper(scheme 1)	this paper (scheme 2)
Withdrawal	704 bytes	213 bytes	384 bytes
Single Spend	1.9 kB	596 bytes	640 bytes
Batch Spend ($n > 1$ coins)	N/A	$702 + 43n$ bytes	$682 + 43n$ bytes
Compact Spend (k coins)	N/A	383 bytes	491 bytes
Deposit	Same as respective Spend protocols		
Bank's Store (per spent coin)	0.3 kB	64 bytes	64 bytes

Fig. 1. Space Efficiency of different protocols

4.4   Extensions

Our schemes can be extended to support full coin tracing using the same method as in [8]. It can also be extended to support arbitrary wallet size. Due to space limitation, these extensions are shown in the full version of the paper[2].

4.5   Security Analysis

Proofs of the following theorems can be found in the full version [2].

Theorem 1. *Our first scheme is secure under the q-SDH assumption and the k-DDHI assumption in the random oracle model.*

	CHL	this paper (scheme 1)	this paper (scheme 2)
Single Spend			
User	18ME	17ME + 2P	24ME +8P
Merchant	11ME	10ME + 4P	6ME +20P
Bank	11ME	10ME + 4P	6ME +20P
Batch Spend ($n > 1$ coins)			
User	N/A	$(4n + 18)$ME + 2P	$(4n + 11)$ME + 10P
Merchant	N/A	$(2n + 11)$ME + 6P	$(2n + 5)$ME + 25P
Bank	N/A	$(2n + 11)$ME + 6P	$(2n + 5)$ME + 25P
Compact Spend			
User	N/A	10ME + 1P	17ME + 4P
Merchant	N/A	6ME + 2P	4ME + 13P
Bank	N/A	6ME + 2P	4ME + 13P

Fig. 2. Computational Cost of Spend protocols. (ME=Multi-based Exponentiation, P=Pairing).

Theorem 2. *Our second scheme is secure under the LRSW assumption and the k-DDHI assumption in the random oracle model.*

5   Concluding Remarks

We introduced the idea of compact spending and batch spending into compact e-cash, presented security model to accommodate the new idea, and gave efficient and secure constructions. One problem of our system is that since BBS+/CL+ (or CL) signatures do not support concurrent signature generation, withdrawal must be done in a sequential manner. The same drawback is also present in the original compact e-cash [8]. It remains an open problem to design a secure compact e-cash scheme which supports concurrent withdrawal.

Acknowledgments

We would like to thank Colin Boyd and the anonymous reviewers of ACISP 2007 for their helpful comments and suggestions.

References

1. Au, M.H., Susilo, W., Mu, Y.: Constant-Size Dynamic k-TAA. In: De Prisco, R., Yung, M. (eds.) SCN 2006. LNCS, vol. 4116, pp. 111–125. Springer, Heidelberg (2006)
2. Au, M.H., Susilo, W., Mu, Y.: Practical compact e-cash. Cryptographic eprint archive (2007)
3. Au, M.H., Wu, Q., Susilo, W., Mu, Y.: Compact e-cash from bounded accumulator. In: Abe, M. (ed.) CT-RSA 2007. LNCS, vol. 4377, Springer, Heidelberg (2006)

4. Boneh, D., Boyen, X.: Short signatures without random oracles. In: Cachin, C., Camenisch, J.L. (eds.) EUROCRYPT 2004. LNCS, vol. 3027, pp. 56–73. Springer, Heidelberg (2004)
5. Boneh, D., Boyen, X., Shacham, H.: Short group signatures. In: Franklin, M. (ed.) CRYPTO 2004. LNCS, vol. 3152, pp. 41–55. Springer, Heidelberg (2004)
6. Boneh, D., Lynn, B., Shacham, H.: Short Signatures from the Weil Pairing. In: Boyd, C. (ed.) ASIACRYPT 2001. LNCS, vol. 2248, pp. 514–532. Springer, Heidelberg (2001)
7. Brickell, E., Gemmell, P., Kravitz, D.: Trustee-based Tracing Extensions to Anonymous Cash and the Making of Anonymous Change. In: SODA '95: Proceedings of the Sixth Annual ACM-SIAM Symposium on Discrete Algorithms, Society for Industrial and Applied Mathematics, pp. 457–466 (1995)
8. Camenisch, J., Hohenberger, S., Lysyanskaya, A.: Compact e-cash. In: Cramer, R.J.F. (ed.) EUROCRYPT 2005. LNCS, vol. 3494, pp. 302–321. Springer, Heidelberg (2005)
9. Camenisch, J., Lysyanskaya, A.: A Signature Scheme with Efficient Protocols. In: Cimato, S., Galdi, C., Persiano, G. (eds.) SCN 2002. LNCS, vol. 2576, pp. 268–289. Springer, Heidelberg (2003)
10. Camenisch, J., Lysyanskaya, A.: Signature Schemes and Anonymous Credentials from Bilinear Maps. In: Franklin, M. (ed.) CRYPTO 2004. LNCS, vol. 3152, pp. 56–72. Springer, Heidelberg (2004)
11. Canard, S., Traoré, J.: On fair e-cash systems based on group signature schemes. In: Safavi-Naini, R., Seberry, J. (eds.) ACISP 2003. LNCS, vol. 2727, pp. 237–248. Springer, Heidelberg (2003)
12. Chaum, D.: Blind Signatures for Untraceable Payments. In: McCurley, K.S., Ziegler, C.D. (eds.) Advances in Cryptology 1981 - 1997. LNCS, vol. 1440, pp. 199–203. Springer, Heidelberg (1999)
13. Chaum, D.: Security without identification: Transaction systems to make big brother obsolete. Communications of the ACM 28(10), 1030–1044 (1985)
14. Dodis, Y., Yampolskiy, A.: A verifiable random function with short proofs and keys. In: Vaudenay, S. (ed.) PKC 2005. LNCS, vol. 3386, pp. 416–431. Springer, Heidelberg (2005)
15. Furukawa, J., Imai, H.: An efficient group signature scheme from bilinear maps. In: Boyd, C., González Nieto, J.M. (eds.) ACISP 2005. LNCS, vol. 3574, pp. 455–467. Springer, Heidelberg (2005)
16. Lysyanskaya, A., Rivest, R.L., Sahai, A., Wolf, S.: Pseudonym systems. Selected Areas in Cryptography 184–199 (1999)
17. Maitland, G., Boyd, C.: Fair Electronic Cash Based on a Group Signature Scheme. In: Qing, S., Okamoto, T., Zhou, J. (eds.) ICICS 2001. LNCS, vol. 2229, pp. 461–465. Springer, Heidelberg (2001)
18. Micali, S., Rabin, M.O., Vadhan, S.P.: Verifiable random functions. In: FOCS, pp. 120–130 (1999)
19. Pedersen, T.P.: Non-interactive and information-theoretic secure verifiable secret sharing. In: CRYPTO, pp. 129–140 (1991)
20. Teranishi, I., Furukawa, J., Sako, K.: k-Times Anonymous Authentication (Extended Abstract). In: Lee, P.J. (ed.) ASIACRYPT 2004. LNCS, vol. 3329, pp. 308–322. Springer, Heidelberg (2004)
21. Teranishi, I., Sako, K.: k-times anonymous authentication with a constant proving cost. Public Key Cryptography, pp. 525–542 (2006)

Use of Dempster-Shafer Theory and Bayesian Inferencing for Fraud Detection in Mobile Communication Networks

Suvasini Panigrahi[1], Amlan Kundu[1], Shamik Sural[1], and A.K. Majumdar[2]

[1] School of Information Technology
[2] Department of Computer Science & Engineering
Indian Institute of Technology, Kharagpur, India
{Suvasini.Panigrahi@sit,kunduamlan@sit,shamik@sit,
akmj@cse}.iitkgp.ernet.in

Abstract. This paper introduces a framework for fraud detection in mobile communication networks based on the current as well as past behavioral pattern of subscribers. The proposed fraud detection system (FDS) consists of four components, namely, rule-based deviation detector, Dempster-Shafer component, call history database and Bayesian learning. In the rule-based component, we determine the suspicion level of each incoming call based on the extent to which it deviates from expected call patterns. Dempster-Shafer's theory is used to combine multiple evidences from the rule-based component and an overall suspicion score is computed. A call is classified as normal, abnormal, or suspicious depending on this suspicion score. Once a call from a mobile phone is found to be suspicious, belief is further strengthened or weakened based on the similarity with fraudulent or genuine call history using Bayesian learning. Our experimental results show that the method is very promising in detecting fraudulent behavior without raising too many false alarms.

Keywords: Mobile communication networks, fraud detection, Dempster-Shafer theory, Bayesian learning.

1 Introduction

The telecommunications industry has expanded dramatically in the last few years with the development of affordable mobile phone technology. With the increasing number of mobile phone subscribers, global mobile phone fraud is also set to rise. Telecommunication fraud occurs whenever a perpetrator uses deception to receive telephony services free of charge or at a reduced rate. It is a worldwide problem with substantial annual revenue losses for many companies. Mobile communication fraud, which is the focus of this work, is particularly appealing to fraudsters, as calling from the mobile terminal is not bound to a physical location and it is easy to get a subscription. This provides a means for illegal high-profit business for fraudsters requiring minimal investment and

J. Pieprzyk, H. Ghodosi, and E. Dawson (Eds.): ACISP 2007, LNCS 4586, pp. 446–460, 2007.
© Springer-Verlag Berlin Heidelberg 2007

relatively low risk of getting caught. Mobile phone fraud is defined as the unauthorized use, tampering or manipulation of a mobile phone or service.

Although actual figures are not available, according to the Communications Fraud Control Association, the mobile telecommunications industry suffers loss of $35- $40 billion annually, due to fraud in its networks [1]. Telecom and Network Security Review reports that in USA, the financial losses account for about 2 percent to 6 percent of the total revenue of network operators, thus playing a significant role in total earnings. As noted by Barson et al. [2], the true losses are expected to be even higher and it is difficult to give precise estimates, since the telecommunication companies are reluctant to reveal figures on fraud losses. Furthermore, fraudulent attacks cause lots of inconveniences to the victimized subscriber which might motivate the subscriber to switch to a competing carrier. Since operators are facing increasing competition, the reputation of a network operator may suffer from an increasing number of fraud cases since potential new subscribers would be very reluctant to switch to a carrier which is troubled with fraud. From the above discussion, it is clear that the losses caused by fraud acts as the primary motivation for fraud detection in mobile telecommunication networks. In addition to financial losses, fraud may also cause distress, loss of service, and loss of subscriber confidence [3]. Thus, mobile telecommunication fraud is a significant problem which needs to be addressed and detected in the strongest possible manner.

There are many different types of telecom fraud and these can occur at various levels. The two most prevalent types are - *subscription fraud* and *superimposed* or *surfing fraud*. Subscription fraud occurs when the fraudster obtains a subscription to a service, often with false identity details, with no intention of paying. This is at the level of a phone number and all calls from this number will be fraudulent. Superimposed fraud is the use of a service without having the necessary authority and is usually detected by the appearance of phantom calls on a bill. It involves a legitimate account with some legitimate activity, but also includes some superimposed illegitimate activity by a person other than the account holder. Superimposed fraud will generally occur at the level of individual calls and the fraudulent calls will be mixed with the legitimate ones. Superimposed fraud can remain undetected for a long time. It is particularly expensive and prevalent in major cities throughout the USA. Superimposed fraud poses a bigger problem for the telecommunications industry and for this reason we focus on identifying this type of fraud.

The early fraud detection systems examined whether two instances of one subscription were used at the same time (overlapping calls detection mechanism), evidencing card cloning. While this procedure efficiently detects cloning, it misses a large number of other fraud cases. A more advanced system is a velocity trap which detects card cloning by using an upper speed limit at which a mobile phone subscriber can travel. Subsequent calls from distant places provide evidence for card cloning. Although a velocity trap is a powerful method of detecting card cloning, it is ineffective against new forms of fraud. Therefore, there is a need for the development of dynamic and adaptive fraud detection mechanisms, based on the behavioral modeling of calling activity.

2   Related Work

In this section, published work with relevance to fraud detection in mobile telecommunication networks is reviewed.

Moreau et al. [4] describe a rule-based system, which accumulates number or duration of calls that match specific patterns in one day and calculate the average and standard deviation of the daily values. Moreau et al. [5] have used supervised neural networks for detection of fraud in mobile telecommunication networks. Burge et al. [6] represent short-term behavior by the probability distribution of calls made by a subscriber in one day. The "Current User Profile" (CUP) is examined against the "User Profile History" (UPH), which is the average of the CUPs generated by that subscriber. Taniguchi et al. [7] have presented three approaches, namely, a supervised feed-forward neural network, Gaussian mixture model and Bayesian networks to detect fraud in communication networks. Fawcett and Provost [8] have combined data mining and machine learning techniques for detecting fraudulent usage of cellular telephones based on profiling subscriber behavior. Murad and Pinkas [9] use three profile levels - call profile, daily profile and overall profile to represent subscriber behavior. Any significant deviation from the subscriber's normal behavior is detected as fraudulent. Rosset et al. [10] illustrate rule-based fraud detection by using two separate levels of data, subscriber-level data and behavior-level data. Burge and Shawe-Taylor [11] have introduced an unsupervised neural network technique for developing behavior profiles of mobile phone subscribers for use in fraud detection. Grosser et al. [12] have focused on the problem of detecting unusual behavioral changes of mobile phone subscribers by building data structures corresponding to current and history profile of subscribers. Briotos et al. [13] have detected subscribers who are using their mobile phones in a disloyal way. Kou et al. [14] present a comprehensive review of current techniques used in fraud detection in different domains. Bolton and Hand [15] have described the tools available for statistical fraud detection.

Usually, the more advanced a service is, the more is its vulnerability to fraud. In the future, operators will need to adapt rapidly to keep pace with new challenges posed by fraudulent subscribers. While conventional approaches to fraud detection and analysis may be sufficient to cope with some current types of fraud, they are less able to handle new possibilities. It is well-known that every subscriber has certain calling behavior which establishes an activity profile for him. A particular usage pattern may be normal for one subscriber while abnormal for other subscribers. In addition, there may be changes in subscriber behavior owing to personal or seasonal needs. Due to progress of technology, fraudsters can also adopt new fraud techniques resulting in new usage patterns. Hence, systems that cannot evolve or "learn", soon become outdated resulting in large number of false alarms. Thus, there is a need for FDSs which can combine multiple evidences including patterns of genuine subscribers as well as fraudsters, learn their calling patterns, and adapt to the changes in their behavior. In this paper, we propose a unique FDS that combines different evidences using Dempster-Shafer theory. In addition, Bayesian learning takes place by applying prior knowledge and observed data on suspicious calls. To the best of our knowledge, this is the first ever attempt to develop a mobile phone FDS using information fusion and Bayesian learning. In this paper, we use the terms call and transaction interchangeably since a subscriber's call results in a transaction updating the service provider's database.

The rest of the paper is organized as follows. We propose a mobile phone FDS and describe its components in Section 3. In Section 4, we discuss the results obtained from extensive simulation with stochastic models. Finally, we conclude in Section 5 of the paper.

3   Proposed Approach

We propose an FDS which monitors behavioral patterns of a mobile phone subscriber by comparing his most recent activity patterns with past usage patterns. The proposed FDS may be abstractly represented as a 5-tuple $< M, P, \Psi(T_{j,\rho}^{M_i}), \theta_{LT}, \theta_{UT} >$, where:

1. $M = \{M_1, M_2, ..., M_n\}$ is the set of mobile phones on which fraud detection is performed.
2. $P = \{P(M_1), P(M_2), ..., P(M_n)\}$ is the set of profiles, where each $P(M_i)$ corresponds to the profile of the subscriber of the mobile phone M_i. The subscriber behavior information, which facilitates reliable fraud detection, is derived from the toll tickets (TT) provided by the network operator. TT contains details of the call made by a subscriber. We have used 6 components of a TT to generate subscriber profiles which are considered to be the most relevant fraud detection features. Each subscriber profile may be represented as a 6-tuple: $< IMSI, Destination\_No, Call\_Duration, Call\_Type, Call\_Date, Call\_Time >$
   - IMSI: International Mobile Subscriber Identity which identifies a subscriber uniquely.
   - $Destination\_No$: the number that was called.
   - $Call\_Duration$: the duration of the call in seconds.
   - $Call\_Type$: the type of the call (local, national, international). We represent the various call types as: local: 0, national: 1, international: 2.
   - $Call\_Date$: starting date of the call.
   - $Call\_Time$: starting time of the call. We have partitioned the start time into 4 time windows (morning, daytime, evening, night).
3. $\Psi(T_{j,\rho}^{M_i})$ is the suspicion score of a call $T_{j,\rho}^{M_i}$ and ρ is the time gap between successive calls of a particular type on the same mobile phone.
4. θ_{LT} is the lower threshold, where $0 \le \theta_{LT} \le 1$.
5. θ_{UT} is the upper threshold, where $0 \le \theta_{UT} \le 1$.

3.1   FDS Components

The proposed FDS has the following 4 major components:

- Rule-based Deviation Detection Component (RBDDC)
- Dempster-Shafer Combination Component (DSCC)
- Call History Database Component (CHDC)
- Bayesian Learning Component (BLC)

Rule-Based Deviation Detection Component (RBDDC)

RBDDC consists of generic as well as subscriber-specific rules which classify an incoming call as seemingly genuine or seemingly fraudulent with a certain probability. The probability value is termed as the suspicion score of the incoming call. The suspicion score measures how the call's behavior deviates from the normal usage profile of the mobile phone subscriber. We compute suspicion score for each call on a mobile phone and the score is updated whenever there is a new call on that particular mobile phone. We briefly discuss two of the rule-based techniques below.

- **Breakpoint Analysis** (R_1)

  Break point analysis is an unsupervised outlier detection tool that is used for behavioral fraud detection. It is a tool that identifies changes in spending behavior based on the call information in a single account [16]. The term "break point" signifies an observation or time where anomalous behavior is detected. For the mobile telecommunication application, recent calls on a mobile phone are compared with previous usage patterns to detect sudden changes in the behavior of a subscriber. In this method, a sliding window of fixed length is used such that as a call occurs, it enters the window and the oldest call in the window is removed. Calls in the most recent part of the window are then compared with those in the early part of the window to find if a change in calling behavior has occurred. Statistical tests are employed to see if the recent calls conform to the 'normal behavior' of the subscriber or if they follow a different pattern when compared to the older calls. We have used *Call_Duration* attribute as the comparison criterion. Suppose the sliding window W contains Z calls in all: X calls to form the profile and the next Z - X calls to test for an increase in *Call_Duration*. Mean values of *Call_Duration* in each window are compared using a simple t-test for computational efficiency. The t-test assesses whether the means of two groups are statistically different from each other. The formula for the t-test is given as:

  $$t_{value} = \frac{meanprofile - meantest}{\sqrt{\dfrac{varprofile}{nprofile} + \dfrac{vartest}{ntest}}} \tag{1}$$

where, *meanprofile*: Mean of the calls that form the profile, *meantest*: Mean of the calls that form the test data, *varprofile*: Variance of the calls that form the profile, *vartest*: Variance of the test calls, *nprofile*: Number of calls that form the profile, *ntest*: Number of test calls.

Depending on positive or negative t_{value} we can define the degree of variation ($d_{variation}$) of test calls from the normal profile calls as given by Eq. (2):

$$d_{variation} = \begin{cases} 1 - \dfrac{abs(meanprofile - meantest)}{max\_call\_duration} & if \ t_{value} > 1 \\ 0 & otherwise \end{cases} \quad (2)$$

where, $max\_call\_duration$ is the maximum call duration among all calls in W .

- **Frequency Deviation Detection** (R_2)

  We have used another rule to detect excessive activity on an account in terms of frequency of calls and the corresponding call type. An example of high activity could be excessive number of international calls in a day. To identify the sudden increase in frequency of calls of a particular call type we build a profile of subscriber's calling frequency along with each transaction's call type. We monitor behavioral patterns of a mobile phone by comparing its most recent activity with the history profile of its usage. We compute the frequency deviation (fd) of a subscriber by the following expression:

$$fd = \begin{cases} 1 - \dfrac{abs(dailyavg - monthlyavg)}{max\_frequency} & if \ dailyavg > monthlyavg \\ 0 & otherwise \end{cases} \quad (3)$$

where, $dailyavg$: average frequency of calls of type t per day, $monthlyavg$: average frequency of calls of type t per month, $max\_frequency$: maximum frequency of calls of type t per day in a particular month.

Dempster-Shafer Combination Component (DSCC)

The role of the DSCC is to combine evidences from the rules R_1 and R_2 at RBDDC in order to compute suspicion score of a call. Dempster-Shafer theory (D-S theory) is a mathematical theory of evidence based on belief functions and plausible reasoning. The D-S theory assumes a Universe of Discourse U, also called Frame of Discernment, which is a set of mutually exclusive and exhaustive possibilities. Wang et al. [17] have presented a distributed intrusion detection system which uses D-S theory to combine information. They have shown that multi-sensor data fusion scheme gives much better performance than single sensor. Chen and Venkataramanan [18] have applied Dempster-Shafer approach to distributed intrusion detection in Ad Hoc networks. They have combined data from multiple nodes in a distributed intrusion detection system to estimate the likelihood of intrusion.

We have used the D-S theory in the context of mobile phone fraud detection as follows. For every incoming call $T_{j,\rho}^{M_i}$, the rules R_1 and R_2 share their independent observations about the behavior of the call. These observations, which serve as evidences, are combined to form a decision about the call's genuineness. The main advantage of Dempster-Shafer approach is that no a priori knowledge is required, making it potentially suitable for anomaly detection of a previously unseen pattern. The Dempster's rule of combination gives a numerical procedure for combining observations from the RBDDC to compute suspicion score of a call. If two basic probability assignments (BPA's) $m_1(h)$ and $m_2(h)$ are given, they combine into a third basic probability assignment $m(h)$ defined by the following expression:

$$m(h) = m_1(h) \oplus m_2(h) = \frac{\sum_{x \cap y = h} m_1(x) * m_2(y)}{1 - \sum_{x \cap y = h} m_1(x) * m_2(y)} \tag{4}$$

For the mobile phone fraud detection problem, the frame of discernment U consists of two possible values for any suspected call $T_{j,\rho}^{M_i}$ which is given as: $U = \{fraud, \neg fraud\}$. For this U, the power set has three possible elements: hypothesis $h = \{fraud\}$ implying that $T_{j,\rho}^{M_i}$ is fraudulent; hypothesis $\overline{h} = \{\neg fraud\}$ that it isn't; and universe hypothesis U that $T_{j,\rho}^{M_i}$ is either fraudulent or isn't (suspicious). The basic probability assignments for the two rules R_1 and R_2 can now be given as follows:

– BPA for R_1: A call that is detected as a breakpoint, have the following basic probability assignments according to the measure of degree of variation as given by Eq. (2):

$$m_1(h) = 1 - \frac{abs(meanprofile - meantest)}{max\_call\_duration}$$
$$m_1(\overline{h}) = 0 \tag{5}$$
$$m_1(U) = 1 - \left(1 - \frac{abs(meanprofile - meantest)}{max\_call\_duration}\right)$$

– BPA for R_2: A call for which frequency deviation is detected, the following basic probability assignments is done according to the measure of frequency deviation as given by Eq. (3):

$$m_2(h) = 1 - \frac{abs(dailyavg - monthlyavg)}{max\_frequency}$$
$$m_2(\overline{h}) = 0 \tag{6}$$
$$m_2(U) = 1 - \left(1 - \frac{abs(dailyavg - monthlyavg)}{max\_frequency}\right)$$

Here the zero in the basic probability assignment of $\overline{h}$ means that rule R_i gives zero degree of belief regarding the trustworthiness of the call $T_{j,\rho}^{M_i}$. Hence, evidences of both R_1 and R_2 give no support to the belief that call $T_{j,\rho}^{M_i}$ is genuine. Following the Dempster's rule for combination as given by Eq. (4), the combined belief of R_1 and R_2 in h denoted by $P(h)$ is calculated as: $P(h) = m_1(h) \oplus m_2(h)$. Based on the suspicion score $P(h)$, the call on a particular mobile phone can be detected as normal, abnormal, or suspicious. Since $P(h)$ and $P(\overline{h})$ add to unity, $P(\overline{h}) = 1 - P(h)$.

Call History Database Component (CHDC)

Huge amounts of mobile phone history call data are collected and warehoused in the CHDC for extracting useful information about subscribers' usage which facilitates the detection of any anomalous activity on the mobile telecommunication network. The calls that are labeled as suspicious by the DSCC are passed to the CHDC for strengthening or weakening of the belief based on the similarity with fraudulent or genuine call history. Once a mobile phone is labeled as suspicious, further calls on this mobile phone are allowed but each call is checked by the FDS. This is done to avoid troubling the legitimate subscribers with occasional high level of activity. Since the expected behavior of a fraudster is to gain as much as possible in a limited time, any malicious behavior can be detected by monitoring the $Call\_Gap$ (ρ) of calls on a mobile phone along with each call's $Call\_Type$. For accomplishing this, we have built a "Subscriber Profile History" (SPH) for individual subscribers and a "Generic Fraud History" (GFH) for comparing the new calling behavior to profiles of generic fraud. SPH is built from past calling pattern of individual subscribers and GFH is built from past fraud data. The call detail summaries are updated in real time so that the fraud can be detected as soon as it occurs.

In our framework, we define 12 mutually exclusive and exhaustive events by partitioning $Call\_Gap$ into 4 time slots and considering each of the three call types. Each event D_{xy} depends on the particular time slot (x) in which it occurs, where $x \in \{1, 2, 3, 4\}$ and the $Call\_Type$ (y), where $y \in \{0, 1, 2\}$. The set of events is given by: $D = \{D_{10}, D_{20}, D_{30}, D_{40}, D_{11}, D_{21}, D_{31}, D_{41}, D_{12}, D_{22}, D_{32}, D_{42}\}$. The event D_{10} is defined as the occurrence of a call on the same mobile phone M_i within 8 hours of the last call ($x = 1$) of local $Call\_Type$ ($y = 0$) which can be expressed as:

$$D_{10} = True | \{\exists T^{M_i}_{j,\rho} \wedge ((0 < \rho \le 8) \wedge Call\_Type = 0)\} \tag{7}$$

In a similar way, the events D_{20}, D_{30} and D_{40} can be expressed as:

$$D_{20} = True | \{\exists T^{M_i}_{j,\rho} \wedge ((8 < \rho \le 16) \wedge Call\_Type = 0)\} \tag{8}$$

$$D_{30} = True | \{\exists T^{M_i}_{j,\rho} \wedge ((16 < \rho \le 24) \wedge Call\_Type = 0)\} \tag{9}$$

$$D_{40} = True | \{\exists T^{M_i}_{j,\rho} \wedge ((\rho > 24) \wedge Call\_Type = 0)\} \tag{10}$$

The definition of the remaining events follows from the above. It may be noted that we have empirically chosen the above definitions of $D'_{xy}s$. Other events could be similarly defined. We next compute the values of $P(D_{xy}|h)$ and $P(D_{xy}|\bar{h})$ from the SPH and GFH respectively. $P(D_{xy}|h)$ measures the probability of occurrence of D_{xy} given that the call is originating from a fraudster and $P(D_{xy}|\bar{h})$ measures the probability of occurrence of D_{xy} given that the call is originating from a legitimate subscriber. We have created two look-up tables FCFT (Fraud Call Frequency Table) and GCFT (Genuine Call Frequency Table) to determine the values of $P(D_{xy}|h)$ and $P(D_{xy}|\bar{h})$. The likelihood functions $P(D_{xy}|h)$ and $P(D_{xy}|\bar{h})$ are computed by the following expressions:

$$P(D_{xy}|h) = \frac{No.\,of\,occurrences\,of\,D_{xy}}{No.\,of\,calls\,in\,GFH} \tag{11}$$

$$P(D_{xy}|\bar{h}) = \frac{No.\,of\,occurrences\,of\,D_{xy}\,on\,M_i}{No.\,of\,calls\,in\,SPH\,on\,M_i} \tag{12}$$

Using Eqs. (11) and (12), $P(D_{xy})$ can be computed as follows:

$$P(D_{xy}) = P(D_{xy}|h)P(h) + P(D_{xy}|\bar{h})P(\bar{h}) \tag{13}$$

Bayesian Learning Component (BLC)

BLC is used to update the suspicion score obtained from the DSCC in the light of the new evidence from the CHDC. Whenever new information D_{xy} is available, we revise our initial belief using Bayes Rule which can be written as:

$$P(h|D_{xy}) = \frac{P(D_{xy}|h)P(h)}{P(D_{xy}|h)P(h) + P(D_{xy}|\bar{h})P(\bar{h})} \tag{14}$$

The goal of Bayesian Learning is to find the most probable hypothesis h_{map} given the training data. This is known as the Maximum A Posteriori Hypothesis (MAP Hypothesis) given by:

$$h_{map} = \max_{h \in H} P(h|D_{xy}) \tag{15}$$

For applying MAP hypothesis, we calculate the posterior probability for hypothesis $h : fraud$ as:

$$P(fraud|D_{xy}) = \frac{P(D_{xy}|fraud)P(fraud)}{P(D_{xy}|fraud)P(fraud) + P(D_{xy}|\neg fraud)P(\neg fraud)} \tag{16}$$

Similarly, the posterior probability for hypothesis $\bar{h} : \neg fraud$ is calculated as given by Eq. (17):

$$P(\neg fraud|D_{xy}) = \frac{P(D_{xy}|\neg fraud)P(\neg fraud)}{P(D_{xy}|fraud)P(fraud) + P(D_{xy}|\neg fraud)P(\neg fraud)} \tag{17}$$

Depending on which of the posterior value is greater, the future actions are decided by the FDS.

3.2   Methodology

The flow of events in our FDS has been depicted by the block diagram in Figure 1. We explain the steady-state operation of the FDS starting at any arbitrary j^{th} call $T_{j,\rho}^{M_i}$ on mobile phone M_i. The call is first handled by the RBDDC. Based on the suspicion score $\Psi(T_{j,\rho}^{M_i})$ of this call, it is categorized as genuine, suspicious or fraudulent. If $\Psi(T_{j,\rho}^{M_i}) < \theta_{LT}$, the call is considered to be genuine. On the other hand, if $\Psi(T_{j,\rho}^{M_i}) > \theta_{UT}$ then the call is declared to be fraudulent and manual confirmation is made with the legitimate subscriber. In case $\theta_{LT} \leq \Psi(T_{j,\rho}^{M_i}) \leq \theta_{UT}$, then the mobile phone M_i is labeled as suspicious and further calls on this mobile phone are investigated. The purpose is to lower false positives and at the same time not to compromise with true positives.

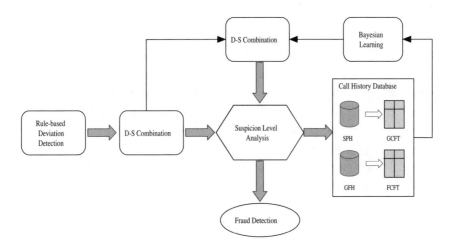

Fig. 1. Block diagram of the FDS

A suspicious behavior on a mobile phone may occur due to some isolated calls occasionally made by a legitimate subscriber or it could be really committed by a fraudster. When the $(j+1)^{\text{th}}$ call $T_{j+1,\rho'}^{M_i}$ occurs on the same mobile phone M_i, it is again passed through the RBDDC. In case the call is again found to be suspicious, the call is further analyzed by the FDS by passing it to the CHDC. Depending on the call gap ρ' and the *Call_Type*, the FDS determines which of the events D_{xy} has occurred and retrieves the corresponding $P(D_{xy}|h)$ and $P(D_{xy}|\overline{h})$ values from the tables FCFT and GCFT respectively.

The value of $P(D_{xy})$ is then calculated using Eq. (13) and the initial belief about the mobile phone is updated using Eq. (14). After computing the posterior beliefs, if $P(h|D_{xy}) \geq P(\overline{h}|D_{xy})$ then we again apply the D-S theory for combining the posterior belief $P(h|D_{xy})$ of the jth call and the $P(h)$ value of the $(j+1)^{\text{th}}$ call on mobile phone M_i, else we output only $P(h)$ value of the $(j+1)^{\text{th}}$ call. Based on the overall belief $\Psi(T_{j+1,\rho'}^{M_i})$ thus obtained, it is checked to see to which of the three categories viz. genuine, suspicious, or fraudulent the $(j+1)^{\text{th}}$ call belongs and the cycle repeats. The progression of the above method continues until the suspicion score goes down and finally falls below the lower threshold θ_{LT} or goes up and ultimately exceeds the upper threshold θ_{UT}.

4   Simulation and Results

We demonstrate the effectiveness and usefulness of our FDS by testing it on large scale data. Due to unavailability of real life mobile phone call data for testing, we developed a simulator to model the behavior of genuine subscribers as well as that of fraudsters. In this section, we first describe the components of our transaction simulator and then we analyze the performance of the proposed FDS. The simulator has the following three components as shown in Figure 2.

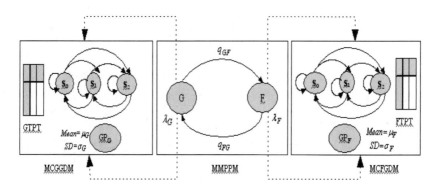

Fig. 2. Transaction simulator

- Markov Modulated Poisson Process Module (MMPPM):A Markov-modulated Poisson Process is a Poisson process that has its parameter λ controlled by an underlying Markov process. The proposed MMPPM has two states: good state G and fraud state F with arrival rates λ_G and λ_F, respectively. Transition from G to F takes place with probability q_{GF} and the transition from F to G takes place with probability q_{FG}.
- Markov Chain Genuine Gaussian Distribution Module (MCGGDM): This block consists of a finite Markov chain having three states S_0, S_1 and S_2 corresponding to the three call types local, national and international, respectively. The transition probabilities among the states, represented by q_{ij} where $i \in \{0, 1, 2\}$ and $j \in \{0, 1, 2\}$, are given in a genuine transition probability table (GTPT). The Markov chain captures the changes of $Call\_Type$ of genuine calls based on the profile of the subscriber. We have also used Gaussian distribution to generate $Call\_Duration$ for genuine subscribers since it is the most commonly observed probability distribution in many natural processes. It is represented by a Gaussian process GP_G having mean μ_G and standard deviation σ_G as shown in Figure 2. The simulator can handle different subscriber profiles by varying μ_G and σ_G.
- Markov Chain Fraud Gaussian Distribution Module (MCFGDM): This component is used to generate synthetic $Call\_Type$ and $Call\_Duration$ for fraudsters and is similar to MCGGDM. The values associated with the fraud transition probability table (FTPT) are changed to capture the changing

behavior of fraudsters. The values of μ_F and σ_F are also varied to capture different categories of fraudsters during generation of fraudulent calls.

We have used standard metrics to study the performance of the system under different test cases. True positives (TP) are the fraudulent calls caught by the system and false positives (FP) are the genuine calls labeled as fraudulent (also called false alarms). Different possible cases were considered over a large number of calls. The performance of the FDS is dependent on lower threshold (θ_{LT}) and upper threshold (θ_{UT}). In Table 1(a), we show the variation of TP/FP at different values of θ_{LT} and θ_{UT}. It is seen that as θ_{LT} increases, TP decreases. The same trend is true for θ_{UT} also. If θ_{UT} is set too high, then most of the frauds will go undetected whereas if θ_{UT} is set too low then there will be a large number of false alarms leading to serious denial-of-service. Similarly, high value of θ_{LT} will pass most of the frauds and on the other hand low value of θ_{LT} will lead to unnecessary investigation of large number of genuine calls. Hence, selection of θ_{UT} and θ_{LT} has an associated tradeoff. It is seen that $\theta_{LT} = 0.3$ and $\theta_{UT} = 0.7$ is a good operating point with sufficiently high TP rate and reasonably low FP rate.

Table 1. Variation of TP/FP (%) with (a) θ_{LT} and θ_{UT} (b) λ_G and λ_F

θ_{UT}	θ_{LT}			
	0.2	0.25	0.3	0.35
0.7	95/10	93/9	93/5	90/5
0.75	94/9	91/7	89/5	88/4
0.8	92/8.5	90/6	86/3.5	84/2
0.85	88/7	87/4	83/3	82/1

(a)

λ_F	λ_G			
	0.2	0.25	0.3	0.35
6	92/5	91/7	88/8	84/10
7	93/3	92/5	90/6.5	87/8
8	95/3	92.5/4	91/4.5	89/7
9	96/2	94/3	91/4	90/6

(b)

The arrival rate of calls can also influence the performance of the FDS. In Table 1(b), we show the variation of TP/FP at different values of λ_G and λ_F, while keeping $\theta_{LT} = 0.3$ and $\theta_{UT} = 0.7$. It shows that with increase in λ_G, TP decreases and FP increases due to increase in number of genuine calls. As the Poisson arrival rate in fraud state λ_F increases, TP increases and FP decreases due to increase in number of fraudulent calls.

As the state transition rate q_{GF} increases at constant q_{FG}, it increases the number of fraud calls resulting in increasing TP and decreasing FP as shown in Figure 3(a). Similarly, by increasing the state transition rate q_{FG} at constant q_{GF} we obtain an outcome opposite to that of the previous case which is shown in Figure 3(b).

The variation of TP and FP with mean μ_G is shown in Figure 4(a). As μ_G increases at fixed value of μ_F, the behavior of the genuine subscriber resembles that of fraudsters, which causes TP to decrease and FP to increase. Similarly, increasing mean μ_F, at fixed value of μ_G, causes large behavioristic deviation from normal profile resulting in increasing TP and decreasing FP as shown in Figure 4(b).

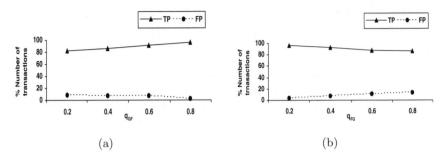

Fig. 3. Variation of TP/FP with (a) q_{GF} (b) q_{FG}

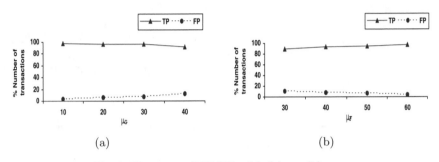

Fig. 4. Variation of TP/FP with (a) μ_G (b) μ_F

5   Conclusions

Mobile phone fraud has become a high priority problem on the agenda of most mobile network operators since fraud is the significant source of lost revenue to the mobile telecommunications industry. Furthermore, it lowers subscribers' confidence in the security of their calls. Efficient fraud detection systems can save operators from financial loss and also help restore subscribers' confidence. In this paper, we have introduced a novel approach for fraud detection in mobile communication networks by integrating three approaches, namely, rule-based techniques, Dempster-Shafer theory and Bayesian learning. The Dempster's rule is applied to combine multiple evidences from the rule-based component for computing suspicion score of each call. The suspicion scores are updated by means of Bayesian learning using history database of both genuine subscribers as well as fraudsters. In this work, we have built fraud model from profiles of generic fraud. Any other validated fraud model may also be suitably used. Stochastic models were used to generate synthetic calls for analyzing the performance of our proposed FDS. The simulation yielded up to 96% TP and less than 10% FP. Based on the results, we conclude that fusion of multiple evidences and learning are the appropriate approaches for addressing this type of real world problems where the patterns of behavior are complex and there may be little or no knowledge about the semantics of the application domain.

Acknowledgments. This work is partially supported by a research grant from the Department of Information Technology, Ministry of Communication and Information Technology, Government of India, under Grant No. 12(34)/04-IRSD dated 07/12/2004.

References

1. Fraud Analytics for Telecom (February 2007) http://www.fairisaac.com/ Fairisaac/Solutions/Product+Index/Fraud+Analytics +for+Telecom/
2. Barson, P., Field, S., Davey, N., McAskie, G., Frank, R.: The Detection of Fraud in Mobile Phone Networks, Neural Network World, pp. 477–484 (1996)
3. Hoath, P.: Telecoms Fraud, The Gory Details, Computer Fraud & Security, pp. 10–14 (January 1998)
4. Moreau, Y., Preneel, B., Burge, P., Shawe-Taylor, J., Stoermann, C., Cook, C.: Novel Techniques for Fraud Detection in Mobile Telecommunication Networks. In: ACTS Mobile Summit (1997)
5. Moreau, Y., Vandewalle, J.: Detection of Mobile Phone Fraud using Supervised Neural Networks: A First Prototype. In: Proceedings of the International Conference on Artificial Neural Networks (1997)
6. Burge, P., Shawe-Taylor, J.: Detecting Cellular Fraud Using Adaptive Prototypes. In: Proceedings of the Workshop on AI Approaches to Fraud Detection and Risk Management, pp. 9–13 (1997)
7. Taniguchi, M., Haft, M., Hollmen, J., Tresp, V.: Fraud Detection in Communication Networks using Neural and Probabilistic methods. In: Proceedings of the IEEE International Conference on Acoustics, Speech, and Signal Processing, Pages, pp. 1241–1244 (May 1998)
8. Fawcett, T., Provost, F.: Combining Data Mining and Machine Learning for Effective User Profiling. In: Proceedings of the Conference on Knowledge Discovery and Data Mining (1996)
9. Murad, U., Pinkas, G.: Unsupervised Profiling for Identifying Superimposed Fraud. In: Proceedings of the $3^{\rm rd}$ European Conference on Principles of Data Mining and Knowledge Discovery, pp. 251–261 (1999)
10. Rosset, S., Murad, U., Neumann, E., Idan, Y., Pinkas, G.: Discovery of Fraud Rules for Telecommunications - Challenges and Solutions. In: Proceedings of the Conference on Knowledge Discovery and Data Mining, pp. 409–413 (1999)
11. Burge, P., Shawe-Taylor, J.: An Unsupervised Neural Network Approach to Profiling the Behavior of Mobile Phone Users for Use in Fraud Detection. Journal of Parallel and Distributed Computing 915–925 (2001)
12. Grosser, H., Britos, P., Garcia-Martinez, R.: Detecting Fraud in Mobile Telephony Using Neural Networks. In: Proceedings of the 18th International Conference on Industrial and Engineering Applications of Artificial Intelligence and Expert Systems, pp. 613–615 (2005)
13. Britos, P., Grosser, H., Sierra, E., Garcia-Martinez, R.: Unusual Changes of Consumption Detection in Mobile Phone Users. Special Issue in Neural Networks and Associative Memories Research in Computing Science, pp. 195–204 (2006)
14. Kou, Y., Lu, C.T., Sirwonqattana, S., Huanq, Y.P.: Survey of Fraud Detection Techniques. In: Proceedings of the IEEE International Conference on Networking, Sensing and Control, pp. 749–754 (2004)

15. Bolton, R.J., Hand, D.J.: Statistical Fraud Detection: A Review. Journal of Statistical Science 235–255 (2002)
16. Bolton, R.J., Hand, D.J.: Unsupervised Profiling Methods for Fraud Detection. In: Proceedings of the Conference on Credit Scoring and Credit Control (September 2001)
17. Wang, Y., Yang, H., Wang, X., Zhang, R.: Distributed Intrusion Detection System Based on Data Fusion Method. In: Proceedings of the 5th World Congress on Intelligent Control and Automation, pp. 4331–4334 (June 2004)
18. Chen, T.M., Venkataramanan, V.: Dempster-Shafer Theory for Intrusion Detection in Ad Hoc Networks. In: Proceedings of the IEEE Internet Computing, pp. 35–41 (December 2005)

On Proactive Perfectly Secure Message Transmission

Kannan Srinathan[1], Prasad Raghavendra[2],
and Pandu Rangan Chandrasekaran[3]

[1] International Institute of Information Technology
Gachibowli, Hyderabad - 500032
srinathan@iiit.ac.in
[2] University of Washington
Seattle, WA
prasad@cs.washington.edu
[3] Indian Institute of Technology, Madras,
Chennai-600036, India
rangan@cs.iitm.ernet.in

Abstract. This paper studies the interplay of network connectivity and perfectly secure message transmission under the corrupting influence of a Byzantine *mobile* adversary that may move from player to player but can corrupt no more than t players at any given time. It is known that, in the stationary adversary model where the adversary corrupts the same set of t players throughout the protocol, perfectly secure communication among any pair of players is possible if and only if the underlying synchronous network is $(2t + 1)$-connected. Surprisingly, we show that $(2t + 1)$-connectivity is sufficient (and of course, necessary) even in the proactive (mobile) setting where the adversary is allowed to corrupt different sets of t players in different rounds of the protocol. In other words, adversarial mobility has no effect on the possibility of secure communication. Towards this, we use the notion of a Communication Graph, which is useful in modelling scenarios with adversarial mobility. We also show that protocols for reliable and secure communication proposed in [15] can be modified to tolerate the *mobile* adversary. Further these protocols are round-optimal if the underlying network is a collection of disjoint paths from the sender S to receiver R.

Keywords: Proactive security, Perfectly Secure Communication.

1 Introduction

Consider two players, a sender **S** and a receiver **R**, who want to "talk" to each other via an underlying communication network that they do not trust. Note that if **S** and **R** are connected directly via a private and authenticated link (like in the generic solutions for secure multiparty computation [2,4]), secure communication is trivially guaranteed. However, in reality, it is not economical to directly connect *every* two players in the network.

J. Pieprzyk, H. Ghodosi, and E. Dawson (Eds.): ACISP 2007, LNCS 4586, pp. 461–473, 2007.
© Springer-Verlag Berlin Heidelberg 2007

The sender's distrust in the underlying communication network is usually modeled by a virtual entity called the *adversary* that can corrupt some of the players (nodes) in the network. There have been a variety of adversary models used in the literature, each one catering to a different real-life setting. Dolev *et al* [7], who introduced and studied the problem of perfectly secure communication assume that the adversary can corrupt up to any t players in the network and that the adversary is non-mobile, that is, a player once corrupted remains so subsequently. More recent efforts using the same (non-mobile) adversarial model for the problem of perfectly secure communication include [10,9,6].

However, as first noticed in [14], the non-mobile model implicitly assumes that the number of dishonest players in the network is independent of the protocol's execution time. This is usually not true in practice. Furthermore, since a corrupted player could be corrected given sufficient time, [14] proposed the mobile adversary model wherein the adversary could move around the network whilst still corrupting up to t players at any given instant. Subsequently, extensive research efforts on tolerating mobile adversaries have resulted in what is now well-known as *proactive security*[12,11,8,1].

1.1   Contributions

We completely characterize the set of (mobile) adversaries that can be tolerated over a given communication network. Specifically, let G be a communication network under the influence of a mobile adversary who is capable of corrupting up to t nodes in any round. We prove that the necessary and sufficient condition for the existence of a perfectly secure communication protocol between every pair of players is that the underlying network must be $(2t+1)$-connected. When viewed conjointly with the extant results in the literature, we conclude:

Perfectly *secure* message transmission tolerating a **mobile** adversary is possible
if and only if
Perfectly *reliable* message transmission tolerating a **static** adversary is possible.

In other words, neither the additional requirement of *secrecy* nor the extra adversarial power of *mobility* affects the set of tolerable adversaries! We show that the secure message transmision protocol proposed in [15] can be used to obtain a protocol tolerating a mobile adversary. Further, if the network is a collection of disjoint paths from the sender to the receiver, then we show that our protocol is round-optimal.

2   Model

Consider a synchronous network $\mathcal{N}(\mathcal{P}, \mathcal{E})$ represented by an undirected graph G where $\mathcal{P} = \{P_1, P_2, \ldots, P_N\} \cup \{\mathbf{S}, \mathbf{R}\}$ denotes the set of players (nodes) in the network that are connected by 2-way communication links as defined by $\mathcal{E} \subset \mathcal{P} \times \mathcal{P}$. The players $\mathbf{S}$ and $\mathbf{R}$ do not trust the network connecting them.

Nevertheless, the sender **S** wishes to *securely* send a message to the receiver **R** through the network. Security here means that **R** should receive exactly what **S** sent to him while other players should have no information about it, even if up to t of the players (excluding **S** and **R**) collude and behave maliciously. This problem, known as *perfectly secure message transmission* (PSMT), was first proposed and solved by Dolev *et al.*[7]. In the problem of *perfectly reliable message transmission*, the sender **S** wants to send a message to **R** such that receiver receives the message sent irrespective of the actions of the adversary. However the condition of secrecy of the message is removed.

Any protocol execution is assumed to take place in a sequence of rounds. At the beginning of each round the players send messages to their neighbors. The messages sent by a player in round k reaches the neighbor at the beginning of round $k + 1$.

The distrust in the network is modeled by a mobile Byzantine adversary $\mathcal{A}$ who can corrupt t players in each round. The adversary can change the set of corrupted parties once every ρ rounds. In this paper, we assume the worst case that of $\rho = 1$,[1] which means the adversary can change his set of corrupted parties every round. More formally before the beginning of a round k, the adversary can corrupt any subset $\mathcal{P}_{corrupt}$ consisting of t players. Then the adversary has access to the messages sent to the players in $\mathcal{P}_{corrupt}$ in round $k - 1$ and can alter the behavior of the players in $\mathcal{P}_{corrupt}$ arbitrarily in the round k. However note that on corrupting a player P in a round k the adversary does not obtain information about the messages to and from the player P in all the previous rounds.

3   Communication Graph

Graphs have been used as a very powerful abstraction of the network by modeling the physical link between two players as an edge between the corresponding vertices of the graph. However in this kind of modeling of the network, the edges of the graph only indicate the link between two spatial locations. It does not contain any temporal information. Hence we propose a representation that contains both spatial and temporal information.

Specifically we use a communication graph G^d to study the execution of a protocol that has run d rounds. In the communication graph G^d, each player P is represented by a set of nodes $\{P^0, P^1, P^2 \dots P^d\}$. The node P^r corresponds to the player P at round r. For any two neighboring players P and Q and any $1 \leq r \leq d$, a message sent by P to Q in round $r - 1$ is available to Q only at round r. Hence there is an edge in G^d connecting the node P^{r-1} to the node Q^r for all $1 \leq r \leq d$.

Note that the connection graph is a directed graph, because of the directed nature of time. So the edges between the nodes at consecutive time steps are always oriented towards increasing time.

---

[1] Without loss of generality, one can assume that ρ is a positive constant greater than or equal to one since otherwise, there exists another adversary $\mathcal{A}'$ with $t' = \frac{t}{\rho}$ that simulates the same scenario.

Definition 1. *Given a graph $G = (V, E)$ and a positive integer d, the Communication Graph G^d is a directed graph defined as follows*

- *Nodes of G^d belong to $V \times \{0 \ldots d\}$. Let us denote the node $(P, r) \in V \times \{0 \ldots d\}$ by P^r.*
- *The edge set of G^d is $E^d = E_1 \cup E_2$ where, $E_1 = \{(P_a^{r-1}, P_b^r) \,|\, (P_a, P_b) \in E \text{ and } 1 \leq r \leq d\}$ and $E_2 = \{(P_a^{r-1}, P_a^r) | P_a \in V \text{ and } 1 \leq r \leq d\}$*

Notions similar to the Communication graph have appeared in [5,3]

Let $\mathcal{P}^r$ denote the set of nodes corresponding to players at round r, $\mathcal{P}^r = \{P_a^r \,| P_a \in V\}$.

Let $\mathcal{A}_{mobile}$ be a threshold mobile adversary acting on a network G that can corrupt any t players in a single round. Consider an execution Γ of a d-round protocol on G. Suppose $\mathcal{A}_{mobile}$ corrupts a set of nodes $A_r = \{a_1, a_2, \ldots a_t\}$ in round r in G, then the same effect is obtained by corrupting the nodes $A^r = \{a_1^r, a_2^r, \ldots a_t^r\}$ in the communication graph G^d. Hence the effect of $\mathcal{A}_{mobile}$ on execution Γ can be simulated by a static general adversary who corrupts $\bigcup\limits_{r=0}^{d-1} A^r$ on G^d. Stating the above result formally we have,

Lemma 1. *Mobile threshold adversary $\mathcal{A}_{mobile}$ acting on the original network graph G can be simulated by a static general adversary given by the adversary structure $\mathcal{A}_{static}^d = \{A_1 \cup A_2 \cup A_3 \ldots \cup A_d | A_r \in \Pi_t(\mathcal{P}^r), 1 \leq r \leq d\}$ on the Communication graph G^d, where $\Pi_t(P^r)$ denotes the set of all subsets of cardinality t of the set $\mathcal{P}^r$.*

4   Characterization of Proactive Perfectly Reliable Communication

In this section we characterize graphs on which perfectly reliable communication is possible tolerating a mobile adversary who can corrupt up to t players in each round.

Theorem 1. *Perfectly reliable communication between any two players in the network G tolerating a mobile adversary that can corrupt at most t players in any round, is possible if and only if G is $(2t + 1)$-connected.*

It has been shown in [7], that with a static adversary perfectly secure communication is possible if and only if the graph G is $2t + 1$ connected. Hence clearly Perfectly reliable message transmission with mobile adversary is possible only if G is $2t + 1$-connected. In order to prove the sufficiency of $2t + 1$ connectivity, we modify the communication graph for the problem of reliable communication.

Definition 2. *Given a graph G with nodes S and R, and a positive integer d the modified Communication Graph $\mathcal{G}^d$ is the graph G^d along with two additional nodes $\mathcal{S}$, $\mathcal{R}$. $\mathcal{S}$ is connected to all $S^r, 0 \leq r \leq d$ and $\mathcal{R}$ is connected to all R^r, $0 \leq r \leq d$. Further the edges between (S^{r-1}, S^r) and (R^{r-1}, R^r) for $1 \leq r \leq d$ are removed.*

Definition 3. *Two paths Γ_1 and Γ_2 between the nodes S and R in the Modified Communication graph $\mathcal{G}^d$ are said to be securely disjoint if the only common nodes between the two paths are S^a and R^b for various values of a and b. That is,*

$$\Gamma_1 \cap \Gamma_2 \subset \{S^0, S^1, S^2 \ldots S^d\} \cup \{R^0, R^1, R^2 \ldots R^d\}$$

Definition 4. *Given a path $\Gamma = \{S, P_1, P_2 \ldots P_{m-1}, R\}$ from S to R in the underlying graph G, the space-time path Γ^i in graph $\mathcal{G}^d$ is defined as*

$$\Gamma^i = \{\mathcal{S}, S^i, P_1^{i+1}, P_2^{i+2}, \ldots P_{m-1}^{i+m-1}, R^{i+m}, \mathcal{R}\} \quad 0 \le i \le d - m$$

Lemma 2. *For any path Γ of length m from S to R in G, the paths $\Gamma^i, 0 \le i \le d - m$ are pairwise securely disjoint. Further, for any two vertex disjoint paths Γ_1, Γ_2 and for any i, j the paths Γ_1^i and Γ_2^j are securely disjoint.*

Proof: Suppose for a path Γ and $0 \le a < b \le d - m$, the two paths Γ^a and Γ^b are not disjoint. Let P_i be the vertex of Γ corresponding to a common vertex between Γ^a and Γ^b. Further let P_i be the kth vertex of Γ. Then by definition, Γ^a passes through P_i^{a+k} and Γ^b passes through P_i^{b+k}. Since the paths intersect at P_i we get $a = b$. A contradiction.

The other part of the claim is trivially true, since if Γ_1^i and Γ_2^i have a common vertex P_a^b then the vertex P_a is common between Γ_1 and Γ_2.   □

Lemma 3. *Let n be the number of vertices in G. For all $d > (2t+1)n$ there are at least $2td + 1$ securely disjoint paths from S to R in $\mathcal{G}^d$ of which the adversary can corrupt at most td.*

Proof: Since the underlying graph G is $2t + 1$ connected, there are $2t + 1$ vertex disjoint paths $\{\Gamma_1, \Gamma_2, \ldots \Gamma_{2t+1}\}$ in G. Then consider the set of paths $\{\Gamma_i^j | 1 \le i \le 2t + 1, 0 \le j \le d - n\}$ in $\mathcal{G}^d$. All these $(2t + 1)(d - n)$ paths in this set are secure disjoint by claim 2. Further since the adversary can corrupt at most td nodes in $\mathcal{G}^d$, at most td of these secure disjoint paths can be corrupted. As $d > (2t + 1)n$, we have $(2t + 1)(d - n) > 2td$ and thus the result follows.   □

To finish the proof of Theorem 1, observe that from lemma 3 the single phase protocols for reliable communication proposed in [7] can be executed on $\mathcal{G}^d$ for $d > (2t + 1)n$. Further since any protocol on $\mathcal{G}^d$ can be simulated on G in d rounds, we obtain d round protocols for reliable communication.

5   Round Optimal Proactive Reliable Communication

We first prove a graph-theoretic result that is useful in the design of round-optimal protocols tolerating a mobile adversary. In order to state the result we make the following definition.

Definition 5. *The reliable-diameter D of a $2t + 1$ connected graph G is the smallest positive integer such that $\mathcal{G}^D$ satisfies the condition that removal of any two sets of vertices in $\mathcal{A}_{static}^D$ does not disconnect S and R.*

Recall that $\mathcal{A}^D_{static}$ denotes the static adversary structure on G^D that can simulate the mobile adversary A. Henceforth we use $\mathcal{A}^D$ to denote the adversary $\mathcal{A}^D_{static}$ on G^D.

From lemma 3 we know that the reliable diameter of a graph G is bounded by $D \leq (2t+1)n + 1$.

Theorem 2. *Given a graph G that is a collection of disjoint paths between S and R, if D is the reliable-diameter of the graph G, then the graph G^D contains $2t(D-1) + 1$ secure disjoint paths from S to R such that the adversary can corrupt at most $t(D-1)$ of the paths.*

The proof of the theorem is deferred to the appendix A.1.

Theorem 3. *Let D be the reliable diameter of a network G, then D is the optimal round complexity for a reliable communication protocol on the network G.*

Suppose there exists a protocol Π that runs in $d < D$ rounds and realizes perfectly reliable communication tolerating a mobile adversary. Then consider a network that is identical to $\mathcal{G}^d$ with the static adversary $\mathcal{A}^d$ acting on it. The players in $\mathcal{G}^d$ can simulate the execution of protocol Π as follows.

- The player P_i^j in $\mathcal{G}^d$ emulates the execution of player P_i in round j of the protocol Π.
- The messages sent by P_i to P_l in round j in protocol Π are sent by P_i^j to P_l^{j+1}.
- In addition to the protocol messages, P_i^j sends to P_i^{j+1} the state information of player P_i at the end of the jth round. This information is necessary for the player P_i^{j+1} to emulate the behavior of P_i in the $j+1^{st}$ round.

The protocol Π is a perfectly reliable communication protocol over G and any behavior of the static adversary $\mathcal{A}^d$ can be simulated by the mobile adversary on G. Therefore the above emulation is a perfectly reliable communication protocol on $\mathcal{G}^d$. But since $d < D$ there are two sets in $\mathcal{A}^d$ the removal of which disconnects S and $\mathcal{R}$. This is a contradiction to the well known theorem [13] which states that reliable communication on a graph is possible if and only if the network is not disconnected by the removal of any two adversarial sets.

By definition of reliable diameter, the adversary structure $\mathcal{A}^D$ satisfies the condition that the removal of any two adversarial sets does not disconnect $\mathcal{G}^D$. Thus the protocol for reliable communication in [13] can be executed on $\mathcal{G}^D$. Further since any protocol on $\mathcal{G}^D$ can be simulated on the real network in D rounds, we obtain a protocol on G that runs in D rounds. Although this protocol is round-optimal, it could have exponential communication complexity in the worst case.

In order to obtain an efficient protocol, we use the result of theorem 2. Given a graph G that is $2t+1$ connected, there are $2t+1$ disjoint paths from S to R in G. Let H be the subgraph of G consisting of only the $2t+1$ disjoint paths from S to R. On applying theorem 2 on H, we obtain D such that there are $2t(D-1)+1$

disjoint paths in $\mathcal{H}^D$ of which the adversary can corrupt at most $t(D-1)$. Let us denote the $2t(D-1)+1$ paths by $\Gamma_1, \Gamma_2, \ldots, \Gamma_{2q+1}$, where $q = t(D-1)$. We describe the protocol on the graph $\mathcal{H}^D$ and show how it can be executed on the real network G.

Protocol REL: Round-Optimal Reliable Message transmission of **m** .

- The sender S sends the message **m** along all the paths Γ_i, $1 \le i \le 2q+1$.
- All players P_a^b along a path Γ_i just forward the message to the next player along Γ_i.
- The receiver on receiving the values along all the paths and takes the majority value as the message **m**.

In order to emulate the above protocol on the graph G, if a player P_1^b and P_2^{b+1} are consecutive nodes in $\mathcal{H}^D$ along some path Γ_i, then P_1 on receiving the message **m** along a path Γ_i at the beginning of round b sends it to the player P_2 at the end of round b.

The protocol has a communication complexity of $O((2tD^2|\mathbf{m}|)$ bits and this is polynomial in n since $D \le (2t+1)n+1$. Further if the underlying graph G itself is a collection of disjoint paths from S to R, then the protocol is round-optimal.

6 An Efficient Secure Protocol

Let H be the subgraph of the network G consisting of $2t+1$ disjoint paths from S to R. On applying theorem 2, we know that there exists a D such that in the modified Communication graph $\mathcal{H}^D$, there are at least $2t(D-1)+1$ vertex disjoint paths from the sender to the receiver (and by symmetry, from the receiver to the sender) of which the adversary $\mathcal{A}^D$ can corrupt at most $t(D-1)$ paths. However note that it is not possible to abstract out these paths as wires between S and R since unlike wires each of these paths can be used at most once. Therefore most secure communication protocols tolerating a static adversary, cannot be modified to protocols tolerating a mobile adversary.

In this section, we show that the protocol for perfectly secure message transmission proposed in [15] can be modified to tolerate mobile adversaries. The protocol runs in just two phases, and since no single phase protocol can exist [7], the modified protocol is phase optimal.

We now present the 2-phase protocol. We show the protocol execution on $\mathcal{H}^{2D}$. This can be easily converted to a protocol on G in a straightforward manner as was done for the case of reliable communication.

In a single round, a player can send messages to his neighbors and in one phase that consists of D rounds the sender S can send a message to the receiver R or vice-versa.

Let us assume that the message **m** is an element of a sufficiently large field $\mathbb{F}$. In the graph $\mathcal{H}^{2D}$, the first phase is executed in the first D rounds and the second phase using the next D rounds. We refer to the nodes corresponding to the first D rounds as the first half, and the nodes corresponding to the last D rounds as the second half. For purposes of presentation let $q = t(D - 1)$. Let $\Gamma_i^{(1)}, 1 \leq i \leq 2q + 1$ be $2q + 1$ disjoint paths from $\mathcal{R}$ to $\mathcal{S}$ in the first half. Let $\Gamma_i^{(2)}, 1 \leq i \leq 2q+1$ be $2q+1$ disjoint paths from $\mathcal{S}$ to $\mathcal{R}$ in the second half of $\mathcal{H}^{2D}$.

Code for the Receiver: Phase I

1. The receiver selects at random $2q + 1$ polynomials p_i, $1 \leq i \leq 2q + 1$ over a finite field $\mathbb{F}$, each of degree q. He sends through each of the $2q+1$ securely disjoint paths, say $\Gamma_i^{(1)}$, $1 \leq i \leq 2q + 1$, the polynomial p_i and the set $\{r_{ij} = p_j(i)\}_{1 \leq j \leq 2q+1}$.

Code for the Sender: Phase II
The sender receives a polynomial p_i' and $2q + 1$ values r_{ij}' along each path $\Gamma_i^{(1)}$.

1. The sender creates the contradiction graph on $2q+1$ nodes as follows: he adds the edge (i, j) if $p_j'(i) \neq r_{ij}'$ or $p_i'(j) \neq r_{ji}'$.
2. The sender creates a $2q + 1$ degree polynomial $Q(\cdot)$ with the constant term as his message **m** and the coefficient of x^i being $p_i'(0)$.
3. The sender perfectly reliably sends using $\Gamma_i^{(2)}$ the following to the receiver using the reliable communication protocol discussed earlier on the second half of $\mathcal{H}^{2D}$:
   (a) For each edge in the contradiction graph, the values $(p_j'(i), r_{ij}', p_i'(j), r_{ji}')$.
   (b) For $a = 1$ to $q + 1$, the value $q(a)$.

Message Recovery by the Receiver
The receiver finds all the faults that occurred in Phase I using the values $p_j'(i), r_{ij}', p_i'(j)$ and r_{ji}' received from the sender and the values $p_j(i), p_i(j)$. There can be at most q faults in Phase I. From the $q + 1$ equations, he can solve for these $\leq q$ possibly modified coefficients along with the message **m**.

Lemma 4. *The receiver R can recover the message sent by sender S.*

Proof: Firstly note that the receiver R can detect all corruptions that occurred during Phase I. Each of the polynomials p_i are of degree q. If the adversary changes the polynomial p_i to p_i', then for at least one of the honest wires $\Gamma_j^{(1)}$ there will be a contradiction $p_i'(j) \neq r_{ij}$. Thus the sender will broadcast the 4-tuple $(p_j'(i), r_{ij}', p_i'(j), r_{ji}')$ and the receiver will detect that p_i has been corrupted in Phase I. The receiver can thus determine the set of paths $\Gamma_i^{(1)}$ for which $p_i = p_i'$. As there are at least $q + 1$ such paths the receiver knows at least $q + 1$ coefficients of the polynomial Q. Thus from the $q + 1$ values along polynomial Q, R can solve for the modified coefficients and also the message **m**. $\square$

Theorem 4. *The adversary gains no information about the message.*

Proof: First we note that at the end of the first phase, the adversary has no information about $p_i(0)$ for each honest path $\Gamma_i^{(1)}$. This is because p_i is a random polynomial of degree q and the adversary has seen only q points on it (one corresponding to each faulty wire). Furthermore, the adversary gains no new information in Phase II. This can be seen as follows: phase II involves broadcast of the 4-tuple $(p'_j(i), r'_{ij}, p'_i(j), r'_{ji})$. Since either path $\Gamma_i^{(1)}$ or path $\Gamma_j^{(1)}$ is faulty, this information is already known to the adversary. Further the adversary knows at most q coefficients of the polynomial Q, and hence obtains no information about the message. $\square$

7 Conclusion

We have shown that adversarial mobility does not affect the feasibility of perfectly secure communication. However, tolerating a mobile adversary does not seem to be free of cost. Though we have presented efficient protocols for reliable and secure communication for every tolerable adversary, we are able to show that the round optimal protocols are efficient only for a special class of networks. It is an interesting open problem to design (or prove the non-existence of) an efficient round optimal protocol for secure communication for all possible networks.

References

1. Backes, M., Cachin, C., Strobl, R.: Proactive secure message transmission in asynchronous networks. In: PODC '03: Proceedings of the twenty-second annual symposium on Principles of distributed computing, pp. 223–232. ACM Press, New York (2003)
2. Ben-Or, M., Goldwasser, S., Wigderson, A.: Completeness Theorems for Non-cryptographic Fault-tolerant Distributed Computation. In: Proceedings of the 20th Symposium on Theory of Computing (STOC), pp. 1–10. ACM Press, New York (1988)
3. Brandes, U., Corman, S.R.: Visual unrolling of network evolution and the analysis of dynamic discourse. In: INFOVIS '02: Proceedings of the IEEE Symposium on Information Visualization (InfoVis'02), Washington, DC, USA, p. 145. IEEE Computer Society, Los Alamitos (2002)
4. Chaum, D., Crepeau, C., Damgard, I.: Multi-party Unconditionally Secure Protocols. In: Proceedings of 20th Symposium on Theory of Computing (STOC), pp. 11–19. ACM Press, New York (1988)
5. Collberg, C., Kobourov, S., Nagra, J., Pitts, J., Wampler, K.: A system for graph-based visualization of the evolution of software. In: SoftVis '03: Proceedings of the 2003 ACM symposium on Software visualization, p. 77. ACM Press, New York (2003)
6. Desmedt, Y., Wang, Y.: Perfectly Secure Message Transmission Revisited. In: Knudsen, L.R. (ed.) EUROCRYPT 2002. LNCS, vol. 2332, pp. 502–517. Springer, Heidelberg (2002)
7. Dolev, D., Dwork, C., Waarts, O., Yung, M.: Perfectly secure message transmission. Journal of the Association for Computing Machinery (JACM) 40(1), 17–47 (1993)
8. Frankel, Y., Gemmell, P., MacKenzie, P.D., Yung, M.: Proactive RSA. In: Kaliski Jr., B.S. (ed.) CRYPTO 1997. LNCS, vol. 1294, pp. 440–452. Springer, Heidelberg (1997)
9. Franklin, M., Wright, R.N.: Secure Communication in Minimal Connectivity Models. Journal of Cryptology 13(1), 9–30 (2000)
10. Franklin, M., Yung, M.: Secure Hypergraphs: Privacy from Partial Broadcast. In: Proceedings of 27th Symposium on Theory of Computing (STOC), pp. 36–44. ACM Press, New York (1995)

11. Herzberg, A., Jakobson, M., Jarecki, S., Krawczyk, H., Yung, M.: Proactive Public Key and Signature Systems. In: Proceedings of 4th Conference on Computer and Communications Security, Zurich, Switzerland, April 1997, pp. 100–110. ACM Press, New York (1997)

12. Herzberg, A., Jarecki, S., Krawczyk, H., Yung, M.: Proactive Secret Sharing, or: How to Cope with Perpetual Leakage. In: Coppersmith, D. (ed.) CRYPTO 1995. LNCS, vol. 963, pp. 339–352. Springer, Heidelberg (1995)

13. Kumar, M.V.N.A., Goundan, P.R., Srinathan, K., Pandu Rangan, C.: On perfectly secure communication over arbitrary networks. In: Proceedings of the 21st Symposium on Principles of Distributed Computing (PODC), Monterey, California, USA, July 2002, pp. 193–202. ACM Press, New York (2002)

14. Ostrovsky, R., Yung, M.: How to Withstand Mobile Virus Attacks. In: Proceedings of the 10th Symposium on Principles of Distributed Computing (PODC), pp. 51–61. ACM Press, New York (1991)

15. Sayeed, H.M., Abu-Amara, H.: Efficient perfectly secure message transmission in synchronous networks. Inf. Comput. 126(1), 53–61 (1996)

A   Proof of Theorem 2

A.1   Results on Paths

We need some definitions and results on paths in the proof of theorem 2. We derive those results in this section.

Let Γ be a path of length L from S to R in G. Let F denote the graph consisting of just the path Γ from S to R. Let $\mathcal{F}^d$ denote the modified communication graph for F for d rounds.

For each of the $S^r, 0 \leq r \leq d$ there is a copy of the path Γ starting at S^r. If r is less than $d - L$ then the copy of Γ starting at S^r is completely contained in $\mathcal{F}^d$ else it is truncated. Let us call these paths as *straight paths*. In fact for every node v in $\mathcal{F}^d$ there is a unique straight path that passes through v. Let $T(v)$ for a vertex v in $\mathcal{F}^d$ denote the round to which v corresponds.

Definition 6. *Let $k < d$ be an integer, then a k-straight cut is a set of vertices C of $\mathcal{F}^d$ that satisfy the following properties*

- *For each $\Gamma(S^r)$ such that $0 \leq r < k$ and $\Gamma(S^r)$ is not truncated in $\mathcal{F}^d$, there is exactly one vertex C_r of C present on $\Gamma(S^r)$. The path $\Gamma(S^r)$ is said to be cut at C_r.*
- *Paths are cut in increasing order of time, more formally $T(C_r) \geq T(C_{r-1})$, $1 \leq r < k$.*
- *All vertices in C are contained in the first k rounds of $\mathcal{F}^d$, i.e $T(v) \leq k, \forall v \in C$.*

Definition 7. *Let us denote the straight path passing through a vertex v as $\Gamma(v)$. Further given a k-straight cut C, let $T_C(v)$ denote the round corresponding to the vertex at which $\Gamma(v)$ is cut by C. Formally $T_C(v) = T(C_r)$ where C_r is the vertex of $\Gamma(v)$ present in C.*

Definition 8. *For a straight cut C, a path in $\mathcal{F}^d$ that does not contain any vertex of C is said to be C-disjoint.*

Lemma 5. *If C is a k-straight cut, and v is a vertex such that $T(v) \leq k$ and there is a C-disjoint path Γ' from $S^r, 0 \leq r < k$ to v then $T_C(v) > T(v)$.*

Proof: We prove by induction on the length of the path $|\Gamma'|$. For a path Γ' of length 0, the vertex v is S^r for some $0 \leq r < k$. Since the path $\Gamma(S^r)$ starts at S^r and C does not contain S^r, it immediately follows that $T_C(S^r) > T(S^r)$. Now suppose the result is true for all $|\Gamma'| = l$.

Let v be a vertex such that Γ' is a path of length $|\Gamma'| = l+1$. Let u denote the vertex just before v on Γ'. By induction hypothesis we know that $T_C(u) > T(u)$. Further we know $T(v) = T(u) + 1$ since there is an edge from u to v. Now there are two cases

- **Case 1**: Both u and v correspond to the same node in F but at consecutive rounds. Suppose u lies on $\Gamma(S^r)$, then v lies on $\Gamma(S^{r+1})$. Thus from the definition of k-straight cut, we know $T_C(v) \geq T_C(u)$. But as $T_C(u) > T(u)$ we get $T_C(v) \geq T(u) + 1 = T(v)$. Further since Γ' is C-disjoint v does not lie on C, i.e $T_C(v)$ is not equal to $T(v)$. Hence $T_C(v) > T(v)$.
- **Case 2**: u and v correspond to consecutive vertices on the path Γ in F. In this case, u and v lie on the same straight path, i.e $\Gamma(u) = \Gamma(v)$. From $T_C(u) > T(u)$ we know that $\Gamma(u)$ is cut after u. Further since Γ' is C-disjoint neither u nor v belongs to C. Hence $\Gamma(v)$ is cut after v which implies $T_C(v) > T(v)$. □

Lemma 6. *If C is a k-straight cut, then in $\mathcal{F}^d$, there is no C-disjoint path from any of the vertices in $\{S^r | 0 \leq r \leq k - 1\}$ to any of the vertices $\{R^j | 0 \leq j \leq d\}$.*

Proof: Suppose there existed a C-disjoint path from $S^r, 0 \leq r \leq k - 1$ to $R^j, 0 \leq j \leq k$ then by claim 5 we have that $T_C(R^j) > j$. This is a contradiction since the path $\Gamma(R^j)$ terminates at R^j, and there cannot be a vertex on $\Gamma(R^j)$ after R^j.

Suppose there is a C-disjoint path Γ' from $S^r, r < k$ to vertex $R^j, j > k$ then there will exist a vertex u on Γ' at round k. This because the path Γ' starts before round k and ends after round k. By claim 5 we know that $T_C(u) > T(u) = k$. This implies that the path $\Gamma(u)$ is not cut by C before round k. But this is a contradiction since C is a k-straight cut. □

A.2 Main Proof

Theorem 5. *Given a graph G that is a collection of disjoint paths between S and R, if D is the reliable-diameter of the graph G, then the graph $\mathcal{G}^D$ contains $2t(D - 1) + 1$ secure disjoint paths from S to R such that the adversary can corrupt at most $t(D - 1)$ of the paths.*

Proof : By definition of reliable diameter we know that the reliable diameter D satisfies the condition that the removal of union of any two sets in $\mathcal{A}^D$ does not disconnect $\mathcal{S}$ and $\mathcal{R}$ in $\mathcal{G}^D$. Further any subset V' of nodes of $\mathcal{G}^D$ that contains at most $2t$ nodes corresponding to each round, can be expressed as the union of two sets in $\mathcal{A}^D$. We shall show that if $\mathcal{G}^D$ contains less than $2t(D-1)+1$ disjoint paths then there exists a subset V' of vertices, such that it contains at most $2t$ vertices at any round, and disconnects $\mathcal{S}$ and $\mathcal{R}$. A contradiction.

In order to prove the existence of such a V', we give an algorithm that produces V' from $\mathcal{G}^D$. But before that we need to define some notation.

Let $\{\Gamma_1, \Gamma_2, \ldots \Gamma_k\}$ be the disjoint paths between S and R in G. Thus $k \geq 2t+1$ and the graph G is the union of all the $\{\Gamma_i, 1 \leq i \leq k\}$. Let l_i be the length of the path Γ_i. Let Π_i denote the following set of paths in $\mathcal{G}^D$,

$$\Pi_i = \{\Gamma_i^j | 0 \leq j \leq D - l_i\}$$

Further let Π denote the union of Π_i for all $1 \leq i \leq k$. Since all the Γ_i are disjoint in G, from lemma 2 we know that all paths in Π are secure disjoint. Let F_i denote the subgraph of G containing the path Γ_i, $1 \leq i \leq k$. Further $\mathcal{F}_i^D$ denote the modified communication graph of D rounds for the graph F_i. It is clear that the graph $\mathcal{G}^D$ can be expressed as $\mathcal{G}^D = \bigcup_{i=1}^{k} \mathcal{F}^D$.

Definition 9. *A path Γ_i^j in Π is said to be* active *in round r if and only if $j < r < j + l_i$ i.e there exists a node other than S and R through which Γ_i^j passes at round r.*

Let Π' be a sorted list of paths in Π in increasing order of round at which they reach R, or in other words in increasing order of the round at which the paths terminate. In the following algorithm Π' at any iteration contains all the paths Π' that are not yet cut in the previous rounds and C contains the set of cut vertices chosen till that instant.

Greedy Algorithm-GA

For each round r from 1 to D do

- If there is a path in Π' that terminates at R^r then terminate.
- If there are $\geq 2t$ active paths in Π' remove the first $2t$ active paths from Π', and cut all those paths in the current round. Update the cut-set C.
- If there are less than $2t$ active paths in Π', then remove all the active paths from Π' and cut all of them in the current round. Update the cut-set C.

Lemma 7. *For any two paths Γ_i^a and Γ_i^b in Π with $a < b$ the algorithm cuts Γ_i^a before Γ_i^b.*

Proof : The result is trivially true since the paths are cut in the order in which they are found in the list Γ' which is sorted according to termination times of paths.   □

Lemma 8. *The algorithm GA cuts exactly $2t$ paths at each round until it terminates.*

Proof : Suppose the algorithm GA cuts less than $2t$ paths in a round r, then it implies that the number active paths in Π' at round r was less than $2t$. Since the algorithm has not terminated till round r, it implies that there has not been a path that started earlier than round r and has terminated without being cut by the algorithm. As there are less than $2t$ active paths at round r, it implies that the algorithm cuts all the paths that started before round r by the end of round r. So consider any $\mathcal{F}_i^D$ for some $1 \leq i \leq k$. Consider the set of vertices $C' = C \cap F_i^D$. For each $\Gamma_i^a 0 \leq a \leq r - 1$ there is exactly one vertex of Γ_i^a in C'. This along with lemma 7 imply that C' is a r-straight cut for $\mathcal{F}_i^D$. Hence by lemma 6 there is no C' disjoint path from an $S^a, a < r$ to any $R^b, 0 \leq b \leq D$ in $\mathcal{F}_i^D$.

Thus on removal of set C, there is no path from $S^a, a < r$ to $R^b, 0 \leq b \leq D$. In other words, removal of vertices of C completely disconnects the sender's action corresponding to first $r - 1$ rounds. Also note that C does not contain any vertex of a round greater than r. But if such a C existed, then for any integer m, in $\mathcal{G}^{mr}$ by repeatedly removing C we can disconnect all sender vertices from receiver vertices. A contradiction to the fact that D is finite.   □

Lemma 9. *The algorithm GA does not terminate before round $D - 1$*

Proof: If the algorithm terminated at a round $r < D - 1$ then it means that there exists a path Γ in $\mathcal{G}^D$ which terminated at the rth round without being cut before. From lemma 8 we know that C is of size $2t(r - 1)$ at this round. Hence the algorithm has cut $2t(r - 1)$ paths all of which are disjoint from each other. Further since Γ terminates by round r and the algorithm cuts paths in increasing order of termination time, all the paths that are cut terminate before round r. So including Γ and all the paths that were cut, there are at least $2t(r - 1) + 1$ disjoint paths that terminate in the first r rounds. Note that the adversary can corrupt at most $t(r-1)$ of these paths. This implies that $\mathcal{G}^r$ satisfies the property that the union of any two sets in the adversary does not disconnect $\mathcal{S}$ and $\mathcal{R}$. A contradiction to minimality of D.   □

Proof of theorem 2: If all paths in Π are cut by the end of the algorithm, then following the same argument as in proof of lemma 8 we can show that C is a D-straight cut for each $\mathcal{F}_i^D 1 \leq i \leq k$. Thus the removal of C would disconnect all the sender vertices S^a from the receiver vertices R^b. Note that C contains at most $2t$ vertices at any round, and hence can be expressed as the union of two sets of the adversary $\mathcal{A}$. A contradiction to the fact that D is the reliable diameter. Hence there exists a path in Π that is not cut by C. From lemma 8 we know that the algorithm cut exactly $2t$ paths in Π in every round. So clearly there are at least $2t(D - 1) + 1$ paths in Π.   □

Author Index

Al-Hinai, Sultan Zayid 11
Aono, Hiroshi 259
Araki, Toshinori 122, 133
Au, Man Ho 431
Aumasson, Jean-Philippe 184

Babbage, Steve 1
Baltatu, Madalina 107
Bao, Feng 171
Bhattacharya, Debojyoti 29
Billet, Olivier 82
Birkett, James 274
Brands, Stefan 400
Bringer, Julien 96

Chabanne, Hervé 96
Chang, Donghoon 59
Chu, Cheng-Kang 323
Cid, Carlos 1

Dahmen, Erik 245
Damgård, Ivan 416
Dawson, Ed 11
De Decker, Bart 400
Demuynck, Liesje 400
Deng, Robert H. 171
Dent, Alexander W. 274
Ding, Jintai 158

Finiasz, Matthieu 184

Geisler, Martin 416
Golić, Jovan Dj. 107

Hayashi, Ryotaro 200
Henricksen, Matt 11
Hong, Seokhie 59, 143
Hongo, Sadayuki 259
Hu, Lei 158
Huang, Qiong 215
Huang, Xinyi 308

Ishihara, Takeru 259
Iwasaki, Terutoshi 45
Izabachène, Malika 96

Jeong, Kitae 143
Ji, Wen 158

Krøigaard, Mikkel 416
Kundu, Amlan 446
Kunihiro, Noboru 45
Kurokawa, Takashi 370

Lamberger, Mario 68
Lee, Changhoon 143
Lee, Sangjin 59
Lim, Jongin 143
Liu, Fen 158
Lv, Shuwang 158

Majumdar, A.K. 446
Meier, Willi 184
Mu, Yi 308, 431
Mukhopadhyay, Debdeep 29

Naito, Yusuke 45
Nakazato, Junji 370
Neven, Gregory 274

Obana, Satoshi 122
Ohta, Kazuo 45
Okeya, Katsuyuki 230, 245

Panigrahi, Suvasini 446
Pasini, Sylvain 338
Peyrin, Thomas 82
Pointcheval, David 96
Pramstaller, Norbert 1, 68
Pyshkin, Andrei 158

Raddum, Håvard 1
Raghavendra, Prasad 461
Rangan Chandrasekaran, Pandu 461
Reyhanitabar, Mohammad Reza 385
Rijmen, Vincent 68
Robshaw, Matt J.B. 82
RoyChowdhury, D. 29

Safavi-Naini, Reihaneh 385
Saha, Dhiman 29
Sasaki, Yu 45
Schepers, Daniel 245
Schuldt, Jacob C.N. 274
Shikata, Junji 259

Shimoyama, Takeshi   45
Simpson, Leonie   11
Srinathan, Kannan   461
Sung, Jaechul   59, 143
Sural, Shamik   446
Susilo, Willy   308, 431

Tanaka, Keisuke   200
Tang, Qiang   96
Tartary, Christophe   293
Tzeng, Wen-Guey   323

Vaudenay, Serge   184, 338
Vuillaume, Camille   230

Wang, Huaxiong   293
Wang, Shuhong   385
Weinmann, Ralf-Philipp   158
Wong, Duncan S.   215, 308
Wu, Wei   308
Wu, Yongdong   171

Yajima, Jun   45
Yamamura, Akihiro   370
Yasuda, Kan   355
Yoshino, Masayuki   230
Yung, Moti   59

Zimmer, Sébastien   96

Printing: Mercedes-Druck, Berlin
Binding: Stein+Lehmann, Berlin

Lecture Notes in Computer Science

For information about Vols. 1–4489

please contact your bookseller or Springer

Vol. 4600: H. Comon-Lundh, C. Kirchner, H. Kirchner (Eds.), Rewriting, Computation and Proof. XVI, 273 pages. 2007.

Vol. 4595: D. Bošna\vcki, S. Edelkamp (Eds.), Model Checking Software. X, 285 pages. 2007.

Vol. 4592: Z. Kedad, N. Lammari, E. Métais, F. Meziane, Y. Rezgui (Eds.), Natural Language Processing and Information Systems. XIV, 442 pages. 2007.

Vol. 4591: J. Davies, J. Gibbons (Eds.), Integrated Formal Methods. IX, 660 pages. 2007.

Vol. 4590: W. Damm, H. Hermanns (Eds.), Computer Aided Verification. XV, 562 pages. 2007.

Vol. 4589: J. Münch, P. Abrahamsson (Eds.), Product-Focused Software Process Improvement. XII, 414 pages. 2007.

Vol. 4588: T. Harju, J. Karhumäki, A. Lepistö (Eds.), Developments in Language Theory. XI, 423 pages. 2007.

Vol. 4587: R. Cooper, J. Kennedy (Eds.), Data Management. XIII, 259 pages. 2007.

Vol. 4586: J. Pieprzyk, H. Ghodosi, E. Dawson (Eds.), Information Security and Privacy. XIV, 476 pages. 2007.

Vol. 4584: N. Karssemeijer, B. Lelieveldt (Eds.), Information Processing in Medical Imaging. XX, 777 pages. 2007.

Vol. 4583: S.R. Della Rocca (Ed.), Typed Lambda Calculi and Applications. X, 397 pages. 2007.

Vol. 4582: J. Lopez, P. Samarati, J.L. Ferrer (Eds.), Public Key Infrastructure. XI, 375 pages. 2007.

Vol. 4581: A. Petrenko, M. Veanes, J. Tretmans, W. Grieskamp (Eds.), Testing of Software and Communicating Systems. XI, 379 pages. 2007.

Vol. 4578: F. Masulli, S. Mitra, G. Pasi (Eds.), Fuzzy Logic and Applications. XVIII, 693 pages. 2007. (Sublibrary LNAI).

Vol. 4577: N. Sebe, Y. Liu, Y. Zhuang (Eds.), Multimedia Content Analysis and Mining. XIII, 513 pages. 2007.

Vol. 4576: D. Leivant, R. de Queiroz (Eds.), Logic, Language, Information, and Computation. X, 363 pages. 2007.

Vol. 4574: J. Derrick, J. Vain (Eds.), Formal Techniques for Networked and Distributed Systems – FORTE 2007. XI, 375 pages. 2007.

Vol. 4573: M. Kauers, M. Kerber, R. Miner, W. Windsteiger (Eds.), Towards Mechanized Mathematical Assistants. XIII, 407 pages. 2007. (Sublibrary LNAI).

Vol. 4572: F. Stajano, C. Meadows, S. Capkun, T. Moore (Eds.), Security and Privacy in Ad-hoc and Sensor Networks. X, 247 pages. 2007.

Vol. 4570: H.G. Okuno, M. Ali (Eds.), New Trends in Applied Artificial Intelligence. XXI, 1194 pages. 2007. (Sublibrary LNAI).

Vol. 4569: A. Butz, B. Fisher, A. Krüger, P. Olivier, S. Owada (Eds.), Smart Graphics. IX, 237 pages. 2007.

Vol. 4566: M.J Dainoff (Ed.), Ergonomics and Health Aspects of Work with Computers. XVIII, 390 pages. 2007.

Vol. 4565: D.D. Schmorrow, L.M. Reeves (Eds.), Foundations of Augmented Cognition. XIX, 450 pages. 2007. (Sublibrary LNAI).

Vol. 4564: D. Schuler (Ed.), Online Communities and Social Computing. XVII, 520 pages. 2007.

Vol. 4561: V.G. Duffy (Ed.), Digital Human Modeling. XXIII, 1068 pages. 2007.

Vol. 4560: N. Aykin (Ed.), Usability and Internationalization, Part II. XVIII, 576 pages. 2007.

Vol. 4559: N. Aykin (Ed.), Usability and Internationalization, Part I. XVIII, 661 pages. 2007.

Vol. 4549: J. Aspnes, C. Scheideler, A. Arora, S. Madden (Eds.), Distributed Computing in Sensor Systems. XIII, 417 pages. 2007.

Vol. 4548: N. Olivetti (Ed.), Automated Reasoning with Analytic Tableaux and Related Methods. X, 245 pages. 2007. (Sublibrary LNAI).

Vol. 4547: C. Carlet, B. Sunar (Eds.), Arithmetic of Finite Fields. XI, 355 pages. 2007.

Vol. 4546: J. Kleijn, A. Yakovlev (Eds.), Petri Nets and Other Models of Concurrency – ICATPN 2007. XI, 515 pages. 2007.

Vol. 4545: H. Anai, K. Horimoto, T. Kutsia (Eds.), Algebraic Biology. XIII, 379 pages. 2007.

Vol. 4544: S. Cohen-Boulakia, V. Tannen (Eds.), Data Integration in the Life Sciences. XI, 282 pages. 2007. (Sublibrary LNBI).

Vol. 4543: A.K. Bandara, M. Burgess (Eds.), Inter-Domain Management. XII, 237 pages. 2007.

Vol. 4542: P. Sawyer, B. Paech, P. Heymans (Eds.), Requirements Engineering: Foundation for Software Quality. IX, 384 pages. 2007.

Vol. 4541: T. Okadome, T. Yamazaki, M. Makhtari (Eds.), Pervasive Computing for Quality of Life Enhancement. IX, 248 pages. 2007.

Vol. 4539: N.H. Bshouty, C. Gentile (Eds.), Learning Theory. XII, 634 pages. 2007. (Sublibrary LNAI).

Vol. 4538: F. Escolano, M. Vento (Eds.), Graph-Based Representations in Pattern Recognition. XII, 416 pages. 2007.

Vol. 4537: K.C.-C. Chang, W. Wang, L. Chen, C.A. Ellis, C.-H. Hsu, A.C. Tsoi, H. Wang (Eds.), Advances in Web and Network Technologies, and Information Management. XXIII, 707 pages. 2007.

Vol. 4536: G. Concas, E. Damiani, M. Scotto, G. Succi (Eds.), Agile Processes in Software Engineering and Extreme Programming. XV, 276 pages. 2007.

Vol. 4534: I. Tomkos, F. Neri, J. Solé Pareta, X. Masip Bruin, S. Sánchez Lopez (Eds.), Optical Network Design and Modeling. XI, 460 pages. 2007.

Vol. 4531: J. Indulska, K. Raymond (Eds.), Distributed Applications and Interoperable Systems. XI, 337 pages. 2007.

Vol. 4530: D.H. Akehurst, R. Vogel, R.F. Paige (Eds.), Model Driven Architecture- Foundations and Applications. X, 219 pages. 2007.

Vol. 4529: P. Melin, O. Castillo, L.T. Aguilar, J. Kacprzyk, W. Pedrycz (Eds.), Foundations of Fuzzy Logic and Soft Computing. XIX, 830 pages. 2007. (Sublibrary LNAI).

Vol. 4528: J. Mira, J.R. Álvarez (Eds.), Nature Inspired Problem-Solving Methods in Knowledge Engineering, Part II. XXII, 650 pages. 2007.

Vol. 4527: J. Mira, J.R. Álvarez (Eds.), Bio-inspired Modeling of Cognitive Tasks, Part I. XXII, 630 pages. 2007.

Vol. 4526: M. Malek, M. Reitenspieß, A. van Moorsel (Eds.), Service Availability. X, 155 pages. 2007.

Vol. 4525: C. Demetrescu (Ed.), Experimental Algorithms. XIII, 448 pages. 2007.

Vol. 4524: M. Marchiori, J.Z. Pan, C.d.S. Marie (Eds.), Web Reasoning and Rule Systems. XI, 382 pages. 2007.

Vol. 4523: Y.-H. Lee, H.-N. Kim, J. Kim, Y. Park, L.T. Yang, S.W. Kim (Eds.), Embedded Software and Systems. XIX, 829 pages. 2007.

Vol. 4522: B.K. Ersbøll, K.S. Pedersen (Eds.), Image Analysis. XVIII, 989 pages. 2007.

Vol. 4521: J. Katz, M. Yung (Eds.), Applied Cryptography and Network Security. XIII, 498 pages. 2007.

Vol. 4519: E. Franconi, M. Kifer, W. May (Eds.), The Semantic Web: Research and Applications. XVIII, 830 pages. 2007.

Vol. 4517: F. Boavida, E. Monteiro, S. Mascolo, Y. Koucheryavy (Eds.), Wired/Wireless Internet Communications. XIV, 382 pages. 2007.

Vol. 4516: L. Mason, T. Drwiega, J. Yan (Eds.), Managing Traffic Performance in Converged Networks. XXIII, 1191 pages. 2007.

Vol. 4515: M. Naor (Ed.), Advances in Cryptology - EUROCRYPT 2007. XIII, 591 pages. 2007.

Vol. 4514: S.N. Artemov, A. Nerode (Eds.), Logical Foundations of Computer Science. XI, 513 pages. 2007.

Vol. 4513: M. Fischetti, D.P. Williamson (Eds.), Integer Programming and Combinatorial Optimization. IX, 500 pages. 2007.

Vol. 4511: C. Conati, K. McCoy, G. Paliouras (Eds.), User Modeling 2007. XVI, 487 pages. 2007. (Sublibrary LNAI).

Vol. 4510: P. Van Hentenryck, L. Wolsey (Eds.), Integration of AI and OR Techniques in Constraint Programming for Combinatorial Optimization Problems. X, 391 pages. 2007.

Vol. 4509: Z. Kobti, D. Wu (Eds.), Advances in Artificial Intelligence. XII, 552 pages. 2007. (Sublibrary LNAI).

Vol. 4508: M.-Y. Kao, X.-Y. Li (Eds.), Algorithmic Aspects in Information and Management. VIII, 428 pages. 2007.

Vol. 4507: F. Sandoval, A. Prieto, J. Cabestany, M. Graña (Eds.), Computational and Ambient Intelligence. XXVI, 1167 pages. 2007.

Vol. 4506: D. Zeng, I. Gotham, K. Komatsu, C. Lynch, M. Thurmond, D. Madigan, B. Lober, J. Kvach, H. Chen (Eds.), Intelligence and Security Informatics: Biosurveillance. XI, 234 pages. 2007.

Vol. 4505: G. Dong, X. Lin, W. Wang, Y. Yang, J.X. Yu (Eds.), Advances in Data and Web Management. XXII, 896 pages. 2007.

Vol. 4504: J. Huang, R. Kowalczyk, Z. Maamar, D. Martin, I. Müller, S. Stoutenburg, K.P. Sycara (Eds.), Service-Oriented Computing: Agents, Semantics, and Engineering. X, 175 pages. 2007.

Vol. 4501: J. Marques-Silva, K.A. Sakallah (Eds.), Theory and Applications of Satisfiability Testing – SAT 2007. XI, 384 pages. 2007.

Vol. 4500: N. Streitz, A. Kameas, I. Mavrommati (Eds.), The Disappearing Computer. XVIII, 304 pages. 2007.

Vol. 4499: Y.Q. Shi (Ed.), Transactions on Data Hiding and Multimedia Security II. IX, 117 pages. 2007.

Vol. 4498: N. Abdennahher, F. Kordon (Eds.), Reliable Software Technologies – Ada Europe 2007. XII, 247 pages. 2007.

Vol. 4497: S.B. Cooper, B. Löwe, A. Sorbi (Eds.), Computation and Logic in the Real World. XVIII, 826 pages. 2007.

Vol. 4496: N.T. Nguyen, A. Grzech, R.J. Howlett, L.C. Jain (Eds.), Agent and Multi-Agent Systems: Technologies and Applications. XXI, 1046 pages. 2007. (Sublibrary LNAI).

Vol. 4495: J. Krogstie, A. Opdahl, G. Sindre (Eds.), Advanced Information Systems Engineering. XVI, 606 pages. 2007.

Vol. 4494: H. Jin, O.F. Rana, Y. Pan, V.K. Prasanna (Eds.), Algorithms and Architectures for Parallel Processing. XIV, 508 pages. 2007.

Vol. 4493: D. Liu, S. Fei, Z. Hou, H. Zhang, C. Sun (Eds.), Advances in Neural Networks – ISNN 2007, Part III. XXVI, 1215 pages. 2007.

Vol. 4492: D. Liu, S. Fei, Z. Hou, H. Zhang, C. Sun (Eds.), Advances in Neural Networks – ISNN 2007, Part II. XXVII, 1321 pages. 2007.

Vol. 4491: D. Liu, S. Fei, Z.-G. Hou, H. Zhang, C. Sun (Eds.), Advances in Neural Networks – ISNN 2007, Part I. LIV, 1365 pages. 2007.

Vol. 4490: Y. Shi, G.D. van Albada, J. Dongarra, P.M.A. Sloot (Eds.), Computational Science – ICCS 2007, Part IV. XXXVII, 1211 pages. 2007.